Testaments of Toluca

Nahuatl Studies Series
Number 8

UCLA Latin American Studies

Volume 90

Testaments of Toluca

Edited and translated
with commentary and an introductory study
by

Caterina Pizzigoni

Stanford University Press
UCLA Latin American Center Publications
2007

Stanford University Press
Stanford, California

Printed in the United States of America on acid-free, archival-quality paper

Library of Congress Cataloging-in-Publication Data

Testaments of Toluca / edited and translated with commentary and an introductory study by Caterina Pizzigoni.
p. cm.—(Nahuatl studies series ; no. 8)
Includes bibliographical references.
ISBN-13: 978-0-8047-5607-5 (cloth : alk. paper)
ISBN-10: 0-8047-5607-4 (cloth : alk. paper)
1. Nahuas—History—Sources. 2. Nahuas—Mexico—Toluca de Lerdo—History—Sources. 3. Wills—Mexico—Toluca de Lerdo. 4. Toluca de Lerdo (Mexico)—History—Sources. I. Pizzigoni, Caterina.

F1221.N3T48 2007
972'.5300497452—dc22 2006031889

Contents

List of Notaries in the Corpus

The notaries are given alphabetically by second name, disregarding *de* and/or the article. (T) and (C/T) denote that the notary is from the Toluca area or Calimaya/Tepemaxalco; a more specific designation is given just thereafter, still within the parenthesis. The numbers and dates of wills written by the notary follow, and, if applicable, the page where he is discussed in the introductory study. Some remark about each notary's writing will be found in the document introduction to each of his testaments.

Antonio, Juan (T, San Juan Bautista). No. 34, 1757.
Antonio, don Juan (C/T, central Tepemaxalco). No. 41, 1710.
Aquino, Tomás de (C/T, central Calimaya). No. 75, 1701.
Bartolomé, Santiago (T, Santa Ana). No. 36, 1737.
Benavides, Anastasio de (C/T, Tepemaxalco, San Lucas Evangelista). No. 47, 1731. Discussed p. 42.
Bernardo, Juan (C/T, Tepemaxalco, Santa María de la Asunción). No. 68, 1783.
Constantino, Juan Manuel de (C/T, Santiago Apóstol Quaxochtenco). No. 95, ca. 1730.
Cruz, Andrés de la (T, San Luis). No. 4, 1716.
Cruz, don Bernardo de la (C/T, Tepemaxalco, Santa María de la Asunción). No. 56, 1692.
Cruz, Francisco de la (T, San Pedro Tototepec). Nos. 26, 27, 1733 and 1735. Discussed p. 41.
Cruz, Francisco de la (C/T, Santa María Nativitas). No. 88, 1678.
Cruz, Francisco de la (C/T, Santiago Apóstol Quaxochtenco). No. 94, 1697 and 1703/1709. Discussed p. 45.
Cruz, Juan de la (T, San Pedro Tototepec). No. 25, 1728.
Cruz, don Juan de la (C/T, central Tepemaxalco). No. 42, 1654.
Cruz, Leonardo de la (C/T, Tepemaxalco, San Lucas Evangelista). No. 48, 1735.
Cruz, Marcelo de la (T, different tlaxilacalli). Nos. 7 and 11, 1740 and 1737. Discussed p. 40.
Cruz, Matías de la (T, different tlaxilacalli). Nos. 12, 21, 1737 and 1738. Discussed p. 41.
Cruz, don Martín de ? (C/T, Santiago Apóstol Quaxochtenco). No. 94, 1703.
Cruz, Pedro de la (C/T, central Calimaya). No. 83, 1759.
Cruz, don Pedro de la (T, San Francisco Calixtlahuaca). No. 19, 1737.
Cruz, Tomás de la (T, various tlaxilacalli). Nos. 8–10, 20, 1701 to 1711. Discussed p. 40.
Cruz, Vicente de la (T, place unknown). No. 37, 1732.
Diego, Agustín (C/T, central Tepemaxalco). No. 44, 1762.
Fabián, Sebastián (C/T, Tepemaxalco, San Lucas Evangelista). Nos. 52–55, 1759 and 1762. Discussed p. 43.
Francisco, Andrés (T, San Juan Bautista). Nos. 29 and 32, 1737 and 1736. Discussed p. 42.
Francisco, Antonio (T, place unknown). No. 38, 1737.
Francisco, don Juan (C/T, central Calimaya). Nos. 79, 80, 1734 and 1739. Discussed p. 45.
Gerónimo, Pascual (T, Transfiguración Capultitlan). No. 17, 1737.
González, Bartolomé (T, San Luis). No. 3, 1699.
Gregorio, Juan (T, Santa Ana). No. 35, 1728.
Hernández, Francisco (T, San Bartolomé Tlatelolco). No. 22, 1715.
Hernández, Pedro (C/T, central cluster). Nos. 43 and 84, 1762 and 1760. Discussed p. 42.
Jiménez, don Bernardino (C/T, Calimaya, San Antonio de Padua). No. 86, 1733.
Josef, Adrián (T, San Juan Bautista). No. 33, 1756.
Juan, Felipe (C/T, Santa María Nativitas). Nos. 91–93, 1759 and 1760. Discussed p. 45.
Juan (y Colidris?), Gregorio (C/T, Calimaya, San Antonio de Padua). No. 87, 1737.
Martín, Diego (T, Santa María de los Angeles Huitzillan). No. 18, 1741.
Martín, Diego (C/T, Calimaya, San Antonio de Padua). No. 85, 1717.
Martín, Luis (C/T, Tepemaxalco, Santa María de la Asunción). Nos. 57–61, 1759, 1760, and 1762. Discussed p. 43.
Martín, Pedro (C/T, Tepemaxalco, San Lucas Evangelista). No. 51, 1759.
Matías, Agustín (C/T, Santa María Nativitas). No. 90, 1759.
Matías, don Diego ? (C/T, central Tepemaxalco). No. 69, 1737.
Matías, Francisco (T, San Miguel Totocuitlapilco). No. 16, 1652.
Mejía, Domingo (T, San Bartolomé Tlatelolco). No. 23, 1731.
Nicolás, Diego. (T, San Bartolomé Tlatelolco). No. 24, 1737.

Pablo, Juan (C/T, Santiago Apóstol Quaxochtenco). No. 97, 1761.
Pascual, Jacinto (C/T, Santiago Apóstol Quaxochtenco). No. 96, 1760.
Pérez, don Pedro (T, San Cristóbal). No. 15, 1732.
Ramos, Domingo (C/T, Tepemaxalco, San Lucas Evangelista). Nos. 49 and 50, 1736 and 1726. Discussed pp.42–43.
San Juan, (don) Miguel de (C/T, Tepemaxalco, Santa María de la Asunción). Nos. 62–66, 1737 to 1762. Discussed pp. 43–44.
Santiago, Andrés de (C/T, central Tepemaxalco). No. 40, 1693.
Santiago, Bernardo de (T, various tlaxilacalli). Nos. 2, 5, 13, 30, 1717 to 1733. Discussed pp. 39–40.
Santiago, Cipriano de (T, Santa María Cozcatlan). No. 6, 1731.
Santiago, don Domingo de ? (C/T, central Calimaya). No. 77, 1759.
Santiago, Juan Antonio de (C/T, Santa María Nativitas). No. 89, 1737.
Santiago, Salvador de (T, San Juan Bautista). Nos. 28, 31, 1710 and 1731. Discussed pp. 41–42.
Santos, (don) Hipólito de, (C/T, central Calimaya). Nos. 70–74, 76, 81, 82, 1738 to 1763. Discussed p. 44.
Santos, Pedro de los (C/T, central Calimaya). No. 78, 1712.
Santos, Santiago de los (T, San Cristóbal). No. 14, 1732.
Silverio, (don) Antonio (C/T, Tepemaxalco, Santa María de la Asunción). Nos. 57 and 67, 1762 and 1758. Discussed p. 44.
[Tapia], Gregorio de (T, Santa Bárbara Mixcoac). No. 1, 1671.

List of Testaments in Clusters

[1]Nos. 3 and 4, the wills of Juana Francisca, 1699, and Ana María, 1716, both of San Luis, pp. 55–57, are probably a mother-daughter cluster.

Acknowledgments

MY GREATEST DEBT is to Stephanie Wood and Jim Lockhart. Without them, as will be seen from my remarks at the beginning of the introductory study, there would have been no book like the present one. To them above all goes my gratitude, along with my appreciation of a unique opportunity and my deep affection and attachment.

During my work on this project I have been at the Institute for the Study of the Americas in London, where for part of the time I have held a Leverhulme fellowship. I thank all my colleagues for the stimulating environment, and for their support and friendship. It is a wonderful community indeed! In particular I thank James Dunkerley for being such a solid guide and friend in these years, and Linda Newson for having introduced me to advanced study in the field of early Latin American history. (I have of course not forgotten my first beginnings in the field with Professor Daniele Pompejano.)

My gratitude goes also to the personnel of the Archivo Histórico del Arzobispado de México for their help and for the special space they gave me, and on behalf of Stephanie I thank their counterparts at the Archivo General de la Nación and also at the Newberry Library.

When the book was approaching its final stages, I was staying in Zacatecas, and I am most thankful to John Sullivan and the native speakers at the Instituto de Docencia e Investigación Etnológica there for their friendship as well as for sharing their knowledge and helping with doubts.

I must also thank Bob Haskett for a superb reader's report on the book, which helped greatly with its publication, and Rebecca Horn for her enlightened proofreading. And Norris Pope at Stanford deserves special mention for his kindness and his belief in the project.

I dedicate my efforts in this enterprise to my mother Giovanna, my father Giuseppe, my brother Mauro, and my grandmother Giudy, for whom no words could express my love and gratitude; and to Anna Lundeby, an angel, who would have liked so much to do a PhD. I will always remember some of her final words: "I hope that you all have a goal, a dream, an idea, something you would like to do . . . and that you do it."

C. P.
London, March 2006

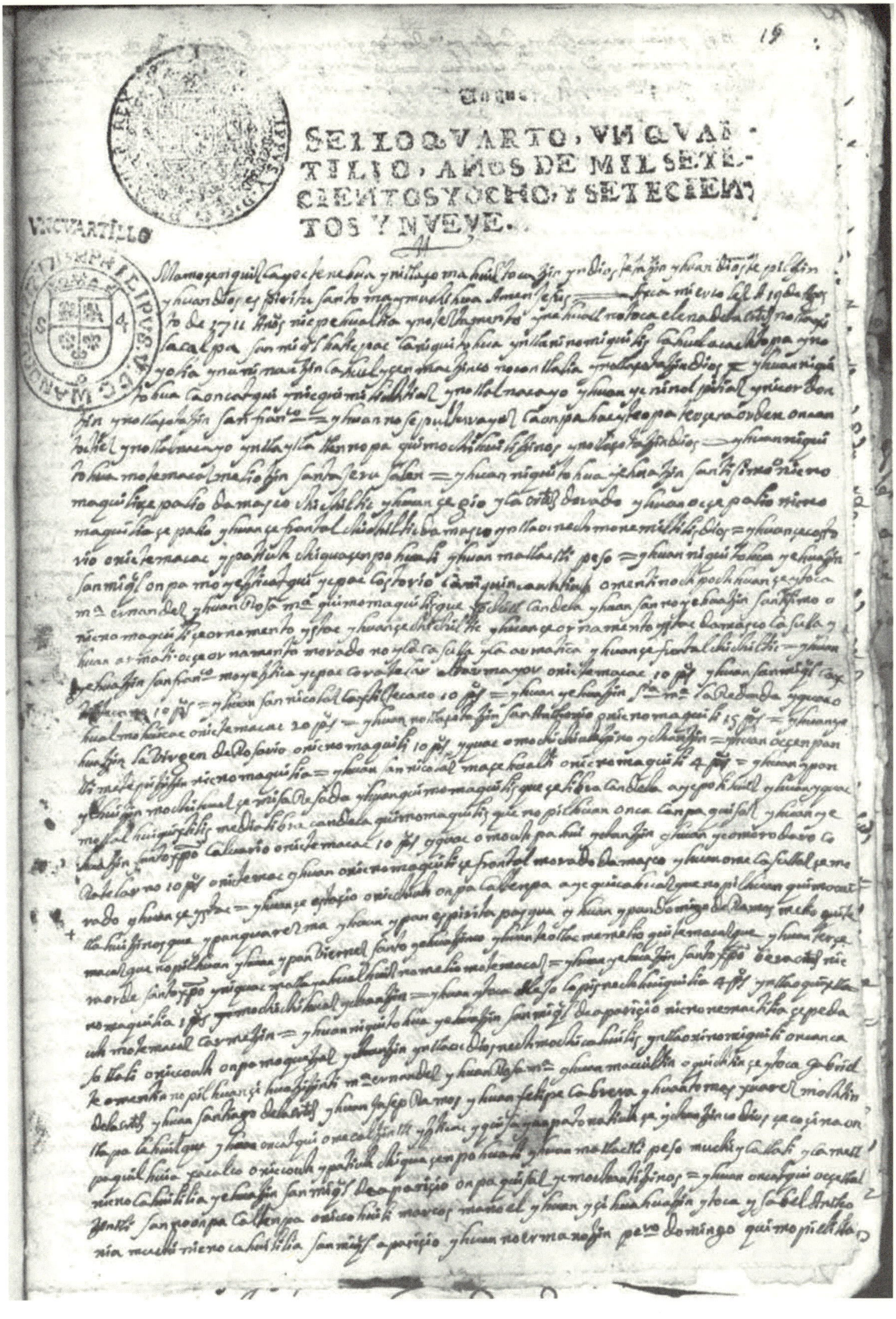

SELLO QVARTO, VN QVAR-TILLO, AÑOS DE MIL SETE-CIENTOS Y OCHO, Y SETECIEN-TOS Y NVEVE.

FIGURE 1. Testament of Elena de la Cruz, San Miguel Aticpac, 1711 (No. 10), written by Tomás de la Cruz, p. 1. Courtesy of the Archivo Histórico del Arzobispado de México.

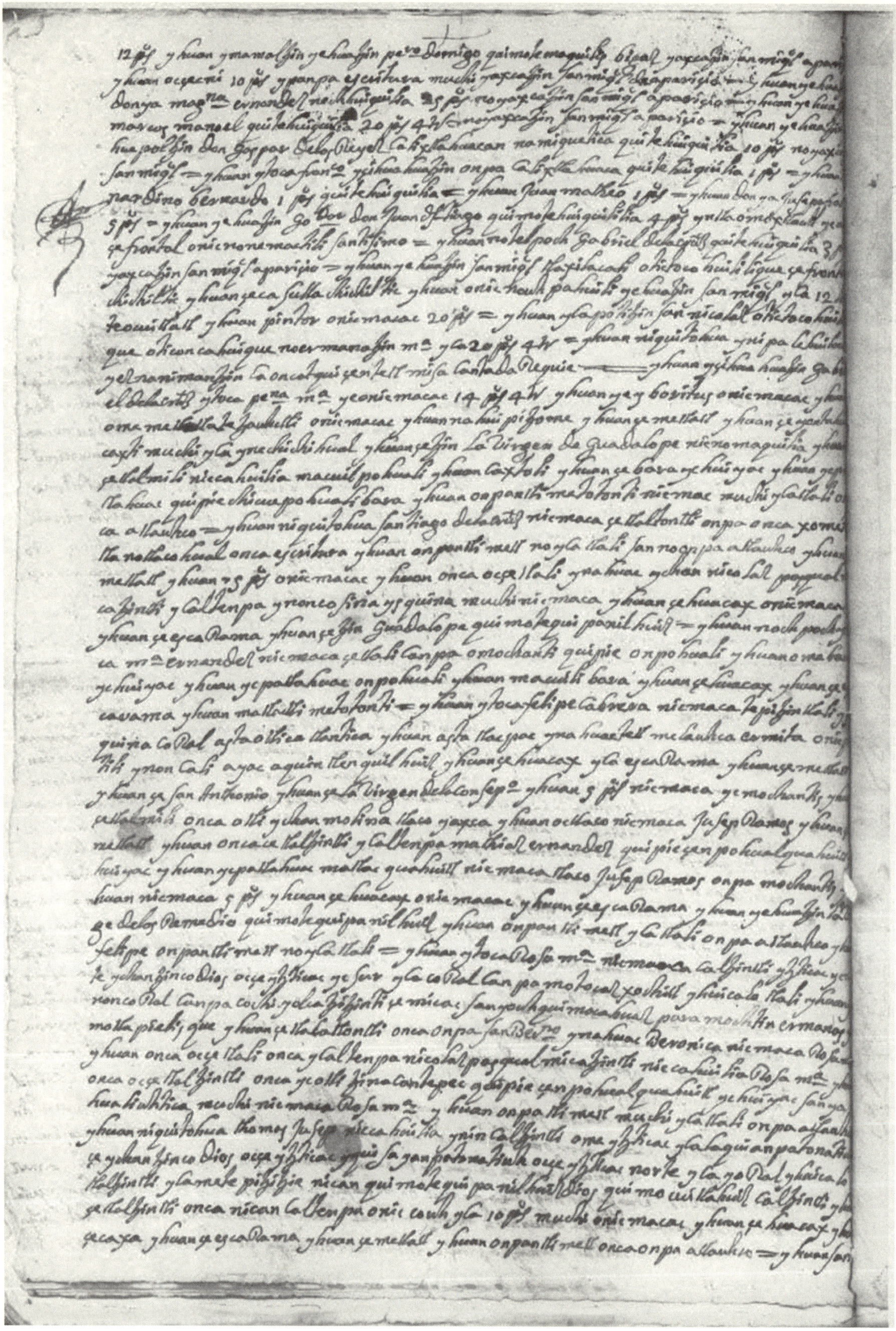

FIGURE 2. Testament of Elena de la Cruz, p. 2.

FIGURE 3. Testament of Elena de la Cruz, p. 3.

Introductory Study

Amo Aqui mictlapa nechtzoteconehuas
No one is to cause me headaches in the land of the dead.
Melchora María, San Bartolomé Tlatelolco (Toluca area), 1737 (No. 24)

NAHUATL TESTAMENTS can give the impression of being extremely intimate documents; when reading them it can seem as if we are privileged to watch something we would not normally be permitted to see. But after all, if we look at the documents closely, the truly intimate touches are rare. Perhaps what the wills really give us is a sense of great immediacy and reality, much of which comes from their almost always being issued when the testator is expected to die very soon, probably that day, creating a unique moment in a life, a very special perspective on it. In the area of Calimaya/Tepemaxalco in the Toluca Valley, a native term is often used toward the end of a will to describe the testament—*nococoxcatlatol*, "my sick person's statement"—and we can almost see the testator lying in bed at home, where the document was usually prepared.[1]

The will is a distillation of a life only in certain basic respects—family, property, some economic activity, death rituals—but it is dramatized for us by the imminent end of that life, the realization that the testator is about to let go of the connections we are just discovering. Indeed, a Nahuatl will is even more dramatic than the type of testament we are familiar with from Europe and the United States nowadays, and not only because it is made in extremis, but because it is almost theater. An audience is present, whether it be relatives and friends, or most often officials, and the testator talks to them; that is why he or she is always saying "my statement is to be realized," or "no one is to take it away from my child," and sometimes, despite the convention of using the third person, he or she even speaks directly to the witnesses or one of them.[2]

I was not the first person to become interested in indigenous wills. The interest has come out of the general social history of early Spanish America, out of the desire to study the social reality and everyday life of indigenous people, and when we look for sources in indigenous languages which would show that dimension, we always come up with wills.[3] That is precisely what happened to me in the Archivo Histórico del Arzobispado de México (AHAM). I was thinking of the wills as material for a dissertation and later monograph on gender and everyday life in the indigenous world of the Toluca Valley in the eighteenth century. I went ahead to do the dissertation using a fairly limited corpus of wills, only provisionally transcribed and translated, a practical necessity which permitted good preliminary results.[4]

As my thoughts turned toward a future monograph, I realized how much more was to be learned from further study of individual wills, and also of the whole body of them. Facing the many subtleties of the corpus—the two cultures involved, Hispanic and indigenous; the changes over time; the marked variation from place to place; the connections between specific documents—I came to understand a great deal more about each document and each situation, which would gradually come to life and deliver more information both about the testator and about the general context than I at first would have imagined possible. I began to write informal commentaries to give concrete form to these insights before going on to the next stage. At the same time, I was hoping to make all this information available to others, to enable them first to share the actual experience of the indigenous peoples' expression, and second to use these rich materials and my comments about them for various kinds of research. And because the wills are from different writers in different districts, I became aware of the importance of the notaries, the intermediaries between the testators and us, and in my commentaries I began to discuss what

[1]In Nahua wills of many times and places, the testator speaks of the house "where I lie," a formulation that is found only once or twice in the Tolucan wills, but frequently we see the words "this home of mine," or "this house," telling us equally well that the testator lies sick at home.

[2]See the passage in No. 80 where the testator suddenly begins to speak in the second person to her nephew, wanting him to take care of her daughter for her.

[3]The first published collection of Nahuatl mundane documents, Anderson, Berdan and Lockhart 1976, has a prominent first section devoted to testaments. Other collections with indigenous wills followed, such as Cline and León-Portilla 1984, Reyes García et al. 1996, Rojas et al. 1999–2002, and, to an extent, Kellogg and Restall 1998.

[4]Pizzigoni 2002.

I noticed about their lives and work.

In sum, I imagined a publication in which each and every testament would have the following: to aid future research, a very exact and careful transcription; for readers of all kinds, a translation which is both accurate and readable; and to save for the public the knowledge I had gained only through a long process of deduction, intuition, and comparison with other documents, a document introduction—a substantial item which not only highlights and interprets the most salient points in the testament, but reconstructs the whole situation of the testator, and also adds an analysis of some characteristics of the notary. With this apparatus, these precious life-documents could speak to us today and convey a great deal about a world now largely disappeared, but still fresh, fascinating, and significant.

As it happens, it was not necessary to invent everything from scratch, for over the past few decades others have been coming face to face with similar situations regarding various types of Nahuatl texts. An increasingly analytical kind of philology has evolved, leading to publications which, though they are editions, are also like monographs and make the same sorts of contributions that monographs do.[1] In particular, the collection *The Testaments of Culhuacan* was a model, a source of perspective, and a point of departure for further developments.[2]

In light of the above considerations, I decided on a publication that features a collection of wills (98 of them) carefully transcribed and fully translated, with many notes, and for each one an interpretive introduction that is sometimes longer than the original document. This introductory study that you are now looking at attempts to give the reader needed information about the corpus and how to deal with it, while also setting forth a large number of important findings in a provisional way.

I have now told you the genesis and rationale of this book at an intellectual level. I believe it will add to your understanding if I also say some words about the more tangible history of the project. In the years 1999–2001 I did research in Mexico City toward a dissertation at King's College, London, with emphasis on gender and everyday rural life among indigenous people in the late colonial period. My explorations centered on the archiepiscopal archive (AHAM). In addition to the litigation in Spanish that I found, I came upon some wills in Nahuatl from the Toluca region and soon began collecting all I could find, even though at that time the Nahuatl language was a mystery to me.

In the summer of 2000 I attended a Nahuatl course at Yale University, where I got a good foundation in the language.[3] It so happened that James Lockhart took over the class for a week, and knowing that he had worked with older Nahuatl documents and even specifically with Toluca, I brought photocopies of some of my wills to class, where one of them was studied by the group. By good fortune the one chosen, that of Melchora María (quoted above), now No. 24 in this volume, gave excellent examples of the role of women in forming networks and bringing up children, topics then at the center of my interest, and by even better fortune, the will contained the remark here quoted, open evidence that the Nahuas interpreted everything including religion in their own way, based on their own heritage. From that time forward I have worked with Jim at long distance on the transcription, translation, and interpretation of the Nahuatl wills; he became my dissertation adviser, although informally, with the chapters of my 2002 dissertation that were based on Nahuatl documents and that were the beginning of some of the approaches used here.

Even during my dissertation campaign, Jim saw the relevance of another effort to collect Nahuatl wills from Toluca, made quite a few years before by Stephanie Wood. Using mainly the Archivo General de la Nación (AGN), as well as the Newberry Library and some other repositories, Stephanie had put together a collection of testaments much larger than my own, had written essential notes from the archival dossiers in which they were contained, and above all had completed by hand on the photocopies the important portions of the documents that are lost in the right margins in the binding at the AGN. Jim contacted Stephanie, whom I already knew, and it

[1]Karttunen and Lockhart 1987; Lockhart 1993; Sousa, Poole and Lockhart 1998. Publications such as these are at the heart of what is often called the New Philology. As it happens none of these books deals with testaments, but the principle is the same with any kind of older Nahuatl documentation.

[2]Cline and León-Portilla 1984. A publication of Yucatecan Maya wills, Restall 1995, takes advantage of the *Testaments of Culhuacan* and develops its methods further. It also contains much material that would be useful for comparative purposes, but in the name of practicality I will for now remain within the Nahua sphere.

[3]I take the occasion to thank Jonathan Amith for his excellent instruction.

was agreed that she would make her photocopies and notes available for use in my dissertation as needed, and that at some future time a volume or volumes of the wills collected by both of us would be published. We were thinking of a joint editorship. As it turned out, the Nahuatl wills were crucial both to my dissertation and to my plans for a future monograph, so they have taken up a very large proportion of my life and time, whereas Stephanie has been occupied with her fascinating recent book[4] and a large number of other pressing academic activities. As the book began to take final shape, in an unparalleled act of generosity she declined to be credited as co-editor of the present volume.[5]

Looking ahead, I see this book partly as a large step toward a monograph on life among indigenous people of the Toluca Valley in the eighteenth century.[6] But I think that it is something of great permanent value on its own, and I hope that both Nahuatl experts and other readers will open their minds and hearts to it, becoming aware of the almost inexhaustible richness of its original materials.

1. Characteristics of the Corpus

ONCE THE CORPUS of available Nahuatl testaments from the Toluca Valley was narrowed to the 98 included in the present collection,[7] the parallels with the Testaments of Culhuacan became clearer, as well as a number of very significant differences. It is in relation to the Culhuacan testaments that one can get a first appreciation of the nature of the body of documents employed here and of the significance of the present publication. The present corpus is considerably larger (including informative but unfinished wills, there are about 60 in the Culhuacan collection), but each one is large enough to demonstrate significant patterns. The Culhuacan documents are from the Valley of Mexico, the Toluca materials from the first major valley to the west, still in the central area of the country but a bit more removed from the capital. The Culhuacan documents are dated ca. 1580, in the heart of a hundred years of evolution that are sometimes called Stage 2, whereas the Toluca materials are from later, the second half of the seventeenth and above all the eighteenth centuries, falling into Stage 3.[8] Temporal comparisons between the two bodies of documents are called for, especially since the later period is still less studied in terms of such documents than the earlier.

A strength of the Culhuacan testaments is that they were a unified collection from their very inception. The corpus here was assembled from scattered sources, but through concentration on certain areas, much of the same unity was achieved, and at the same time, spreading over a much longer period and

---

[4]*Transcending Conquest*, Wood 2003. See her work based on the corpus of Toluca Valley testaments in Wood 1991, 1994, and 1997, and in Wood and Haskett 1997.

[5]Through Loera Chávez 1977 and 1981 I have become aware that another collection of Nahuatl wills from Calimaya and Tepemaxalco may be in existence, and I intend to explore this possibility in the near future.

[6]I am not the first to take this path. Sarah Cline followed *The Testaments of Culhuacan* with a monograph on Culhuacan in the same years (Cline 1986). In that case, the documentary publication and its commentary stand to this day beside the monograph as something of equal value with distinct characteristics and potential, and I hope that the same will be true in my case.

[7]I presently have about the same number of wills from the Toluca Valley not included in this book, a good many of which are already transcribed and translated in preliminary fashion. I will be using them in monographic research in which I am now engaged, but it may be many years before they are published as a second volume. They could prove useful not only in adding numbers to the corpus, but in contributing to our understanding of cultural unity and variety in the region, showing whether the rest of the valley is more like Toluca, more like Calimaya/Tepemaxalco, or quite distinct from either.

[8]The stages of postconquest evolution of the Nahuas were first discussed in Karttunen and Lockhart 1976 in regard to linguistic phenomena specifically and were developed as a broader theory of social and cultural change in Lockhart 1992. Stage 1 (to about 1540 or 1545) is the first postconquest generation, during which the Nahuatl language hardly changed. In Stage 2 (from then until the middle of the seventeenth century), Nahuatl took a myriad of words from Spanish, but mainly nouns, while other aspects of the language were unaffected. Finally, during Stage 3 (from then on, including the time investigated here) Nahuatl took words other than nouns, created equivalences between Nahuatl and Spanish words, and added Spanish sounds to its phonology. In Lockhart 1999, p. 209, the cultural implications of the stages are succinctly summarized, calling Stage 1 a generation of little cultural change; Stage 2 a hundred years when change affected predominantly corporations, and Hispanic elements entered Nahua frameworks as discrete items; and Stage 3 a time of personal interpenetration of the two societies, with more intimate, structure-altering change.

containing documents from a variety of places, the present corpus allows study of temporal and regional variation within its own quite broad boundaries of time and space. Aspects such as patterns of possession and inheritance, funeral practices, and many others can be tested in multiple localities and over several decades. Cultural subareas can be discerned as well as unities across the larger region, and even the idiosyncrasies of some individual *tlaxilacalli* can be studied. The Culhuacan collection, with so many wills made in the same year in the same altepetl, contains several invaluable clusters of wills by relatives. But the documentation in this volume, as a result of the regional concentration and the archival practice of including several wills in the same dossier, also contains clusters, and in fact even more of them. Reconstructing the clusters has been a sort of detective work that was both difficult and fascinating. Some of the associated wills were in the same dossiers, but others were not, and it was only by recognizing internal crossreferences that many could be identified. I wish I could convey to the reader the sense of successful puzzle solving, of reality, that I felt as one after another of the clusters emerged, sometimes from the merest hints at first, and I hope that the reader too can have that experience in studying them in this book.

Chronology

LET US EXAMINE some of the prime characteristics of the corpus in more detail, starting with the chronological framework. At the same time it is necessary to say something about the regional distribution, to which I will devote more space below. Briefly, the corpus is divided into two main parts regionally, first Toluca proper with its immediate surroundings, and second the area of the double altepetl Calimaya/Tepemaxalco; discussion of temporal distribution in the collection must take this regional division into account. Overall, the testaments concentrate in the eighteenth century up until 1763; there is only one document from later (1783). Far fewer, just 10 of the 98, come from the second half of the seventeenth century (from 1652 to 1699); nevertheless, they are crucial in defining evolution over a longer time and in distinguishing the eighteenth century from what preceded it, identifying the changes that took place later. Many of the testaments concentrate in specific years, particularly 1737, 1759–60, and 1762. Although a large number of variables have been involved in the preservation of testaments and their appearance in this volume, it does seem that these concentrations correspond to years in which more people died as a result of epidemics (smallpox in 1737, *matlaçahuatl* [typhus] in 1762).[1]

The table on p. 5 gives the number of testaments in the present corpus by decade for the Toluca area and Calimaya/Tepemaxalco, with totals.

The testaments from Toluca proper are in the main from relatively early in the eighteenth century, concentrating around the decade of the 1730s, with 10 in the first three decades and only 2 as late as the 1750s. The majority of the testaments from Calimaya/Tepemaxalco, 35 out of 60, concentrate in the 1750s and 1760s; indeed, 31 of them are from the short period 1758–63. Thus the reader of the book may form the impression that the coverage for the Toluca area is mainly earlier than for Calimaya/Tepemaxalco. In a sense that is true, but note also that the latter group actually has more seventeenth-century wills than Toluca and displays a reasonable selection from the first half of the eighteenth as well, 18, concentrating in the 1730s just as in Toluca proper.

The division between seventeenth and eighteenth century in this context seems meaningful to me, and surely there are several phenomena which can be detected primarily only in one or the other. Yet I have also noticed that the documents of the 1690s share much with those of the first decade or two of the next century, and further that the numbers pick up with that decade. One way to look at the matter would be that the "early eighteenth century," and the core of the corpus, begins with the 1690s.

Temporal patterns of change will be discussed below in a number of specific categories of interest. Here let me make a more general remark about the temporal patterning that can be discerned because of the relatively even distribution of the documents over more than a hundred years. All of the documents in the corpus fall within Stage 3 as generally conceived, that is, after the dividing line of 1640 or 1650. To a great extent all belong to that stage linguistically and in other ways. From the begin-

[1]Rojas 1999–2002 (vol. 1, p. 26) contains a graph with the comment that in the whole AGN there are more Nahuatl testaments from 1737 than from any other year early or late. See also Márquez Morfín 1993 and Florescano and Malvido 1992, 1: 171–76. My thanks to Linda Newson for these references.

DISTRIBUTION OF THE CORPUS OF WILLS

Date	Toluca	Calimaya/Tepemaxalco	Totals
1650–59	1	1	2
1660–69	—	—	—
1670–79	1	1	2
1680–89	—	1	1
1690–99	1	4	5
Totals 17th century	3	7	10
1700–09	3	2	5
1710–19	5	3	8
1720–29	2	1	3
1730–39	21	12	33
1740–49	2	—	2
1750–59	2	19	21
1760–69	—	15	15
1770–79	—	—	—
1780–89	—	1	1
Totals 18th century	35	53	88
Totals overall	38	60	98

ning, for example, they contain loanwords for close kin like siblings and nieces/nephews. But the three stages of postconquest Nahua evolution have not yet been defined closely, year by year, in many categories, or within specific regions. What is seen in the present corpus is that many facets often thought of as characteristic of Stage 2 persist in the Toluca Valley, at least to some degree, through most of the seventeenth century and are still present in certain documents even in the first couple of decades of the eighteenth.

Regional distribution, sociopolitical organization, and order

FOR CONSIDERATIONS of time and space, it was not possible to put the entire approximately 200 testaments collected from the Toluca region in a single volume. My choice, as already mentioned, was to concentrate on two main areas. First, the immediate area of Toluca (38 testaments), including Toluca proper with its constituent tlaxilacalli, as well as the tlaxilacalli that surrounded it and were in some way associated with it. Second, the double altepetl of Calimaya/Tepemaxalco (60 testaments), to the south of Toluca in the Valley, half way between Metepec and Tenango del Valle.[2] The areas were chosen not for any preconceived attributes but because they delivered the largest concentrations of documents, and so many important cultural elements can be studied when there is a sufficient supply of texts from the same places, with related people and practices, and the same notaries. The testaments from the Toluca area mainly correspond to holdings of the AHAM that were collected by myself, while those from Calimaya/Tepemaxalco are principally from the AGN and were collected primarily by Stephanie Wood.

In the early stages of my Toluca project it was far from my mind that I might discover significant cultural differences between the subareas of the Toluca Valley. In my dissertation, based more on the materials from Toluca proper, I tended to assume that what I was finding was common to the whole valley at that time. Now, after close work with documents from both subareas, I realize that al-

[2]I imagine that most readers of this volume are already acquainted with the terms *altepetl* and *tlaxilacalli*. Here I will say only that the local states of central Mexico, seen by the Spaniards in the light of municipalities and called *pueblos*, were called *altepetl* in Nahuatl both before and after the conquest, and that they consisted of separate constituent parts called *tlaxilacalli*, usually arranged symmetrically in an order of rotation and precedence.

though there are many significant commonalities, the two also constitute distinct cultural regions in some quite important respects, and that some of the interesting things I found in Toluca were entirely absent in Calimaya/Tepemaxalco; some features of the latter were also missing in the former. The result is a more differentiated picture of evolution and an opportunity for fascinating comparisons within a regional setting. I will point out many below, but I am sure that additional distinctions remain to be discovered, and I also imagine that there were other cultural subareas in the valley.

With the documents for the volume once identified and grouped into the two different areas, the question arose of how to order them logically and usefully in the book, a matter naturally related to their organization in actuality, so that I will discuss the two things at the same time. To an extent I have followed Nahua sociopolitical principles (and indeed, if all the relevant information were available, I would have followed them much more closely). The large categories are based on the altepetl and the secondary categories on the tlaxilacalli that compose them. I immediately faced problems in that the organization of the altepetl of Toluca is not well studied, whereas Calimaya and Tepemaxalco are a complex, interwoven double altepetl, somewhat better studied but still mysterious, and sometimes it is not clear which of the larger entities a given tlaxilacalli belongs to.

I started with Toluca, the largest population center of the valley and the hub of its economy. Works on the area, based entirely on Spanish sources it seems, make a distinction between tlaxilacalli that they call barrios of Toluca and other tlaxilacalli more outlying but somehow still associated with Toluca. I followed this order, putting first the "barrios" (15 wills) and then all the other testaments belonging to the area (23).[1] The individual tlaxilacalli in both groups come in a random order here, because nothing is presently known about their order of precedence or rotation, and the works do not even always agree about which category a given entity belongs in. In the wills themselves there is very little to document the existence of two categories. Nearly all of the documents name the tlaxilacalli only and no larger entity. In both of them testators often have church bells rung for them (not a known practice in Calimaya/Tepemaxalco), and in both they are often buried at the *huei teopan*, "the great church," apparently meaning the establishment built by the Franciscans on the main square of Toluca city.

As for Calimaya/Tepemaxalco, in this case too much information is lacking about internal organization. The two were paired altepetl sharing the same basic territory, and also the same parish and central church, but they had separate sets of tlaxilacalli, separate cabildos and separate governors. We have virtually no knowledge of exactly how the territories of the two related to each other. We do know that both had various tlaxilacalli in the central settlement cluster now known as Calimaya. In one case, it is known that an outlying Calimaya tlaxilacalli, San Antonio de Padua (la Isla), was the northern part of a single cluster, San Lucas Evangelista (Tepemaxalco) the southern.

It is strongly to be presumed that Calimaya was the senior of the two. Not only did it ultimately give its name to the whole, but the patron saints were San Pedro for Calimaya, coming first, and San Pablo for Tepemaxalco, coming second. San Antonio is today much larger and more prosperous than the adjoining San Lucas and has a much bigger and more luxurious eighteenth-century church. Yet no explicit, conclusive information is available about the order of the two altepetl. Even being aware of the fact that Calimaya is no doubt senior, I have put Tepemaxalco first in the volume because there are many more documents from there (31 against 18 from Calimaya), and because, as we will see, its internal order is better understood. There are some cases in which it is not certain whether a tlaxilacalli belongs to Calimaya or Tepemaxalco, and these documents have been placed at the end of the book (11 wills).

A set of tribute lists extant for Tepemaxalco from 1658 to 1665[2] allows a certain insight into the internal organization of that altepetl, for not only do the lists go by tlaxilacalli, their order is unvarying from one list to the next, just as in traditional Nahua sociopolitical organization. Also traditional is the fact that there are exactly eight tlaxilacalli. They are as follows:

[1]See Romero Quiroz 1973, pp. 135–43.

[2]Museo de Antropología e Historia, Archivo Histórico, Colección Gómez de Orozco 185.

1. Teocaltitlan Tlatocapan (also sometimes called Teopanquiyahuac)
2. Pasiontitlan
3. San Francisco Pochtlan
4. Tlatocapan
5. Mexicapan
6. San Lucas (Evangelista)
7. Santa María de la Asunción
8. Santiago

Not all of these actually appear among the tlaxilacalli of the testaments in the present corpus (Pasiontitlan, San Lucas, and Santa María are definitely represented, with a reference in one will to Pochtlan), and one Tepemaxalco tlaxilacalli in the corpus, San Juan Bautista Yancuictlalpan, is not on the tribute list. Nevertheless, I have followed the order as far as it is applicable, putting the wills from the missing tlaxilacalli last. In the corpus there appear some wills from an entity called Santiago Apóstol Quaxochtenco. It is conceivable that this is the eighth tlaxilacalli of Tepemaxalco. In dossiers it is identified as belonging to the larger Calimaya parish (which does not exclude Tepemaxalco), but since the modifying words Apóstol and Quaxochtenco are very prominent in the wills and their dossiers, and they are entirely lacking in the tribute lists, I have classified Santiago Apóstol Quaxochtenco for now as uncertain between Calimaya and Tepemaxalco.

Working with the corpus has made me aware of a distinction within each of the two altepetl. Each of them had several tlaxilacalli in the same central, apparently somewhat nucleated settlement. Wills from these tlaxilacalli almost always try to identify the respective altepetl. But wills from outlying settlements, such as San Lucas and Santa María de la Asunción in Tepemaxalco, do not identify any overarching altepetl; sometimes the tlaxilacalli itself is called an altepetl. Santiago Apóstol Quaxochtenco appears to be one of these outliers, not giving any larger altepetl framework and making identification harder.

With Calimaya, essentially nothing is known about the organization of the tlaxilacalli, and probably there were some that have not yet been identified. As it happens, Calimaya too had a tlaxilacalli named Pasiontitlan, and I have put it first because it was ranked high in Tepemaxalco, but for the rest the order of Calimaya tlaxilacalli is random except for putting the outlying San Antonio de Padua last within Calimaya. A tlaxilacalli Santa María Natividad known to be within the parish and general jurisdiction possibly belongs to Calimaya (it at least borders some Calimaya areas), but as with Santiago Apóstol Quaxochtenco, information is insufficient for a definitive classification, and here the tlaxilacalli is put at the end among those unclassified within Calimaya/Tepemaxalco.

The whole question of dual organization and parallel altepetl within the same jurisdiction is challenging and significant, and I believe that I have made here some contribution to the topic, but many aspects of it remain a mystery. Several wills of the corpus even contain hints that the people of the time were themselves becoming somewhat confused, and that some earlier distinctions may have fallen by the wayside.[3] But the materials make clear that even as late as the 1760s, the two altepetl were functioning separately side by side.

Reflecting indigenous sociopolitical organization when feasible is important to me, but even more important is putting similar material together in one place for the benefit of the reader. All the documents from each tlaxilacalli will be found together, and within that all the documents prepared by a given notary; I maintain a general progression forward in time within each entity. Nevertheless, in the case of clusters of relatives in the same tlaxilacalli, I put their wills together regardless of the other principles. The result is something of a compromise, but I hope it will make the materials as usable as possible, and by crossreferences I have tried to point the reader to similar or connected materials which are located far apart.

Gender

A VITAL ASPECT of the corpus is the gender ratio, how many testaments were issued by men and how many by women. In the immediate Toluca area, women represent roughly 37% of the testators and men the remaining 63%. In Calimaya/Tepemaxalco the aggregate percentage is similar. But when data are split into subentities, we find a surprising predominance of women in the altepetl of Calimaya, women representing almost 56% of the total, against 44% for the men. In the overall total for the double altepetl, this exceptional female predominance is outweighed by the data from the better

[3]See Nos. 42 and 43 among other testaments.

represented Tepemaxalco and from the tlaxilacalli that do not belong clearly to one altepetl or the other. In the entire combined corpus, 38 testaments were issued by women against 60 by men, meaning that women are about 39% of the testators and men about 61%.

The ratio is surprisingly consistent with that in some other collections. Counting all wills in the Testaments of Culhuacan including fragments with named testators, women are nearly 38%. In the Rojas collection of testaments, four different sub-collections have ratios for women of 41%, 35%, 27%, and 38% respectively.[1] The norm seems to be less than half but more than a third. That male testators were more numerous could have been expected, since men had easier and more frequent access to document production and public officials (despite some notable exceptions in this very corpus), and as family heads they generally had more property to bequeath. But the proportion of female testators is still relatively high, telling us that their role in the ownership and transmission of property was active and significant.

We should not forget that females are frequently mentioned in the testaments of males, and vice versa. No doubt that tends to be true of all wills; it is outstandingly true in the testaments of Toluca.

Clusters

ANALYSIS OF MANY kinds of patterns, notably those involving more than one generation, are greatly facilitated when we can study not merely a single will, however rich, but two or three connected wills of relatives. Family clusters are a great asset to scholarship, something that the field learned already in the Testaments of Culhuacan. As said before, the wills of the present corpus were scattered in different archives, branches, and dossiers, so that recognizing clusters was often quite a challenge, but a highly rewarding one. A total of 13 clusters have been identified and studied, 8 in the Toluca area and 5 in Calimaya/Tepemaxalco.[2] No less than 32 testaments are involved in some cluster, almost a third of the corpus.

In the majority of cases (at least 8), parent and child are linked, although in 4 instances another kind of relationship is involved as well, particularly husband and wife or siblings.[3] It is important to notice the presence of women in these parent-child relationships, either as mothers or as daughters. The other clusters are built around various kinds of relationships: brothers, husband and wife, grandfather and granddaughter. One cluster includes the peculiar combination of son-in-law, father-in-law, and relative of the latter, with considerable light thrown on the woman who was wife of one and daughter of another, crossing tlaxilacalli lines to marry.[4] In another the relationship is not clearly stated, but is likely either father-son or grandfather-grandson. Among the 8 cases of parent-child relationship there is a very complex cluster, with wills from a mother, a daughter, a distant in-law, and the in-law's husband.[5]

Readers who come searching for immediate insights and human color (such as father and son both being buried under a copal tree in Nos. 22 and 23) could do no better than to read some of the clusters first of all.

2. The Wills and What They Tell Us

THIS CENTRAL SECTION of the introductory study is dedicated to an analysis of the different parts of a testament as they are seen in the corpus here, following the order in which they appear in an actual document. In this way I attempt to give the reader a good grasp of the organization of the testaments and at the same time present an in-depth discussion of their contents. The overall structure of these mainly

[1] Vol. 1, pp. 59-60.

[2] A page in the front matter, "List of Testaments in Clusters," specifies and numbers each cluster, also giving the relationship of those involved. Nos. 3 and 4 are also probably a cluster, not to speak of another potential but unproven one, Nos. 26 and 27. The testator of No. 26 makes his executor his *consuegro* Francisco de la Cruz, and the testator of No. 27 is Francisco de la Cruz, but he says nothing that would confirm the connection. The situation is even more confusing because the two testaments have a Francisco de la Cruz as notary. Besides, Francisco de la Cruz is such a common name that it could possibly be another person altogether.

[3] Parent/child clusters are in Nos. 5–6 in the Toluca area and 22–23, 28–29, and 30–31 in Calimaya/Tepemaxalco. Nos. 35 and 36 also may constitute a parent/child cluster. Clusters in which other relatives are added to the parent and child are, in the Toluca area, Nos. 10–13, and in Calimaya/Tepemaxalco, 39–41, 47–49, and 85–87.

[4] Nos. 72, 78, 79.

[5] Nos. 10–13.

eighteenth-century wills of the Toluca Valley is very much like that of other indigenous testaments in New Spain from the sixteenth century forward; the major components and their order remain the same. New features and variety within the corpus are found in the contents of each part and in the forms of expression.

In discussing each consecutive part of a testament I will give some attention to how it corresponds to the general tradition of Nahuatl wills. Sometimes this amounts to comparing it with the Testaments of Culhuacan, the classic collection of the late sixteenth century. In this way we can begin to understand developments over the postconquest centuries as a whole, the evolution from Stage 2 on into Stage 3. But I am even more concerned to discuss variation and uniformity within the corpus itself. A major category of interest is how much or how little change is observed over the more than a hundred years between 1652, date of the first document, and 1763, date of the last but one. Even more central is to show some of the dimensions of the subregional variation that has emerged in the course of this project, the differences in each consecutive topic between the immediate Toluca area and Calimaya/Tepemaxalco. And where evidence exists, I will point out variation even within these two cultural subregions, at the tlaxilacalli level. Yet I do not lose sight of the extent to which both subregions were uniform, and the larger Toluca Valley, at least as far as these two regions exemplify it, possessed important commonalities.

Preamble

FROM THEIR FIRST inception in the mid-sixteenth century under the direction of mendicant philologists through their further evolution in the hands of Nahuatl notaries, wills in Nahuatl always began much like their Spanish counterparts, with a formulaic doctrinal statement varying little in the practice of any particular notary, though not entirely the same from one notary to the next, one settlement to the next, or across time. Starting in the sixteenth century, mention of the Trinity was extremely common, as well as invocation of the Virgin Mary to pray for the testator's soul. Other common material, not all of it always included in any particular example, was reference to the ill health of the body and the soundness of the mind, to the inescapability of death, to giving the soul to God (who should come to receive it) and the body to the earth of which it was made, often ending with a brief endorsement of the beliefs of the Roman Catholic church. In Stage 2 wills, rarely would the preamble contain mention of any saint other than the Virgin Mary.

In the Toluca corpus, all the Stage 2 formulas can be found in some text or other, but one soon notices that they are most fully represented in the oldest wills, or in especially conservative writers, or in outlying settlements. The Toluca wills as a whole move in the direction of a new style or styles.

Generally speaking, perhaps the easiest, quickest way to identify Stage 3 Nahuatl wills as opposed to those of Stage 2 is the presence at the very top of mention of the holy family, Jesus, Mary, and Joseph; in Stage 2 wills the holy family is lacking. Some general directive of church officials must have been at the root of the change, but it becomes a diagnostic trait. In the Toluca Valley corpus we do indeed find the holy family in a prominent role. They are missing in the first two documents, of 1652 and 1654, but are present from 1678 forward.

Both subareas were strongly affected by the trend, but a regional difference can be detected. Toluca seems, as so often, more conservative, more often putting the holy family after the Trinity than before it, and in a large number of cases only Jesus is named. In Calimaya/Tepemaxalco the names of the full holy family are at the very beginning of almost every testament; then they may be repeated after the Trinity, and sometimes for good measure after the whole preamble as well.

The preamble phrase *ma in mochihua amen*, "may it be done, amen" (the "may it be done" is of course a translation of "amen") is also probably a Stage 3 trait. It is entirely absent in the Testaments of Culhuacan. Just when it becomes common in Nahuatl wills generally is not presently well established. It is a standby of the Toluca Valley corpus, most often immediately after mention of the Trinity and sometimes at the end of the preamble as well. It is equally predominant in both subregions, though not universal.[6] In Calimaya/Tepemaxalco the phrase is from the beginning sometimes in

[6]The notary Sebastián Fabián of San Lucas Evangelista, for example, does not use it at all in his four testaments (Nos. 52–55).

Nahuatl only, without the "amen." In that form it is present in Calimaya/Tepemaxalco from 1654 (No. 42), but the three seventeenth-century wills from the Toluca area lack it, which may or may not be significant.

The three elements—the holy family, the Trinity, and "amen"—often stand as a sort of heading preceding the preamble proper, and this too seems a new feature since Stage 2. In Stage 2 wills the testator usually started by saying "in the name of" (*ica in itocatzin*, etc.) the Trinity, or expressed belief in it. These ways and similar ones (such as *icatzinco ninomachiotia*, "I take as my sign") are still seen in the Toluca corpus, above all in earlier documents or ones from certain outlying tlaxilacalli, but there is movement toward a new dominant phrase, that of praising the Trinity. The term used is *cenquizcayectenehua*, "to praise entirely, wholly, perfectly." Still missing in the earliest testaments, it becomes dominant in the Toluca area after 1700 and in Calimaya/Tepemaxalco by the 1690s.

Despite this commonality, regional nuances also assert themselves. Some tlaxilacalli of Calimaya/Tepemaxalco never adopted the praise formula at all (San Antonio de Padua, Santa María Nativitas, Santiago Apóstol Quaxochtenco). It was predominant in the Toluca area in a form that was grammatically standard, the reflexive used as passive (*mocenquizcayectenehua*), but we also notice a form (in almost a third of the cases in the whole corpus) not compatible with normal Nahuatl grammar, in which the active reflexive is combined with the passive ending (*mocenquizcayectenehualo*). In Calimaya/Tepemaxalco the nonstandard form at first glance seems greatly predominant, but a count for the whole double altepetl shows that the standard and nonstandard forms are about equal in frequency. Closer examination reveals that the nonstandard form was hugely predominant only in the central settlement cluster, in both the Calimaya and the Tepemaxalco halves, while it was hardly present in the outlying tlaxilacalli. One such tlaxilacalli, San Lucas Evangelista, in the early 18th century lacks the praise formula, but when it adopted it in the 1750s, it uniformly took a standard but reverential form (*mocenquizcayecteneuhtzinoa*); in neighboring Santa María de la Asunción that very same form was the only one used, and may have started earlier.

Coming to the main body of the preamble, we find that an almost universal feature, continuing from earlier wills, is mention of the soul. It has been believed that in many regions the Spanish loanword *-anima(ntzin)*, "one's soul," gradually displaced the accompanying Nahuatl equivalent term *-yolia*, "spirit," by Stage 3, but if so that surely had not happened in the Toluca Valley. In the great majority of cases in both subregions, from first to last, both terms are still seen side by side within the preamble.

But otherwise, a large regional divide expresses itself in the body of the preamble. In both Toluca proper and Calimaya/Tepemaxalco the heading is followed by identification of the testator and the sociopolitical entity, which will be dealt with below. In Calimaya/Tepemaxalco there is a movement toward elaboration in what follows, especially involving saints, whereas in the Toluca area the rest of the preamble is reduced or even nonexistent.

If we look back to the Testaments of Culhuacan, whose preambles were not especially elaborate for the time, after the Trinity and self-identification they usually (with some variation and in various orders) move on to invoke the Virgin Mary as intercessor, speak of the state of mind and body, place the soul in the hands of God, and issue an abbreviated credo. The immediate Toluca area in this corpus has preserved the Trinity in the heading, and often added the holy family and amen, but severely curtailed the rest. The predominant style is simply to place the soul in the hands of God, omitting everything else, including even the invocation of Mary. Many wills lack even this much, going straight to the ringing of bells, the shroud, etc., so that in a way there is only a heading and no preamble at all. No saints are ever invoked in the preambles of Toluca, in which aspect the Stage 2 style is preserved.

Calimaya/Tepemaxalco was moving in the opposite direction. It too was shedding such things as mention of the state of mind and body, and the credo, but it retained not only giving the soul to God but also the invocation of Mary to pray for the soul, and it added many helpers in that enterprise. Often included were whole collections of named saints, at least some of whom were important in Calimaya/Tepemaxalco specifically; the recital might start with the patrons San Pedro and San Pablo, name as many as three or four more saints, then perhaps go on to the guardian angel and a general mention of "all the male and female saints" in heaven, sometimes ending with a picture of celestial bliss and praise of the deity.[1]

This style was not there uniformly from the beginning; the earliest wills from Calimaya/Tepemaxalco lack it, being more like those of the Toluca area. In the central cluster, it picks up starting in the 1690s and gathers strength in the early eighteenth century, reaching a mature form perhaps in the 1730s. But like some other phenomena, it concentrates in the central settlement, in both halves, whereas it is less well developed in the outlying tlaxilacalli. Despite a quite full example or two, San Lucas and Santa María de la Asunción mainly invoke only the Virgin Mary. Santa María Nativitas (ironically) does not even invoke the Virgin.

We will see that many of the largest wills recording the most property were issued by male testators, and that male names showed greater variety than those of females, but it could not be said that preambles of male testators are overall more elaborate. The degree of elaboration seems to have varied with the region, the notary, and probably the notary's fee, but the most elaborate preambles seen in the corpus are in a series of testaments of women prepared by Hipólito de los Santos of Calimaya in the 1750s and 1760s.

Personal names

MOVING FROM the formulas to other elements of the preamble, we find that a universal item, usually placed soon after the heading, is the testator's self-identification, achieved simply by stating his or her name (sometimes accompanied by information on marital status, which I will discuss just below). As is well known by now in the philology of ethnohistory, names are an essential and powerful tool for studying the status and connections of a given person (testator or not), and also of his/her family and other individuals within the setting of a certain community. Thus I will take this opportunity to discuss naming patterns in the present corpus.

The great majority of personal names in the corpus consist of only two elements, the first name and then what I call not a surname but a second name, for in most cases it is not handed on to the next generation; a given nuclear family will usually have a miscellany of different second names. This is a general characteristic of the Nahuas from the early sixteenth century forward, and it is very well reflected in the present corpus, although the higher a family group's status, the more it was inclined to preserve the same second name across generations. First names were not markedly different by status; it is generally speaking the second name and its use that tells us so much.

The naming system is largely as we already expect for this time.[2] Indigenous names are in effect a thing of the past, and the most common appellations consist of two names of a saint or first names, such as Gregorio Juan or Lucía María. The status implications of such a name are the lowest of all in the repertoire, but can be raised by the addition of "de San," as happens a few times in the corpus (for example with Esteban de San Juan [No. 16], who when young might have been known as simple Esteban Juan).[3]

In addition to sharing the double first names, both males and females can have religious second names not derived from saints, such as de la Encarnación, de la Trinidad, de los Santos, and de los Angeles. The general tradition in central Mexico was that such names connoted a somewhat higher status, but when we look at all the testators in the present corpus it is not clear that they actually separated those so named from the mass, with the exception of de la Cruz, which I will comment on a bit later. We see an abbreviation of some such names through omission of "de" and the article; thus testator No. 63 is Josefa Trinidad, not Josefa de la Trinidad as the name should be by its origin. Earlier in time this truncation would have reduced the status implications, but in the present corpus, after such names had been in use for generations, that may no longer have been a consideration.

In another type of name both elements are taken whole from some famous source: Baltasar de los Reyes from one of the Magi; Domingo Ramos, a play on Palm Sunday; Tomás de Aquino after the famous saint. Women too could have such names (such as Catarina de Sena), but none seem to appear

[1]See testament No. 70 written by Hipólito de los Santos as a full example, discussed in the document introduction there. There was a certain emphasis on archangels, with frequent mention of San Miguel, San Rafael, and San Gabriel.

[2]See Lockhart 1992, pp. 121–30.

[3]The important name Santiago (discussed further below) is a frozen example of this phenomenon, with the "San(t)" and the saint's name amalgamated, so that it always requires "de" and by its structure alone has some connotations of prestige, aside from its very specific history.

in the present corpus.[1] Names of this kind have a higher tone than double first names, but they do not normally become the source of a lineage name.[2]

In many parts of central Mexico by the time of our corpus or before, second names which were established Spanish surnames were the most prestigious name type in the indigenous world. There were two levels, first patronymics and other originally plebeian names, like Hernández or García, and second, for the top level, names with prestige among Spaniards, like Guzmán or Mendoza. This aspect of the naming system exists in our corpus, but is not as well developed as we might expect. The highest-ranking among the testators and other people in the wills do not uniformly have Spanish second names. We can discern Estrada, an excellent Spanish surname, in the governorship of Calimaya, and similar names surface from time to time (Guzmán in an early example, Tapia, Vicuña, Mendoza, Villanueva, Alcántara).[3] Spanish surnames at a lower level are also seen as appellations of indigenous people of above average rank (Hernández, González, García, Mejía, Jiménez, Sánchez). But almost all of the wealthiest and highest-ranking testators bear names of the types mentioned before, belonging to the system first devised for indigenous people specifically and evolving over centuries. I am not presently equipped to analyze this phenomenon. For whatever reason, second names that in many parts of the Valley of Mexico would have implied intermediate rank attained the highest level in the Toluca area and Calimaya/Tepemaxalco.

The higher a family's wealth and status, the more it would retain the same name across generations, generally more with males, although full consistency is lacking. Women do have better chances of receiving a lineage name in high-status families. The peak of this trend is reached with the immensely wealthy former governor don Juan de la Cruz (No. 39), who passes his second name on to all of his many children, female as well as male.[4] In cases where the family has not yet quite reached the top, some of the children may have one of the parents' second names, while others do not. At a lower level, some lineage continuity is expressed at times by reversing the names of parent and child for both genders, or by retaining the female's more humble second name for female children.[5]

Analyzing gender differences more broadly, it can be said that men's names are much more varied; the difference is heightened by men's receiving the honorific title "don" along with the higher local offices. Normally, though not invariably, the title is retained for the rest of the person's life.[6] The don transforms even the humblest name, such as Francisco Pedro. The corresponding title for women, "doña," is extremely rare and is never attributed to a female testator, not even to María Micaela, *principala* and *cacique*. It shows up only in early testaments, mainly with the wives of governors, the best example being the de la Cruz family of Tepemaxalco.[7]

The name of this gubernatorial family leads us to another matter, the high concentration of the names de la Cruz and Santiago among prominent people in both Toluca proper and Calimaya/Tepemaxalco.

[1]The name Mateo Juárez is of this type; though I do not know the model, the majority of indigenous people named Juárez across a wide range of times and regions had the first name Mateo. See Lockhart 1992, p. 512, n. 139.

[2]That holds true in the corpus as a whole, yet it does seem that the second element of some such names was beginning to be handed on in families separately at times, especially de los Reyes and Ramos. Of those with the second name Juárez, only two were Mateo, and the other three had different first names.

[3]The second name Serrano, sometimes as an additional second name, so to speak, was associated with governing families in Calimaya/Tepemaxalco. Possibly it came directly from Spanish, where it would be a quite good surname. But possibly it derived from a famous Nahuatl interpreter of the Toluca Valley in the late sixteenth century, a Juan Serrano del Valle whose name seems to have been concocted especially for him (see Lockhart 1991, pp. 219–20).

[4]Another case is María Ana de Morales (No. 9), with two daughters with the same second name.

[5]See Mauricia Josefa and don Francisco Pedro (Nos. 37 and 38), whose daughters all have Josefa and sons all Francisco as second names, and also the case of Francisco de la Cruz (No. 27), whose wife is Pascuala María, with the daughters María Salomé and María Magdalena.

[6]The corpus does not deliver absolute proof, but it appears that no one in our areas bore the don before holding high office.

[7]The testament of María Micaela is No. 43. Only two references to doñas are from the Toluca area, both in the testament of Elena de la Cruz (No. 10); the other cases are from Calimaya/Tepemaxalco and are to be found in the following testaments: don Juan de la Cruz (No. 39, 1691), three doñas, all wives of governors; María Salomé (No. 42, 1654), two doñas, the executor and a witness; Agustín de la Cruz (No. 72, 1755), casual reference to a property-owning doña who may not be indigenous.

These two names were spread all over central Mexico by the beginning of Stage 3 and probably before; for the most part they connoted an intermediary level between common double first names below and Spanish names above. However, in the Toluca Valley in our time they tend to indicate high social status, often related to the highest public offices of governor, alcalde, and fiscal (as well as others, and especially notary). The names played a similar role in both subareas, except that de la Cruz was much stronger in Calimaya/Tepemaxalco, numerically and in the proportion of high offices, according to a provisional count I have made. Another difference was that by my count only 2 women bore the name de la Cruz in the Toluca area as opposed to 16 in Calimaya/Tepemaxalco, showing that the name was being used much more for lineage purposes in the latter area.[8]

To conclude, it can be said that except for a larger or smaller emphasis on de la Cruz, no general differences emerge between the Toluca area and Calimaya/Tepemaxalco. One may see hints of a particular name becoming strong in a particular tlaxilacalli; for example it appears that an officeholding clan with the name Juan held forth in Santa María Nativitas (see No. 93). There is also little change across time, though further research may show that there was a certain evolution in the style of first names.

Marital status

RIGHT AFTER THE testator's name, early in the preamble, comes a slot for the testator's marital status, but it is by no means always filled. In a provisional count less than a third of the testators give marital information at this point, though sometimes it emerges elsewhere in the will. Intensive investigation could doubtless determine the exact or probable status of the testator in a great many more cases, and I have often made deductions or speculations about the matter in the individual document introductions. Women and men have a fully symmetrical position here, giving the same kind of information with about the same frequency and using categories which are direct counterparts of each other. No major subregional differences have been detected in this matter.

The largest category is for married people, and indeed it is clear enough that the vast majority of indigenous people of both genders married. The most common formula is "my wife's name is . . ." or "my husband's name is . . ."[9] The words used after 1700, *-namic(tzin)* for "husband" and*-cihuahuatzin* or *-cihuauh* for "wife," showing gender differentiation, are to my present knowledge special to this time and region, and I will discuss them in more detail as part of a treatment of kinship terms further below.

Widows and widowers, when they indicate their status, usually use the Spanish loanwords *viuda* and *viudo*, sometimes specifying the deceased partner's name (*nonamictzin catca, nocihuahuatzin catca*). Occasionally the latter expression alone gives the information, without using *viuda/viudo*. The primary categories used are the ones we would expect, for the loanwords had generally replaced the indigenous counterparts (*icnocihuatl* and *icnooquichtli*) even in advance of Stage 3 (the indigenous terms are still used in the Testaments of Culhuacan, however).

The corpus contains one single declared case of a woman never married, designated not by the usual loanword *soltera* but as an *ichpocatl* (No. 43, 1762). The phenomenon was rare enough that in all likelihood she was in truth the only unmarried woman testator. No male declares himself a *soltero*, "bachelor," and there may well have been none (though the word is used once for an heir, in No. 39, 1691).

Unit names

AFTER IDENTIFYING THE testator, Nahuatl wills from all times and places normally go on to identify the testator's sociopolitical unit: the altepetl, the tlaxilacalli, or both. The Toluca area almost always names the tlaxilacalli alone, apparently taking the overarching altepetl as a given, as was often the case in the Nahua tradition when the altepetl was large and complex (the Testaments of Culhuacan are of this type). Only two documents mention Toluca as a point of reference; an early one (No. 1, 1671) calls Toluca both *altepetl* and *ciudad*, "city," which was its rank by that time within the Spanish system. A later testament (No. 14, 1732) from San Cristóbal calls that unit a dependency of the ciudad of Toluca. The most interesting feature is that San Cristóbal, though sometimes considered to be one of the

[8]No women at all bore the name Santiago in either subarea, possibly because it was by origin a male saint's name.

[9]In the Toluca area, men sometimes (3 cases) say "married to . . ." (*casado ica*) rather than naming the category for wife. Women do not do the same in the corpus.

"barrios" of Toluca, is here itself called an altepetl. Without more context such as that available for Calimaya/Tepemaxalco, it would be hard to give an interpretation for this instance.

The term *barrio* fails to appear in any of the testaments from the Toluca area, depriving us of a possible way of distinguishing the supposed "barrios" from the outlying tlaxilacalli. The great majority of all the Tolucan wills give the tlaxilacalli and nothing else, using the indigenous word.

In Calimaya/Tepemaxalco we find a much more differentiated situation, with distinctions of various kinds between the central cluster (in both halves) and the outlying tlaxilacalli. In the central settlement the name of the altepetl (San Pedro Calimaya or San Pablo Tepemaxalco, with some cases of apparent confusion) is usually, though not without exception, specified in addition to the tlaxilacalli. Of all the testaments from outlying tlaxilacalli, the name of the overarching altepetl is given in identification only once (No. 58, Santa María de la Asunción, 1759).

The loanword *barrio*, absent in the Toluca area, does appear in Calimaya/Tepemaxalco, but it is used only in reference to tlaxilacalli in the central cluster. Sometimes it appears instead of *tlaxilacalli*, sometimes in addition. The two may not be pure equivalents. The outlying tlaxilacalli sometimes use the native term, but they never use *barrio*. Thus for entities in the central cluster *tlaxilacalli* may retain its traditional sense, while *barrio* would say in addition that they are in that cluster and not outlying. Here is the distinction sought in the Toluca area and not found.

The outlying entities seem to be in some sense asserting independence from the larger altepetl and the central cluster. As we have just seen, they usually avoid mention of the larger altepetl, and all those represented in the corpus call themselves altepetl at some point (and sometimes tlaxilacalli in the same breath). San Lucas does not mind simply calling itself a tlaxilacalli in the traditional manner much of the time, but Santa María de la Asunción and Santa María Nativitas avoid the word completely and generally use only the proper name of the unit as identification.

It is possible that *altepetl* as used in the corpus is affected by the Spanish word *pueblo*, for the Spaniards had long called any identifiable indigenous settlement a pueblo whether it was part of a larger entity or not. The connection becomes quite apparent when the word is used meaning the part of an entity where most of the people live, not in the traditional Nahuatl meaning, which embraced the entire entity. (Instances are in Nos. 57, 58, 61, and 68.) Nevertheless, *pueblo* is never seen as a loanword in the corpus, though it is known to occur in some Stage 3 Nahuatl documents of other regions.

Funeral arrangements

THE WILLS IN THE CORPUS contain no term such as "funeral," although it could be that the occasionally seen loanword *entierro*, literally "burial," could be given a broader interpretation. Here I discuss all the dispositions directly related to the testator's death, not only the mass and burial, but offerings of various kinds. This material, a universal of the Nahuatl testament tradition, normally comes early in the document in the Toluca Valley corpus, either incorporated into the preamble or as individual items immediately following; offerings to cofradías are sometimes put near the end.

Mass. The great majority of testators in both subregions (85 of the 98) request a mass to help the soul. It is of interest that though in the preamble, when the testator places the soul in the hands of God, the predominant phrase is *-yolia -anima(ntzin)*, "spirit and soul," in this position the loanword for "soul" stands alone more often than not (a trend which has been often observed in testaments of the late period in other regions, but for testaments as a whole and not just a certain section).

It may be that a mass was implied even by some of those who did not specifically request one. In both subregions testaments issued in the late seventeenth century often lack any mention of a mass; yet a mass had been at the core of the reason for making wills since their inception among the Nahuas. The corpus documents one case in which a person not asking for a mass received one nevertheless.[1] In other cases poverty seems to be the reason for the absence, and there may in reality have been no mass. In one tlaxilacalli, San Antonio de Padua in Calimaya, no mass is requested, only responsory prayers; with just three examples, it is hard to say whether the reason is the testators' poverty, which they declare, or some tlaxilacalli policy.

[1]Andrés Nicolás (No. 1), 1671.

Relatives are often made responsible for seeing that the mass is performed, and also for looking after the burial and all the rest. The duty goes especially to the main heirs in return for what they have received, or in their absence to the spouse, or less frequently a parent or a collateral relative.[2] Some such requests are made specifically because of the testator's poverty, but most do not seem to carry that implication. Usually no more than one mass is requested, with only three exceptions, all from Tepemaxalco, all early, and all involving wealthy testators.[3] In the wills of some times and places, one frequently sees the sale of land to pay for a mass; in this corpus it is rare, with only one full-scale example,[4] though sometimes magueyes, clothing, and animals are to be sold for the purpose, or retrieved debts to be used the same way.

In all the above the Toluca area and Calimaya/Tepemaxalco represent a unit, but in one respect they part ways. Tolucan wills often speak of a high mass or a high mass of requiem and never mention a responsory prayer; wills from the other subregion mention only masses with responsory prayer, never a mass of requiem. I am at present not entirely sure whether this difference is in language only or represents a difference of actual practice in the two parishes.[5]

Shroud. Almost half the testaments in the corpus include specific mention of a shroud. Proportionately more are from the Toluca area than from Calimaya/Tepemaxalco. The date seems unrelated to the frequency. A hint of evolution across time is that two early wills, one from each area, ask for burial in humble ordinary clothing, something rarely seen later.[6] Another such hint is the increasing use of the Spanish loanword for shroud.[7]

In the Toluca area, shrouds are mentioned more in certain tlaxilacalli than others, with some concentration on San Juan Bautista, San Pedro Tototepec, and San Miguel Aticpac. A relation between the shroud and wealth is seen in the fact that its mention tends to correspond with the request for the bells to be rung. Less than a fourth of the requests are by women. Some women simply ask for a shroud, usually with the rope of San Francisco; two specify the habit of the Virgin of Carmen, and one requests the habit of the Virgin of Merced. Men request either a generic shroud with the rope of San Francisco or the actual Franciscan habit, but in three cases from San Juan Bautista and one from Santa María de los Angeles Huitzillan, they ask for the habit of Carmen like the women (in the last case accompanied by the rope of San Diego; the only other instance of a rope of San Diego is a man from Santa Ana).

In Calimaya/Tepemaxalco, because of the large concentration of women testators in the central cluster and especially in the Calimaya half, the ratio of women to men is reversed. Here, and more according to expectations, only women, mainly from Calimaya, request the habit of the Virgin of Carmen. Among men the habit of San Francisco is very common, accompanied by its rope. A startling and revealing fact is that all of those in Calimaya/Tepemaxalco, male or female, in either altepetl, who request a habit as a shroud are located in the central cluster, with none at all in any of the outlying tlaxilacalli.

The evolution of the term used to designate the habit is the opposite of that with the shroud; here

[2]In two tlaxilacalli, San Bartolomé Tlatelolco in the Toluca area (Nos. 22–24), and San Lucas in Tepemaxalco (Nos. 47–55, with one exception), the priest is mentioned in this connection, as helping the testator, doing a favor, etc., but the reference in these cases is clearly to the performance of the mass and not to arranging and paying for it.

[3]Don Juan de la Cruz (No. 39), 1691; Polonia María (No. 41), 1710; María Salomé (No. 42), 1654.

[4]No. 74, María Clara, Pasiontitlan (Calimaya), 1763. Actually the land is to be sold for both burial and mass. In No. 16, dated 1652, land is to be sold "to be used for me," which may amount to the same thing; the order was canceled, however.

[5]I had wondered if a mass with responsory prayer was in fact equivalent to a high mass, but two examples refer specifically to a high mass accompanied by responsory prayer: María Salomé (No. 42), 1654, and Rosa Francisca (No. 84), 1760.

[6]Esteban de San Juan (No. 16), Toluca area, 1652, in his cloak ("notilma"), and Antonio de la Cruz (No. 88), Calimaya/Tepemaxalco, 1678, in his "rags" ("notzotzoma"), which may well mean his ordinary clothing.

[7]In the large majority of cases native vocabulary based on the verb *quimiloa*, "to wrap," is used, but in the Toluca area from 1735 to 1741 5 wills speak of *nomortaja*, "my shroud," using the Spanish loanword. In Calimaya/Tepemaxalco we find 12 examples, two of them from the 1730s and all the rest from the period 1758–1763, all in the central cluster, by four notaries, with Hipólito de los Santos alone responsible for 8 of the 12. No example appears in any of the outlying tlaxilacalli of Calimaya/Tepemaxalco.

the loanword gives way to an indigenous term.[1]

Burial. As one would expect, references to the burial of the testator are standard in the whole corpus. By my count only 5 testators in Toluca fail to mention the burial place, whereas the corresponding number in Calimaya/Tepemaxalco is 30. But this gives a false impression, for several outlying tlaxilacalli there leave out the burial place entirely, apparently by policy and custom.[2] In the central cluster of Calimaya/Tepemaxalco the situation is much as in Toluca proper. The word for the grave site is the loan *sepultura* in both regions, but though "opening" the grave (using the verb *tlapoa*) is a commonplace in Calimaya/Tepemexalco, the phrase is never used in the Toluca area.

Only in the Toluca area do we find references to burial in the great church, apparently the Franciscan church on the main square of the town, which was the senior establishment in the whole valley. In both subregions three or four times as many people request burial inside the church as ask to be buried outside in the churchyard. It appears that nearly half of the whole group was buried in the church, with that possibility existing also for cases of not mentioning the burial place, especially in tlaxilacalli which never did so. One conclusion is that the group of testators contains many people of means, by indigenous standards. It would seem to follow that the relatively small minority buried in the churchyard would have been poorer, but some notably wealthy people requested burial outside, so the matter remains in doubt.[3]

A large proportion of all requesting burial inside the church went on to request a specific site, oriented to some saint's image or chapel. In Toluca far the most popular saint for this purpose was San Francisco.[4] Next most popular were Jesús Nazareno and the Christ of the Santa Vera Cruz. Only two burials were at places devoted to the Virgin.

In Calimaya/Tepemaxalco many testators wish to be buried close to an image of the Virgin or of a female saint (Santa María de la Asunción, Nuestra Señora de la Candelaria, Nuestra Señora de Guadalupe, Santa María Magdalena). About as many request burial close to a male saint, with San Antonio the most popular. The emphasis on San Francisco seen in Toluca is lacking; he attracts only one burial. All the requests for burial close to an image are from the central cluster except for one (No. 46, from San Lucas in 1681).

One naturally wonders to what extent testators wished to be buried next to a saint of their own gender. The situation in this respect is somewhat equivocal (when there was a family tradition, gender had to be left unconsidered), but some things can be said. In the Toluca area, burial next to a male saint (including Jesus in this category) was the trend, and this outweighed any gender preference. Of the 15 requests for special sites in Toluca proper, only 2 mention female saints. Of the female testators relevant here, only one chose burial close to a female saint. With the males the ratio was heavily in favor of male saints.

In Calimaya/Tepemaxalco things were a bit different. Of the 14 such requests (not less than Toluca proportionately if we consider that essentially only the central cluster comes into question), only a third of the men were buried close to female saints, and a majority of the women were, so that in both cases there was a gender correspondence for the majority, but clearly no rigid rule on the matter existed.

In the whole corpus 6 testators (4 of them in the immediate Toluca area) say that they wish to be buried next to a family member. Most such requests involve parents or a husband. It is here that human interest reaches a peak, especially because we often

[1]The loanword *habito* ceded to the indigenous word *-tlaquentzin*, "one's garment, garb." The phenomenon also has a strong regional dimension. The loanword was used in the Toluca area in the early examples (1671 and 1717); then during the 1730s the indigenous word became dominant (5 examples to 3), and the three examples after that are all indigenous. In Calimaya/ Tepemaxalco the same thing happened, but earlier and more overwhelmingly; a single example (1654) has the loanword, and all the others, starting in 1691, have the indigenous term.

[2]The burial place is unmentioned in the 13 wills of Santa María de la Asunción, in the 3 of San Antonio de Padua, in the 6 of Santa María Nativitas, and in 3 of 4 in Santiago Apóstol Quaxochtenco (the fourth is dubious). Note that here Santa María de la Asunción departs from the practice of San Lucas Evangelista, which it often resembles.

[3]There is also the unresolved question of whether some people buried near doors were on the inside or the outside.

[4]I leave to future research the task of unraveling the terminology for these burials that is used in the wills. They speak of the Tercera Orden (of San Francisco) at the great church, of a chapel of San Francisco, and a shrine (*hermita*) of San Francisco at the church. It is possible that all of these are the same thing. It is also not entirely clear what may have been inside the great church and what an independent building standing outside.

learn the true circumstances piecemeal. In No. 5 Luis Francisco asks for burial at the great church behind the holy cross, where his father lies buried; in No. 6 Isabel María also asks to be buried behind the holy cross, not saying what we gradually gather, that her husband and her recently deceased son both lie there already. Finally we grasp that Isabel is showing a strong family solidarity. Another attractive episode (already mentioned above, p. 8) features a father and son being buried together under a copal tree (Nos. 22 and 23).

The Jerusalem fund. No clear chronological trends emerge in the things we have just been discussing, although it may be that a specific mention of the burial was more nearly obligatory earlier than it was later. The next item to which I turn shows both chronological and regional variation. At some point church officials in New Spain began urging or requiring testators to contribute to a fund to support Christianity in Jerusalem. Early in its history this fund had become a royal sinecure, and by the time we are studying, the money probably stayed somewhere within the church organization of New Spain. Contributions to Jerusalem are not ordinarily seen in Stage 2 wills (they are lacking in the Testaments of Culhuacan), but they become a prominent feature of Stage 3 wills in many places. In our corpus, Jerusalem is lacking in both subregions from the wills issued from 1652 through 1678, but appears prominently in Tepemaxalco in the 1690s. After 1700 it is a standard feature of wills in both subareas; 59 testaments of the total 98 mention it.

Yet a strong regional distinction enters in. In the Toluca area the contribution is uniformly half a real, in Calimaya/Tepemaxalco twice that, a full real, with equal uniformity. The difference must go back to local ecclesiastical directives but still may have sociocultural meaning. One possible reason for the difference is that the indigenous population of Calimaya/Tepemaxalco may have been wealthier than that of the immediate Toluca area. No one in the whole area ever overpaid the standard contribution, with the exception of the unusually wealthy and ostentatious don Juan de la Cruz of Tepemaxalco (No. 39, 1691), who quadrupled it.

Although the Jerusalem fund seems to have been intended as obligatory after it was instituted, it does not, as we have seen, appear in each and every testament even after 1700. Since money is involved, the absence of mention in certain cases probably means that the contribution actually was not given. Some such cases seem to correspond to the testator's poverty. And not only certain individuals omitted the Jerusalem fund, it was left out in whole tlaxilacalli of Calimaya/Tepemaxalco; we do not see a word about it in the testaments from the Tepemaxalco tlaxilacalli of San Lucas, and also not in the three testaments from the immediately adjacent Calimaya tlaxilacalli of San Antonio.

Bells. Here we have a major feature of the funeral complex that is manifested in only one of the two subregions, the immediate Toluca area. No less than 23 of the 38 testators of the Toluca area ask for bells to be rung at their death, whereas the word "bell" never occurs in a single testament of Calimaya/ Tepemaxalco.[5] Did the Calimaya area not have bells? Or is it possible that they were rung but not mentioned in testaments? That hardly seems likely in view of the substantial contributions given to ring them. In any event, in Toluca proper the practice had deep roots, extending from the earliest will in 1652 to the latest ones of the 1750s. A total of 9 women and 14 men had the bells rung, sometimes giving no further details, sometimes mentioning their own tlaxilacalli specifically, but in most cases asking for the bells to ring in at least two tlaxilacalli in addition to the one of residence. The most popular places for bell ringing were San Sebastián, San Juan Bautista, Santa María de los Angeles Huitzillan, San Diego, San Bartolomé Tlatelolco, and Santa Clara Cozcatlan; the "great church" is not mentioned in this connection.[6] The fee or donation was half a real for each church at which the bells were rung. Testators who made wills for funeral purposes only and who listed no assets did not have the bells rung; doing so correlates with the possession of property and monetary resources.

[5]In 10 cases the word used in the Toluca area is *miccatepoztli*, literally "dead-person iron," in 7 cases the simpler variant *tepoztli*, "iron," and in 6 cases the loanword *campana*. A temporal or other trend is not immediately apparent, other than that *campana* is used in all three testaments from San Bartolomé Tlatelolco, and the loanword is not seen in the corpus after the 1730s.

[6]Further analysis of the combinations could probably help to establish affinities between tlaxilacalli and contribute to the question of whether there is really any difference between the "barrios" and the other tlaxilacalli, or if they are all in the proper category.

Cofradías. It is sometimes said that cofradías (lay sodalities) were important in the funerals of indigenous people, arranging or financing masses and burials for their members. That may be true for other times and regions, but not for the two subregions of the present corpus in the time represented. Cofradías are mentioned in the wills primarily in order to give offerings to them. Only three testators expect benefits such as a mass and burial from a cofradía. A cofradía of the Sangre de Cristo in Quauhtitlan has two adherents, both females: one in the Toluca area (No. 2, 1733), the other in Calimaya in the central cluster (No. 80, 1739). The first seems in necessity and in any case does not count on the cofradía for everything, asking a grandchild to help; the second is well off and seems to have full expectations of receiving benefits. In 1678 a man in an outlying tlaxilacalli of Calimaya/Tepemaxalco (No. 88) expects an unnamed cofradía to help him with the funeral; he seems to be in economic difficulties. The examples are too few to extrapolate trends from them, except that cofradías are not a major source of support for death ceremonies in the corpus.

In surveying the corpus one soon notices that nearly all the donations to cofradías are in the Toluca area. Even there they are not seen in the majority of wills, far less than bell ringing. Counting the instances presents some problems because sometimes only a saint is named, or in the case of the Toluca hospital the donation could be directly to the hospital rather than to the cofradía based in it (though in one case the cofradía is specifically mentioned). Using my best judgment, I find 13 instances of donations in Toluca proper, only four of them by women, who tend to be wealthy, in one case (No. 10) spectacularly so. The only explanation at hand is that male testators often had more resources for offerings. The offering to each cofradía may be a maguey or two, or half a real or a real, with a very few cases of greater generosity by both genders. Bernardino de Santiago (No. 26) offers an egg-laying hen. Santísimo Sacramento and Animas stand out among the cofradías, but they are numerous.[1]

Calimaya/Tepemaxalco presents only three testators (2 male, 1 female) with donations to a cofradía, all in the central settlement. The offerings are of the usual kind, and a cofradía of San Antonio stands out as common to all three. The puzzle is that there are so very few instances in 60 documents from the double altepetl. Calimaya/Tepemaxalco probably lacked a hospital like the one in Toluca, but we cannot believe that it lacked cofradías. Some of the outlying tlaxilacalli had a mayordomo of a cofradía as an important official, and a cofradía in San Antonio de Padua even employed a notary. Nevertheless, here is another striking example of cultural differentiation between the two subregions.

One wonders if the variation can be understood as a chronological trend, but even the Calimaya/Tepemaxalco wills which are contemporary with the bulk of the Toluca examples have only one donation. The difference, then, appears more regional than temporal, with Calimaya/Tepemaxalco simply not attuned to cofradía donations.

It is possible that when testators wished to be buried close to a certain image or altar, they were in effect declaring an allegiance to that saint's cofradía. In one case that is made explicit (No. 39, with San Antonio), but sufficient evidence is lacking otherwise.

Undocumented aspects. Not all the ceremonies and expenses surrounding death got recorded in the wills. Some we can glimpse from occasional mentions. A few seventeenth-century wills refer to donations or payments to the singers; this feature is widely seen in other times and regions, and it may not have stopped as an actual practice, but it ceased to be recorded in wills in the corpus after 1700.[2] A few times a monetary donation for the grave site is mentioned; it was likely paid in many other cases as well.[3] And of course it is well known that feasting accompanied funerals in the indigenous central Mexican tradition as in many others worldwide. An unusual memorandum by a testator's nephew (No. 94) shows not only the cost of a mass and candles but large expenses for food and drink. It also shows that the nephew continued to have additional masses and responsory prayers performed over a period of years, though the testator's will had not specifically

[1]They include Sangre de Cristo, Santísima Cruz, Santo Monumento, some manifestations of Mary, San Francisco, San Diego, and several other saints, as well as the hospital.

[2]No. 16, Toluca area, 1652 (*cuicanime*); No. 39, Tepemaxalco, 1691 (*cantores*).

[3]See for example No. 19 (Toluca area, 1737), which speaks of buying the grave, and No. 88 (Santa María Nativitas, 1678), where an offering of 1 real is made.

requested them (other than asking to be remembered). Something similar may have applied in many other cases, especially with wealthy testators.

Kinship terms, the order of heirs, and inheritance patterns

STILL FOLLOWING the structure of the testament, after the funeral arrangements the reader will see substantive bequests mainly to close relatives and above all to children when there are any. Before entering into that realm we need to understand some of the subtleties of the use of kinship terminology, which does not correlate closely with any particular part of the will. I began an analysis of this vast and complex topic in my doctoral dissertation and plan to develop it fully in a future monograph; here I intend only to present a sketch that will help with the reader's comprehension of the corpus.

Kinship terms seem uniform in the two subareas of Toluca and Calimaya/Tepemaxalco, and they essentially conform to expectations for Stage 3, with loanwords used for same-generation kin including in-laws, and also for collateral relatives in the preceding and following generations, while native terms are retained for relatives of other generations in the direct line. Perhaps this statement is not graphic enough for some readers. More tangibly, the standard terms in the corpus are *-hermano*, "brother"; *-hermana*, "sister";[4] *-primo hermano*, "first cousin, male"; *-prima hermana*, "first cousin, female"; *-cuñado*, "brother-in-law"; *-cuñada*, "sister-in-law";[5] *-sobrino*, "nephew"; *-sobrina*, "niece"; *-tio*, "uncle"; *-tia*, "aunt." Father, mother, and grandchild are as in Nahuatl traditionally, *-tatzin*, *-nantzin*, and *-xhuiuh*.[6]

The terms for children and spouses retain indigenous vocabulary, but represent some new de–velopments in comparison to earlier generations. Traditionally, as can be seen in the Testaments of Culhuacan, children were not differentiated by gender when still small, being generally called by the term *-pil* (usually in the reverential, *-piltzin*, to avoid a monosyllabic word), *-pilhuan* in the plural. Once they grew up, gender-specific terminology could be used, although it was not always applied in fact: *-telpoch* (the unpossessed form means "young man") for a son and *-chpoch* (the unpossessed form means "young woman") for a daughter. This system can still be seen at work in the Toluca corpus, but by the eighteenth century some changes had appeared and operate in many if not most of the documents where children are mentioned. Although not universal, they betray important influences on the language.

Now some testators mark the gender distinction even with small children by using *-telpochton*, "little son," and *-chpochton*, "little daughter."[7] A related but somewhat different tendency appears to be even more widespread. The traditional nongendered term, *-piltzin*, is used for the son and the gendered *-chpoch* for the daughter.[8] This change parallels one taking place with the terminology for spouses that I will discuss below. Both of them seem to point to Spanish gender distinctions reaching into areas of Nahuatl kinship terminology that had previously not been affected.[9]

---

[4]The traditional term *-teiccauh*, for the relationship between an older male brother/cousin and a younger sibling/cousin of either gender, occurs as an undercurrent in Nos. 7, 27, 62, 88, none from after the 1740s.

[5]The term *–huepol*, one's same-generation in-law of the opposite gender, occurs once, in No. 10, dated 1711.

[6]Parents-in-law and children-in-law are also called by the traditional indigenous terms: *-monta*, "father-in-law"; *-monnan*, "mother-in-law"; *-mon*, "son-in-law"; *-cihuamon*, "daughter-in-law."

[7]Nos. 25, 1728, and 27, 1735, from the Toluca area. One or the other term is found in many more testaments.

[8]Examples in No. 38 (1737) in the Toluca area, and in the Calimaya/Tepemaxalco area Nos. 54 (1759), 56 (1692), 74 (1763), and 94 (1703). These examples do not use diminutives, so one could get the impression that this mode is used only for grown children, but in No. 45 (1695) it is used for children specifically called small. Many more examples are from the Calimaya/Tepemaxalco area than from Toluca, but my impression remains that the two subareas are basically quite uniform; I will investigate possible subregional variation at a future date. Notice that two of the examples are from the 1690s. I believe that all the new developments had been evolving through the second half of the seventeenth century; another way to view the data, however, would be that it reinforces my perception that the 1690s virtually belong to the eighteenth century.

[9]The corpus contains a number of examples of the term *-coneuh*, "child of a woman"; *-piltzin* was originally "child of a man," though long before the time of the Toluca testaments women too might call their children *-piltzin* (some examples are in the present corpus). *-Coneuh* often implied a very young child or infant, and like all the older terms for offspring before adulthood, it was used for both genders. The examples available here do not suffice to answer certain questions definitively. It is not always possible to estimate the age of the child involved. All the children in the collection whose names are specifically given are male (with one of unspecified gender). It is easy to imagine that *-coneuh* like *-piltzin* was now being appropriated for the male only, but we cannot be sure. In some instances the word is used for not having children, which would imply that it applies to either gender.

Because of the above, my translation policy is very complex; *-piltzin* is translated as "son" when it is consistently contrasted with *-chpoch* for daughter in a document, but otherwise as "child."[1]

When testators list various children as heirs, they normally go from the oldest first to the youngest last, usually without making their procedure explicit. This aspect of the wills becomes important in my interpretation of them and can be helpful to the reader in perusing and understanding them. I defer absolute proof for the future, but consider the will of don Juan de la Cruz (No. 39, 1691), who mentions the eldest first, goes on with other married children, then comes to one who was married after his first wife's death, then to an adult child not yet married, and finally to small children still living in the house, the last of whom is specifically called the youngest. The terms *yacapantli*, "eldest," and *xocoyotl*, "youngest," occur from time to time in the text and can often be useful in our orientation.[2]

Grandchildren are less frequently found in the testaments; nevertheless, they appear not only when all the testator's children have died, but may at times get a substantial inheritance even when some of the children are alive, standing in for a child who has died already. They are always called by the traditional term *-xhuiuh*, with no distinction of gender or age, so no change in this respect took place in the eighteenth-century Toluca Valley.

Collateral relatives are also not the most frequent heirs, but at times we find relatively wealthy testators who provide members of their original family with some inheritance, or remember some nephew or niece with a small donation, perhaps in the name of the relationship they had with their own siblings. When all the potential heirs in the direct line are dead, they may receive more. So may in-laws, godchildren, and stepchildren.[3]

In reading a testament we are of course interested in how the heirs in each of the above categories tended to fare in the division of the inheritance. I will devote some space to this matter below under houses, lands, and animals, but it does deserve a few words of more unified discussion. Yet this topic, in a sense embracing most of the others dealt with here, will require much systematic research in the future in order to do it justice. Here I make only a few relevant statements as a provisional guide. It is clear in the corpus that parents intended all children of both genders to get something or other, especially when they were beyond first infancy. Females receive important bequests. The overall strategy, however, seems to have been that men were being set up as household heads, with the eldest as the successor of the present head of the family, whereas women were being set up to marry other men who would be the household heads. Thus men normally get more of almost everything and especially things specifically related to making an agricultural living.

Despite the preference given to males, in the texts we will see many exceptions, with females receiving large bequests of houses and lands, and not only, as we can easily understand, when they are the only child left alive. A strong factor here is that apparently children often received their principal inheritance at the time of marriage; this way of doing things is made specific in the will of don Juan de la Cruz just referred to, can be inferred in part from the will of the wealthy Elena de la Cruz (No. 10, 1711), and can be glimpsed or guessed in many other cases. Since the other children had already taken their part, those still at home, including females, sometimes received surprising bounty. Remember that in the wills testators felt no obligation to mention anyone who did not receive a bequest.

Terminology for spouses is the other area in which significant change can be traced from the patterns of Stage 2 despite the retention of indigenous words. While in the Testaments of Culhuacan the term *-namic*, "spouse," was used for both genders equally, in Toluca Valley texts of the eighteenth century it normally means "husband" only, and it is paired with another, gendered term, *-cihuahuatzin*, "one's woman," which now means "wife."[4] As we

[1]Yet *-piltzin* as "son" is near enough to dominance (and I will not here go into some indications that even plural *-pilhuan* sometimes seems to have meant "sons") that I translate it as "son" in *itlaçopiltzin* or *tepiltzin* in the ubiquitous phrase for the Trinity, whereas in a Stage 2 text one would not hesitate to translate it as "child."

[2]For another example of *xocoyotl*, see No. 8, 1701, from Toluca.

[3]Godchildren of either gender were called by two older indigenous terms, *teoyotica -coneuh*, "one's child through sacrament," or *-tlaquatequil*, "a person one has baptized." The relationship between the biological parent and the godparent was expressed with the loans *compadre* and *comadre;* those so named might be called on for help or to raise children, but do not appear as heirs.

[4]In Toluca proper this term is always reverential, while in Calimaya/Tepemaxalco it is often plain *-cihuauh*.

have seen happens with the terms for children, *-piltzin* and *-chpoch*, the traditional nongendered term is appropriated for the male only, while a gendered term indicates the female. The new system gives Toluca Valley Nahuatl a close equivalent to the pair of words in the Spanish of that time for a married couple: *marido* and *mujer*.

Some examples can be found in the corpus of men referring to their wives as *-namic*, but one is in the very earliest text, No. 16, dated 1652. Another is in No. 85, which though dated past 1700 is a conservative, old-fashioned document among a set of three such from San Antonio de Padua.[5] If we look to Toluca Valley documents beyond Toluca proper and Calimaya/Tepemaxalco, as I did in my doctoral dissertation, it appears that the transition from *-namic* to *-cihuahuatzin* was gradually occurring across the second half of the seventeenth century and was essentially complete by 1700. In the present corpus, No. 46, of 1681, uses *-cihuahuatzin*. Especially revealing is a document of 1662, not included here, in which a wife is called *-namic* three times, but also once *-cihuahuatzin*.[6]

Spouses do not usually play an important role as heirs, the testator generally preferring blood kin of the following generation. They are not invariably mentioned even when alive. However, they become important as custodians for minor children, especially the wife, and in this capacity the wife often receives a large part of the inheritance with the understanding that she will hand it on to the children later. When normal heirs are entirely absent, the spouse may benefit correspondingly.

Perorations

I NOW TURN to another topic needed for a good comprehension of the bequests in the whole central part of the testament. Nahuatl wills are known for a feature absent in their Spanish and other European counterparts, a phrase of exhortation or admonition coming at the end of a command or bequest, sometimes called a peroration because of that position. Such phrases seem to derive from the nature of the Nahuatl testament as a staged, oral performance before an audience, though it is realized that the statements are to some extent stylized and abstracted from the actual utterances of the testator. The tendency was barely discernible in the earliest documents, which were still closer to the Spanish model. Even in the Testaments of Culhuacan of ca. 1580, the majority of the examples have at most an isolated such phrase or two, though in a few of the later ones the tendency becomes stronger, and one of 1583 (Doc. 60) has some statement of this kind after most bequests. With time, perorations become ever more widespread and more consistent within the body of the testament, though the temporal dimensions of the evolution are not yet well understood.

The present corpus belongs to the time of the fully developed peroration. The tradition is not manifested in every single document; many lack a single such indication, among them not only short texts devoted to funeral arrangements, but some full-scale testaments. Some peroration-like statements are seen in the majority of the wills, however, and in many they take on the aspect of a refrain which is repeated consistently after each item, emphasizing the ultimately oral nature of the statement, giving it a rhythm, also punctuating, telling the listener that one item is finished and now the next is to be expected.

No marked overall trend in variation can be readily discerned. The very earliest document (No. 16, 1652) has a fully consistent refrain, *ayac quitlacoz*, "no one is to go against it," and we find an approximation of a refrain also in the very latest (No. 68, 1783). Wills without perorations are also found both early and late. No overall regional difference surfaces either. Perorations predominate, while some wills lack them, in both the Toluca area and in Calimaya/Tepemaxalco. The latter's central cluster does not differ visibly from the outlying tlaxilacalli, as it does in so many cases. Even many of the particular phrases used are shared between the two major subregions.[7]

In some cases the peroration is double, as in No. 25, 1728, in the Toluca area: "no one is to cause me

[5]The very latest document in the corpus, No. 68, dated 1783, uses *–namic* in reference to the wife, but it seems part of a consciously archaic vocabulary which even includes an unparalleled preconquest-style way of giving the calendar year.

[6]See Pizzigoni 2002, pp. 132–34. The document referred to is in AHAM, box 56:24.

[7]Some of the phrases (perhaps all of them) had long been in the testament repertoire. Already in the Testaments of Culhuacan we see *ayac tlein quitoz* ("no one is to say anything"), *ayac quiquixtiliz* "no one is to take it from him/her"), *ayac quixtoquiliz* ("no one is to claim it from him/her"), *ayac quichalaniz* ("no one is to dispute it"), all of which appear in the Toluca Valley corpus.

worry [about it] in the future; my will is to be carried out." The same thing is seen in Calimaya/Tepemaxalco (see No. 79, 1734). The effect is reminiscent of a feature of Nahuatl song, where each verse ends in vocables or nonsense syllables, often first a set of syllables specific to the verse, and then a more general one common to the whole song.

Some subtle differences are to be observed between the two subregions. In the Toluca area the primary positive exhortation is *neltiz notlanequiliz*, "my will is to be realized or carried out," which is never seen in just that form in Calimaya/Tepemaxalco. The phrase is quite often found toward the end of the preamble (a position where a peroration is rare in Calimaya/Tepemaxalco), even when the will contains no other such phrases. In Calimaya/Tepemaxalco the most popular exhortation is *neltiz notlatol mochihuaz*, "my statement is to be carried out and done." (The *mochihuaz*, "it is to be done," is sometimes omitted.)

Idiosyncrasies can be observed at the local level. The perorations in the many Calimaya testaments written by Hipólito de los Santos have a particular style and hardly vary from one to the next, and the same is true of the work of other notaries as well. It becomes clear that each writer used his own conventions and did not take pains to reproduce the testator's words exactly.

We see tlaxilacalli conventions too. All three documents from San Bartolomé Tlatelolco in the Toluca area use the peroration *neltiz notlatol*, "my statement is to be carried out," though that was not the dominant phrase in the area overall. In the Tepemaxalco tlaxilacalli of Santa María de la Asunción, the two main notaries use a refrain not seen elsewhere, "my sick person's statement is to be carried out before God" (compare Nos. 61 and 62).

Houses and saints

AFTER THE FUNERAL arrangements, the next thing we expect to see in the Toluca Valley corpus, as in other Nahuatl wills, is the first substantive bequest, which typically concerns the house of residence of the testator, if he or she owns such a property. Most do, and indeed, 62 testators out of 98 mention at least one house in their will.[1] A majority are house-owners in both of the subregions that we have been considering, but the proportion is higher in Toluca proper. More male than female testators mention a house.

If Toluca and Calimaya/Tepemaxalco are similar in terms of the numbers of testators bequeathing a house, striking differences appear between the two areas in the matter of description of homes. Testaments of Toluca often deal with the buildings one by one; those of Calimaya/Tepemaxalco never do so.

It is generally understood that Nahua houses of the sixteenth and seventeenth centuries were complexes consisting of separate structures, each of which might be used by a nuclear family, arranged around a patio. Each building was described by its orientation to a cardinal direction, with the central patio as an unspoken reference point.[2] Now, thanks to the testaments from the Toluca area, it is possible to reconstruct how a household compound looked at a later time. Most things remain the same. Each building is still indicated as facing in a certain direction onto an unmentioned patio. Most common are ones facing east (still *iquiçayampa tonatiuh*, "where the sun comes out"), thus on the west side of the patio, or west (still *icalaquiyampa tonatiuh*, "where the sun goes down"), on the east side, using the traditional indigenous phrases for the solar directions.[3] Buildings can also face north and south, and in that case the Spanish loans *norte* and *sur* may be used, or places that are located in the corresponding direction may be given in the traditional indigenous fashion for non-solar directions. Buildings facing north are the rarest, since the front is never in the sun; a few houses in the corpus face north nevertheless.

In addition to specifying the orientation of the buildings, the Toluca subregion often gives them specific names. The one most commonly mentioned, and also normally named first, is called *ichantzinco dios*, "the home of God" (10 times), or *oratorio*, "oratory" (7 times), using a loanword. After enough experience the reader finally grasps that these names describe the main residential structure of the complex, which also contains an altar or altars

[1]The two subregions differ in house terminology in that in Toluca proper a house is almost always called *caltzintli*, with the reverential, while in Calimaya/Tepemaxalco the simple term *calli*, without the reverential, is much more common. At times *-chan*, "one's home," is also found in both areas, either together with *calli* or alone.

[2]See Lockhart 1992, pp. 59–69. The Testaments of Culhuacan contain many examples of such complexes.

[3]In one case (No. 6, 1731) the west is given as *poniente*, using the Spanish loanword.

with the saints. A separate building for the saints (the *santocalli*, "saint-house") was apparently no longer common as it had been in earlier centuries. The ichantzinco dios was normally on the east or west of the patio, less frequently facing south, and only in one case facing north (No. 10). Then there often was a kitchen, called *cocina* using the loanword, normally opposite the ichantzinco dios.[4] Despite a tendency for the two primary buildings to face east and west, there was no definitive position for the elements of a compound; any building could, though less commonly, stand on the north, and even less commonly on the south.[5]

The structures mentioned above were probably of a single story, but there is one case in which a building is described as being on top of another, giving us an example of a rare two-story construction (No. 17). The household compound as described in the testaments from Toluca proper can then be completed by a corral or pen for animals, though in one case flowers were grown in it.

In a great many cases the piece of land on which the house is built is also specifically bequeathed, being referred to most frequently as *ihuicallo tlalli*, "the land going with (the house)." Though it is different in form, the thinking behind this term is the same as with the traditional Nahuatl word for the piece of land attached to the house as the family's main sustenance, *callalli*, "house-land." In fact, *callalli* appears once in the Toluca-area corpus (No. 10). The Spanish loan *solar*, "lot," is far less frequently seen in Toluca-area testaments.

In the testaments of Calimaya/Tepemaxalco, everything is just the opposite. The orientation of the buildings of the complex is not given, nor are any separate buildings named. The compound is not described at all except as a *calli*, "house," which in Nahuatl can mean either one building or several. Not even a corral is mentioned. One important element is present in many cases, however, which is entirely lacking in the Toluca area. This is the indigenous structure for storing maize, the *cuezcomatl* (with different spellings), which I translate as "corncrib" because of the function. It is sometimes mentioned as though it were in conjunction with the house, but on other occasions it is bequeathed in a detached way with no reference to a house compound.

Such a uniform and striking difference between the two subareas in the matter of house descriptions in testaments must be considered in itself a major fact of cultural history, showing two separate traditions at work, each dominant in its own realm, despite the geographical, social, and cultural proximity of the two. At present I am not sure of the further significance of the phenomenon, though I hope to approach closer to it in future research. I suspect that the home compounds in Calimaya/Tepemaxalco may have shared many of the elements made explicit in the wills of the Toluca area even if it was not the custom there to name them in wills. And can it be that there were no corrals in Calimaya/Tepemaxalco? The testators did not lack animals. Can it be that there were no corncribs in the Toluca area? More than a few testators there had oxen who plowed their lands to grow maize, which must have been stored somehow. Calimaya/Tepemaxalco may have been in an agriculturally richer part of the valley, or the markets and businesses of Toluca may have detracted to an extent from agricultural pursuits, but the difference still arouses puzzlement and curiosity.

If house complexes are described in a strikingly different way in the two subregions under study, when it comes to bequeathing houses, testators across the entire regional spectrum behave in a similar fashion. It is difficult to make precise statements, for some cases are ambiguous about the relationship between the testator and the heir, and also some testators leave more than one house to various heirs. However, it can be said relatively safely that in a large number of cases both male and female testators leave the house to a son, perhaps most frequently the eldest, but at times also the youngest, or to a grandson when no son is available. Daughters and granddaughters receive a house in far fewer cases, at times only in order to raise a younger male sibling (as in No. 24). Through the vagaries of mortality, marriage, and their own efforts, however, females not infrequently become the possessors of houses and even main family residences. Only Elena de la Cruz and don Juan de la Cruz (Nos. 10 and 39) are wealthy enough to provide basically all their many children with a house.

It seems that children are the preferred heirs when

[4]In many cases in which only the orientation toward the east or the west is specified, and not the use, the buildings could easily be kitchens.

[5]In the Testaments of Culhuacan the first and in a sense principal building in a complex is usually on the north.

it comes to the house complex; even in the cases in which a wife or husband receives a house, it is usually as custodian, in order to raise small children and then pass the property on to them.[1] In far fewer cases the house goes to a nephew or niece, a daughter-in-law, a wife but without the custodial function, or to a sibling or mother. Unique in the corpus is María Josefa (No. 12), who has accumulated large debts and orders her house sold to pay them, not leaving it to either of her living children.

The saints—that is, what we today might call sacred images kept at home—become a major consideration in a discussion of indigenous households in the Toluca Valley. Saints were virtually the symbol of the home, and the writer of a memorandum in Spanish tellingly lists one collection as household furnishings (*ajuar de casa*) (No. 82). They are usually bequeathed together with the house, and house and saints become a standard pair. At times (as in No. 72) they are called residents or householders (*chanecatzitzintin*), on a par with the members of the family. When saints are mentioned without a house, we suspect that a house is implied, though sometimes we learn that it is not. Roughly half of the testaments in the corpus, in both subareas, contain some mention of saints being bequeathed either in specific reference to a house or not. One inherited the house to serve the saints.

It might seem from the language of the corpus, which never includes a word meaning image, that people believed the saints were the same as the ones in heaven and not a representation. This is a complex matter, but the texts in several ways show a clear awareness of a distinction between the household saints and the originals. They speak of them as objects, giving "a" San Antonio to someone, and another San Antonio to someone else; they speak of someone buying a saint for a certain price.[2] The term "saint" was usually divided into male (*santo*) and female (*santa*), even when speaking of groups of them. It included personae beyond those seen by the church as saints. Christ and even sometimes God could be saints in this sense, not distinguished from the rest. Félix de Santiago (No. 81) left two female saints and "two little Christs" to his son. Antonio de Santiago (No. 50) left to a son "two saints, a San Isidro and a God the Father." Saints could be represented as paintings on canvas or as statues and statuettes of various dimensions.[3]

The reference to saints can be very general, merely a recommendation to serve all the male and female saints that are in the house, at times with a reminiscence of the traditional ritual of sweeping and providing incense, candles, and flowers (these details are mentioned only in San Lucas Evangelista, with one case in Tlamimilolpan). Or names of specific saints can be listed, and these vary greatly, depending on local practice and personal devotion. No straightforward connection can be established between the gender of testators and that of saints possessed or received, but the documents show that men possessed sacred images more commonly than women and in a greater variety, corresponding to their ownership of more houses.

As I said above, saints are normally bequeathed with the house, so in many cases the eldest son is the one who gets them. However, some testators distribute saints among various heirs. The more images testators have, the wealthier they are; indeed, saints are a good indicator of wealth. The best examples are those of don Juan de la Cruz, who leaves at least one saint to each of his eight children, and Elena de la Cruz (Nos. 39 and 10). At times saints are left to heirs who bear their name, such as a Juana getting San Juan, or an Ignacio San Ignacio.[4]

Some saints stand out from the others, probably the largest, most expensive, best decorated of the lot, as well as the most loved, and they are found only in families with certain resources. We see two expressions of such a status. The first and more common is that a piece of land is devoted to the service of the saint, with an heir who is made custodian and in effect owner, though the saint is imagined as the owner. Second, a few household saints were actually taken to the church to stay, either still belonging to the family or being donated to the community.[5]

I have touched upon saints in the preambles of

[1]In a certain number of cases testators leave a house to a child and also to some other kind of relative, or to two children of both genders in an equal way.

[2]Some clear examples are in Nos. 9, 50, 78, and 79, but there are many more cases through the whole corpus.

[3]Images of this kind, not found in early testaments such as the ones from Culhuacan, are generally described in Wood 1991.

[4]These examples come from No. 39; see also Nos. 48 and 78.

[5]Examples can be found in Nos. 11, 36, 56, and 57.

testaments, in the choice of burial sites, and now in households, but all that still does not exhaust their role in the lives of the testators and their families. They can be from the beginning expressions of the community as well as the family. Not only do household saints sometimes end up with the larger community; in one prominent case (Nos. 56 and 57), the symbol of the family was at the same time the patron saint of the tlaxilacalli. The same sentiments and kinds of support extend to a whole world of saints outside the home, often (though by no means necessarily) connected with the local sociopolitical entity. Elena de la Cruz (No. 10) is the best developed example. She leaves saints to her children for their homes, but more notable are her huge donations including whole immensely valuable properties to the tlaxilacalli saint, San Miguel de Aparicio. Ornaments, masses, candles, and donations of magueyes or of money are also lavished on a most impressive list of saints, apparently including all those to whom local cofradías, whether of indigenous people or of Spaniards, are dedicated. We must assume that similar devotion existed among those who for lack of resources were less able to express it; partial evidence to that effect is found throughout the corpus.

Land

ALONG WITH HOUSES and saints, the kind of property that is most seen in the Toluca testaments is surely land. After the first substantive bequest of a house, a will typically goes over to bequests of land when the testator has any to bequeath. The great majority of testators (75 out of 98) prove to be landowners of some kind. Whenever anyone possessed much land, it was, as we find among indigenous people all over central Mexico in the postconquest centuries, scattered here and there in separate parcels,[6] and thus bequests of land often make up the bulk of a testament.

What appears clear from the beginning is that the vocabulary used to describe landholdings varies between the two subareas of Toluca proper and Calimaya/Tepemaxalco. The difference begins with the land associated with the house complex. Toluca stays closer to the traditional indigenous concept of arable land that happens to be associated with the dwelling, most often, as we have seen, using the expression *tlalli ihuicallo caltzintli*, "the land that goes with the house." In Calimaya/Tepemaxalco that language is never used; rather the house is on a *solar*, a Spanish term and concept implying even subdivision of an urban area specifically to create lots to build houses on. (The term *solar* is used in a minority of cases in the Toluca area too, however.)

Nahuatl generally has a well established distinction between *milli*, a piece of land under active cultivation, and *tlalli*, land in general, or a piece of land without further qualification (and in other meanings earth, soil, land as a country, etc.) Both terms are found in the corpus in the usual senses. But whereas *milli* is much used in Calimaya/Tepemaxalco, in Toluca it is rarer, and more common is another word never seen in Calimaya/Tepemaxalco: *tlalmilli*, literally "land-field," which to my knowledge has never been well defined. From the context of its use I have formed the impression that it refers to a cultivated field devoted most likely to maize and not to specialty crops like the *memilli*, "maguey field." From the fact that the tlalmilli plus the milli in Toluca amount to a proportion of the landholdings somewhat similar to the plain milli in Calimaya/Tepemaxalco, I deduce that *tlalmilli* is virtually another word for *milli*. Uncertainties remain, however. To guide the reader concerning the use of the terms in the original texts, in the translations I have consistently rendered *tlalli* as "land," *milli* as "cultivated field," and *tlalmilli* simply as "field."

It is tempting to think of the milli as more valuable than the tlalli, which could be undeveloped, whereas a milli by definition is under current development. Occasionally we can be sure of the situation because of some added words in the text; thus in No. 8 a plot is called *çan tlalli*, "just land." But it gradually emerges that in many cases the fact that a parcel is called *tlalli* does not mean that it is not a milli as well. Some writers seem to prefer one term, some the other. In No. 79, a series of tlalli later

[6]The sites are often described as in a known settlement or sociopolitical unit, or on the road to one. Often the name of the place is of the type that could easily refer to a unit but has not been identified as such, so that it could be an actual physical description. Sometimes in such cases I have given the word as a place name in the translation, with the literal meaning in parenthesis, or vice versa. A frequent word of this type is *ixtlahuatenco*, literally "at the edge of the plain," used very liberally in the texts, and rendered literally by Spanish translators, so I finally decided that there was no doubt that the literal meaning was intended. In a similar case, *quauhtenco*, "at the edge of the woods," I was not so sure and continued to put both versions.

appear collectively as milli. In No. 87 we read "se pedaso tlali nomil," "a piece of land (tlalli) which is my cultivated field (milli)." Because of this usage, and since urban plots are called *tlalli* in the Toluca area and not in Calimaya/Tepemaxalco, we can hardly treat *tlalli* as a statistical category.

The terminology of land measurement is an important issue that divides the two subareas even more distinctly. All over central Mexico from before the conquest, land had been measured in a unit of usually seven to ten feet, varying locally, with several names, of which *quahuitl*, literally "stick," was the most common. The basic one-family plot typically measured 20 quahuitl square, and larger parcels measured in multiples of 20. This system is found in all its purity in the Toluca area but is absent in the texts from Calimaya/Tepemaxalco, which do not show the word *quahuitl* a single time, early or late.

In Toluca 20 quahuitl is the most common measurement of a parcel; bigger holdings measure in multiples up to 80 quahuitl, and holdings of 20 may be divided in half for the heirs, resulting in two pieces of 10. As in the traditional system, only one measurement is usually given; in earlier times it had often been understood that the second measurement was 20, and that may be the case here too. Occasionally it is specified that the plot is square, or 10 may be given as the width, presumably as the result of splitting. Other measurements exist but are secondary. In some cases we find use of the *surco*, "furrow," which seems to be smaller than the quahuitl and appears at times in both major subareas.[1] The Spanish-based system used in Calimaya/Tepemaxalco was known in the Toluca area but hardly employed in the documents of our corpus.[2]

In the Calimaya/Tepemaxalco area, from the earliest to the latest texts, from all localities, *quahuitl* never appears. The system used is based rather on the Spanish *fanega*, a grain measure, and the *almud*, one twelfth of a fanega, indicating the size of a piece of land by saying how much grain (often specifically maize seed) it would take to sow it.[3] Actually, an equivalence existed between the two types of measurement; an almud was 10 quahuitl. Thus one might imagine that the same system was operating in both subareas, merely slightly disguised. But such is not the case. Plots of 2 almudes (20 quahuitl) do not have the clear dominance seen in the Toluca area. Nor do large fields measure 8 almudes (80 quahuitl). Rather large fields typically measure a fanega (120 quahuitl) or half (60), or three-fourths (90). It is true that some fields of 2 almudes are seen, but ones of 3 are more prominent, achieved by dividing a fanega in half and then in half again. The most basic unit of Calimaya/Tepemaxalco was thus the fanega, whose 120 quahuitl would have been an odd number in the traditional system.

Throughout the corpus the testator sometimes gives an exhortation to the heir of a given piece of land involving the phrase *ipan tequiti*. Here *ipan* is the relational word *-pan*, "in, on, etc." in crossreference to the land, and *tequiti* is a verb meaning various things: among others, to work, to perform duties in general, or to perform tribute duties in particular. In testaments of earlier times and other regions, *ipan tequitiz in tlalli* sometimes can be shown to mean "he or she is to perform tribute duties on the basis of having the land." It has never been established, however, that that is the only possible meaning; many cases remain ambiguous. The meaning could be "he/she is to work on the land," or "he/she is to do the duties related to working the land." The ambiguity applies fully to the present corpus. Spanish translators sometimes render the phrase as "hará los trabajos," "he/she will do the work."

In certain cases we can be sure of the meaning. When the phrase is closely associated with the word *tlacalaquilli*, "tribute in kind or in money," we can be sure that tribute duties associated with the land in question are meant. Without that guide, we remain

[1]Numbers of measurements given in furrows are much larger than those given in quahuitl. It seems that furrows were used to achieve more exactness, which could be done with a smaller unit. Quahuitl are usually in even 20s, sometimes 10s from division, occasionally 5s from redivision, but not less than that or more uneven. Furrows can come in any odd number, though they too all in all stay somewhat even, and possibly there were two of them to a quahuitl. The indigenous word *cuemitl* appears once in the Calimaya/Tepemaxalco area (No. 94, 1703) in the same meaning; I am not sure whether it or *surco* was the original term.

[2]In both major subareas the Spanish *vara* was often used for properties in more or less urban situations. A vara is a Spanish yard, a little less than three English feet, and it is less than half of a normal quahuitl. The only example in which it is used for larger pieces of rural land instead of urban lots is in Elena de la Cruz (No. 10).

[3]Very occasionally for greater exactness the *cuartillo* is used, one-fourth of an almud.

uncertain. I have sometimes given the translation "he/she is to do the duties," leaving it open whether they are duties for the municipal corporation or the duties of cultivation. Sometimes I have added a specific footnote, sometimes not. In the future, making use of a larger corpus, I intend to investigate exhaustively the question of the meaning of the phrase and its variation with time, region, and context.

On the matters of the possession and inheritance of land I am not yet prepared to make definitive statements. With the uncertainties about the meaning of land categories and their arbitrary use in the corpus, plus the facts that for many plots measurements are not given, that the relationship of testator and heir is often not known, and much land was distributed in advance of the testament, a full assessment of this crucial matter must await further investigation. Especially it will require a great deal of close situational analysis as well as an expansion of the corpus. Thus I will confine myself here to some brief provisional statements. Perhaps the most important of them is that I do not yet find a difference in patterns of land possession and inheritance between the two major subareas. It is as though certain basic aspects of indigenous life, including kin terminology as well as the possession and inheritance of property, developed uniformly across the whole region at the same time that noticeably different local cultures were evolving.

Women represent a substantial proportion of the testators who bequeath landed property (26 cases); of course male testators remain the majority and usually possess more pieces of land, while women typically have only one or two parcels. However, some women (6 of them) are very land-wealthy by indigenous standards.[4] In general, while men are in a privileged position in terms of possessing and inheriting land, by their presence female testators show that women can assume an active role in inheritance within their families and communities. It would be extremely complicated and probably not very productive to measure the rather muddled and varying land categories we have just seen (*solar, milli, tlalmilli, tlalli*) by gender of possessor. The same is true with inheritance of land. It may be useful to say that men seem to inherit more land in all major categories than women.[5] Landholding is common among women nevertheless, since many of them inherit land from male and female testators in their role of daughters and granddaughters, or less commonly wives, nieces and siblings.

A fascinating question related to land has to do with magueyes. In Toluca proper *memilli*, "maguey fields," are mentioned a few times, indicating that some testators possessed land that was dedicated exclusively to the cultivation of magueyes. Also we see quite a few other instances of pieces of land or lots with magueyes on them, and some of them too were used exclusively for magueyes, for they are said to be planted in them (*meyotoc*). These descriptions and expressions are not seen in the texts from Calimaya/Tepemaxalco. As with similar differences, we are left wondering whether maguey cultivation was actually stronger in the Toluca area, as I am inclined to believe, or whether the difference is part of the two different traditions of testament writing.

Magueyes could be possessed independently of land. María Salomé (No. 42) bequeaths an impressive number of maguey plants that are said to be on other people's lots, many of which she has bought even though the land still belongs to someone else.

The ownership of magueyes seems quite common among both female and male testators, although quantities vary greatly. Sometimes we see impressive amounts hinting at commercial activity for production of alcoholic beverages; in this depart-

[4]Elena de la Cruz (No. 10), Melchora María (No. 24), Ana Teresa (No. 51), María Clara (No. 74), and Pascuala de la Cruz (No. 80). And Pascuala María (No. 57), though possessing directly only one large parcel, arranged the disposition of other holdings of her prominent family.

[5]Again I must make a disclaimer, that this whole topic will require separate full-scale investigation, which I do plan to carry out in the future. One important and difficult matter needing consideration here is the fact that women are a minority, though a large one, of the testators. Should we compute the ratio of the amount of land held to the number of testators to achieve a just comparison? Or should we assume that anyone who had any land issued a testament, and that our corpus is a good direct sample of the whole situation? I am somewhat shy about rushing into matters of this nature. In the corpus used for my dissertation, it was the case that a larger proportion of the recipients of the developed milli were men than with the possibly less developed tlalli, whereas women received a higher proportion of tlalli than milli. That finding does not hold true for the present collection, and I now believe that it may have been the result of using a smaller and differently constituted corpus rather than evidence of a tendency to give the most valuable properties to men (though such a tendency may well have existed).

ment women are more numerous than men in the corpus despite being a minority of the testators (6 against 4 in the possession of large quantities). Much more numerous in both subareas are the cases of testators bequeathing magueyes without a clear relation to land, a few plants to be dedicated to saints or given to particular heirs. Again Toluca proper predominates.

The question of whether or not women had a special position in the field of maguey cultivation, using it at times to compensate for a lack of lands, is of the greatest interest and calls for further research, though the problems in reaching firm conclusions are many.

Animals

THE TOLUCA VALLEY was famous for introduced Spanish livestock from the sixteenth century forward. Thus although lands are far more prominent in the corpus of testaments than animals, livestock are significantly present. They do not have their own section of the will, as lands in effect do. Usually they are scattered among the bequests to different heirs who receive land and perhaps a house, though sometimes they come toward the end as an afterthought, or have an entire separate memorandum devoted to them. The stock in question are above all oxen, but also cows and some horses, with a few mules and donkeys.

Large livestock are present in the wills of both major subareas. In the Toluca area 11 testaments mention such animals, compared to 9 (or possibly only 8) in Calimaya/Tepemaxalco.[1] This makes the proportion considerably greater in Toluca. No chronological bias is immediately apparent; if anything, animals are more prevalent in the earlier part of the time covered.

The term *yolcatl*, known elsewhere in the meaning of a large domestic animal, beast, is used for both ox and horse here and is of frequent occurrence, but only in the Toluca area. Also restricted to the Toluca area in the corpus is the word *huacax* (from *vacas*, "cows," with a plural analyzed as singular), usually meaning ox and occasionally cow. *Buey* does turn up for ox in two Toluca documents, however. Cows are mainly called *vaca*.

In Calimaya/Tepemaxalco, an ox is generally *buey*, a cow is *vaca* or some diminutive thereof, and *huacax* is unattested. Only in the 1691 will of don Juan de la Cruz is an ox called anything other than *buey*: *quaquahue*, an early indigenous neologism which was long the main word for the animal in Nahuatl.

Oxen most often come in yokes of two for working the land.[2] A testator might own one or two such teams, but the wealthier may have several, and the unequaled don Juan de la Cruz mentions eighteen yokes of oxen, as well as eight riding horses.

Horses in indigenous families of central Mexico were often associated with local commerce and the transportation of goods, and there is one case in the corpus (No. 75) in which that might apply, but more often horses (called *caballo* as usual) are mentioned with a saddle, thus intended for riding. More clearly for the transportation of goods were mules (*macho* for male mule, *mula* for the female), for which at times carrying gear is specified, and which at times were rented out. The use of a few donkeys (*burros*) in the corpus is not clear.

Smaller domestic animals are rarely mentioned, which probably does not mean they did not play an important role in the indigenous economy. Pigs and chickens make an occasional appearance; the vocabulary used is *pitzotl*, "pig," *cochinito*, "piglet," *tlatlazqui*, "egg-laying hen," and *pollo*, "chicken for eating." Sheep, in the Spanish system called *ganado menor* as opposed to horses and cattle, are seen in two documents only, called *ichcatl* as usual. Pigs and sheep are mentioned in the Toluca area only. I imagine pigs were equally widespread in Calimaya/Tepemaxalco, but it is known that sheep were raised primarily in the northern part of the valley.[3]

Of the about 20 testators who possess large animals, only 3 are women, so it is apparent that livestock did not usually stay long in the hands of women even though they inherited quite a few. Elena de la Cruz (No. 10) is extremely wealthy in almost everything, so it does not surprise us that she owns at least 7 oxen as well as some donkeys

[1]In No. 55, the form "yehuana" can plausibly be read as *yegua*, "mare," but the interpretation is not certain.

[2]The function of working the land is specifically mentioned at times and often implied. Whether ox-carts were also in use among the indigenous people is unknown; I see no evidence of it.

[3]See the testaments of don Ramón de Santiago (No. 7), don Felipe de Santiago (No. 25), Elena de la Cruz (No. 10), Pascual Antonio (No. 36), Bernardino de Santiago (No. 26), and Mateo Serrano (No. 94). For some words on sheep in the valley see Lockhart 1991, pp. 210–11.

and pigs. The other two female testators have only a couple of cows or a horse.[4] In the inheritance of animals, when wealthy testators possess a large number of them, all the children are included in the bequest, sometimes on a basis of full equality. The exceptional don Juan de la Cruz left yokes of oxen and riding horses to all his sons and daughters alike. However, we observe a tendency to give yokes of oxen to sons, and single oxen and cows to daughters, no doubt because the yokes were employed in agricultural tasks that fell in men's realm.[5] Wives receive working oxen in default or as custodians, however. In the best documented example (No. 38) of dividing a large number of cows among all the children both male and female, males receive more than females. Horses go to female heirs almost as frequently as to males, though when we look at testators the picture is very different.

Debts

AT TIMES TESTATORS include in their wills some reference to uncollected debts owed to them, hoping that the heirs will be able to arrange payment. The proceeds are sometimes to go for funeral expenses, and such was probably often the intention even when not specified. These debt-related statements usually come almost at the end of the testament, often with the flavor of an afterthought, and sometimes as an actual addendum after the signatures. Instances are not numerous in the present corpus; they seem to concentrate mainly in the Toluca area (11 cases, against only 3 cases in Calimaya/Tepemaxalco) and in an early period, from the second half of the seventeenth century to the 1730s. Perhaps the practice of using a late portion of the testament to deal with the liquidation of debt, which had Spanish precedent and had been a part of the genre from its first inception, was getting progressively lost in the eighteenth century.[6]

Some of the debts concern some item of clothing that the testator had previously lent or hocked, such as a jacket, a huipil, a skirt, or a cape.[7] In one case, the testator wants the value of a lost axe to be passed on to his son (No. 46). More commonly the testator is claiming money, usually just a few pesos, in debts of whose origin we know nothing.

In a few cases the debts are on a larger scale, and then they tend to enter into the main body of the testament. Outstanding is our famous and wealthy Elena de la Cruz (No. 10), who expects to collect different amounts of money from a large group of people, for a total of almost 90 pesos; it seems that even a governor, some doñas, and a couple of Spaniards, at least judging by their names, are in debt to her. Here we have grounds to think that she was an important moneylender or advanced sums for business purposes, opening up vistas for further research on the role played by indigenous women in the local economy.

Another instance, although far less astonishing, is that of Esteban de San Juan (No. 16), who has borrowed 4 pesos from various people, including a governor, even outside his tlaxilacalli, and who at the same time hopes to collect 4 pesos owed him by others. He too appears to have been in some sort of business and to have had dealings with Spaniards. Thus it seems that business and monetary networks existed that went beyond the limits of each person's own district. Finally, María Salomé (No. 42) had paid the substantial sum of 12 pesos for her son, and now claims them back in her testament. This case is typical in that quite a few of the debts seen in the corpus are between relatives, hinting at family connections as a way to solve cash problems or do business. But other debts, and indeed the majority, seem to lack the family aspect.

The end of the testament

THE WILLS OF THE Toluca Valley corpus are like others in the Nahuatl tradition in having a well defined concluding section, consisting in the fullest cases of a statement that the will is coming to an end, the appointment of an executor or executors, and the naming of witnesses, who often include a variety of local indigenous public officials. I will discuss each of these matters in turn.

Ending the body of the will. As in Nahuatl wills from many times and regions, the Toluca Valley testaments are careful to say that the main part of the will—the substantive bequests and com-

[4]Isabel María (No. 6), and Dominga Melchora (No. 75).

[5]See for example don Baltasar de los Reyes (No. 46) and don Juan Alonso (No. 56).

[6]I do not deal here with the practice of hocking land, a form of debt of which there are a few examples in the corpus; I expect to collect more cases and take on the topic systematically at a later time.

[7]See the testaments of Luis Francisco (No. 5), Isabel María (No. 6), María Ana de Morales (No. 9), and Salvador Cayetano (No. 35).

mands—has ended. The phenomenon seems to go back originally to the oral nature of the whole proceeding. Nahuas had long used a particular phrase to indicate that a substantial speech had come to an end and that a few formulaic words would now top off the occasion. That phrase—the straightforward *(ca) ye ixquich*, "that is all"—was then used to end testaments and can be seen in the Testaments of Culhuacan. It is popular in the present corpus as well, but in the slightly different form *(ca) çan ixquich.* The phrase with *çan* (literally "just") instead of *ye* (literally "already") is almost universal in the corpus, in the two major subareas and in both the center and the outlying tlaxilacalli of Calimaya/Tepemaxalco.[1]

Several regional differences emerge, however. We see the phrase used much more consistently in Calimaya/Tepemaxalco than in the Toluca area. In Toluca, usually either *ca çan ixquich* stands by itself or is supplemented by "that I say." In Calimaya/Tepemaxalco it is usually followed by the statement that the testator is concluding the testament, using the verb *tzonquixtia*, which is nearly missing in the texts from the Toluca area. Much of the time instead of using Spanish loan terminology for the testament at this point, the writers of Calimaya/Tepemaxalco put an interesting indigenous equivalent, *nococoxcatlatol*, "my sick person's statement." Styles vary with tlaxilacalli, but the expression at least appears almost everywhere. Again the word is entirely missing in the Toluca area.

Executors. Next in order is appointing an executor of the testament (using the usual loanword *albacea*, with a circumlocution here and there). The characteristics of the person chosen as executor, as shown by the name and any other attributes given or surfacing in other documents, are of much help in attempting to assess the status of the testator.

The appointment of executors varies greatly by region. In the Toluca area they are the norm; 31 testaments have them, only 7 do not, and of these, three or four use phrases such as *nopan tlatoz*, "will speak for me," which virtually define what an executor is. In Calimaya/Tepemaxalco, however, only 24 testaments have executors, and an impressive 36 do not. As so often in this subregion, we see a large contrast between the central cluster and the outlying tlaxilacalli. In the center (both halves), 20 testaments have executors, only 4 do not, a result much the same as in the Toluca area, whereas in the outlying tlaxilacalli there are only 4 testaments with executors, 32 without. Thus it appears that executors were much more common in major settlement centers.

The testator might choose two executors instead of one, and this choice too has a marked regional dimension. In the Toluca area over a third of the wills have two executors, while in Calimaya/Tepemaxalco only 2 of the 24 have more than a single executor.

The rank of the executor seems to have been an important consideration for the testator. In a provisional count I found that nearly half the executors in Calimaya/Tepemaxalco bore the don, in the Toluca area close to a third. Sometimes their offices or former offices (including the highest, governor) are specified, or we know from other sources that they have been officeholders. Relatives, especially brothers and nephews, also appear in this role, and one compadre. A Spanish friar also appears as executor once (No. 36, Toluca area, 1737).

The vast majority of executors in the corpus are male, but there are a few interesting exceptions. One of the earliest wills, that of María Salomé in Tepemaxalco, dated 1654 (No. 42), has a female executor with a title and a very prestigious second name, doña María de Guzmán. Female solidarity seems to play a role here, and looking at the two names we can suspect that María Salomé was the protegé of doña María de Guzmán more generally. The early date makes us wonder if at that time female executors were more common. The will of Lucas de la Cruz, also of Tepemaxalco, dated 1695 (No. 45), still seventeenth century but approaching the time of the bulk of the corpus, also has a female executor. This time the appointment crosses genders, and the name of the woman, María de la Encarnación, does not betray high rank; the testator himself was of quite high status. It must simply be registered that such a situation was possible and acceptable.

Both of these examples predate 1700 and are from Calimaya/Tepemaxalco. A third, No. 10, is from the Toluca area and is dated 1711. In this case the testator, Elena de la Cruz, a woman of great wealth by indigenous standards, appoints her two

[1]No. 87, from San Antonio de Padua, 1737, is the only document in the corpus to use *ye ixquich*.

daughters as her executors even though she has living sons and doubtless many other connections. Female solidarity certainly comes into play in this case, and it will be seen in their testaments that this whole line of women was exceptionally independent and uninclined even to mention the men in their lives.

No woman executor is found after 1711, and the function was thereafter left entirely to males.

Witnesses. Like the executor, the witnesses are a clue to the status of the testator, and even a richer one. I judge by their rank, name types, and number, but in each case one must take into consideration the practice of the particular tlaxilacalli, for some of them routinely assembled public officials for the occasion, and others did not. The loanword *testigo*, "witness," had been in the language for generations, and is universal in the corpus. In Stage 2 wills, of which the Testaments of Culhuacan can again be the example, often many more witnesses were called than in the Spanish tradition, and they routinely included women, frequently equal in numbers to the men, whereas it was not the general practice among Spaniards to use women as witnesses. In Stage 3 wills generally speaking across central Mexico, witnesses grow fewer in number, women are reduced to the disappearing point in this function, and often local officials are the predominant if not the only witnesses.

All of these things happen in the Toluca Valley corpus. One does, however, find some vestiges of the earlier tradition. Some of the early wills are little different from the Culhuacan testaments. In the just cited will of María Salomé of Tepemaxalco, dated 1654 (No. 42), we see no less than nine witnesses. Some are high male officials, it is true; but no less than four are women, one of them a doña. The will of Andrés Nicolás of Toluca, dated 1671 (No. 1), has five witnesses, of whom three are women, the other two being men without don or any named office. From these examples we could imagine that the Stage 2 tradition was still in full force. But there is other evidence. The very earliest will, from the Toluca area in 1652 (No. 16), has only three witnesses, all male officials.

The last example of the old style in the corpus is the will of Mateo Serrano in the Calimaya/Tepemaxalco area, dated 1703 (No. 94). Here we find six witnesses, three of them women; the men include two officials and a person with no named office (a relative of the testator judging by his second name). One final woman witness appears in a woman's will of Calimaya dated as late as 1759 (No. 77). She is apparently the only personal witness to the document; all the others are male officials. She may have been brought in for friendship and female solidarity, or, given the rarity of the phenomenon and the lack of other personal witnesses, she may have been a last resort. No other female witnesses appear in the corpus.

A difference between personal witnesses—associates specifically called by the testator—and local public officials who are present in the line of duty is seen in both major subregions, with the distinction sometimes made explicitly, other times implicitly. Depending on the tlaxilacalli, however, the rank and number of the officials present can reflect something about the testator.

It does not seem to be the case that the numbers of witnesses to testaments are reduced drastically during the years covered by the Toluca Valley corpus. We cannot arrive at a conclusion merely by counting, because humbler people would often have very few witnesses, apparently unable to assemble more. Perhaps we can see a certain tendency for wills to have three witnesses, the Spanish norm and legal minimum. But important people standardly had more than that, and some tlaxilacalli seem to have brought together as many officials as could be located on such occasions.

Tlaxilacalli traditions varied sharply. In the three wills from San Bartolomé Tlatelolco in the Toluca area, the witnesses are always men holding church offices, with no other witnesses listed. In all the wills from San Pedro Tototepec in the same area, the witnesses are always a mixture of church and cabildo officials, with no one else. In the two Tepemaxalco tlaxilacalli of San Lucas Evangelista and Santa María de la Asunción, the tradition was to bring together a large number of cabildo and church officials, though San Lucas was somewhat more consistent in actually assembling them. As in many other things, these two entities run closely parallel. Both also lacked executors of wills, and one must wonder if the conjunction of the absence of executors and the presence of so many officials meant that the officials took an active part in administering wills.

Officials. Since so many witnesses were officials, the witness lists are a prime source for finding out something about local officialdom—what the offices were, what individuals or family groups held them, what their ranks were. We can tell very little about their actual duties. The titles are largely the same in the two major subareas; many more examples are available from Calimaya/Tepemaxalco, however. There are two hierarchies, the cabildo and the church organization, which for the most part are intermingled in the lists, though in a few tlaxilacalli only the church officials appear as witnesses. The highest office is that of the governor, presiding over the indigenous cabildo, as is well known, but our notion of the position is borne out by the wealth and connections of past governors in the corpus. The only ones for which there is any substantial information are those of the twin altepetl Calimaya and Tepemaxalco. The governor, the main fiscal of the church in a given unit, and the holder or holders of the office of alcalde in the civil hierarchy were the only ones always accorded the title of don (after about 1700, at least); these three positions may simply be called the high offices.

The head of the indigenous church organization was the fiscal or chief steward of a given church; sometimes in the documents the distinction between *fiscal mayor* and *fiscal teniente* is made. The fiscal appears in more testaments than any other kind of official other than the notary. Beneath him were various positions such as *temachti* or teacher of the Christian doctrine, *tepisque* (the Spanish form of *tepixqui*, "one in charge of people"), and *topile*, literally "holder of a staff," at the lowest level of authority in this scheme. One also sees the *mayordomo*, once or twice related specifically to a cofradía, and the *diputado*, literally "deputy," who may also be a cofradía official, but in lists both are readily included in the church hierarchy. The mayordomo and the temachti have enough prestige that sometimes they receive the title of don; the latter sometimes functions as notary or even is one concurrently. Sometimes the term *maestro* appears; it might mean a choir director, but in the case or two where it is expanded to *maestro de doctrina* we see that it is about the same thing as the temachti. Indeed, in our sample the word *temachti*, so frequently seen in Calimaya/Tepemaxalco, does not appear in the Toluca area. As the reader will see, for the purpose of exact identification of these offices, many of which have no close English equivalent, I retain the Spanish or Nahuatl in translations for all except the governor, who is usually given in English in the literature, and the notary (*escribano*).

In the larger centers it is hard to say much about how many alcaldes there are. The reader will understand that the office was that of a first-instance judge belonging to municipal government. In outlying tlaxilacalli, circumstantial evidence seems to indicate that there was only one at a time, roughly on a par for prestige and precedence with the local fiscal; some tlaxilacalli tend to put one of them first in lists, others the other one. There would normally be no governor in an outlying tlaxilacalli. Beneath the alcalde were, in some tlaxilacalli at least, councilmen called *regidor mayor* and sometimes *regidor menor*, an *alguacil mayor* or chief constable, and lesser officeholders such as a *merino*. The regidor mayor was at times considered high enough to receive the don, but consistency is lacking.

The official named last in the will was normally the notary who wrote it, who in many cases would later occupy higher offices, but I will say more on this point in a whole section about notaries.

It is clear not only from their being intermingled in witness lists, but from the same individuals in succession appearing in both hierarchies, that the two acted in close conjunction and were occupied by essentially the same individuals and families. Those holding the lower offices in each hierarchy often advanced to higher posts; it is not yet clear what the limits on such advance were, if any.

3. Language and Orthography

THE LANGUAGE IN WHICH the Toluca Valley corpus is cast represents a significant topic transcending the individual parts of a testament as reviewed in the section just above. Although the subject tends to become too technical for some readers, it yields vital insights into culture, and also relates to the question, which is so central here, of commonality versus variety within the region. Then too, a reader accustomed to other kinds of Nahuatl can use some guidance in dealing with Toluca Valley texts. In the following I treat first the Spanish influence seen in the texts, and then the language more generally, but concentrating above all on some sound changes that had a strong effect on the appearance of Nahuatl documents in the Toluca Valley in the time of the corpus.

Phenomena of contact with Spanish

THE MOST IMPORTANT diagnostic traits of Stage 3 in Nahuatl, which begins around the middle of the seventeenth century in central Mexico as a whole, are: the presence of loan verbs; the presence of loan particles;[1] the use of loans for close blood relatives not in the direct line; equivalence relationships, in which a Nahuatl word can represent any meaning of a particular Spanish word; calques or loan translations, in which native vocabulary is used to represent Spanish idioms; plurals of inanimate nouns.[2]

The present corpus contains examples of all of the above traits and thus in a way fits the existing picture of Stage 3 Nahuatl quite well. We must, however, ask the question of how uniformly these characteristics appear. Are they present in the documents from the seventeenth century? Do those early texts show evidence of Stage 3 phenomena?

The answer must be somewhat equivocal. One of the signs, loanwords for close blood relatives like brother, sister, niece, or nephew, is indeed strongly present in the seventeenth-century documents. However, no loan verb appears, and only three cases of particles, whereas they are more numerous after 1700. The loan *hasta* meaning "as far as" occurs in a will of 1654 (No. 42) from the central part of Tepemaxalco. The loan *para* is found in a text of 1692 from Santa María de la Asunción (No. 56) in the meaning "in order to," used with an indigenous verb. A spectacular instance of a loan particle occurs in a document of 1697 from Santiago Apóstol Quaxochtenco (No. 94), which has *ni* not once but twice in a sequence, so that the meaning is "neither . . . nor" and the phrase structure is from Spanish.

A couple of quasi-calques are seen in the seventeenth-century part of the corpus, instances which combine native and loan vocabulary to reproduce a Spanish idiom. In a 1681 will from San Lucas Evangelista (No. 46) we find "quitzaqua quenta," "he closes out the account," with the native verb *tzaqua*, which would hardly have originally had this special sense, and the popular loan *cuenta*, "account." A will from Tepemaxalco in 1691 (No. 39) has the very mixed utterance "niquipie noyermanos y ermanas," "I have brothers and sisters." Here native *pia* is used as an equivalent of Spanish *tener*, "to have (in many senses)," while "brothers and sisters" are loanwords. The Nahuatl possessive prefix is used with "brothers," reflecting an ancient way of speaking of having relatives, but it is not repeated with "sisters," rather *hermanos* and *hermanas* are connected by the Spanish conjunction *y*, as if the two are considered an indivisible unit, and the writer had switched in mid-phrase to Spanish. These two examples suffice to show the general closeness of Spanish conversation that we expect in Stage 3.

Other typical phenomena of Stage 3 seem absent from the seventeenth-century documents. We are now presented with some puzzles. In such a small corpus, consisting of 10 wills (a document type with restricted, formulaic, traditional vocabulary in which many contact phenomena are not very likely to surface) and one bill of sale, is it reasonable to expect that all the speech phenomena of the time would be represented? Loan verbs despite their diagnostic importance are rare in Nahuatl documents even in Stage 3. Might some of them not have circulated in the Nahuatl of the region in the seventeenth century despite their absence here? I consider it likely, but I cannot give a definitive answer.

Notice also that two of the loan particles are from the 1690s. Does this mean that perhaps they had first been introduced in this possibly crucial decade? In view of the 1654 instance, I doubt it, but it remains a possibility until we have more texts from earlier in the seventeenth century.

Notice further that the examples of loan particles and the Spanish-influenced phrases cited above are almost all from Calimaya/Tepemaxalco. In a moment we will see that in the following decades loan particles are proportionately more numerous in that area than in the area of Toluca proper. Had the distinction already existed in the seventeenth century? Possibly, but the numbers are too small to say.

[1]The term "particle" is used here in the same sense as in the writings of Karttunen and Lockhart, meaning any Nahuatl word which does not inflect, is invariant. In Spanish the loans referred to would be called prepositions, conjunctions, and adverbs.

[2]The criteria given here are as in Lockhart 1992, pp. 304–18, the findings, approach, and terminology of which I follow closely in this section, drawing also on Lockhart 1991, pp. 122–40. The same is true of section 4 here.

Adoption of Spanish sounds is also important but hard to measure with certainty in the written texts. Loanwords and Spanish names written with typical Nahuatl sound substitutions show that at least a good proportion of speakers in the Toluca Valley had not yet fully assimilated the Spanish phonetic repertoire by the time of the corpus.

Let us turn then to the eighteenth-century part of the corpus, 88 of the 98 wills, and continue with the topic of loan particles, specifically with the most popular one by far, *para*. Multiple examples occur in both major subareas. In both we find the two primary uses of the word in Spanish, both clause-introductory as in the example already cited, and with a noun complement, as in "para nopiltzi," "for my child" (No. 74). Only in Calimaya/Tepemaxalco, perhaps by chance, do we find *para* in the quasi-calques *para ic tlacpac*, "in an upward direction, above," based on Spanish *para arriba*, and *para ic tlatzintlan*, "in a downward direction, below," based on Spanish *para abajo*.[1]

Looking at the whole corpus, we soon see that *para* is much better represented in Calimaya/Tepemaxalco than in the Toluca area. In the latter it appears in four of the decades represented, for a total of 7 times. In Calimaya/Tepemaxalco it is seen no less than 45 times, 44 of them in the eighteenth century. We might be inclined to think that given the overall later dates of the Calimaya/Tepemaxalco sample, the difference has to do with the time factor as Spanish influence grew ever stronger, but 17 of the 45 examples from Calimaya/Tepemaxalco are from before 1740, even though that subarea is not as well represented in the corpus in that time as Toluca. I do not mean to make too much of the difference in a sample of this size. Consider the fact that no less than 19 of the 45 examples in Calimaya/Tepemaxalco were produced by a single writer, Hipólito de los Santos. Yet one cannot help being impressed by the quantitative difference between the two subareas.

A loan particle rivaling *para* in popularity in central Mexico generally is *hasta*, "until, as far as, etc." But in the present corpus the loan appears only 5 times, in 3 documents: one of them in the Toluca area (No. 10, 1711), with the spatial meaning, and the others in Calimaya/Tepemaxalco, with the spatial meaning in one case (No. 42, 1654) and the temporal meaning in the other (No. 80, 1739). All of the other loan particles in the corpus are from Calimaya/Tepemaxalco: *mientras*, "while"; *siempre*, "always"; *desde*, "since"; *fuera de*, "aside from"; *entre*, "among"; *por*, here meaning "as."[2] Again it seems that these words may have been more used in Calimaya/Tepemaxalco than in the Toluca area in our period, as well as increasing over time.

With loan verbs, the picture is more equal. The first impression is that the verbs are much rarer than the loan particles and barely suffice to meet one's minimal expectations for a corpus of Stage 3 texts. Toluca has 3 attestations in 3 different documents. One of the verbs, used twice, is *cobraroa*, from Spanish *cobrar*, "to collect" (Nos. 5 and 6, 1731), and the other is *doraroa*, "to gild" (No. 10, 1711). Calimaya/Tepemaxalco has more attestations, 7 in 7 different documents, but not more proportionately, and again only two verbs (not the same ones as Toluca). The dates are spread across the years 1717 to 1763. The remarkable thing is that all but one of the instances involve *cruzaroa*, from Spanish *cruzar*, "to cross," in reference to roads crossing. Five of the six come from San Lucas Evangelista and the contiguous San Antonio de Padua. The other verb, from central Calimaya, is *constaroa*, "to be recorded."[3]

In order not to tire the reader with examples, I will merely say that in both subareas calques or at least semi-calques continue to appear at times in much the same fashion as those illustrated for the seventeenth century.

The seventeenth-century texts do not show clear examples of equivalence relationships. In those after 1700 it several times seems as if *ica*, "through it, etc.," is the equivalent of Spanish *con*, "with," as it was in Stage 3 central Mexican texts more generally. The clearest example is perhaps the identification phrase *casado ica*, "married to," which in Spanish is *casado con*.[4] Nor do we see in the seventeenth century any examples of native nouns which would not have had a plural ending in traditional Nahuatl being given one in the Spanish fashion; but some exam-

[1]In these phrases *para* and *ic* are duplicatory; the phrases mean the same thing even without *para* and are actually sometimes seen in the corpus in that form.

[2]The loans are found in Nos. 65 (1760), 77 (1759), 78 (1712), 81 (1738), 82 (1762), and 84 (1760). The words *de*, "of, from," and *y*, "and," appear frequently in the corpus, but they are virtually always part of a set Spanish phrase and cannot be considered separate loanwords. At times *y* looks like a true loan, however, as in "temaxtin y escribano," "temachti and notary" (No. 79, 1734). A bit different, but close to this class of loans is *primeramente*, "first" (No. 78, 1712).

[3]*Cruzaroa*: Nos. 50 (1736), 52 (1759), 53 (1759), 81 (1738), 85 (1717), 87 (1737). *Constaroa*: No. 74 (1763).

[4]In Nos. 5 (1731), 13 (1733), and 32 (1736), all from the Toluca area.

ples surface after 1700, in both subareas, especially having to do with lands and fields.[5]

Thus the texts from the eighteenth century show all the normal signs of Stage 3 Nahuatl, though the Stage 3 phenomena could not be said to dominate them. The seventeenth-century texts show some of the signs, but others are missing; it remains to be seen whether the language at that time was in transition, running temporally somewhat behind the Valley of Mexico, or the lack is due merely to the small sample.

Beyond the diagnostic traits of Stage 3, the Spanish loanwords in the testaments are standard fare in such documents; they constitute a quite short list of nouns (though frequently repeated in the texts), many of which had been included in testaments from the mid-sixteenth century. Almost all of them could readily be imagined in texts of Stage 2, though such loans continued to accumulate in Stage 3 as well. No marked difference in this majority of the loanwords emerges between the seventeenth- and the eighteenth-century documents in the present corpus. One eighteenth-century loan betrays an awareness of usage in Spanish and thus has a Stage 3 flavor. The Nahuatl word *tlalli*, "land," was used traditionally to mean a particular plot of land, and that meaning is still seen throughout the corpus. But the Spaniards never said "a land," always "a piece of land," and so in both subareas we sometimes see *pedazo* accompanying *tlalli*, or even *pedacito*, with a Spanish diminutive attached.[6] Interesting in another way is the retention of an earlier popular loan, *quixtiano*, derived from *cristiano* but meaning a person of Spanish ethnicity. The two examples come from the Toluca area only.[7]

Toluca Valley Nahuatl, orthography, and phonology

SOME OF THE TEXTS in the corpus closely resemble contemporary documents from the Valley of Mexico in every way that one at first notices. Others are so different that a reader accustomed to the more standard mode has a very hard time understanding them. They may even seem rather hilarious. Eventually it becomes clear that the difference is almost all in an orthography reflecting different pronunciations: more specifically, weakening of syllable-final consonants. If one carries out the exercise of rewriting some of the most difficult or deviant texts in a more standard orthography, it becomes apparent that in every other way, at least to a superficial view, they too differ little from texts of the Valley of Mexico at the same time, whether in content, vocabulary, morphology, or syntax.

Here I will mention the transcription policy used in this volume, which is normal for works of this type, retaining all the original letters unchanged, reproducing all abbreviations and overbars as nearly the same as print allows, manipulating the original only by spacing the letters as words by modern grammatical criteria. In one way I veer a bit from what is usually seen in comparable works. I had considered marking obvious errors or extremely deviant spellings by "[*sic*]" and by frequent explanations in footnotes as well, but there are so many variations and departures from the usual standard, as well as so many omissions and repetitions of syllables and words, that the more usual policy would have filled the book with "[*sic*]" and footnotes. I do not imagine that the transcriptions are without some error on my part, but I have exercised extreme care, and I ask the reader to take it that all phenomena in the transcription, however outrageous or erroneous, are really there in the original.

I will also take this occasion to explain that in the translation and in my own commentary all Nahuatl names and other words that I might use appear in a standard orthography, while Spanish names and words are given in the modern fashion. When something from a transcription is reproduced literally as it is, it appears in quotes. I have found it best to keep the names of churches and saints in Spanish generally speaking.

Though on first exposure to the Toluca Valley corpus it may occur to one that we have here some radically different or simplified version of the Nahuatl language, such turns out not to be the case.

[5]See Nos. 7 (1740), *tlalmilme;* 72 (1755), *tlalme;* 79 (1734) *milme*. Some examples of *miltotontin* (Nos. 38, 1737, and 80, 1739, among others) could be viewed differently because Nahuatl even in earlier times sometimes showed plural endings on any word with the diminutive *-ton*.

[6]In the Toluca area, Nos. 24 (1737) and 28 (1710); in Calimaya/Tepemaxalco, Nos. 43 (1762), 68 (1783), 72 (1755), 80 (1762), and 87 (1737).

[7]In No. 4 (1716), "quixtiano"; in 8 (1701), "ce quixtianoto," "a little Spaniard, a Spanish boy." Note that the word was distinct from the less transformed loanword meaning a person who believes in Christianity; in No. 39, 1691, we see "nichristiano," "I am a Christian."

The range of expression does not seem more restricted than in similar Valley of Mexico texts. Toluca Valley Nahuatl was no simplified language intended only for intergroup communication. I am not familiar with Otomanguean languages (varieties of Otomanguean had once dominated the valley and are spoken there to this day), and I cannot be sure that Nahuatl was the first language for all the writers and speakers represented in the corpus; but it surely seems so. Everything in the texts can be accounted for either by Nahuatl-internal developments such as the weakening of final consonants which was in operation everywhere, or by the pervasive Spanish influence. No other factor can be detected.

If we search systematically for any signs that Toluca Valley Nahuatl was in some way deteriorating or incompetent, we find little—although perhaps something. A great many essential prefixes and suffixes are missing in the texts, but I do not take this for some transformation or loss of grammatical structure. Rather I see it as a result of the constant inadvertent syllable omissions seen in the corpus, a feature of all Nahuatl writing but especially marked in the Toluca Valley.

The only pervasive phenomenon that might arouse concerns about the state of Nahuatl in the valley has already been mentioned (p. 10): that a large number of documents, some of them by the most professional notaries, begin a will with the phrase *ma mocenquizcayectenehualo*, "may it be entirely praised," which contains two incompatible ways of rendering a verb passive, used at the same time. In normal Nahuatl grammar, the verb can be made in effect passive by use of the reflexive prefix; that would give *mocenquizcayectenehua*. Or the passive suffix *-lo* can be used, causing the removal of any specific object prefix: *cenquizcayectenehualo*. In the Nahuatl grammar of central Mexico of that time, either way eliminates the other. This is an extremely basic aspect of the grammar of the language. I cannot explain how so practiced and knowledgeable a writer as Hipólito de los Santos of Calimaya can have used the nonstandard phrase. As we have noticed above, it is seen more in the more sophisticated and up-to-date center of Calimaya/Tepemaxalco than in the provincial and old-fashioned outlying tlaxilacalli. Thus it seems to have been considered a refinement or ornament. Possibly the reflexive as passive had become so dominant (for it increased everywhere as time went on) that the true passive had become vestigial and people of the Toluca Valley were no longer very familiar with it. Yet the texts contain a few examples of correct passives. And no similar anomalies appear with any other words or utterances.[1]

One case of true incompetence is seen in the corpus, the inability of a writer to produce a correct version of "our savior," or even to sort out what forms of the agentive can be possessed and what forms not. A writer in San Lucas Evangelista in the Calimaya/Tepemaxalco area (No. 50, 1726), seems to fumble between the root meaning "savior" and another meaning "teacher or preacher" and also gives a possessed form of an agentive in *-ni*, impossible in normal Nahuatl grammar. Other writers produce "our savior" flawlessly in the standard manner, however.[2]

The Nahuatl of the texts here, although in most respects it belongs to the variety of the language spoken in the Valley of Mexico, also shows certain signs of affinity with peripheral Nahuatl, which did not share some of the innovations of the central dialects. But in all these cases we find both variants, not a complete agreement with one side or the other. Only central Nahuatl had the distinct first person reflexive prefixes *no* (sing.) and *to* (pl.); peripheral Nahuatl retained *mo* for all persons and numbers. In the texts one will see a constant variation between one and the other, as in *ninomiquiliznequi* versus *nimomiquiliznequi*, "I am about to die." Often both variants can even be found in a single text by a single writer. Central Nahuatl elided more vowels than did peripheral Nahuatl; in the texts one sees both modes, above all with the word for "soul" contained in almost every will: *nanimantzin* versus *noanimantzin*, "my soul." In central Nahuatl, when a subject prefix ending in *i* is followed by *c* object prefix and *on* directional, the *i* standardly becomes *o*, thus *nicon* becomes *nocon*. In the Toluca Valley texts both ways are seen, especially in the common

[1]In western Nahuatl the nonactive *-lo* is sometimes used as a plural. The same might happen in the Toluca Valley, but the subject of the verb, *in itocatzin*, "the name of," is grammatically singular. No hint of a *-lo* plural is found in any other phrase in the corpus.

[2]See n. 3 to No. 50. Standard possessed preterit agentives with the word "savior" *(totemaquixticatzin)* are in Nos. 22 (1715) and 31 (1731).

phrase "I place it (the soul)": *nicontlalia* or *nocontlalia*.[3]

Now let us turn to the matter that tends to make some of the texts of the Toluca Valley an impenetrable forest for the uninitiated reader: the substitution of other letters for those of standard orthography in response to a radical weakening of syllable-final consonants.[4] Such weakening was occurring also in the Valley of Mexico at this time, and there were even some orthographic adjustments to it, so the Toluca Valley is not unique, but it seems to have gone much further.

First let me speak briefly of a matter of this kind which Toluca and the Valley of Mexico share. Even in otherwise very standard documents of the central valley, across the whole time when Nahuatl was written, one will often find the letter *n* treated very differently than in grammars. Apparently because syllable-final *n* was the weakest consonant written down, it was constantly being omitted ("nonatzin" for *nonantzin*, "my mother"), and more puzzling for the reader, it was forever being intruded after a vowel where by standard notions it did not belong ("canlli" for *calli*, "house"). This phenomenon is identical in the Toluca Valley corpus. Since readers of other kinds of texts are probably already familiar with it, it will not be mentioned further.[5]

In the following I will simply list the other syllable-final consonants and explain how they may be treated in the corpus. I am not a linguist, and this volume is directed to a wider audience than linguists, but to have some order in my list I speak first of the stops from front to back, then the fricatives, the affricates, the liquid, and the relevant glide. Let it be understood from the beginning that the substitutions are not carried out consistently, not even by a given writer.

Syllable-final *p* [p] is very rare in Nahuatl, but the word *huiptla*, "the day after tomorrow," is of frequent occurrence in the phrase *moztla huiptla*, "in the future." In the corpus the *p* often becomes *c* or occasionally is omitted: "huictla, huitla."

Final *t* [t] is also rare. It may be omitted or replaced by *c*: *Quitta*, "he sees it," can become "quita" (as often in the Valley of Mexico too) or "quicta."

Syllable-final *tl* [t^l] occurs only at the very end of a word in Nahuatl. The most obvious sign of Tolucan Nahuatl, something hardly occurring in the Valley of Mexico, is that the [t] attack is omitted and the *tl* is written as *l*. Thus *nehuatl*, "I," becomes "nehual."

Final *c* [k] is often omitted, another feature often seen also in Valley of Mexico texts: *nicchihua*, "I do it," becomes "nichihua." Especially characteristic of Tolucan writing is that *c* is used instead of other weakened final consonants: *-p* and *-t* as seen above, very often instead of *-uh* [w], and often in the place of the generally unwritten consonant that was historically a glottal stop but may have been [h] by this time, as in most varieties of Nahuatl today.

Final *s* [s], which in conservative writing appears as *z*, is often simply omitted, especially at the end of a word. Thus many future forms can be recognized only by deduction. For *nicmacatiaz*, "I am leaving it to him, I am going to leave it to him upon dying," one may see "nicmacatia" or "nimacatia."

Final *x* [sh] is often omitted, or we may see *s* as a substitute: instead of *axcan*, "today, now," one will find "aca" or "asca."

Final *tz* [ts] is weakened to [s] and often written *s*, as in "mestli" instead of *metztli*, "month." This phenomenon is commonly seen in the Valley of Mexico as well.

Final *ch* [tsh] was apparently often weakened to [sh] in speech; it is found written as *x* or *s*, or omitted. The forms of *nochpoch*, "my daughter," are many: "nopox," "noxpos," "nospo," and many more.

Final *l* [l], that is, *l* in standard Nahuatl, as opposed to the *l* used in Tolucan Nahuatl for standard *tl*, seems the most stable of the syllable-final con-

[3]The *o* assimilation was not universal even in the Valley of Mexico, though only that version had good tone. With elision, the idiosyncrasy of the Toluca Valley may be limited largely to the one word *-animantzin*. Elision is never seen with the loanwords for brother and sister, but that tends to be true in the Valley of Mexico as well. The constantly seen form "my daughter," *nochpoch*, though it is written in many unorthodox ways, always has the standard elision, *i* being omitted after *o*. We could take it that the *o/i* elision is standard, the *o/a* elision problematic in general, for we find the forms "noamatlacuilol" and "noaxca."

[4]This matter is treated in Lockhart 1991, pp. 122–40, using three texts also included in this volume (Nos. 47–49, above all 47). The developments are discussed in greater specificity there than here; at that time it was not fully realized how widespread the phenomena were, but the analysis still mainly holds true in regard to nonstandard orthography in the entire corpus here.

[5]See Lockhart 2001, pp. 112–14.

sonants, but it is sometimes omitted, as in "nopihua" for standard *nopilhuan*, "my children."

Final *uh* [unvoiced w] is often omitted or even more characteristically written as *c*; "nitlatlactilia" for *nictlatlauhtilia*, "I implore him/her (to pray for me)," becomes almost as much a signal-word for Tolucan-style deviance as "nehual" for *nehuatl*. At the very end of a word, *uh* is apparently more likely to be omitted entirely than to have a substitute; for *noxhuiuh*, "my grandchild," we very often see "noxhui."

Many of these substitutions are further complicated by hypercorrection. That is, when *ch* [tsh] has been weakened to [sh], not only will it be written *x*, but since its pronunciation has merged with that of *x*, *ch* will be written instead of *x* at times; we will see for *axcan* "achca." Just so *tl* is used for *l*, as in "fiscatl" for *fiscal*, and even prevocalically, as in "de tla crus" for de la Cruz. We often see *tz* for *s/z* as well.

The most characteristic phenomenon of nonstandard Tolucan writing is something I am not aware of in the Nahuatl texts of other areas, though I imagine it is possible: the insertion of an *i* [i] after a vulnerable syllable-final consonant to preserve it in speech and writing. Thus for *ixquich*, "all," we may see "ixiquichi." This feature I have come to call the "Tolucan *i*" (meaning "Tolucan" in the broader sense of the whole valley). The phenomenon can spread beyond *i* [i] to other vowels, however. With a few writers and one in particular (Sebastián Fabián, Nos. 52–55), one may see such a form as "nehuala" for *nehuatl*, "I," in which because of the contiguous *a* in the stem, *a* is inserted instead of *i*.

Tolucan texts of this time can represent a formidable challenge to a reader coming from the mainline corpus of Nahuatl documentation. I hope that the above remarks can be a guide and help, but I know from my own case that only long experience brings any facility with these materials.

I must emphasize again that the nonstandard things I have been discussing do not dominate every text in the corpus, far from it. Some texts show few of the signs mentioned; others only some slight hint. What are the principles of variation? I must await future more systematic research to give definitive answers and full explanations. For now I will make some general observations and discuss a couple of individual phenomena more completely. Overall, I perceive that texts are more likely to have a standard appearance, approximating contemporary texts of the Valley of Mexico, first the earlier they are, second the more professionally trained the notary is, and third more in Toluca proper than in Calimaya/Tepemaxalco.[1] Those writers of the seventeenth and early decades of the eighteenth century who write *c/ç/z* instead of *s* and organize their items using the marginal sign v̲ often tend to a more standard writing. But none of these trends are at all consistent, and I will go no further for now.

I will, however, give an example of the variation in the writing of a single word, *huiptla*, "the day after tomorrow," already mentioned above. As we saw, the main nonstandard version is "huictla," with *c* for *p*. Only three pre-1700 texts in the corpus contain the word, two in Calimaya/Tepemaxalco and one in the Toluca area. All are written in the standard fashion, with *p*. Comparing the two subareas overall, one can get somewhat different proportions according to whether one counts attestations, documents with attestations, or writers. Counting writers seems to give the most significant results. In the Toluca area, 7 writers use the standard *p*, 2 use *c*, and 3 are nonstandard in some other way, so that over half are standard. In Calimaya/Tepemaxalco it turns out the opposite; 7 write nonstandard *c*, 3 are nonstandard in some other way, and only 3 write *p*. Among them is the most professional writer of the area, Hipólito de los Santos, and if we counted attestations only, he alone would bring *p* nearly to the same level as *c* in Calimaya/Tepemaxalco. Both areas are alike, then, in having both standard and nonstandard versions; only the proportions vary.

I will also attempt to give some notion of the distribution of the "Tolucan *i*" to preserve final consonants, a feature which generally correlates with the most nonstandard writers in all respects. The phenomenon is seen in both subareas. One hesitates whether to concentrate on the cases in which it is pervasive or on all those in which it surfaces at least once. If we take the first tack, the Toluca area has extreme examples in No. 3 (1699), Nos. 12 and 21 (1737, both by the same writer), and No. 38 (the memorandum, ca. 1738). Calimaya/Tepemaxalco

[1]Certain outlying tlaxilacalli of Calimaya/Tepemaxalco, notably San Antonio de Padua, tend to have quite standard forms as part of a general old-fashioned conservatism, but in others nonstandard writing reaches its height.

has equivalents in No. 47 (1731) and four documents done by one writer in 1759 and 1762 (Nos. 52–55). Looking for documents with at least one Tolucan *i* or equivalent, I find 8 in the Toluca area, 19 in Calimaya/Tepemaxalco. In the latter one sees very little of the phenomenon in the central cluster, in either half, so that it is concentrated mainly in the outlying tlaxilacalli and above all in the contiguous San Lucas Evangelista and Santa María de la Asunción, which have both the most extreme examples and the largest number of cases.

The nonstandard variants thus do not seem to separate the language of one subarea from the other in any basic way, but to relate to a common facet of language in the larger region. Although the texts of notaries such as Bernardo de Santiago and Tomás de la Cruz in the Toluca area could almost pass for Valley of Mexico products, even among them we will find an occasional slipping back into the characteristic deviances of the Toluca Valley.

4. Notaries

ALL THAT WE KNOW about the testators and their heirs and associates comes to us through the notaries who, using their own vocabulary and conventions, wrote the documents that we read. It is only by a close study of the characteristics and procedures of the notaries that we can begin to get some notion of where the testator begins and the notary leaves off. At times we may get the impression that the notary is following the testator word for word, but in many cases we know that is not true. Much will remain unknown about the relationship of the two. But the situation is not hopeless, for the notaries themselves are authentic members of the communities we wish to study. They accurately reflect, for example, the subregional variations of which we have seen so many.

On all counts, then, attention should be paid to the notaries. Here, as a gesture in that direction, I discuss those notaries in the corpus who are responsible for more than one will, (briefly mentioning, because of his extreme orthography, one who has only a single will in the collection); I arrange them according to the first document they have in the volume.[1] I mention what can be discovered about their careers, for it was common and natural that a notary should also at some time occupy the post of temachti, teacher of religious doctrine, and the more successful of them went on to the higher offices of alcalde and fiscal, attaining the don as a result (for the office of notary did not in itself usually have the don as a prerogative). As it happens, the majority of that sort of information in the corpus concerns Calimaya/Tepemaxalco. Many things might explain why such data are rare in the Toluca-area portion of the corpus, and I will not speculate; I am not yet willing to believe that notaries there did not frequently advance to higher posts. Occasionally the writers call themselves notary of the church, occasionally of the commonwealth or municipality (*república*). It would be most interesting to follow these clues further and see to what extent the two posts were separate, to what extent combined, but since most writers are called notary pure and simple, I leave the question for future research.

With each notary I discuss the preamble style he uses, which is to be understood in the context of the section on preambles above (pp. 9–11). I make a general statement on the nature of his orthography, whether it is more conservative or more unorthodox, and I say a word on anything particularly striking about his vocabulary, either traditional or Spanish-influenced. Recognizing that technical discussion of orthographic variation will go beyond the interests and capacities of many readers, I relegate this matter, important though it is to the cultural articulation and evolution of the region, to a footnote for each writer, in which his tendencies are listed in a sort of telegraph style. These notes are to be interpreted in the light of the section on language just preceding this one.

Toluca area

BERNARDO DE SANTIAGO is responsible for four testaments dated from 1717 to 1733 (Nos. 2, 5, 13, 30); he served people in four different tlaxilacalli: San Juan Bautista, Santa Clara Cozcatlan, San Juan Evangelista, and San Miguel Aticpac. It cannot go unmentioned that he produced the most beautiful pages in the entire corpus, with large, exquisitely formed letters evenly spaced. His preambles are extremely uniform from one will to the next; they

[1] It would be well to discuss every single notary, including those represented only once, and to compile and analyze the information, but considerations of time and space prevent that at present.

fit within the usual, quite rudimentary Toluca pattern but retain some conservative formula too, such as the body returning to the earth of which it was made. Yet he is not devoid of modernity; he contributes one of the few loan verbs in the Toluca-area corpus, and he uses the semi-calque *casado ica*, "married to," from Spanish *casado con*; he also employs the loanword *mortaja* for "shroud."

Overall, Bernardo de Santiago's orthography is almost implausibly standard for someone writing in the Toluca Valley in the eighteenth century. It would be very hard to distinguish him from the better writers of his time or earlier in the Valley of Mexico. In the majority of his texts, only his prefix string *nicon* instead of *nocon* veers somewhat from the standard, and it is a minor sin. In his earliest text, however, in just one phrase he falls into a nonstandard Tolucan mode. He omits a final *c* and twice inserts an epenthetic *i* at the end of a word to preserve a consonant, the famous "Tolucan *i*."[1] Perhaps Bernardo de Santiago's standard Nahuatl usage and orthodox orthography were the result of careful instruction, an overlay, so that he was capable of slipping back into more local modes.[2]

MARCELO DE LA CRUZ was the writer of two Toluca-area wills of 1737 and 1740 (Nos. 11 and 7), serving people in the tlaxilacalli of San Miguel Aticpac and Santa Clara Cozcatlan. His preamble format is close to that of Bernardo de Santiago just above. He writes most of the final consonants most of the time, but he is far more affected than his colleague by Toluca-style orthography. He tends to much omission and some repetition of syllables. We see a great deal of influence of Spanish speech in his texts; he uses plural suffixes on native vocabulary ("tlalmilme," "fields"; "meme," "magueyes"), has the particle *para*, and writes "pedaso tlali," "a piece of land." His phrase *mocahua ica* may be a calque for Spanish "se queda con," "he/she keeps." But once he uses the conservative *-teiccauh*, "younger sibling of a male" (though he also has *-hermano*).[3]

TOMÁS DE LA CRUZ is a rival of Bernardo de Santiago for the position of premier notary of the Toluca area in the corpus, though they were not strict contemporaries, Tomás de la Cruz coming earlier. He was responsible for four wills from 1701 to 1711, done for people in Santa Bárbara Xolalpan or Solarpan, San Sebastián, and San Miguel Aticpac (Nos. 8–10, 20). His preambles follow the usual simple style of the Toluca area. His calligraphy is excellent even if his pages are not quite as stunning as those of Bernardo de Santiago. His orthography is similar too, preserving the great majority of the final consonants, but Tomás de la Cruz is less conservative and less regular. He gives a few words in highly irregular forms. His reproduction of Spanish words often shows letter substitutions. He seems to have merged Spanish [r] and [d] in speech, and also [r] and [l]; thus "costorio" for *custodio*, "omorodaro" for *omodoraro*, "coratelar" for *colateral*, and both "Belnarda" and "Bernarda."

His vocabulary is cosmopolitan, rich in both older native terms and up-to-date echoes of Spanish. We have just noted his use of a loan verb; he can write such a phrase as "yc ysquina cosina," "at the corner of the kitchen"; he uses not only *para* but *hasta*, in the latter case the only writer from the Toluca area to do so. Yet he also includes some traditional terms seen nowhere else in the corpus: *callalli*, "house-land," and *-huepol*, "one's same-generation in-law of the opposite gender."[4]

---

[1]"Cenpohualquahuitli yc patlahua Macuilquahuitli," standard *cempohualquahuitl ic patlahuac macuilquahuitl.*

[2]Orthography: Has *no* first person reflexive and "nanimantzin" consistently. Retains *-uh, -ch, -x, -c, -z, -tl* with full consistency. Is rare in the corpus in writing *-lli* more often than *-li* ("tlalli" rather than the predominant "tlali"). His use once of "ceuhpa" instead of "ceppa" implies that [w] was weak in his pronunciation even though he writes the full-*uh* wherever it is standard. Often writes *h* in the position traditionally occupied by glottal stop, as some of the best writers of the Valley of Mexico also had long done. Even retains *-n* in the great majority of cases and virtually never intrudes it. Uses mainly final *-z* instead of *-s*, a conservative trait.

[3]Orthography: Has *no* first person reflexive, but *nicon* and "noanimantzin." Consistently writes *-l* for *-tl*. Sometimes *-s* is missing; may use *-s* for *-tz*, *-c* for *-t*. Has a substitution seen most frequently in Calimaya/Tepemaxalco, *-c* for *-uh*. His hallmark is hypercorrect *-ch* for *-x*: "yachca" for *iaxca*. Writes "mostla huictla" with *c*, not the standard *p* of Bernardo de Santiago. Has much intrusive *-n*. Uses mainly *-s* rather than *-z*.

[4]Orthography: Has *no* first person reflexive consistently, as well as "nanimantzin"; varies between *nocon* and *nicon*. The final consonants are virtually always present in standard form, including *-tl*; *-c* is omitted just once. Reproduces more final *-n* than most writers in the corpus. Varies between *-s* and *-z*, with some hypercorrection: "dioz, teztamento." Always writes *-li*, never *-lli* like Bernardo de Santiago. Writes the strange metathesis "yhuicatlapan" for *icuitlapan*, "behind it." The verb *chipahua*, "to clean, " seems to take the form "-uhpahua."

MATÍAS DE LA CRUZ, a Toluca-area notary, has two wills in the corpus, written in 1737 and 1738 for people in San Miguel Aticpac and San Sebastián (Nos. 12, 21). His preambles are of the simple type prevalent in the Toluca area. His writing is not without some standard elements, but it is outstanding for unorthodox forms of a type seen both in the Toluca area and in Calimaya/Tepemaxalco. His two texts are an extreme example of the Tolucan *i*, containing over 30 occurrences, from "axica" for *axcan*, "now," to much more complex instances. Matías de la Cruz is notable for writing a hypercorrect consonant, then an *i* to preserve it, then an intrusive *n* after the *i*, giving a result that only a very experienced reader of such texts could decipher (see n. 5 below). In one testament a garbled Spanish phrase accompanies the final signatures, making one wonder about the notary's competence, though his performance is all in all within the normal range except for his orthography. Like many writers in the corpus, Matías de la Cruz has both up-to-date and archaic language: the Spanish particle *para* and the poetic old *xamani*, "to be shattered, disintegrate."[5]

FRANCISCO DE LA CRUZ is represented by two testaments from San Pedro Tototepec in the Toluca area, from 1733 and 1735 (Nos. 26, 27). His preambles conform to the Tolucan style, with only the Trinity and placing the soul in God's hands, but they stand out because unlike most testaments in Toluca proper they use the nonstandard double passive of the verb "to praise," and to render "entirely in the hands of (God)," they use the rare phrase *ce imactzinco* instead of the usual *icenmactzinco*. When we examine No. 25 from 1728, also written in San Pedro Tototepec, but by a different notary, and find both of these features the same, we realize that they are a tlaxilacalli convention more than a personal style and must have been handed from one notary to the next. That becomes even more clear when we see, in the place where the word *memoria*, "memorandum (of testament)" sometimes occurs, the strange form "metario," which must have arisen through some notary's misapprehension of a Spanish word, and then see that it too is present in No. 25. The two Tototepec notaries also share formulas about the sick and praying for the soul and even specific spellings, "chani" for *chane*, "resident," and "omochique" for *omochiuhque*, "they became" (and this despite the fact that Francisco de la Cruz otherwise writes *-uh* in the orthodox way).

The writing gives a quite standard impression, undermined somewhat by the fact that there is an overbar over almost every single *y* whether it is associated with an *n* or not. Except for the special tlaxilacalli word "metario" the only notable thing about the vocabulary in these wills is the single occurrence in the collection of the word *-huexiuh*, "one's fellow parent-in-law," an exception to the general use of loanwords for same-generation in-laws in the corpus.[6]

SALVADOR DE SANTIAGO of the Toluca area has two wills in the collection, from 1710 and 1731 (Nos. 28, 31), both done for people in San Juan Bautista. Despite the small number of texts, the stretch of years between them implies a significant career. He uses the usual reduced preamble of Toluca. Although he writes *-s* instead of *-z*, the main impression is of very orthodox, conservative writing, with all of the final consonants unchanged. He even writes *-lli* rather than *-li* part of the time. One is put in mind of Bernardo de Santiago and wonders if the two could be related, but too many notaries are named Santiago and Cruz for such speculation to be fruitful. Close observation discovers a few hints in the orthography of Tolucan-style nonstandard features. The vocabulary is not striking, though we do see the very Hispanic "pedaçito tlalli," "a bit of land," and Salvador de Santiago is rare in the corpus in using the older expression "noamatlacuilol," "my writing on paper,"

[5]Orthography: Has "nanimatzin" and *nicon*. Writes one standard *-tl*; has no *-l* for *-tl*, but avoids it by use of the *i:* "nehuatli" for *nehuatl*. Most final *-tl* in his texts is ironically for *-tli*, thus "çoçomatl" for *tzotzomatli*, "rags." Sometimes writes standard *-uh* rather than using the Tolucan *i*. May hypercorrect *-x* to *-ch*. Once uses epenthetic *e* rather than *i*, in "ninconetlalia" for *nicontlalia*. Has some *e* for *i* in *-tli:* "huetzintle" for *huentzintli*. An example of the extreme form in the text above, which occurs several times, is "mochihuatzin," in which the *tz* is hypercorrect for *-z* or *-s*, the *i* is the Tolucan epenthesis, and the *n* is intrusive in addition, so that the word is equivalent to *mochihuaz*, "it is to be done." Abounds in superficially strange forms, such as "m[a?]quilicquahui," in which apparently the *qui* is for *cui*, a Tolucan *i* is followed by an intrusive *c*, and final *-tl* is missing, so that the form is the equivalent of *macuilquahuitl*, "5 quahuitl."

[6]Orthography: Has *no* first person reflexive, "nanimatzin," *nicon*. Has consistent *-l* for *-tl*. Writes most final *-uh, -c, -ch, -x, -tz;* uses final *-s*, sometimes hypercorrected to *z*, as in "dioz." Once *-x* replaces *-ch*. Omits *-l* a few times. In *moztla huiptla*, writes the second word "huiphtla."

"my document," for the testament in the concluding words.[1]

ANDRÉS FRANCISCO has two wills in the collection, from 1736 and 1737 (Nos. 29 and 32), both done for people in the Toluca-area tlaxilacalli of San Juan Bautista. He lacks a high profile. His preambles are in the usual abbreviated Toluca style; his hallmark is the phrase *cemanahuac teotlatoani*, "universal divine ruler," using the abbreviation "C̄m̄h." He mainly retains the final consonants in their standard form despite some weakening and omission here and there. The effect is spoiled a bit by many missing syllables and some omission and intrusion of *n*, though not nearly as extreme as with some writers. He is one of those who uses the semi-calque *nicasado ica,* "I am married to."[2]

Calimaya/Tepemaxalco

PEDRO HERNÁNDEZ is the author of two testaments of 1760 and 1762 (Nos. 43 and 84). He is the only notary in the corpus to officiate in both Tepemaxalco and Calimaya, and also the only one to give himself the fancy title "royal and public notary." His preambles are in the central Calimaya/Tepemaxalco style, with invocation of several saints popular in the area, but differ in not featuring praise of the Trinity. His writing is fluent and skilled, giving a first impression of being quite standard, but it has many local characteristics, along with the very individual trait of mainly writing *z* for prevocalic *tz*, especially in *-zin* for the reverential element *-tzin*. As with many writers, he has both some traditional traits, such as using more native vocabulary than usual in giving the date, and phrases close to Spanish, as in "por albasea," in which *por* has the idiomatic meaning "as."[3]

ANASTASIO DE BENAVIDES of San Lucas Evangelista wrote only one of the documents in the corpus (No. 47, 1731), but he is included here because he rivals another notary or two as the most complete and extreme example in the collection of unorthodox writing in the style of the Toluca Valley. He also illustrates, along with Antonio Silverio of Santa María de la Asunción, that conventional writing skills were not essential to the advance of a notary, for both of them later acquired the don (Benavides as fiscal, and Silverio probably also). His preamble and some other parts of the will that he wrote closely resemble others from his tlaxilacalli in general structure and vocabulary, but the way he handles the matter of the witnesses implies that he was not very familiar with the testament genre. He not only weakens almost all the final consonants or follows them with the Tolucan *i*, of which he is a prime example, but he has other unrelated orthographic idiosyncrasies not otherwise seen in the corpus, including *chu* for *hu* and *R* for *cr*. A whole article has been devoted mainly to his orthography for those who should be interested in studying it in detail.[4]

DOMINGO RAMOS of San Lucas Evangelista is represented in the corpus by two wills, of 1726 and 1736 (Nos. 49, 50). He has an almost archaic preamble formula, quite extensively carried out and well executed in one case. He gives a general impression of writing much more standardly than his San Lucas colleague Anastasio de Benavides, with many final consonants unchanged. Yet at one point or another he also does all the unorthodox things typical of the Toluca Valley and especially of San Lucas. He is much given to syllable omission. He is the writer discussed above (p. 36) who was unable to get the word for "savior" right. With Domingo Ramos it surely seems that standard writing was an overlay, something to which he had been very meaningfully

---

[1]Orthography: Has *no* first person reflexive and *nocon*, varies on elision or nonelision with *-animantzin*. Consistently writes final *-tl*, usually also *-c, -s, -x, -tz, -ch, -uh*. Writes *p* in *moztla huiptla*. Sometimes omits *-c*, once *-s*. His "metztiyetz" for *moyetztiyez* has a hypercorrect *-tz* for *-z/-s* implying that he merged [ts] and [s] in speech.

[2]Orthography: Has *no* first person reflexive prefix, writes "nanimantzin," but has *nicon*. Has *-tl, -c, -s, -tz, -ch, -uh*. Sometimes weakens *-tz* to *-z*, occasionally omits *-c*. Omits *-uh* once before *tz*, but that was something done on occasion by very orthodox writers in the Valley of Mexico. Once writes the inventive metathesis "puihtla" for *huiptla*.

[3]Orthography: Varies between *no* and *mo* as first person reflexive; has unassimilated *nicon*; mainly writes "noanimanzin" but also elides the *o* once. Has, in addition to *z* for *tz*, *-c* for *-uh*; tends to write *-l* instead of *-tl* but has an occasional *-tl*; usually writes *-x* or *-h* for *-ch*. Sometimes has standard *cui*, but also *qui* ("oquimoquili" for *oquimocuili*).

[4]Lockhart 1991, pp. 122–40. Benavides writes *-l* for *-tl*, omits *c* or writes *-qui*, omits *-ch* or writes *-x* or *-chi*, omits *-x* or writes *-xi*, and omits *-uh* (never replacing it with *-c* or writing *-hui*). He consistently retains standard *-l* and *-s*.

exposed, but he was constantly falling back into unorthodox local ways.[5]

SEBASTIÁN FABIÁN of San Lucas Evangelista authored four short wills in the corpus, from 1759 and 1762 (Nos. 52–55). He writes a standard preamble for San Lucas in his time, with praise of the Trinity (the verb being in the orthodox reflexive reverential as usual at that time and place) and invocation of Mary. In most ways he is a normal, competent, notary, but his texts look highly non-standard and can be hard to understand because of his very generous use of the Tolucan *i* to preserve final consonants (plus other unorthodoxies). He also frequently extends the principle of the Tolucan *i* to other vowels which harmonize with vowels in the stem: thus *a* at the end of "nehuala" for *nehuatl*, and *e* in "setele" for *centetl*. In both these cases *-tl* was already weakened to *-l*, but still needs epenthesis to be preserved. The epenthetic vowels *a* and *e* are quite common in his texts, but he also has *o* in "noCo-Catlatolo" for *nococoxcatlatol*, "my sick person's statement."

There is little of special note in Sebastián Fabián's vocabulary, but once he retains an old formula in ending a passage with "That is all with which I kiss his hands and feet" (No. 54).[6]

LUIS MARTÍN of Santa María de la Asunción wrote five of the testaments in the collection, from 1759, 1760, and 1762 (Nos. 57–61). Once he adds "de Francia" to his name, indicating pretensions and ambitions for higher office, but he seems not to have fulfilled them yet by 1762. He is contemporary with another notary of Santa María, Miguel de San Juan. From our corpus it appears that the two of them were the main notaries of the tlaxilacalli in the later 1750s and early 1760s, but Miguel de San Juan has a much earlier document in the volume and advanced to high office earlier; possibly he served as a model for Luis Martín. At any rate, they share a great deal. Luis Martín's preamble formula is very close to Miguel de San Juan's, consisting mainly of praise of the Trinity (using the correct reflexive reverential) and invocation of the Virgin (though in his last document he adds some of the local saints popular in the central cluster of Calimaya/Tepemaxalco). Both have the very same unique peroration (see above, p. 22). But most of Luis Martín's texts look much less standard, with more substitutions, and he omits and repeats more syllables. Overall there is nothing too striking about his vocabulary, although his "tlen oora," apparently based on a phrase like *en cualquier hora*, "at whatever time," is of interest.

Except in one case where he did the writing for the less capable official notary, Luis Martín seems to have had mainly humble clients. In this too he is like Miguel de San Juan; it may reflect the tlaxilacalli more than a particular notary.[7]

MIGUEL DE SAN JUAN of Santa María de la Asunción has five testaments in the corpus, from 1737, 1752, 1759, 1760, and 1762 (Nos. 62–66). By 1762 he had acquired the don, was fiscal, and had already been alcalde (see No. 66); as fiscal he still wrote and authorized testaments. I have already spoken of his main characteristics in comparing him with his junior colleague Luis Martín, just above. In his writing he uses most of the same unorthodox forms as Luis Martín, but the proportions are different, and Miguel de San Juan is capable of giving a general impression almost as orthodox as Bernardo de Santiago of Toluca. Signs of Spanish speech in his texts, though not numerous, are striking: "desde tepitzin," based on Spanish "desde pequeño," "since he was little," and *parejo*, "equal," an adjective, used almost as an adverb. Older terminology is also in

[5]Orthography: Has some cases of the Tolucan *i*, as in "ynemaqui" for *inemac*. Consistently writes *-l* for *-tl*. Although virtually all the other final consonants are present in standard form at times, he often omits *-uh* or writes *-c* instead, as so often in Calimaya/Tepemaxalco. He may omit *-ch* or write it as *-x* or *s*. He may omit *-s* and *-c* and weaken *-tz* to *-s*. Sometimes he writes *qui* for *cui* and *que* for *cue*. Sometimes uses *-uh* through hypercorrection instead of *-c* to represent a weak syllable-final sound, as in "auhque" for *aquen*, where there was historically a glottal stop after the *a*.

[6]Orthography: Has mainly *mo* first person reflexive, but also once *no*; writes both "nanima" and "noanimantzin." Many of the final consonants including *-l* are sometimes missing, and he has some of the usual substitutions indicating weakening (uses both *-s* and *-x* for *-ch*, and *-s* also for *-x*), though he does not use the *-c* for *-uh* so often seen in Calimaya/Tepemaxalco. Often omits *-r* in loanwords. There are also hypercorrections, including *-tl* for *-l*. These texts would reward much more study.

[7]Orthography: Has both *no* and *mo* first person reflexive, both "nanimantzin" and "noanimantzin." Almost always writes *-l* for *-tl*, but has one *-tl*. Never has *-uh*, usually *-c* instead. For *-ch* often writes *-h*, sometimes *-x*; may also write *-h* for *-x*. Has one case of Tolucan *i*, "ixiquih" for *ixquich*. Often writes *-n* in the position of historical glottal stop. In *moztla huiptla* has "huictla." Sometimes writes *ll* for *y*.

evidence: *-teiccauh*, "younger sibling of a male," and *tequitcatlalli*, "tribute land."[1]

ANTONIO SILVERIO of Santa María de la Asunción has his name on two testaments, though he wrote only one of them, in 1758 (No. 67); he was official notary again in 1762, by then don Antonio Silverio, but in No. 57 of that year he had Luis Martín, discussed above, do the actual writing. After we have read the will he wrote, we realize why.

From the tiny sample of No. 67, a short will for a person already deceased, Silverio seems one of the least skilled, least knowledgeable notaries in the whole corpus, though he writes individual letters clearly. His preamble includes praise of the Trinity with a basically correct reflexive reverential verb, along with invocation of Mary, typical for the tlaxilacalli. But he is one of the worst omitters of syllables in the corpus. He has a strange *-zn* for the *-tzin* reverential, the only example in the collection. In this short text he has three examples of the Tolucan *i*. At the end he uses the abbreviation of the word *alcalde* as a contentless rubric, perhaps never having understood what it meant.[2]

HIPÓLITO DE LOS SANTOS of Calimaya is the best represented notary in the collection, with no less than eight wills written between 1738 and 1763 (Nos. 70–74, 76, 81, 82). He officiated in the various tlaxilacalli of the central settlement of Calimaya—we have examples from Pasiontitlan, Teopantonco, and Tlamimilolpan—but never in outlying tlaxilacalli or in Tepemaxalco. By the 1750s and 1760s he seems to have been the dominant notary in the core of Calimaya, with a mainly wealthy clientele and outstanding connections among the official community.

From the beginning he was temachti, teacher of the doctrine, as well as notary; generally he is seen as notary alone, and sometimes as temachti alone. Once he calls himself the church notary (*escribano de la santa iglesia*), and once the municipal notary (*escribano de la república*). He first appears as don Hipólito de los Santos in 1758, then is inconsistent with the title during a two-year period, and after 1759 is consistently don. He had probably held the office of fiscal at some point in the late 1750s.

De los Santos is an extremely fluent, practiced writer with a fine hand. His texts give an impression of professionalism and even of orthodoxy, though in fact they contain many nonstandard features. In him these features seem to take on the aspect of a new local orthodoxy.

Starting with a preamble form that had evolved by the 1730s in writers such as don Juan Francisco, just below, de los Santos develops a special list of saints who are invoked in each will, though he may abbreviate it with lesser clients, and he had not yet determined its definitive shape in his first will of 1738.[3] He uses the nonstandard double passive of the verb "to praise" in the first sentence of the preamble, perhaps thereby giving it the final stamp of approval on the local scene.

De los Santos takes a middle path between a conservative orthography and an expression of local idiosyncrasies. Even though he writes most of the final consonants in a standard way at times, and is unusual in Calimaya/Tepemaxalco in consistently writing the *p* in *moztla huiptla*, he also uses some of the typical letter substitutions of the area, in some cases without or almost without exception. Though he has full command of all the native vocabulary used in the region, he is at the same time unusually close to Spanish. He has many more examples of *para* than any other writer, as well as the only compound particle (*fuera de*) and one of the two loan verbs in the Calimaya/Tepemaxalco texts (*constaroa*), and he frequently uses the semi-calque *nicchihuilia cargo*, equivalent to *le hago cargo*, "I charge him with."[4]

[1]Orthography: Has both *no* and *mo* first person reflexive, has both "nanimatzin" and "noanimantzin." Almost all of the final consonants are standard at times, including *-tl* and *-uh*. But writes more *-l* than *-tl*. Sometimes has *-c* for *-uh* in the popular way in Calimaya/Tepemaxalco, and also has *-uh* for *-c* as a hypercorrection. May weaken *-ch* to *-x*, *-x* to *-s*. Has "huictla" in *moztla huiptla*. May leave *ll* unassimilated, as in "notlalyo nosoquio," "my body (my earth and clay)."

[2]Orthography: In addition to *-zn* for *-tzin*, consistently has *-l* for *-tl*. Omits *-uh*, often omits *-c*. Has *h* for prevocalic *ch*, otherwise not seen. Omits a syllabic vowel in *mahuiz-* to give "mahus-" and *huel* to give "hul," which may reflect a speech phenomenon but is rare in the corpus. Has *qui* for *cui*: "onitlaquilo" for *onitlacuilo*. His examples of the Tolucan *i* are "ixiquichi" for *ixquich* and "imixipaznco" for *imixpantzinco*.

[3]See No. 70, with an example of the full form and a more detailed discussion of the saints. The 1738 will is No. 81.

[4]Orthography: Varies between *no* and *mo* first person reflexive, has mainly "noanimantzin," but also "nanimantzi" once. Also in native vocabulary once writes unelided "noaxca," "my property." Within a (*cont'd*)

DON JUAN FRANCISCO of Calimaya has two testaments in the corpus, from 1734 and 1739 (Nos. 79, 80), both done in the central-cluster tlaxilacalli of Tlamimilolpan. Like Hipólito de los Santos just above, he acquires the don and is simultaneously temachti and notary (of the church); in one document he is called temachti alone, though he still produces the testament.

Indeed, don Juan Francisco can be seen as a sort of prototype of de los Santos. Like him he has the nonstandard form of the verb "to praise" at the beginning. He invokes many saints in his preambles, already very close to the list used by de los Santos, with only minor variation. His texts are less standard in appearance than those of de los Santos; he tends to have many of the same local unorthodoxies without the standard variants that de los Santos also uses. He also commits more omissions, repetitions, and simple mistakes. He gives his work an archaic and to us charming touch of oral spontaneity by using the second person possessor with the name of the Trinity, "your name," thus speaking directly to the deity, and he once allows a testator to speak directly to her nephew in the body of the will. There is nothing especially striking about his vocabulary in the context of the corpus.[5]

FELIPE JUAN of Santa María Nativitas has three short testaments in the corpus, dated 1759 and 1760 (Nos. 91–93). He belonged to a local officeholding family with the second name Juan.

His preambles have the Trinity but lack the praise formula, and indeed lack anything else other than placing the soul in the hands of God; thus they approximate the style of the Toluca area. The reason could be that the wills are so brief and rudimentary, but more likely it has to do with a tlaxilacalli style. In orthography Felipe Juan has both a standard and a nonstandard version of many things. He would probably show a broader range if we had a longer document; here there is no occasion for certain final consonants even to come into play.[6]

FRANCISCO DE LA CRUZ of Santiago Apóstol Quaxochtenco has no testaments in the corpus, but he produced two documents associated with No. 94: a bill of sale of 1697 and a memorandum of 1709, of which the first part may have been written in 1703. Under these circumstances such things as his treatment of preambles cannot be discussed. His orthography shows many tendencies of the Calimaya/Tepemaxalco area already well developed in the late seventeenth century. He has both an extreme Spanish loan, the double particle *ni . . . ni*, "neither . . . nor," and some traditional vocabulary, calling the officials elders and his fathers.[7]

5. Some Concluding Remarks

IN REVIEWING the successive parts of the texts included in this collection we have seen that Nahuatl testaments written in the Toluca Valley in the late seventeenth and the eighteenth centuries were true successors of those of earlier times and other places. Not only do they have the same constituent parts, in the same order, but also much of the same vocabulary, from *misa*, "mass," to *albacea*, "executor," and *testigo*, "witness." And this statement holds true for all of the documents in the present corpus, as well as for other wills of the Toluca Valley that I have seen in the course of my research. The corpus of testaments also reflects some strong social and cultural continuities in the indigenous world more generally. For example, it is just as true here as it was in the Testaments of Culhuacan, which I have

---

framework of writing a large number of final consonants standardly, he has *-l* for *-tl* consistently. Usually writes *-c* for *-uh* (plus like many simply omitting it at the end of a word), and also uses *-c* in the slot of the historical glottal stop. Mainly has *-h* or *-x* for *-ch*. Sometimes writes *qu* for *cu* before front vowels: "yquitlalpa" for *icuitlapan*, "quesContontli" for *cuezcontontli*.

5Orthography: Uses only *mo* first person reflexive, has only "noanimatzin," never elided. Writes "mostla huictla" with *c* rather than the standard *p* of de los Santos. Either omits *-uh* or puts *-c* instead. Often omits *-c*; also uses *-c* in the slot of the old glottal stop or just intrudes it. Often has *-x* for *-ch* and *qui* for *cui*, as in "quitlahuia" for *cuitlahuia*. Has a "Tolucan *e*" in "grabiele" for Gabriel.

6Orthography: Has mainly *no* first person reflexive, but also *mo* once; has "-animantzin" unelided. Writes both *-tl* and *-l* instead, more the latter. Once has a hypercorrect *-tl* for *-l*. Mainly writes *-h* for *-ch*, but sometimes retains *-ch*. Sometimes omits *-c, -x, -s*. There is no test of his treatment of *-uh*.

7Orthography: Has *no* first person reflexive. Has consistent *-l* for *-tl*. Writes *-h* and *-x* for *-ch, -s* for *-tz*. Omits *-t* or replaces it with *-c*. Has a quite rare *-c* for word-final *-uh*, "ypatic," for *ipatiuh*, "its price," but also retains word-final *-uh* as in "onicchiuh," "I did it." Writes a triple *l, lll*, which seems to represent [ly]: "melllo" for *medio*, usually "melio" in the corpus; "polllo" for *pollo*.

been systematically using as a point of comparison, that landholding is scattered in many comparatively small parcels and constantly redispersed through inheritance patterns; it is equally true that male names are more varied and often more prestigious than female names. And there are important differences at this level as well. Household saints are as pervasive in the present corpus as houses and land, but they are virtually absent from the Testaments of Culhuacan; kinship terminology is quite transformed from one corpus to the other.

But such unqualified generalizations are hard to formulate about the material in this collection because of a number of interrelated factors and perspectives which are themselves of the greatest interest. Thus the testaments of the present corpus, in addition to their underlying similarity, as texts, to the Testaments of Culhuacan, show many signs of post-sixteenth-century change. One is justified in calling the present collection overall a body of Stage 3 wills, with typical characteristics such as the holy family in the heading, the presence of the fund for Jerusalem, the disappearance of women as witnesses and the predominance in that function of local officials, completely aside from Stage 3 kinship terms and many signs of the language and orthography of that stage more generally. A very significant feature of the corpus, however, is that the diagnostic characteristics of the late period are often missing in the wills of the seventeenth century; at times they are absent even in the earlier texts of the eighteenth century, and also, to an extent, in some of the outlying tlaxilacalli of Calimaya/Tepemaxalco for as far forward in time as the corpus reaches. We seem to see that the set of symptoms or developments that can be abbreviated as Stage 3 was not in full force, as far as the form of wills is concerned, until considerably later than is imagined for the Valley of Mexico or central Mexico as a whole, and the same may be true of the language itself, though here the evidence is not yet sufficient. And though the typical Spanish loanwords of Stage 3 for close kin are present in the testaments from the first, an undercurrent of traditional kin terminology continues into the first decades of the eighteenth century.

Going beyond the testamentary genre, but staying with the theme of chronological trends in the corpus, one detects the development of a feature of Stage 3 kinship terminology not yet noticed elsewhere.[1] In the post-1700 period the Toluca Valley wills, from both main subareas in the corpus, while not going over to loanwords for the very closest of kin in the direct line, use native vocabulary to introduce gender distinctions very much on the Spanish model for small children and also for spouses. It appears that these new distinctions were just beginning to take hold in the late seventeenth century and did not become standard until close to 1700 (though in the corpus the evidence is better about the chronological trend with spouses than with children).

The greatest obstacle to uniform substantive generalizations about the present corpus is an aspect of it—regional variation—which at the same time opens up new and valuable perspectives on the evolution of indigenous society. I have been talking about things that unite the whole corpus of documents and that demonstrate marked characteristics uniform in both major subareas, and in all likelihood in the entire valley. In the end there will probably prove to be a Toluca Valley regional culture among indigenous people distinct from that of other comparable large central Mexican basins. Meanwhile, the present corpus reveals a startling number of differences between the two subareas of Toluca proper and Calimaya/Tepemaxalco. And the distinctions do not stop there. It is true that each major subarea—defined with Calimaya/Tepemaxalco as the jurisdiction of two paired altepetl, and in the Toluca case apparently as a parish, with the connections to the indigenous altepetl of Toluca not yet fully understood—displays many aspects that are uniform throughout that subarea and at the same time distinct from the other. But within each of the two are individual tlaxilacalli that may have features peculiar to themselves, or may fall into patterns of variation as blocks. The Toluca area is relatively homogeneous, but in Calimaya/Tepemaxalco we see again and again that a central settlement cluster, which includes components from both of the constituent altepetl, is distinct from the outlying tlaxilacalli, again of both altepetl.

Let us review some of the subarea-wide distinctions. We see them first as what we might call testamentary culture, aspects of the development of a genre which vies with historical annals as the most important avenue of Nahua self-expression in the

[1] Other than in Pizzigoni 2002, pp. 132–34, 145–49.

centuries after Spanish contact. Toluca-area testaments put less emphasis on the holy family than their counterparts in Calimaya/Tepemaxalco. Requests for bell ringing and cofradía donations occur only in Toluca. The donation for Jerusalem is half a real in Toluca, a full real in Calimaya/Tepemaxalco. All over Calimaya/Tepemaxalco the testaments often speak of "opening" the grave (using *tlapoa*), an expression never seen in Toluca. Both areas are very similar overall as to perorations, but only the Toluca area tends to put one at the end of the preamble, and the favorite or dominant perorations of the two are somewhat different. Detailed descriptions of the house complex occur only in Toluca, whereas the *cuezcomatl* or corncrib is mentioned only in Calimaya/Tepemaxalco.

These last items bring up an important question to which, with the present materials, I cannot always provide a certain answer. To what extent are these differences limited to a certain form of expression and to what extent do they reflect a broader reality? I view the tradition of preparing testaments as an important aspect of local culture, even when nothing else is involved. For one thing, it helps map two separate cultural traditions when we find that the main peroration in Toluca is *neltiz notlanequiliz*, "my will is to be carried out," and in Calimaya/Tepemaxalco *neltiz notlatol mochihuaz*, "my statement is to be carried out and done," and that neither subarea ever uses the other's version. In various districts of Calimaya/Tepemaxalco, as part of the concluding formula, the will is called *-cocoxcatlatol*, one's "sick person's statement," an expression that is absent in Toluca.

But many of these differences appear in testaments because of actual differences in phenomena in the broader world. I have no doubt that in Toluca people in point of fact paid half a real for Jerusalem, and in Calimaya/Tepemaxalco a full real. In other cases we are left in some doubt. As I wondered above, do the differences in house descriptions in the two areas imply any actual differences in the house complexes, and did the people around Toluca really not have corncribs? In these cases I much doubt that the difference in actuality was as great as in the literary tradition. Similar questions are whether or not maguey cultivation is actually stronger in Toluca, as it seems to be in the wills, whether large animals were more common in Toluca and sheep missing in Calimaya/Tepemaxalco, and whether Toluca was more active in borrowing and lending.

Looking more broadly within the corpus, we find many other cases in which we can hardly doubt, though still merely intuitively, that a given phenomenon goes beyond testaments. The word *huacax*, meaning ox and sometimes cow, is well attested in the wills of Toluca while entirely missing in those of Calimaya/Tepemaxalco, and I cannot seriously entertain the notion that this word for an important animal was used in testaments only. Likewise the fact that there are so many more Spanish loan particles in the wills of Calimaya/Tepemaxalco than in those of Toluca, even when the time difference is neutralized, is surely not something characteristic of testaments alone, but relates to the language spoken in the two subareas generally.

An important difference of this kind, that must be reflected in social and cultural reality beyond testaments, has to do with land. The category *tlalmilli* for a certain kind of field occurs only in Toluca, almost replacing the *milli* predominant in central Mexico generally, whereas in Calimaya/Tepemaxalco *milli* is the only term used. These words must have originated with the testators and be what they called their lands in everyday life. Even more important is the question of measurements. It also reflects life more broadly that Toluca stayed with the traditional quahuitl as a unit, whereas Calimaya/Tepemaxalco never used the quahuitl at all, employing instead the Spanish-based system of almud and fanega. And the difference is not merely in traditional versus Spanish terminology. In Toluca the traditional 20-quahuitl plot was the basis of everything, whereas in Calimaya/Tepemaxalco the fanega (equivalent to 120 quahuitl) gave the framework, causing the 3-almud plot, one fourth of a fanega (30 quahuitl), to be as common as plots of one or two almudes (10 and 20 quahuitl).

All the differences I have been discussing apply uniformly or nearly so across the two subareas. Others operate within subareas. The most striking trend is a difference between the central cluster of Calimaya/Tepemaxalco and all the outlying tlaxilacalli, regardless of which of the two altepetl is involved. We seem to see that in basic ways the two-altepetl structure is being undercut, with an ever more unified center standing out more clearly from ever more independent outlying tlaxilacalli. Also it often turns out that the center is more like Toluca, while the outlying tlaxilacalli are different from both the center and Toluca. Thus the overall picture of naming executors seems sharply different in the two subareas taken as a whole. But when we separate center and outliers, we find that the appointment of executors of wills was reasonably similar in Toluca and the center of Calimaya/Tepemaxalco, while it was in the outlying tlaxilacalli of Calimaya/Tepemaxalco that executors were hardly named.

The nonstandard double passive verb for praising the Trinity *(mocenquizcayectenehualo)* is much more characteristic of Calimaya/Tepemaxalco than of Toluca, where it is barely present, but in truth it is barely present in the outliers of Calimaya/Tepemaxalco either, and concentrates in the center of the double altepetl. Likewise the two major subareas seem to have a strikingly different style of preamble of the will, with Toluca favoring a stripped-down form and Calimaya/Tepemaxalco invoking a myriad of saints, many with local connotations. But again we see that the many saints are only in the center, and that preambles in some of the outlying tlaxilacalli are as plain as in Toluca. Being buried in the habit of an order is quite common in Toluca and in the center of Calimaya/Tepemaxalco, but it is never mentioned in the latter's outlying tlaxilacalli. In various ways we glimpse the picture of a wealthier, more sophisticated and up-to-date center as against a poorer and more old-fashioned outlying area.

I do not mean to imply that the outlying tlaxilacalli of Calimaya/Tepemaxalco act entirely as a unit (though when it comes to the tlaxilacalli of the center, I am unable to perceive any differences among them). Each one has a somewhat different style of testament, in some cases markedly so. San Lucas Evangelista seems to have been a hotbed of unorthodox orthography. We also see affiliations between certain individual tlaxilacalli. Thus within Tepemaxalco, San Lucas and Santa María de la Asunción, which from various hints appear to be contiguous, share features such as the form of the verb for praising the Trinity and the use of a collection of local officials as the primary witnesses. Although the tlaxilacalli of the Toluca area are harder to distinguish from one another, it is precisely there that we see one of the most marked cases of an individual style, with different notaries using a whole array of vocabulary and formulas rarely found elsewhere, and one erroneous Spanish loanword ("metario"), that is seen nowhere else and that they must have copied from one another as an element of tlaxilacalli culture.

Within this framework I wish to devote some words to the topic of gender, for when I first approached these materials my interest was primarily in gender in everyday life, and indeed specifically in certain aspects of the role of women in it. My interest in these topics is as keen as ever, but the Toluca Valley materials have taught me to see them within a broader context. I gradually grasped that one learns as much about women and gender from men's wills as from women's wills, on which I at first concentrated exclusively.

Gender matters seem to be among the aspects that do not vary much with tlaxilacalli or major subarea but are uniform throughout the corpus. In the corpus overall, in both subareas, we find fully confirmed the general understanding that in the indigenous world women's names were less differentiated and humbler than those of men. Things in this department do evolve over time, however, often running parallel with ever-increasing Spanish influence of various kinds. We see women functioning as witnesses and executors in the earlier wills and disappearing in those functions from the later ones, and we see in addition that from the seventeenth century into the early eighteenth and then later decades, ever fewer women have the doña or high-ranking names like Guzmán. But not everything new was to the direct disadvantage of females, as in the Spanish-inspired trend to recognize gender in naming spouses and small children that is dominant by 1700.

An analytical, point-by-point approach to the testamentary genre such as I have adopted here brings to one's awareness that by formal criteria the genders are treated with full equality. Self-identification modes are the same, preambles are the same, as well as donations and rituals; there is no kind of property that cannot under certain circumstances be held by either gender; both name executors and call on the same kind of witnesses. Without a doubt, however, despite the prominent role of women that we see in maguey cultivation, the data support preference for males or male dominance in many respects; females have fewer houses (and hence fewer saints), less land, fewer animals. They never hold any local office. Nevertheless, as we have seen, a large minority of the wills is issued by women, and female heirs are found again and again even when there are males too. The generally weaker showing does not do justice to the fact that some of the wealthiest and most influential people in the corpus are women. Sometimes it occurs to an extent by default, as in the case of Pascuala María (No. 57), with most of the men of a generation dying before her, so that she became the very active head of an important local family and functioned in a network with female relatives. But sometimes female prominence seems to arise more spontaneously, as when Elena de la Cruz (No. 10) names her two daughters executors despite having male sons and other male connections. Sometimes women seem to inherit the family house because elder males have already married, left, and received their inheritance.

This whole aspect—not so much of the overall picture of the genders, but of how individual women can be put in remarkable positions at times—is one of the main points requiring further research, both refining the statistical aspect and going yet further with reconstructing the subtleties of specific situations.[1] Much the same is true for the question of the inheritance of lands and of houses in general, and all these topics are of course intimately related.[2] There seems to have been a common overall vision of the strategy of inheritance that both genders to a large extent shared.

The differences and similarities across the wider Toluca region as seen in this corpus are of such complexity and diversity that we cannot doubt that we are dealing with a spontaneous, unconscious evolution. Some individual elements, it is true, may be the result of conscious policy. Decisions of Spanish ecclesiastics must have been involved in the different donation for Jerusalem in the two subareas (parishes). Possibly someone once undertook a reorganization of the lands of the Calimaya/Tepemaxalco area using the fanega and the almud as the basis. But surely no one directed the people of the central cluster to use a nominally incorrect verb to praise the Trinity, or told the people of San Pedro Tototepec that there was such a word as "metario." And the broader changes in the direction of a more gendered kin terminology are also something that no one would have tried to achieve by decree. With a body of wills such as these, each with its own coefficient of time and place, we can go far toward reconstructing a hitherto unknown process of regional and subregional cultural evolution.

I am not unmindful, however, of the utility of going beyond a corpus even as rich as this one in search of larger perspectives on regional variation and uniformity. Above (p. 3, n. 7) I already briefly speculated on the potential of treating the remaining extant Toluca-Valley testaments of this time—a body of material at least as large as the present corpus—in the same fashion as here. Surely such study, which in some form I will be undertaking in the near future, will approach closer to the question of the existence of a unitary culture among the indigenous people of the valley, distinct in some ways from that of the people of the Valley of Mexico or the Cuernavaca basin, and help establish whether or not there are other subareas in the valley as well defined as the two illustrated here, or whether perhaps one of our two types of subculture dominates much of the area.

Certain difficulties are to be anticipated. Above I stated that in laying out the criteria for setting up the present collection, the reason for choosing the Toluca area and Calimaya/Tepemaxalco was that they presented the thickest concentrations of documents, in which trends and uniformities can be observed and multiple examples can be found from a single tlaxilacalli. The remaining material is thinner, more scattered, and the redundancy seen here, with all its side effects, will often be lacking. Yet with the two subcultures already well established, it will be much easier to place a single document or a few of them within the Toluca Valley framework than it would have been before the Toluca area and Calimaya/Tepemaxalco had been studied.

Consider an isolated will issued in 1795 in Metepec, which I use as an example because it has already been published.[3] We immediately see familiar things universal in our present corpus: the holy family, the Jerusalem fund, the use of *-cihuauh* for "wife." But the formula of praise for the Trinity is missing, as in only older or old-fashioned items in the present collection. The preamble lacks the saints

[1] I am especially interested in using such techniques to develop a better picture of women's role in economic activities like pulque production (see pp. 27–28 above) and moneylending (see the hint on p. 29).

[2] I am considering in particular what research strategy to employ to determine more closely the extent of continuities and changes in the household complex between the Testaments of Culhuacan and the Toluca area as shown in the present corpus, as well as to find out more about complexes in Calimaya/Tepemaxalco and the rest of the Toluca Valley.

[3] Anderson, Berdan and Lockhart 1976, Doc. 6, testament of Miguel Gerónimo.

of central Calimaya/Tepemaxalco. Despite the late date, land is measured in quahuitl in numbers based on 20, and most of the final consonants are preserved in the orthography. The Jerusalem fee is half a real. All in all, things are more like the Toluca area than Calimaya/Tepemaxalco.

It is my belief that regional and subregional variation in the indigenous world was not confined to the Toluca Valley. It would be most desirable to expand comparisons with other regions and times beyond the Testaments of Culhuacan that have been used so much here. A problem is first that published materials have often not been edited in such a fashion that they are strictly comparable with those here, and second that they are often highly scattered in time and place, which has many advantages but works against regional and subregional specificity. I do note that the Rojas collection contains a most promising set of testaments from Ocotelolco, a part of Tlaxcala, in the late sixteenth and early seventeenth centuries, and that a collection published by Luis Reyes et al. is restricted to Mexico City in the sixteenth century.[1] If closely examined, these two sets could add much to our perspective. I can only wish, however, that other scholars would undertake broad searches for mundane Nahuatl documents, testaments specifically, from other areas known to be rich in such things, including perhaps Chalco, Coyoacan, Tetzcoco, and Xochimilco, and produce critical editions of the documents collected as a basis for ever wider and more comprehensive regional and temporal comparisons. I would hope that some of this activity would include Stage 3—the later seventeenth and the eighteenth centuries—which still has not received its due relatively speaking.

The reader will perhaps have noticed that with an exception or two I have not commented on the extent to which patterns seen in the corpus here are of indigenous versus Hispanic origin, or represent a convergence or amalgamation. It is not that I do not think of such matters; rather I consider them fascinating and important, especially in questions of inheritance, landholding, and family structure, and I believe that they have much to do with the pattern of evolution across time. The problem is that we lack one whole side of the picture. Editions and studies of wills in Spanish issued in New Spain at any time from the sixteenth century to independence are nowhere to be seen. It is only out of such materials, and not the pronouncements of ecclesiastics and high governmental officials, that we can form a picture truly comparable with what emerges from collections such as the present one. I believe that voluminous resources exist, probably for the Toluca Valley itself as well as other regions, and one of my projects for the future is to enter this area, but I should not be the only person to do so.[2]

I thus hope that the exploration of regional and subregional variation that I have begun here with a fortunately constituted collection of Nahuatl testaments can lead to similar perspectives on a larger stage.[3]

---

[1]Rojas et al. 1999–2002, vol. 1; Reyes García et al. 1996.

[2]I am thinking here of wills issued by people who belonged to the Hispanic world. A different but related problem is that testaments in Nahuatl are increasingly scarce after about 1770. Many wills even of indigenous people are in Spanish, often a seemingly strange and opaque Spanish that comes to life when we reconstruct the Nahuatl syntax and terminology that underlies it. This resource too should be systematically exploited.

New finds as this book goes to press, however, begin to make it appear that the Nahuatl testamentary tradition may have lasted longer than is often imagined. Miriam Melton-Villanueva has discovered two substantial collections of Nahuatl testaments from parts of the Toluca Valley in the first three decades of the nineteenth century, and she and I are planning to publish a joint article on them in the near future.

[3]During 2007 my article "Region and Subregion in Central Mexican Ethnohistory: The Toluca Valley, 1650–1760" will appear in the *Colonial Latin American Review*. The article complements the present book by going more deeply into the theme of regional and subregional variation which runs through the introductory study. It actually was written well before the appearance of the book, and some of the sections here are derived from it.

Testaments of Toluca

Transcription, Translation, and Commentary

1. Andrés Nicolás, Santa Bárbara Mixcoac, city of Toluca, 1671

(AGN, Hospital de Jesús 326, exp. 13)

HERE THE testator, who may be a widower, since he mentions no wife, takes the unusual step of dividing his main household complex between a niece and his daughter, actually mentioning the niece first, though the daughter's inheritance may be more substantial. Another house with its land—whether in the same complex or not is not clear—goes to a nephew. The nephew's bequest is conditional upon his returning home to live, a motif seen from time to time in the corpus. Andrés Nicolás shows a devotion to San Francisco in his burial garments and more especially in requesting burial before the saint's shrine.

This testament is from an early date, thirty years before the corpus picks up in numbers in the first decade of the eighteenth century. Some of its value is that it shows things already functioning as they did later, as in requesting the bells to be rung in three barrios of Toluca proper, including Andrés Nicolás's own, or in having structures of the household oriented to cardinal directions. Other things are more special to this earlier time. In the post-1700 corpus, in the immediate Toluca area the main residence is usually called *ichantzinco Dios*, the home of God; here the Spanish term *oratorio* appears in the Nahuatl, and we also see *icaltzinco Dios*, the house of God. Thus it appears that one of the dominant phrases of this subarea in the time after 1700 was still in gestation here. In later wills from Toluca proper, no mention is made of the larger municipal entity; here it is prominent, called both altepetl and *ciudad* because Toluca by this time had the rank of city in the Spanish system. Later wills usually have officials as witnesses; here, in an earlier pattern, we see apparently common citizens instead, and it is especially notable that there are women among them, actually more numerous in this case than the men, as in sixteenth-century wills.

In many respects the writing and the language are the same as they would be later in the Toluca region, but we do find some conservative traits, such as a frequent period or dot to punctuate, and tendencies to write *ç/z* instead of *s*, as well as to retain unchanged the orthography of final *n*, *tl*, *ch*, and *uh*. Crucial loanwords such as those for niece and nephew are already in evidence, and even *hábito* for a religious habit, whereas later the indigenous *-tlaquentzin* mainly took over. Some conventions were different from later; here we begin "in the name of" the Trinity, whereas the later typical phrase spoke of its praise; here we see mention of the "precious revered rope" of San Francisco, whereas later those honorific adjectives are not often applied to this item. The loanword *maestro* at the end seems to be the equivalent of the *temachti* seen in later texts, a teacher of religious doctrine, sometimes acting as notary, but possibly the word means choirmaster. The frequent intrusive *n* in the text is shared with many later documents.

[*f. 21*]

Ynca yn itlaçomahuiztoncatzin yn santicima trinidad. yn dios tentatzin yn dios tenpi[. . .] dios Espū Santon Ame Jesus — Axcã miercoles A 23 de Enero yhua xiuhtlapohuali . de 1671 anos nicpehualtia . noteztanmento y nehuatl. notocan Adres nicolas. auh notlaxilacalpan San Bar^{ra} mixcohuac yn ipann altepetl çiudad tolonca. yntla Oninomiquilin in opan nechmomachiyotiliz. y tt^{o} dios yxpatzin San fran^{co} hermita Onpan nitoctiez yhua. Oncatqui yc moquimilos y notlalnacayo. ABiton çayal. yhua yc ninolpititas yn itlaçomahuizcordotzin notlaçotatzin San fran^{co} yhua noSantacofrandia Espital mocahuatiuh Ome tomitzi. yhua Santa Bar^{ra}. San Ju^{o} Euagelizta . Santa clara. nopanpa tzinliniz micatepoztli mocahuatiuh memeliotzintzin neltiz notlanequiliz —

[*f. 21*]

In the precious revered name of the most holy Trinity, God the father, God the son, and God the Holy Spirit, amen. Jesus. — Today Wednesday the 23rd of January in the year count of 1671, I named Andrés Nicolás, in my tlaxilacalli of Santa Bárbara Mixcoac in the altepetl and city of Toluca, begin my testament. When I have died, our lord God is to designate [a grave site] for me facing the shrine of San Francisco; there I am to lie buried. And the means exist for my earthly body to be shrouded, a habit of sackcloth [or serge], and I am to go girt with the precious revered rope of my precious father San Francisco. And 2 reales are to be delivered to my holy cofradía at the hospital. And the bells are to be rung for me at Santa Bárbara, San Juan Evangelista, and Santa Clara; half a real each is to be

yhuā niquitohua. yn caltzintli çentetl ytzticac yn iquiçayapan tonatiuh nicahuilitiaz yn noçoBrina yn itonca. maria sanlome yhua yn quexquch ynic mantincan tlalli yhuicalo tlalpātli conannaz ayac aqui quixtoquiliz y moztla huiptla capa titz[. . .]

delivered. My will is to be realized. —
And I say that I am leaving a house facing east to my niece named María Salomé, and she is to take however much land, flattened earth, that goes with it. No one is to claim it from her in the future.

yhua y nochpoch yn intocan Felipah de la Crūz nicnomaquilintiuh y caltzintli. çentetl ytztica yn incalaquiya tonnatiuh Oc çentetl ytzticac yn ihuiccopan tonlon[tzin?][1]. Onca yez Auh ynn oratorio yn itlaçomahuizcaltzin ttº dios. ça cemicac ychatzinco yez ayac aqui quimoyaxcatiz. Auh y çano yuhqui ynic catqui caltzintli yn ihuicalo tlaltzintli yyaxca yez. Amo aqui tley quitoz yn capan titztihui yhua yc tequitizq̄ quiocahuizq̄ yn ipito[2] Aic tle yc mochalanizq̄. y moztla huiptla neltiz notlanequiliz =

And I am giving to my daughter named Felipa de la Cruz a house with one building facing west and another facing toward Toluca;[1] she is to be there. And the oratory, the precious revered house of our lord God, is to be her home forever; no one is to appropriate it. And it is to be the same with the land going with the house, it is to belong to her. No one is to say anything in the future. And she and her [elder female cousin?][2] are to share working with it. They are not to argue over anything in the future. My will is to be realized. =

yhua noçoBrino. yn itonca SenBastia mīn. Ocatqui. Sentetl caltzintli ytztincac yn iquiçaanpan tonnatiuh yzquina Otli[3] canpa. yn iyaxca yez. yntla hualmocuepaz yn capa nemi macoz [. . .][4] çano yhuicalo caltzintli macoz

And as to my nephew named Sebastián Martín, there is a house facing east [at the corner of the road][3] that is to be his property, that is to be given to him if he returns here from where he is living. [. . .][4] [land] going with the house is likewise to be given to him.

yhuā çenca niquinotlatlauhtiliayan yehuatzintzin diego lois yhuan miḡl de la crūz yehuatzintzin. quimoCuitlahuizq̄. y notlalnacayo ypan motlatoltizq̄[5] ytla yuhqui quimochihuilizq̄. ca Dios quinmotlaxtlahuiliz —

And I greatly implore Diego Luis and Miguel de la Cruz to take care of my earthly body and see to it.[5] If they do, God will reward them. —

Omochiuh teztamento. Onotzaloq̄. yehuantin yn imixpan teztigos. mari franca franco de la Crūz = Jusanya maria = Juceph de la Crūz - Joseph franca[6] teztigos Auh nixpan gregorio De [tanpia] maestro Santa ygleçia[7]

The testament was done before witnesses who were summoned, who are María Francisca, Francisco de la Cruz, Susana María, Josef de la Cruz, Josefa Francisca,[6] the witnesses. And before me, Gregorio de [Tapia], teacher at the holy church.[7]

---

[1]The meaning is apparently to the south.
[2]Apparently "yn ipito" includes *-pi*, which covered a female's older sister or older female cousin. However, the word belongs to an older generation of kinship terminology little seen in the present corpus, and ought to have had the *-tzin* suffix rather than *-ton*, so uncertainties remain. "Her little child," *-pilton*, remains a strong possibility.
[3]Or with a corner on the road?
[4]Here a fold in the paper obscures perhaps three words.
[5]These two are apparently the general executors of the will, though the usual terminology is not used.
[6]I presume that in view of the feminine Francisca, the feminine form of Josef was also intended.
[7]A note in Spanish says that a mass was performed for Andrés Nicolás on the 18th of March of 1671 by fray Esteban García, although no mass is mentioned in the will itself.

2. María de la Encarnación, San Juan Evangelista, 1733

(AHAM, Box 47:24, Juzgado Eclesiástico de Toluca)

WE HAVE here an example of a testament issued purely to make funeral arrangements. The testator is a widow and seems to lack family connections, for the only family member mentioned is a granddaughter. María de la Encarnación mentions no property at all, makes no bequests, makes no specific requests about her funeral, and there are no witnesses or executors, all of which together would lead us to think that she is destitute. Another indication is her calling upon a cofradía to provide shroud, burial, and mass, for though many testators make donations to cofradías (as María does not), few mention any burial benefits they expect from them. Over and above the cofradía, María requests her granddaughter to help. We cannot be certain whether this means that no male relatives were alive, or that she was relying on a network of solidarity among women in the same family. There was more to the story than is contained in the will, for despite the lack of mention of an executor, a note informs us that one later paid for her mass.

The testament is beautifully written, with a quite standard and conservative orthography, by the notary Bernardo de Santiago, whose tendencies are described in the introductory study (pp. 39–40). Note that the day here is given in Nahuatl words, while by this time it is most often seen expressed in Arabic numbers and sometimes in Spanish words. A phrase of interest is *viuda ica*, which translates "widow of" but more literally says "widow through." By this time *ica* was often a substitute for Spanish *con*, "with," and this construction may have been influenced by the quite common *casado ica*, "married to," based on Spanish *casado con*, literally "married with."

Ma mocenquizcayectenehua yn ytlaçomahuiztocatzin in Dios tetahtzin yhuan Dios ytlaçoPiltzin yhuan Dios Espiritu Santo Ma yuh mochihua Amen Jesus.
Axcan Lunes ye ic Cempohualli yhuan yei tonatiu mani Metztli Nouiembre yhuan Xiuhtlapohualli de 1733 años, Nicchihua noMemoria in Nehuatl Maria de la encarnacion Viuda yca Matheo de la cruz notlahxilacalpa San Juan Evangelista. Niquitohua yntla moztla huiptla ninomiquiliz. Ca huel acachtopa yn noyolia Nanimantzin Ca huel ycenmactzinco nicontlalia in notlaçomahuiztahtzin Dios. Ma quihualmanili, ca ytlachihualtzin. Auh in notlalnacayo Ca ytech nicpohua in tlalli, ca ytech oquiz yc ochihualoc yhuan niquitohua yn noMortaxa yez, Ca quimotemaquiliz, nocofradia Sangre de Christo de huauhtitlan[1] yhuan ytech quizaz. Noentierro yhuan Nomissa, yhuan tlen polihuiz tomin ypampa noMissa, ca tlapalehuiz noxhuiuh ytoca Anastacia Leonor,
Bernardo de Santiago Escriuano[2]

May the precious revered name of God the father, God his precious son, and God the Holy Spirit be entirely praised. May it be done, amen. Jesus.
Today Monday the 23rd day of the month of November in the year count of 1733, I María de la Encarnación, widow of Mateo de la Cruz, make my memorandum [of testament] in my tlaxilacalli of San Juan Evangelista. I say that if I die in the future, first of all I place my spirit and soul very entirely in the hands of my precious revered father God; may he come take it, for it was made by him. As for my earthly body, I assign it to the earth, for from it it emerged and of it it was made. And I say that my cofradía Sangre de Cristo of Quauhtitlan[1] will provide what is to be my shroud, and from it will come [payment for] my burial and a mass for me. My grandchild named Anastasia Leonor is to help with what is spent on account of the mass for me.
Bernardo de Santiago, notary.[2]

---

[1]That the testator of No. 80 belongs to a cofradía in Quauhtitlan makes clear the intention of "huauhtitlan" here.
[2]On the back is a note in Spanish saying that the mass was performed by a friar on February 20, 1734, and the executor made the payment.

3. Juana Francisca, San Luis, 1699

(AHAM, Box 21:79, Juzgado Eclesiástico de Toluca)

IN THIS document a married woman leaves her possessions—a field, a lot with magueyes, and a wooden vessel—to her daughter. Since no house is mentioned, the buildings in which she lived were probably her husband's property. Though she seems to have no other children and has no other choice, she shows no hesitance in leaving everything she has to a female. The testament is very simple, not providing much information, and funeral arrangements are also minimal. No executor is named, and the witnesses are two apparently common citizens plus the nearly obligatory fiscal of the church. We gather that Juana Francisca is not of high status. On the other hand, what is mentioned is only what belonged to her personally, and the family holdings may have been more extensive. Her husband paid a substantial amount for her burial and even went beyond the normal single mass to be said for her.

The many differences between this writer's orthography and what would be seen in a typical document of the Valley of Mexico make a strong impression and almost render the document incomprehensible at first for the reader of ordinary Nahuatl texts, but they are for the most part deviances common in the Toluca Valley and are discussed in the introductory study. However, *gua* for *hua* is rare, most often found in the writing of secular Spaniards not very knowledgeable about Nahuatl. And only occasionally do we see *s* for standard *ch*, as in "nopos" for *nochpoch*, "my daughter." The writer seems to have been quite unpracticed; "xichi" for *ixquich*, "all," contains some common phenomena of Toluca Valley writing, but taken as a whole construction, it is an anomaly or mistake and would be unintelligible without the context. Perhaps the intention was "xiquichi."

Jesus maria y Jocephe
Axca lune a [3?] y mani mestli de ene^{ro} ygua ypa yni xihul de 1699 años ca nicmahiotin yn tenpitzin numemoria ca negual nutoca Juana fran^{ca} nunami ytoca miguel de la crus tlaxilacal[. . .] San Luys ca melagua niguitogua yxipatzinco dios ca amun tle nipiye ypanpa nica nesi amapan —
ygua niquitoguan sentel numisan mitos yn ipaleguiloca yes nanima noyolia [yca yca?][1] ca melagua niquitoa yxipa^{to}co dios ca ce nopos yto ana maria nicaguilia se mili ygua niguitoa sanu yegual nospos ytoa ana maria nicagualia ce guaxicali nicagualia y se solar yca metototli nicagualia nospos ytoca ana maria —

ca san xichi oniguito hipatzin^{to}co dios ygua nutestigo Luys manu[. . .]l ygua Juan del crus fiscal mayor pablo fabela
escriBano Bartolome gosale[2]

Jesus, Mary, and Joseph.
Today, Monday the [3rd] of the month of January in this year of 1699, I named Juana Francisca [in the] tlaxilacalli of San Luis record this little memorandum [of testament] of mine; my husband's name is Miguel de la Cruz. I say truly before God that I have nothing, wherefore it appears here on paper. —
And I say that a mass is to be said for me, to be the help of my soul and spirit. [Therefore?][1] I say truly before God that I leave to a daughter of mine named Ana María a cultivated field, and I say that likewise to that daughter of mine named Ana María I leave a wooden vessel; I leave it to her. And I leave to my daughter named Ana María a lot with small magueyes. —
That is all that I have said before God and my witnesses, Luis Manuel and Juan de la Cruz, and the fiscal mayor, Pablo Fabela.
Notary Bartolomé González.[2]

---

[1]Possibly "yca" is repeated inadvertently, but the letters are not clear, and it is also possible that *yeica*, "wherefore, therefore" is intended.
[2]At the back of the will it is reported that the husband paid 8 pesos for the burial of his wife, including a mass to be said for her. In addition, he paid 3 pesos for another mass.

4. Ana María, San Luis, 1716

(AHAM, Box 28:20, Juzgado Eclesiástico de Toluca)

THE TESTATOR, a married woman, leaves half a lot with magueyes to her son, and also a field that he is to share with her husband. Perhaps the son is still very young and needs the help of his father; in fact, Ana María refers to him as her *-coneuh*, which while it applies to any child of a woman, has connotations of affection, and is especially likely to be used for small children. As in the previous will, no great amount of property is seen, no house is mentioned, and funeral arrangements are basic. Here too the woman seems not to be of high status. No executor is specified; of the various witnesses, two are indicated as such and appear to be ordinary citizens; two more added at the end of the testament are officials.

The testator's name is very common, yet several things point to her being the daughter mentioned in No. 3 just above, the will of Juana Francisca. Beyond the same tlaxilacalli and a congruence of the dates, the testator possesses just what was left to the daughter in No. 3, a field and a lot (or part of one) with magueyes. The two wills also have a witness in common, Luis Manuel. That it is the same Ana María in both cases is perhaps not absolutely certain, but it is highly probable.

If we compare this testament with No. 3 as two documents from San Luis, we can see that some of the formulas are similar or identical, even if the two notaries use different spellings. It is uncommon that the testator names her child right at the beginning, as part of her self-introduction; usually children are mentioned only when it comes to bequests. An interesting honorific term is applied to Luis Manuel here: "tlatuane," for standard *tlatoani*. Originally designating a preconquest-style ruler of an altepetl, the word was then applied also to the postconquest altepetl governor and to some other holders of high office. By the mid-seventeenth century (Stage 3), however, the word begins to disappear from ordinary Nahuatl documentation, especially in the singular; nowhere in our present corpus will the governor be seen called *tlatoani*. In everyday speech, however, the term continued in use, gradually becoming merely a term of politeness. In the Nahuatl of some places today, *tlatoani* is the equivalent of Spanish *señor*. Perhaps that was already the effect in our present example. Generally speaking, however, in the Toluca corpus *señor* is reserved mainly for Spaniards, or to very high ranking and well born indigenous officials. Possibly "tlatuane" here is an approximate equivalent of *señor* but indicating that the person is not Spanish. Since the example is unique, one cannot be certain. Nor is it possible to make many deductions about the status of this testator and the preceding one on the basis of their having Luis Manuel as a witness.

The original of this testament is in a very unusual format, extremely small; the orthography, while typical for Toluca, is less extreme in its deviance than that of the preceding document even though both are from the same tlaxilacalli.

Jesus ma^{a}

yca ytocatzi dios tetatzin yn dios tepiltzin yn dios espiritu s.^{to} yeyntintzintzi personas auh ca san se huel neli teotl dios —

Axca martes a 3 de nobiembre y mani mestli yhua ypa yni xihuitl de 1716 años nica nicmahiotia yni tepitzi nomemoria ca nehual notoca ana ma^{a} notlaxilacalpa s. Luis nonamictzi ytoca fran^{co} mateo onicpix se noconeh ynahuac ytoca migel nicolas yhua niquitohua ca nicmaca y noanima y noyolia yn yehuatzi nodios auh nonacayo nicmaca yn tlali yhua niquitohua ca niccahua se misa mitos ypalehuiloca yes y noanima y noyolia ca yoqui notlanequilis notlatol niccahua —

yhua niquitohua yni noconeh migel nicolas niccahuilia tlaco solar yca metl onca ynahuac ysolar tlatuane[1] Luis manuel yhua nicahuilia se tlalmili onca yc tiahui yha[2] quixtiano [Juliamo?] concahuisque yca nonamictzin fran^{co} mateo Ca yoqui no ca yoqui notlanequilis notlatol niccahua ayac quixtoquilis mostla huiptla — ca san ixquih oniquitic yc yxpantzinco nodios camo tlen oc se nicahua panpa nica ne[*verso*]sis amapa ca oncan ca notestigo Luis manuel yc ome notestigo agustin migel yehuanti tlaneltocasque ypa yni nomemoria mostla huiptla —

fiscal mayor don nicolas de olibares fiscal tiniente Juan de la cruz e.c.bano andres de la Cruz[3]

Jesus and Mary.

In the name of God the father, God the son, and God the Holy Spirit, three persons but only one very true deity God. —

Today, Tuesday the 3rd of the month of November in this year of 1716, I named Ana María record here this small memorandum [of testament] of mine in my tlaxilacalli of San Luis. My husband is named Francisco Mateo; I have had one child by him named Miguel Nicolás. And I say that I give my soul and spirit to my God, and I give my body to the earth. And I say that I leave a mass to be said to be the help of my soul and spirit, for such is my will and my statement that I leave. —

And I say that to this child of mine Miguel Nicolás I leave half a lot with magueyes, close to a lot of [. . .][1] Luis Manuel. And I leave him a field where one goes to the home[2] of the Spaniard [Juliamo?]; he is to share it with my husband Francisco Mateo, for such is my will and my statement that I leave. No one is to claim it from him in the future. — That is all that I have said before my God, for I leave nothing else, as will be seen here [*verso*] on paper. My witness is there, Luis Manuel; my second witness is Agustín Miguel. They will verify this memorandum of mine in the future. —

Fiscal mayor don Nicolás de Olivares. Fiscal teniente Juan de la Cruz. Notary Andrés de la Cruz.[3]

---

[1]At this point the text has a hard-to-translate honorific term, "tlatuane" for standard *tlatoani*. See the discussion of the word in the document introduction.

[2]"Yha" stands for *ichan*, "his home."

[3]At the back is a notation that a high mass was said for the testator in 1717.

5. Luis Francisco, Santa Clara Cozcatlan, 1731

(AHAM, Box 45:47, Juzgado Eclesiástico de Toluca)

THOUGH A married man, Luis Francisco entrusts his three little children and his property to his mother. We might imagine his wife dead, but from the mother's testament, No. 6 here, we learn for sure that the wife was still alive when the testament was issued. It is very uncommon in the corpus for a man with small children not to put them in his wife's charge if she is alive and present. It is possible that some problem or tension existed between husband and wife. Another possibility, however, is that since the mother of the testator, Isabel María, was still living in the same house as the others, she simply occupied a dominant position through seniority and was the natural person to whom to turn first. In the later will, the dying mother leaves the property to the wife as custodian after all. Here the testator asks the mother to hand the house and lot on to the only son when she dies; by the order in which the names are mentioned, we can presume that the son was the eldest, but he is also the only male, and it was a common practice for the eldest son to get the core of the property, as happens in this case. Note that the name of the testator is echoed in the names of two of his children, Francisco Javier and Gregoria Luisa.

Another peculiarity of this will is that the testator not only asks to be buried in a specific place, which we quite often see among substantial citizens who can afford it, but that he wants to be buried where his father lies. In the corpus it is quite rare for testators to request burial close to their parents. Yet when we look at Isabel María's testament, we see that she asks something similar, to be buried with her husband, Luis Francisco's father. These facts betray a strong family cohesion and also a certain position, although no large landholdings are in evidence.

This is another testament beautifully written by notary Bernardo de Santiago, who apparently served more than one barrio of Toluca. It has several traits in common with No. 2, for instance the day given in Nahuatl words, or the expression *casado ica*, "married to," parallel to the *viuda ica*, "widow of," that we saw before. The will also contains the most interesting loan verb *cobraroa*, from Spanish *cobrar*, "to collect." Loan verbs from Spanish are one of the primary diagnostic traits of Stage 3, and they do occur in the eighteenth-century Toluca corpus as expected, but they are also rarer than one would have imagined. A full treatment of this notary will be found in the introductory study, pp. 39–40.

Ma mocenquizcayectenehua yn itlaçomahuiztocatzin in Dios tetahtzin yhuan Dios ytlaçoPiltzin yhuan Dios Espū Santo Ma in mochihua Amen Jesus = Axcan Lunes ye ic Cempohuali yhuan Chicome tonatiuh mani Metztli Agosto yhuan Xiuhtlapohualli de 1731, Nicpehualtia notestamento in nehuatl. Luis fran.co casado yca Christina Ana notlaxilacalpa Santa Clara Ca huel ninococotica niquitohua yntla moztla huiptla ninomiquiliz Ca huel acachtopa in noyolian Nanimantzin Ca ycenmac.co nicontlalia in notlaçomahuiztahtzin Dios Ma quihualmanili Ca ytlachihualtzin Auh in notlalnacayo Ca ytech nicpohua in tlalli Ca ytech oquiz yc ochihualoc. yhuan niquitohua in noSepultura yes Ca ompa huey teopa yc ycuitlapan.co Santa Cruz yc cani motoquiltitica notlaçotahtzin onca toctiez in notlalnacayo yntla onechmonochili in notlaçomahuiztahtzin Dios: yhuan Santa Jerusalen motemacaz meliotzin huentli. yhuan niquitohua yn ypalehuiloca yez nanimantzin ce Missa Cantada nopampa mochihuaz. yhuan niquitohua Ca oncate yeintin nopilhuantoto yn ce ytoca

May the precious revered name of God the father, God his precious son, and God the Holy Spirit be entirely praised. May it be done, amen. Jesus. = Today, Monday the 27th day of the month of August, in the year count 1731, I Luis Francisco, married to Cristina Ana, in my tlaxilacalli of Santa Clara, begin my testament. I am very ill; I say that if I die in the future, first of all I place my spirit and soul entirely in the hands of my precious revered father God; may he come to take it, for it was made by him. And my earthly body I assign to the earth, for from it it came and of it it was made. And I say that my grave is to be at the great church, behind the holy cross, where my precious father is buried; there my earthly body is to lie buried when my precious revered father God has summoned me. And half a real is to be given as an offering for Holy Jerusalem. And I say that the help of my soul is to be a high mass to be performed for me. And I say that I have three little children, one named Francisco Javier,

fran.co Xavier yhuan oc ce ytoca Alberta Ma.a Oc ce ytoca Gregoria Luisa nican niquincauhtiuh ynahuac.co notlaconantzin Ysabel maria quinmohuapahuiliz. Auh intla moztla huiptla momiquiliz notlaçonantzin, nopiltzin fran.co Xauier quimocahuililitehuaz yn Caltzintli Ce ytzticac yc ycalaquianpa tonatiuh yhuan oc ce ytztica yc Sur yhuicalo tlaltzintli onca quimotequipanilhuiz in tto Dios, yhuan niquitohua Ca huel nicnotlatlauhtilia yehuatzin Pedro de Santiago Ca yehuatzin noAlbacea metztiez nopan motlahtoltiz. yhuan ynic Onic onicchiuh notestamento onotzaloque testigos Pedro Martin Don Mathias Andres Lorenzo hipolito = yhuan niquitohua ompa huitzila ynn itoca Manuel de los Santos nechhuiquilia ce coton coyotl,[1] yancuic yca ce tomin prenda onictlali mocobraros
Bernardo de Santiago Escriuano

another named Alberta María, another named Gregoria Luisa. I leave them here with my precious mother Isabel María, who is to raise them. And if my precious mother dies in the future, she is to leave to my child Francisco Javier the house, [of which] one [building] stands looking west and the other south, [and also] the land that goes with it. There he is to serve our lord God. And I say that I greatly implore Pedro de Santiago to be my executor and speak for me. And as I have made my testament witnesses were summoned: Pedro Martín; don Matías Andrés; and Lorenzo Hipólito. = And I say that in Huitzillan a person named Manuel de los Santos owes me a new jacket [in mixed style].[1] I hocked it for a real; it is to be collected.

Bernardo de Santiago, notary.

[1]"Coton coyotl" would be *cotón coyote* in Spanish. A *cotón* was a short tight jacket often said to be typical of indigenous dress of the time; *coyote* was sometimes applied to things of a mixed style or in which the Spanish element was predominant.

6. Isabel María, Santa Clara Cozcatlan, 1731

(AHAM, Box 45:62, Juzgado Eclesiástico de Toluca)

DYING AT the end of August, 1731, Luis Francisco (No. 5) left his mother Isabel María in charge of his children and his property. Now, hardly more than two months later, the mother herself is dying, and she leaves the property to Cristina Ana, her daughter-in-law and Luis Francisco's widow, to be handed on to the children. The property is the same that Luis Francisco had given to his mother for the benefit of his children, though she makes no mention of the fact; the house complex still consists of two buildings with the same orientation. Cristina Ana receives more than Isabel María's own daughter, Teresa Francisca: the family house and the land that goes with it, in addition to some magueyes. (Note that the daughter bears the same second name as the son, derived from their father Marcos Francisco, Isabel María's deceased husband.) This preference must be due to Cristina Ana's being the widow of the eldest son and having children. Only two children are mentioned, whereas there were three in Luis Francisco's testament; in all likelihood one had succumbed in the meantime. The death in quick succession of father, grandmother, and child leads us to imagine that an epidemic was raging in this particular year.

In contrast to Cristina Ana's house and lot, Isabel María's daughter Teresa Francisca receives only the mother's special saint, Isabel, and two rows of magueyes which were probably the mother's personal property. The mother's personally felt cult passes on in the direct line of descent and not to the in-laws. For the rest, daughter-in-law and daughter are treated equally, each receiving some clothing and a cow. Large livestock were not a common possession of women in the Toluca Valley. The testator may have been wealthy in her own right despite (as with her son) a lack of impressive landholdings. Further evidence of wealth comes from the funeral arrangements: not only does Isabel want to be buried behind the cross, the same place where her husband lies, but she also requests bells to be rung and a particular shroud, the habit of Carmen with the rope of San Francisco. This shroud seems to have been quite popular in some barrios of Toluca and neighboring districts; it may be related to the fact that the Carmelites had a church in Toluca proper.

Note by the way that Isabel María's two executors were also witnesses for her son's testament.

The orthography of notary Cipriano de Santiago is quite standard, a bit reminiscent of the style of Bernardo de Santiago in No. 5. Most of the date is still given in Nahuatl words. The Spanish loan verb *cobraroa* is there again, and from a combination with Spanish comes also the expression *iztica poniente*, "looking west," with a loanword for west, which is not common in the corpus, since with the solar directions the traditional Nahuatl equivalent is generally used. It is interesting that *-teoticaconeuh*, literally "child through holy things," a Nahuatl way of rendering the concept of godchild through baptism since the sixteenth century, is still retained here, though the original expression was usually *teoyotica -coneuh.*

Ma mosenquizcayectenehua ytlazomahuiztocatzin Dios tetatzin yhuan Dios ytlazopilzin yhuan Dios Espiritu Santo Ma yuh mochiua Amen Jesus Maria y Josephe —
Axcan sabado yeic tonatiuh Mani Meztli de Nobiembre yhuan Xiuhtlapohualli de 1731 a^{os} Nicpehualtia notestamento Nehuatl Notoca ySalvel Maria nibiuda yca Marcoz francisco Notlaxilacalpan Santa clara Cozcatlan Niquitoa ca hel ninococohua yntla nechmonochilis notlazotatzin Dios ca hel ySemactzinco nicontlalia noyolian nanimantzin yn notlazotatzin Dios yhuan yc quimiliuhtiaz Notlalnacayo yca abito del Carme sayal yhuan yc ninolpitiaz yca yCordontzin Notlazotatzin San francisco yhuan nosepultura yes onpa huey teopan yquitlapantzinco Santa Cruz onpa nechmomachiotilis yn notlazotatzin Dios yhuan niquitohua Ypalehuiloca Noyolian Nanimantzin Ce missa cantada de Requi Ca ye oncatqui yhuan Niquitohuan Nopanpa tzilinis tepoztli notlaxilacalpan yhuan Niquitoa motemacaz Melio Santa gerusalen yhuan Niquitohua nopanpa tzilinis tepoztli Sta Maria de los Angeles huitzilan yhuan San Juan Bap.^{ta} yhuan San Diego yhuan San Sevastian Motemacaz Memeliotzitzin neltiz notlanequilis yhuan Niquitohua Nicnomaquilia yehuatzin las Animas çe metontli = yhuan Niquitohua Nozihuamon ytoca Christina hana nicCahuilia Çe tzomiqueitl yamancayo yhuan Niquitohua nocpoc tereça francisca Niccahuilia Çe huipili yamanqui yhuan Niquitohua NoÇihuamon ytoca Christina hana nican niccahua Calitic nican tlatequipanos yca Noxhuihuan omentin Çe ytoca Xabiel francisco oc çe ytoca gregoria luisa nican mocahuazque tlatequipanosque yca yehuantintzintzin Santos yhuan Santas yn Caltzitli yztica yc Sur ychantzinco Dios oc Çe yztica puniente niccahuilia Mochi yca tlali yhuan yCa metotontin yhuan Niquitohua Nochpoc ytoca teresa fra^{ca} nicnocahuililia Santa ySavel quimotequipanilhuiz yhua niquitohua niccahuilia Ome Surco metotontin onca tecpani otlica = yhua niquitohua noteoticaconeuh ytoca Maria de la O. niccahuilia ome metotontin = yhuan Niquitohuan oc Çe noteoti-

May the precious revered name of God the father, God his precious son, and God the Holy Spirit be entirely praised; may it be done, amen. Jesus, Mary and Joseph. —
Today, Saturday the 3rd day of the month of November of the year count of 1731, I named Isabel María, widow of Marcos Francisco, begin my testament in my tlaxilacalli of Santa Clara Cozcatlan. I say that I am very ill; if my precious father God calls me, I place my spirit and soul very entirely in the hands of my precious father God. And my earthly body is to be wrapped in a habit of Carmen of serge, and I will be girt with the rope of my precious father San Francisco. And my grave is to be in the great church behind the holy cross; there my precious father God will designate a place for me. And I say that the help of my spirit and soul is a high mass of requiem, which is already [provided for?]. And I say that the bells are to be rung for me in my tlaxilacalli, and I say that half a real is to be given for Holy Jerusalem. And I say that the bells are to be rung for me in Santa María de los Angeles Huitzillan, San Juan Bautista, San Diego, and San Sebastián; half a real is to be given for each. My will is to be carried out. And I say that I give to the [cofradía of] Animas one little maguey. = And I say that to my daughter-in-law named Cristina Ana I leave a soft wool skirt, and I say that to my daughter Teresa Francisca I leave a soft huipil, and I say that I leave my daughter-in-law named Cristina Ana here in the house. Here she is to work with my two grandchildren, one named Javier Francisco and the other Gregoria Luisa, who are to stay here. They are to serve the male and female saints. The house that looks south is the home of God, the other looks west; I leave them [to Cristina Ana as custodian] together with the land and some small magueyes. And I say that to my daughter named Teresa Francisca I leave Santa Isabel; she is to serve her. And I say that I leave her 2 furrows of small magueyes [lined up?] along the road. = And I say that to my godchild named María de la O I leave two small magueyes. = And I say that to an-

caconeuh ytoca tribusio niccahuilia Ome metl yhuan niquitohua Onca Çe huipili Coyotl[1] Onicmacac nahui peso Mocobraros yc mochihuaz Nomissa[2] yhuan niquitohua ca huel niquinnotlatlauhtilia nopan motlatoltizque yehuantzin Don Mathias Andres = yhuan Lurenzo ypolito [*verso*] Yehuantintzin noAlbasea meztiesque yntla quali quimochihuilisque Ca Dios quimoxtlahuiliz h[. . .] yhuan Niquitoa Ca Amo tlein ninopil[. . .]a Ca huel ninotolinia yhuan onozaloque testigos Pedro de Sta Maria testigo = testigo Diego Antt^{o} Martines = testigo Juaquin Benito = testigo Nicolas de S.tiago = Yhuan niquitoua Oncate Ome yolcame huacaxtin ce conanas teresa fran^{ca} conanas Costicatontin[3] Oc Christina hana Conanas ynon pinti[c]co Yhuan Nehuatl Nixpan Ess$^{\underline{no}}$ = Cipriano de S.tiago[4]

other godchild of mine named Tiburcio I leave two magueyes. And I say that there is a huipil [in mixed style][1] that I gave four pesos for; [the money] is to be collected, and with that the mass for me is to be performed.[2] And I say that I greatly implore those who are to speak on my behalf, don Matías Andrés and Lorenzo Hipólito, [*verso*] who are to be my executors. If they do it well, God will reward them. And I say I have nothing; I am very poor. And the witnesses who were called are Pedro de Santa María, witness; witness Diego Antonio Martínez; witness Joaquín Benito; and witness Nicolás de Santiago. = And I say there are two animals, cows. Teresa Francisca is to take the small yellow cow;[3] Cristina Ana is to take the other, the little mottled one. Before me the notary, Cipriano de Santiago.[4]

[1]See n. 1 in No. 5 (p. 59).

[2]Either she has not yet actually received the huipil, or she means to give it back.

[3]If taken literally the Nahuatl seems to say that both cows are small and yellow.

[4]At the end of the testament a note in Spanish says that a high mass was celebrated on November 16. A high mass was paid for in the following January, it not being clear if this was in payment of the mass already celebrated or was for a second mass.

7. Don Ramón de Santiago, Santa Clara Cozcatlan, 1740

(AHAM, Box 56:55, Juzgado Eclesiástico de Toluca)

HERE WE see a wealthy testator, with the common but quite prestigious second name Santiago (not treated, however, as a family surname), plus the title don to underline his status. The amount and variety of his possessions give a measure of his wealth: houses, different kinds of land, magueyes, oxen, sheep, and tools; purchased land is mentioned prominently, as well as associated notarial documents. Don Ramón has an extended family, mentioning many heirs, but in some cases there is no indication of their relationship with the testator, so that it is hard to analyze the inheritance pattern.

The primary heir is a Tomás de San Juan, young enough to need others to watch over him, whom we would ordinarily take to be don Ramón's son, but nothing is said to that effect. And a significant amount of property goes to three other relatives, including Santiago de los Angeles, a younger brother or cousin (called by the traditional term *-teiccauh*, rare in these texts), who also serves as assistant executor; Simón Florencio, a nephew; and Petrona Francisca, relationship unknown. A great deal of valuable movable property and even some real estate is left jointly, in some cases to be permanently undivided, to Tomás de San Juan and the other three. Don Ramón's unnamed wife and her three small female children, whose names are given, get only one small piece of land with some magueyes on it.

One theory to account for these facts would be that Tomás de San Juan is don Ramón's eldest child and Petrona Francisca his second; the other children receive virtually nothing because they are both female and very small. The collateral relatives are brought in heavily because their help with don Ramón's children is expected. Or one might think that all the main heirs including Tomás de San Juan are collateral relatives, that don Ramón had been the eldest of several siblings, received the bulk of the inheritance, and now is making a broader distribution (he is clearly acting in this capacity in the case of his nephew Simón Florencio). If he had no male heir, such a policy might have suggested itself. But if the three little girls are his only children, surely they would have received more. Perhaps we must give much weight to the fact that don Ramón speaks of the children as his wife's and not as his, so that he would have no children at all. However these things may be, with this relatively well-off extended family we see a strong solidarity in matters of inheritance.

The testator has a special attachment to San Francisco, as indicated by the arrangements for his grave and shroud, and he makes quite a few offerings to cofradías, another sign of his wealth.

As for the orthography, although more standard than in some of the preceding testaments, it shows some conventions typical of Toluca Nahuatl. For example, it has the *l* for final *tl* so typical of the region. Note the use of the Spanish preposition *para*, common in Stage 3 Nahuatl, as we will see in other testaments, as well as other Spanish terms. On the other hand, a very traditional expression that has become rare by this time is still there, *huehuetlalli* for "patrimonial land," as well as the already mentioned *-teiccauh*. The notary Marcelo de la Cruz is discussed in the introductory study, p. 40.

Ma mosenquisCayectenehua yn itlasomahuistocatzi yn dios tetatzin yhuan dios ytlasopiltzin yhuan dios espirito santo m[. . .] yn mochihuan Amen Jesus — Axcan Jueues A 24 de marso yhuan xiuhtlapohuali de = 1740 a^{os} nicpehualtia notestamento nehual notoca D$^{\underline{n}}$ ramon de Santiago notlaxilacalpan santa clara ca niquitohua yntla y tlen nopan quim[. . .]chihuis yn notlasomahuistatzin dios yn n[. . .]yoliantzin Ca ysenmactzinco niconnotlalilia ma quihualmanili ca oquimochihuili ca yAxcatzin yhua niquitohua yn canpa tocties yn notlalnacayo ca yxpantzinco notlasomahuistatzin san fransisco ycapillatzin onca nechmomachiotilis yhuan niquitohuan yc quimiuhtias notlanacayo ytlaquentzin notlasomahuistatzin san fran^{co} yhuan ycordontzin yc ninolpitas yhuan ypalehuiloca yes yn noAnimantzi se misa cantada mocchihuas deliJensia yhuan motemacas meliotzin Jerusalen neltis notlanequilis yhuan = niquitohua niccahuilia to tomas de S$^{\underline{n}}$ Ju^{o} caltzintli ychantzin dios ysticac yquisayanpa tonatiuh yn quenami oquimocahuili yn notlasotatzin yhuan no[S]onantzi santos yhuan santas ca onca quinmotequipanilhuis yhuan niquitohuan amo quicahuasque quitasque Atatla oquinamictique yquac yno yehuantzitzi quimomachiltia yhua oc se caltzintli ysticac ycalaquianpa tonatiuh mochi mocahua yca yhuan se tlaltontli tlalmili yhuan yhuan no mocahua ynahuactzinco yhuan huehuetlali mochi mocahua y tomas de S$^{\underline{n}}$ Ju^{o} yhuan meme huehuey yhuan tepitzin naucanpa quisas quimochelhuisque petrona fransisca yhuan Santiago de los anJeles yhuan toma de S$^{\underline{n}}$ Ju^{o} yhuan simon Florensio nosoBrino neltis notlanequilis amo Aquichanis yn mustla huictla capa tistihui — [*verso*]

yhuan niquitohua moCahua se yonta yc motequipanosque quinauhcahuis amo aquin quitlasotlas[1] neltis notlanequilis mocahua matlactli ychcame san-

May the precious revered name of God the father, God his precious son, and God the Holy Spirit be entirely praised. May it be done, amen. Jesus. — Today, Thursday the 24th of March and the year count of 1740, I named don Ramón de Santiago begin my testament in my tlaxilacalli of Santa Clara. I say that, if my precious revered father God should bring something upon me [if I die], I place my spirit entirely in his hands; may he come and take it, for he made it and it belongs to him. And I say that, as to where my earthly body will lie, it is in front of the chapel of my precious revered father San Francisco; there he is to designate [a place] for me. And I say that my earthly body is to be wrapped in the habit of my precious revered father San Francisco, and I am to be girt with his rope. And the help of my soul will be a high mass; steps are to be taken. And half a real is to be given for Jerusalem; my will is to be carried out. = And I say that I leave a house, the home of God, facing east, to Tomás de San Juan, as my precious father and [precious] mother left it; there he will serve the male and female saints. And I say that they are not to leave him, they are to look after him; [when] they have arranged his marriage [in Atlauhtlan], at that time they will decide [what to do]. And another house faces west; it is all left to him, and a small piece of land, a field, is also left to him, and the patrimonial land is all left to him; it is all left to Tomás de San Juan. And the magueyes, large and small, are to be in four parts; Petrona Francisca, Santiago de los Angeles, and Tomás de San Juan, and Simón Florencio my nephew are to divide them among themselves. My will is to be carried out, no one is to dispute it in the future. — [*verso*]

And I say that a yoke [of oxen] is left with which they are to work; the four of them are to share it. Nobody is to make it expensive;[1] my will is to be carried out. Ten sheep are left; they are likewise to

---

[1]What is meant is probably that nobody is to put a price on it, i.e., charge the others for using it.

no ycqui nauhcanpa quichtisque quimochechelhuisque y uareta mocahua sanno yocqui quinauhcahuisque yc motequipanosque yhuan ome asadones sanno notlanequilis petrona fra^{ca} mocahua yca tlalmilme ome pedaso tlali yhuan oc se tlaltzintli meyotoc quipie macuilquahuil niccahuilia petrona fransisca neltis notlanequilis oc se tlaltontli quipie matlauhquahuil yca senpantli yhuan tlaco metepitzin niccahuilia nosihuahuatzi[. . .] yca yeyintin ypilhuantoton se ytoca nicolasa ma,^{a} oc se ytoca ma,^{a} uentura oc se ytoca serafiana yhua niquitohuan huehuey meme mocahua yca santia onca quimichiquis yhuan ynon tepitzitzin quinquichtis santhia ca yntlatocAl amo aquinquichtilis = Ayc motlayeliuhtasque[2] oc se tlactzintli mocahua santa ma,^{a} de los anJeles yachca santiago de los anJeles tlalcohuali onca escritura = se xiuhtica motemaca chiquasen to[3] oc se tlaltzintli mocahua ynahuac Santhiago de los anJeles meyotoc nauhpan quiquichtisque quimochechelhuisque metepitzitzin neltis nonotlanequilis oc se tlaltzintli oncacqui santa ma,^{a} de los anJeles tlalcohuali oquimotemaquilitia Julian de santiago niccahuilia tomas de S^{n} Ju^{o} quimoxelhuisque simon florension oncacqui escritura oriJinal mocacti memoria mocauhti para motamachihua Amo quitzonteconehuas miccatzitzintin ca huel quitamachihuasque neltis notlanequilis omocauhquc omcntin ytclpochhua yhuan ysihuatzin yehuanti quimacas escritura [*f.* 2]

put them in four parts, they are to divide them among themselves. A crowbar is left; the four of them are likewise to share it and work with it; and it is likewise my will [that the four of them are to work with and share] two hoes. Petrona Francisca is left with some fields, two pieces of land, and I leave to Petrona Francisca another small piece of land planted in magueyes that measures 5 quahuitl. My will is to be carried out. I leave another small piece of land that measures 10 quahuitl with a row and a half of small magueyes to my wife with her three small children, one named Nicolasa María, another named María Ventura, and another named Serafiana. And I say that the big magueyes are left to Santiago, he is to harvest them there; and Santiago is to remove those small ones, [because it is something sown by them]. No one is to take them away from them. = They are never to go along dividing[2] another piece of land at Santa María de los Angeles that is left, the property of Santiago de los Angeles. It is bought land, and there is a notarial document. = Six reales are given out every year.[3] Another piece of land is left to Santiago de los Angeles, planted in magueyes; they are to make four parts of it and divide the small magueyes. My will is to be carried out. There is another piece of land at Santa María de los Angeles, bought land, Julián de Santiago left it; I leave it to Tomás de San Juan, he is to divide it with Simón Florencio. There is an original notarial document; a memorandum is being left for the measurement. It is not to give a headache to the dead, for they are to measure it well. My will is to be carried out. Two sons of his [of Julián de Santiago, presumably] were left, and his wife; they are to issue him a notarial document. [*f.* 2]

simon florensio omocahua yca se tlalmili yhua oc se pedaso tlali meyotoc metepitzitzin yaxca ytlasotatzin yhuan ytlasonantzin quimichimachilisque tlaxilacalyacanque miguel Ju^{o}chin oc se tlaltzintli oncacqui san Ju^{o} Buahtista camino real tlalcohuali oncacqui escritura mocahua ynahuac petrona fransisca sann ichquich quimotema sesexiuhtica ome tomi huentzintli oc se tlaltzintli oncacqui san seuastiantzin yca se caltzintli ychantzinco dios ysticac ycalaquianpa tonatiuh oc se cosina ysticac yquisanpa tonali niccahuilia simon florensio yca ydestamento ysiticatzin

Simón Florencio was left with a field and another piece of land planted in magueyes, small magueyes, the property of his precious father and precious mother; the tlaxilacalli leaders, [including] Miguel Joaquín, are to recognize it. There is another piece of land at San Juan Bautista on the highway, bought land; there is a notarial document. It is left to Petrona Francisca. [The land or its owner] gives an offering of only 2 reales each year. There is another piece of land at San Sebastián with a house, the home of God, facing west, and another, a kitchen, facing east; I leave it to Simón Florencio in ac-

2For "motlaxeliuhtasque," "they are to go along dividing it."

3This passage might mean that six reales a year are still being paid for the price of the land, but more likely that six reales a year are donated from the land to Santa María de los Angeles.

nicolasa ma,[a] y mocahuan se mel santisimo yhuan santa omel nicnocahuililia santa chara se mel sangre de cristo se mel yhuan santo monimento[4] oc se mel san fran[co] oc se mel las animas oc se mel yhuan noaluasea mesties ca yehuatzin D[n] pedro de santa ma,[a] ca yehuatzin nopan motlatoltis yntla quali quimochihuilis ca dios quimotlachtlahuilmaquilis yhuan yehuatzin noteccautzin santiago de los anJeles yhuan onotzaloque testigos ynmichpa ochi testigo D[n] Ju[o] de santiago testigo = D[n] Ju[o]chin Beneto

Ess=criuano marselo de cruz

cordance with the testament of his grandmother Nicolasa María. And one maguey is left to the Santísimo [Sacramento] and Santa [. . .], and I leave [two] magueyes to Santa Clara, one maguey to the Sangre de Cristo, and another maguey to the Santo Monumento,[4] to San Francisco another maguey, to Animas another maguey. And my executor will be don Pedro de Santa María, he is to speak for me; if he does it well God will give him his reward, along with my younger sibling Santiago de los Angeles. And witnesses were summoned; [it was done] before witnesses, including don Juan de Santiago; witness don Joaquín Benito.

Notary Marcelo de la Cruz.

[4]The *monumento* was a church-like edifice of wood, essentially a catafalque for very grand funerals, that was set up in front of the main altar for Easter and the death of kings or viceroys; here it would mean the one for Easter, or in this case no doubt a cofradía devoted to it.

8. Juan Crisóstomo, Santa Bárbara Xolalpan, 1701

(AHAM, Box 22:5, Juzgado Eclesiástico de Toluca)[1]

JUAN CRISÓSTOMO is without doubt a wealthy man, as shown by his property: two house complexes and several pieces of land, including large fields with maize and smaller ones with magueyes. His largest field, 80 by 40 quahuitl, would hold eight of the normal 20 by 20 plots, and some of his holdings were purchased. He leaves a house and two large fields to his son, probably the eldest and in any case the only male. However, the daughters also get some land, including, interestingly enough, almost all the fields that are related to maguey cultivation. The testaments of the Toluca Valley indicate a predominance of women in the possession and cultivation of magueyes; in this case, Juan Crisóstomo owns various maguey fields, being one of the few men to do so (see also No. 7), but he passes them on mainly to females. Besides entrusting his wife with possessions that are to be used to raise his youngest daughters, including the family's main residence and the land it is on, he also leaves a maguey field and another field to her as her personal inheritance. In the corpus, it is common for male testators to leave some property to their wives to take care of small children, but it is rarer for them to bequeath anything for the wife's personal use.

The various offerings, the funeral arrangements, the membership in several cofradías, and more specifically the burial in the chapel where his parents lie are further hints of Juan Crisóstomo's high status. It is significant that he names both his parents, for otherwise whenever similar references to burial are made in the corpus, only the father is mentioned. It is as if they functioned together as a household, and the same happens when the testator refers to a house that both his parents had bought for a Spanish boy who was to become a priest. This is an extraordinary detail suggesting close relationships between the ethnicities, and also the importance that indigenous people gave to the role of the priest. Another element that reveals the presence of Spaniards in this testament is the term *señor* preceding one of the witnesses' names. It seems that this family had strong connections with people of Spanish origin living in the district.

A moving detail is Juan Crisóstomo's concern for the difficulties his wife may have in meeting his burial expenses because his long illness has depleted his resources. The concern seems genuine and not the formulaic "I have nothing" that we often see at the end of testaments; yet though liquid assets may be lacking, the testator has preserved more than a sufficiency to bequeath to his heirs.

This is another fine example of a beautifully written testament; the work of notary Tomás de la Cruz is analyzed in the introductory study (p. 40). Note that here, in the usual Toluca-area style, land is

[1]The testament is accompanied by a contemporary Spanish translation. Xolalpan is from *solar*.

mainly measured in the indigenous quahuitl, in multiples or fractions of 20, as opposed to the predominant use of the Spanish fanega and almud in Calimaya/Tepemaxalco, yet the Spanish fashion is also used with one large holding. Notice also the expression *çan tlalli*, "just land," implying that the land is undeveloped and perhaps confirming implications of the term *tlalli* more generally.

Ma moçenquizCayectenehua yn itlaçomahuiztocatzin yn dios tetatzin yhuan dios tepiltzin yhuan dios espiritu Santo ma y muchihua Amen Jesus —
Axca Sabado A 14 de mayo de 1701 Años nicpehualtia y notestamento y nehuatl notoca Juan Crisostomo notlaxilacalpa Santa Barbara xolalpa Ca niquitohua yntla ninomiquilis Ca huel acachtopa y noyolia y nanimantzin Ca huel yçenmactzinco nocontlalia y notlaçotatzin dios = yhuan niquitohua oncatqui ynic quimiliuhtiaz y notlalnacayo yhuan yc ninolpitiaz yn icordontzin y notlaçotatzin San franco = yhuan noSepultura yez Ca nican huey teopa yCapillatzin Rosario Canin tocticate notlaçotatzin yhuan notlaçonantzin oncan toctiez y notlalnacayo yntla ytla nopan quimochihuilitzinos y notlaçotatzin dios = yhuan niquitohua motemacaz meliotzin Santa Jerusalen = yhuan hospital motemacaz 1 ts = yhua niquitohua nopanpa tzilinis tepostli Onpa Cacalomaca yhua San Anthonio yhuan San Buenabentora yhuan Santa Barbara yhuan S[. . .] matheo ocosacaticpa . motemacaz huentzintli memeliotzitzin neltis notlanequilis = yhua niquitohua yntla ninomiquilis Ca nican catqui nocihuahuatzin ytoca maria Belnarda yn quenin nechmotoquilis Camo tlen nicnopielia Ca ye macuilxihuitl onipeuh ninococohua Ca mochi tlacatl quimomachiltitica = yhuan niquitohua y noConfradia Santisimo = yhuan San Anthonio = yhuan San franco = yhuan Animas = yhuan la virgen de los dolorez = yhuan Sangre de xpo niquinnomaquilia hoome metl = yhua niquitohua Oncatqui ce caltontli Onpa Cacalomaca yhuicalo tlaltzintli yCa quezqui metl nauhpohualquahuitl yc huiyac yc patlahuac Onpohualquahuitl niccahuilia notelpoch ytoca Juan Anthonio ypan tlacalaquiz yhuan çe tlalmili niccahuilia Canin motoca media yhuan yey almo tlaoli yhuan niquitohua oncatqui çe memiltontli quipie çenpohualquahuitl yhua oc çecann iSaliuhca no çenpohualquahuitl San tlali niccahuilia nochpoch ytoca thomaSa Juana ypan tequitis – yhua niquitohua Oncatqui oc çe memiltontli quipie çenpohualquahuitl yc huiyac yc patlahuac Caxtolquahuitl tlaco niccahuilia noçihuahuatzin yhua oc tlaco niccahuilia nochpoch ytoca Rita Juliana = yhuan oc çe nochpoch ytoca nicolasa ma xocoyotl

May the precious revered name of God the father, God the son, and God the Holy Spirit be entirely praised. May it be done, amen. Jesus. —
Today, Saturday the 14th of May of the year 1701, I named Juan Crisóstomo begin my testament in my tlaxilacalli of Santa Bárbara Xolalpan. I say that if I die, first of all I place my spirit and soul very entirely in the hands of my precious father God. = And I say that I have the means with which my earthly body will be shrouded, and I am to be girt with the rope of my precious father San Francisco. = And my grave is to be here at the great church in the chapel of the Rosario where my precious father and precious mother lie buried; there my earthly body is to lie buried if my precious father God brings something upon me. = And I say that half a real is to be given for Holy Jerusalem. = And a real is to be given for the hospital. = And I say that the bells are to be rung for me at Cacalomacan, San Antonio, San Buenaventura, Santa Bárbara, and San Mateo Ocoçacaticpac. An offering of half a real each is to be given. My will is to be carried out. = And I say that if I die, here is my wife named María Bernarda. [I do not know?] how she is to bury me; I have nothing, for I began to be sick five years ago, and everyone knows it. = And I say that my cofradías are Santísimo Sacramento, San Antonio, San Francisco, Animas, Virgen de los Dolores, and Sangre de Cristo; I give them two magueyes each. = And I say that there is a little house at Cacalomacan and the land that goes with it, with a few magueyes, 80 quahuitl long and 40 quahuitl wide; I leave it to my son named Juan Antonio; he is to pay tribute on it. And I leave him a field where half a fanega and 3 almudes of maize are sown. And I say that there is a little maguey field measuring 20 quahuitl, and another abutting on it, also of 20 quahuitl, just land; I leave it to my daughter named Tomasa Juana; she is to do tribute duty on it. – And I say that there is another little maguey field measuring 20 quahuitl long and 15 quahuitl wide; I leave half to my wife, and I leave the other half to my daughter named Rita Juliana. = And I leave to another daughter of mine named Nicolasa María, the youngest, another piece

niccahuilia oc çe tlali yCa quezqui metotonti quipie çenpohualquahuitl yc huiyac yc patlahuac matlaquahuitl = yhuan Oncatqui oc çe memiltontli titoquaxochnamiqui tereSa tlacohuali quipie Caxtolquahuitl yc huiyac yc patlahuac matlacquahuitl niccahuilia noçihuahuatzin ytoca m[a] Bernarda = yhuan Oncatqui çe tlalmili quipie Caxtolquahuitl yc huiyac yc patlahuac matlacquahuitl niccahuilia nochpoch thomasa Juana – yhua oncatqui oc çe tlali titoquaxochnamiqui Saluador quipie matlacquahuitl yc huiyac yc patlahuac macuilquahuitl niccahuilia oc çe nochpoch Rita Joliana = yhua niquitohua Oncatqui oc çe caltzintli nican Cani ticate yntlacohual notlaçotatzin yhua notlaçonantzin ypan testamento oquimitalhuitiaque oquimocahuililiaya çe quixtianoto yntla quimonemiltilisquia dios tla mochihuazquia teopixqui Ca conanazquia auh ynin queni omomiquili nehuatl oniconan axca niquitohua Ca niccahuilia noçihuahuatzin yc quihuapahuaz nochpoch xocoyotl ytoca nicolasa maria çentetl ytzticac yquisayanpa tonatiuh ychantzinco dios oc çe ytzticac yCalaquianpa tonatiuh oc çe ytzticac norte yhuicalo tlaltzintli meyotoc quipie çenpohualquahuitl San yahualtic ayac aquin quimohuaxcatis = yhua niquitohua onicnocohui çe tlaltontli nican ypan tlaxilacali San Juan euang[ta] nopal[*verso*]yotoc YCa quezqui metotonti quipie Caxtolquahuitl niccahuilia noçihuahuatzin ytoca m[a] Bernarda ayamo mochihua escritura Ca san ixquich = yhua niquitohua Ca huel çenca niquinnotlatlauhtilia y noalbaSea yezque don Gaspar de S.tiago fiscal mayor yhua pasqual de los Reyez Ca yehuantzitzin nopan motlatoltisque yntla quali quimochihuilisque Ca dios quinmotlaxtlahuilis = yhua onotzaloque ymixpan onicchiuh y noteztamento teztigos Sr Juan Gonsales testigo manuel hernandez testigo Juan Bas[ta] testigo marcos d S. pe[ro]
es[no] thomas de la Cruz

of land with a few little magueyes, measuring 20 quahuitl long and 10 quahuitl wide. = And there is another little maguey field bordering on [land of] Teresa, that was purchased, measuring 15 quahuitl long and 10 quahuitl wide; I leave it to my wife named María Bernarda. = And there is a field measuring 15 quahuitl long and 10 quahuitl wide; I leave it to my daughter Tomasa Juana. – And there is another piece of land bordering on [land of] Salvador, measuring 10 quahuitl long and 5 quahuitl wide; I leave it to another daughter of mine, Rita Juliana. = And I say that there is another house here where we are, purchased by my precious father and my precious mother. In the testament they said they were leaving it to a Spanish boy, that if God gave him life and he would become a priest, he would take [the house]. Well then, since he died, I took it. Now I say that I leave it to my wife with which to raise my daughter, the youngest, named Nicolasa María; one [building] looks east and is the home of God, another looks west, another looks north, and the land that goes with it, planted in magueyes, measuring 20 quahuitl on all sides. No one is to appropriate it. = And I say that I bought a little piece of land in the tlaxilacalli of San Juan Evangelista planted in nopal cactus [*verso*] with a few magueyes, measuring 15 quahuitl. I leave it to my wife named María Bernarda. A notarial document [for the sale] has not yet been made. That is all. = And I say that I very greatly implore those who are to be my executors, don Gaspar de Santiago, fiscal mayor, and Pascual de los Reyes, to speak for me; if they do it well, God will reward them. = And those who were summoned, before whom I made my testament, the witnesses, are señor Juan González; the witness Manuel Hernández; the witness Juan Bautista; the witness Marcos de San Pedro.
Notary Tomás de la Cruz.

9. María Ana de Morales, San Miguel Aticpac, 1707

(AHAM, Box 24:30, Juzgado Eclesiástico de Toluca)[1]

HERE A WOMAN, a widow from a statement in a notation at the end of the will, leaves most of her property to her two daughters, while there is also a grown-up male member of the family, a grandchild. In fact, the two daughters inherit a house each and some of its land, while the grandson only gets a bit of land. A Tomás García is also mentioned among the heirs, though receiving only a saint's image; maybe he is married to one of the daughters, or perhaps is a son who already received most of his inheritance. Note a quite rare reference to some clothes to be collected from the person holding them.

The funeral arrangements and offerings lead us to think that María Ana de Morales had ample re-

[1]The testament is accompanied by a contemporary Spanish translation.

sources and was of quite high status even though she does not list extensive property. In addition, her second name is in the Spanish style and is passed on to both her daughters and to the grandchild, in the same fashion as with Spaniards, though with wealthy indigenous people too at times. Also the hypothetical son-in-law has a Spanish second name. Perhaps these details hint at some sort of family connection with Spaniards, and the hypothesis is strengthened by the fact that a witness is a *señor*, a Spaniard, and bears the name Morales that has been assumed by the whole family. It is quite likely that some of the Morales family are racially mixed, though we cannot be sure, and they are still functioning as indigenous people and using Nahuatl. Dividing up a household complex and giving various independent parts of it to various heirs, as is done here, is also strongly in the Nahua tradition.

The language and orthography are unusually standard for the Valley of Toluca and characteristic of notary Tomás de la Cruz, who is discussed in the introductory study (p. 40). However, note the strong Spanish influence in the expression *ic esquina cocina*, "at the corner of the kitchen."

Ma moçenquizcayectenehua yn itlaçomahuiztocatzin yn Dios tetatzin yhuan Dios tepiltzin yhuan Dios Espiritu Santo ma y muchihua Amen JeSus = Axca Juebez a 10 de mayo de 1707 Años nicpehualtia y noteltamento y nehuatl notoca M$^{\underline{a}}$ Ana de moralez notlaxilacalpa San Mig̅l haticpa Ca niquitohua yntla ninomiquilis Ca huel acachtopa y noyolia y nanimantzin Ca huel yçenmactzinco nocontlalia y notlaçotatzin Dios = yhuan niquitohua Ca nechmotlaocolilia noxhuiuh ytoca manoel de moralez ynic quimiliuhtias y notlalnacayo yhuan y ninolpitias yn icordontzin y notlaçotatzin San Fran$^{\underline{co}}$ = yhua noSepoltura yez canpa huey teopa ermita San Fran$^{\underline{co}}$ calitic oncan toctiez y notlalnacayo yntla ytla tlen nopan quimochihuilitzinos y notlaçotatzin Dios yhuan niquitohua motemacaz meliotzin Santa JeroSalen = yhuan yehuantzin SantiSimo nicnomaquilia 1 t$^{\underline{n}}$ yhuan Animas nicnomaquilia çe metontli = yhuan niquitohua nopanpa tzilinis teposti nican notlaxilacalpa San migl yhuan San Juan Bas$^{\underline{ta}}$ yhuan Calvario yhuan San Ber$^{\underline{no}}$ notemacaz huentzintli memeliotzitzin neltis notlanequilis = yhuan niquitohua yn ipalehuiloca yez nanimantzin ca nechmotlaocolilia nopilhuan omenti çe ytoca Jusepa de moralez yhuan brigida de moralez çentetl miSa Cantada Requien = yhuan niquitohua yn itoca Juan diego nechhuiquilia çentetl tzomihuipili yhuan çenSotl[2] tzomicueytl motlanilis notech monequiz yn tzomicueytl quipie nahui bara = yhuan oncatqui çe caxa ysoltic monamacaz = yhuan niquitohua yn itoca = thomas garçia nicnocahuililia çe Santo $\overline{xpo}$ = yhuan yn itoca Jusepa de moralez nicnocahuililia no Se San $\overline{xpo}$ = yhuan niquitohua oncatqui yn cal-

May the precious revered name of God the father, God the son, and God the Holy Spirit be entirely praised. May it be done, amen. Jesus. = Today Thursday the 10th of May of the year 1707, I named María Ana de Morales begin my testament in my tlaxilacalli of San Miguel Aticpac. I say that, if I die, first of all I place my spirit and soul very entirely in the hands of my precious father God. = And I say that my grandchild named Manuel de Morales is doing me the favor that my earthly body is to be shrouded and I am to be girt with the rope of my precious father San Francisco. = And my grave will be at the great church, in the shrine of San Francisco, inside the building; there my earthly body will lie buried, if my precious father God brings something upon me; and I say that half a real will be given for Holy Jerusalem. = And to the [cofradía of] Santísimo Sacramento I give 1 real, and to [the cofradía of] Animas I give a small maguey. = And I say that the bells are to ring for me here in my tlaxilacalli of San Miguel, and in San Juan Bautista, at the Calvario, and in San Bernardino; an offering of half a real each will be given. My will is to be carried out. = And I say that the help of my soul will be a high mass of requiem that two children of mine, one named Josefa de Morales and [the other] Brígida de Morales, are favoring me with. = And I say that one named Juan Diego owes me a huipil of wool and a skirt of wool of one standard length;[2] it is to be requested from him and used for me. The wool skirt measures 4 varas. = And there is an old chest, it is to be sold. = And I say that to the one named Tomás García I leave a Santo Cristo. = And to the one named Josefa de Morales I also leave a Santo Cristo. = And I say that there is a house

---

[2]From *çotl*, originally a quarter-length of a full tribute cloth.

tzintli ytzticac yc Sor yhuan o oc çe[3] niccahuilia Jusepa de moralez = yhuan oc çe cali yzticac yquisayapa tonatiuh niccahuilia Brigida de moralez yhuan yhuicalo tlaltzintli quipie matlacquahuitl San yahualtic yexcan moxelhuizque nopilhuan yhuan yc yhuicatlapan cali onca tepitzin tlali yc yzquina cosina niccahuilia yn itoca marçel de moralez[4] onpa quimotoquitis quezqui metotontin yhuan niquitohuan Ca huel çenca nicnotlatlauhtilia y noalbasea yez don Juan de los Reyes fiscal mayor Ca yehuatzin nopan motlatoltis yntla quali quimochihuilis ca Dios quimotlaxtlatlahuilis = yhuan onotzaloque yn imixpan onicchiuh y noteztamento teztigos Sr marçel de moralez teztigo[5] marçel de moralez
ezno thomas de la C†.[6]

looking toward the south,[3] which I leave to Josefa de Morales. = And another house looking toward the east I leave to Brígida de Morales. And as to the land going with it that measures 10 quahuitl on all sides, my children are to divide it in three parts. And behind the house there is a little land at the corner of the kitchen that I leave to the one named Marcel de Morales;[4] he is to plant a few little magueyes there. And I say that I very greatly implore him who is to be my executor, don Juan de los Reyes, fiscal mayor, to speak on my behalf; if he does it well, God will reward him. = And the witnesses before whom I made my testament were summoned: señor Marcel de Morales;[5] witness Marcel de Morales.
Notary Tomás de la Cruz.[6]

[3]*Oc ce* would mean "another," but it seems to be a mistake here, influenced by another part of the text; no account is taken of the phrase in the Spanish translation.

[4]"Marcel" is apparently an error for the Manuel above, influenced by the name of the witnesses who follow; the Spanish translator made the same deduction and simply put Manuel.

[5]It is not certain whether there is one Spaniard named Marcel de Morales and another witness with the same name, or whether the two are the same person.

[6]At the back of the testament it is reported in Spanish that the testator was a widow and that a high mass was sung for her in April 1708.

10. Elena de la Cruz, San Miguel Aticpac, 1711

(AHAM, Box 54:1, Juzgado Eclesiástico de Toluca)[1]

THE TESTAMENT of Elena de la Cruz is the first of a cluster of four wills, three by women and one by a man (Nos. 10 through 13). They include Elena's daughter María Hernández and a María Josefa, a more distant relation (to be precise, she was the sister of the second husband of the widow of María Hernández's son). These wills were all part of a lawsuit over inheritance. The man, Adrián Josef, was María Josefa's husband, and his will was found separately.

The present testament far exceeds the usual in its size as well as in the amount of information it contains and in the value of its bequests, and Elena de la Cruz is equally unusual (though in many ways still representative), being perhaps the clearest example of a wealthy and independent woman found in the Toluca Valley corpus. She has an impressive amount of real estate, with no less than 17 pieces of land listed. The holdings include house lots in town, scattered agricultural land, and a major maguey-producing plot. Elena has purchased at least several of the properties herself. In addition to the land, she lists two complexes of houses, one worth 130 pesos, an exceptional amount for a property held by a provincial indigenous person, plus magueyes and at least seven oxen, as well as some donkeys and pigs. She does not speak of her parents or of any inheritance from them, so the impression given is of a woman rising in wealth and status through her own efforts. If Elena's husband had any part in her success, it is hidden from us; she fails even to mention him.

Elena makes bequests to her children in a relatively even-handed way, though showing some preference for the heirs of her eldest son. (There is actually some ambiguity in the will, which unlike most may have been written over several days or longer, about whether this son, Gabriel de la Cruz, is still alive or not; perhaps he has died very recently.) More characteristic of Elena's female independence is the regard she shows for her two daughters in naming them first in the list of her children, whereas according to the order in the bequests they were not the eldest; in entrusting to them the worship of an image of San Miguel associated with an expensive monstrance; and above

[1]The testament is accompanied by a contemporary Spanish translation.

all in choosing them as her executors. It is extremely rare to find women as executors in the Toluca testaments.

The children generally bear second names that reflect the relatively high family status, an exception being Rosa María. Two males carry on their mother's second name, but a universal surname for all the descendants, as with the very highest ranking lineages, has not yet been attained. Neither Elena nor any of her close relatives bears the don or doña or is shown holding a municipal or church office, though Elena has business dealings with such people, and one of them is among the witnesses. Note that the youngest son is once called Tomás Juárez and another time Tomás Josef, a less impressive combination.

The funeral arrangements underline Elena's high status and also her attachment to San Francisco. Her religious bequests, several of which have been made earlier and are now being recapitulated, go beyond anything else in our corpus. She shows great devotion to saints in general, bequeathing five household images and leaving large donations to many more in churches (or to their cofradías), but her largesse to the tlaxilacalli saint San Miguel Aparicio exceeds all bounds; the 130 pesos for a monstrance and donation of a house complex bought for the same amount are exceptional. No less than 77 pesos of debts currently owed her are to go for San Miguel; they show not only her dedication to the saint, but also that she is a businesswoman on a large scale.

The notary Tomás de la Cruz demonstrates once again his beautiful style and relatively standard orthography (see Nos. 8, 9 and the introductory study, p. 40). The terms referring to the decoration of altars and saints' images are highly influenced by Spanish, including the loan verb *doraroa*, "to gild," from Spanish *dorar*. In the actual form in the text, "omorodaro," *d* and *r* are reversed, showing that in this writer's speech the two consonants were not yet fully differentiated. The text contains attestations of the common loan prepositions *para* and *hasta*. This is the only case in the corpus where large pieces of agricultural land are measured in Spanish varas, usually used for urban lots. Yet some old-fashioned indigenous words occur too. Throughout the Toluca corpus we see evidence of land attached to the house in the traditional Nahua manner, but only this document contains the traditional Nahuatl term *callalli*, "house-land," to designate it. Also, the old term *-huepol*, in-law of the same generation but opposite sex, appears here for the only time in the corpus instead of the otherwise universal *cuñado/a*.

Note that the old loanword *huacax*, a reanalyzed plural (from *vacas*, "cows"), which most often means "cow" in the Nahuatl of various times and regions, and seems to have that meaning in No. 6 above, in this document repeatedly has the meaning "ox," and the same will be seen in some other documents in the corpus.

[*f.* 15]

Ma moçenquizCayectenehua yn itlaçomahuiztocatzin yn dios tetatzin yhuan dios tepiltzin yhuan dios espiritu Santo ma y muchihua Amen Jesus = Axca miercolez A 19 de Agosto de 1711 Años nicpehualtia y noteztamento y nehuatl notoca elena de la cruz notlaxilacalpa San mig̃l haticpac Ca niquitohua yntla ninomiquilis Ca huel acachtopa y noyolia y nanimantzin Ca huel yçenmactzinco nocontlalia y notlaçotatzin dios = yhuan niquitohua Ca oncatqui ynic quimiliuhtiaz y notlalnacayo yhuan yc ninolpitiaz yn icordontzin y notlaçotatzin San franco = yhuan noSepultura yez Ca onpa huey teopa terçera orden oncan toctiez y notlalnacayo yntla ytla tlen nopa quimochihuilitzinos y notlaçotatzin dios = yhuan niquitohua motemacaz meliotzin Santa JeruSalen = yhuan niquitohua yehuatzin SantiSimo onicnomaquili çe palio damasco chichiltic yhuan çe gio yCa

[*f.* 15]

May the precious revered name of God the father, God the son, and God the Holy Spirit be entirely praised. May it be done, amen. Jesus. = Today Wednesday the 19th of August of the year 1711, I named Elena de la Cruz begin my testament in my tlaxilacalli of San Miguel Aticpac. I say that if I die, first of all I place my spirit and soul very entirely in the hands of my precious father God. = And I say that I have the means with which my earthly body will be shrouded, and I am to be girt with the rope of my precious father San Francisco. = And my grave is to be at the great church, at the [chapel of] the Tercera Orden; there my earthly body is to lie buried if my precious father God brings something upon me. = And I say that half a real is to be given for Holy Jerusalem. = And I say that I gave to the Santísimo Sacramento a canopy of

cruz dorado yhuan oc çe palio nicnomaquilia çe palio yhuan çe frontal chichiltic damasco yntla oc nechmonemiltilis dios = yhuan çe costorio onictemacac ypatiuh chiquaçenpohuali yhuan matlactli peso = yhuan niquitohua yehuatzin San mig̅l onpa moyetzticatqui ycpac Costorio Ca niquincauhtiuh omenti nochpochhuan çe ytoca m^{a} ernandez yhuan Rosa m^{a} quimomaquilisque xochitl Candela yhuan Sanno yehuatzin SantiSimo onicnomaquili çe ornamento ystac yhuan çe chichiltic yhuan çe ornamento ystac damasco CaSula yhuan armati oc çe ornamento morado no yCa CaSulla yCa armatica yhuan çe frontal chichiltic = yhuan yehuatzin San fran^{co} moyetztica ycpac coratelar altar mayor onictemacac 10 p^{o}s yhuan San mig̅l Caxtilteca no 10 p^{o}s = yhuan San nicolaz Caxtilteca no 10 p^{o}s = yhuan yehuatzin Sta m^{a} la Redonda yquac ohualmohuicac onictemacac 20 p^{o}s = yhuan notlaçotatzin San Anthonio onicnomaquili 15 p^{o}s = yhuan yehuatzin la Virgen de Rosario onicnomaquili 10 p^{o}s yquac omochichiuhtzino ychantzin = yhuan oc çenpantli metepitzitzin nicnomaquilia = yhuan san nicolaz maçehualti onicnomaquili 4 p^{o}s = yhuan ypan ylhuitzin mochihuaz çe miSa ReSada yhuan quimomaquilisque çe libra Candela ayc polihuiz yhuan yquac motlalhuiquixtilis media libra candela quimomaquilisque nopilhuan onca Canpa quiSaz yhuan yehuatzin Santo x̄p̄ō Caluario onictemacac 10 p^{o}s yquac omouhpahui[2] ychantzin yhuan yc omorodaro coRatelar no 10 p^{o}s onictemac yhuan onicnomaquili çe frontal morado damasco yhuan ome CaSullas çe morado yhuan çe ystac = yhua çe estaçio onicchiuh onpa Caltenpa ayc quicahuazque nopilhuan quimocuitlahuitzinosque ypan quarezma yhuan ypan espiritu pasqua yhuan ypan domingo de Ramos melio quitemacazque nopilhuan yhuan ypan viernez Santo yohuatzinco yhuan teotlac memelio quitemacazque yhuan terçera orde Santo x̄p̄ō yn iquac motlayahualhuiz no melio motemacaz = yhuan yehuatzin Santo x̄p̄ō bera crus nicnomaquilia 1 p^{o}s yc mochichihuaz ychantzin = yhuan ytoca Alejo lopis nechhuiquilia 4 p^{o}s yntla oquixtlauh motemacaz carmetzin = yhuan niquitohua yehuatzin San mig̅l de apariçio nicnonemactilia çe pedaso tlali oniccouh

crimson damask and an ensign with a gilded cross, and I am giving it another canopy, and an altar hanging of crimson damask, if God allows me to live a while longer. = And I provided a monstrance costing 130 pesos. = And I say that as to the San Miguel on top of the monstrance, I am leaving behind two daughters of mine, one named María Hernández and [the other] Rosa María. They are to provide it with flowers and candles. And I likewise gave to the Santísimo Sacramento a white ornament, a crimson one, and an ornament of white damask, a chasuble with a vestment; and another purple ornament, also with a chasuble with a vestment, and a crimson altar hanging. = And I gave 10 pesos for the San Francisco on top of the side altar at the main altar, and for the San Miguel of the Spaniards also 10 pesos. = And for San Nicolás of the Spaniards also 10 pesos. = And for Santa María la Redonda when she came I gave 20 pesos. = And to my precious father San Antonio I gave 15 pesos. = And to the Virgen del Rosario I gave 10 pesos when her home [chapel] was fixed up. = And I am also giving her a row of small magueyes. = And to San Nicolás of the indigenous people I gave 4 pesos. = And on his feast day a low mass is to be performed, and they are to give him a pound of candles, which are never to be lacking, and when he has a feast day my children are to give him half a pound of candles; it is from them that the money is to come. And I gave 10 pesos for Santo Cristo del Calvario when his home [chapel] was cleaned,[2] and for gilding the side altar I also gave 10 pesos. And I gave him an altar hanging of purple damask and two chasubles, one purple and one white. = And I set up a station of the cross at the entry [to my home]; my children are never to abandon it; they are to take care of it; at Lent and the feast of the Holy Spirit, and Palm Sunday, my children are to provide half a real, and they are to provide half a real in the morning and again in the afternoon on Good Friday, and also when the Santo Cristo of the Tercera Orden goes in procession, they are to provide half a real. = And to the Santo Cristo de la Vera Cruz I give a peso for his home [chapel] to be fixed up. = And a person named Alejo López owes me 4 pesos; when he has paid it, it is to be given for Carmen. = And I say that I donate to San Miguel de Aparicio a piece of land that I bought; there his home [chapel] is to be erected if God

[2] "Omouhpahui" is a form of *chipahua*, "to clean something." The same spelling occurs in a later instance.

onpa moquetzaz ychantzin yntla oc dios nechmochicahuilis yntla oninomiquili oncan cate omentin nopilhuan çihuatzitzinti m$^{\underline{a}}$ ernandez yhuan Rosa m$^{\underline{a}}$ yhuan macuiltin oquichtin çe ytoca Gabriel de la crus yhuan Santiago de la crus yhuan Jusep Ramos yhuan felipe Cabrera yhuan tomas xuarez mochtin tlapalehuizque yhuan oncatqui ome caltzintli ytzticac yquisayanpa tonatiuh çe ychantzinco dios çe coçina onpa quilhuia xacalco oniccouh ypatiuh chiquaçenpohuali yhuan matlactli peso muchi y Callali yCa metl nicnoCahuililia yehuatzin San mig̃l de apariçio onpa quisaz yc mochantitzinos = yhuan oncatqui oc çe tlaltzintli Sanno onpa Caltenpa oniccohuili marcos manoel yhuan yçihuahuatzin ytoca ySabel Anthonia muchi nicnocahuililia San mig̃l apariçio yhuan noermanotzin pe$^{\underline{ro}}$ domingo quimopielilia [*f. 15v*] 12 p^{o}s yhuan ymamaltzin yehuatzin pe$^{\underline{ro}}$ domigo quimotemaquilis bigaz yaxcatzin san mig̃l apariç[. . .] yhuan oc çecni 10 p^{o}s ypanpa escritura muchi yaxcatzin San mig̃l de apariçio yhuan yehuatz[. . .] donya mag$^{\underline{na}}$ ernandez nechhuiquilia 25 p^{o}s no yaxcatzin San mig̃l apariçio = yhuan yehuatz[. . .] marcos manoel quitehuiquilia 20 p^{o}s 4 t^{s} no yaxcatzin San mig̃l apariçio = yhuan yehuatzin [. . .]huepoltzin[3] don gaspar de los Reyez Calixtlahuacan namiquetica quitehuiquilia 10 p^{o}s no yaxca[. . .] San mig̃l= yhuan ytoca fran$^{\underline{co}}$ yçihuahuatzin onpa Calixtlahuaca quitehuiquilia 1 p^{o}s = yhuan [. . .]nardino bernardo 1 p^{o}s quitehuiquilia = yhuan Juan matheo 1 p^{o}s = yhuan donya Jusepaha 5 p^{o}s = yhuan yehuatzin Go$^{\underline{dor}}$ don Juan de Stiago quimotehuiquililia 4 p^{o}s yntla omoxtlauh yca[. . .] çe frontal onicnonemactili SantiSimo = yhuan notelpoch Gabriel de la cruz quitehuiquilia 3 p[. . .] yaxcatzin San mig̃l apariçio = yhuan yehuatzin san mig̃l tlaxilacali otictocohuililique çe fronta[. . .] chichiltic yhuan çe caSulla chichiltic yhuan onicnouhpahuili yehuatzin San mig̃l yCa 12 [. . .] teocuitlatl yhuan pintor onicmacac 20 p^{o}s = yhuan yCapotitzin San nicolaz otictocohuili[li]que oticoncahuique noermanatzin m$^{\underline{a}}$ yCa 20 p^{o}s 4 t^{s} = yhuan niquitohua yn ipalehuiloc[. . .] yez nanimantzin Ca oncatqui çentetl miSa Cantada Requie = yhuan yçihuahuatzin Gabr[. . .]el de la cruz ytoca pe$^{\underline{na}}$ m$^{\underline{a}}$ ye onicmacac 14 p^{o}s 4 t^{s} yhuan yey boritus onic-

still gives me health. When I have died, there are my two female children, María Hernández and Rosa María, and five males, one named Gabriel de la Cruz, and Santiago de la Cruz, Josef Ramos, Felipe Cabrera, and Tomás Juárez; they are all to help. And there are two houses facing east, one the home of God and one a kitchen [at the place they call Xacalco?]; I bought it at the price of 130 pesos. I leave it including the house-land with magueyes to San Miguel de Aparicio; from there is to come the means to build his home. = And there is another piece of land also outside the house that I bought from Marcos Manuel and his wife named Isabel Antonia; I leave it all to San Miguel de Aparicio. And my brother Pedro Domingo has [*f. 15v*] 12 pesos, [as a result of which] he is charged with providing beams belonging to San Miguel Aparicio. And another 10 pesos on account of a notarial document, all of it belongs to San Miguel Aparicio. And doña Magdalena Hernández owes me 25 pesos, which also belongs to San Miguel Aparicio. = And Marcos Manuel owes 20 pesos and 4 reales, which also belongs to San Miguel Aparicio. = And [the sister-in-law of][3] don Gaspar de los Reyes, who is married in Calixtlahuaca, owes 10 pesos, which also belongs to San Miguel. = And the wife of a person named Francisco at Calixtlahuaca owes 1 peso. = And Bernardino Bernardo owes 1 peso. = And Juan Mateo 1 peso. = And doña Josefa 5 pesos. = and the governor don Juan de Santiago owes 4 pesos; when it is paid [it is to go toward?] an altar hanging that I donated to the Santísimo Sacramento. = And my son Gabriel de la Cruz owes 3 pesos, which belongs to San Miguel Aparicio. = And we bought for the San Miguel of the tlaxilacalli a crimson altar hanging and a crimson chasuble, and I had San Miguel cleaned up, with 12 [ounces of ?] gold, and I gave 20 pesos to the painter. = And we bought a cloak for San Nicolás, my sister María and I did it together, for 20 pesos and 4 reales. = And I say that for the help of my soul there is a high mass of requiem. = And to the wife of Gabriel de la Cruz named Petrona María I already gave 14 pesos and 4 reales, and I gave her three little donkeys, and two *magueyes*

[3] I take it that what is missing here is the third person singular possessor prefix crossreferring with don Gaspar de los Reyes, and since *-huepol* designates a person of the opposite sex of the possessor, the person meant must be a woman, a sister-in-law. It would seem that Elena de la Cruz is taking this means of identifying the person because she has forgotten her name, much as in the following bequest. Other interpretations of the phrase are possible, however.

macac yhu[. . .] ome metl tlatetzauhctli[4] onicmacac yhuan nahui pitzome yhuan çe metlatl yhuan çe yonta hu[. . .]caxti muchi yCa ynechichihual yhuan çetzin La Virgen de Guadalope nicnomaquilia yhuan çe tlalmili niccahuilia macuilpohuali yhuan Caxtoli yhuan çe bara yc huiyac yhuan yc patlahuac quipie chicuepohuali bara yhuan onpantli metotonti nicmac muchi yCa tlali onca atlauhco = yhuan niquitohua Santiago de la cruz nicmaca çe tlaltontli onpa onca xomet[. . .]tla notlacohual onca escritura yhuan onpantli metl no Yca tlali Sanno onpa atlauhco yhuan [?] metlatl yhuan 5 p^{o}s onicmacac yhuan onca oc çe tlali ynahuac ychan nicolaz pasqual [. . .]catzintli yCaltenpa ynon coSina ysquina muchi nicmaca yhuan çe huacax onicmacac yhuan çe escaRama[5] yhuan çetzin Guadalope quimotequipanilhuiz = yhuan nochpoch yt[. . .]ca m$^{\underline{a}}$ ernandez nicmaca ce tlali Canpa omochanti quipie onpohuali yhuan ome bar[. . .] yc huiyac yhuan yc patlahuac onpohuali yhuan macuili bara yhuan çe huacax yhuan çe escarama yhuan matlactli metotonti = yhuan ytoca felipe Cabrera nicmaca tepitzin tlali ysquina CoRal asta otli ca tlantica yhuan asta tlacpac ynahuac tetl melauhca ermita onicp[. . .]tili ynon Cali ayac aquin tlen quilhuiz yhuan çe huacax yCa escaRama yhuan çe metlatl yhuan çe San Anthonio yhuan çe la Virgen de la conSep$^{\underline{o}}$ yhuan 5 p^{o}s nicmaca yc mochantis yhu[. . .] çe tlalmili onca otli ychan molina tlaco yaxca yhuan oc tlaco nicmaca Jusep Ramos yhuan ç[. . .] metlatl yhuan onca ce tlaltzintli yCaltenpa mathiaz ernandez quipie çenpohualquahuitl y[. . .] huiyac yhuan yc patlahuac matlacquahuitl nicmaca tlaco Jusep Ramos onpa mochantis yhuan nicmaca 5 p^{o}s yhuan çe huacax onicmacac yhuan çe escaRama yhuan yehuatzin la V[. . .]ge de los Remedio quimotequipanilhuiz yhuan onpantli metl yCa tlali onpa atlauhco yh[. . .] felipe onpantli metl no yCa tlali = yhuan ytoca Rosa m$^{\underline{a}}$ nicmaca caltzintli ytzticac yc [. . .]te ychantzinco dios oc çe ytzticac yc Sur yca coRal Campa motocaz xochitl yhuicalo tlali yhuan ynon coRal Canpa cochi yolcatzitzinti çemicac San youhqui mocahuaz para mochtin ermanos Y [. . .] motlapielisque yhuan çe [tlalatlontli?] onca onpa San Ber$^{\underline{no}}$ ynahuac Beronica nicmaca Rosa m[. . .] yhuan onca oc çe tlali onca

capones,[4] and 4 pigs, and a metate, and a yoke of oxen with all their tackle, and I give her a Virgen de Guadalupe, and I leave her a field 116 varas long and 160 varas wide, and I give her two rows of little magueyes along with the land, at the ravine. = And I say that to Santiago de la Cruz I give a little piece of land at Xometitlan, that I purchased, and there is a notarial document [to prove it], and two rows of magueyes also with the land, likewise at the ravine, and a metate, and I gave him 5 pesos, and as to another piece of land next to the home of Nicolás Pascual, deceased, outside the kitchen, at the corner, I give it all to him. And I gave him an ox with an *escaramán*,[5] and a Guadalupe that he is to serve. = And to my daughter named María Hernández I give a piece of land where she made her home, that measures 42 varas long and 45 varas wide, and an ox with an escaramán, and 10 little magueyes. = And to the one named Felipe Cabrera I give a bit of land at the corner of the corral as far as the road, where it ends above, next to a stone, going straight to the shrine; I gave him that house to keep. No one is to say anything to him. And I give him an ox with an escaramán, and a metate, and a San Antonio, and a Virgen de la Concepción, and 5 pesos with which to make himself a home, and a field at the road going to the home of Molina, half as his property, and the other half I give to Josef Ramos, along with a metate, and a piece of land outside the place of Matías Hernández measuring 20 quahuitl long and 10 quahuitl wide, and I give half to Josef Ramos; there he is to make his home, and I give him 5 pesos, and I [already] gave him an ox with an escaramán, and a Virgen de los Remedios that he is to serve, and two rows of magueyes with the land, at the ravine. And [I give] two rows of magueyes, also with the land, to Felipe. = And to the one named Rosa María I give the house facing [north], the home of God, and another facing south, with the corral [or pen] where flowers are to be sown, and the land going with it, and that corral where the large animals sleep is always to stay as it is for all the brothers and sisters; they are to keep [their animals] there. And a [little piece of land?] at San Bernardino next to Verónica I give to Rosa María, and another piece

[4]The form "tlatetzauhctli" corresponds to standard *tlatentzauctli*, from *tentzaqua*, to block the aperture of something, thus a maguey whose aperture has been blocked. The more technical meaning is not yet apparent; in the Spanish term used in my translation, taken from the Spanish translation, *capón* refers to something castrated or cut.

[5]I am grateful to Eliazar Hernández for informing me (in June 2005) that today an *escaramán* is a kind of large, heavy harrow pulled by oxen and used in preparing the soil for sowing. The meaning here is probably similar.

yCaltenpa nicolaz pasqual micatztintli niccahuilia Rosa mª yhu[. . .] onca oc çe tlaltzintli onca yc otli tzinacantepec quipie çenpohualquahuitl yc huiyac San yahualiuhtica muchi nicmaca Rosa mª yhuan onpatli metl muchi yCa tlali onpa atlauh[. . .] yhuan niquitohua thomas Jusep niccahuilia ynin caltzintli ome ytzticac yCalaquianpa tonatiuh çe ychantzinco dios oc çe ysticac yquiSayanpa tonatiuh oc çe ytzticac norte yca yoRal yhuicalo tlaltzintli yca metepitzitzin nican quimotequipanilhuiz dios quimocuitlahuiz caltzintli yhu[. . .] çe tlaltzintli onca nican Caltenpa oniccouh yCa 10 p^{o}s muchi onicmacac yhua çe huacax yhu[. . .] çe caxa yhuan çe escaRama yhuan çe metlatl yhuan onpantli metl onca onpa atlauhco = yhuan san [*f. 16*] yhuan san migl apariçio nicnomaquilia onpantli metl nican onca tlacpac = yhuan nanoel Anthonio nicmaca ynon tlaltontli Canpa oquitocac ymetoton San quenami[6] Sentecpantli yhuan San Juan de dios nicnomaquilia yey metl tepitoton yhuan Santo xpo bera cruz nicnomaquilia yey metl tepitoton yhuan Animas Caxtilteca nicnomaquilia çe metl tepiton = yhuan Santo xpo SanGre de xpo nicnomaquilia ome metl tepitoton = yhuan San nicolas Caxtilteca çe metl tepiton yhuan merçedez çe metl tepiton yhuan San Anthonio yey metl tepitoton yhuan Animas çe metl San nicolaz ome metl yhuan la Virgen de los dolores çe metl = yhuan niquitohua nopanpa tziliniz tepoztli San migl yhuan Santa Barbara yhuan San Ber$^{\underline{no}}$ yhuan caluario motemacaz huentzintli memeliotzitzin neltiz notlanequiliz = yhuan niquitohua Ca huel cenca niquinnotlatlauhtilia omentin nochpochhuan mª ernandez yhuan Rosa mª yehuanti noalbaSea yezque yntla quali quimochihuilizque Ca dios quinmotlaxtlahuiliz = yhuan onotzaloque yn imixpan onicchiuh y noteztamento teztigos don mathiaz de la cruz Go$^{\underline{dor}}$ teniente testigo Ber$^{\underline{no}}$ bernardo testigo diego pasqual testigo pe$^{\underline{ro}}$ domigo

ez$^{\underline{no}}$ thomas de la cruz

of land outside the place of Nicolás Pascual, deceased, I leave to Rosa María, and another piece of land on the road to Zinacantepec that measures 20 quahuitl long and is the same on all sides; I give it all to Rosa María, along with two rows of magueyes including the land, at the ravine. And I say that I leave to Tomás Josef this house with two [buildings], one a home of God facing west, and another facing east, and another facing north, with the corral and the land going with [the house], with little magueyes; here he is to serve God and to take care of the house, along with another piece of land here at the entrance to this house that I bought for 10 pesos; I have given it all to him. [I give him] in addition an ox, a chest, an escaramán, a metate, and two rows of magueyes that are at the ravine. = And [*f. 16*] to San Miguel de Aparicio I give two rows of magueyes that are here above; to Manuel Antonio I give that little piece of land where he planted his small magueyes, about twenty of them;[6] to San Juan de Dios I give three small magueyes, to the [cofradía of] Santo Cristo de la Vera Cruz I give three small magueyes; and to the [cofradía of] Animas of the Spaniards I give a small maguey; to the [cofradía of] the Sangre de Cristo I give two small magueyes; and to San Nicolás of the Spaniards I give a small maguey, and to [Nuestra Señora de la] Merced a small maguey, and to San Antonio 3 small magueyes, and to [the cofradía of] Animas 1 maguey, to San Nicolás 2 magueyes, and to the Virgen de los Dolores 1 maguey. = And I say that the bells are to be rung for me at San Miguel, Santa Bárbara, and San Bernardino, and at the Calvario; an offering of half a real each is to be given. My will is to be carried out. = And I say that I greatly implore my two daughters, María Hernández and Rosa María, to be my executors. If they do it well, God will reward them. = And those were summoned before whom I made my testament, the witnesses: don Matías de la Cruz, deputy governor; witness, Bernardino Bernardo; witness, Diego Pascual; witness, Pedro Domingo.

Notary Tomás de la Cruz.

[6]*Quenami* is equivalent to Spanish *como*, and the meaning might be "como veinte," i.e., "about twenty," or possibly it could be "as they are, in a row."

11. María Hernández, San Miguel Aticpac, 1737

(AHAM, Box 54:1, Juzgado Eclesiástico de Toluca)[1]

FROM THE property listed in this testament, it is apparent that María Hernández is not as wealthy as her mother, Elena de la Cruz (No. 10), and yet she is by no means impoverished. Her holdings show a strong degree of continuity, for twenty-six years after her mother's death she still has and passes on to heirs the house, land, and maguey plantings that her mother had left her. She also possesses some land and images of saints that were not mentioned in her mother's testament, probably an acquisition through her marriage (which she, like her mother, fails to mention). Moreover, attached to the testament is a short memorandum in Spanish, in which some possessions not included in the actual will are listed, such as cloaks, skirts, blouses, wool and cotton (enough perhaps to imply that she produced textiles for sale), some magueyes, a substantial maize supply, 4 pesos in cash, and some tools, including an escaramán, perhaps still the same one that her mother had left her.

She bequeaths the house and land to a grandchild, and some more land to another, doubtless because her own son, their father, has already died. Actually, she does not mention her son and does not refer to her grandchildren as such, simply reporting their names, but the relationship is known through the dossier in which the testaments of this cluster were found.

In terms of funeral rituals, María Hernández is to be buried at the chapel of the Franciscan Tercera Orden, like her mother, another sign of continuity and of a strong relationship between mother and daughter. The other details of funeral and burial are similar, apart from the ringing of bells, which is missing here. In addition, María Hernández requests a specific shroud, the habit of the Virgin of Carmen. Missing are the mother's huge religious donations; it is curious to see that no reference is made to devotion to the tlaxilacalli saint, who had been so important for María's mother.

The testator names two executors, one of them being defined as a *señor*, whom we can therefore assume to be a Spaniard.

The notary, Marcelo de la Cruz, is the same who produced the will of don Ramón de Santiago (No. 7). Here as there, his orthography is relatively standard for Toluca; but here, much more than there, he leaves out large numbers of syllables and letters.

[*f.* 2]

ma mosenquisCayecnehuan Ytlasomahuitocatzin yn dios tetatzin yhuan dios ytlapiltzin yhuan dios espirito santo ma yn mochihua Amen Jesus ma$^{\underline{a}}$ y Joseph Axcan miercoles A 20 de noBienBre yhua xiuhtlapohuali de = 1737 a^{os} nicpehualtia notestamento yn nehual notoca ma^{a} hernandis nican nichane San miguel Aticpac ca niquitohuan yntla ytla tle nopan quimochihuilitzinos yn notlasomahuiztatzin dios ca huel ysenmactzincon niconnotlalilia yn noyoliantzin Ca yAxcatzin ma quihualmani ca oquimochihuili yhuan niquitohua yn canpa tocties yn notlalnayo ca onpa Calten terser orde onca nechmomachiotilis yhuan nitohuan yc quimiliuhtias yn notlalnacayo ca ye oncacqui ytlaquitzin la uirJe del carme yhuan yc ninolpitias ycordontzin San fran^{co} yhuan motemacas meliotzin Santa Jerusales neltis notlanequilis yhuan ypalehuiloca yes yn noAnimantzin mochihuas deliJensia se misan cantada yhua

[*f.* 2]

May the precious revered name of God the father, God his precious son, and God the Holy Spirit be entirely praised. May it be done, amen. Jesus, Mary, and Joseph. Today, Wednesday the 20th of November in the year count of 1737, I named María Hernández, citizen here in San Miguel Aticpac, begin my testament. I say that if my precious revered father God should bring something upon me, I place my spirit very entirely in his hands, for it belongs to him; may he come get it, for he made it. And I say that as to where my earthly body is to lie buried, it is at the entrance to [the chapel of the] Tercera Orden; there [a place] is to be designated for me. And I say that as to what my earthly body is to be wrapped in, there is already a habit of the Virgen del Carmen, and I am to be girt in the rope of San Francisco. And half a real is to be given for Holy Jerusalem; my will is to be carried out. And the help of my soul will be that steps will be taken so that a

---

[1]The testament is accompanied by a contemporary Spanish translation.

niquitohua ynin cali ysticac ychantzin dios niccahuilia Ju^{o} estasion yhuan oc se ysticac ylaquianpa tonatiuh mochi yca coral yhuan oc se cosinita[2] yhua niquitohuan yca se pedaso tlali yhuilancauh cali meyotoc mochi conanas Ju^{o} estasio Amo aquichani yn mostla huictla yn canpa tistihui yhuan niquitohua la uirje de los dores mohuicas carme mochtzi Santos yhuan Santo[3] mocactzinohua calitic ca yehuatzin chanecatzitzitin onca quimotepanihuisque Ju^{o} estasion yhuan ytlasonantzin ytoca polonian Antt,^{a} yhua niquitohuan niccahuilia oc se tlaltontli tepito niccahuilia Rafael Antt,^{o} onca Caltenpa huehuecalco yhuan niquitohuan oc se pedaso onpa ycuipan caluario tlalmili calaqui sentlaxeloli[4] tlaoli concahuisque yermano amo Aquitlanis yn mostla huictla can tistihue [*f. 2v*] yhuan niquitohuan oc se tlali yc otli ychan molina tetep[. . .]tzin niquincahuilia oc sepa Ju^{o} estasio yhuan rafael Antt^{o} concahuisque amo Aquinchalanis y mostla huictl[. . .] yhuan niquitohuan y[cua?] omochi[5] notestamento onotzaloque testigos D^{n} seuastian fiscal teniente de la san yglesia testigo señor Ju^{o} manuel serano yhuan yhuatzin yn noAluasea mesties ytocatzin nicolas saluador ca hue senca nicnotlatlauhtilia Ca yhuatzin nopan motlatoltzinos yntla cuali quimochihuilis ca dios quimotlachtlahuilmaquilis —

yhuan yehuatzin señor Ju^{o} manuel Serano ca yehuatzin nopan motlatoltisque y mostla huictla —
E=ss=^{no} marselo de la cruz

high mass will be sung. And I say that I leave this house facing [east], the home of God, to Juan Estacio, along with another facing west, together with a corral and another little kitchen.[2] And I say that Juan Estacio is to take all of a piece of land going with the house, planted in magueyes. No one is to dispute with him in the future. And I say that the Virgen de los Dolores is to go [to be in the church of] Carmen. All the [other] male and female saints[3] are to stay in the house and be residents; Juan Estacio and his precious mother named Polonia Antonia are to serve them there. And I say that I leave another little piece of land to Rafael Antonio, outside the patrimonial house. And I say that another piece behind the Calvario, a field into which one measure[4] of maize fits, is to be shared by him and his brother. No one is to demand it from them in the future. [*f. 2v*] And I say that I am leaving another little piece of land on the road to Molina's home to Juan Estacio and Rafael Antonio; they are to share it. No one is to dispute with them in the future. And I say that my testament was [well?] made.[5] The witnesses called were don Sebastián, fiscal teniente of the holy church, and señor Juan Manuel Serrano as a witness, and the person named Nicolás Salvador is to be my executor; I very greatly implore him to speak for me; if he does it well, God will give him his reward. —

And señor Juan Manuel Serrano is also to speak for me in the future. —
Notary Marcelo de la Cruz.

[2]By the usual disposition of buildings in the Toluca subarea, we would expect the one facing west, opposite the "home of God," to be the kitchen. The fact of the existence of another little kitchen would seem to confirm it. Yet the Spanish translator says: "tengo una casa y se compone de oratorio, sala y cocina," or "I have a house consisting of an oratory, a living room, and a kitchen."

[3]The word should be "Santas," according to the formula normally found in testaments.

[4]The Spanish translator renders this as "vn quartillo," a cuartillo or fourth of an almud.

[5]The intention may be *qualli omochiuh*, "it was made well." Since the writing is unclear, an alternative might be *inic omochiuh*, "as to how it was made," (witnesses were called), for that phrase too is sometimes found at this position in a will.

12. María Josefa, San Miguel Aticpac, 1737

(AHAM, Box 54:1, Juzgado Eclesiástico de Toluca)[1]

MARÍA JOSEFA orders her house to be sold to pay her large debts related to the maguey harvest and remains with practically no property apart from a number of magueyes; these along with the size of the debts hint at her large-scale involvement in their cultivation and the production of alcoholic beverages. Like some other women of the Toluca region who were involved in the pulque business, she mentions no land. Having a productive activity of her own may have provided her much independence, and in fact some evidence in that direction is her autonomous arrangement to sell the house. In

[1]The testament is accompanied by a contemporary Spanish translation.

addition, if we look ahead at her husband Adrián Josef's testament (No. 13), from four years earlier, 1733, we can see that he mentions no building, thereby confirming that the family house was María Josefa's property.

She leaves the magueyes equally to her two sons, Juan Crisóstomo and Antonio, the latter being born of a common-law marriage—any reference to which was interestingly eliminated in the Spanish translation. The father of the child is not mentioned, nor is María Josefa's (previous?) marriage to Adrián Josef.

An interesting detail is the appearance in the document of a member of the local clergy, a fray Domingo, in the role of a person whom the testator entrusts with the delicate task of taking care of the sale of valuable property; curiously, there is no mention of him in the Spanish translation.

Compared to the two previous documents, María Josefa's testament is less specific on funeral and burial. She does say, however, that she wishes to be shrouded in the unusual habit of the Virgin of Merced, the only example in the whole corpus of testaments. Her burial is to be in the central church of Toluca, but no mention is made of the chapel of the Tercera Orden as with her distant relatives of Nos. 10 and 11.

Despite her present economic emergency, her general status must have been high; that all the witnesses are Spanish is a sign of it, together with the instructions left for the funeral, and the size of her debts for pulque production is another indication.

In terms of orthography and language, the notary Matías de la Cruz combines some traditional and standard forms with more deviant traits typical of eighteenth-century Toluca. "Atiquipanqui" for Aticpac is a fine example of the extra *i* of Toluca, representing an epenthetic [i] in speech to make a preceding consonant pronounceable. It occurs again and again throughout the document, leading to some initially almost unrecognizable forms (explained in the introductory study, p. 41). Note the unusual loan term *matrimonio natural* for common-law marriage, and also the substitution of *g* for *d* in "noConmagere" for *nocomadre*, "my comadre or ritual comother."

[*f.* 22]
Ma mocenquisCayectenehua yn itlaçomahuistoCatzin Dios tetatzin yhua Dios ytlaçopilitzin yhua Dios Espirito Santo ma ye m[a]chihua Ame Jesus maria y Joseph[ā] —
AxCan Jebes ynic Caxtoli tonatiuh mani Metzintli Angosto yhuan xiuhtlapohuali de 1737 años niquipehualtia notestamento nehuatl notoCa maria Josepha notlaxilaCalpa San miguel atiquipanqui yhua niquitohua ytla ocnechimotlaçotili y cenmanahuaqui y tlatohuani Dios Ca huel achtopā ycenmatzin^{co} niContlalia noyoliatzin nanimatzin yhuan niquitohua yqui moquimilus y notlanaCayo ca ytlaquetzin la Virgen la mercē[?] chipahuaqui çoçomatl[2] yhuā niquitohua yni Caltzintli monamaCatzin ypāpā tle niquitehuiquilia yteConpatzinCon frāȳ Domigo y quimonamaCatzin yhua niquitohua ytla ytla omocahui para nomisSā Sā mochihuatzin ypalehuiloCatzin noyoliatzin nanimatzin yhuā niquitohuā niquitehuiquilia opohuali yhuā yey p^{s} 403[3] p^{s} ypāpā tlachiquitli yhuā niquitohuan niquitehuiquilia Caxtoli yhua cen p^{s} yhua niquitohua niquinohui-

[*f.* 22]
May the precious revered name of God the father, God his precious son, and God the Holy Spirit be entirely praised. May it be done, amen. Jesus, Mary, and Joseph. —
Today Thursday the 15th day of the month of August in the year count of 1737, I named María Josefa begin my testament in my tlaxilacalli of San Miguel Aticpac. And I say that when the universal ruler God has shown me his love [brought about my death], first of all I place my spirit and soul entirely in his hands, and I say that what my earthly body is to be shrouded in is the habit of the Virgen de la Merced, a clean cloth.[2] And I say that this house is to be sold on account of what I owe, at the orders of fray Domingo; he is the one who is to sell it. And I say that if anything is left for a mass for me, it is to be performed as the help of my spirit and soul. And I say that I owe 43 pesos[3] on account of the maguey harvesting [literally scraping], and I say that I owe another 16 pesos. I say that I owe to my comadre

---

[2]Apparently "çoçomatl" is the equivalent of standard *tzotzomatli*, "rag, cloth."

[3]Despite the use of Arabic numbers, the figure "403" for 43 retains the structure of the Nahuatl *ompohualli omei*, "forty plus three."

quililia noConmagere biestatzin niquinohuiquililia yenye pe.^{so} yhua nitohua noConnehui ytoCa Juan quirisosto niquicahuilia sepohuali yhuā matlatli memetotoli tepitoto yhuān oC oncen noConnehui ytoCa Antt^{o}nio matremonio natoralal niquiCahuilia Antt^{o} sepohuali yhuā matlatli metotoli tepitoto yhua niquitohuā yehuātzin Roque de S$^{\underline{tta}}$ Ma^{a} niquinocahuilila nonehui ytoca Juan quirisosto yhuā niquitohua Ca huel quimoSanTzinlilitzin[4] yhuā niquitohua Salbadro de Stigo no quimoSantzinlilitzin ypāpā ome tlaCatli quisantzinliz yhua niquitohua ca huel niquinotlatlatlaAuhtilia noAlbasea yehuātzin Salbador de Stigo yhua niquitohua ytla quali quimochihuilitzin Ca Dios quimotlaxitlahuiliz yhua niquitohua y noSepoltura yes Ca opā hue teopa Calitiqui nechimomachiyotiliz Dios yhua niquitohuā texipa omochihui notestameto testigo espānol S^{r} fran^{co} seRano testigo Nicolas diasi[5] testigo espānol Raf$^{\underline{ael}}$ Gonmiz finis por este forma de [?]
Nicolas diasi fines por este forma fran$^{\underline{co}}$ seRano fines por este forma Rafael Gonmis[6]
esn̄o mathias de la cruz

Vicenta 3 pesos. And I say that I leave to my child named Juan Crisóstomo 30 small magueyes, and to another child of mine named Antonio, of a common-law marriage, I leave 30 small magueyes. And I say to Roque de Santa María that I leave to him my child named Juan Crisóstomo, and I say that he is to discipline him well,[4] and I say that Salvador de Santiago is also to discipline him, so that two people will discipline him. And I say that I greatly implore my executor Salvador de Santiago [to accept the task], and I say that if he does it well God will reward him. And I say that my grave is to be at the great church, inside; God will designate [a place] for me. And I say that my testament was made before people: the Spanish witness señor Francisco Serrano; witness Nicolás Díaz;[5] and the Spanish witness Rafael Gómez.

Nicolás Díaz. Francisco Serrano. Rafael Gómez.[6]

Notary Matías de la Cruz.

[4] Literally, "really shout at him." The Spanish translator has "que lo cuyde y le enseñe loables costumbres," "that he should take care of him and teach him praiseworthy customs."

[5] By his name the middle witness is most likely a Spaniard as well, though we cannot be sure. The Spanish translator took it that all three witnesses were Spanish.

[6] Each of the three signatures, actually copied out by the notary with an appropriate rubric for each one, is preceded by a phrase in garbled Spanish which I have not managed to understand fully. It appears to be "fines por este forma" (once "finis"), with in one case "de" added at the end. Possibly "forma" was for *firma*, "signature." The main Spanish formulas used at this point were *por testigo*, "as a witness", and *lo firmé por él a su ruego*, "I signed for him at his request." The Spanish translation ignores the three phrases.

13. Adrián Josef, San Miguel Aticpac, 1733

(AHAM, Box 47:23, Juzgado Eclesiástico de Toluca)

THE TESTATOR is the husband of María Josefa (No. 12), dying four years before her. He mentions no house or land, so apparently he has been living in the house of his wife; however, he has some expensive possessions, specifically a horse and two large paintings of saints. He bequeaths them to his son Juan Crisóstomo, who is still a small child, according to his wife's testament some years later, but Adrián leaves nothing to her to take care of the child. Since it is rare for a husband to leave no property to his wife when she has to look after small children, his neglect to make any provision may show that María Josefa is already well off on her side of the family and so needs no support, or that the couple has had some trouble, perhaps related to María Josefa's other child outside marriage, as we have seen in her testament (though we do not know whether that child was born before or after Adrián's death).

Funeral arrangements are quite standard, but it can be taken as a sign of status that Adrián requests a high mass and that it was paid for shortly after his death, as reported at the back of the testament. Often there is much more delay, and the promptness hints at ready money for the offering. Adrián's burial close to the chapel of the Tercera Orden at the main church of Toluca reminds us that Elena de la Cruz and María Hernández of Nos. 10 and 11 were buried similarly, but we cannot be sure that there is a connection. The relatively large debt of 10 reales owed to Adrián, and the fact that two of his special witnesses bear the don, testify further to his position.

The language and writing of the testament show no characteristics of Toluca Nahuatl except for the unassimilated "nicontlalia," "I place it," instead of *nocontlalia*; it is a standard Nahuatl, even with the use of older-style punctuation, typical of notary Bernardo de Santiago, who is discussed in the introductory study (pp. 39–40). *Casado ica* (literally "married with," a form influenced by Spanish) appears, as happens in other testaments by this notary.

Ma mocenquizcayectenehua yn itlaçomahuiztocatzin in Dios tetahtzin yhuan Dios ytlaçoPiltzin yhuan Dios. Espu Santo Ma in mochihua Amen Jesus = Axcan Jueues ye ic Macuili tonatiuh mani Metztli Marzo, yhuan Xiuhtlapohualli de 1733 años Nicchihua. noMemoria yn Nehuatl, Adrian Joseph. Casado yca Maria Josepha; notlahxilacalpa San Miguel Aticpac, Ca huel ninoCocotica Niquitohua ytla moztla huip ninomiquiliz Ca huel acachtopa i noyolian Nanimantzin Ca ycenmac$^{\underline{co}}$ nicontlalia yn notlaçomahuiztahtzin Dios; Ma quihualmanili Ca ytlachihualtzin: Auh in notlalnacayo Ca ytech nicpohua yn tlalli, ca ytech oquiz yc Ochihualoc = yhuan niquitohua; yn Nosepultura yez Ca ompa huey teopa ythualco yc yxpan.^{co} teocalli. Tercera Orden. onca toctiez yn notlalnacayo. intla oninomiquili = yhuan niquitohua yn ipalehuiloca yez Nanimantzin Ce Missa Cantada nopampa Mochihuaz = yhuan Santa Jerusalen motemacaz Meliotzin huentzintli; yhua Niquitohua ce Nopiltzin ytoca Juan Chrisostomo NicnoCahuililia Ce la Virgen Santissima de la Assumpcion, de Lienzo. quimopielia ome baras. yhuan yehuatzin San Joseph, de Lienzo quimopielia ce bara yhuan Ce quarto. mochi nicnoCahuililia nopiltzin = yhuan niccahuilia Ce yolcatl. Cauallo yca ynechichihual; yhuan niquitohua yn itoca Gabriel ymontzin Juan Ramos. Nechhuiquilia Mahtlactomin: yhuan niquitohua Ca huel nicnotlatlauhtilia yehuatzin, Antt.^{o} de la cruz Ramires ca yehuatzin noAlbacea, metztiez. nopan motlahtoliz, intla yuhqui quimochihuiliz ca Dios. quimotlaxtlahuilmaquiliz. yhuan ynic onicchiuh noMemoria Onotzaloque testigos. Don Marcos Manuel. yhuan Don Diego Pasqual = Domingo Lazaro =
Escriuano Bernardo de Santiago[1]

May the precious revered name of God the father, God his precious son, and God the Holy Spirit be entirely praised. May it be done, amen. Jesus. = Today, Thursday the 5th day of the month of March in the year count of 1733, I Adrián Josef, married to María Josefa, make my memorandum [of testament] in my tlaxilacalli of San Miguel Aticpac, for I am very sick. I say that if I die in the future, first of all I place my spirit and soul entirely in the hands of my precious revered father God; may he come to take it, since it was created by him. And my earthly body I assign to the earth, for from it it came and of it it was made. = And I say that my grave is to be at the great church, in the patio [churchyard], facing the chapel of the Tercera Orden; there my earthly body is to lie buried when I have died. = And I say that the help of my soul will be a high mass to be performed for me = And half a real is to be given as an offering for Holy Jerusalem. And I say that I leave to my child named Juan Crisóstomo a Virgen Santísima de la Asunción, on canvas, measuring two varas, and a San José on canvas, measuring a vara and a quarter; I leave it all to my child. = And I leave him a beast, a horse with its gear. And I say that a person named Gabriel, the son-in-law of Juan Ramos, owes me 10 reales. And I say that I greatly implore Antonio de la Cruz Ramírez, who is to be my executor, to speak for me; if he does it God will give him his reward. And I made my memorandum [before] witnesses who were called: don Marcos Manuel, don Diego Pascual, and Domingo Lázaro.

Notary Bernardo de Santiago.[1]

[1] At the back of the testament a note in Spanish says that a mass for the testator was paid for in April.

14. Juan Rafael, San Cristóbal, 1732

(AHAM, Box 46:54, Juzgado Eclesiástico de Toluca)

ALTHOUGH THE affiliation of the testator, Juan Rafael, is omitted from the will, his brother Agustín Pedro (No. 15) indicates in his testament that he lives in San Cristóbal, a dependency of the city of Toluca, and we can assume that they are both residents in the same entity. The place is not the only problematic thing about the present testament; important matters related to property and heirs are also left in doubt. Juan Rafael mentions a daughter Petrona María and a brother Agustín Pedro, but it is not entirely clear which of the two is going to inherit a yoke of oxen. (An escaramán and an axe are to be sold for candles.) It may be that he is essentially leaving everything to his brother as custodian for his daughter, a plan soon to be blocked by dramatic developments, for Agustín will die just under a month later. Given that he has oxen and at least one saint, Juan Rafael must have a house and some land, but again these details remain obscure.

Funeral arrangements are completely omitted, common formulas are ignored, a sentence is left hanging, and an afterthought about an axe is inserted in an entirely inappropriate place, not to speak of a good deal of syllable omission, plus the lack of clarity on crucial matters that we already observed. Either the notary was virtually incompetent, or the testament was done in great haste. Perhaps for these reasons it was apparently not validated, as the Spanish words at the end of it testify.

Note that don Pascual Fabián, a witness here, is executor of the will of Juan Rafael's brother (No. 15); there he proves to be a past alcalde.

Generally speaking the orthography and language of the notary Santiago de los Santos fall within the normal range for Toluca of the time, though note the unusual *tz* for *z* even before vowels and the even rarer form of the verb *yectenehua*, "to praise," at the beginning, adding an agentive ending to the already unorthodox double passive (see p. 36.) Spanish influence is not unusual here, but the phrase *yuntita bueyes*, "a little yoke of oxen," hints at the closeness of Spanish conversation.

---

ma moCenquisCaYectenehualoni YCa[1] YtlatzotoCatzin dios tetatzin dios in itlatzoPiltzin yhua dios EsPiritu santos ma Y mochihua Am Jesus maria Y JosPhe Ax YPan CenPuali Yhuan Ce tonatiu de otubre Yhua xitlaPuali de 1732 años Ca niCa nicPehualtia nomemorial nehual notoCa Juan rafael Ca niCa niCautiYa Ce nohPos YtoCa Petrona maria Yhua noErmano YtoCatzi agustin Pedro Ca niCa nicCautiya[2] YCa notlatzotatzin Santo S^{an}n antonio Para nehmoCuitlahuilis Ca niCa nicCahuilia Ce Yuntita Bueyes YCa quitequiPanos notlatzotatzin San atonio Yhua niquitohua Ce EsCaraman Para YCa motemos tle monequi Para tePitzi Candela[3] Yhua amo aqui[4] testigos oc Ce noErmano Yhua oc Ce acha[5] YaCaPantli Ytocatzi JosePhe Ernandes testigos D^{n} PasCual fabian
nosPa nehual NiEsCriBano S^{an}tiago de lo Santos
Este testam^{to} no pasa[6]

May the precious name of God the father, God his precious son, and God the Holy Spirit be entirely praised.[1] May it be done, amen. Jesus, Mary, and Joseph. Today on the 21st day of October in the year count of 1732, I named Juan Rafael begin here my memorandum [of testament]. I am leaving here a daughter of mine named Petrona María along with my brother named Agustín Pedro. I leave [him?][2] here with my precious father holy San Antonio to take care of [her?] for me. I leave here to [him?] a little yoke of oxen with which [he?] is to serve my precious father San Antonio. And I say that [there is] an escaramán to seek out what is needed for a little candle.[3] And no one . . .[4] Witnesses: another brother of mine, the eldest, named Josef Hernández. And another axe.[5] Witness don Pascual Fabián.
Before me, the notary Santiago de los Santos.
This testament is not issued.[6]

---

[1]The word "yca," *ica*, an instrumental relational word in the third person, does not seem to fit in this sentence.

[2]The object of the verb is shown as singular and could be either the daughter or the brother; and since number is not marked consistently in this corpus, the object could also be both of them. Taking "Yhua" to mean "along with" leads to the interpretation in the translation above. If it were taken simply as "and," the possibilities would be wider. Beyond semantics and grammar, the practical probabilities do seem to favor the brother as the referent, since he is a more likely candidate as custodian and as operator of a yoke of oxen. But this crucial part of the testament remains ambiguous. It is not impossible that the one being taken care of is the saint.

[3]I.e., the escaramán is to be sold for candles; these would probably be for Juan Rafael's funeral, but there remains the possibility that he is speaking of the candles that were kept at household saints' altars, in this case San Antonio's.

[4]These words are left hanging. The intention was no doubt to say that no one should interfere with the testator's command.

[5]The words "Yhua oc Ce acha," "and another axe" (meaning apparently "and also an axe," for no other axe appears in the text), were an afterthought inserted in the middle of the phrase naming the testator's older brother as a witness. The intention seems to be that the axe also should be sold for candles.

[6]It is not clear whether this Spanish statement is in the hand of the Nahua notary Santiago de los Santos or not.

15. Agustín Pedro, San Cristóbal, 1732

(AHAM, Box 46:53, Juzgado Eclesiástico de Toluca)

THE TESTATOR, a married man, issues his testament for the purpose of funeral arrangements only, concentrating on the way he wishes his burial to be carried out. We glimpse a relatively high status in the shroud, burial, offerings, and the high mass, for which he makes his wife responsible; his witnesses and his executor are all of high rank. No property is mentioned; yet it is hard to believe that Agustín Pedro is destitute. We learn nothing more about the cloudy matter of whether or not his brother Juan Rafael (No. 14) left him a yoke of oxen and some tools, at least in custody. The impression is that Agustín Pedro, who so recently was charged with caring for his brother's child, fell ill and died suddenly, so that there was no time to write a proper testament and itemize his possessions. Two such deaths in quick succession in the same family make us think of epidemic disease.

Note that San Cristóbal, generally considered a barrio or tlaxilacalli, is called an altepetl here, while Toluca, though it ranked as an altepetl, is here called by its Spanish designation, *ciudad.*

The notary in this case, don Pedro Pérez, may be of higher than usual status for a person in that position, for he not only bears the don as very few notaries did, but he has a Spanish surname as a second name. One cannot see on the printed page that his calligraphy is large and careful, and he has a true capital *F*, unlike any other writer in the corpus. His orthography is unexceptional by Toluca standards, although he writes *u* for *uh* and also almost always for *hu*.

Ma mosenquiscayectenehualo yn itoCatzin Dios tetatzin Dios yn itlazoPiltzin Dios Espiritu S^{n}to Ma in mochiua AMe Jesus M^{a} y Jose —
Axca Juebes Ypan 13 tonatiu Y mani meztli de Nobienbre Yhuan xiutlapuali de 1732 nican nictlalia notestamento nehual notoca Agustin Pedro nociuauatzin Ytoca Maria nicolasa nican tichanique Yn ialtepetzin notlazotatzin S^{n} xptobal Yuilanca Siudad S^{n} Jose tolocā Ca niquitohua Yntla nixmotitlanililis yn iJustoJustisiatzin[1] Y notlazotatzin Dios ninomomiquilis Ca motemacas meliotzin S^{n}to Jerusalen Yhuan ome tomintzin tlalcoaloni[2] Yhuan Ycan YCordontzin notlazotatzin S^{n} F.^{co} yc ninolpitias Yhuan YCan Sentel ayatzintli Yc moquimilotias Yn notlalnacayo Yhuan nosepultura Yes puertatenco tiopa Yhuan Yn iPaleuiloca yes Y noAnimantzin Ycan Sentel Missa Cantada de Requie Ca nixmotlaocolilis nociuauatzin Ytoca Maria nicolasa Ca nican teixpa onitlacuilo testigo fiscal de la S^{n}ta Yglecia D^{n} tomas de los S^{n}tos testigo alcalde actual D^{n} tomas nicolas noalbasea Yes alcalde Pasado D^{n} Pascual fabian Yhuan tla cuali quimochiuilis ca Dios quimoxtlauililis Ess.^{no} D^{n} Pedro Perez[3]

May the name of God the father, God his precious son, and God the Holy Spirit be entirely praised. May it be done, amen. Jesus, Mary, and Joseph. —
Today Thursday on the 13th day of the month of November and the year count of 1732, I named Agustín Pedro issue here my testament; my wife is named María Nicolasa, and we are citizens here in the altepetl of my precious father San Cristóbal, a dependency of the city of San José Toluca. I say that if my precious father God sends his justice[1] on me and I die, half a real is to be given for Holy Jerusalem, and two reales for purchasing land,[2] and I am to go girt with the rope of my precious father San Francisco. And my earthly body is to be wrapped in a poor cloak. And my grave is to be beside the church door. And the help of my soul is to be through a high requiem mass that my wife named María Nicolasa is to favor me with. I did the writing here before people: the witness don Tomás de los Santos, fiscal of the holy church; witness don Tomás Nicolás, present alcalde. My executor is to be don Pascual Fabián, past alcalde, and if he does it well, God will reward him. Notary don Pedro Pérez.[3]

[1]In the form "iJustoJustisiatzin" it is not clear whether "Justo" is a failed first effort to write *justicia*, or whether it is meant (minus gender agreement) as an adjective "just," modifying "justice," in which case it would be unparalleled. The phrase about God sending his justice upon one, as a euphemism for death, is one of the formulas of testamentary Nahuatl.

[2]Apparently the land referred to is the burial plot. An analogous item in the 1737 will of Vicenta Teresa, No. 19, speaks specifically of the grave site, "nocepulturacohualoni," and the fee there is also two reales.

[3]A Spanish notation at the end reports that at least one high mass was celebrated within a month, being paid for in late January.

16. Esteban de San Juan, San Miguel Totocuitlapilco, 1652

(AGN, Civil 1207, exp. 11)[1]

LIKE THE FIRST testament in this collection, that of Andrés Nicolás of 1671, this one of 1652 gives us a glimpse of the condition of things and the manner of expressing them in a time well before the bulk of the corpus, which dates from after 1700, and indeed it takes us an additional twenty years back. As in the other case, much is familiar, yet some differences are also to be observed. In the 1671 will, it seemed that the dominant term in the Toluca subarea for the primary residential building in the household complex after 1700, *ichantzinco Dios*, "the home of God," had not yet jelled, other formulations being used. Here, in 1652, the term is used once, but it means a church, not a household building, reinforcing our impression that the standard post-1700 meaning of the expression is a relatively late development. In the 1671 will, it was noteworthy that in an older pattern, ordinary citizens including women were the witnesses rather than officials, but here, though the date is even earlier, the witnesses are male officials, as so often in the later time.

A major characteristic of eighteenth-century Toluca Valley Nahuatl is that a man's wife is referred to normally as his *-cihuahuatzin*, "his woman," and the term *-namic*, originally meaning one's spouse of either gender, is reserved for the husband of a woman. Here in 1652 the testator refers to his wife exclusively as *-namic*, in the older pattern, using the word a total of three times. For this circle of Nahuatl speakers the post-1700 pattern of use of spousal terms had clearly not yet been established.

The testament included here is only the most intelligible part of a larger body of obscure papers which represent two or three separate attempts to write Esteban de San Juan's will. That explains perhaps why it does not open with a traditional formula, the identification of the entity in which the will is issued, and the self-introduction of the testator, which is known only from the Spanish translation and from some of the other papers.

Apart from that, Esteban de San Juan follows a familiar pattern in bequeathing his property, giving most of it to Nicolás de los Santos, in all probability his son. His wife, who gets much less, is to raise a little daughter who gets nothing, but her mother is probably expected to pass her bequest on to her once she grows up. The wife clearly remains in the household complex even though it formally goes to the son, and she may even be in charge there. The testator gives her the responsibility of paying some of his debts, making it seem that she may have been active in his business.

Esteban shows a special devotion to Santa María and San Nicolás, leaving a field for their worship. Note that his son's name may derive from this devotion. The funeral ceremony and offerings are described in detail, giving the impression that the testator is of relatively high status. There is even some money for the church cantors, which is generally uncommon in the corpus; perhaps their mention is mainly a trait of an earlier time. Esteban seems to request a burial by charity, but this may be a mere formula; the statement is immediately followed by a small offering anyway. A larger offering is given for his vigil, and in addition there is a crossed-out line in which a cow and its calf, very valuable property, are to be sold to pay for the vigil.

The numerous sums of money that are owed to Esteban de San Juan and are owed by him to others imply that he was in some sort of business. Many different communities are mentioned in this connection. His business associate and executor Juan de Vicuña has a name like a Spaniard, and there are some other Spanish surnames, though more ambiguous, among those with whom he has dealings. It seems likely that Esteban was involved in low-level cross-community trade of the kind that often involved both Spaniards and indigenous people.

Francisco Matías, the notary as emerges from the Spanish translation, writes in a relatively conservative style, just as we would expect from the early period compared to the rest of the corpus (note the retention of *ç* before vowels, as well as final *z*, *uh*, and *tl*). He also includes a series of typical letter substitutions in loanwords betraying Nahuatl-style pronunciation, to a greater extent than we usually see in later documents.

---

[1]The testament is accompanied by a contemporary Spanish translation in very bad condition.

[*f. 5*]
Axca biernes ypa meztli de març̧o a i 1652 años

v[2] yhua niquitohua ytla Dios quimonequiltia nopa tzimliniz capana mocahuatiuh huentli meº ayaquitlacoz -

v yhua niquitohua nosepoltura ynahuac Sata yclesia mocahuatiuh huetztli ayaquitlacoz - i to -

v yhua niquitohua noquimiliuhca ca ça yca notilma yez ayaquitlacoz -

v yhua niquitohua vca mocehuiz notlalnacayo par amol te tios nicchihua mocahuatiuh huetli meº ayaquitlacoz

v yhua nitohu[. . .] Sa miguel yhua totlaçonatzin Sata maria mocahuatiuh huetzin[. . .] i to

v yhua nitohu[. . .] [tl?]a onaci ychatzinco y Dios nopa mitoz bixilia mocahuatiuh huetzintli ayaquitlacoz - 4 to

v yhua niquitohua macozque Cuicanime - 2 ayaquitlacoz

v yhua nitohua cocoxcatzintzinti macozque i to meº ayaquitlacoz

v yhua nitohua baca yhua yconeuh monamacazque notech monequi [?. . .] nobixilia yez ayaquitlacoz[3]

v yhua niquitohua nictechtia cali ytoca nicolas de lo Satos yhua ynatzin quihuapahuaz ytoca marcarita ayaquitlacoz

v yhua niquitohua mili monamaca[c?] cepohua ytla monamacac notech monequi

v yhua niquitohua nictechtia y nonamic çano opa cepohuali yc mani ayaquitlacoz

v yhua niquitohua çanopa ce tlapatl oteco cepohuali ypa macquahuitl nictechtia ytoca Nicolas de lo Satos ayaquitlacoz

v yhua niquitohua pº hernadez quipie[4] mili cepohuali oteco tlatzintla nictechtia totlaçonatzin Sata maª yhua Sato Sa nicolas cocahuia ayaquitlacoz

v yhua niquitohua otictlane tomi capoltitla nonamic

[*f. 5*]
Today Friday the 1st of the month of March of the year 1652

v [2] And I say that, if God desires it, the bells are to be rung for me; an offering of half a real is to be delivered. No one is to go against it. -

v And I say that my grave [is to be] close to the holy church; an offering of 1 real is to be delivered. No one is to go against it. -

v And I say that my shroud will just be with my cloak. No one is to go against it. -

v And I say that my earthly body is to rest there; I do it by charity. An offering of half a real is to be delivered. No one is to go against it.

v And I say that to San Miguel and to our precious mother Santa María an offering of 1 real is to be delivered.

v And I say that when [my body] reaches the home of God [the church], a vigil is to be said for me; an offering of 4 reales is to be delivered. No one is to go against it.

v And I say that the singers are to be given 2 [reales]. No one is to go against it.

v And I say that the sick will be given 1 real and a half. No one is to go against it.

v And I say that a cow and its calf are to be sold; [the proceeds] will be used for me for my future vigil. No one is to go against it.[3]

v And I say that I assign the house to Nicolás de los Santos, and his mother is to raise the one named Margarita. No one is to go against it.

v And I say that a cultivated field of 20 [quahuitl] is to be sold; when it has been sold it will be used for me.

v And I say that I assign [a field or piece of land] to my spouse, also there; it is 20 [quahuitl]. No one is to go against it.

v And I say that also there is a piece at the side of the road, 30 quahuitl; I assign it to the one named Nicolás de los Santos. No one is to go against it.

v And I say that Pedro Hernández holds[4] a cultivated field of 20 [quahuitl] at the edge of the road, below. I give it to our precious mother Santa María and holy San Nicolás; they share it. No one is to go against it.

v And I say that we borrowed money at Capultitlan;

---

[2]The first eight entries have the word *oneltic*, "it was carried out," in the left margin; the notations seem to have been added afterwards.

[3]This entry was marked out.

[4]Here the verb *pia* seems to have its older meaning to hold, have custody of.

quixtlahuaz ce i ps^{o} 4 to yhua p^{o} lopiz ytech ca i ps^{o} 4 to ayaquitlacoz
v̲ yhua niquitohua Sa peliphe nichuiquilia 2 b^{o}s [n?] ytoca Ana yhua x̄p̄oual Rafael quixtlahuaz - 2 ps^{o} ayaquitlacoz
v̲ yhua niquitohua tlacotepec nichuilia ytomi Cobernatol 2 ps^{o} quixtl[. . .]huaz non[. . .]c[5] ayaquitlacoz [*f. 5v*]
v̲ yhua niquitohua nechhuiquilia i ce ps^{o} ytoca Grabiel [a ?] sa loreço quixtlahu[. . .] Ayaquitlacoz

v̲ yhua niquitohua Sa Sebastia mili colaltitla Dios - oquimotlapopolli do Juah? [. . .]do oquimonamaquilitia yehuatl oquicouh Jua te bicoya matlactli p^{o}s 4 to ca nicno[. . .]tiz ayaquitlacoz

v̲ yhua niquitohua ytla onechmopolhui y notlaçomahuiztatzin y Dios At^{o} Feliciano yhua Jua de bicoya y noalhuaciales yehuatl quimocuitlahuizque y tley nictecpanaz yn itoca textameto auh ytla [y?. . .]qui quimochihuilique Dios quimo[tla?]tlaxtlahuilizque yhua nehuatl nixpa
miguel de stiago fiscal

†	†	†
diego juarez tifotatos	fran^{co} matias	miguel gar^{a} tifotatos

my spouse is to pay 1 peso and 4 reales; and Pedro López owes 1 peso. No one is to go against it.
v̲ And I say that at San Felipe I owe 2 pesos to one named Ana; and Cristóbal Rafael is to pay 2 pesos. No one is to go against it.
v̲ And I say that in Tlacotepec I owe money to the governor, 2 pesos; my spouse[5] is to pay it. No one is to go against it. [*f. 5v*]
v̲ And I say that one named Gabriel [in] San Lorenzo owes me 1 peso; he is to pay it. No one is to go against it.
v̲ And I say that don Juan ? [. . .], whom God removed, at death sold a cultivated field in San Sebastián, next to a corral [or at Corraltitlan]; Juan de Vicuña bought it [for] 10 pesos and 4 reales. I will [. . .] it. No one is to go against it.
v̲ And I say that, when my precious revered father God has destroyed me [when I die], Antonio Feliciano and Juan de Vicuña are my executors; they are to take care of what I will order in what is named the testament. If they do so, God will reward them. Before me,
Miguel de Santiago, fiscal.

Diego Juárez, diputado; Francisco Matías; Miguel García, diputado.

[5]The original was no doubt "nonamic."

17. Marcos Francisco, Transfiguración Capultitlan, 1737

(AHAM, Box 113:66, Juzgado Eclesiástico de Toluca)[1]

MARCOS FRANCISCO gives no details about his marital status, although we know that he has two daughters and probably a son; he may be a widower, or his wife may be omitted from the testament because all the children are grown up and are not in need of custodial action to guard their property. The testator divides most of his possessions between the two daughters, Gerónima Francisca and Petrona Ana (at times with the name inverted, Ana Petrona). Each gets a house, and while the former is assigned a lot, some magueyes and a field (*tlalmilli*), the latter gets two such fields. Something is left also to Cristóbal de Santiago, probably Marcos's son even if nothing is said to that effect; he inherits a house and is put in charge of a considerable quantity of magueyes dedicated to Ecce Homo. Thus Marcos Francisco shows no preference for the son, while the daughters occupy the preeminent place in the bequests and are even entrusted with some landed property that is more often reserved to males. This leads us to think that Cristóbal de Santiago, though an adult, was the youngest son, leaving the older females in a better position this time. It is very difficult to establish with certainty who was the eldest, since both daughters are treated in a very similar way, but the principal order of mention is Gerónima Francisca, Petrona Ana, and Cristóbal, and it seems that offspring are normally listed in order of seniority in the wills of the Toluca Valley.

The testator possesses a quite large household complex, with a building facing east and another facing north, which has an upper story (both the location on the south of the patio and the two stories are very uncommon in the corpus of testa-

[1]The testament, which is accompanied by a contemporary Spanish translation, is quite deteriorated, torn in some places and illegible in others.

ments from the Toluca area), in addition to yet another apparently looking south. He also owns a large number of maguey plants, most of them being dedicated to the worship of Ecce Homo; probably he was involved in the business of raising magueyes and producing alcoholic beverages, which is quite unusual for men, at least in the Toluca corpus.

All the witnesses are officials or past officials bearing the title don, which seems at least to put Marcos Francisco in touch with high-status members of his community. By his property and the funeral arrangements he might belong somewhere in that group himself, but he has a humble name and lacks the don, and the same is true of his executor Marcos Bernabé; probably neither has held high municipal or church office.

Notary Pascual Gerónimo writes in a quite standard Nahuatl, apart from a profusely used extra *n* that often coincides with a glottal stop. In this document as in some others the Spanish word *oratorio*, "oratory," appears in the Nahuatl with the same meaning as *ichantzinco dios*, "the home of God," or the main residence. This usage may have actually preceded the development of the Nahuatl term (see No. 1 above, dated 1671), and it continued in the eighteenth century as an alternative (it is used also in No. 18, dated 1741). Of further interest is the form "caltzintzintin," "houses" with plural marking as in Spanish, whereas Nahuatl generally represents inanimate nouns only in the singular, and that tends to be the dominant mode in the Toluca corpus as well.

Ma senquiscayectenehualon yn itlasonmahuistocantzin y dios tetantzin yua dios yn itlasonpiltzin yua dios epiritu santo ma y mochihua Amen Jesus maria y – Joseph = Axcan lunes en 10 de Julio yua xihuitl = de 1737 a^{os} nictlalia nomemoria testamento y nehua nicocoxcatzintlin notocantzin marcos fran.^{co} nican notlanxilacalpan trasfigurasion capultitlan yu- [. . .] niquintoa y noyoliatzin y nanimantzin ca huel içenmactzincon nicnomaquilia y notlasonmahuist[. . .]tzin dios = yua niquinto[. . .] ca motemacas santa J[. . .]rusa[. . .] meliotzin = yua ynic nimoquimilos nomortaxa ca nechmotlaocolilis nochpontzin = yua yn icordontzin y notlanesontantzin san fran^{co} yc nolpintias neltis notlanequilis = yua ca onpa calintic nosepultura yes = yua yn ipalehuilocatzin y nanimantzin ca sentel missa cantada de Requie neltis notlanequilis = yua niquitoa ca oncatqui se oratorio yztican yquisayan tonatin yua oc se yztican yc norte oc se sano ycpa tlachie yc no ome caltzintzintin conanas nochpoch = Geronima Fran.^{ca} yno tlachie y norte = yua oratorio yua oc çe caltzintlin yztican yquisayan tonatin conanas nocpoch ytoca Petrona An = yua oc çet yzti caltzintlin yc tepemaxalcon[2] conanas christobal de santiago neltis notlanequilis [yua mo aquix?tinis y notlatol];[3] = yua niquintoa yni solar yhui[. . .]lon solar meyontoc niccahuilia nochpoc yn itoca Geronima Fran.^{ca} yc

May the precious revered name of God the father, God his precious son, and God the Holy Spirit be entirely praised. May it be done, amen. Jesus, Mary, and Joseph. = Today, Monday, the 10th of July of the year of 1737, I the sick person named Marcos Francisco issue my memorandum of testament here in my tlaxilacalli of Transfiguración Capultitlan. And I say that I give my spirit and soul very entirely into the hands of my precious revered father God. = And I say that half a real will be given for Holy Jerusalem. = And what I am to be wrapped in, my shroud, my daughter is to favor me with. = And I will be girt with the rope of my precious father San Francisco. My will is to be carried out. = And my grave will be inside the [church] building. = And the help of my soul is a high requiem mass; my will is to be carried out. = And I say that there is an oratory facing east, and another [house] facing north, and another on top of it likewise facing north, [so that] there are two houses [in one building]; my daughter Gerónima Francisca is to take those that face north. = And my daughter named Petrona Ana is to take the oratory and another house that looks toward the east. = And Cristóbal de Santiago is to take another house toward Tepemaxalco;[2] my will is to be carried out, and no one is to undo my statement.[3] = And I say that I leave this lot that goes along with [the houses]—the lot is planted in magueyes—to my daughter named Gerónima Francisca; with it

---

[2]The meaning is probably facing south.

[3]The intention seems to be *ihuan amo ac quixitiniz in notlatol*, "and no one is to undo my statement," but part of the sheet is missing here.

quimotequipanilhuisquen santontzitzin yua yno metzitzintin[4] toloncan otlin sano calintic mocahua yca yenhuatzin santo ycsiomo = yua sanocan sentlapal oncatquin chiuhnahui tecpantlin metzitzintin sa yehuatzin santo ycsio[m]o yua ca yenhuatl christobal de san santiago quimoquitlahuis yno metzintlin = yu[. . .] yno metzintlin ypa ysolar diego Antonio tlancon solar sano yenhuatzin santo ycsiomo nicnomaquilia sano yehual christobal de santiago quimoquitlahuis yno metzitzintin = yua nepatla oc oncatquin quesquin metzitlin sano yenhuatzin s[. . .]to ycsiomo nicnoma?quilia sa christobal quimoquitlahuis yno metzintlin yua ca oncatqui se tlalmilin yc [sang?uatzin] otlin nicmacatin nochpoch = Geronima Fran.ca yua nohpoch Ana petrona nicmacatin se tlalmilin ypan loma guac se tlalmilin oncatquin y tolocan otlin sano yenhual nicacatin Ana petrona = yua ca yenhuatzin marcos berabel mochiuhtzinos noalbaseatzin nicnocahua nopan motlantoltis ytla qualin quimochihuilis ca ios quitlaxtlahuilis yua ca onotzalonquen testigos ynic micchiuh notestamento testigo Dn Leon Pedro [*verso*] Fiscal de la santa ygle[s]ia tioo Santiago de la Cruz Regidor manyor testi[. . .] Dn Juan Pasqual Alcalde pasado esno de la santa yglesia Pasqual Geronimo[5]

they are to serve the saints. And those magueyes[4] on the road to Toluca likewise stay in the house [with the family], with holy Ecce Homo. = And at the same place, on one side there are 180 magueyes likewise for holy Ecce Homo, and Cristóbal de Santiago is to take care of those magueyes. = And as for those magueyes on the lot of Diego Antonio, half the lot, I give them likewise to holy Ecce Homo; Cristóbal de Santiago is to take care of them likewise. = And in the middle there are a few more magueyes, likewise I give them to holy Ecce Homo; Cristóbal is to take care of those magueyes [likewise]; and there is a field on the road to San Juan that I am giving to my daughter Gerónima Francisca, and to my daughter Ana Petrona I am giving a field on the slope; and there is a field on the road to Toluca, I am giving it to Ana Petrona likewise. = And Marcos Bernabé is to become my executor, and I leave him [as such]. He is to speak on my behalf; if he does it well, God will reward him. And the witnesses were summoned [before whom?] my testament was done. Witness don León Pedro, [*verso*] fiscal of the holy church. [Don?] Santiago de la Cruz, regidor mayor. Witness don Juan Pascual, past alcalde. Notary of the holy church Pascual Gerónimo.[5]

[4]Since *-tzitzintin* can serve as diminutive, the meaning here and below may be that the magueyes were small.
[5]A note in Spanish reports that a mass was celebrated.

18. Felipe de Santiago, Santa María de los Angeles Huitzillan, 1741

(AHAM, Box 57:51, Juzgado Eclesiástico de Toluca)

HERE THE TESTATOR, Felipe de Santiago, entrusts the house and saints to his wife and his mother, leaving them also a horse or mule each, while no mention is made of children. Practically all his property is shared between the two women in equal parts, which is quite unusual. The absolute absence of references to children probably means that Felipe de Santiago did not have any, or at least any surviving. In most testaments, even when children are too small, or already grown up and married somewhere else, they get something. In addition, the role of the testator's mother stands out. It is not the first case that we have seen of (doubtless widowed) mothers as survivors of testators; these cases, in which they may be put in charge of looking after property and junior family members, hint at the important role they retained in their children's families even while all the children were still alive. Felipe's possession of equine animals and valuable clothing and at the same time lack of land may point to his making a living in local trade, though if so he seems not to have flourished in it.

If we consider funeral arrangements, Felipe de Santiago appears to be of a relatively high status. He requests the shroud of the Virgin of Carmen, which we have already seen with testators coming from specific barrios of Toluca, and the very unusual rope of San Diego. An interesting detail is that he leaves some pants to be sold to pay for his funeral; clothes are quite rarely found in the testaments of this corpus, but when they are mentioned, it is often because they are used as security for a loan or to pay for one's funeral expenses.

The notary here is Diego Martín, also one of the two executors of the will; his writing is quite standard and conservative for the period. He uses the reverential *tlaço-*, "precious," any time he mentions the testator's mother, in the traditional vein of respect for the elders. Note the Spanish influence in *calzones blancos*, "white pants," (also *calzones encima*, "pants worn on top") while the adjective for the same color is given with native vocabulary, *iztac*, in describing an animal.

Ma moçenquisCaYectenehua yn itlaçomahuistoCatzin Yn D^{s} tetatzi[. . .] yhuan D^{s} ytlaçomamahuispiltzin yhuan D^{s} espirito Santo m[. . .] y mochihua Amen Jesus maria y JoSeph —
AxCan domingo En 3 de DiSienBre yhuan xiuhtlapohuali de 1741 Año nicChihua notestamento nehuatl notoCa fel[. . .]pe de Santiago notlaxilaCalpan Santa ma^{a} de losS angeles hu[. . .]tzila: Ca niquitohua achtopa nictlalia ySenmactzinCo noyoli[. . .]tzin nanimantzin notlaçotatzin D^{s}: tla ninomiquilis nopa[. . .] tzilinis miCatepostli niCan notlaxilaCalpan Santa ma^{a} de losS a[. . .]geles huitzila: yhuan San Ba^{ta} yhuan San Sebastian = yhu[. . .] San Diegotzin = motemaCas memeliotzitzin huentzintli = yni[n?] neltis notlanequilis = yhua niquitohua nomortaxa yes ytl[. . .]quentzin: notlaçomahuisnantzin la Birgen del Carmen = yhu[. . .] ynic ninolpitias yCordontzin San Diego = yhuan niquitohua noSepultura es in onpa huey teopan yxpantzinCo Santo Bera Crus ompa nechmachitilis Notlaçotatzin D^{s} = yhuan niquitohua yn ipalehuiloCa yes noyoliantzin ^{a}tzin Se misa Cantada de Requien: MonamaCas quesqui metotontin niquinnopielia = ma[. . .] yhuan niquitohua Nocihuahuatzin ytoCa tomaSa quiteria yhuan Notlaçonantzin ytoCatzin Bernarda getrudes: niquinNoCahuilia ytic Caltzintli ynehuantzitzin quenamen OmCan Cal Se yztiCac yCalaquianPa tonatiuh oratorio yhuā oc Se yztiCac yquiSayāpa tonatiuh: niquinnoCahuililia mochi yCa Santos = quename omCa Caltzintli amo aquin tlen quitos mostla huiptla = yhuan niquitohua Se yolCatl nicCahuilia noçihuahuatzin çe tliltic = yhuan notlaçonantzin = nicnCahuililia Se yolCatl yStac = yhuan niquitohua se Calsones BlanCo = yhuan çe Calsones EnSiman monamaCas = ypalehuiloCa yes noyoliatzin nanimantzin = yhuan niquitohua Ca San ixquich Camo tlen nicnopielia Ca huel ninotolinia = yhuan Ca huel cenCan nicNotlatlauhtilia noalBaSeatzin metztiees yehuan Atonio Fele yhuan Diego martin = YhuaN testigos yn imixpantzinCo omochiuh notestamento: Don toriBio de la Cruz Alcalde pasado yhuan yehuatzin Don Domigo Ramos = yhuan fisCal de la Santa ygleSia Don migel geronimo

May the precious revered name of God the father, God his precious revered son, and God the Holy Spirit be entirely praised. May it be done, amen. Jesus, Mary, and Joseph. —
Today Sunday the 3rd of December of the year count of 1741, I named Felipe de Santiago make my testament in my tlaxilacalli of Santa María de los Angeles Huitzillan. First I say that I place my spirit and soul entirely in the hands of my precious father God. If I die, the bells are to be rung for me here in my tlaxilacalli of Santa María de los Angeles Huitzillan, San Juan Bautista, San Sebastián, and San Diego. = An offering of half a real each is to be given. = This my will is to be carried out. = And I say that my shroud is to be the habit of my precious revered mother the Virgen del Carmen. = And I am to be girt with the rope of San Diego. = And I say that my grave is to be at the great church, facing the Santa Vera Cruz; there my precious father God will designate [a place] for me. = And I say that the help of my spirit and soul will be a high requiem mass; a few little magueyes that I have are to be sold [to pay for it]. = And I say that I leave my wife named Tomasa Quitería and my precious mother named Bernarda Gertrudis jointly inside the house. As to how the house is, one [building], an oratory, faces west; the other one faces east. I leave it to them, including the saints. = No one is to say anything in the future about how the house is. = And I say that I leave an [equine] beast to my wife, a black one. = And to my precious mother I leave a beast, a white one. = And I say that a pair of white hose [pants] and a pair of hose worn on top are to be sold [to contribute to paying for] the help of my spirit and soul. = And I say that that is all. I have nothing, for I am very poor. = And I greatly implore those who are to be my executors, Antonio Félix and Diego Martín, [to accept the task]. = The witnesses before whom my testament was made are don Toribio de la Cruz, past alcalde; don Domingo Ramos. = And the fiscal of the holy church, don Miguel Gerónimo.

Es$^{\underline{No}}$ Diego martin[1]

Notary Diego Martín.[1]

[1]At the back it is reported in Spanish that at least two high masses were celebrated in 1741.

19. Vicenta Teresa, San Francisco Calixtlahuaca, 1737

(AHAM, Box 67:17, Juzgado Eclesiástico de Toluca)[1]

VICENTA TERESA leaves her husband Juan Miguel in charge of their house and the small piece of land it is on, entrusting to him the care of their four small children, two male and two female. Only the names of the two sons are given, and it is specified that they are to share the land. Thus it seems that the husband's function is purely custodial and that the property will eventually be the children's. Even though the testator is female, the names of the female children are not given, and nothing is said about any inheritance for them; probably the males were older. The house plot is tiny in any case; either the husband has other land, or the family is extremely land-poor.

As small as it is, the land is very interesting. It was acquired through Vicenta Teresa's comadre, who initially donated it (apparently after her husband was dead, for she is spoken of as the sole donor), then changed her mind, and the plot had to be paid for after all. We get the impression of a woman-to-woman relationship and transfer of property, and it is strengthened by the fact that the testator now feels empowered to give her husband charge of it and to name the heirs to the land. Yet we are told that the land was first given to both spouses, and that both of them later bought it. Even so, one is left with the feeling that the house and its land are mainly Vicenta Teresa's. At any rate, we see the importance of the relationship between two comadres and how basic the originally Spanish institution of ritual coparenthood had become.

Despite declaring relatively little property, the testator (or someone for her) seems to have quite a little money to put into a shroud of the Virgin of Carmen (typical of this part of the Toluca Valley, as we have seen), a burial in the chapel, a high mass, and various offerings. These details seem to make Vicenta Teresa, or at least the family, relatively well off. One can also deduce from the fact that she is to be buried next to her father in a chapel that he was a person of substance and that the continuity of the testator's line is still felt despite Vicenta Teresa's marriage. The witnesses to the testament constitute a most impressive list of high local officials.

The notary don Pedro de la Cruz is a distinguished person too, as indicated by the don and his position of past alcalde. The testament is written in conservative style, with only a few details typical of Toluca Nahuatl. It is quite carelessly done; syllables or whole words are omitted at times, there are some mistakes such as "minomiquilis" for "ninomiquilis" or "nimomiquilis," "I will die," and also some repetitions. Such slips make it impossible to say for sure whether the passage where the writer speaks of the holy Trinity "and" God the father, God the son, and God the Holy Spirit represents one of these careless errors or confusion about a basic point of Christian doctrine.

Jesus, M$^{\underline{a}}$ y Josephe Ame —
Ma mocequizcayectenehualoni yn itlasomahuiztocatzin y S$^{\underline{n}}$tisima tridad yhua Dios tetatzin yhua Dios yhua Dios ytlaçopiltzin yhua Dios Espiritu – Sancto Ma yuh mochichihua Ame Jesus
Axca miercoles en 27 de febrero de 1737 a^{os} Nic-Pehualtia notestamento nehual notoca Vicenta Theresa notlaxilacalpa S$^{\underline{n}}$to S$^{\underline{n}}$ Fran$^{\underline{co}}$ calixtlaguaca niquituhua yntla minomiquilis ca huel acachtopa noyolia nanimantzin ycemactzinco notlaçotatzin Dios yhua niquitoua ca ocatqui yn iquimiliuhca yez yn itlaquentzin la Virgen del Carme yhua yc ni-

Jesus, Mary, and Joseph. Amen. —
May the precious revered name of the most holy Trinity and God the father, God his precious son, and God the Holy Spirit be entirely praised. May it be done, amen. Jesus.
Today Wednesday the 27th of February of the year of 1737, I named Vicenta Teresa begin my testament in my tlaxilacalli of holy San Francisco of Calixtlahuaca. I say that if I die, first of all [I place] my spirit and soul entirely in the hands of my precious father God. And I say that there is a shroud [for my body] that is to be the habit of the Virgen del Car-

[1]The testament is accompanied by a contemporary Spanish translation.

molpitias yn icordontzin notlaçotzin Sn Franco yhua niquituhua canpa nopultura yez ca onpa yyecmacopatzinnco notlaçotatzin oncatca tispiez[2] notlalnacayo yhua niquitohua ca motemacas Ome temacas Ome tomintzin nocepulturacohualoni yhua meliotzin Snta Jerosale yhua niquitohua Ca Oncatqui yn ipalehuisloca yez y n[. . .]yoliantzin y nanimantzin cetel Missa Cantadan Requien yhua niquituua ca nopapa tzilitniz tepustli notlaxilacalpa Snto Sn Franco calisxtlaguaca yhua niquitohua nonamictzin yn itoca Juan miquel nica niccauhtehuas ca nica nicnopielia ome caltzintli yxpātzinnco yztica yquisayanpa tunatiuh yhua cosina yztica yc Xocotitla[3] yhuicalo [*verso*] Tlaltzinntli ca san otechmotlaolili noconmadre ytoca Melchora de los renyez ynamictzin difuto felis Manuhuel oc cenpa Omotencue[. . .]tzinno nocomadre Oc cepa Oticcohuililique yca nahui peso tlaltzinntli ypatiuh yc huiyac yequahuill yhua yhua yc patlahuac onquahuill ca niquitohua nonamictzin ytoca Juan Miguel yhua niquitohua yntla ninomiquilis ca quinmocuitlahuiz nahuiti nopilhuatoto yhua Ometi Oquichtototi ce toca Juo Diego oc ce ytoca Palu Franco = yhua quimotlacoxelque yn iquiyahuac yhua niquitohua ca neltis notlanequilis —

yhua niquihua ca huel cenca nicnotlatlauhtilia noalbaceal yez ytoca Dn ysidro Lopez ca yehuatzin nopa motlatooltis yntla quali q̄mochihuilitzinnos yn inahuactzinco Dios yhua satepa nehual ca Dios quimotlaxtlashuilis = yhua onotzanloque ynmixpa tlatoque onicchiuh noteztamento —

testigo fiscal de la Sancta yGlesia D.n Lenō—toribion testigo fiscal teniente ygnasio de la Cruz testigo Alcalde Actual D.n Bernabel de Sn.tiago testigo teninte Alcalde Lorenzo de la Cruz [*f.* 2] Testigo Alcalde Passado D.n Manuel de la Cruz
Essno ~~all~~ pado D.n Peo de la Cruz

men, and I am to be girt with the rope of my precious father San Francisco. And I say that as to where my grave will be, my earthly body is to lie buried[2] on the right-hand side of my late precious father. And I say that 2 reales are to be given for buying my grave, and half a real for Holy Jerusalem. And I say that the help of my spirit and soul is a high requiem mass. And I say that the bells are to ring for me in my tlaxilacalli of holy San Francisco of Calixtlahuaca. And I say that I am leaving my husband named Juan Miguel here; here I have two houses; the one in front faces east, and a kitchen faces Xocotitlan,[3] [with] the land going with it. [*verso*] My comadre named Melchora de los Reyes, whose deceased husband was Félix Manuel, gave it to us. My comadre changed her mind again, and we bought the land from her again for a price of 4 pesos; it is 3 quahuitl long and 2 quahuitl wide. And I say that my husband named Juan Miguel—I say if I die he is to take care of four small children of mine, and two are little boys, one named Juan Diego and the other named Pablo Francisco. = They are to divide in halves [the land] that is outside [the house]. And I say that my will is to be carried out. —

And I say that I very much implore my future executor named don Isidro López to speak on my behalf. If he does it well in relation to God and secondly to me, God will reward him. = [The witnesses] were summoned; I made my testament before the gentlemen [or officials]. —

Witness fiscal of the holy church don León Toribio; witness fiscal teniente Ignacio de la Cruz; witness present alcalde don Bernabé de Santiago; witness alcalde teniente Lorenzo de la Cruz. [*f.* 2] Witness past alcalde don Manuel de la Cruz.
Notary don Pedro de la Cruz, past alcalde.

[2]The form "tispiez" seems unintelligible; what would have been expected is *toctiez*, "will lie buried," and the Spanish translator rendered it accordingly.

[3]The Spanish translator understood Xocotitlan as to the north.

20. Will issued by Pascual de los Reyes for María Inés, San Sebastián, 1703

(AHAM, Box 23:9, Juzgado Eclesiástico de Toluca)

THIS TESTAMENT is unusual because a man issues it on behalf of his deceased sister; there is only one other similar case in the corpus, No. 34. Thus when a person dies without leaving a testament, a close relative may decide to issue one on her/his behalf, and the validity of the procedure remains unchallenged. With some testaments in the corpus that are short and incomplete and have clearly been written in haste, the suspicion arises that they might have been issued by someone else after the testator's death. But here as in No. 34, all ambiguity is excluded by an explicit statement made by the relative at the beginning of the will. Yet other wills are issued openly by persons in authority on behalf of the deceased, as in No. 60.

Pascual de los Reyes lists the items that his sister's deceased husband had bequeathed to a daughter, Gregoria, adding that María Inés herself did not leave anything because she sold everything she had to get medical treatment. No house or land is mentioned; thus the family appears to be presently poor, but that may be a recent development resulting from the sale of assets because of the illness, for Gregoria inherited from her father two chests and a most impressive array of saints: two large paintings, one in a gilt frame, and a statue. Also, Pascual was able to pay for a grave, a shroud, a high mass and offerings.

Pascual's human concern can be perceived in the words used whenever he refers to his sister and her poor health. In a further touching detail he affirms that he is going to take care of the young daughter, keep the property safe, and hand it on to her when she grows up. Indeed, quite a few years later he stepped in to protect Gregoria's rights, as emerges from the records of a lawsuit in which the present testament was found.

The notary is once again Tomás de la Cruz, whom we have already found in previous testaments from Santa Bárbara Xolalpan and San Miguel Aticpac; he was clearly serving several barrios of Toluca and settlements in the neighboring area. More details about him are included in the introductory study (p. 40).

Ma moçenquizCayectenehua yn itlaçomahuiztocatzin yn dios tetatzin yhuan dios tepiltzin yhuan dios espiritu Santo ma y muchihua Amen Jesus
Axca martez A 26 de Junio de 1703 Años nicchihua ynin memoria nehuatl notoca pasqual de los Reyez ytechcopa noermanatzin micatzintli ytoca m^a^ ynez totlaxilacalpa San Sebastian quenami San cocoxcatzintli ocatca oquimacac ynon Cocoli San çemi youhqui omocauh[1] omomiquili Ca oquimoteochihuili totatzin dioz ypan yBulatzin yhuan oquimomachiotili Ca niquitohua oncanontzin Cani oncatqui poerta perdon oncan toctiez yn itlalo ySoquiyo Ca ye nican onicnotlaocolili yquimiliuhca yhuan yCordontzin totlaçotatzin San fran^co^ yc molpitiaz = yhuan motemacaz meliotzin Santa JeruSalen = yhuan tictotlaocolilia çe misa Cantada ynic palehuilos yanimantzin = yhuan niquitohua Ca oquimopieliaya çe ychpochto ytoca Gregori[. . .] Ca oquimocahuililitia ytlaçotatzin ocatca ytoca pe^ro^ ViSente ome caxa yhuan San JuSep quimopielia çe bara yhuan tlaco yCa ymarcotzin teocuitlayo yhuan Santa Getrodez motlacaquetzinotica = yhuan yehuatzin la Virgen del Rosario quimopielia çe bara ayac tlen quimopieliaya quenin San cocoxqui ocatca mochi oquinamacac yn tlen quimopieliaya yc mopatiaya Ca nehuatl nicpielis ynin tlen oq[. . .]mocahuilili ytatzin notoca pasqual de los Reyes yntla quimohuapahuilis dios nicmacaz = yhuan niquitohua Ca nehuatl ninochihua albaSea nicnopalehuilis nicnocuitlahuiz yn canin toctiez yn itlalnacayo = ymixpan testigos ynic om[. . .]chiuh ynin memoria Gaspar de

May the precious revered name of God the father, God the son, and God the Holy Spirit be entirely praised. May it be done, amen. Jesus.
Today, Tuesday the 26th of June of the year 1703, I named Pascual de los Reyes make this memorandum [of testament] in our tlaxilacalli of San Sebastián concerning my deceased sister named María Inés. Since she was sickly, [God] gave her that complaint, and suddenly she was left in such a state[1] that she died. Our father God has blessed her in his bull, and he has designated [a place for her burial]; I say that there where the door [church portal] of pardon is is where her earthly body is to lie buried. I have given her as a favor a shroud and a rope of our precious father San Francisco with which she is to be girt. = And half a real is to be given for Holy Jerusalem. = And we are giving her as a favor a high mass so that her soul will be helped. = And I say that she had a little daughter named Gregoria. Her late precious father named Pedro Vicente left her two chests, a San José measuring a vara and a half, with a frame covered with gold [or silver], a Santa Gertrudis in the round, and a Virgen del Rosario measuring a vara. No one had anything. Since she [María Inés] was sick, she sold everything she had to get treatment. I named Pascual de los Reyes will keep for her these things that her father left her [Gregoria], and if God raises her [if she grows up] I will give them to her. = And I say that I make myself executor; I will help her and take care of where her earthly body will lie buried.= This memorandum was made in the pre-

---

[1]Aspects of the translation of the passage from "quenami" to "omocauh" are speculative.

la Cruz fiscal testigo Ber^{no} de los Santos testigo Saluador de los Reyes testigo melchor de los Reyez testigo don Gaspar de S.tiago fiscal mayor
Es^{no} thomas de la Cruz

sence of witnesses: Gaspar de la Cruz, fiscal; witness, Bernardino de los Santos; witness, Salvador de los Reyes; witness, Melchor de los Reyes; witness, don Gaspar de Santiago, fiscal mayor.
Notary Tomás de la Cruz.

21. Tomasa Gertrudis, San Sebastián, 1738

(AHAM, Box 54:31, Juzgado Eclesiástico de Toluca)

THE WIDOW Tomasa Gertrudis mentions no relative other than a nephew, Juan Antonio, to whom she bequeaths a house with a small piece of land. Probably she has no surviving children. She also entrusts to Juan Antonio the worship of the Virgin of Guadalupe inside her house. The fact that the image is defined as standing leads us to think that it was a statue; however, it is also true that the verb "to stand" was used to describe standing figures in a painting, so we cannot be sure.

If bequests occupy a small portion of the testament, funeral arrangements seem to be central. Tomasa Gertrudis asks for a shroud of the Virgin of Carmen, a specific burial place in the church, and bells to be rung in three districts. In addition, her nephew is to provide for a high mass (in return, no doubt, for receiving the house and land). The executor and two of the witnesses are prominent individuals in the community, as seen in their title of don. Thus despite the lack of large amounts of property, the testator appears to be of a relatively high status.

Matías de la Cruz is the same notary as in No. 12, and here he shows some of the same characteristics, especially the extra *i* to preserve the pronounceability of a syllable-final consonant. As there, he omits some syllables and characters, but in some ways this document is a bit more standard than the other one, though they were written little more than a year apart. Note the use of the verb *xamani*, "to be shattered, to come apart into small pieces" in reference to the body after death, a hint of the traditional Nahuatl rhetoric emphasizing the ephemeral nature of human life, as seen in earlier collections of Nahuatl song such as the Cantares Mexicanos. On the other hand, as in Nos. 17 and 18, dated close to the same time, the Spanish loanword *oratorio*, "oratory," is used as a designation for the main residence instead of the locally predominant *ichantzinco Dios*, "the home of God."

Ma mocemquiscayectenehua yn intlaçomahuistocatzin y Dios tetatz[in] yhua Dios ytlaçopilitzin yhua Dios Espirito Santo ma ye mochihua Ame Jesus Maria y Joseph — Axca mierconlis yninqu[i?] chinahui tonatiuh mani Metztli nobienbre yhua siuhtlapohuali de 1738 años ninquipehualtia nomemoria nehuatli notoca thomasa Getrodis nivioda notlaxilacalpa Sa SeBastiane yhua niquitohua ytla nechimotlaçotiliz y cemmanahuaquin y tlatt^{o}ni Dios yhua niquitohua ca huel ycematzinc^{o} ninconetlalia noyoliatzin nanimatzin yhua niquitohua caxica chocas tepostl cachitopa notlaxilacalpa Sa Sebastia yhua Sa Juan Ba^{p}ta yhua Sata Maria de los Angel yhua niquitohua neltis notlanequilis motemacas huetzintle memelotzintzi yhua niquitohua yqui moquimilos y notlanacayo ca ytlaqu[e?]quetzin notlaçomahuisnatzin la Virgen del Carme yhua niquitohua yPalehuilocatzin nanimatzin se misa sa catada de Requi nechimotlaquolilia nosobrino ytoca Juan Antonio yhua niquitohua y nosepoltoRa yes ca opa hue teopa ca

May the precious revered name of God the father, God his precious son, and God the Holy Spirit be entirely praised; may it be done, amen. Jesus, Mary, and Joseph. — Today, Wednesday the 9th day of the month of November in the year count of 1738, I named Tomasa Gertrudis, widow, begin my memorandum [of testament] in my tlaxilacalli of San Sebastián. And I say that if the universal ruler God shows me love [brings about my death], I place my spirit and soul very entirely in his hands. I say that now the bells are to sound, first in my tlaxilacalli of San Sebastián, then in San Juan Bautista and Santa María de los Angeles, and I say that my will is to be carried out. An offering of half a real each is to be given. And I say that my earthly body is to be wrapped in the habit of my precious revered mother the Virgen del Carmen. And I say that the help of my soul is a high mass of requiem that my nephew named Juan Antonio is favoring me with. And I say that my grave is to be at the great church before

xipatzincon Santo quichrito de bera cruz ca opa nechimomachiyotiliz Dios ca opa chamatos[1] y notlanacayo yhua niquitohua caltzintle ytzintica yquisayapa tonatiuh ninquicahuilia oratorio nosobrino Juan Antonio yhua niquitohua mochica tlali m[a?]quilicquahui quipieye yhua niquitohua yehuatzin la Virge de huadalope micatzinnohua calitiqui oca quimotequipanilhui[s] yhua niquitohua ca huel niquinotlatlauuhtiliya yehuatzin Dn Antonio de tapia yehuatzin S noAlbaseametzin yes yhua niquitohua ytla quali quimochihuilis ca Dios quimo[m?]tlaxitlahuiliz yhua niquitohua ca texipa omochihui nomemoria testigo don Bernadin fran^co^ testigo Antonio GosSaleles fisCal de [la?] Sta ygelecia Dn Juan de la cruz Es^no^ Mathias de la Cruz

Santo Cristo de la Vera Cruz; there God will designate [a place] for me, and there my earthly body will lie shattered.[1] And I say that as to a house facing east, an oratory, I leave it to my nephew Juan Antonio, and I say that it includes the land, measuring 5 quahuitl. And I say that he is to serve the Virgen de Guadalupe that stands inside the house. And I say that I greatly implore don Antonio de Tapia to be my executor, and I say that if he does it well God will reward him. And I say that my memorandum was done in the presence of people: don Bernardino Francisco, witness; Antonio González, witness; fiscal of the holy church don Juan de la Cruz.
Notary Matías de la Cruz.

[1] "Chamatos" is standard *xamantoz*, containing *xamani*, "to be shattered," plus the auxiliary verb *onoc*, to lie.

22. Ambrosio Lorenzo, San Bartolomé Tlatelolco, 1715

(AHAM, Box 28:21, Juzgado Eclesiástico de Toluca)

THE WIDOWER Ambrosio Lorenzo is clearly well off, holding quite a few pieces of land (often hovering near the traditional 20-quahuitl plot), scattered in different places in the classic pattern. He distributes them among his four children, Antonia María, Gregorio Juan, Josef de los Angeles, and Tomasa Francisca; the two males receive much more land than the females, but Antonia María inherits the family house in addition. Mentioned first, she was possibly the eldest child, but also it may have been a factor that the two sons were already married by then (as we see in the mention of two daughters-in-law, one of them confirmed in No. 23 as the wife of Gregorio Juan). Tomasa Francisca must have been the youngest.

The testator also leaves some land apparently to be shared by all the children, and two lots, one to his grandchildren, and the other to people whose relation to him is not clear. One of the lots had been the property of the testator's mother, and it is worthy of note that Ambrosio passes it on to his grandchildren despite having four living children. One of the grandchildren, Andrés Juan, gets some land on his own; in No. 23 we learn that Gregorio Juan had a son of that name. Gregorio is apparently the elder of Ambrosio's two male children and somewhat favored over his younger brother Josef de los Angeles. Ambrosio Lorenzo also possesses some magueyes; he leaves a few of them to two daughters-in-law, while dedicating the rest to his funeral expenses.

A few days after the testament was issued, the same notary added a note that the local priest, in the presence of the fiscal of the church, divided a small lot between two women. The relationship of the testator with these women is not established (we are told only that one of them is a widow), nor is it clear whether the lot in question is one of those mentioned in the testament proper. In any case, we see an example of the active role occasionally given to the local priest in the administration of testators' estates (See No. 12 for another instance).

It is possible that the testator has close connections with the local indigenous church hierarchy, but inconsistencies and under-identification of individuals leave us without certainty on this point. One of Ambrosio's executors is a Josef de la Cruz, without title; could this be the same person as the fiscal of the church with the same name except that the notary twice not only calls him don but gives him the rarer title of señor? Is the Domingo Julián who inherits part of a lot from Ambrosio the same as the church topile of that name who is a witness?

Funeral arrangements are typical for a well-off individual, even if no shroud is mentioned. A very unusual element, however, is the burial under a copal tree, rather than in the church near some religious image as might be expected with a person of Ambrosio Lorenzo's standing; his wish almost seems to be more in line with ancient beliefs than with Christian ritual.

Unusual also is the opening of the testament, with a little prayer directly to God, cast in the traditional masculine vocative. More generally, the notary Francisco Hernández uses traditional and quite elaborate formulas, in line with the style of sixteenth-century testaments (see for example the whole preamble, or the formula for the executors, explaining so clearly that they are to expect their reward in heaven, not here and now). Apart from that, his writing definitely falls within the framework of eighteenth-century Toluca Nahuatl and contains many personal irregularities. In one aspect he goes to the extreme, omitting so many syllables that comprehension becomes difficult or impossible at certain crucial points.

Jesus maria hi Joseph
tonteCuiyoen diosSe ma ynpapa yn imachi[. . .] y Crűz ma xitechmomaquixtilitzino yn ihui[. . .]pa y toAhua y niCa ninomachiyotia yn ica ytoCatzi y dios tethatzi yhua dios tepiltzi yhua d[. . .]os espirito Sato yeytzintzin yn personas y[. . .] Sa çe huel neli teotl dios auh ca nica nicpeuhhualtia y nodestameto nehuatl notoca Abosio loReço Auh Ca nica nochatziCo Sato S. bar$^{\underline{me}}$ tl[. . .]tilolCo auh y noÇihuahuatzi Yn itoCa maria CoSepsio difuta — v yhua niQuitohua Ca techtziCo Nipohqui y notlaçomahuisnatzi Sata maria Sopsio — v Yhua niquito y nanimatzi Ca San pactiCatqui Caque Catqui y notlalnaCayo Ca huel moconcotiCatqui Ca Sa niCa nicChixtiCatq[. . .] yn itlaSomahuismiquilitzi y notlaSomahuistem[. . .]quixtiCatzi tt^{o} JeSus xpo que tlaCahuas yn itlaç[. . .]yolotzi yhua niquitohua Ytla ninomiquilis Ca nopapa tzilinis Capana Satha Jerosale huetztlin[. . .]

v yhuan ihua niquitohua y noSepoltoRa yes yc to[. . .]locacopa ytzitla copalquauhuitl neltis notlatol —

v yua niquitohua nechmotlaocolilisque Çetetl vigilia neltis y notlantol huetzintli — 1 me^{o}

v yhua niquitohua y notlasoteopixCatzi nechmotlaoncolilis çe miSan neltis notlatol huetzitli — 5 ps^{o}

v yuã niquitohua y nopiltzi yn itoca Atonia mar[. . .]a nicahuili CalCatzitli neltis notlatol — [*verso*]

v yhua niquitohua niCahuiliti Sepohuali Sorco Solar neltis

v yhua niquitohua y nopiltzi ytoca gregurio Joa nicmati mochica yn ixacal totlatiCatiCa otli ca neltis —

v Yhua niq̃tohua y nopiltzi yn itoca Joçeph de los Agelis no nicCahuilia ynic Can iCha yno tlaltotli neltis

v Yhuan niquitohua Ca oca matlatli Yhuan ome

Jesus, Mary, and Joseph.
O our lord God, for the sake of the sign of the cross save us from our enemies. Here I take as my sign the name of God the father, God the son, and God the Holy Spirit, three persons but only one really true deity God. Here I named Ambrosio Lorenzo begin my testament; my home is here in holy San Bartolomé of Tlatelolco, and my deceased wife's name is María Concepción. — v And I say that I belong to [the cofradía of] my precious revered mother Santa María de la Asunción. — v And I say that my soul is healthy and nothing is the matter with it; my earthly body is very sick. I am just awaiting here the precious revered death of my precious revered savior our lord Jesus Christ and his precious decree. And I say that if I die the bells are to be rung for me. [There will be an] offering for Holy Jerusalem.

v And I say that my grave will be toward Toluca, under the copal tree. My statement is to be carried out. —

v And I say that they are to favor me with a vigil. My statement is to be carried out. Offering — half a real.

v And I say that my precious priest is to favor me with a mass. My statement is to be carried out. Offering — 5 pesos.

v And I say that I am leaving the house to my child named Antonia María. My statement is to be carried out. — [*verso*]

v And I say that I am leaving her the lot, of 20 furrows. It is to be carried out.

v And I say that I am giving to my child named Gregorio Juan [land] together with the straw hut on it, on the [?] road. It is to be carried out. —

v And I say that I leave to my child named Josef de los Angeles that little piece of land for a place for his home on it. It is to be carried out.

v And I say that there are 12 magueyes that are to

metl 2 notech poquih yes neltis y notlatol —

v Yhua niquitohua y noÇihuamo ÇebastiAna fran^{ca} nicmati ome metl 2 neltis notlatol —

v Yhua niquitohua Sano nosihuamo ytoca Agelina JuÇepha nicmati ome metl 2 neltis notlatol —

v yua niquitohua y nopiltzin itoCa gregorio Jua nicCahuiliti tlali Çepohualpa ynic huiyac onpohualpa ynic patlahuac neltis notlatol —

v Sano yehuatl nopiltzi Gregorio Jua nicCahuiliti tlali tlapechco opohualpa neltis

v yhua niquitohua Sano nopiltzi Joceph de los agelis nicmati tlali tlatosCac Sepohualpa Ynpa matlacquah neltis notlatol —

v yhua niquitohua Sano yehuatl Joseph de los Agelis nichuiliti tlali tlatic neltis tlatol —

v yhua niquitohua Sano yehuatl Juceph nicmati tlali yxtlahuaCan Sepohuali neltis notlatol

v yhua niquitohua nochpoch Atonia maria y nicmati tlallin çepohuali Soco neltis notlatol —

v Yhua niquithohua Sano nochpoch ytoca tomaSan fra^{ca} nicmacati tlali tlatosCaC neltis — [*f.* 2]

v Yhua niquitohua Sano nochpoch ytoca tomaSam fra^{ca} nicmaCati tlali tlatosCac Sepohualpa neltis notlatol[1]

v Yhua niquitohua nicmati tlali xoloco matlacquahutl ytocac notzi gregurio joa neltis notlatul

v Yhua niquituhua yn itoca biatris Juçepha Ca huehue co nel ynic quis ynic tla cruz ynic tuloCapa[2] neltis y notlatol —

v Yhua niquitohua yno solar yn iaxca nonatzi catca niquicahuiliti ynoxhuihua yn ithoca Adres Joa yhuan itoCa Salbador neltis notlatul —

v Yhua niquitohua y noxhuin ithoCa Adres Joa niccahuili tlali Çepohualpa neltis notlatol —

v Yhua niquito tlali tlatosCa quicatomatisas quicahuili[3] nopilhua netis notlatol —

belong to me [be used for my expenses]. My statement is to be carried out. —

v And I say that I am giving to my daughter-in-law Sebastiana Francisca 2 magueyes. My statement is to be carried out. —

v And I say that I am likewise giving to my daughter-in-law named Angelina Josefa 2 magueyes. My statement is to be carried out. —

v And I say that I am leaving to my child named Gregorio Juan land of 20 [quahuitl] long and 40 wide. My statement is to be carried out. —

v Likewise I am leaving to my child Gregorio Juan land at Tlapechco of 40. It is to be carried out.

v And I say that to another child of mine, Josef de los Angeles, I am giving land at Tlatozcac, of 30 quahuitl. My statement is to be carried out. —

v And I say that I am likewise leaving land at Tlatic to Josef de los Angeles. My statement is to be carried out. —

v And I say that I am likewise giving Josef land on the plain, of 20. My statement is to be carried out.

v And I say that I am giving to my daughter Antonia María land of 20 at Tzonco. My statement is to be carried out. —

v And I say that I am likewise giving to a daughter of mine, Tomasa Francisca, land at Tlatozcac. It is to be carried out. — [*f.* 2]

v And I say that I am likewise giving to my daughter Tomasa Francisca land of 20 at Tlatozcac. My statement is to be carried out.[1]

v And I say that I am giving land at Xoloco of 10 quahuitl to my child Gregorio Juan. My statement is to be carried out.

v And I say that the person named Beatriz Josefa [. . .] since [. . .] left [. . .] cross [. . .] toward Toluca.[2] My statement is to be carried out. —

v And I say that I am leaving that lot that was the property of my mother to my grandchildren named Andrés Juan and Salvador. My statement is to be carried out. —

v And I say that I leave to my grandchild named Andrés Juan land of 20. My statement is to be carried out. —

v And I say that [I?] am leaving land at Tlatozcac [. . .?][3] to my children. My statement is to be car-

---

[1]Possibly these two entries, one at the end of a page, the second at the beginning of the following one, are the same, referring to the same land.

[2]Probably because of extensive syllable omission, substantial parts of this passage remain unintelligible.

[3]Again probably because of syllable omission, a string of letters in the Nahuatl has not yet been satisfactorily analyzed.

v Yhua niquitohua yno Solar yn ipa motlalisque yn ixhū[. . .]tin y mochiti Domigo Julia ynhua tomasan fra^{ca} yhua Joliana JoÇepha quimoxexelhuisque

v Yhua niquitohua Ca ye onictzōquixti y nodestameto abocio loso v Yhua niquitohua y nohualvasiahua yesque huatzinzti Do bernaVel niColas yhua JuÇeph de la Cruz ytla qualli quimocuitlahuisque y naMatlacuilol Ca dios quimotlaxtlaliliz camo nica quimotilisque yn itlaxtlahuiltzi Ca opa yn ilhuiCatli quimotilisque yn itlaxtlahuiltzi Ca dios quimotlaxtlahuililis yn imixpatziCon onitlacuilo yehuatzintzin S^{r} Do Joceph de la cruz fiscal de la Sa^{ta} yJelisia yhua diego de Sa cru difutado yhua nicolasn marti teoyotica tepixqui yhua domigo Jolia topile [*f.* 2*v*] destigos

v Axca mierColes a 23 dias del mes de octonbre yhua yn ipa xihuitl de 1715 años —

v es^{no} fra^{co} hernades

v Axca lones a 28 dias del mes de octobcr motlanahuatili toteopixcatzi temachtiani oquimotlatequili Solarto Cocahuisque yn itoca beniCan losia bioda yhua niColas maria —

v yxpatzi Sr Do Juceph de la Cruz fiscal de la Satha ygelsia

es^{no} fra^{co} hernades

ried out. —

v And I say that as to that lot on which [. . .] are all to settle—Domingo Julián, Tomasa Francisca, and Juliana Josefa—they are to divide it among themselves.

v And I say that now I, Ambrosio Lorenzo, have concluded my testament. v And I say that those who are to be my executors are don Bernabé Nicolás and Josef de la Cruz. If they take good care of my document, God will reward them. They will not see their reward here, for they will see their reward in heaven. God will reward them. I did the writing in the presence of señor don Josef de la Cruz, fiscal of the holy church; Diego de la Santa Cruz, diputado; Nicolás Martín, church tepisque; and Domingo Julián, topile, [*f.* 2*v*] witnesses.

v Today, Wednesday the 23rd day of the month of October in the year of 1715. —

v Notary Francisco Hernández.

v Today, Monday the 28th day of the month of October, our priest the preacher ordered that he [divided ?] the small lot. One named Beni[t?]a Lucía, widow, and Nicolasa María are to share it. —

v In the presence of señor don Josef de la Cruz, fiscal of the holy church.

Notary Francisco Hernández.

23. Gregorio Juan, San Bartolomé Tlatelolco, 1731

(AHAM, Box 45:48, Juzgado Eclesiástico de Toluca)

DYING SIXTEEN YEARS after his father Ambrosio Lorenzo (No. 22), Gregorio Juan seems at first glance to bequeath less; on closer examination one sees that though the son mentions fewer pieces of land, some of them are larger, and the difference is not great. The father mentions land in the amount of 200 quahuitl (by the traditional 20, it seems), plus a few odd pieces whose measurements are not given. The son mentions nearly as much, 180, though in his case the unmeasured part is restricted to a small house lot. We cannot be sure how much of the land presently held by Gregorio is the same that came to him from his father, but we do know that he in some fashion improved upon the more than 70 quahuitl the father left him in his testament. It is interesting to note that the house in question is not the one that Ambrosio Lorenzo left to one of his daughters, but must have been acquired before the father's death, probably at the time of Gregorio Juan's marriage to Angelina Josefa, who already appeared in the father's testament.

A son Antonio receives the lion's share of Gregorio Juan's estate: the house, half the lot, and 120 quahuitl of land, three times as much as his brother Andrés Juan. Gregorio's granddaughter Felipa inherits 20 quahuitl and is to get a portion of the lot to build herself a house on; it is hard to tell which of the brothers was her father. Looking back to Ambrosio Lorenzo's will, we are presented with some problems. From the present testament, it would seem clear that Antonio is the eldest child, followed by Andrés Juan. Yet in their grandfather's will, Andrés Juan alone is mentioned, receiving 20 quahuitl of land. Could there have been two grandchildren named Andrés Juan, one dying before now and another named the same, as sometimes happened? The Andrés Juan mentioned in Ambrosio's will would now be at least 16 years old, probably older, and it would seem strange for Gregorio Juan to leave specific directions about such a late teenager's being "raised." We must also consider that Gregorio's granddaughter Felipa must have had some child of his for a parent, and surely not someone who still needed to be brought up.

Nothing is left to Gregorio's wife, Angelina Josefa, although she is given the responsibility of raising the children with the help of unnamed others, probably the executors.

But if Gregorio Juan has lands comparable to those of his father, in other ways we see signs of fewer resources and lower standing. The funeral arrangements are more modest, and no offerings are given; whereas the father had at least one don among his executors, the son does not (the witnesses, however, are the same church officials in both cases). But we see his continuing identification with his father in the fact that he asks to be buried with him next to the copal tree, a striking detail illustrating a practice now traditional in the family.

Although notary Domingo Mejía shows some of the typical traits of Toluca Nahuatl, his work is much more standard and easily intelligible than that of his colleague Francisco Hernández in the same tlaxilacalli sixteen years earlier. He does, however, still preserve the by now rather archaic initial paragraph markers, as in the earlier testament. Perhaps the fact that both use the word *solarton*, "little lot," has something to do with speech in this micro-locality. Among the witnesses in both cases is a lower church official called a *tepixqui*, or *tepisque* as the Spaniards said; earlier a common term, it is little seen in the eighteenth-century Toluca corpus.

---

ynca in itlasonmahuistocatzi yn Dios tetatzi yhua Dios tepiltzi yhua dios espirito santo —	In the precious revered name of God the father, God the son, and God the Holy Spirit —
v ca nica nicpehualtiya in notestameto nehual notoca Gregorio jua nosihuahuatzi Agelina jusenpa = ca nica nicha[. . .] santo san Barme tlatilollco ca ytetzico nipochqui notlas[. . .]mahuisnatzi santa mariya asopsio – ca huel mococotica[. . .]qui y notlalnacayo anhu i noanimatzi ca san pactica qe quimonequiltitzinos y tto Dios ytla ninomiquilis ca nopapan tzilinis capana neltis notlatol —	v Here I named Gregorio Juan begin my testament; my wife is Angelina Josefa. I am a citizen here in holy San Bartolomé of Tlatelolco and I belong to [the cofradía of] my precious revered mother Santa María de la Asunción. – My earthly body is very sick, but my soul is healthy as our lord God would wish it. If I die, the bells are to be rung for me. My statement is to be carried out. —
v ynhua niquitohua y nosepoltora yes ynahuactzico notlasotatzi mesticatca ynahuac copalquatl neltis —	v And I say that my grave is to be close to my precious late father, next to a copal tree. It is to be carried out. —
yhua niquitohua y notlasoteopixcatzi ca nopa quimochihuilis setetl misan resanda neltis notlatol —	And I say that my precious priest is to perform a low mass for me. My statement is to be carried out. —
v yhua niquitohua yni caltzitli yhua tlaco ynn isolarto y niccahuiliti nopiltzi attonio neltis notlatol —	v And I say that I am leaving this house and half of its little lot to my child Antonio. My statement is to be carried out. —
v yhuan oc tlaco solarto niccahuilitiuh nopiltzi adres jua neltis notlatol — oca quihuapahuasque ynatzin[1]	v And I am leaving the other half of the little lot to my child Andrés Juan. My statement is to be carried out. — There [their? his?] mother and others are to raise [them? him?].[1]
v yhua niquitohua noxhui felipa ponrisia oncan ic quixelhuisqe qexquich yc mochatis ytla monemitis neltis notlatol	v And I say that there they are to distribute to my grandchild Felipa [Florencia?] as much [land] as needed to make herself a home, if she lives. My statement is to be carried out.
v yhua niquitohua se tlali opohualpa quactla otlica	v And I say that I am leaving a piece of land of 40

[1]The last sentence here seems to be an afterthought. Since the omission of *n* is so common in the corpus, the reference can be to both of the children or to Andrés Juan alone. The plural verb with only the mother given as subject tells us that others are to take part, though we do not know who they are.

niccahuilitiuh nopiltzi adres jua neltis notlatol —

v yhua niquitohua ca oc sepohualpa tlali niccahuilitiuh noxhui felipa neltis notlatol —

v yhua niquitohua oc se tlali onpohuapa niccahuilitiuh nopiltzi attonio neltis notlatol —

v ynhua niquitohua se tlali nauhpohualpa niccahuilitiuh nopiltzi atonion neltis notlatol — [*verso*]

v ynhua niquitohua yn nosobrino matias nechtlaoncolis se peson yhua tlacamo quimonequiltiya quimoCuepilisqe macuili pesos nechmomaquili[2]

v ynhua niquitohua y noalbasiashua yesque ca yehuatzi jua tomas yhua yehuatzi felipe de santiyaGon : ytla quali quimochihuilisqe ca Dios quimotlaxtlahuilis —

v yhua ca ye onictzoquixti y notesntameto : ymispa notestigos ca yehuatzi fiscal de la santa yglesia Do pasqual ramos fiscal teniyete jasito atonio : teoyotica tepixqui pedro nicolas

Es^{no} DomiGon meginya

axca sabada en 14 de julio de 1731 a^{os}[3]

[quahuitl] on the Quauhtla road to my child Andrés Juan. My statement is to be carried out. —

v And I say that I am leaving another piece of land of 20 to my grandchild Felipa. My statement is to be carried out. —

v And I say that I am leaving another piece of land of 40 to my child Antonio. My statement is to be carried out. —

v And I say that I am leaving a piece of land of 80 to my child Antonio. My statement is to be carried out. — [*verso*]

v And I say that my nephew Matías is to favor me with 1 peso. And if he doesn't want to, he is to return 5 pesos, he is to give it to me.[2]

v And I say that my executors are to be Juan Tomás and Felipe de Santiago. If they do it well, God will reward them. —

v And now I have concluded my testament before my witnesses: don Pascual Ramos, fiscal of the holy church; Jacinto Antonio, fiscal teniente; Pedro Nicolás, church tepisque.

Notary Domingo Mejía.

Today Saturday the 14th of July of the year 1731.[3]

[2]The implication here seems to be as follows: Gregorio Juan is willing to forgive the rest of Matías's 5-peso debt if the latter comes up with 1 peso; otherwise he will have to pay the whole amount. The form "nechmomaquili" is here interpreted as a future with a missing *s*.

[3]At the back of the will it is reported in Spanish that Gregorio Juan, married to Angelina Josefa, died on the 16th of July of 1731 (two days after the testament was issued) and that a low mass was performed, though just when is not clear.

24. Melchora María, San Bartolomé Tlatelolco, 1737

(AHAM, Box 52:20, Juzgado Eclesiástico de Toluca)

QUITE OFTEN we see that a wife is left in charge of certain property with the responsibility of using it to raise her children. Here an older daughter is cast in a similar role. The widow Melchora María has a daughter María Francisca who seems to be grown, and a son Juan Valeriano (the namesake of his father) who appears to be still a small child. The difference in age of the two children leads one to wonder if the son is the product of a second marriage. The mother's solution, which shows strong cooperation between female relatives faced with a family emergency, is to charge the daughter with raising the little son and to leave much of the inheritance to her despite the general preference for males. We cannot compare sizes, but María Francisca receives two and a half pieces of land, Juan Valeriano only one and a "little piece of a lot." The daughter does not quite inherit the house and saints formally, but Melchora María "leaves her inside the house," the same expression used when mothers are left in charge of a house and their own children. It is left open or unclear whether the house will later go to Juan Valeriano or not. A certain Antonio gets half of a piece of land along with the daughter; possibly he is the Antonio Nicolás who is the testator's executor, and if we exercise our imaginations yet further, he might even be married to the daughter.

At the end of her will, Melchora María says that she does not want to create trouble between her children, highlighting a very common problem, squabbling over inheritance among the various family members. In addition to that, she uses a remarkable expression when she says that no one is to cause her headaches in *mictlan*, "the land of the dead" (in the

will as *mictlampa*, with a suffix indicating "toward"). This passage illustrates a potentially important point of a rare kind about the penetration of Christian doctrine in indigenous minds, for the use of the term is not orthodox. Preconquest religion did not know a full dichotomy between hell and heaven; mictlan was the land of the dead in general. In postconquest Christian vocabulary, the word meant hell specifically. In expecting to be in mictlan after death, was Melchora María retaining the full preconquest meaning and ignoring the Christian conception of a distinct heaven and hell? Such usage may hint at a very incomplete penetration of Christian notions in Nahua communities after all.

Melchora requests bells to be rung for her and burial at a specific place inside the church, which are arrangements typical of relatively high-status individuals. However, the high mass that traditionally accompanies them is lacking; she only requests that a low mass be celebrated. Also, high-status connections are absent other than the church officials who standardly acted as witnesses in San Bartolomé Tlatelolco.

Notary Diego Nicolás writes in a quite typical but not extreme Toluca Nahuatl style; he is especially fond of inserting an extra *n* in syllable-final position. Note the deviant form "tifotado" for *diputado*, "deputy" (a similar case is on p. 83), yet the individual letter substitutions are in the standard range. We see the influence of Spanish conversation in the expressions *pedazo tlalli*, "a piece of land," and *pedacito solar*, "a little piece of a lot."[1] Nahuatl traditionally spoke simply of "a land," whereas Spanish like English usually feels the necessity of something like "a piece of land."

Ca ninomachiotia Yn ica ytoCatzi Y Dios tentatzin yhua Dios tenpiltzin yhua Dios Espiriton santo Auh ca ni Nicpenhualtia y notestameto nehuatl notoca merchora maria bio[?]da nonamictzin catnca Jua balenriano Ca nica tichaneque Santo San Sa Bar$^{\underline{me}}$ tlatilolco Ca ntetzico nipoqui notlasomahuisnatzi Santa maria la cosephSio Ca huel moConcoticatqui y notlalnacayo Auh noanimatzin Ca Sa pacticatqui que quimonequiltis y tt^{o} D̄s ytla ninomiqulis ca nopapa tzilinis capanatzi neltis notlatol yhua niquitohua nosepoltora yes ynahuac tosequiscanatzin teopacalictic neltis notlatol — yhua niquitohua ytic yni Caltzitl oca nicauh nochpoch maria fra$^{\underline{ca}}$ oca quihuapahua nocone Jua baleriano mochica satoti neltis notlatol yhua notlasoteopixcatzi nopa quimochihuilis Se misa resada neltis notlatol yhua niquitoa se tlali cr$\overset{+}{o}$ztitlan nicahuiliti maria fra$^{\underline{ca}}$ neltis notlatol yhua niquitohua oc se pedaso tlali calbario nicmacati Sa ye no ye nochpoch maria fra$^{\underline{ca}}$ yhua niquitohua oc Se tlali Solar monepatlaxelotica tlaco conanas Atonio tlaco Conanas maria fra$^{\underline{ca}}$ neltis notlatol yhua niquitohua Se tlali xometitlan sepoalmani nicmacati nocone Jua baleriano yhua niquitoa oc Se pedasito Solar texocotitla nic[*verso*]macati sa

I take as my sign the name of God the father, God the son, and God the Holy Spirit. Here I named Melchora María, widow, begin my testament; my husband was Juan Valeriano. We are citizens here in holy San Bartolomé of Tlatelolco, and I belong to [the cofradía of] my precious revered mother Santa María de la Concepción. My earthly body is very sick, but my soul is healthy, as our lord God would wish it. If I die, the bells are to be rung for me; my statement is to be carried out. And I say that my grave is to be next to our consummate Mother, inside the church building; my statement is to be carried out. — And I say that I am leaving inside this house my daughter María Francisca; there she is to raise my child Juan Valeriano; [I leave it] together with the saints; my statement is to be carried out. And my precious priest is to perform a low mass for me; my statement is to be carried out. And I say that I am leaving a piece of land at Cruztitlan to María Francisca; my statement is to be carried out. And I say that I am giving another piece of land at the Calvary to my same daughter María Francisca. And I say that another piece of land, a lot, is being divided equally; Antonio is to take half, and María Francisca is to take half; my statement is to be carried out. And I say that I am giving a piece of land at Xometitlan, of 20 [quahuitl], to my child Juan Valeriano. And I say that I am giving another little piece

---

[1]Despite the fact that both *pedazo* and *solar* are from Spanish, this is a Nahuatl phrase with the relation between the two nouns indicated by simple conjunction, without the Spanish *de*.

ye no yehua Juan Baleriano neltiz notlatol yhua niquitohua notepatlatoca noalbasia yes notepatlatoca mochihuas yehuatzin Atonio nicolas ytla quali quimochihuil Ca Dios quimotlaxtlahuilis Ca yonictzoquixti y notestameto Camo tle y netequipacholi nitemacatias yn ipa nocha mochica nochpoch maria fra<u>ca</u> yhua Jua hua baleria Amo Aqui mictlapa nechtzoteconehuas amo Aqui tle nichuiquilia ca nicnoCuititica ymixpa notestigos yehuatzi Fiscal Du Joseph de Santiago Fiscal teniete pasqual de lu rreyes tifotado Gancobo Asensio teoyotica tepixqui salbador de los aJeles escribano de la sata yglesia Diego nicolas Axca Dumigo [l? e?] 1 de SephtieBre yn ipa xihuitl de 1737 Anos —

of a lot at Texocotitlan [*verso*] to the same Juan Valeriano; my statement is to be carried out. And I say that my intercessor, my executor, is to be Antonio Nicolás, who is to be made my intercessor; if he does it well, God will reward him. I have concluded my testament. I am not to go away giving people trouble in my home, and that includes my daughter María Francisca and Juan Valeriano. No one is to cause me headaches in the land of the dead. I owe nothing to anyone. I am making my declaration before my witnesses, fiscal don Josef de Santiago, fiscal teniente Pascual de los Reyes, diputado Jacobo Asencio, and church tepisque Salvador de los Angeles. Notary of the holy church, Diego Nicolás. Today, Sunday the [1st?] of September in the year of 1737. —

25. Don Felipe de Santiago, San Pedro Tototepec, 1728

(AHAM, Box 39:17, Juzgado Eclesiástico de Toluca)

THE TESTATOR don Felipe de Santiago reverses the custom of bequeathing the house and the land that goes with it to the eldest son; in fact, he leaves them to a little son Baltasar, often affectionately called Baltasarillo here, who is apparently the youngest of the males, while three grown-up sons get only a farming animal each and a piece of land to share. Baltasarillo also gets a little cow. In all likelihood the three grown-up sons have already married and established their homes, so that the family residence is left for the youngest. Note that one of the sons has the same second name as the father, while two others share another second name, de la Cruz. Santiago and Cruz were the most common second names in the Toluca Valley at this time for people of medium to high status. No second name is given for Baltasarillo, probably because he is so young.

Don Felipe also has two little daughters, Sebastiana María and Andrea Beatriz, to whom he leaves a small cow and a little sheep respectively (though no land). Indeed, the testator possesses a considerable number of large animals, which is not very common in the corpus. The fact that farming animals and land are left only to the sons is consonant with the understanding that men are more active in farming. In the end don Felipe mentions his wife, Angelina María, but only to say that she is to take care of the children.

Apart from his livestock, the burial at the main altar and the title don speak of don Felipe's high status. The don is very common also among the witnesses, who include cabildo members as well as the more often seen church officials; the executor too is a don. Thus don Felipe de Santiago is very well connected among the prominent individuals of his community. He makes various offerings of money and whole loads of shelled maize and beans, which testify to the availability of cash and resources. (Little Baltasar is to provide the mass, probably not making the arrangements personally in view of his age, but being financially responsible because he inherited the house.)

A question raised by the testament is how it is that such a clearly influential and wealthy person, who possesses farming animals and farming products beyond the norm, bequeaths only one piece of agricultural land. Unless it is a vast holding, of which there is no sign, don Felipe would appear to be poor in land. Could he operate on rented lands? Has he already given most of his holdings to his grown sons? There is no way of knowing, but what appears in this testament cannot have been the entirety of his assets at the height of his career.

Notary Juan de la Cruz appears to be greatly influenced by Spanish in the opening formula, using the whole Spanish phrase "en el nobre" for "in the name," something which is not seen in any other testament of the corpus. We see many traits that are typical of Toluca Nahuatl, such as for example the replacement of *-uh* with *-c*, as well as some inadvertent repetitions that might give the impression of carelessness and confusion. We see also some classic or conservative characteristics. The most outstanding thing about the document, however, is the way that it shows several features of a pronounced tlaxilacalli style which is discussed under No. 26.

Ssa pedro D^{n} phelipe de S^{n}tiago[1] Missa Catada — En el nobre Jesus Ma^{a} y Juseph Ma mosequiscayectehualo yn itlaSomahuistoCatz[. . .] y dios tetatzin yhua y dios yn itlaÇopiltzin yhua yhua y dios Espirito Sato Ma y mochihua Amen JeSus Maria y Juseph —
Axcan domigo a 15 de febrero de 1728 Anos Ca ni-Ca nicpehualtian y nometario test[. . .]Meto y nehual y notoca Do felipe de S^{n}tiago y notlaxilaCalpa Sato Sa pedro tototepec yhua niquitohuan huel acachtopa Se ymactzinCo niCotlalia y noyoliatzin yhua y nanimatzin Se imactzinco nicotlalia y notlaÇotatzin dios[2] yhua niquitohuan ytla itla nonpa quimochihuilis y notlaÇotatzin dios Ca oCacqui ynic quimilictias y notlalnaCan[. . .] yhua ynic ninolpitias yn itlaÇoMahuisgordotzin y notlaÇotatzin Sato Sa fran^{co} yhua niquitohuan ytla OnicnomaSehuitzinno yn itlaÇomahuisMiquilitzin y notlaÇotantzin dios y noSepultura yes Can Opa Calitic teopatzintlin Artar Mayor Opa tocties yn notlalnaCayo hua yhua niquitohuan Ca motemaCas Mcliotzin Sata Jerusale yhua yspitar MotemaCas Meliotzin yhua CoCoxCatzintzinti MaCosquen Meliotzin ynic nopa quimotlatlactilisquen y notlaÇotatzin dios — yhua ynquac ytla OnicnomaSehuitzinnos yn inMiquilitzin y notlaÇotatzin dios yCan Missa nimotoCastzinnos yehual bartesal quixtlanhuas y nomissan yhua niquitohuan yn ichatzinco y notlaÇotatzin dios ystiCa yquiSayapa tonaltzintli yhua Oc Se Caltzintli ystiCa ycalaquiyapa tonaltzintlin yhua yhuiCalo tlaltzintlin yehual y notelpochto yn itoCa BarteSarillo yehual chani yes Amaqui nechMaquilis netequipacholisn y mostla huiphtla neltis y notlanequilis yhua niquitohuan Se baquilla nicCahuilitias Sano yehual y notelpochto bartesarillo neltis y notlanequilis yhua niquitohua Oc Se notelpoch yn itoCan pasqual de S^{n}tiago ynhua Juan de la Cruz yhua Att^{o} de la Cruz Se tlatzintli yc Otli metepec niquiCahuilitias quiYeCahuisquen mocti yeiti Sa parejo Moxexelhuisque neltis y notlanequilis Sano yehua pasqual de S^{n}tiago n[. . .] nicCahuilitias yolCatzintli yelemiquin yhua Oc Se

San Pedro Don Felipe de Santiago[1] High mass — In the name of Jesus, Mary, and Joseph. May the precious revered name of God the father, God his precious son, and God the Holy Spirit be entirely praised. May it be done, amen. Jesus, Mary, and Joseph. —
Today, Sunday the 15th of February of the year 1728, I named don Felipe de Santiago begin my memorandum of testament here in my tlaxilacalli of holy San Pedro of Tototepec. And I say first of all that I place my spirit and soul entirely in the hands of my precious father God,[2] and I say that if my precious father God brings something upon me [if I die], there is the means with which my earthly body will be shrouded, and I will be girt with the precious revered rope of my precious father holy San Francisco. And I say that when I have attained the precious revered death of my precious father God, my grave is to be inside the church, at the main altar; there my earthly body is to lie buried. And I say that half a real is to be given for Holy Jerusalem, and half a real is to be given for the hospital, and half a real is to be given to the sick so that they will pray to my precious father God for me. — And when I have attained the death of my precious father God I am to be buried with a mass. Baltasar is to pay for my mass. And I say that as to the home of my precious father God [the principal building] facing east and another building facing west, along with the land that goes with it, my little son named Baltasarillo is to be the householder. No one is to cause me worry [about it] in the future; my will is to be carried out. And I say that likewise I am leaving to my little son Baltasarillo a little cow; my will is to be carried out. And I say that I am leaving to another son of mine named Pascual de Santiago, [and others named] Juan de la Cruz and Antonio de la Cruz a piece of land on the road to Metepec; the three of them are to share it; all three are to divide it among themselves equally. My will is to be carried out. And I am likewise leaving to Pascual de Santiago a beast for cultivation of the land, and to

---

[1]The word "testamento" appears to have been inserted later at this point.
[2]The Nahuatl, apparently inadvertently, makes much of this statement twice, which is ignored in the translation.

notelpoch Jua de la Cruz nicCahuilitias Sano Se yolcatzintli Sano yelemiq̃ yhua tt^{o}n de la Cruz nicCahuilias Sen YolCatzintlin Amaqui quiquixtili y motla huiptla nelti notlanequilis yhua niquitohua Oc Se nochpochto yn itoCa Sebastiana Ma^{a} nicCahuilitias Se baquilla neltis y not[. . .]nequilis yhua niquitohua Oc Se nocpochto yn itoCa Andrea biatris nicCahuilitias n[. . .] Se ychCatotlin neltis y notlanequilis yhua niquitohua y noSihuahuatzin Yn itoCa Angelina Ma^{a} quihuapahuasque yn ipilhua Amaqui nechmaquilis netequipacholin y mostla huiptla neltis y notlanequilis - yhua niquitohua Ca huel nicnotlatlactiliya yhuatzin D^{n} Juseph Angusti Ca yehual nopa motlatoltis noalbasia yes [. . .] ytla quali quimochihuilis Ca dios quimotlaxtlahuilis yhua Onotzaloque Omo Omochique testigos Ca yehual D^{n} Gr^{mo} de la Cruz Alcalde Actual testigo D^{n} mig[l?] de S^{n}tiago teniete alCalde testigo - yhua D^{n} Manuel de la Cruz fisCal de la Santa yGleSian testigo Jua de S^{n}tiago AlhuaSil Mayor testigo — do Jusep de S^{n}tiago Regido[. . .] Mayor testigo —

yhua niquitohua Se Carga tlaOtli yhua se Carga Anbas ninohuetias para SatiSimo Sacrameto neltis y notlane[. . .]
Jua de la Cruz es^{no}

another son of mine, Juan de la Cruz, I likewise am leaving a beast, likewise for cultivation, and to Antonio de la Cruz I am leaving a beast. No one is to take them from them in the future; my will is to be carried out. And I say that to a little daughter of mine named Sebastiana María I am leaving a small cow; my will is to be carried out. And I say that to another little daughter of mine named Andrea Beatriz I am leaving a little sheep; my will is to be carried out. And I say that my wife named Angelina María [and others] are to raise her children. No one is to cause me worry in the future; my will is to be carried out. – And I say that I greatly implore don Josef Agustín to speak for me and be my executor. If he does it well, God will reward him. And those who were summoned to become witnesses were don Gerónimo de la Cruz, present alcalde, as a witness; don Miguel de Santiago, alcalde teniente, as a witness; and don Manuel de la Cruz, fiscal of the holy church, as a witness; Juan de Santiago, alguacil mayor, as a witness; don Josef de Santiago, regidor mayor, as a witness. —
And I say that I am making an offering for the Santísimo Sacramento of a load of shelled maize and a load of beans [*habas*]. My will is to be carried out.
Juan de la Cruz, notary.

26. Bernardino de Santiago, San Pedro Tototepec, 1733
(AHAM, Box 50:2, Juzgado Eclesiástico de Toluca)

AS WE WOULD EXPECT, Bernardino de Santiago, a married man, leaves his house with its lot and the saints to the only male child, Marcos de Santiago, who bears the same second name. But when it comes to inheriting land, the son does not have the same clearly predominant position. He receives one piece of land whose size is not specified; the largest piece whose measurements are given[1] goes to the wife, and without instructions to raise any child with it or leave it to one later. In addition, the testator distributes four equally-sized pieces of land, apparently carved out of a single larger piece, to four daughters, while only Tomasa Francisca, the second child in line, gets an additional piece, possibly to live on. (Note that one of the daughters may have gotten her first name from a particular devotion to the Santa Ursula that is kept in the house, and all the daughters have Francisca as their second name, giving them the equivalent of a unified female lineage name that is otherwise not seen in the corpus.) Continuing with his generosity to heirs beyond his son, Bernardino gives bits of land to a grandchild and a sister. Thus he seems wealthy in land. Nevertheless, he claims to be very poor and moreover says that the tlaxilacalli leaders know it; if this statement has more than formulaic significance, it must mean that he is relatively poor in cash.

A further detail confirming his wealth is the number of offerings that he leaves, although he entrusts his children with providing a shroud and a requiem mass, and requests burial outside the church. Among the offerings another kind of animal makes its appearance in the corpus: an egg-laying hen to be offered to a cofradía, the only example that has been

[1]The unit of measurement used in this document is the *surco*, or furrow; I have not yet determined its exact relation to the more frequently seen quahuitl except that it was smaller, but since all the measurements given are in terms of it, comparisons can be made on a firm basis.

found in the Toluca Valley testaments.

Bernardino de Santiago's good connections within his local society are illustrated by his witness list, a collection of high secular and church officials all bearing the title don. He himself, however, despite a good position, does not seem to be of quite that rank; he lacks the don and probably has never held a high local office. The same is true of the person he chooses as executor, his fellow father-in-law Francisco de la Cruz, who may actually be the testator of No. 27, though possibly he is the notary of the present document.

It seems that notary Juan de la Cruz, of No. 25, and notary Francisco de la Cruz, here and in No. 27, share a body of conventions and formulas that are typical of San Pedro Tototepec. Note, for instance, the way of beginning the testament with a heading containing the place name, the testator's name and the type of mass, or the mention of the hospital, little seen elsewhere, or the somewhat more elaborate version of *ichantzinco dios*, "the home of God," for the principal residence. Another shared peculiarity is the expression *ce imactzinco* instead of *icenmactzinco* for "entirely in his hands." Most puzzling is a word "metario," which appears in exactly the same place as *memoria*, "memorandum (of testament)," in the corpus generally, and I have translated it as memorandum simply on the strength of its position. Conceivably it evolved from an expression such as *memoria testamentaria*; but whatever its origin was, it is testimony to the sometimes quite distinct evolution of vocabulary and phraseology in each small indigenous unit.

Another interesting phrase in this testament, whether special to Tototepec or not, is rare in the corpus; the expression *notlatocahuan tlaxilacalyacanque*, "my rulers the leaders of the tlaxilacalli," is a remnant of older Nahua public rhetoric.

San Pedro – Bernadino de Stiago Missa de Requien

Ma mosequiscayectenehualo yn itlaçoMahuistocatzin ȳ la SantisiMa trinidad ȳhua dios tetatzin ȳhua dioz dioz tepiltzin ȳhua dioz espiritu Santo Ma ȳ mochihua Ame Jesus Ma^{a} y Juceph — Axca Sabado a 22 de agusto de 1733 Años – Ca nica nicpehualtia ȳ nometario testaMeto ȳ nehual ȳ notoCa Bernadino de Stiago ȳ notlaxilacalpa Santo San pedro tototepec – Ca niquitohua huenl acachtopa Se imactzinco nicotlalia ȳ noyoliatzin ȳhua ȳ naniMatzin Se imactzinCo niContlalia ȳ notlaçoMahuistatzin dioz ȳnhua niquitohua ȳtla itla nopa quiMochihuilitzinos ȳ notlaçotatzin Dioz Ca nechMotlaocolilisque ȳ nopilhua ȳ nomortaJan yes ȳhua ȳnic ninolpitias yn itlaçogordotzin ȳ notlaçotatzin Santo San fra^{co} ȳhua niquitohuan ytla onicnoMaSehuitzinos yn itlaçomiquilitzin ȳ notlaçotatzin Dioz ȳ nosenpultura yes Ca opa teopa ȳthualCo Opan puerta Mayōr Opa toctiyes ȳ notlalnacayo neltis notlanequilis – ȳhua niquitohua MotemaCas Meliotzin Santa JeruSale ȳhua yZpitar MotemanCas Meliotzin = ȳhua niquitohua ca nichuechiuhtias Se tlatlasqui ȳnahuactzinCo las aniMas neltis notlanequilis = ȳhua niquitohuan Ca nechMochihuilis Setel Misa de Requie ȳ notelpoch ȳn itoCa marÇos de Stiago – Camo tle nicnopielia Ca huel ninotolinia ȳn ixpatzinCo ȳ notlaçotatzin dioz Ca ye nechmactilitiCate ȳ notlatoCahua tlaxilacalyacaque neltis notlanequilis = ȳhua niquitohua ȳ caltzintli yn ichatzinCo y notlaçotatzin dioz ytzticac

San Pedro — Bernardino de Santiago Requiem mass

May the precious revered name of the most holy Trinity and God the father, God the son, and God the Holy Spirit be entirely praised. May it be done, amen. Jesus, Mary, and Joseph. — Today Saturday the 22nd of August of the year 1733, here I named Bernardino de Santiago begin my memorandum of testament in my tlaxilacalli holy San Pedro of Tototepec. – I say that first of all I place my spirit and soul entirely in the hands of my precious revered father God, and I say that if my precious father God should bring something down upon me [if I die], my children are to do me the favor of supplying what will be my shroud and that with which I will be girt, the precious rope of my precious father holy San Francisco. And I say that if I attain the precious death of my precious father God, my grave will be in the churchyard, at the main door; there my earthly body will lie buried. My will is to be carried out. – And I say that half a real is to be given for Holy Jerusalem, and half a real is to be given for the hospital. = And I say that I am making an offering of an egg-laying hen to [the cofradía of] Animas. My will is to be carried out. = And I say that my son named Marcos de Santiago is to have a requiem mass performed for me. – For I have nothing; I am very poor before my precious father God; my rulers the tlaxilacalli leaders know it about me. My will is to be carried out. = And I say that I am leaving the

ȳquiSanyapa tonati ȳhua Oc Se caltzintli ytzticac ȳcalaquiapa tonati ȳhua ȳhuiCalo tlaltzintli nicCahuilitias ȳ notelpoch ȳn itoCa marÇus de Stiango yehual chani yes quimotequipanilhuis ȳ notlasotatzin Sato Sa diego ȳhua yehuatzin señora Sata urÇula Amo aqui quixtoquilis ȳ mostla huiptla neltis notlanequilis – yhua niquitohua ȳ nochpoch yn itoCa thomasa fraca nicCahuilitias Caxtoli ÇorCo neltis notlanequilis = yhua niquitohua oc Se tlaltzintli ȳc ȳteCo Al nicCahuilitias ȳ notelpoch yn itoCa marÇus de Satiago neltis notlanequilis = ȳhua niquitohua Oc Se tlaltzintli yc mani yc Otli Sa Loreçotzin nicCahuilitias ȳ nocihuahuantzin napohuali ȳhua matlactli ȳhua chiCome ÇorCo Amo aqui quixtoquili ȳ mostla huiptla neltis notlanequilis = ȳhua niquitohua ȳ nochpoch ȳn itoca melchora fraca nicCahuilitias Sepohuali ȳhua nahui ÇorCo neltis notlanequilis – ȳhua niquitohua ȳ nochpoch yn itoca urçolan fraca nicCahuilitias Sepohuali ȳhua nahui ÇorCo neltis notlanequilis – ȳhua niquitoa ȳ nochpoch yn itoCa thomaSan fraca nicCahuilitias Sepuhuali ȳhua nahui ÇorCo neltis notlanequilis ȳhua niquitohua ȳ nochpoch ȳn itoCa pasquala fraca nicCahuilitias Sepohuali ȳhua nahui ÇorCo neltis notlanequis – ȳhua niquitoa ȳ noxhuito ȳn itoCa Jua Juceph nicCahuilitias ȳntlanMia ȳ miltzintli[2] Mochi Conanas Amo aqui quiquixtilis ȳ mostla huiphtla neltis notlanequilis = ȳhua niquitohua Se miltotli ȳnahuac erMita nicCahuilitias ȳ noermanatzin ȳn itoCa Juçepa LuȳSa neltis notlanequilis = yhua niquitohua ȳ nopriMoerMano ȳn itoCa Jua niColas nechhuiquilia Se peso Motlanilis = ȳhua niquitohua Ca huel nicnotlatlauhtia ȳehuatzin y nohuexiuhtzin fraco de la Cruz ȳehuatzin nopa motlatoltiz noAlbasia yes ȳtla quali quiquimochinhuilis ca dioz quimoxtlahuilis yhua Onotzaloque Omochique testigo = Dnn aloço nicolas Alcade testigo – Dn diego nicolas fiscal mayor testigo – Dn Simo de los anJeles fiscal teniete testigo – Dn Jua de la cruz teniete Alcade testigo

fraco de la Cruz esnos

house which is the home of my precious father God, looking east, and another house looking west, and the land that goes with it, to my son named Marcos de Santiago; he is to be the householder and serve my precious father holy San Diego and señora Santa Ursula. No one is to claim it from him in the future. My will is to be carried out. – And I say that I am leaving to my daughter named Tomasa Francisca 15 furrows [of the same lot?]. My will is to be carried out. = And I say that I am leaving another piece of land at the edge of the water to my son named Marcos de Santiago. My will is to be carried out. = And I say that I am leaving another piece of land on the San Lorenzo road, with 97 furrows, to my wife. No one is to claim it from her in the future. My will is to be carried out. = And I say that I am leaving to my daughter named Melchora Francisca 24 furrows. My will is to be carried out. – And I say that I am leaving to my daughter named Ursula Francisca 24 furrows. My will is to be carried out. – And I say that I am leaving to my daughter named Tomasa Francisca 24 furrows. My will is to be carried out. And I say that I am leaving to my daughter named Pascuala Francisca 24 furrows. My will is to be carried out. – And I say that I am leaving to my little grandchild named Juan Josef the end of the cultivated field;[2] he is to take all of it. No one is to take it from him in the future. My will is to be carried out. = And I say that I am leaving a little cultivated field close to the shrine to my sister named Josefa Luisa. My will is to be carried out. = And I say that my first cousin named Juan Nicolás owes me 1 peso; it is to be requested from him. = And I say that I really implore my fellow father-in-law Francisco de la Cruz to speak for me and be my executor; if he does it well, God will reward him. Those who became witnesses were summoned: don Alonso Nicolás, alcalde, witness; don Diego Nicolás, fiscal mayor, witness; don Simón de los Angeles, fiscal teniente, witness; don Juan de la Cruz, alcalde teniente, witness.

Francisco de la Cruz, notary.

[2]The basic meaning seems to be what is left over after what is given to the daughters. The daughters' portions were apparently all sections carved out of a single large field.

27. Francisco de la Cruz, San Pedro Tototepec, 1735

(AHAM, Box 51:3, Juzgado Eclesiástico de Toluca)[1]

ALTHOUGH definite proof is lacking, the testator Francisco de la Cruz may be the fellow father-in-law whom Bernardino de Santiago (No. 26) names as executor. The two testaments are very similar in terms of formulas and funeral arrangements, so that some common pattern is in operation, though it is hard to know whether to attribute it to traditions shared within a familial group, to customs general within the tlaxilacalli, to the habits of the notary, or, most likely, to a combination of all three. The testator's strategy with bequests is quite surprising. He mentions first his youngest son, Josef de Santiago, who gets the house and the land that goes with it. Then the eldest son receives the same amount of land, followed by two other males, Ignacio Nicolás and Felipe de Santiago, who get less (note the persistence of the second name Santiago in the family, perhaps connected with the Santiagos of Nos. 25 and 26). The testator is therefore reversing the custom of bequeathing the house and lot to the eldest son, exactly as happens with don Felipe de Santiago, No. 25, from the same tlaxilacalli. Once again, the reason may be that the youngest son is the only one still needing a house, while the others have already married and gone away. It does seem at times in the Toluca corpus that the youngest child has a special position, but the materials are insufficient to define it further. Francisco de la Cruz also has two small daughters, to whom he leaves very little land compared to the sons; and the wife, Pascuala María, gets a piece of land on her own (as also happens in No. 26).

Note the reference to a sibling, Miguel de la Cruz, for an issue related to some bordering land. It is also of interest that the traditional term *teiccauh*, meaning a younger same-generation relative of either gender, a sibling or cousin, is used instead of the Spanish *hermano* usually seen in the corpus. Miguel bears the same second name as the testator, which is quite common in high status families. In addition, the fact that the executor and the witnesses, who are all officials, show the title don indicates Francisco's connection with prominent individuals in the tlaxilacalli.

Funeral arrangements are surprisingly similar to those of Bernardino de Santiago (No. 26), with the shroud being provided by the children and the requiem mass by a son, while the testator leaves various offerings to cofradías. The only detail that seems different is the burial in the church. This appears to point to similar funeral practices among people of a similar social status within a tlaxilacalli, though again one must wonder if the notary had some role in the similarity.

Francisco de la Cruz is also the name of the notary in this case, the same one who wrote the immediately preceding will. Several unusual words and phrases are used in both testaments and to a considerable extent in the other testament from Tototepec (No. 25), as is dealt with under No. 26. Another interesting feature in both of Francisco de la Cruz's wills is that in the opening line he uses an "and" between the Trinity and the three manifestations of God; this formulation might just be a result of the broad and loose use of *ihuan*, "and," that we see in some testaments, or it might show a complete lack of comprehension of what the Trinity is, making it a fourth entity. Since the writer repeats it across different wills, it is not, however, a result of simple carelessness and confusion, as we might have expected in the similar formulation in a will of much the same time in a different Toluca tlaxilacalli (No. 19). The notary Francisco de la Cruz is not without his idiosyncrasies and omissions, but on the whole, by Toluca standards, he is a conservative, consistent writer.

S.n pedro – Fra.$^{\underline{co}}$ de la crus – Misa de Requie – Ma mosequiscayectenehualo ӯn itlaçoMahuistocatzin ӯ la satiMa trinidad ӯhua dios tetatzin ӯhua dios ӯn itlaçopiltzin ӯhua dios espiritu sato ma ӯ mochihua Ame Jesus Ma$^{\underline{a}}$ y Juceph — Axca doMigo e 3 de abril de 1735 Años — ca nica nicpehualtia ӯ nometario testanMeto ӯ nehual notoca Fra$^{\underline{co}}$ de la crus y notlaxilacalpa Santo Sa pedro tototepec ca niquitohua huel acachtopa se imactzinco nicotlalia ӯ noyoliatzin ӯhua ӯ naniMatzin ӯhua se imactzinco nicotlalia ӯ notlaçotatzin dios ӯhua niquitohua ӯtla

San Pedro – Francisco de la Cruz – requiem mass – May the precious revered name of the most holy Trinity, and God the father, God his precious son, and God the Holy Spirit be entirely praised. May it be done, amen. Jesus, Mary and Joseph. — Today, Sunday the 3rd of April of the year 1735, here I named Francisco de la Cruz begin my memorandum of testament in my tlaxilacalli holy San Pedro of Tototepec. I say that first of all I place my spirit and soul entirely in the hands of my precious father God; and I say that, if my precious father God brings

[1]The testament is accompanied by a contemporary Spanish translation.

itla nopa quiMochihuilitzinos ȳ notlaçotatzin dios ca nechmotlaocolilisque ȳ nopilhua ȳ nomortaja yes ȳhua ynic ninolpitias ȳn itlaçogordotzin ȳ notlaçomahuistatzin Sato Sa Fra^{co} ȳhua niquitohua ȳtla onicnoMasehuitzinos ȳn ytlaçomiquilitzin ȳ notlaçotatzin dios ñ nosepultura yes ca opa teopa yehual ca opa tocties y notlalnacayo neltis notlanequilis — ȳhua niquitohuan motemacas meliotzin sata Jerusale ȳnhua ȳzpitar motemacas meliotzin ȳhua niquitohua cocoxcatzintzinti macosque meliotzin ȳnic nopapan quimotlatlauhtilisque ȳ notlaçotatzin dios — ȳhua niquitohua y SatiSimo Sacrameto Meliotzin nicnoMaquilitias ȳhua las anima nicnomaquilitias Meliotzin neltis notlanequilis = ȳhua niquitohua ȳ notelpochto yn itoca Juceph de Satiago noxocoyo — ca yehual nechmochihuilis setel misa de requie ȳhua niquitohua Sano yehual xucuyo chani ȳes — ȳ caltzintli yzticac yc xocotitla[2] — ȳhua yhuicalo tlaltzintli Opohuali ȳhuan ome çorco niccahuilitias amo aqui quiquixtilis ȳ mostla huiphtla neltis notlanequilis — ȳhua niquitohua oc Se notelpoch yacapatli ȳn itoca Juceph de satiago[3] nicCahuilias Sano opohuali ȳhuan ome çorco — neltis notlanequilis — ȳhua niquitoa oc Se notelpoch yn itoca ȳnasio nicolas nicCahuilitias — caxtoli ȳhua ȳei çorco Amo aqui quiquixtilis — neltis notlanequilis — ȳhua nitohua oc Se notelpoch yn itoca phelipe de satiago niccahuilitias caxtoli yhua nahui çorco — yhua niquitohua ȳnotzin matlactli çorquito corneja niquicahuilitia ȳn nochpochtohua yn itoca ma^{a} Salome niccahuilitias macuili çorquito — oc Se nochpochto yn itoca ma^{a} madalena Macuili çorquito niccahuilitias neltis notlanequilis = ȳhua niquitohua oc Se tlaltzintli ȳxtlahuateco niccahuilitias ȳ nosihuahuantzin ȳn itoca pasquala ma^{a} amo aqui quiquixtilis — ȳhua niquitohua Ca huel nicnotlatlauhtilia ȳ noAlbasia quimelahuactlalis ȳ quanxoxtli ȳn oquitilana ȳ noteccatzin miquel de la crus neltis notlanequilis — ȳhua niquitohua ȳ notelpoch ȳacapatli ȳc tlatzintla quiquetzan Caltzintli Sa ȳyuca caltzintli neltis notlanequilis — ȳhua niquitohua ca nechhuapanhuilisque ȳtlaçonatzin amo nechmaquilisque netequipacholi ȳ moctla huiphtla neltis notlanequilis Ȳhua ca huel nicnotlatlauhtilia yehuatzin do

something upon me [if I die], my children are to grant me what will be my shroud and that with which I will be girt, the precious rope of my precious revered father holy San Francisco. And I say that when I shall have attained the precious death of my precious father God, my grave will be at the church; there my earthly body is to lie buried. My will is to be carried out. — And I say that half a real is to be given for Holy Jerusalem, and half a real is to be given for the hospital; and I say that the poor sick people are to be given half a real so that they will pray to my precious father God for me. — And I say that I am giving half a real to the Santísimo Sacramento, and I am giving half a real to Las Animas [both cofradías]. My will is to be carried out. = And I say that my little son named Josef de Santiago, my youngest, is to arrange a mass of requiem for me; and I say that likewise the youngest will be the householder in the house looking toward Xocotitlan,[2] and I am leaving to him the land that goes with it, 42 furrows; no one is to take it from him in the future. My will is to be carried out. — And I say that I am leaving to another son of mine, the eldest, named Josef de Santiago,[3] 42 furrows; my will is to be carried out. — And I say that I am leaving to another son of mine named Ignacio Nicolás 18 furrows; no one is to take it from him; my will is to be carried out. — And I say that I am leaving to another son of mine named Felipe de Santiago 19 furrows. — And I say that I am leaving to my small daughters those 10 small furrows at the corner; to the one named María Salomé I am leaving 5 small furrows, and to another small daughter of mine named María Magdalena I am leaving 5 small furrows. My will is to be carried out. = And I say that I am leaving to my wife named Pascuala María another piece of land at the edge of the plain; no one is to take it from her. — And I say that I greatly implore my executor to set the border straight that my younger sibling Miguel de la Cruz marked; my will is to be carried out. — And I say that my son, the eldest, is building a house below; the house is by itself. My will is to be carried out. — And I say that [the executor?] and his precious mother will raise him for me; they are not to give me any concern in

[2]The Spanish translation specifies the location as to the north.

[3]That both the youngest and the eldest seem to bear the same name would appear to be a mistake of the writer. Though it was not unheard of to name a child after another full sibling who had already died, in the eighteenth century one can hardly imagine two living sons with exactly the same name. However, given the distinction of youngest and eldest and separate bequests, we cannot doubt that two sons were involved.

diego nicolas ȳehuatzi nopa motlatoltis noAlbasia ȳes ȳtla quali quimochihuilis ca dios quimoxtlahuilis — ȳhua onotzaloque omochique testigo — Dn salbador de lo satos # fiscal maȳor testigo Dn manuhuel de la crus # Alcade testigo — Dn abrosio nicolas # teniete fiscal testigo — Dn domigo Ra[?]Mos # teniete Alcade testigo —

Fraco de la cruz Esno[4]

the future; my will is to be carried out. And I greatly implore don Diego Nicolás to speak on my behalf and be my executor; if he does it well, God will reward him. — Those who became witnesses were called: don Salvador de los Santos, fiscal mayor, witness; don Manuel de la Cruz, alcalde, witness; don Ambrosio Nicolás, fiscal teniente, witness; don Domingo Ramos, alcalde teniente, witness.
Francisco de la Cruz, notary.[4]

[4]At the back of the testament it is said in Spanish that a high mass was performed, and the executor gave 3 pesos. Also, on the other side, it is reported that a mass was sung in 1748 for "Josef de Santiago Xocoyotl," who died when he was 10 years old; a nephew paid 3 pesos for the mass, and "el pueblo le apropio el pedazo de tierra," of 44 furrows, clearly the same piece that is given as 42 furrows in the present will.

28. Pascual Francisco, San Juan Bautista, 1710

(AHAM, Box 25:29, Juzgado Eclesiástico de Toluca)[1]

HERE THE TESTATOR Pascual Francisco follows the quite common pattern of leaving his main possessions, a house and a piece of land, to his wife Francisca Teresa so that she will have resources to raise three small children. More unusually, she also gets a yoke of oxen, an asset that is generally passed on to males, since it is strictly related to agricultural tasks. But another piece of land, where one would think the oxen might have been useful, goes to Pascual Francisco's mother, and she in turn is instructed to leave it to his brother when she dies. So we are dealing with a standard property description but apparently relatively little land, since both pieces are called small. It is interesting to note that the testator dedicates part of it to his original family, which is not very common, and that though a brother will be the ultimate heir, for now he gives preference to his mother. Indeed, for the present everything goes to females. In the end, one of the children, Pedro, will remain in the house, as his will, issued 27 years later (No. 29), testifies.

If the property seems somewhat meager, the various offerings and the funeral arrangements hint at a relatively high status. In addition to the shroud and a specific place of burial in the church, Pascual has some magueyes and some money for saints, cofradías, bells to be rung, and a high mass. However, when it comes to executor and witnesses, the testator does not show any particular connection with officials and high ranking members of the community; only one witness bears the title don.

The testament is generally well written, and the notary Salvador de Santiago (discussed on pp. 41–42), probably due to the early date of the will, preserves many conservative traits, both in his orthography and in his phraseology; for example, he retains the old expression *in tlalli in çoquitl*, "the earth and clay," in speaking of the corpse.

[*f. 1*]
S. Juā Bapta Pasqual frco
// Ma moçequizCayectenehua yn itlaçomahuistocatzin yn dios tetatzin yn dios tepiltzin yoā yn dios Espo S.to ma y mochihua Amē Jesos —
// AxCan domingo A 21 de diçienbre yoā xiuhtlapohualli D. 1710 Nicpehualtia notestamento nehuatl notoca Pasqual frco notlaxilacalpa S. Juā Bapta Ca niquitohua yntla Onechmopopolhui y notlaçotatzin Dios yoā niquitohua Ca oncatqui ynic moquimilos yn tlali çuquitl yoā yc ninolpitias yn icordōtzin y

[*f. 1*]
San Juan Bautista. Pascual Francisco.
// May the precious revered name of God the father, God the son, and God the Holy Spirit be entirely praised. May it be done, amen. Jesus. —
// Today, Sunday the 21st of December of the year count of 1710, I named Pascual Francisco begin my testament in my tlaxilacalli of San Juan Bautista. I say that when my precious father God has effaced me, I say that I have the means with which my earthly body will be shrouded, and I will be girt with

[1]The testament is accompanied by a contemporary Spanish translation.

notlaçotatzin San fr$^{\underline{co}}$ yoā niquitohua Ca onpa nitoctos huey teopa ycuitlapa [. . .]tzin[2] yhua Ca nopāpa tzilinis miccatepostli yexcāpa huel achtopa notlaxilacalpa San Juā Bap.^{ta} yoā San Sebastia yhuā S$^{\underline{ta}}$ ma^{a} de los angeles huitzila yoā motemacas memeliotzitzi yoā motemaca meliotzin Jerosale yoā niquitohua motemacas çe tomintzin noconfr$^{\underline{a}}$ Espital yni neltis notlanequilis – yoā niquitohua yn ipalehuiloca yes y nohuanimantzin Ca Oncatqui Çe misSa Cantada de Requi yoā niquitohua yn caltzintli çe ytztica ycalaquiyanpa yn tonatiuh Oratorio Oc çe ytztica yquiSayanpa yn tonatiuh Coçina mochica tlalli çe pedaçito niccahuilia noçihuahuatzin ytoca fr$^{\underline{ca}}$ teresa Onca quinhuapahuas yeytin nopilhuantoto çe ytoca pedro - Oc çe ytoca Orçola – Oc çe ytoca Joliana yni neltiz notlanequilis yhua niquitohua Ca niccahuilia çe yota huaCaxti Sano yehuatzin noçihuahuatzin yhua niquitohua Ca nicnocahuililia Santissimo çe metl Oc çe metl San Diego – Oc çe metl yehuatzin trançitatzin yhua niquitohua Ca nixelhuia nonantzin tepitzin tlalli quimopielis yntla mostla huiptla quimonochilis yn dios ca quimocahuililis nohuermanotzin ytoca Joçep manohuel Ca San ixquich y niquitohua neltis notlanequilis yhua niquitohua yntla Onechmopopolhui y notatzi y notatzin Dios - Ca huel çenca nicnotlatlauhtilia y nohualbaçea metztiyetz ca yehuatzin diego ernades yhuā yn imixpa^{co} omochiuh y notestamento testigos don miguel yhuā testigo P$^{\underline{o}}$ loca yntla quali quimochihuilis ca dios quimotlaxtlahuilis fiscal de Sāta ygleçia gr$^{\underline{o}}$ de S.tiago –

Es^{no} S.l$^{\underline{or}}$ de S.go

the rope of my precious father San Francisco. And I say that I am to lie buried at the great church, behind [Jesús Nazareno].[2] And the bells are to be rung for me in three places, first of all in my tlaxilacalli of San Juan Bautista, in San Sebastián, and in Santa María de los Angeles Huitzillan, and half a real is to be given for each of them. And half a real is to be given for Jerusalem. And I say that a real is to be given for my cofradía [at?] the hospital. This my will is to be carried out. – And I say that the help of my soul will be that there is a high requiem mass. And I say that I leave the house, [consisting of] one [building] facing west, an oratory, and another facing east, a kitchen, together with a little piece of land, to my wife named Francisca Teresa. There she is to raise my three small children, one named Pedro, another named Ursula, another named Juliana. This my will is to be carried out. And I say that I leave a yoke of oxen likewise to my wife. And I say that I leave a maguey to the Santísimo Sacramento, another maguey to San Diego, and another maguey to [Nuestra Señora del] Tránsito. And I say that I distribute to my mother a little bit of land; she is to keep it. If God summons her in the future, she is to leave it to my brother named Josef Manuel. That is all that I say. My will is to be carried out. And I say that when my father God has effaced me, I very greatly implore the one who is to be my executor, Diego Hernández, [to accept the task]. My testament was done before witnesses: don Miguel and the witness Pedro Lucas. If [Diego Hernández] does [his task] well, God will reward him. Fiscal of the holy church, Gregorio de Santiago.

Notary Salvador de Santiago.

[2]The original is torn at this point, and at the corresponding place the Spanish translation has "detras de la capilla de Jesus Nazareno."

29. Pedro Pablo, San Juan Bautista, 1737

(AHAM, Box 54:30, Juzgado Eclesiástico de Toluca)[1]

PEDRO PABLO, a widower, is a quite rare case of a male testator dividing his possessions equally between children of both genders. Miguel Gerónimo, his son, and Eugenia Gertrudis, his daughter, are to share the house that Pedro Pablo inherited, the piece of land that goes with it, and also some more land and magueyes. The children must be small, since he entrusts them to his sister Ursula María, together with the worship of four images of saints that are to remain inside the house. Other saints are assigned a maguey for their cult, among them the tlaxilacalli saint; also two female godchildren are given a plant each. These details hint at a probable role of the testator in the cultivation of magueyes. Thus, apart from the house, Pedro Pablo owns both magueyes and pieces of land, whereas, as we have already seen, female testators involved in the cultivation of the plant usually had no landed property.

[1]The testament is accompanied by a contemporary Spanish translation.

The testator's sister Ursula plays an essential role, since she is to raise his children and in all probability administer their property until they reach the age to do so for themselves. Later, in the litigation in which this will was found, she was to claim to be Pedro's executor, but in this document Pedro names his brother Santos de la Cruz as one of his executors. Therefore Pedro's original family seems to have great importance here. He also leaves something to two godchildren of his; indeed, this is a case of extended connections, beyond the nuclear family proper.

The testator's original family is partially documented elsewhere in the corpus. Pascual Francisco of the same tlaxilacalli, who made his will in 1710 (No. 28), was Pedro Pablo's father, for there he names three small children, including a Pedro and an Ursula who is the Ursula María already mentioned. It is interesting that Pedro is still living in the house his father left so many years previously; we find in the 1710 will, however, that the father did not leave the house and land directly to Pedro, but to Pedro's mother. At least so the language reads. The case is instructive, for it shows that it was probably understood among those involved that Pedro would eventually get the house from his mother, and this even though he had two sisters. The father's will also puts Pedro's brother Santos de la Cruz in a different light, for the latter was not included among Pascual's three children; perhaps he is a half brother by a subsequent marriage of their common mother. Another connection between the two generations has to do with saints; the father was buried close to an image in the church of Jesús Nazareno; the son is buried elsewhere in the church, but in his house is still an image of Jesús Nazareno illustrating a continuing family devotion and helping explain the father's choice of a burial site.

The funeral arrangements are in line with the perception of the testator as a quite wealthy individual. He requests the shroud of the Virgin of Carmen, a specific burial place, a high mass, and bells to be rung. However, among the executors and the witnesses there is only one high-status official with the title don, the fiscal, and he may be present more in an official capacity than as a personal associate.

The notary Andrés Francisco (discussed on p. 42) is quite prone to leaving out syllables or elements of a sentence. However, the spelling is rather conservative, especially for the time and place. In the expressions *niviudo*, "I am a widower," and *ihabitotzin*, "his habit," strikingly Spanish constructions and words are combined with very traditional aspects of Nahuatl grammar. Note also *-tlaquatequil*, literally "one's person who is baptized," for one's godchild, an old term not often seen in this corpus.

San Juan Bap^{ta} pedro y pablo[2]
Ma mocenquiscayectenehua yn intlaçomahuistoc[. . .] yn Santissima trinidad yn dios tetatzin yhua dı[. . .] ytlaçopiltzin yhua dios espirito Santo ma yn mochihua Amen Jesus m^{a} Joseph —
Axcan sabado diez yn seis de março de 1737 a[. . .] y nictla notestamento nehuatl notoca pedro y pab[. . .] niviyodo notlaxilaCalpan san Juan Bap^{ta} ca niquitoa ytla nechmotlaçotilis yn ~~cmh~~[3] tto dios Ca huel yncenmactzinco nicontlalia y noyoliantzin y nanimantzin yhua niquitoa ynic nopanpa tzinlinis miccatepustli yexcanpa S^{n} Juan Bap^{ta} sant[. . .] maria de los angeles San sebastian motemaca[. . .] huentzintli memeliotzitzin yhua motemacas mel[. . .] Santa Jerosalen yhua niquitoa vncatqui noquim[. . .]uhca yn yaBitotzin la virJen del carme yhua niqui[. . .]a y

San Juan Bautista. Pedro y Pablo.[2]
May the precious revered name of the most holy Trinity, God the father, God his precious son, and God the Holy Spirit be entirely praised. May it be done, amen. Jesus, Mary, and Joseph. —
Today Saturday the 16th of March of the year 1737, I named Pedro [y] Pablo, widower, issue my testament in my tlaxilacalli of San Juan Bautista. I say that if our universal[3] lord God shows me his love [brings about my death], I place my spirit and soul very entirely in his hands. And I say that the bells are to be rung for me in three places, San Juan Bautista, Santa María de los Angeles, and San Sebastián; an offering of half a real each is to be given. And half a real is to be given for Holy Jerusalem. And I say that I have a shroud, the habit of the

---

[2]The notary twice gives the form "Pedro y Pablo," with a *y* that was doubtless not part of the name as ordinarily used, but comes from association with the paired saints often referred to as "San Pedro y San Pablo," who must have provided the basis for the name. The Spanish translator gives the name the same way as I understand it, Pedro Pablo.

[3]The abbreviation stands for *cemanahuac*, "universal or concerning the entire world."

nosepultura yez yxpantzin tersera orden ep[. . .][4] oc se puerta vncatqui ce misa cantada de Reque y palehuilos y naniniamantzin yhua niquitoa ynin Caltzintli onechmocahuililitia notlaçotatzin pa[. . .]cual fran^co^ axca niccahuilia omenti nopilhua ynto miguel Geronimo yhua ogenā Getrudes y[. . .] caltzintli ce ytztica ycalaquianpa tonatiuh orato[. . .]o oc ytztica ynquisayapa tonatiuh cosina niquincahuilia nopilhua mochica tlali maCuilquahui[. . .] amo aquichalanis yn mostla yn puihtla y onCan y tiztihui hua metototi niquincahuilia huel nepatla mox[. . .] ynhua tlali yxtlahua vnpuhualmani Cocahuisque nepan-[. . .] moxelos nicnocahuilia noermanatzin vrsula m[. . .] yehuatzin quimocuitlahuitzinos yhua yehuatzin Jesus nasa[. . .]no yhuatzin la virgen de guadalupe yhua yehuatzin Sann antonio yhua oc setzin la Virgen de guadalupe linso mochintitzintzin mocatzinonoa Calitic yhua niquitoa [*verso*] yehuatzin San Juan Bapta nicnocahuililia çe metl oc se metl nicnomaquilia San diego yh[. . .] la Vir de loreto ce metl ynhua niquia notlaqua[. . .]quil[5] ytoca osebia trinidad niccahuilia ce metl oc se intoca ystebania nicahuilia no ce metl ynhua niquitoa huel çenca nicnotlaltla[. . .]tilia yehua noermanotzin santos de la cruz yhua y[. . .]huatzin santiago de los santos ca yehuatzitzin nopan motlatoltisque ca yntla quali quimochihuilisque ca dios quimotlaxtlahuilitzinos Auh ynic onictlali notestamento testigo Gregorio Antt^o^ yhua fiscal de santa ynGlesia D^n^ luis Bap^ta^
Es^no^ Andres fran^co^

Virgen del Carmen, and I say that my grave is to be in front of the Tercera Orden[4] [next to another door?]. There is a high requiem mass by which my soul is to be helped. And I say that as to this house that my precious father Pascual Francisco left me, now I leave it to my two children named Miguel Gerónimo and Eugenia Gertrudis; of the houses, one faces west, an oratory, and another faces east, a kitchen. I leave them to my children together with land of 5 quahuitl. No one is to dispute it in the future. And I leave the small magueyes to them, to be divided absolutely equally between them, and land on the plain, of 40 [quahuitl], that the two of them are to share and divide in half. I leave my sister Ursula María to take care of them, along with Jesús Nazareno, a Virgen de Guadalupe, a San Antonio, and another Virgen de Guadalupe on canvas; all of them stay inside the house. And I say [*verso*] that I leave to San Juan Bautista a maguey; I give another maguey to San Diego, and a maguey to the Virgen de Loreto. And I say that I leave a maguey to my godchild[5] named Eusebia de la Trinidad, and I also leave a maguey to another named Estebanía. And I say that I greatly implore my brother Santos de la Cruz and Santiago de los Santos to speak for me; if they do it well God will reward them. And witnesses to how I issued my testament were Gregorio Antonio and the fiscal of the holy church, don Luis Bautista.
Notary Andrés Francisco.

[4]Possibly the missing word is some form of *españoles*; there could have been two divisions of the Tercera Orden, one for Spaniards and one for indigenous people.

[5]The missing letters are *te* to make "notlaquatequil."

30. Pascuala Melchora, San Juan Bautista, 1717

(AGN, Hospital de Jesús 326, exp. 2)[1]

THE TESTAMENT of Pascuala Melchora, in all probability a widow, contains many details of great interest in terms of women's activities and relationships within the family. She leaves the home complex to apparently the elder of two daughters, Micaela Sebastiana, while Micaela and the younger Catalina Martina are to share the piece of land on which the house is built. She also has a son, Sebastián de Santiago (testament No. 31 here), who is left out, probably because he is already well established or has received his share. Originally, the testator intended to leave the house to Juana María, but she is now disowned after a quarrel; the relationship is not given, but most likely she was the eldest daughter. Here we have a rare and touching description of the relationship between mother and daughter and some problems in it, which is reinforced by a memorandum added at the end of the testament. There Pas-

[1]The testament is accompanied by an undated contemporary Spanish translation, which contains quite a few analytical and explanatory remarks of great interest, in some cases giving the impression that the translator personally knew or interviewed the testator and some of the principals. Yet the remarks are very likely mere extrapolations and could be unreliable, so I do not report them in detail.

cuala Melchora apparently wants to show that she did all that could possibly be expected for Juana María, paying her health expenses, burying her husband and little daughter, spending money on helping her with land, giving her large numbers of magueyes. It seems that in this case a strong mutual help network of females within the same nuclear family has finally broken down.

The memorandum indicates a great deal of family solidarity but above all it shows large resources on the part of Pascuala Melchora; she seems to have spent 49 pesos and 7 reales on her daughter, a very significant sum for an indigenous person even if it was spread out over some years, and the magueyes would have been worth a lot too. The plants are described with a specific vocabulary confirming a deep knowledge of their management. Thus the testator seems to be a substantial maguey entrepreneur; like many individuals who are involved in maguey cultivation and pulque production, she lacks extensive holdings of land, or any other property apart from the house and its lot. A further detail confirming Pascuala Melchora's involvement with magueyes is the business controversy she has with Pascuala Ursula over 5 pesos that were used to buy some plants; in this case the testator seems to be seeking to repudiate a purchase which now can be of no advantage to her.

Funeral arrangements are another sign of the testator's wealth; she mentions a shroud of the Virgin of Carmen, a specific burial place, a high mass, bells to be rung and offerings to several saints, including the tlaxilacalli saint, in which magueyes play an important role once again. The mass is to be paid for by three children, indicating that providing a mass was often considered the duty of children and heirs even when the testator had the necessary means. In addition, the status of the executor, an alcalde and a don, attests to Pascuala Melchora's connections with the high levels of her local society, even if some of the other witnesses are less impressive.

We have already seen various testaments (Nos. 2, 5 and 13) produced at a considerably later date by the notary Bernardo de Santiago, who is broadly discussed in the introductory study (pp. 39–40). It seems that he served not only the barrios of Toluca proper but also some tlaxilacalli in the surroundings of the city (admitting that the distinction between the two types of entity remains somewhat unclear).

[*f. 1*]

Ma mocenquizcaYectenehua yn itlaçomahuiztocatzin yn Dios tetahtzin yhuã Dios ytlaçoPiltzin yhuã Dios Espiritu S^{to} Ma in mochihua Amen Jesus Ma^{a} y Joseph —

Axcan lunes ye ic Chicnahui tonatiuh mani Metztli de Agosto yuã xiuhtlapohuali de 1717 a^{os} Nicpehualtia yn Notestamento yn Nehuatl - notoca Pasquala Melchora niCan notlahxilacalpa S. Ju^{o} Baup^{ta} Ca niquitohua yntla moztla huiptla ninomiquiliz Ca huel acachtopa yn noyolia Nanimantzin Ca huel yCenmac^{co} niContlalia yn notlaçomahuistahtzin Dios = yhua niquitohua ynic quimiliuhtiaz yn notlalnacayo Ca oncatqui Abito del Carme Zayal yuã yc ninolpintiaz yn iCordontzin notlaçotahtzin Sn fran^{co} – yuãn yn noSepultu yez Ca onpa huey teopa yxpan^{co} Sta Vera Cruz onca nechmomachiotiliz yn notlaçotahtzin Dios = yuã niquitohua Motemacaz Meliotzin huentzintli Sta Jerusalen yuã niquitohua yehuatzin S. Ju^{o} Bap^{ta} nicnomaquilia ce metontli – yuã yehuatzin S. Diego ce metontli – yhuã notlaçonantzin trancito ce metontli yuã yehuatzin S. Antt^{o} nicnomaquilia Ce metontli – yuã niquitohua No-

[*f. 1*]

May the precious revered name of God the father, God his precious son, and God the Holy Spirit be entirely praised. May it be done, amen. Jesus, Mary, and Joseph. —

Today, Monday the 9th day of the month of August and the year count of 1717, I named Pascuala Melchora begin my testament here in my tlaxilacalli of San Juan Bautista. I say that if I die in the future, first of all I place my spirit and soul very entirely in the hands of my precious revered father God. = And I say that to shroud my earthly body there is the habit of Carmen of serge, and I will be girt with the rope of my precious father San Francisco. - And my grave is to be at the great church, facing the Santa Vera Cruz; there my precious father God will designate [a place] for me. = And I say that half a real is to be given as an offering for Holy Jerusalem. And I say that to San Juan Bautista I give a small maguey, and to San Diego a small maguey, and to my precious mother of Tránsito a small maguey, and to San Antonio I give a small maguey. – And

panpa chocaz tepostli Nican notlahxilacalpa S. Ju^{o} Baup^{ta} yuā Sta Ma^{a} de los Angeles huitzila yuā S. Sebastian motemacaz huentzintli Meliotzitzin Neltiz notlanequiliz = yuā niquitohua yn ipalehuiloca yez Nanimantzin Ca nechmotlaocolilia nopilhuan yeintin Ce ytoca Sebastian de Stiago yuā Micaela Sebastiana yuā Catalina Martina nechmotlaocolilia Ce Missa cantada de Requie = yuā niquitohuan Ca onicMacac Macuili pesos Pasq^{la} Vrsula Oniccohuili macuili metl Capones[2] Axca Ca quitemacaz Ca çan Onicpielti = yuān niquitohua Ca oncatqui Ce huehue calli yChan^{co} Dios - ytztica yc ycalaquianpa tonatiuh – yuā oc ce Cosina Ytztica yc yquizayanpa tonatiuh yhuicalo tlaltzintli quipie yc y huiac Cenpohualquahuitli yc patlahua Macuilquahuitli – Niccahuilia nochpoch Micaela Sebastiana auh yn tlaltzintli quimonepantlaxelhuizque Catha^{na} Martina Concahuizque yuā Niquitohua Juana Ma^{a} Ca nicCahuiliaya yn Caltzintli Auh yn axca Ca ahmo nicCahuilia ypanpa Onechtlaxilico Nahui tomin yuā Onechylhui Axca ximiqui Nozo ahmo ximiqui Ximotoca nozo ahmo Ximotoca Ca ahmo niMitzyximati ynMixpa nopilhua Oquito = yuā niquitohua Ca huel cenca nicnotlatlauhtilia noAluacea Metztiez Ca yehuatzin D^{n} Diego de la O Alc^{de} Ordinario – yuān onotzaloque testigos ynmixpa onicchiuh notestam^{to} testigo Baltazar de los S^{tos} Saluador de la Cruz testigo yhuan Yehuatzin fiscal D^{n} Lucas Ximenes

I say that the bells are to sound for me here in my tlaxilacalli of San Juan Bautista, and at Santa María de los Angeles Huitzillan, and at San Sebastián; an offering of half a real each will be given; my will is to be carried out. = And I say that the help of my soul will be that my three children, one named Sebastián de Santiago, [and the others] Micaela Sebastiana and Catalina Martina, are providing me a high mass of requiem. = And I say that I gave 5 pesos to Pascuala Ursula; I bought five *magueyes capones* from her.[2] Now she is to give it up; I only gave it to her to keep [or lent it to her]. = And I say that there is an old [or patrimonial, inherited] house, the home of God, looking west, and in addition a kitchen looking east. A piece of land going along with it measures 20 quahuitl long and 5 quahuitl wide. – I leave it to my daughter Micaela Sebastiana, and she and Catarina Martina are to divide the land in half and share it. And I say that I was going to leave the house to Juana María, but now I am not leaving it to her, because she came and knocked four reales out of my hands and told me, "Now die or don't die, get buried or don't get buried, I don't know you [am not related to you]." She said it in front of my children. = And I say that I very greatly implore the person who is to be my executor, don Diego de la O, alcalde ordinario, [to do his task]. – And the witnesses who were summoned, before whom I made my testament, are Baltasar de los Santos, witness; Salvador de la Cruz, witness; and the fiscal don Lucas Jiménez.

Nehuatl - Nixpan Es^{no} Bernardo de S^{n}tiago es^{no} de la Sta Yglesia [*f.* 2]

Before me, the notary Bernardo de Santiago, notary of the holy church. [*f.* 2]

Memorial ytechcopa Pasq^{la} Melchora de 1717 a^{os}

Memorandum concerning Pascuala Melchora, year of 1717

yhuan niquitohua ca ye onicmacac Nochpoch Ju^{a} Ma^{a} huel Achtopa Onicpahti yCa huel mic tomin Cenpohuali yuā macuili pesos. Onicpohpolo omococo ychan ju^{o} nicolas — 25 p^{s}

I say that as to what I gave my daughter Juana María, first of all I had her treated with a very great deal of money, 25 pesos that I spent on various occasions. She was sick at the house of Juan Nicolás. — 25 pesos.

yuā oc ceuhpa nochan Omococo yuā ynamic omococo yuān omomiquili Onictocac Onicquimilo yuā Onicchihuili Missa — 7 p^{s} 4

And another time she was sick at my home, and her husband was sick and died. I buried him and supplied the shroud and had a mass performed for him. — 7 pesos, 4 reales.

yuān Oc ceuhpa Omomiquili ychpochto Onictocac

And another time her little daughter died; I buried her

[2]In the testament, some magueyes are defined as "capones," which would refer to being cut in some way, possibly for the draining of the juice, some others as "maiden," *ichpochtli* in Nahuatl, explained in the Spanish translation of the testament as just reaching maturity; finally the 25 magueyes are said to have stalks, *quiquiyo* in Nahuatl, or *quiyotes* in Spanish. In the testament of Elena de la Cruz (No. 10), the Spanish translation has *magueyes capones*, while the Nahuatl has the form "tlatetzauhctli," for a maguey whose aperture has been blocked.

Onicquimilo — 2 ps 3
yuā Onicnemili ytlal onpa S$^{\underline{ta}}$ Cruz Onicpopolo Mahtlactli pesos — 10 ps
yhua Onicmacac Juana M$^{\underline{a}}$ Cenpohuali yuā Macuili Metl . quiquio Oquich —
yhuā Oc cempohuali yuā mahtlactli meme ychpopochti mochi ocona —
Nixpa Nehuatl - D$^{\underline{n}}$ Diego de la O Alc$^{\underline{de}}$ ordinario OnicCac ynin tlahtoli —
Es$^{\underline{no}}$ Ber$^{\underline{o}}$ de S^{tiago}

and supplied the shroud. — 2 pesos, 3 reales.
And I [looked into?] her land at Santa Cruz; I spent 10 pesos. — 10 pesos.
And I gave Juana María 25 magueyes with stalks; she harvested them. —
And as for 30 "maiden" magueyes, she took them all. —
Before me, don Diego de la O, alcalde ordinario; I heard this statement. —
Notary Bernardo de Santiago.

31. Sebastián de Santiago, San Juan Bautista, 1731

(AHAM, Box 45:46, Juzgado Eclesiástico de Toluca)

THE TESTATOR, probably a widower, leaves all his limited property, a house and a small piece of land, to be divided between his daughter Ana de los Santos and a grandchild, Juan del Carmen. The latter seems to be in a privileged position in inheriting part of the property at present, even if he is of the second generation, rather than waiting to receive it from his mother; the reason is probably that he is the only living male heir in the testator's line.

It seems likely that the testator here is the same Sebastián de Santiago briefly mentioned in the 1717 will of Pascuala Melchora (No. 30) of the same tlaxilacalli. Although the documents were found in different repositories and irrefutable evidence is lacking, nevertheless the burial arrangements of the two are highly suggestive. Pascuala Melchora requests burial before the Santa Vera Cruz; Sebastián de Santiago wishes to be buried before the Santo Cristo de la Vera Cruz. The second formulation not only explains the first, making it clear that we are dealing with an image of Christ on the true cross; the agreement between the two makes it look very much like a case of a son requesting burial close to his mother in a place of common devotion.

With the house and a bit of land as the only possessions mentioned in the testament, Sebastián de Santiago does not appear wealthy even by indigenous standards. However, his funeral arrangements seem to indicate a quite high status; in fact, there are bells to be rung, a high mass, and the shroud of the Virgin of Carmen, in addition to the specific burial place inside the church. The shroud and the name of the grandchild mentioned above hint at a special devotion to the Virgin of Carmen in the testator's family. But when it comes to executors and witnesses, Sebastián's profile once again appears to be quite low, since neither of his executors bears the don, and there is only one don among the witnesses.

The notary Salvador de Santiago produced No. 28 also, and here despite the passage of quite a few years we can find the same conservative characteristics and very similar expressions, including the phrase *in tlalli in çoquitl*, "the earth and clay," although written here with the possessive *no-*, "my," and an additional ending, which was actually the more frequent form when this idiom was in vogue.

Ma mosenquisCayectenehua ytlasomahuistoCatzin dios tetatzin yua dios tepiltzin yua dios espirito Santo ma y mochihua Ame Jesos maria y Joshep —

May the precious revered name of God the father, God the son, and God the Holy Spirit be entirely praised. May it be done, amen. Jesus, Mary, and Joseph. —

AxCa mierColes a 31 de otobre yua xiuhtlapohuali de 1731 - nicchihua notestameto nehuatl notoCa SeBastia de S.tiago notlaxilaCalpa S$^{\underline{n}}$ Jua Bauhtista Ca niquitoa ytla nechmonochilis y notlaSotatzin dios Ca huel achtopa ysemactzinCo noConnoCotlalia y noyoliatzin nanimatzin yua niquitoa nopanpa tzinlinis miCatepostli notlaxilaCalpa San Jua

Today Wednesday the 31st of October of the year count of 1731, I named Sebastián de Santiago make my testament in my tlaxilacalli of San Juan Bautista. I say that if my precious father God calls me, first of all I place my spirit and soul entirely in his hands. And I say that the bells are to ring for me in my tlaxilacalli of San Juan Bautista, San Sebastián,

Bauhtista yua Sa SeBastia yua S$^{\underline{n}}$ta Ma$^{\underline{a}}$ de loS ang$^{\underline{s}}$ motemaCas memeliotzintzin yni neltis notlanequilis yua niquitoa ytla nechmonochilis y notatzin dios Ca oCatqui y tlen ic moquimilos y notlalo nosoquiyo ytlaquetzin notlasomahuisnatzin la Birgen del Carme nechmomaquilia noxhuiuh ytoCa Jua del Carme yua nochpontzin ytoCa Ana de lo Santos yua niquitoa ypalehuiloCa y noyoliatzin nanimatzin oCatqui Se misa Catada de Requie Sano yehuatitzintzin nechmomaquilia yua niquitoa ytla nechmonochilis y notatzin dios Capa nechmomachiotilis huey teopa yxpatzinCo notemaquixtiCatzin Santo xpo la Bera Crus yua niquitoa Caltzintli niquiCahuilia Jua del Carme yua Ana de lo Santos quimoxelhuisque mochi Yca tlaltzintli matlaquautl ypan tequipanosque Ca san ixquich Camo tle nicnopielia yCa senCa nicnotlatlauhtilia noalBaSea moetzties yehuatzin Antonio de tapia ytla quali quimochihuilis Ca dios quimotlaxtlahuilis yua ymixpan omochiuh noamatlaCuilol testigo D$^{\underline{n}}$ Jusep de la Cruz yua yehuatzin loys Bauhtista alBaSea moCauhtzinnoa yua testigo fisCal de Santa ygleÇa Jua de lo Reyes —

ES$^{\underline{no}}$ Saluador de Santiago[1]

and Santa María de los Angeles. Half a real is to be given for each. This my will is to be carried out. And I say that if my father God calls me, I have the means to shroud my earthly body, the habit of my precious revered mother the Virgen del Carmen. My grandchild named Juan del Carmen and my daughter named Ana de los Santos are giving it to me. And I say that the help of my spirit and soul is a high requiem mass, which they are likewise giving me. And I say that if my father God calls me, he will designate for me where [I will be buried] at the great church, facing my savior Santo Cristo de la Vera Cruz. And I say that I leave a house to Juan del Carmen and Ana de los Santos; they are to divide it between them, together with the land of 10 quahuitl, on which they are to work. That is all. I have nothing [else]. Therefore I greatly implore the person who is to be my executor, Antonio de Tapia, [to do his task]; if he does it well, God will reward him. My document was done before the witness don Josef de la Cruz, Luis Bautista, who is also being left as an executor, and the witness Juan de los Reyes, fiscal of the holy church. —

Notary Salvador de Santiago.[1]

[1]Outside a note in Spanish reports that the high mass was performed in November of the same year and paid for by the executor Tapia in December.

32. Joaquín Josef, San Juan Bautista, 1736

(AHAM, Box 52:19, Juzgado Eclesiástico de Toluca)

JOAQUÍN JOSEF, a married man, typically leaves his property to his son, Antonio, who is presumably quite young, since the testator's wife, Lorenza Francisca, is asked to raise him. Antonio gets a house complex consisting of the standard two buildings and containing an image of the Virgin of Guadalupe. The testator mentions no other assets. From that and from his plain name, it would seem that Joaquín comes from a low-status family, or at least that he has become indigent because of some adverse event, for he speaks of no landed property at all, not even the lot the house stands on.

The lack of assets seems strange given that the funeral arrangements correspond to those requested by high-status individuals. In fact, Joaquín Josef requests a high mass, a specific shroud, and burial in the chapel of Jesús Nazareno, in addition to providing offerings for bells to be rung and for the fund of Holy Jerusalem (not to speak of additional masses performed for the testator later and possibly paid for by relatives). Moreover, of the four witnesses, three are dons, showing some link with prominent individuals. One of them, the fiscal of the church don Antonio de Tapia, is very likely the same person who five years before served as the executor of Sebastián de Santiago (No. 31), but who at that time had not held high office yet and had not earned the don.

The notary Andrés Francisco is the same as in No. 29 and preserves here the same kind of formulas at the beginning, the abbreviation for *cemanahuac*, "universal," and some inaccuracies with syllables and wording. Also the type of Spanish influence is similar, for example with *nicasado ica*, "I am married to," reminiscent of *niviudo*, "I am a widower," and an even more striking combination of Spanish idiom and traditional Nahuatl syntax.

junsep joanquin
Joseph[1] —
Ma mosenquisyectenehua yn itlaçomahuistocatzin santissima trinidad yn dios tetatzin yhua dios yntlaç[. . .] yhua dios espiritu santo Ma y mochihua Ame[. . .] Jesus maria y Joseph —
AXcan martes a 8 de mayo de 1736 años nic[. . .] y nomemoria nehuatl notoca Joanquin Josep[. . .] nicasado yca lorensan fran^{ca} notlaxilacalp[. . .] San Juan Bap^{ta} ca niquitoa tla nechmotlaço[. . .]tzinos yn Cm̄h teotlatohua tt^{o} dios ca huel ynce[. . .]mactzin nicotlalia y noyoliantzin y naniman[. . .] yhua niquitoa ynic nopanpa tzinlini micatep[. . .]stli yexcanpa san Juan Bap^{ta} santa m^{a} de l[. . .] Angeles san sebastian motemacas huentzin[. . .] memeliotzintzin yhua motemacas meliotzin sa[. . .]ta Jerosalen yhua niquitoa y noquiliuhca yes [. . .] yabitotzin notlacotatzin santo san fran^{co} yhua y[. . .] ninolpitias yn iCordontzin yhua niquitoa y nosepultora vnca ycapillatzin Jesus nasareno vnca n[. . .]chmomachiotilis yn Cm̄h teotlatoani tt^{o} dios yhua niqu[. . .] vncatqui se misa cantada de Reque yc palehuilos yn nanimatzin yhua niquito y nopiltzin yntoca Antt^{o} ca niccahuili ynin caltzintli se ytztica yc ynquisayanp[. . .] tonatiuh ychantzinco dios yhua o se ytztica ycalaquianpa tonatiuh yhua yehuatzin la Virgen de guadalupe vnca quimotequipanilhuis yhua y noçihuahuatzin ytoca loren[. . .] fran^{ca} vnca quinmohuapahuilis yhua niquito ca cen[. . .]notlatlauhtili yehua felis fran^{co} ca yehuatzin no[. . .]pan motlatoltis noalbasea metzties ca yntla quali qu[. . .]chihuilis ca dios quimotlaxtlahuilis Auh Ynic onictlali [. . .] nomemo ymixpantzinco testigos D^{n} Joseph Alunso testi^{o} D^{n} domino de S^{n}tiago testi^{o} Bentuara fran^{co} fiscal de S^{n}ta yglesia Dn Antt° tapia
eS$^{\underline{no}}$ Andres fran^{co}[2]

Josef Joaquín.
Joseph.[1] —
May the precious revered name of the most holy Trinity, God the father, God his precious [son], and God the Holy Spirit be entirely praised. May it be done, amen. Jesus, Mary and Joseph. —
Today, Tuesday the 8th of May of the year of 1736, I named Joaquín Josef, married to Lorenza Francisca, [make] my memorandum [of testament] in my tlaxilacalli of San Juan Bautista. I say that, if the universal divine ruler our lord God shows me his love [brings about my death], I place my spirit and soul very entirely in his hands, and I say that the bells are to ring for me in three places, San Juan Bautista, Santa María de los Angeles, and San Sebastián; an offering of half a real each is to be given, and half a real is to be given for Holy Jerusalem. And I say that my shroud will be the habit of my precious father holy San Francisco, and I am to be girt with his rope. And I say that my grave is at the chapel of Jesús Nazareno; there the universal divine ruler our lord God will designate [a place] for me. And I say that there is a high requiem mass with which my soul is to be helped; and I say that to my child named Antonio I leave this house; one [building], the home of God, faces east, and another faces west; there he is to serve the Virgen de Guadalupe, and my wife named Lorenza Francisca is to raise him there. And I say that I greatly implore Félix Francisco to speak on my behalf and be my executor. If he does it well, God will reward him. I have issued my memorandum [of testament] before the witnesses: don Josef Alonso, witness; don Domingo de Santiago, witness; Ventura Francisco; fiscal of the holy church, don Antonio de Tapia.
Notary Andrés Francisco[2]

[1]Probably all three members of the holy family were originally mentioned here.
[2]At the back there are three sentences written in Spanish on different sides; probably the paper was folded. They report on the performance of various masses for the testator, at least three of them.

33. Juan de los Santos, San Juan Bautista, 1756

(AHAM, Box 76:41, Juzgado Eclesiástico de Toluca)[1]

HERE THE TESTATOR, Juan de los Santos, issues a will exclusively to make dispositions about his funeral and burial; no property whatsoever is mentioned. He is probably a widower, since he entrusts two brothers of his, and not his wife, with looking after his little children; nothing more is said about the children, so we have no clue about their gender and number. It appears likely that the testator was truly indigent; the testament does not seem to have been made in great haste. The names of the brothers are of the most humble type, and though the witnesses are of higher rank, they all may be church

[1]The testament is accompanied by a contemporary Spanish translation.

officials doing their duty rather than associates sought out by the testator.

Thus funeral arrangements are a priority for Juan de los Santos. He requests bells to be rung, the shroud of the Virgin of Carmen, and burial in the chapel of San Juan, the tlaxilacalli saint and also the saint from whom he gets his name. A high requiem mass is to be provided by his mother. The mother here, and the two brothers mentioned above, are hints of a strong connection of the testator with his original family, as well as of his own reduced circumstances.

The notary Adrián Josef still gives the date in a more traditional Nahuatl form, in spite of the fact that this testament is quite late in time, and he retains the old phrase *–tlallo -çoquiyo*, "one's earth and clay," for earthly body. His orthography is quite standard in some respects, but he has the *h* for *ch* and *ll* for *y* not infrequently seen in Nahuatl documents of this time, whether in Toluca or elsewhere. The most unusual general feature is his consistent use of *z* for *tz* even at the beginning of syllables, as in "noteozin" for *noteotzin*, "my deity." His form "nomegcatepos," for *nomiccatepoz*, "my bells," with *e* for *i* and *g* for *c*, is something of an anomaly.

S,n J,n B[. . .]
Ma mosenquiscallectehua yn itlazomahuistocazin yn Dios tetazi yhuan Dios yn itlazopilzi yhuan Dios Espiritu Santo Ma mochihua Amen Jesus
Axca Martes ypan ome thonali mestli Marzo yhuan xiuhtlapuali año de 1756 nicchihua nomemoria Nehuatl notoca Juan de los Santos niquitohua yntla nehmonochilis yn noteozi yn notlatocazi Dios Ca huel ahtopa ysemaczinco nicontlalia yn nollolianzi noanimanzi yhuan zilinis nomegcatepos notlaxilacalpan S,^{n} Juan Baptista Santa maria de los Angeles yhuan S,^{n} Sebastian motemacas memeliozizin neltis notlanequilis yhua niquitohua yntla nehmonochili yn noteozi Dios Ca nehmomachiotilis ompa huey teopa Capilla San Juan yhua yc moquimilos yn notlalo nozoquio ytlaquezi notlazomahuisnanzin la Virgen del Carme yhuan yc ninolpis ycordonzin notlazotazin S,^{r} S,^{n} fra^{co} yhuan se missa cantada de Requie ypalehuiloca y nollolianzi noanimanzi nehmotlaocolilia llehuazi notlazonanzi yhuan Ca huel senca nicnotlatlauhtilia llehuazi nohemanozi Basilio antonio llehuazi mochiuhzinos noalbasea yhuan nohermanozi Joachin Joseph nehymitilisque nopilhuantoto yhuan testigo D,n bernabel Antonio fiscal de la Santa yglecia[2] D,^{n} Fran,^{co} antonio

Es,^{no} Adrian Joseph

San Juan Bautista
May the precious revered name of God the father, God his precious son, and God the Holy Spirit be entirely praised. May it be done, amen. Jesus.
Today, Tuesday on the 2nd day of the month of March in the year count of 1756, I named Juan de los Santos make my memorandum [of testament]. I say that if my deity and ruler God calls me, first of all I place my spirit and soul entirely in his hands. And my bells will be rung in my tlaxilacalli of San Juan Bautista, in Santa María de los Angeles, and in San Sebastián; an offering of half a real each is to be given. My will is to be carried out. And I say that when my deity God has called me, he will designate [a place for my burial] at the great church, in the chapel of San Juan. And my earthly body is to be shrouded in the habit of my precious revered mother the Virgen del Carmen, and I am to be girt with the rope of my precious father lord San Francisco. And my precious mother is to favor me with a high requiem mass as the help of my spirit and soul. And I very greatly implore my brother Basilio Antonio to become my executor, along with my brother Joaquín Josef; they are to look after my little children for me. Witness don Bernabé Antonio; fiscal of the holy church[2] don Francisco Antonio.
Notary Adrián Josef.

[2] It may be that don Bernabé Antonio, not don Francisco Antonio, was the fiscal; the Spanish translator thought so, but there seems no way to be sure.

34. Will issued by María de Guadalupe for Mateo de Luna, San Juan Bautista, 1757

(AHAM, Box 78:6, Juzgado Eclesiástico de Toluca)

HERE A MARRIED WOMAN issues a will in favor of her nephew, Mateo de Luna, in all likelihood because he had died suddenly without being able to make one himself. This is one of only two cases in the corpus (the other is No. 20) of a testament issued by an individual on behalf of somebody else, and it is remarkable that a woman took it upon herself to do it, especially with her husband still alive. Perhaps María was the only living blood relative of Mateo de Luna. In terms of property, she arranges for a house and the land it is on to go to her grandchild Juan Paulino, while mentioning also his first cousin Marcos Antonio, but it is unclear if the two are to share only the piece of land or the whole property. There is also a field, and in this case no doubt is left that it is to be divided between the two heirs. Since María de Guadalupe is acting on behalf of Mateo de Luna, Juan Paulino and Marcos Antonio must be related to him; perhaps the former was his child and the latter his nephew.

Funeral and burial are also taken care of; María gives offerings for the bells to be rung and for a low mass, and she has arranged a grave in the chapel of Jesús Nazareno, which seems to be quite popular among the testators of San Juan Bautista. The mass was actually said, and no one seems to challenge the legality of the proceedings.

María's husband Andrés de Guadalupe is chosen as executor. The second name Guadalupe is otherwise seen in the corpus only once (No. 82), and it is also very unusual for man and wife to bear the same second name as they do here. One is left wondering if the pair originally had more normal names and then both adopted Guadalupe, after the Virgin of Guadalupe, for devotional reasons. Note that Andrés gets the additional title of don only when referred to as the executor; such variation occurs in the corpus mainly when the person is only marginally distinguished, or very new to distinction. The two are in fact likely of quite high status, however. Though Mateo de Luna lacked large assets, his name stands out from the crowd, and the four witnesses to the document all bear the don, showing connections with high-ranking individuals of the community.

The testament is issued in the second half of the eighteenth century, and the notary Juan Antonio reflects many of the characteristics of the Tolucan Nahuatl of that time. However, some traditional expressions are still present, and even one quite archaic term, *xamani*, which speaks of the body breaking apart or shattering in the grave. We also see the bizarre form "palegolos," for *palehuiloz*, "it will be helped," and simple slips and omissions are not rare in the document.

Sn Juan Bauptista Mateo de lona —
Ma mocenquiscallectenehua yn itlasomahuistocatzin yn Dios tetatzin yhua Dios ytlasopiltzin yhua Dios espirito S^{n}to ma yn mochihua amen Jesos Maria y Joseph —
Axcan Juebes Mani mestli de septiembre A 15 yhua xitlapoali año de mil setesientos y sinquenta y siete años nehuatl notoca Maria de goadalope yhua nonamictzin Andres de goadalope nican totlaxilacalpan S^{n} Juan Bauptista nictlalia yi memoria yhua niquitohua nicnotlaocolia nosobrinotzin mateo de lona huetzintli nic chocas micatepostli S^{n}ta maria de los Angeles S^{n} Juan Bauptista S^{n} sebastian [. . .][1] yhua nicnotlaocolia se missa Resada yni palegolos yn illanimantzin yhua niquitohua ysepoltora lles onpa yxpantzinco Jesos de nasareno tocapilla yn canpa tlamis xamanis yn itlalo ysoquio yn canpa quimomachiotitilis yn iteotzin D^{s} yhua niquitohua noxhui Juan paolino niccahuilia caltzintli oratorio tlachi yc xocotitla yhua oc se tlachie ycalaquia [*f.* 2] tonali

San Juan Bautista Mateo de Luna —
May the precious revered name of God the father, God his precious son, and God the Holy Spirit be entirely praised. May it be done, amen. Jesus, Mary, and Joseph. —
Today, Thursday the 15th of the month of September in the year count of 1757, I named María de Guadalupe—my husband is Andrés de Guadalupe, and our tlaxilacalli is here in San Juan Bautista—issue this memorandum [of testament], and I say that I favor my nephew Mateo de Luna with an offering so that the bells will sound at Santa María de los Angeles, San Juan Bautista, and San Sebastián [. . .],[1] and I favor him with a low mass so that his soul will be helped. And I say that his grave will be in front of our chapel of Jesús Nazareno, where his earthly body will end and break apart, where his deity God will designate a place for him. And I say that to my grandchild Juan Paulino I leave a house; [one building], an oratory, looks toward Xocotitlan and another one looks toward the west [*f.* 2], with a

---

[1]The unclearly written letters at this point look somewhat like "y fabia" or "y tabia." They do not appear to designate another place where the bells are to be rung, and they remain puzzling.

yhuan tlaltontli yn ihuilanca caltzintli matlacquahuitl quimonepantlaxelhuisque Marcos Antonio yprimo hermano Juan paolino Moxelohua tlali yc patlahuac yhua niquitohua yno tlamili ytlantzinco hermitatzin sano nepantla moxelos tlaco quicoquis Juan paolino yhua tlaco Marcos Antonio yhua ca huel nicnotlatlatilia nonamictzin D^{n} Andres de goadalope ca llehuatzin ypan motlatoltis yn las animas[2] yhua niquitohua ca teixpan omotlali yni amatlaquiloli testigos D^{n} matias de la cruz D^{n} Juchin belasquis D^{n} Ju de D^{s} fiscal de la S^{n} yglesia D^{n} tomas de villanoeba —

Es^{no} Juan Antonio[3]

little piece of land that goes with the house, of 10 quahuitl. Juan Paulino and his first cousin Marcos Antonio are to divide it equally. The land is to be divided by width. And I say that that field next to the shrine is likewise to be divided in the middle. Juan Paulino is to take half, and Marcos Antonio half. And I greatly implore my husband don Andrés de Guadalupe to speak on behalf of [the soul of Mateo de Luna].[2] And I say that this document was issued publicly. The witnesses were don Matías de la Cruz; don Joaquín Velásquez; don Juan de Dios; and the fiscal of the holy church, don Tomás de Villanueva. —

Notary Juan Antonio.[3]

[2]The phrase Las Animas usually refers to the cofradía devoted to the souls of the dead in purgatory, but perhaps the writer became confused, for executors are always exhorted to speak for the soul of the testator, and the plural form of the word could not be applicable to a single person.

[3]A note in Spanish confirms that this is the memorandum of Mateo de Luna and that a low mass was said.

35. Salvador Cayetano, Santa Ana, 1728

(AHAM, Box 39:18, Juzgado Eclesiástico de Toluca)

POSSESSING BOTH very substantial assets and a distinguished or at least unusual second name, Salvador Cayetano is married to Micaela Inés (later Inés Micaela, for inversion of names does happen at times in these testaments). Apparently they have no surviving children, since he divides his property between a grandchild and another person whose relationship to him is not declared. The grandchild, Vicente Romero, and the other person, a Pascual Antonio, each receive a house complex and 80 quahuitl of land, some of it literally divided between them. Though Vicente inherits one field on his own, much of his portion goes to him jointly with Micaela, probably in the sense that she is to take care of the property until the grandchild is grown up. Basically, Salvador Cayetano treats the two heirs equally, apart from Vicente being associated with his wife and Pascual getting some saints. Perhaps it was merely that Pascual was older and needed no guardian, and on the other hand the house that Vicente got may have had some unmentioned saints. As to Pascual Antonio's status, we can only speculate. Possibly he is another grandchild; he could even be a second son of the testator, with Vicente Romero the child of the now deceased first son. The fact that Vicente is mentioned first may indicate some sort of precedence or preference for him, for order of mention of heirs is generally significant in the corpus. In any case, Pascual seems to be the testator of will No. 36, issued in 1737.

Although Salvador Cayetano lacks the don, several indicators point to a quite high status for him; some people appearing in the will have names more on the Spanish pattern than the indigenous; I have already noted his extensive property for an indigenous person. His executor is a don. He has means for a shroud, a high requiem mass, bells to be rung and some offerings, particularly quite generous ones to cofradías. Moreover, Salvador has a special devotion to the Holy Cross, since besides giving four pesos for its cofradía, he also requests to be buried close to it.

The collection of debts is often relegated to the end of testaments or even comes as an afterthought, as here, after the signature of the notary. Salvador remembers some debts owed him, two of them in other tlaxilacalli, one involving apparently the sale of a cape and another a purchase of magueyes, which could be an indication that he is involved in small business in the immediate Toluca region. As often, proceeds from the debts are to be used for funeral expenses.

The style of notary Juan Gregorio is an even mix of conservative and eighteenth-century Toluca traits, accompanied by a frequent omission of syllables, with some repetitions as well.

Ma çequizcayectenehualo yn itocatzin yn Dios tetatzin y Dios tepiltzin yhua y Dios Esp^{tu} S^{to} Ma y mochihua Amen Jesus —

Axca Sabando a 7. de febro yuã xiuhtlapohuali de 1728 an^{os} Ca nictlalia y notameto y nehuatl notocan Saluador Cayetano yhua nosihuahuatzin Micaela ynes notlaxilacalpan Santa Ana Ca niquitonhua Ytla ninomiquilis Ca huel acachtopan Y noyolia y nanimatzin Ca huel isemactzincon notlalia y notlaçotatzin y tt^{o} Dios yuã Ca niquitoã ytla ninomiquilis Ca ocatqui ynic quimiltias y notlalnacayo yuã yc ninolpitias yn icordotzin y notlaçontatzin San fran.^{co} yuã niquitoã y noçepultura yes Ca ocan yn inahuactzinco Santisima Crus Ca opan toctos y notlalnacayo - yhua niquitoã motemacas Sta Jherosale yuã niquitoa Ca nophapan tzinlinis micatepustli San fra^{co} yuã Sancta maria natibitas - yuã San Diego motemacas memeliotzintzin huetzintli neltis mochihuas yuã niquitoã y nocofradia = Sagre de xp^{to} yuã Santisima Cruz motemacas huetzintli nahui tomitzin Sano yuhqui O sen cofradia no nahui tomi motemacas neltis y notlanequilis = yuã niquitoã in ipalehuiloca yes Ca nitlaolilon setetl — Misan Requie Catada = Ca yehuatl yc nipalehuilos = yuã ninquitoã Ca nitoã Ca ocatqui Caltzintli ytzticac yn icalaquiapan tonati yn ichantzinco yn Dios Oc Sen ytzticac yn iquisapan tonatonati yhuicalo tlali Sepohualmani Ca nicCahuilitiuh noxhuiuh ytocan Bisente romero yca yehuatzin nosihuahuatzin ynes micaela Ca oca quimotequipanilhuisque y tt^{o} Dios yn ca moyetzticate Oc se tlalmili ocatqui xometitla sepohualmani Ca nicCahuilitiuh Bisete Romero Oc se tlalmili ca sano Opan Ocatqui Sano Sepohualmani Sano yehuatl niquicahuilitiuh Bisete Romero Ca nosihuahuatzin Oc Se tlaltzintli Ocatqui yc opan yatica otli San Jeronimo opohualmani sepohualmani Bisete Romero = oc no sepohualmani Ca niccahuilitiuh pasqual Antonio = Oc sen Cali ocatqui yhuicalo tlali sepohualmanani Solar Ca nicCahuilitiuh pasqual Antonio Ca pan tequitis[1] ytla quimonemiltilis y Dios = yuã niquitoã yenhuatzin y yehual huey tlatoani Dios yuã tlaçonsihuapilen del carme yuã San Jua Baptista Ca niccahuilitiuh pasqual Antonio quimotequipanilhuis = yuã Oc Se tlanili ocatqui huey otlica Sepohualmani ypa matlacquahuitl Ca nicCahuilintiuh pasqual Antonio = yuã ocatqui oc se tlali matlacquahuitl Ca yhuicalo yn iCaltzin = yuã

May the name of God the father, God the son, and God the Holy Spirit be entirely praised. May it be done, amen. Jesus. —

Today, Saturday the 7th of February in the year count of 1728, I named Salvador Cayetano issue my testament in my tlaxilacalli of Santa Ana; my wife is Micaela Inés. I say that if I die, first of all I place my spirit and soul very entirely in the hands of my precious father our lord God, and I say that if I die there is the means with which my earthly body will be shrouded, and I will be girt with the rope of my precious father San Francisco. And I say that my grave will be close to the Santísima Cruz; there my earthly body is to lie buried. – And I say that [something] is to be given for Holy Jerusalem. And I say that the bells are to be rung for me at San Francisco, Santa María Nativitas, and San Diego; a half real offering is to be given for each. It is to be done and carried out. And I say that for my cofradía of Sangre de Cristo and for Santísima Cruz an offering of 4 reales is to be given. Likewise 4 reales are to be given for another cofradía. My will is to be carried out. = And I say that the help of [my soul] is to be that I am favored with a high requiem mass; that is what I will be helped with. = And I say that there is a house looking to the west, the home of God, and another looking to the east, and the land that goes with it, 20 [quahuitl]; I leave it to my grandchild named Vicente Romero along with my wife Inés Micaela. There they are to serve our lord God where they are. There is another field at Xometitlan of 20; I am leaving it to Vicente Romero. Likewise there is another field there, likewise of 20; I am likewise leaving it to Vicente Romero [with] my wife. There is another piece of land where the road goes to San Gerónimo, of 40. I am leaving 20 to Vicente Romero and the other 20 to Pascual Antonio. = There is another house and land going with it of 20, a lot; I am leaving it to Pascual Antonio; he is [to do tribute duty on it][1] if God gives him life. = And I say that I leave the great ruler God, the precious lady del Carmen, and San Juan Bautista to Pascual Antonio; he is to serve them. = And there is another piece of land at the highway, of 30 quahuitl, that I am leaving to Pascual Antonio. = And there is another piece of land of 10 quahuitl going with his house. =

[1]Possibly the meaning is rather that he is to work on it.

Ca huel senca nicnotlatlauhtilia y noalvaçeal yes Ca yehuatzin Dn Jua de la Cruz huel nopan motlatoltis ytla quali quimochihuilis Ca Dios quinmotlaxtlahuilis = yuā Onotzaloque testigos yn imixpan omochiuh y notestameto D^{n} fra$^{\underline{co}}$ matias fiscal mayor yuā Ph$^{\underline{e}}$ de Satiago = yuā Domigo hernades —
— Ess$^{\underline{no}}$ Juā Gregorio de bilesia[2]
yuā niqutoā Ca nechhuiquilia Nicolas Santilla Setel Capoti Ca ye quimomachiltia y tleyn ipantiuh axca nitquitoā ma tlaco quimoxtlahuilis tlaco nicpolonhuan —
yhua niquitoā ytocan Aug$^{\underline{ti}}$ Ph$^{\underline{e}}$ ychantzinco S$^{\underline{ta}}$ maria de los ageles huitzinla Ca nechhuiquila se peso nechmomaquilisquia metl axca ma quimoxtlahuili se peso = Ca notech monequis — 1 p.^{s}

yhuan opan Sa lorezo Ca ytocan Diego Ca nechhuiquilia se peso ca quimoxtlahuilis notech monequis — 1 p.^{s}

And I very greatly implore the person who is to be my executor, don Juan de la Cruz, to speak strongly for me; if he does it well, God will reward him. = And witnesses were called before whom I made my testament: don Francisco Matías, fiscal mayor; Felipe de Santiago; and Domingo Hernández. —
Notary of the church[2] Juan Gregorio.
And I say that Nicolás Santillán owes me a cape; he knows what its value is. I say now, let him pay half; I cancel half. —

And I say that a person named Agustín Felipe whose home is Santa María de los Angeles Huitzillan owes me a peso; he was going to give me magueyes. Now let him pay back a peso; it is to be used for me. — 1 peso.
And at San Lorenzo a person named Diego owes me a peso. He is to pay it back; it is to be used for me. — 1 peso.

[2]Though "bilesia" may be a bit hard to recognize, it is one of the many versions seen in the Toluca corpus and elsewhere of Spanish *iglesia*, "church," which caused Nahua speakers much trouble with its [gl] cluster, unpronounceable for them; "gilesia" is quite common, and since some writers switched letters for any two voiced stops, *b* for *g* falls within the normal range. At the back it is reported in Spanish that the executor paid for the mass nine or ten days after the date of the testament.

36. Pascual Antonio, Santa Ana, 1737

(AHAM, Box 52:47, Juzgado Eclesiástico de Toluca)

THE TESTATOR Pascual Antonio (recipient of bequests in will No. 35) follows the common rule of leaving his house and its lot to his son, Pedro de Alcántara, the only heir mentioned in the will. Pedro also gets another piece of land and some magueyes. Note that his second name, Alcántara, is quite unusual and implies a relatively high status, despite the more ordinary name of his father; yet if we look at the broader context including No. 35, we find several high-ranking names in this circle. The son seems to be a little boy, as his father calls him and as can also be deduced from the fact that he is entrusted to the care of the executors, but he inherits the property on his own and not in conjunction with Pascual Antonio's wife, Basilia Antonia (who has the same second name as the testator). The situation with the wife is indeed unclear; it appears possible that she too was on the verge of death (see note 1 below).

It can be said with some certainty that the house with its lot and the piece of land mentioned by the testator were among his inheritance in 1728 from Salvador Cayetano (No. 35), although the exact connection between the two is not known. Pascual Antonio has retained the core of the inherited property, but seems to have lost some of the land, or at least it remains unmentioned. Pascual still has two of the saints that Salvador left him and appears to have acquired a few more during the years; he now requests them to be put in the church, which implies that they are quite impressive artifacts. In addition, Pascual Antonio mentions a type of possession absent in Salvador's will, animals. In fact, he owns a cow and a horse that are to be sold (probably to pay for his funeral), and a male mule and five pigs of his are with his in-laws; these animals are not strictly linked to agriculture, and their possession hints at other kinds of activities, such as trade, transportation, and possibly sale of milk or meat. As with his older relative Salvador Cayetano, we can suspect that Pascual Antonio is involved in some sort of petty local trade. Note that his mother-in-law also owes him some money; there is a strong connection with his wife's family here.

Funeral arrangements are standard, somewhat on the upper side, with a shroud and rope of San Diego (very rare in the whole corpus as opposed to the rope of San Francisco), some offerings, a high mass, and bells to be rung. (Place of burial goes unmentioned.) The witnesses do not tell us much; only the almost obligatory fiscal has the don, but an alcalde is also present. Pascual Antonio's choice of executors is very unusual, since one of the two he names is a friar. The second is the same Nicolás Santillán who owed a cape to Salvador Cayetano in the previous testament; though he lacks the don, he has a high-sounding Spanish second name.

The style of notary Santiago Bartolomé seems to be very much in line with that of Juan Gregorio from the previous testament: a combination of conservative traits and some characteristics of Toluca Nahuatl. In addition, there is some interesting vocabulary for Spanish-introduced animals.

Man mosequiscanyectenehualo yn itlasomahuistocantzin y[. . .] tetantzin yûa Dios tepiltzin yûa Dios espirito S$^{\underline{to}}$ ma y[. . .] mochihua —
Axcan sabado A 2 de nobiebre D 1737 a^{o}s nitlalia notestamento y nehuatl notocan pasqual Antt$^{\underline{o}}$ notlaxilaCalpan S$^{\underline{ta}}$ Anna ca niquitoâ ytla ninomiquilis ca huel acachtopan y noyôlia y nanimantzin ca huel iSemactzinco niconocahuilili y notlasotatzin yûa yûa ca hoca ynic quimiliuhtias y notlalnacay[. . .] yûa y nicnolpitias yn icordotzin y notlasotatzin S^{to} S. Diego yûa ca motemacas meliotzin S$^{\underline{ta}}$ Jherole yûa nopapa tzilinis meuhcatepostli — yûa yn ipalehuiloca yes y noyôlia ca nitlaocolilo Misa cantada = yûa ca hocahqui caltzintli yzticaqui ycalaquiapan tonali oc se yzticacqui yquisanyapa tonali yhuicalo tlalmili solar ca nicCahuilia notelpochto ytoca pedro alcantar yûa Oc se tlalmili sepohualmani solar ca no nicCahuilia notelpochto yûa niquitoâ ca no mochihuas ymisa nosihuahuatzin — Misan cantada ca neltis mochihuas[1] yûa — niquitoâ ca mocalaquisque S$^{\underline{tos}}$ teopan S$^{\underline{to}}$ oesiomo jezos nasareno la birge del carme Sta ynes S$^{\underline{n}}$ marti S^{n}n isidro yûa ca huel nicnotlatlauhtilia noalbasea yes ca yehuantzin frai Juze Serbantes yûa Nicolas Santilla yûa ca honotzaloque testigos marcos ipolito Bentora de santiago — alcalde hoctoal — fiscal mayor don Ju^{o} de satiago testigo yn imixpa omochiuh notestamento

Ess$^{\underline{no}}$ santiago bartolome [*verso*]
se huacax[2] monamacas yhua se cahuayo tliltic mo-

May the precious revered name of [God] the father, God the son, and God the Holy Spirit be entirely praised. May it be done. —
Today, Saturday the 2nd of November of the year of 1737, I named Pascual Antonio issue my testament in my tlaxilacalli of Santa Ana. I say that, if I die, first of all I leave my spirit and my soul very entirely in the hands of my precious Father; and the means exist to shroud my earthly body, and I am to be girt with the rope of my precious father holy San Diego. And half a real will be given for Holy Jerusalem, and the bells are to ring for me. — And the help of my spirit will be that I am favored with a high mass. = And there are [two] houses, one looking toward the west, another looking toward the east, and the field that goes with them is a lot; I leave it to my little son named Pedro de Alcántara. And I also leave another field, of 20 [quahuitl], a lot, to my little son. And I say that a mass is also to be performed for my wife, a high mass; it is to be carried out and realized.[1] — And I say that the saints are to be put in the church, holy Ecce Homo, Jesús Nazareno, the Virgen del Carmen, Santa Inés, San Martín, and San Isidro. And I greatly implore that my executors be fray José Cervantes and Nicolás Santillán. And the witnesses who were summoned are Marcos Hipólito; Ventura de Santiago, present alcalde; and the fiscal mayor, don Juan de Santiago, witness. Before them my testament was done.

Notary Santiago Bartolomé. [*verso*]
A cow[2] is to be sold, and a black horse is to be sold.

[1]The literal meaning of the Nahuatl here seems quite clear, yet many questions arise. It is otherwise unheard of in the corpus for a mass to be requested for a person not already dead or about to die, and in a Spanish notation at the back, dated in May of 1738, a Basilia Antonia is referred to as the widow of Pascual Antonio. One would expect that the testator would have asked his wife to have the mass performed for him. The wording of the notation at the back is so unclear that it could refer to a mass said for Basilia Antonia rather than requested and paid for by her. Although she is called Pascual Antonio's widow there, she may have died before the mass of May 1738, and indeed her death may have been foreseen, for the testator leaves his son in the hands of the executors, not of his wife. Another possibility is that the high mass requested in the will is to be for both wife and husband.

[2]In many of the documents in the corpus, a cow is called a *vaca* (or *baca*, or *vaquilla*, etc.), whereas *huacax*, originally the same word, is often an ox. Thus possibly the reference is to an ox in this case.

namacas yhua nechhuiquilia nomona se peso yhua nahuin yhua se macho onictlaneuhti nomonta yhua nomona yhua macuili cochinitos tepitoto — yhua metototi ca no niccahuilia notelpochto yhua niquitohua ca notelpochto ca mocahua ynahuaqui noalbasea nicolas Satilla yhua fray Juze serbates[3]

And my mother-in-law owes me 1 peso and 4 [reales], and I rented a male mule to my father-in-law and my mother-in-law, and 5 small pigs. — And I also leave to my little son some small magueyes. And I say that my little son is left with my executors Nicolás Santillán and fray José Cervantes.[3]

[3]The section on the verso page seems to be in a different handwriting.

37. Mauricia Josefa, no place, 1732

(AHAM, Box 46:50, Juzgado Eclesiástico de Toluca)

THE PRESENT TESTAMENT and the following one (No. 38) contain a cluster consisting of a married couple and have the interest attaching to such a circumstance. At the same time they present several problems which perhaps had best be discussed for both documents at the beginning.

First, contrary to the general, otherwise almost universal practice, in neither document is the tlaxilacalli (or even the altepetl) of the testator specified. That very fact, plus the connection of the pair, induces one to believe that the two share the same tlaxilacalli; moreover, the two documents are virtually identical for several sentences of the preamble despite being done by two different notaries. Because requesting bells to be rung at someone's death is typical of Toluca and its close surroundings, while it is not to be found in testaments from the Calimaya/Tepemaxalco area, I have classified Nos. 37 and 38 with Toluca. Moreover, the great majority of testaments I have found in the AHAM are from the immediate area of Toluca.

Second, one might wonder about the status of Mauricia Josefa's husband, or even about his identity. Mauricia's will appears to be issued in 1732,[1] and she gives her husband's name as Francisco Pedro without don. The other testament is issued in 1737, and the testator gives his name as don Francisco Pedro. The discrepancy, however, can be resolved. Not only could don Francisco have attained his title in the intervening five years by holding some high office, but his status was marginal in some way, leading to vacillating usage. In both documents, unlike most holders of the title, he appears both with and without the don. On the back of his own will, in which he appears as don, the friar making an annotation omits the title, and on the other hand though his name appears without it in his wife's will proper, the Spanish annotation there, by the same friar a few days earlier, accords him the don.

An additional mystery has to do with the spectacle of someone paying for his wife's mass five years after her will was issued. Did she not die at that time after all? Or was don Francisco tardy in fulfilling his obligation, and did so only as his own death approached, for he paid for the mass only a week before his testament was issued? Though a low mass was originally requested, he had a high mass sung, as though to salve his conscience. In his will, don Francisco calls Mauricia Josefa his wife, with no implication that she had died; in the Spanish notation he was first listed as married to Mauricia, then that was crossed out and he was called *viudo*, "widower," instead.

No connection appears between the married pair in terms of possessions. All that Mauricia Josefa bequeaths comes from her late brother, who left her the house and magueyes that she now passes on to Micaela Josefa, apparently her small daughter, but some doubt remains on this point (see note 3 below). The magueyes are to be dedicated to the worship of the Virgin, the use to which Mauricia has already been putting them. The house may not have been the main residence of the large nuclear family, but an additional house that was Mauricia's exclu-

[1]Since the husband appears in person to arrange for Mauricia Josefa's mass, and the date of his action is clearly given as 1737, one must at least suspect that Mauricia's will was also issued in 1737. To pay for the primary mass so long after the death of the testator is otherwise unparalleled in the corpus. The irregularities concerning these two wills lead one to wonder if some form of connivance or falsification was involved. Not only do both, despite listing different notaries, start out with wording and spelling that are close to identical in stretches, but it is hard to tell any difference between the handwritings. It would be unusual in the corpus for the fiscal mayor and fiscal teniente of a tlaxilacalli to be identical over a five-year interval. Yet no motive for falsification is apparent, and we have seen in other cases that local traditions can lead to very similar products by different notaries.

sive property. It is worth noting that, as in other cases of women involved in the cultivation of magueyes, Mauricia has no landed property.

It is hard to assess Mauricia Josefa's social standing. Though she is not independently wealthy, sometimes women in high-ranking families had relatively little property of their own, and Mauricia at least has a house. No witnesses to the will are mentioned at all, unless we take as such the fiscal mayor and fiscal teniente who were most likely simply officiating. Yet Mauricia's deceased brother had the don, and her executor has an uncommon, potentially distinguished Spanish second name.

Other than the formulas common to this unknown tlaxilacalli, notary Vicente de la Cruz gives us little to comment on; for bells he, like his colleague of No. 38, writes *campana* instead of the more common *(micca)tepoztli,* which uses native roots. His writing is reasonably conservative but does share a few of the general characteristics of eighteenth-century Toluca Nahuatl.

---

testamento maurisia Josepha de 1732 años

Axca sabado en [1?]8 de abril nipehualtia notestamento notoca maurisia Josepha yhua nonamictzi yn itoca fran$\underline{^{co}}$ pe$\underline{^{o}}$ y nica ninomachiotia yn ica yn itlasomahuistocatzin y — yn dios tetatzin yn dios yntlaçopiltzin yhuan dios es̄ s$\underline{^{to}}$ yn sa se huel neli teol dios —

y niquitohua yntla nicnomasehuitzinos yn itlasomahuismiquilitzi notlasomahuistatzin dios nopan tlatzilinis canpana yhua motemacas santa gerusale ynic neltis yhuan niquitoa nechmomachiotilisque nosepoltura yes fiscaltin onpa huei theopa yhua niquitohua yn ipalehuiloca noyolia nanimantzin ninotechtia missa ye resada ynic neltis —

yhua niquitohua onechmocahuilitia noermanotzin catca D̄ lucas ynin canli yhua metl yni yaxcatzin notlasomahuisnantzi ynic onnicnotequipanilhuitzino notlasonantzin[2] axca nicnocahuilitias nopito[3] micaela Josepha yehuatzin quimocuitlahuitzinos ynon ynon cali yhua metl ynic neltis — yhua niquitohua y noalhuasealeshua yehuatzin Juan mexia nopan motlatoltis quimocuitlahuitzinos notestamento mostla huictla quimotlaxtlahuilis yn t^{o} dios [*verso*]

fiscal manyor D̄ fran^{co} eligio fiscal teniente nicolas fran$\underline{^{co}}$

es$\overline{no}$ bisente de la crus

Testament of Mauricia Josefa of the year of 1732.

Today, Saturday the [1?]8th of April, I named Mauricia Josefa begin my testament; my husband is named Francisco Pedro. Here I take as my sign the precious revered name of God the father, God his precious son, and God the Holy Spirit, only one very true deity God. —

I say that if I attain the precious revered death of my precious revered father God, the bells are to be rung for me, and [an offering] is to be given for Holy Jerusalem, so that it will be carried out. And I say that the fiscales are to designate [where] my grave will be at the great church. And I say that the help of my spirit and soul is that I assign to myself a low mass so that it will be carried out. —

And I say that my late brother don Lucas left me at death this house and the magueyes that belong to my precious revered mother, with which I have served my precious mother.[2] Now I am leaving here my [small child][3] Micaela Josefa; she is to take care of that house and the magueyes, so that it will be carried out. — And I say that as to my executors, Juan Mejía is to speak on my behalf, he is to take care of my testament. Our lord God will reward him in the future. [*verso*]

Fiscal mayor don Francisco Eligio. Fiscal teniente Nicolás Francisco.

Notary Vicente de la Cruz.

---

[2]The reference in both cases is apparently to an image of some manifestation of the Virgin Mary.

[3]If *-pilton,* "child," is meant, the form "nopiton" is puzzling not only because of the apparent missing *l,* but because women often used the term *-coneuh* for their offspring, especially the very young. Yet in an associated document in No. 38 the root *pil* is again given as *pi.* The root *pi* does in fact appear in some traditional Nahuatl kin terms, of which the most apropos here would be *-pi,* older sister of a female. But not only is *-hermana* otherwise universal in the corpus, the suffix *-tzin* would be demanded rather than *-ton.* Even so, the absence of a Micaela Josefa in don Francisco Pedro's will makes one wonder if she could not have been a sister or some other relative rather than a daughter; Mauricia Josefa had other daughters who are unmentioned here. In an allocation in No. 38, a Micaela Gerónima who is not in don Francisco's will proper turns up getting some animals. Variation in second names was not unheard of (as with a son of Elena de la Cruz, No. 10), so conceivably this person could be a collateral relative and the same as the Micaela Josefa of No. 37.

38. Don Francisco Pedro, no place, 1737

(AHAM, Box 52:21, Juzgado Eclesiástico de Toluca)

THE COMPLEX and sometimes puzzling commonalities and connections between this testament and No. 37, issued by don Francisco Pedro's wife Mauricia Josefa, are discussed at length in the introduction to that document and should be read first in order to understand fully what follows.

Don Francisco not only leaves it unclear whether his wife is alive or dead, and mentions no property of hers, he also ignores the apparent small daughter Micaela Josefa whom his wife left in charge of a house. Perhaps she died when she was still very little, shortly after her mother, if the 1732 date of her will is really authentic. Don Francisco's large holdings go to other children. He proves to be wealthy beyond the ordinary in land, with an 80-quahuitl field at San Lucas and a confusing blur of small holdings around his house lot, plus yet other fields. In distributing the land among his children he favors the males over the females. Two sons, Josef and Antonio (everything indicates that simple Antonio and Antonio Francisco are the same person), are to share the house and its lot, while providing a place to settle there for another son, Gabriel. The three of them, with a grandchild named Pedro, are also to share the 80-quahuitl field at 20 quahuitl each. Antonio gets the biggest portion of his father's lands, 50 quahuitl in total plus an extra 10 quahuitl that he is to share with another son, Matías. Josef and Gabriel get 30 quahuitl each.

The testator also mentions two daughters, Inés Rosa and Francisca Josefa (note the same second name as the deceased mother), but they get little compared to the sons, just 10 and 20 quahuitl each. To conclude the impressive list of the testator's landed property, he leaves a field of 20 quahuitl to the Virgin of Guadalupe, and two small fields around the house lot to be held in common among his children and dedicated to the worship of the saints.

From another document related to the will, a division among the heirs of property not mentioned in it, we learn that don Francisco's wealth is not confined to land. He also owns both livestock—cows and oxen—and magueyes on quite a large scale. The pattern of inheritance remains much the same in this domain, though a new heir or two appear as if from nowhere. I include the document because of the light it throws on the testator's affairs and more basically because it seems that much movable or ephemeral property may have escaped mention in most wills and that additional allocations of the kind shown here were a common practice.

Despite being a very wealthy man, don Francisco chooses not to display his status through his funeral. In fact, funeral arrangements are just standard, and closely resemble those requested by his deceased wife Mauricia Josefa. Also the witnesses seem to be the same as in Mauricia's will, and do not hint at any connection with high-ranking individuals, the only don being the fiscal, while the executor, as with his wife, bears a Spanish second name but has no title. As we have seen in No. 37, the testator was at this stage of his life being called don only about half the time; his eminence must have been either very new or somewhat dubious. Note that without the don his name is entirely undistinguished, and the same seems to hold true for all his children as their names are given in the will; not even the so common Cruz and Santiago are to be seen. In the allocation of other goods, however, we find that at least several of the sons have the same second name, Francisco, possibly taken from the father's first name. The Matías barely mentioned in the will proves to have the only truly distinguished name in the lot, Serrano.

The notary Antonio Francisco uses exactly the same formulas as the writer of testament No. 37, in the testator's self-introduction as well as in speaking of bells to be rung, offerings, mass, and the fiscales to designate a burial place. An interesting word is "comonidar," a version of the Spanish *comunidad*, "community." This loanword was standard fare in referring to the altepetl as a community, as in *caja de comunidad*, the "community chest or treasury," but here it has developed into something almost like an adverb, "in common." The memorandum is in a different hand, with less orthodox orthography.

---

testamenton D fran^co^ pedro — de 1737 años
Axca miercoles a ocho de mayo nicpehualtia notestamento notoca D francisco pedro yhua nosihuahuatzin

Testament of don Francisco Pedro — year of 1737
Today Wednesday the 8th of May, I named don Francisco Pedro begin my testament; my wife's

ytoca maurisia Josepha y nica ninomachiotia yn ica yn itlasomahuistocatzin yn dios tetatzin yn dios yn itlasopiltzin yhuan dios espiritu santo yn san se huel neli teol dios — yhua niquitohua yntla nicnomasehuitzinos yn itlasomahuismiquilitzi notlasomahuismiquilitzin notlasomahuistatzin dios nopan tlatzilinis canpana yhuan motemacas santa gerosale yhua nechmomachiotilisque nosepoltora yes fiscalti onpa huei teopan yhua niquitohua yn ipalehuiloca noyolia nanimantzin ninotechtia misa cantada ynic nechmotoquilis teopāecatzintlin[1] ynic neltis yhua niquitoa ynin caltzintli yhuan solar caxtolquahuil ihuan matlaquahuitl niquincahuilitias nopilhua ometi Joseph yhua antonio concahuitiyesque ynin cali yhua oc se nopiltzin grabiel motlalis nican tlatzintla quimacasque canpa yc motlalis yhua niquitoa nopiltzin antonio franco nictechtia matlacCuahuitl onicohuili yhua ynon cali amo tlen colinilisq̄e yhua niquitohua nica oc Sentlapal solar matlacquahuitl nictechtia nopiltzin Joseph ynic neltis yhua niquitohua nican tlacpac matlacquahuitl solar niquintechtia omentin nopilhua se yntoca anto yhua matias motlacoxelhuisque ynic neltis yhua niquitohua oc se mili Sa nica quaxochtenco Senpohualmani nicnomaquilia notlasonantzin guadalupetzin yhua niquitohua yxtlahuaca oc Se mili senpohualmani matlaccuahuitl nictechtia nopiltzin anto yhua matlacquahuitl nictechtia nopiltzin grabiel ynic neltis yhua niquitoa oc Se mili Sa lucas senpohualmani nictechtia nopiltzin Joseph yhua niquitoa Sano onpa San lucas senpohualmani nictechtia nopiltzin grabiel yhua niquitoa oc Senpohualmani nictechtia nopiltzin anto yhua niquitoa oc Senpohualmani nictechtia noxhui pedro yno napohualmani oniquinomaquili moxelhuisque SeSenpohualmani ynic neltis yhua niquitoa oc Se mili San sebastiantzi senpohualmani nictechtia nopiltzin antonio franco yhua matlaccuahuitl nictechtia nochpoch ynes rrosa yhua oc no matlacCuahuitl nictechtia nochpoch franca Josepha ynic neltis yhua niquitoa oc Se mili Sentlapal quaxochtenco matlacCuahuitl nictechtia nochpoch franca Josepha ynic neltis —

name is Mauricia Josefa. Here I take as my sign the precious revered name of God the father, God his precious son, and God the Holy Spirit, only one very true deity God. — And I say that if I attain the precious revered death of my precious revered father God, the bells are to be rung for me, and [an offering] is to be given for Holy Jerusalem. And the fiscales are to designate [where] my grave will be at the great church. And I say that as the help of my spirit and soul I assign to myself a high mass so that the person in charge of the church[1] will bury me, so that it will be carried out. And I say that I am leaving this house and the lot of 15 by 10 quahuitl to my two sons Josef and Antonio; they are to be sharing this house. And another son of mine, Gabriel, is to settle [build himself a dwelling] here below; they are to give him a place to settle. And I say that to my son Antonio Francisco I assign 10 quahuitl that I bought [for him?], and that house. They are not to start [trouble] against him. And I say that here on the other side of the lot I assign 10 quahuitl to my son Josef, so that it will be carried out. And I say that here above, I assign 10 quahuitl of the lot to two sons of mine named Antonio and Matías; they are to divide it in half, so that it will be carried out. And I say that I give another cultivated field here at Quaxochtenco, of 20 quahuitl, to my precious mother Guadalupe. And I say that of another cultivated field on the plain, of 20 quahuitl, I assign 10 to my son Antonio, and I assign [the other] 10 quahuitl to my son Gabriel, so that it will be carried out. And I say that I assign another cultivated field at San Lucas, of 20 quahuitl, to my son Josef. And I say that likewise at San Lucas I assign to my son Gabriel 20 quahuitl. And I say that I assign another 20 quahuitl to my son Antonio. And I say that I assign another 20 quahuitl to my grandchild Pedro. They are to divide those 80 quahuitl that I have given them, 20 each, so that it will be carried out. And I say that I assign another cultivated field at San Sebastián, of 20 quahuitl, to my son Antonio Francisco. And I assign 10 quahuitl to my daughter Inés Rosa, and another 10 quahuitl I assign to my daughter Francisca Josefa, so that it will be carried out. And I say that I assign another cultivated field on one side of Quaxochtenco, of 10 quahuitl, to my daughter Francisca Josefa, so that it will be carried out. —

[1]This term, which I have not seen elsewhere to date, literally means the owner or master of the church.

yhua niquitoa oc Se mili Sa nica solar maCuilquahuitl yhua niquitoa Sa nican tlacpac matlaccuahuitl solar yno miltotonti san comonidar y quimoteuipanilhuisque santoti ynic neltis notlatol —

And I say that there is another cultivated field, right here at the lot, of 5 quahuitl, and I say that here above the lot is one of 10 quahuitl. And I say that with those little cultivated fields they are just in common to serve the saints, so that my statement will be carried out. —

yhua niquitoa y noahuasialeshua ca yehuatzin tomas meleres yehuatzin quimocuitlahuis notestamento —
fiscal mayor D fran^{co} eligio fiscal teniente nicolas fran^{co}
escribano antonio fran^{co}[2]

And I say that as to my executors, Tomás Meléndez is to take care of my testament. —
Fiscal mayor don Francisco Eligio. Fiscal teniente Nicolás Francisco.
Notary Antonio Francisco.[2]

de 1738 añoS[3]
Axca domigo matlatli yhua chiCuey tonatih mestli mayo omotzotec yni tlatoli yn itehcopa testameto D, fra^{co} pedro ypihua atonio fran^{co} omacoc opohuali metli yhua Joseph fran^{co} omaCoc chiCome tecpatli metli yhua bacas chiCuase yhua se se yota bues y santoti yyaxiCatzin opuhuali yhua nahui- [. . .] oquiseli Joseph fran^{co} yhua ynes rosan omaCoc opuhuali metli yhua ometi nobilos yhua miCaela Jeronima omaCoc sepuhuali metli yhua ome bacas yhua [. . .]tonio fran^{co} omaCoc chicome tepatli metli yhua santoti metli opuhuali yhua nahui metli y quimotequipanilhuisque yhua bacas ometi se tlaliqui[4] boyes yhua Grabiel fran^{co} omaCoc metli yei tecpatli yhua ome bacas yhua se yota bueyes yhua fran^{ca} Josepha omaCoc sepuhuali metli yhua se baquita yhua Jeronima maria omaCoc sepuhuali metli yhua ynasio felipe omaCoc sepuhuali metli yhua ometi Bacas yhua matias serano omaCoc metli sepuhuali yhua yeiti [torito] yhua se baCa

Year of 1738[3]
Today Sunday the 18th day of the month of May this statement was pronounced concerning the testament of don Francisco Pedro. Of his children, Antonio Francisco was given 40 magueyes, and Josef Francisco was given 140 magueyes, 6 cows, a yoke of oxen, and the saints that belong to him. Josef Francisco received 44 [magueyes], and Inés Rosa was given 40 magueyes and two steers [or young bulls], and Micaela Gerónima was given 20 magueyes and 2 cows, and Antonio Francisco was given 140 magueyes and saints, plus 44 magueyes with which he is to serve them, and 2 cows and [a yoke?][4] of oxen. And Gabriel Francisco was given 60 magueyes, 2 cows, and a yoke of oxen. And Francisca Josefa was given 20 magueyes and a small cow [calf?]. And Gerónima María was given 20 magueyes. And Ignacio Felipe was given 20 magueyes and 2 cows. And Matías Serrano was given 20 magueyes, three [little bulls?], and a cow.

1738
Bacas

atonio fran^{co}	111
Joseph fran^{co}	111111
Matias serano	111
MiCaela Jeronima	11 ?
ynes rosa	11
ynasio felipe	11
fran^{ca} Josepha	1
Grabiel fran^{co}	111

1738
Cows:

Antonio Francisco	3
Josef Francisco	6
Matías Serrano	3
Micaela Gerónima	2 ?
Inés Rosa	2
Ignacio Felipe	2
Francisca Josefa	1
Gabriel Francisco	3

[2]At the back a note in Spanish confirms that a mass was sung and paid for on May 13, 1737. As mentioned in the introduction to No. 37, the annotation is important because it does not use the don with the testator's name and because what appears to have been *casado con*, "married to," Mauricia Josefa is marked out and replaced with *viudo*, "widower." A word after Mauricia's name, which is also marked out, has the right shape to have been *difunta*, "deceased."

[3]This document is on separate paper and in a different hand than the testament. The year stands to one side as though perhaps done later, and though there can be no certainty, it would seem likely that the allocation actually took place on May 18, 1737, which would have been only ten days after the will.

[4]The letters "tlaliqui" are quite clear, but the analysis is not. In an analogous position elsewhere the word has been *yunta*, "yoke," and one must suspect that this term is equivalent. Or it might mean "for working with the land."

Athonio fran^{co}	111[5]	Antonio Francisco	3[5]

[5]Apparently the same Antonio Francisco as above, making him equal with his brother.

39. Don Juan de la Cruz, San Pablo Tepemaxalco, 1691

(AGN, Tierras 2533, exp. 5)[1]

THIS IS ONE of the richest and most complex testaments in the whole Toluca Valley corpus. Don Juan de la Cruz has served as the governor of the altepetl of San Pablo Tepemaxalco, and he is extremely wealthy by indigenous standards.[2] The property listed in his testament is impressive; it includes several houses and at least eight probably large pieces of land,[3] numerous magueyes, seventeen yokes of oxen, and eight riding horses. Almost as impressive is the number of relatives, especially children, who are mentioned. It is very unusual that don Juan begins by giving details about his family of origin: who his parents were, how they arranged his marriage, and the names of his brothers and sisters. Note that none of them bear the same second name, apart from don Juan and his mother,[4] and they seem from that to be a relatively modest family. His parents had property to divide among the children and were able to arrange their marriages, yet the inheritance don Juan received was not large. It strikes one that don Juan's father had a humble name, whereas his mother was among a minority of women who bore a second name such as de la Cruz. Here the usual picture, in which the husband might have a name of some distinction but the wife only two saints' names, is reversed.

What made the difference for don Juan was his marriage to doña Josefa Francisca, whose parents were don Pedro de la Cruz, a famous governor of Tepemaxalco and an immensely wealthy man, and his wife doña Ana Juana. One cannot but wonder if don Juan's mother had some kin connection with the governor, and that was instrumental in the marriage. Things took another fortunate turn for our don Juan when don Pedro's male children died early and he essentially made his son-in-law his principal heir, which seems to have led also to the latter's succession in the governorship.[5] Don Juan and doña Josefa inherited don Pedro's main residence with his patron saint San Pedro, a large corncrib, a large piece of land, and in all likelihood other assets left unmentioned; at some time after don Pedro's death, the pair were able to arrange the marriage of doña Josefa's sister and give her substantial property.

After the information on his family and in-laws, don Juan gets to the core of the will, describing the division of a remarkable amount of property among his children. Apart from Jacinto de la Cruz, the eldest, who inherits only part of a field, possibly because arrangements for him were made long ago,[6] there are Josefa, Juana, Pedro, and María (all of them with de la Cruz as a second name) whose inheritance is more or less the same in each case: nothing less than a house (all but María) with some saints, some land, a corncrib, some magueyes, two yokes of oxen and a horse with saddle. Note that all the children, not just the males, get oxen and horses, animals that are usually linked to manly tasks. Younger and older, male and female are all treated equally, possibly a trend among the very wealthy who were trying to maintain a whole lineage.

Vast resources on the part of don Juan, compared with those of most other testators here, are implied by his bequests; since it is unlikely that his property in its entirety would provide such a perfect fit with his children, it is evident that his assets are even

[1]The testament is accompanied by a contemporary Spanish translation.

[2]Don Juan himself says here that he served as governor for four years; if there is any doubt that he means of San Pablo Tepemaxalco, it is resolved by the Cruz family papers, where he is seen to have been governor of Tepemaxalco in 1682 and 1683 (Lockhart 1992, p. 137).

[3]In No. 41, the will of Polonia María, widow of Jacinto de la Cruz, don Juan's eldest, it turns out that a field mentioned here, shared by Jacinto and a sister, held a fanega of seed, thus was 120 quahuitl in at least one dimension. This represents an altogether different order of size than the usual fields mentioned in the corpus, which most often amount to 20 or perhaps 40 quahuitl, often less. If the fields given to other heirs were comparable, the total of don Juan's lands was huge by indigenous standards.

[4]In this context it is quite likely that don Juan originally had a humbler second name and assumed the de la Cruz only as he was being groomed as the principal heir of don Pedro de la Cruz.

[5]See Lockhart 1992, p. 136.

[6]Yet in his testament (No. 40), Jacinto seems to own no other land than this very piece.

larger. If we look closely at the wording of what appear to be bequests for the older children, we will see that most of the verbs of giving are in the past tense. The transfer of the property, or at least an allocation in principle, happened in the past, probably on the occasion of the marriage of each of the children, and is now only being formalized or confirmed, much as Elena de la Cruz in No. 10 goes back over past religious donations. In this so descriptive document of such a well developed situation, it is likely that we glimpse what was a more general practice, though rarely so explicitly expressed.

Yet don Juan was surely unusual in having the means to provide each of his children with an outstanding start in life, so that he in conjunction with his wife succeeded in arranging a marriage for all of them.[7] Equally unusual is the fact that all the children of both genders bear the same second name coming from their father, a sign of very high status.

María de la Cruz seems to be the youngest of this group of children, and while mentioning her inheritance don Juan gives us an interesting detail by saying that he alone arranged her marriage after his wife had died. The importance given to the wife in arranging the other marriages, and the fact that her absence in that role with this one is thought worth mentioning, are surely significant. Perhaps they point to a strong role of wives in arranging the marriage of children generally; or perhaps they are a reflection of the fact that don Juan's position owed so much to doña Josefa's status as daughter of don Pedro de la Cruz.

After doña Josefa Francisca's death, don Juan married again, to doña Melchora María. We are left uncertain whether or not doña Melchora was the mother of four more children who are listed afterward and all seem to be very young: Agustín, Bernabé, Nicolasa, and Ignacio. Again, they share the same second name de la Cruz. They could equally well have been the youngest children of the first wife, who died when she had the last one. In the testament of the eldest, Jacinto de la Cruz (No. 40), he speaks of his youngest brother, Ignacio de la Cruz, which might seem most natural if they were full brothers; but perhaps he would have said the same even if they were half-brothers. No house is left to the younger set; they are all to share the family house, where they are admonished to stay, probably because they are still living there and are too young to get married. Apart from the house, they receive the same lavish endowment that don Juan has left to the older children: some saints, a corncrib, some magueyes, two yokes of oxen, and a horse with saddle. Ignacio is the one who receives don Juan's saddle, perhaps a sign of affection for the youngest of all his children, or possibly it points to the special position of the *xocoyotl* in Nahua families, of which we occasionally get some glimpse.

In addition to the large bequests to his children, don Juan gives a row of small magueyes to an orphan named Juana. "Orphans" were sometimes illegitimate children of the testator, but we have no particular indication of that in this case. Don Juan also leaves something for his second wife, to be considered her own property: another yoke of oxen, some magueyes and a quite large amount of shelled maize.

Don Juan's wealth and high status cannot but be confirmed by the funeral arrangements. He asks to be shrouded in the habit and rope of San Francisco and to be buried in the church facing an image of San Antonio, patron of the cofradía to which he belongs. He leaves many offerings, often in amounts three or four times the norm, and asks for three masses with responsory prayers to be said for him, much more than is usually found in testaments from the Toluca Valley. Another curious detail comes in as an afterthought at the end, the fact that, probably when he was governor, he bought some chirimías (which could be used in processions and in church music); they seem to have remained his private property, but now he leaves them to the cantors (church musicians including instrumentalists) to worship the Virgin of Guadalupe. As an elder and a former governor who was in a sense in charge of everything in the altepetl, he calls the cantors his children (although it was also an old set expression).

The testament does not end in the usual fashion, since the executor and witnesses are missing, and the notary is not named, which is very strange, especially for an individual of such status; it would

[7]Other testators may have arranged their children's marriages without reporting it, but none were able to manage comparable bequests. So many saddled riding horses in such a context is a staggering feature, not to speak of two yokes of oxen for each child; it is also likely, on analogy with the field shared by Jacinto and Josefa de la Cruz, that their fields were much larger than average.

appear that either the will was not finished, the testator dying first, or some text has been lost (the second folio is on a half sheet). However, don Juan has left us a statement, rare in testaments, about his service as governor. He claims to have delivered all the tribute due and to owe nothing, being especially concerned that the altepetl should not trouble his children with further demands. The somewhat hostile attitude toward the claims of the public and the altepetl are typical of the de la Cruz dynasty and have many parallels in the de la Cruz family papers of the seventeenth and eighteenth centuries, to parts of which the testament apparently refers.[8]

The notary remains unknown, but it can be observed that he displays a beautiful and generally correct standard orthography, with many traditional traits, including the punctuation, that are in line with the early period of this testament compared to the rest of the corpus. Yet the words and phrases are hardly different from what is seen after 1700, and all the kinship terms are already fully the same as later. Some individual words vary somewhat from most later texts; thus here oxen are called by the earlier term *quaquahueque* (although with an unorthodox plural), whereas later in Calimaya/Tepemaxalco we see them called *bueyes*.

[*f. 1*]

Jesus maria y Jusep

v Ma moçenquiscayectenehualo yn itlasomahuistocatzin . yn dios . tetatzin[9] yhuā yn dios Ezpiritu santo = yn yeyntintzintzin perçonās – Auh ca sa huell içeltzin yn huel neli teotl dios santiçima trinidad – ma y mochihua Ame Jesus maria y Josep Etc^{ra} —

v Axcan sabado . a 18 de agosto . ypan xihuitl . de mil y çeysientos - y nobenta y un años - nehuatl - don Ju^{o} de lla C†us . nihuetztoc ninococotican yn tlen cocoli onechhualmihualilitzinno yn ttt^{o} dios . camo nicmati yn tle nōpan mochihuās . yhuā niquitohuā ca nichristiano yhuā nicneltoca . yn santisima trinidad . yn yeytintzintzin teotlacatzintzinti . yn dios tetatzin yy dios ypiltzin . yn dios Espirito santon Auh ca sa huell içeltzin y neli teotl dios - yhuā nicneltoca . yn quexquich y quimoneltoquitia yn tonatzin santa yglesia —

v ynic çentlamatli . niquitohuā . ca notatzin nicolas gaspar - yhuā nonatzin ma^{a} de la C†us - omomiquiliquē ca onechhuāpāuhque yhuā onechmonamictilitiaque - yhuā onechmomaquilitiaque - ompantli me . yhuā niquitohuā niqutohuā ca niquipie noyermanos y ermanas - yacapantli y noermano melchior . fra^{co} y fran^{ca} agellina ysabel martina Ju^{a}na[10] diego de santiago . y notlaçotatzin mochi oquimoxexelhuitia yn tlen inemac niquitohuā ca oninonamicti , yca nosihuahuatzin . donya Jusepa fra^{ca} y nomonta don pē^{o} de la Crus - nomonatzin donya ana Ju^{a}nā - yhuā yn tlalli . yhua calin yn

[*f. 1*]

Jesus, Mary, and Joseph.

v May the precious revered name of God the father, [God his son],[9] and God the Holy Spirit, three persons but really only a single really true deity God the Holy Trinity, be entirely praised. May it be done, amen. Jesus, Mary, and Joseph, etc. —

v Today, Saturday, the 18th of August of the year of 1691, I don Juan de la Cruz am lying sick of the illness that our lord God has sent upon me; I do not know what will happen to me. And I say that I am a Christian and I believe in the holy Trinity, the three divine persons God the father, God his son, and God the Holy Spirit, but really just one true divinity God, and I believe all that our mother the holy Church deems true. —

v First I say that my father Nicolás Gaspar and my mother María de la Cruz have died; they raised me and arranged my marriage before dying, and they left me two rows of magueyes. And I say that I have brothers and sisters; the eldest is my brother Melchor Francisco, [then] Francisca Angelina, Isabel Martina, and Juana,[10] and Diego de Santiago. My precious father left all of their inheritance divided among them. I say that I married with my wife doña Josefa Francisca; my father-in-law was don Pedro de la Cruz and my mother-in-law doña Ana Juana, and the land and houses that my late father-in-law and

---

[8]See Lockhart 1992, pp. 230–32.

[9]The member of the Trinity missing through inadvertence is supplied on the model of the same phrase lower in the text.

[10]The women's names may divide differently than they are given here.

oquimocahuilitia . y nomotatzin yhuā y nomonatzin . omoyetzinoticatca y huecalli . yhuā san^{to} san pedrō - yhuā ce huey cuescomatl . yhuā çe huey tlalli . onpan matica san^{ta} ma^{a} calbariotitla . oconna tlaco yhuā oc no tlaco ocona yhermanā Jusepa de la Crus - yhuā ome yotan quaquahueti . oniquimacac . yhuā çe caballo . ensillado - yhuā yepantli metl . nehuatl . oniquinamictin - don Ju^{o} de la crus yhua nehuatl - donya jusepa frān^{ca}[11] . amo quemania moxicosque yn nopilhua ca noyacapan Jasito de la Crus —

v yhua Jusepa de la Crus . nochpoch . onicmacac çe calin . yhuā santo san pē^{o} - yoā san diegotzin - yhuā tlaco mili cocahuiā Jasinto de la crus . yhuā ce Cuescomatl yhuā ome yota quaquahuetin yhuā çe caballo ensillado . yhua yepantlin metl . Amo aqui tlen quitos yn quemania . tehuati oticnamictiquē yn yn tochpoch - amo aqui moxicos yn quemania —

v yhuā oc no çe nochpoch - ytoca Ju^{a}na de la Crus - onicmacac çe calli . yhuān yehuātzin san^{to} san Ju^{a}ntzin nicnomaquilitiuh . yhuā çe tlalli - onpa matica tequimilteco - yhuā ome yōta quaquahuetin . yhuā çe caballo ensillado yhuā çe cuescomatl . yhuā yepantli metl - yhuā tehuātin oticnamictiquē - amo aqui tlen quitos . yn quemania —

v yhuā notelpoch[12] pē^{o} de la Crus . onicmacac çe calin . yhuā onicnomaquilli Jesus nasarenotzin . yhuā Jesus niyo quimotequipanilhuis . yhuā çe tlallin [*f. 1v*] yhua çe Cuescomatl - yhuā ome yota quaquahuetin . yhuā caballo . ensillado . yhuā yepantli metl . sanno tehuati otiquinamictique . yn topilhuā amo aqui tlen quitos —

v yhuan oc no çe nochpoch - ytoca maria de la Crus - : san noçel onicnamicti . ye omomiquili nosihuāhuātzin omoyetzticatca nicmacatiuh ce cuescoma[. . .] yhua yepantli metl . yhuā nicnomaquilia çe totlaçomahuiznatzin natibi[. . .] yhua çe caballo ensillado . yhuā ome yonta quaquahuetin . yhuā çe tlalin onpa matica otli tenaco - —

v yhuā nitlanahuatia y nopiltzin agustin de lla Crus - soltero . nicnomaquilia Santo San Josep - quimotequipanilhuis . de bultu . yhuā çe cuescomatl : yhua ome yonta quaquahuetin . yhuā ce cabalon enSillado . yhua çe milli . ompa matica Santa maria otli - yhuā . amo quisas . ca nican nicauhti[uh] ytic yni

mother-in-law left were the big house, with a holy San Pedro, and a large corncrib, and a large piece of land at Santa María next to the Calvario [or in Calvariotitlan]. [My wife doña Josefa Francisca] took half, and her sister Josefa de la Cruz took the other half. And I gave [the sister and her husband] two yokes of oxen, a horse with saddle, and three rows of magueyes. I don Juan de la Cruz and I doña Josefa Francisca[11] arranged their marriage. My children are not ever to show envy [try to get her share], [particularly?] my eldest Jacinto de la Cruz. —

v And I gave to Josefa de la Cruz, my daughter, a house and holy San Pedro, and San Diego, and half of a cultivated field that she shares with Jacinto de la Cruz, and a corncrib, two yokes of oxen, a horse with saddle, and three rows of magueyes. No one is ever to say anything. We arranged the marriage of this daughter of ours. No one is ever to show envy. —

v And to another daughter of mine, named Juana de la Cruz, I gave a house, and I am giving her holy San Juan and a piece of land at the edge of the tribute field, two yokes of oxen, a horse with saddle, a corncrib, and three rows of magueyes. And we arranged her marriage. No one is ever to say anything. —

v And to a son of mine[12] Pedro de la Cruz I gave a house, and I gave him Jesús Nazareno and Jesús Niño—he is to serve them—and a piece of land [*f. 1v*], a corncrib, two yokes of oxen, a horse with saddle, and three rows of magueyes. We likewise arranged the marriage of our children [Pedro and his wife]. No one is to say anything. —

v And I by myself arranged the marriage of another daughter of mine named María de la Cruz; my late wife had already died. I am giving her a corncrib and three rows of magueyes, and I give her an Our precious revered mother of Nativitas, a horse with saddle, two yokes of oxen, and a piece of land on the road to Tenango. —

v And I order that to my son Agustín de la Cruz, unmarried, I give a statue of holy San Josef—he is to serve it—, a corncrib, and two yokes of oxen, a horse with saddle, and a cultivated field on the road to Santa María. He is not to leave, for I am leaving him inside this house. And I am giving him three

[11]Here for a moment the deceased wife seems to speak in first person along with the husband.

[12]After "notelpoch" and before "pe^{o}," "do," for the title "don," is marked out. Probably the writer was thinking of don Pedro de la Cruz, the famous governor and grandfather of this heir, then realized his mistake.

calin . yhua yepantli metl - nicmacatiuh . amo tlen aquin quimilhuis yn quemania : —

v̲ yhua nitlanahuatia : oc ce nopiltzin . ytoca bernabel de lla C✝us - nicahuilia notlaçomahuistatzin San^to San āntonio quimotequipanilhuiz . yhua çe Cuesc[. . .]matl . yhua yepantli metl : yhuan çe tlalli - onpa matica . coyohuaca texocotitla - yhua ome yota quaquaheti . yhuā çe caballo - yhuā se silā momacas . yhuā amo quisas . nica yesque ytic yni nochan . amo aqui tl[. . .] quimilhuis —

v̲ yhua nitlanahuatiā . nochpochto - ytoca nicolasa de la C✝us . nicnocahuilia san brernardo quimotequipanilhuis . yhua çe Cuescomatl . momacas - yhuā yepantli metl . yhuā momacas ome yota quaquahuetin momacas - yhuā momacas çe caballo yhuā çe silli : yhuā amo quisas . nica yes - quimotequipanilhuis santoti - amo Aqui tle quimilhuis yn quemania . yhuā çe tlalli onpa matica tepetonco - nicmacatiuh nicolasa de la C✝us - —

v̲ yhuā nitlanahuatia . oc ce noxocyōuh ytoca ynasio de la C✝us . nicnomaquillitiuh . S^to San inasio : yhuā yehuatzin San^ta getrudes - yhua çe Cuescomatl yhua momacas yepantli metl . yhuā yepantli metl - yhuā ome yo[. . .]ta quaquahuetin . yhuā çe tlali . onpan matica huey . atla[13] : yhua çe caballo . yhua y nosilla . ca yehuatl . nicmacatiuh . conanas . amo aquiquixtilis . yn queman[. . .] —

v̲ yhuā y nosihuahuatzin ytoca . donya melchiora maria - nitlanahuatia quima[. . .]que çe yota quaquahueti : yhuā onpantli metl . onpa tlacpac quitititihui . yh[. . .] quimacasque çenpohualli fanega tlaolli . yhua nitlanahuatia . Amo aqui tlen quilhuis . yn quemani —

v̲ yhuā nitlanahuātia y noçepultura . onpa motlapos . yxpantzinco . y notlaçomahuistatz[. . .] Santo San antoniotzin : ca yehuatzintzin quimomachiltitzinohuā : yn ermanōs . ca ytech nipohui Santo Confrandia - yhuā ca nicnomaquilitiuh . macuili metl - Santo San a[. . .]toniotzin - —

v̲ yhuā y noquimiliuhca yes . Santo San fran^co ytlaquetzin nicnohuiquilis . yhuā ynic n[. . .]nocuitlalpitias . San fran^co tzin ycordontzin . — [*f.* 2]

Yhuā nitlanahuatia yey misa yhua yey responsos nopan mitos . ypalehuiloca yes y nani . matzin . - yhuā mocohuas nahui libra candela —

rows of magueyes. No one is ever to say anything to them. —

v̲ And I order that to another son of mine, named Bernabé de la Cruz, I leave my precious revered father holy San Antonio—he is to serve him—, a corncrib, three rows of maguey, a piece of land in Coyohuacan, next to a tejocote tree [or in Texocotitlan], two yokes of oxen and a horse, and he is to be given a saddle. He is not to leave; they are to be here inside this my home. No one is to say anything to them. —

v̲ And I order that to my little daughter named Nicolasa de la Cruz I leave San Bernardo—she is to serve him— and she is to be given a corncrib, and she is to be given three rows of magueyes, and she is to be given two yokes of oxen, and she is to be given a horse and a saddle. And she is not to leave; she is to be here and serve the saints. No one is ever to say anything to them. And I am giving a piece of land at Tepetonco to Nicolasa de la Cruz. —

v̲ And I order that to another [child], my youngest, named Ignacio de la Cruz, I am giving holy San Ignacio, and Santa Gertrudis, and a corncrib, and he is to be given three rows of magueyes, two yokes of oxen, a piece of land at the large body of water,[13] a horse, and my saddle. That is what I am giving him; he is to take it. No one is ever to take it from him. —

v̲ And to my wife named doña Melchora María I order that they are to give a yoke of oxen, two rows of magueyes up above—they are to go show them to her—and they are to give her 20 fanegas of shelled maize, and I order that no one is ever to say anything to her. —

v̲ And I order that my grave is to be opened facing my precious revered father holy San Antonio; the brothers [of the cofradía] are responsible for it, for I belong to the holy cofradía [of San Antonio], and I am giving five magueyes to holy San Antonio. —

v̲ And my shroud is to be that I will wear the habit of holy San Francisco, and I will be girt with San Francisco's rope. — [*f.* 2]

And I order that three masses and three responsory prayers are to be said for me; they will be the help of my soul. And four pounds of candles are to be bought. —

[13] The large body of water might be a lake or a river or stream; the Spanish translation has "en el rio grande," "in the big river."

v̲ yhua nitlanahuatia nictemacatiuh nahui tomi gerusalletzin —
v̲ yhua yehuatzin Santisimo sacrameto nicnomaquilitiuh çe pēsº —
yhua catores niquinmacatiuh - çe pesº —
v̲ yhuā nitlanahuatia yn icnotlacatl . ytoca Juªna nicmacatiuh chicuey metl tepitoto . quitzinehuas . quititisque . —
v̲ yhuan nican teyxpan niquitohua . nahui xihuitl . oninochiuh nigobernador qualli onictemilti tlacallaquilli amo tle nictehuiquilia : amo aqui tlen quimilhuis y nopilhua . yn quemania ca onca Ca : mochi llibrō y canpa mōmomachiontitiuh . yn tlen gasto - opopoliuh amo quemania . quitosque yn altepehuaque - aço ytla niquihuiquilia —
v̲ yhuā onicōuh . chirimeas - ca niquicahuilitīuh nopilhua cantores - yquimotequipanilhuitzinnosque notlaçomahuisnatzin huadallope

v̲ And I order that I am giving 4 reales for Jerusalem. —
v̲ And to [the cofradía of] the Santísimo Sacramento I am giving a peso. —
And to the cantors I am giving a peso. —
v̲ And I order that to the orphan named Juana I am giving eight small magueyes; she is to tear them out; they are to be pointed out to her. —
v̲ And here in public I say that I spent four years as governor; I did well in completing the quota of tribute collected; I owe nothing. No one is ever to say anything to my children, for all the books are there in which is recorded what was spent as expenses. The citizens [or authorities] of the altepetl are never to say that I owe them anything. —
v̲ And I bought some chirimías. I am giving them to my children the cantors; with them they are to serve my precious revered mother Guadalupe.

40. Jacinto de la Cruz, San Pablo Tepemaxalco, Pasiontitlan, 1693

(AGN, Tierras 1501, exp. 3)

THE TESTATOR HERE is the eldest son of the former governor don Juan de la Cruz, who made his will in 1691 (No. 39, just above). Although the connection is not at first evident through his property, due to the fact that Jacinto got little in don Juan's testament, it is made clear through the mention of his youngest sibling Ignacio de la Cruz, also listed as the youngest of the children in No. 39, and through the fact that Jacinto has lent money and clothing to his uncle Diego de Santiago, who appears in No. 39 as the brother of don Juan.

Jacinto de la Cruz is married to Apolonia María, whose testament will follow (No. 41), and they seem not to have any children, or at least any surviving, since everything goes to the wife and a brother. To his wife Jacinto leaves a house and a piece of land on the road to Santa María (de la Asunción, a tlaxilacalli already associated with the family, as we will see). The land, the same piece that don Juan left him in his testament, is to be rented out, nominally to serve San Pedro. Jacinto has already entered into an arrangement of this type with a Spaniard, don Juan de Navarrete, who still owes him some money on the transaction. It seems that Jacinto possesses no other land. He does, however, own two houses, and he leaves the house of his own residence to his youngest brother Ignacio de la Cruz to serve San Pedro, implying that he is to have it because he is the youngest child, who once again seems to enjoy a privileged position.

It is evident that there is a special devotion here to San Pedro, which is a characteristic of the whole family, since it is also stressed in don Juan's testament; it comes doubtless from the fact that don Juan's father-in-law, a famous governor of Tepemaxalco and in effect founder of the line, was don Pedro de la Cruz, who as we see in No. 39 left a large house with a prominent San Pedro in the hands of his daughter and son-in-law.

Our first impression is that Jacinto de la Cruz, though the eldest son, has come far down in status and wealth compared to his father; his total property, at least what is included in the testament, consists of two houses and a piece of land, while even his wife (No. 41), after an interval of some years, seems to possess more. His situation may have been better than appears directly in the will, however. We see that he has been in a position to help out an uncle; we see that though he seems to have only one piece of land, it is large enough or productive enough, or both, that a high-ranking Spaniard is interested in renting it.

Much may be hiding, both here and in don Juan's will, behind the Nahuatl term *calli*, which can be either a whole complex or a single small building within that complex. Don Juan seems to have inherited from his father-in-law a large house (complex) in which a prominent feature was an image of San Pedro; at his death don Juan still lived there and expected his smaller children and second wife to continue to do so. He did not say, however, to whom the large house was to go definitively, and possibly it went after all to his eldest Jacinto, who now lives in it and leaves it with its San Pedro to a brother rather than to his wife in order to keep it within the direct line. Such a sequence of events cannot be considered proved, but it seems possible. Jacinto may have failed to reach something approaching the level of don Juan primarily because he died only two years after him, before time and accumulation could lead him too to greater wealth and the governorship. We know that members of the Cruz dynasty continued as governors in Tepemaxalco all through the following century and beyond.[1]

Jacinto's funeral arrangements reflect high status, since in addition to a mass with responsory prayer he requests burial inside the church, facing an image of Santa María de la Asunción. Here too we see a devotion going back to don Pedro de la Cruz, who was closely associated with both the tlaxilacalli of Santa María de la Asunción and its saint.[2] Moreover, the opening formula is rich in names of saints who are asked to intercede for him, which is not very common yet at this time. He also leaves a standard offering to Jerusalem, although his offerings fall far short of the extravagance of his father.

No executor is appointed, and of the three witnesses only one has the title "don," although two hold public offices. Again, this does not seem to be in line with the predominant status of the family he comes from. The truncation of his father's will unfortunately does not allow us to carry out any comparison.

The notary Andrés de Santiago has a generally standard, conservative style and orthography, probably also due to the early period compared to the rest of the corpus. At times we find an unusual *h* before an initial *i*, as in "hitlaçopiltzin," for "his precious son."[3]

[*f. 15*]
Jesus m^{a}
v Ma çenquiscayectenehualo yn itlaçomahuistocatzin yn dios tetatzin yn dios hitlaçopiltzin yn dios Espirito santo – Ma hi mochihua Ame Jesus maria y Jusep —
Axca sabado: a primero de nobiembre ypann i xihuitl de 1693 Años nican nictlallia nodestamēto nehuatl notoca Jasinto de lla cruz noçihuauh ytoca Ampolonia maria nican nochan san pablo tepemaxalco: notlaxillacalpan: paxiotitlan yn maçihui mococohuā yn notlalo noçoquiyo: Auh y noçialis y notlalnamiquilis camo que ca san pactica: Auh huel achtopa niquitohua yntla onechmolnamiquillitzino yn notlaçomahuistatzin dios yntla oninomiquilli ca hiçenmactzinco nicnocahuillia: y noyolliatzin yn nanimantzin: no nicnotlatlauhtillitzinnohua yn çihuapilli santa maria y mochipa huel neli ychpotzintli yoā yn san pedro yn san pablo: yn san mig[. . .]l arcangel yn san ju^{o} bhtt^{a} yn san franc^{co} yhuā yn ye mochintintzintzin yn santosme yn samtasme yn ilhuicac motemiltiticate: ynic nopanpa: motlatlauhtil-

[*f. 15*]
Jesus, Mary.
v May the precious revered name of God the father, God his precious son, and God the Holy Spirit be entirely praised. May it be done, amen. Jesus, Mary, and Joseph. —
Today Saturday the 1st of November in the year of 1693, here I named Jacinto de la Cruz issue my testament; my wife is named Apolonia María, and my home is here in San Pablo Tepemaxalco, in my tlaxilacalli of Pasiontitlan. Although my earthly body is sick, there is nothing wrong with my will and memory, but they are sound. First of all I say that when my precious revered father God has remembered me and I have died, I leave my spirit and soul entirely in his hands. I also implore the lady Santa María, forever very true virgin, and San Pedro, San Pablo, San Miguel Arcángel, San Juan Bautista, San Francisco, and all the male and female saints who fill heaven to pray for me before our lord God. May it be done, amen. —

[1] Lockhart 1992, pp. 136–37.
[2] Ibid., pp. 232–33.
[3] In Nahuatl any word seeming to start with a vowel derives from one starting with a consonant, which in the older language was still represented in speech by a glottal stop. The letter *h* was the main way to represent the glottal stop, and some writers of older Nahuatl sporadically used it to show the glottal stop word-initially.

litzinosque: yxpantzinco yn tt^{o} dios ma y mochihua
- Ame -

v ynic çentlamatli nitlanahuatia: yntla: onechmocnellillitzinno yn tt^{o} dioz yntla ninomiquilli çe misan yhuã çe Respoços nopan mitos: ypalehuiloca yes y nanimatzin yhuã: nictemacatiuh: çe tomitzin huetzintli Jerusalentzin —

v First I order that when our lord God has befriended me and I have died, a mass with a responsory prayer is to be said for me as the help of my soul, and I am giving a real as an offering for Jerusalem. —

v yhuã nitlanahuatia y noçepultura: ompa motlapos: teopancalintic yxpantzinco açosiontzin —

v And I order that my grave is to be opened inside the church building facing [Santa María de la] Asunción. —

v ynic ontlamantli nitlanahuatia: ynin calli: nicmacatiuh: nohermanillo: ytoca ynasio de la crus xocoyotl: yehuatl iquimotequpanilhuitzinnos santo san pe^{o}: yn ihua y cali yehuatl: ynemac yes: xocoyotl: amo aquin tlen quilhuis yn quemania

v Second I order that I am giving this house to my little brother named Ignacio de la Cruz, the youngest. With it he is to serve holy San Pedro, and the house is to be the inheritance of the youngest. No one is ever to say anything to him.

v ynic yetlamantli: nitlanahuatia yn oc çe: calli yc tlatzintla ycac nicmacatiuh noçihuauh: ytoca Anpollonia maria: yhuan centetl tlallin ompa mantica santa ma^{a}tzin: ontenco: sanno yehuatl nicmacatiuh: noçihuauh: Amo aquin quiquixtilliz yn quemania: quitetlaneuhtitiaz: oncã quistias yni quimotequipanilhuisque santo san pe^{o}: – yhuan niquitohua ynon tlalli onictlaneuhti S^{ro} don Ju^{o} nabarete ynin xihuitl o quitocas yhuan o çe xihuitl quicahuati: yhuan oc nechhuiquili oc chiquaçentomi amo: quimani motencuepas —

v Third I order that I am giving another house, below, to my wife named Apolonia María, and likewise I am giving my wife a piece of land at the side of the Santa María road. No one is ever to take it away from her. She is to go along renting it out, and from that is to come the means with which they will serve holy San Pedro. – And I say that I rented that land to señor don Juan de Navarrete. He is still to sow it this year, and the next year he is to relinquish it. He still owes me 6 reales; he is not ever to go back on his word. —

yhuan nican nimachiotia: notiyo: ytoca diego de Santiago: nechhuiquillia ome pẽs^{o} yhua nahui tomi quixtlahuaz: amo montenCuepas yn quemania yhua çe capote ye yçoltic: onictlaneuhti quixtlahuaz[4] amo motencuepas —

And here I record that my uncle named Diego de Santiago owes me 2 pesos and 4 reales; he is to pay it back, he is not ever to go back on his word. And I lent him a worn cloak; he is to pay for it;[4] he is not to go back on his word. —

Ca san ixquich nictzaqua yni nococoxcatlatol: yxpantzinco: yn tt^{o} dios: yhuan yn imixpan nodestigos yn quineltillizque yni nodestameto yxpatzinco dios
Don pasqual medosan fiscal mañor Nicolas fran^{co} manordom^{o} destigo diego Ramos destigo

That is all. I conclude this my sick person's statement before our lord God and before my witnesses, who will verify this my testament before God.
Don Pascual de Mendoza, fiscal mayor. Nicolás Francisco, mayordomo [of a cofradía], witness. Diego Ramos, witness.

Nehuatl nitlacuilohua ytecopa cocoxqui Andres de santhigo Es^{no} sãta yglesia

I am doing the writing at the command of the sick person. Andrés de Santiago, notary of the holy church.

[4]The cloak is of the type called a *capote*; the verb, if interpreted strictly and in a somewhat old-fashioned way, could mean to give it back rather than to pay for it.

41. Polonia María, San Pablo Tepemaxalco, Pasiontitlan,[1] 1710

(AGN, Tierras 1501, exp. 3)

THE TESTATOR HERE is the widow of Jacinto de la Cruz (No. 40); the Polonia used as her first name is a colloquial version of the Apolonia seen in Jacinto's testament. Dying seventeen years after him, she confirms the fact that the couple had no surviving children, since she leaves most of her property to a

[1]Polonia María's affiliation is deduced from that of her husband, since she still lives where he did.

nephew, Francisco Nicolás. Basically, he gets a house with its lot, a saint, and a fair-sized piece of land, the same things that Polonia inherited from Jacinto de la Cruz. Polonia says that the nephew must share the land with her sister-in-law Josefa de la Cruz, but that is not a new division, for the same land was already divided in half between Jacinto and Josefa in the testament of don Juan de la Cruz in 1691 (No. 39). Polonia María also leaves some saints and a few magueyes to her sister, Bernardina de la Cruz.

Polonia seems to be more wealthy than her husband was; she has preserved all the property that he had left to her, but in addition she has some magueyes, quite a few saints, and possibly some more land, since the lot is not openly mentioned in Jacinto's will. She might have acquired this property after her husband's death, or she might have had some personal possessions coming from her family of origin. It is also conceivable that these assets too come from her husband and simply were taken for granted in his will.

But additional factors point to Polonia's greater wealth. Her funeral arrangements are generally consonant with relatively high status. Some of her dispositions, such as the shroud of the Virgin of Carmen with the rope of San Francisco, are comparable to her husband's, and she requests burial in the church close to him. The introductory formula follows the lines of that of Jacinto, although fewer saints are mentioned. But most importantly, she asks for twice the number of masses he did, and makes more offerings.

Finally, in contrast to Jacinto, Polonia appoints two executors, both of them dons, and has a longer list of witnesses, who seem to be prominent individuals; in fact all but one hold the title don and a public office. A don Juan Antonio, fiscal mayor of the church, acts as notary; in all likelihood he had been an official notary at an earlier time, for the move from notary to fiscal was one of the common patterns in official careers. His style is quite standard, but it also shows some of the characteristics of Tolucan Nahuatl.

[*f. 4*]

Jesus maria y Joseph

Ma çenquisCayectenehualo yn itlaçomahuistoCatzi Dios tetatzin yhuā Dios ytlaçopiltzin yhuā Dios espiritu S^{to} Ma y mochihuā amen Jesus m^{a} y Josehh —

v Axcan domingo a 21 de septiembre de 1710 años nictlalia nomemoria testam^{to} nehual notoca Polonia maria Viuda niCa nichani ypā yaltepetzin S^{to} san pablo tepemaxalCo ahuc yntla Dios nehmoquixtililis y nonemilis nimomiquilis Ca sān imactzinco nicmoCahuililia noyoliantzin nanimantzin notlaçotatzin Dios yhua no nicmotlatlactilitzinoa çihuapili santa Maria yhua moxtitzitzi S Miguel arCangel yhua S Juan Baptista ye moxtitzitzi S.^{tos} yhua Santas yn ilhuicac motemiltiticate nopa motlatoltzinosq̄ yxpantzinco yn tt^{o} Dios —

v huel ahtopā nitlanahuatia y nosepoltura motlapos teopanCalitic yn Cani toctica nonamictzin moesticatca

v ynic ontlamantli nitlanahuatia noquimilicCa yes yn itlaquentzi notlaçomahuisnantzin del Carme yhuan i noCuitlalpitias yn iCordontzin notlaçomahuistatzin S^{to} san fran^{co} —

v ynic yentlamantli nitlanahuatia ome misa yhua ome responço nopa mitos ypalehuiloCa yes noyo-

[*f. 4*]

Jesus, Mary, and Joseph.

May the precious revered name of God the father, God his precious son, and God the Holy Spirit be entirely praised. May it be done, amen. Jesus, Mary, and Joseph.—

v Today, Sunday the 21st of September of the year 1710, I named Polonia María, widow, issue my memorandum of testament; I am a citizen here in the altepetl of holy San Pablo, Tepemaxalco. And if God should take my life from me and I should die, I leave my spirit and soul in the hands of my precious father God, and I also implore the lady Santa María and San Miguel Arcángel and San Juan Bautista and all the male and female saints who fill heaven to speak for me before our lord God. —

v First of all I order that my grave is to be opened inside the church building where my late husband lies buried.

v Second I order that my shroud is to be the habit of my precious revered mother del Carmen, and I am to be girt with the rope of my precious revered father holy San Francisco. —

v Third I order that two masses and two responsory prayers are to be said for me to be the help of my

liantzin nanimatzin yhua nichuenchihuan çe tomi santo Jerusalen —

v no niCa nicmachiotia nicnomaquilitia ome mel notlaçomahuistatzin Jesus de Naçareno yhua oc ome mel nicnomaquiliti notlaçomahuistatzin santo san antonio —

v ynic nahuctlamantli nitlanahuatia yni nocha yCa mochi solar quenami onCa yc tlatzintla Ca yehual nicCahuilia [*f. 4v*] nosobrino fran^{co} Nicolas yhuā Ca nicCahuiliti yn Santo San pedro yhuā St^{o} san diego ca yc nechilnamiquis mostla huictla neltis notlatol mochihuas —

v ynic macuiltlamantli nitlanahuatia çe tlali manti-Ca Santa maria asupCion otli Canpa panohua tenango otli yteh calacqui se anega tlaoli tuctli tlaco nicCahuilia sano yehual noçobrino fran^{co} Nicolas canpa calaqui se media tlaoli tuctli yhuā oc tlaco yaxca nocunyada Josepha de la crus Concahuitiyes amo aqui tle quilhuitinemis quemania —

v yhuā nitlanahuati S^{to} san antonio yhuā santa efigenia Ca yehual niccahuiliti nohermanatzin ytoCa Bernandina de la cruz amo aqui tle quilhuitinemis quemania —

v ynic chiquaçentlamantli nitlanahuatia matlactli mel çano yehual nicCahuilia nohermana bernandina yc nechilnamiquis mostla huictla —

Ca san ixquih nictzonquixtia y nomemoria testamento yn imixpan notestigos yhuā noalbaseas yehuāti tlaneltilisq̄ yxpantzinCo yn tt^{o} Dios nehual notoCa polonia maria Viuda —

D^{n} Juan de la cruz albasea Don Juan nicolas albasea

D^{n} ag^{tin} de S.tiago testigo D^{n} Marcos de S Juan fiscal san fran^{co}[2] testigo D^{n} bisente melchor themaxti testigo D^{n} Marcos de S.tiago Maestro testigo Joseph de la crus teopa topile testigo

D^{n} Juan Antoni^{o} fiscal mayor de la sta yglecia Nehual onitlaCuilo ytecopam cocoxqui

spirit and soul, and I make an offering of one real to Holy Jerusalem. —

v Also here I record that I am giving two magueyes to my precious revered father Jesús Nazareno, and I am giving two more magueyes to my precious revered father holy San Antonio. —

v Fourth I order that I leave this home of mine including the lot, as it is, down below [*f. 4v*], to my nephew Francisco Nicolás, and I am leaving him holy San Pedro and holy San Diego, for with it he will remember me in the future. My statement is to be realized and carried out. —

v Fifth I order that of a piece of land on the Santa María de la Asunción road where the Tenango road crosses, where a fanega of maize seed fits, likewise to my nephew Francisco Nicolás I leave half, where half a fanega of maize seed fits, and the other half is the property of my sister-in-law Josefa de la Cruz; they are to share it. No one is ever to go about saying anything to [Francisco Nicolás].—

v And I order that I am leaving holy San Antonio and Santa Efigenia to my sister named Bernardina de la Cruz. No one is ever to go about saying anything to her. —

v Sixth I order that I am leaving 10 magueyes likewise to my sister Bernardina, with which she is to remember me in the future. —

That is all. I named Polonia María, widow, conclude my memorandum of testament in the presence of my witnesses and my executors; they will verify things before our lord God. —

Don Juan de la Cruz, executor. Don Juan Nicolás, executor.

Don Agustín de Santiago, witness. Don Marcos de San Juan, fiscal for San Francisco,[2] witness. Don Vicente Melchor, temachti, witness. Don Marcos de Santiago, maestro, witness. Josef de la Cruz, church topile, witness.

I, don Juan Antonio, fiscal mayor of the holy church, did the writing at the order of the sick person.

[2]This is the Tepemaxalco tlaxilacalli San Francisco Pochtlan; see Lockhart 1992, pp. 543–44, nn. 103, 109.

42. María Salomé, San Pablo Tepemaxalco, Pasiontitlan, 1654

(AGN, Tierras 2300, exp. 18)[1]

ONE OF THE EARLIEST testaments in the present volume, this document was written half a century before the bulk of the Toluca Valley corpus begins, and some of its many interesting traits were not to be retained in later times. It is included here among the wills of the tlaxilacalli Pasiontitlan in Tepema-

[1]The testament is accompanied by a contemporary Spanish translation.

xalco, for although the notary writes San Pedro Tepemaxalco, we can be pretty sure that he meant San Pablo. In the Calimaya/Tepemaxalco jurisdiction, San Pedro was the patron saint of Calimaya and San Pablo of Tepemaxalco, but here the connection with the latter is evident through the names of prominent witnesses.[2] It appears that there must have been a little confusion with the saint's name; maybe it even represents evidence that the distinction between the two conjoined altepetl was beginning to break down by this time.

María Salomé is in all probability a widow, since the only reference to her husband appears at the end of the testament, in a sort of afterthought and merely in an effort to cement her children's rights to some distant landed property. She divides her possessions mainly among her four children, who all seem to be grown up and possibly already married.

The two sons who play the part of the principal heirs, Josef and Francisco, bear a second name well known in Tepemaxalco, de la Cruz. They are to share two pieces of land, one with magueyes and the other a large piece apparently devoted to maize agriculture. They are also to share some more magueyes that María had bought or cultivated on lots belonging to five different individuals, among them her father, don Pedro Jacobo, and a possible relative who shares the same second name, Sebastián Jacobo. Some furniture and tools also appear, whether because of the fact that such things were mentioned more frequently in wills of earlier times, or because these items are particularly valuable. The sons get a chest each, while Josef receives a lot with magueyes, a plow, and a chisel for himself alone; most likely he is the eldest, followed by Francisco, whose first name is the second name of his father.

Some of the names here are difficult to judge; in post-1700 terms, Salomé and Jacobo are rare second names and might imply distinction, but both had been common in the sixteenth century and possibly still were at the time this will was issued. At least we can be sure that the title don borne by María's father marks high status.

At the end of the testament, María seems to remember that there is more property she wishes to leave to the two sons, in Tenango del Valle at the southern end of the Toluca Valley. The note is a bit confused because this part of the original is badly deteriorated and many words are partly illegible; however, it seems that this property was accumulated by her husband and she is now passing it on to the two sons, or whichever one of them should survive. The outstanding feature is that the holdings are outside the Calimaya/Tepemaxalco area, located in another altepetl altogether and at some distance. Either María's husband Juan Francisco, whose name is not distinguished, was originally from there, or he had important interests there.

The testator also has another son, Gabriel de Santiago, who gets nothing more than a wooden corncrib and is reminded to pay back a quite substantial debt, and a daughter, Luisa María, who receives another wooden corncrib and a metate, as well as some land to share. These children would seem either to be in disfavor or already to have received much of their inheritance. A grandchild of the testator, Leonor, is luckier in the will, since she gets two houses and a piece of land planted in magueyes to be shared with Luisa María, probably because she is still too young to take care of everything by herself. Leonor must be Luisa's daughter, and it is significant here that some important property is passed on to the second generation of heirs through females, with no reference at all to Luisa's husband, who could easily have been entrusted with taking care of the houses and land. At the same time, note that María Salomé follows the same policy as many male testators in favoring males in the central part of the inheritance.

Due to the frequent mention of magueyes and the number of plants involved, at least 32 plus various rows (the standard row included eight plants), we have every reason to assume that the testator's principal activity was the cultivation of the plant and the production of beverages. It is very interesting to notice that María seems to have bought some of the magueyes from other people who still own the land, so that she and her heirs would exploit the plants independently of the land itself. Yet she also had more land of her own than most women who specialized in maguey production.

Thus putting together magueyes, lands and

[2]The first three witnesses are prominent figures of San Pablo Tepemaxalco around the time the will was issued. Don Matías de San Francisco was to be governor there in 1656; don Baltasar de los Reyes, present governor, had been governor before in 1647; don Diego de la Cruz, past alcalde, was to be governor in 1655 (Lockhart 1992, p. 137; see also pp. 128–29). Note that both Calimaya and Tepemaxalco seem to have had a tlaxilacalli Pasiontitlan.

houses, María appears to be a relatively wealthy woman, and she probably was even more so earlier, since at the end of the testament she reports that property of hers was lost when thieves entered her home. All was listed in a document, but unfortunately it is not attached to the testament, so we will never know the nature of what was stolen, but clearly she considered it valuable.

The testator's high status is also evident through the complete and elaborate opening formula and the funeral arrangements. She requests the shroud and rope of San Francisco, burial inside the church, and as many as three high masses with at least two responsory prayers. But what is even more striking is the fact that she names a high-ranking woman as her executor, doña María de Guzmán, thereby indirectly showing her own prominent status. The appointment of women as executors is extremely rare in the Toluca Valley corpus, but it may have been a more common practice earlier in time, during the seventeenth century.

Along the same lines, María has four women in the list of her witnesses, one being another doña, which is practically not seen anywhere else in the Toluca Valley testaments. Female witnesses were present in early testaments such as those of Culhuacan (sixteenth century), but did not correspond to Spanish custom, and the Toluca corpus in general shows that by the eighteenth century indigenous communities of the valley, like those elsewhere, had adopted the Spanish practice. María Salomé might be seen as an exception, but it is more likely that in the seventeenth century the older way still survived in the Toluca region. As for the other witnesses, the three dons who head the list all at some time held the governorship of Tepemaxalco and are powerful evidence of María Salomé's connections.[3]

The notary is a don Juan de la Cruz.[4] His style is much more conservative and standard than that of most later notaries, and his formulas are usually longer and more complete; the whole long preamble (including its lack of Jesus, Mary, and Joseph as a heading) could virtually have been written in the sixteenth century, except for its tendency to use *s* instead of final *z*. We see here the reverential *mahuiz-*, "revered," instead of the doubled *tlaçomahuiz-*, "precious revered" that is so common later. Late in the document the testator addresses the witnesses directly, using the second person plural, also a very archaic trait. It is striking, too, that a person so well endowed mentions no saints; since they are lacking in the preamble as well, the absence may be due to an older style. Nevertheless, the text already contains the loan particle *hasta*, here meaning "as far as."

[*f. 15*]
yca yn imahuistoCatzin yn dios tetatzin yhuan yn dios tepiltzin yhuan yn dios espiritu santo Ma y mochihua nican nicpehualtia yn notestamento nehuatl notoCa ma[a] salomen nican nochan San pedro tepemaxalco notlaxilaCalpan paxioti[. . .] ma quimatican yn yxquichtin quitazque ynin amatl Auh maçihuin mococohua yn notlalnaCayo yec y noyolo y noçialis y notlalnamiquilis ỹ notlacaquia aquin ca san pactica Auh nicchixtiCa yn miquistli yn [. . .]yac huel yxpanpa yehuis yn huel quitlalcahuia yniC niCtlalia ỹ notestamento yc çan tla[. . .]ca yn çan tlatzonco notlanequilis ỹ ye mochipa mopi[. . .] ynic ayac quitlacoz ca yehuatl i yn ys Catqu[. . .] nic-

[*f. 15*]
In the revered name of God the father, God the son, and God the Holy Spirit, may it be done. Here I named María Salomé begin my testament; my home is here in San Pedro Tepemaxalco, and my tlaxilacalli is in Pasiontitlan; may all who see this document know it. Although my earthly body is ill, yet there is nothing wrong with my heart, will, memory, and understanding, but they are sound. I am awaiting death, which no one can flee from or avoid, so that I issue my testament, my last and final will, that is always to be observed, so that no one will violate it. Here it is, as follows; I begin.

---

[3]A witness is listed as fiscal, but he lacks the don. It is hard to know whether this person is fiscal in a minor church, or whether at this time the important fiscal for the altepetl at the main church does not yet ordinarily bear the title.

[4]It would be tempting to think that this person is the same who would later become governor of San Pablo Tepemaxalco and who left us his testament in 1691 (No. 39). But not only is the stretch of years very considerable and the name in its way common, it is not likely that the governor don Juan de la Cruz would have borne the don until he attained high office; he was not governor to our knowledge until the 1680s, and even the founder of the de la Cruz governors was plain Pedro de la Cruz until 1657 (Lockhart 1992, p. 136). In any case, it is quite unusual for a notary to bear the don even after 1700, and even less so earlier. Perhaps this don Juan has already held some higher office.

pehualtia huel achto yehuatl y[. . .] naniman ymactzinCo noContlalia yn tt.^{o} dios Ca o[. . .]imochihuili yhuan ninotlatlauhtilia yn ne[. . .]motlaoColilis nechmopopolhuililis ȳ notlatla[. . .] nechmohuiquilis yn ichantzinCo yn ilhuiCatl [. . .] ȳn iquac naniman quitlalCahuis ȳ nonacayo Ca [. . .]tech nicpohua yn tlalli ca ytech oquis ca tlalli ca [. . .]quitli yhuan notlanequilistica ȳ noquimiliuhca yes san frans^{co} yabitotzin yhuan yCordontzin yc quimiliuhtias ȳ notlalnacayo auh ȳ nose[. . .]ltura onCan toctos ȳ notlalnaCayo te[. . .]ncalitic axCan mani metztli a 19 de no[. . .]bre ypan xihuitl de 1654 Años =

First of all I place my soul in the hands of our lord God, for he made it, and I pray to him that he deign to pardon me my sins and take me to his home in heaven when my soul abandons my body. I assign [my body] to the earth, for from there it came, and it is earth and clay. And by my will my shroud is to be the habit of San Francisco, and my earthly body is to be wrapped with his rope. My grave where my earthly body is to lie buried is inside the church building. Today, in the month of November in the year of 1654. =

<u>v</u> ynic sentlamantli niquitohua yey missa huehuey yn nopanpa mitos au[. . .]n Responsos ome ypalehuiloca yn naman = 3 misas = [?] Responsos –

<u>v</u> First I say that three high masses are to be said for me, with two responsory prayers, as the help of my soul. = 3 masses. = [?] responsory prayers. –

<u>v</u> ynic ontlamantli niquitohua ȳ notelpoch Jose de la Cruz yhuan frans^{co} de la crus niquinmaCa tlalli mani Coyohuaca meyot[. . .]auhpantli metl cocahuisque quiCuisque yhuā yC o[. . .] mani tlali paxiotitlan ome yota Ca no Concahuisque notelpochhuan Juseph de la Cruz yhuan [*15v*] frans^{co} de la Crus yhuan [. . .][5] ynemac Juseph de la Cruz yhuan se escoplo –

<u>v</u> Second I say that I give to my son Josef de la Cruz and to Francisco de la Cruz a piece of land at Coyoacan with magueyes on it, four rows; they are to share it. They are also to take another piece of land in Pasiontitlan, [of a size to be cultivated by] two yokes [of oxen]; my sons Josef de la Cruz and [*15v*] Francisco de la Cruz are to share it also. And [a plow][5] is the inheritance of Josef de la Cruz, and a chisel. –

<u>v</u> ȳnic yetlamantli yn niquitohua ȳ notelpoch gabriel de Santiago se quauhcuescomatl ynemac yhuan ypanpa onitlaxtlauh matlactli omome pesos yn quihuiquilia yehuatl [. . .]imatia ça nechtlaixtlahuilis no[. . .] amo [?] =

<u>v</u> Third I say that a wooden corncrib is the inheritance of my son Gabriel de Santiago. And I paid 12 pesos back on his behalf; [he knew to whom he owed it?]; he is to pay me back without fail [. . .]. =

<u>v</u> ynic nauhtlamantli yn niquitohua ȳ Juseph de la Cruz nicmaCa se solar mani san simon senpantli metl quipia yhuan quiyahuac mani solar mochi meyotoc no ynemac [. . .]man melchior leonardo ysolarpa onicCohuili caxtonli metl no ConCahuiya Juseph de la crus yhuan frans^{co} de la Cruz niman çe tlapal solar onp[. . .]ntli metl no ConCahuia niman ysolarpa notatzin [. . .]on pe^{o} xacobo chicome metl ynnemac no ConCahuia niman sebastian xacobo onicohuili nahui metl ysolarpa no ynemac niman maria mag^{na} biuda oniccohuili nahui metl ysolarpa no ynnemac niman pe.^{o} joachin oniccohuili ome metl ysolarpa no ynemac notelpuchhuan –

<u>v</u> Fourth I say that I give to Josef de la Cruz a lot in San Simón that has a row of magueyes, and outside [the house] the lot is all planted with magueyes that are also his inheritance. Then I bought 15 magueyes from Melchor Leonardo, on his lot; Josef de la Cruz and Francisco de la Cruz are to share them also. Then on one side [of the same?] lot they also share two rows of magueyes. Then on the lot of my father don Pedro Jacobo 7 magueyes are their inheritance; they are to share them too. Then I bought 4 magueyes from Sebastián Jacobo on his lot; they are their inheritance too. Then I bought 4 magueyes on her lot from María Magdalena, widow; they are also their inheritance. Then I bought two magueyes from Pedro Joaquín on his lot; they are also the inheritance of my sons. –

<u>v</u> ynic macuiltlamantli ȳ niquitohua ȳ nochpoch luysa maria ynnemac çe CuauhCuescomatl yhuan se metlatl auh ȳ nocihuamo Angelina ana se metlatl

<u>v</u> Fifth I say that a wooden corncrib and a metate are the inheritance of my daughter Luisa María, and a metate is the inheritance of my daughter-in-law An-

[5]The Nahuatl is not legible; the meaning is taken from the Spanish translation.

ynemac niman noxhuiuh leonor nicmaca ome cali yhuan c[. . .]huaca[6] mani tlalli concahuisque luyssa maria yhuan leonor no meyotoc macuilp[. . .]tli metl —

v ȳnic chiquçentlamantli ȳ niquitohua yn Joseph de la crus yhuan frans^{co} de la crus ome Caxa ynnemac çe huey se tepiton ȳnemac –

niCan nictzonquis[. . .]a yn notzonquiscatlanahuatil yxpan noalbasea doña ma^{a} de gusman ynic quimo-Cuitlahui[. . .]axcan yn notlatqui yhuan mochtin ȳ nopil[. . .]n ȳn oniquinteneuh yhuan naniman [. . .]palehuiloca yntla yuhqui mochi[*f. 16*]huas yn notlanahuatil ca ylhuicatl itic quimotlaxtlahuilmaquilis yn tt^{o} dioz[7]

yhuan ymixpan testigoshuan don matias de san frans^{co} testigo Don Baltasar de los Reyes g.^{or} Don diego de la Crus alld. pasado Doña maria beatris testigo Clara beatris biuda testigo Maria magdalena testigo Catalina bernardina testigo frans^{co} [mg^{l}?] fiscal Juan lucaz teopan top[. . .]

Nehuatl [. . .] Don Juan de la Cruz onitlaCuilo

yhuan ȳn oniqui[. . .]uh[8] yn oquic amixpantzinco ȳn ānotestigohuan [. . .] se amatl mopixtica ynic onitlapolo yni[. . .]laque ychteque nochan yn mochtin nopilhuan [. . .]me yehuantin yn aquin quichicahua yx[. . .]a ametetzacualo[. . .]que [?] – Auh ynin oc centlamantli ȳ niquitohua ȳ nican [. . .]pilhua Joseph de la crus yhuan frans^{co} de la crus saso [. . .]quin quimochicahuilis yn dioz a[?]quinmoxelihuis [?] Tengo en el baye yn ichantzin[. . .] totlaçomahuisna-[. . .] Santa ma^{a} nativitas conanas y [. . .]cali mochi quexquich [. . .]ares onCa moch quiCuis xoco[. . .]li yhuan mochintin [. . .]sta Canin tlantiCac ca ysia-[. . .]miquilistzin [?] y nona[. . .]mictzin Ju^{o} frans.^{co} ayac mostla [*16v*] huiptla quinquixtilis Ca ymaxca yes y nopilhuan Ca tel oncan Catqui yn [. . .]-amatzintli yn tlaneltilis ynic ayac quenmanian quinmaxcatis ynon [. . .] anmetztzinoticate ? [. . .]-notestigohuan yn oquic amixpantzinco noCon[. . .]lli y notlatol Ca nestiCa ast[. . .] Canin tlantiCa [. . .] calli Ca tel onca quaxochtl[. . .] yehuatl tlaneltili yhuan Canin [. . .]tica ca se[. . .] tlacuilonlo ca tel amoixpantzinco macamo mostla hui[. . .] ayac quenmania qu[. . .]maxcatis Ca ynmaxca yes y[. . .] nopilhuan Ca ye [. . .]notzonquis yn [. . .]tlatol

gelina Ana. Then to my grandchild Leonor I give two houses and a piece of land in [Coyoacan];[6] Luisa María and Leonor are to share it. It is also planted in magueyes, 5 rows of magueyes. —

v Sixth I say that two chests, one large and one small, are the inheritance of Josef de la Cruz and Francisco de la Cruz. –

Here I conclude my final commands in the presence of my executor doña María de Guzmán, who is to look after my property and all my children whom I have mentioned, and the help of my soul. If my orders are carried out well [*f. 16*], our lord God will give her her reward in heaven. [It was done on the 9th day of November of the year 1654.][7]

And it is in the presence of [my] witnesses don Matías de San Francisco; don Baltasar de los Reyes, governor; don Diego de la Cruz, past alcalde; doña María Beatriz, witness; Clara Beatriz, widow, witness; María Magdalena, witness; Catalina Bernardina, witness; Francisco [Miguel], fiscal; Juan Lucas, church topile.

I, don Juan de la Cruz, did the writing.

And since I [forgot],[8] [I say] while it is still in the presence of you my witnesses that a document is preserved about what I lost when thieves [entered] my home. All my children [. . .] punished. – And as to another thing that I say, my children here, Josef de la Cruz and Francisco de la Cruz, whichever one of them should live, to them you are to distribute [the following] in Tenango del Valle, the home of our precious revered mother Santa María Nativitas, and he is to take the house[s?] along with however many [lots] there are; he is to take all the fruit and all the [?] until where [the property] ends, for it is the result of the work of my husband Juan Francisco. In future, no one [*16v*] is to take it from them, for it is to be the property of my children, for here are the papers to verify it so that no one will ever appropriate it; you my witnesses [who are here?], since I have [made?] my declaration before you, and it appears how far the [land and ?] house reach, for there are boundaries establishing to where it goes, it is written, so before you [I say], let no one in the future ever appropriate it, for it is to belong to my children. Now I have concluded my statement.

---

[6]The Spanish translation has "coyoaca."

[7]The passage is now missing in the original and is taken from the Spanish translation.

[8]The Spanish translation has "que se me olvido." The Nahuatl must have been "oniquilcauh."

43. María Micaela, San Pablo Tepemaxalco, Pasiontitlan, 1762

(AGN, Tierras 2303, exp. 1)

THIS FASCINATING DOCUMENT presents us with several puzzles, the first and greatest of which is whether the testator is really affiliated with Calimaya or with Tepemaxalco. In No. 42 we saw evidence that the clear distinction between these two entities may have been breaking down for some time, at least in the way they were spoken of. As mentioned in No. 42, San Pedro was the patron of Calimaya and San Pablo of Tepemaxalco. Since Calimaya was the senior of the two paired altepetl and gave the entire double entity its name for Spaniards, it was possible to say San Pedro and San Pablo Calimaya meaning the double jurisdiction as a whole, but it would have been unlikely for someone to say San Pedro and San Pablo Tepemaxalco with the same meaning. Yet that is precisely the formulation that we find used in the testator's self-identification here.

Briefly, there are certain indications in the document that the testator here might in fact belong to Calimaya, not to Tepemaxalco. But after weighing all the factors, I have in the end assigned María Micaela to Tepemaxalco, with the name of the present governor of the altepetl, who is a witness, being decisive. The evidence is considered in detail in the note below.[1]

The testator here is out of the ordinary on two counts. First, she declares herself to be a single woman, one who has never been married, the only such case in the Toluca Valley corpus. Second, she applies to herself some Spanish terms for high-ranking indigenous people in a way that is also unparalleled in the corpus, for either women or men. She calls herself a *principala* and a *cacique*. In New Spain in the sixteenth century the Spanish word *cacique*, taken originally from an indigenous language of the Caribbean, meant the same as Nahuatl *tlatoani*, ruler of an altepetl. *Principal* was virtually equivalent to Nahuatl *pilli*, nobleman, though it could refer to any prominent indigenous person. By the eighteenth century *cacique* sometimes had its original meaning, referring to the head of a dynastic lineage and holder of its rights, but more often it simply meant a person of considerable wealth with high standing in the indigenous community. The exact meaning in the present case is open to speculation.[2]

---

[1]When there is any doubt about which of the two altepetl is meant, one hopes to solve the question by reference to the tlaxilacalli name. But unfortunately for the historian, both Calimaya and Tepemaxalco had a tlaxilacalli with the name used here, Pasiontitlan. Beyond the tlaxilacalli, one hopes for hints in the names of the persons referred to in the testament. With No. 42, that was sufficient to decide the question in favor of Tepemaxalco. Here the evidence points more toward Calimaya, for the testator belongs to or has close connections with the Estrada family, and an Estrada was governor of Calimaya in 1750 (Lockhart 1991, p. 109). On the other hand, the name de la Cruz surfaces prominently here, and Tepemaxalco was long dominated by a de la Cruz dynasty. But one finds people named de la Cruz almost equally prominent in Calimaya, including at least one eighteenth-century governor (see No. 80).

It is clear that the families of the two altepetl were entwined by this time, but it is not yet known to what extent: whether or not the name Estrada appears also in Tepemaxalco in the same way that de la Cruz appears also in Calimaya. Knowledge of the governors of Tepemaxalco and Calimaya in this period is not yet exhaustive, so that the name of the governor does not always confirm the identification. We seem, however, to have a decisive piece of evidence in the name of the present governor who appears as a witness here, don Antonio de la Cruz, since the governor is the same in No. 44, uncontroversially from Tepemaxalco in the year 1762.

Another line of inquiry is to look closely at the tlaxilacalli mentioned in connection with properties. Two of these, Santa María de la Asunción and San Lucas, belong to Tepemaxalco, but the third, San Antonio la Isla, belongs to Calimaya.

The notary is another important factor to be considered. Pedro Hernández, who wrote the present document, was also the notary in a testament of 1760 (No. 84) that can definitely be assigned to Calimaya. Otherwise, notaries do not cross from one altepetl to the other in the corpus. That does not mean, however, that they might not have done so on some occasion, even if it would present difficulties from the point of view of the legality of the document. Nevertheless, this factor is weighty enough that one might be inclined to decide in favor of Calimaya except for the clear and plain presence of the word Tepemaxalco at the crucial juncture and the fact that the present governor is seen elsewhere to belong to Tepemaxalco. These factors are sufficient for me to assign the document to Tepemaxalco, fully aware of some of the signs to the contrary.

[2]For background on the terms see Lockhart 1992, pp. 133–34. The way the words are employed here is of interest. Their use instead of *pilli* (here it would be *cihuapilli*, noblewoman) and *tlatoani* tells us that the indigenous vocabulary is no longer viable for this writer or probably for the testator herself. It is also interesting, though puzzling, that *principal* is properly in the feminine gender by Spanish criteria, *principala*, but *cacique* appears in the masculine form, although *cacica* is frequently seen, at least in Spanish texts.

As an unmarried woman without her own family, María leaves most of her property to a nephew, Josef Trinidad de Estrada, starting with some impressive images of saints, stressing the importance of their worship. Josef also gets a large piece of land, while a small one is left to María's first cousin, Gregorio de Setino. Both Estrada and Setino would be good-sounding surnames even in the Spanish context; also, an Estrada had been governor of Calimaya (see note 1). The executor of the testament is also named Estrada; likely María herself belongs to that lineage. Yet, as frequently happens with the women of important families, her name is not distinguished, nor does María bear the doña. Both Estrada men have rare three-element names.

The saints and the two pieces of land are all the property that María mentions in her testament. Being unmarried, it does not surprise us that she does not have a house on her own; apparently she still lives with relatives. Yet the size of one of the fields and the value of the images reflect high status.

Funeral arrangements also testify to a prominent position, especially the grave inside the church facing the altar of Nuestra Señora de Guadalupe, where her late mother is buried; for her mother she uses the most unusual Spanish expression *señora madre*. The Virgin of Guadalupe is present also in the invocations at the beginning, showing that María had a special devotion to her. The absence of a mass seems to be by inadvertence.

The executor as well as the two witnesses bear the title don; the former has a prestigious name, as we already saw, and the latter share the name de la Cruz, borne by so many governors. One of them is actually the present governor, and the other has the name of a governor of some years previous.[3]

Another puzzle in this testament is how it is that a woman of such standing never married or became a nun as a few indigenous upper-crust women did. Without more context, the reason remains unknown.

The notary is Pedro Hernández (see the introductory study, p. 42), who alone in the corpus defines himself as "royal" and "public." "Royal" strictly meant that one possessed a diploma signed by the Spanish king, and "public" meant that one held one of the licensed notary offices of a Spanish municipality. Pedro Hernández is apparently simply appropriating to himself titles commonly used by the upper rank of Spanish notaries. Despite many Toluca Valley characteristics in his style, he has a relatively standard orthography, as well as some traditional expressions, such as the date given in Nahuatl words, hardly found by this time. Comparison with No. 84, done in the altepetl of Calimaya, leaves no doubt that the same person wrote both wills. The formulas approach the identical, and the orthography is also the same, including the unusual tendency to write *z* for prevocalic *tz*.

[*f. 10*]
Jesus Maria y Josephe
Axcan Viernes yn ipan Sempoali yhuan Macuili tonatic de Junio xihuitl de 1762 anos Ca niCan nictlalia y[. . .]memoria testamento y nehual notoca Maria Micaela yxpocatl = prenSipala = yhuan CaSique = nicha[. . .] ypan yaltepetzin Sr San pedro y San pablo tepemaxa[. . .]co ytex nipohui tlaxilaCali Barrio de paxiutitla [. . .] huel achtopa niquitoa yntla nehmocnelilizinos yn tt^{o} Dios nimomiquilis Ca San ymactzinco nic[. . .]Cahuilia y noyoliantzin yhuan noanimantzin yhua Senca nicnotlatlactilizinoa yn yehuatzin nuestra Señora de guadalupe Sr San Juan B.^{ta} Sr San Josephe de gracia = Sr San Miguel arCangel Santo San grabiel yhuan mochintinzizin Santos yhuan Santas yn ompa yn ilhuiCatl ytic motemiltizinotiCaten ynic nopanpa quimotlatlactilizinosque yn tt^{o} Dios yni momaquixtis y noyoli-

[*f. 10*]
Jesus, Mary, and Joseph.
Today Friday on the 25th day of June of the year of 1762, here I named María Micaela, unmarried woman, *principala* and *cacique*, issue my memorandum of testament; I am a citizen in the altepetl of lord San Pedro and San Pablo, Tepemaxalco, belonging to the tlaxilacalli and barrio of Pasiontitlan. First of all I say that if our lord God does me the good deed that I die, I deliver my spirit and soul into his hands, and I greatly implore Nuestra Señora de Guadalupe, lord San Juan Bautista, and lord San Josef de Gracia, lord San Miguel Arcángel, holy San Gabriel, and all the male and female saints who fill heaven to pray on my behalf to our lord God that he redeem my spirit and soul, etc. =

[3] Lockhart 1992, p. 137.

antzin y noanimanzin e^{tta} =
yhuan nitlanahuatia yntla tt^{o} Dios nehmotlacolilizinos yn itlazomiquiliStzin noSepoltura Motlapos teopancalitic yxpan^{co} yaltartzin n͞r͞a S^{a} de guadalupe = canpa omotoCazino noS^{a} Madre moeStiCatca = yhuan nomortaxa yes yehuatl yn itlaquentzin notlazotatzin Sr San fran^{co} = yCordontzin ynic ninolpitias yhuan Se tomintzin nictemacatia Santo Jerosalen nichuenchihua Ca neltis notlatol mochihuas —
Yhuan nitlanahuatia yehuatzin nuestra señora de los dolores de lienso yhuan yehuatzin Sr San lucas de bulto yhuan Santo angel de la guarda = Ca yehua- [. . .] nicCahuilitia noSobrino Josephe trenidad destrada [*f. 10v*] para quimotequipanilhuizinos ca xochitl [. . .]la[4] ayc polihuis Ca neltis notlatol mochihuas —
yhuan nitlanahuatia Se tlali mili Mantica ala y[. . .]la[5] otli yteh Calaqui Matlactli yhuan Se almo canpa titoCuaxoxoxnamiqui yc tlacpac d^{n} loren[. . .] moesticat ychantzinco Santa Maria la asumpcio Ca yehuatl nicCahuilitia Josephe trinidad destrad[. . .] Ca neltis notlatol mochihuas —
Yhuan nitlanahuatia oc Se pedasito tlali mili m[. . .]ni San Lucas otli ytocayoca Cuequestepec yte[. . .] calaqui ycy almo tlaoli xinaxtli canpa timoCuaxoxnamique Andres ychantzinco San luc[. . .] yc tlatzintla titoCuaxoxnamique D^{n} Miguel C[. . .]yetano moesticatCa = ca yehual niCahuilitia yCa notlanequilis noprimo hermano Gregori[. . .] de [Setino?] Ca neltis notlatol mochihuas —
Ca San yxquix nictzonquistia y nomemoria testame[. . .] yn ixpan^{co} yn tt^{o} Dios = yhuan Sr Gobernador yn itla[. . .]yxpan^{co} omochihua = yhuan noalbaSea D^{n} Juan Antonio destrada yhua notestigos ynic quineltil[. . .]que nomemoria testamento yntla quimochihuil[. . .]zinosque ca tt^{o} D quimotlaxtlahuilizinos =
D^{n} Antonio de la Cruz Gobernador testigo D^{n} Nicolas de la Crz[6] D^{n} Juan Antonio destrada AlbaSea

Nehual onitlacuilo yxpan^{co} noS^{r} G^{or} Pedro hernandes ess^{no} Real y Pu^{co}

And I order that if our lord God favors me with his precious death, my grave is to be opened inside the church building facing the altar of Nuestra Señora de Guadalupe, where my late lady mother was buried. = And my shroud is to be the habit of my precious father lord San Francisco, and I am to be girt with his rope. And I am giving a real that I offer for Holy Jerusalem. My statement is to be realized and carried out. —
And I order that I am leaving Nuestra Señora de los Dolores on canvas and lord San Lucas in the round, and a holy guardian angel to my nephew Josef Trinidad de Estrada [*f. 10v*] to serve them; flowers and [candles][4] are never to be lacking. My statement is to be realized and carried out. —

And I order that I am leaving to Josef Trinidad de Estrada a piece of land, a cultivated field, on the A la Isla[5] road into which 11 almudes fit, bordering above on [land of] the late don Lorenzo from Santa María de la Asunción. My statement is to be realized and carried out. —
And I order that by my will I am leaving to my first cousin Gregorio de Setino [?] another little piece of land, a cultivated field, on the San Lucas road at the place called Cuecueztepec, into which 3 almudes of maize seed fit, bordering on [land of] Andrés from San Lucas, and below bordering on [land of] the late don Miguel Cayetano. My statement is to be realized and carried out. —
That is all. I conclude my memorandum of testament before our lord God. = And it was done in the rulerly presence of the lord governor and my executor, don Juan Antonio de Estrada, and my witnesses who will verify my memorandum of testament. If they do it, our lord God will reward them. =

Don Antonio de la Cruz, governor. Witness, don Nicolás de la Cruz.[6] Don Juan Antonio de Estrada, executor.
I did the writing in the presence of my lord governor, Pedro Hernández, royal and public notary.

[4]The full original here was probably "candela."
[5]San Antonio la Isla (de Padua), belonging to Calimaya.
[6]Whereas in the vast majority of cases the witnesses' "signatures" are written by the notary, this witness actually signed for himself, although in a rather shaky, probably unpracticed hand.

44. Félix Juan, San Pablo Tepemaxalco, Pasiontitlan, 1762

(AGN, Civil 664, exp. 2)

A MARRIED MAN, Félix Juan leaves the house with its lot to his wife Dominga María, together with his son Mariano Josef, saying that the son will eventually be the householder; that means that in all likelihood he is still very small and the wife is put in charge of the property until he grows up. Félix adds that he had bought half of the lot, so the original parcel on which the house was built was smaller, and we can sense that Félix is enterprising in matters of land. Mariano also gets another lot on his own, while Dominga by herself receives two pieces of land amounting to 9 almudes. Thus the testator distributes his landed property between his wife and son, and the former also inherits something on her own, not only in her capacity as mother. But Félix possesses even more land, and he leaves an almud each to three nephews, plus a plot each to his sister and his niece.

Thus the testator seems to be relatively wealthy in terms of landed property, and although his nuclear family receives the greatest share of it, it is interesting to see that he assigns quite significant amounts also to collateral relatives. Note that among the kin group there is a high predominance of the name Antonio/Antonia. In a detail suggesting that he lived above the poverty level, Félix remembers at the very end of the testament that he owns a *binacordia*, a stringed musical instrument of some kind, and leaves it to his sister, saying that it belonged to his late father.

Funeral arrangements are relatively simple, while at the same time showing the existence of some resources: the shroud of San Francisco, an offering to the fund for Jerusalem, a mass with responsory prayer, and a grave outside the church. This last provision arouses some suspicion, since relatively wealthy people usually requested burial inside the church; however, in the Toluca corpus there are quite a few cases of burial in the churchyard even for apparently prominent individuals. Perhaps it was a trend that was forming in the later years of the eighteenth century. And to conclude on religious issues, the reference to the holy Sacrament in the opening formula is very rare and may point to a special devotion.

Félix appoints as executor Manuel Silvestre (with a quite unusual second name) and has three witnesses, one of them being a governor coming from the famous family de la Cruz, the same who is mentioned in María Micaela's will (No. 43). In sum, Félix Juan seems to be an enterprising person, and he has property above the average and signs of good status, but he seems never to have advanced to higher office, and most of the names in his immediate family are not of the type associated with the highest rank.

This is the only testament we have from notary Agustín Diego, and it is written in the characteristic style of the eighteenth-century Toluca Valley. A strange detail is the replacement several times of syllable-final *c* by *t*, especially with *oc* in expressions meaning "more, additional."

[*f. 46*]

Jesus Maria y Joseph

ma mosenquisCayetenetzino yn itlasomahuisnaCayotzi S.tismo S.Cramento yhua D.s. tetatzi D.s. ytlasomahuispiltzi D.s. espiritu s.to ma y mochihua —

Axca sabado a 14 de agosto del año de 1762 a.^{os} Nitlalia Nomemoria testamento Nehual notoca Felis Juan Nosihua ytoca domiga = maria NiCa tichaneque ypa yn ialtepetzi s.to S. Pa tepemaxalco yteh tipohui tlaxilaCali paxiotitla yhua huel axtopa niquitoha Ca huel Niquimotlatlactilia yenhuatzin S.tismo S.Cramento yhua S.^{res} patrones S. P.^{e} s.to S. P^{a} S. Juan Bactistad S. migel arCangel yhua mochi s.tos s.tas yn ilhuiCac motemiltiticate ynic nopapa

[*f. 46*]

Jesus, Mary, and Joseph.

May the precious revered body of the most holy Sacrament and God the Father, God his precious revered son, and God the Holy Spirit be entirely praised. May it be done. —

Today, Saturday the 14th of August of the year of 1762, I named Félix Juan issue my memorandum of testament. My wife is named Dominga María, and we are citizens here in the altepetl of holy San Pablo, Tepemaxalco; we belong to the tlaxilacalli of Pasiontitlan. And first of all I say that I greatly implore the most holy Sacrament and the lords patrons San Pedro and holy San Pablo, San Juan Bautista, San Miguel Arcángel, and all the male and

quimotlatlatilisque y tuteCuio D.s. ytla oNinomiquili ma mochihua —
hul axtopa Nitlanahuatia Nocepultura motlapus tiopaquiahuac yhua noquimilicCa ye ytlaquentzi S.to San Fran^co^ yhua Nichuenchihua se tomi S.to Jerusale yhua se misa yhua se reposos nopa mitos ypalehuiloCa yes y nanimantzi —

yhua Nitlanahuatia yni caltzitlin yCa mochi solar Nicahuilia Nosihua domiga maria yCa se nopiltzi ytoCa mariano Joseph yhua tla D.s. quimomochiCahuilis yehual chaNe yes yhua yhua yni solar tlaCo oniccohui[*f. 46v*]li D marCos Juan oNicnomaquili macuili p^ss^ yhuan ome tomi ypapa matl[. . .] y-huam ome bara yc patlahuac y[. . .] huiat opoali yhua matlactli yhuan om[. . .][1] yca mochi noaxca quichihua senpoali hua nahui amo aqui tle quimilhuis quemania —
yhua Nitlanahuatia solar mantica calvario yteh calaqui yei almo tlao[. . .] Nicahuili nopiltzi mariano Jose am[. . .] aqui tle quil quemania —
yhua Nitlanahuatia ot ce tlali man[. . .]Ca hueyatla yteh Calaqui yei almo tlaoli nicCahuilia Nosihua domiga maria Amo aqui tle quilhus queman[. . .]a yhua Nitlanahuatia ce tlali mani CuiaCa yteh Calaqui se media tlao[. . .] yteh calaqui NiCahuilia Nosihua Ca[. . .]pa Caquis yei almo tlaoli ot yei almo NiquiCahuilia yeiti Nosobrinos cese almo Conanasque luis Anton[. . .] yhua migel aparisio yhua matsim[. . .] Antonio amo aqui tle quimilhuis quemania —

yhua nitlaNahuatia ot se tlali mantica moColoa al yteh Calaqui Na[. . .] almo tlaoli Nitcahuilia Noermana Felipa Antonia amo aqui quiqui[. . .]tilis quemania —
yhua Nitlanahuatia ot ce tlali mantica tlaxomolco yteh Calaqui [*f. 47*] se Cuartillo yhua tlaCo NicCahuilia Nosobrina ytoca Nicolasa Antonia Amo aqui tle quilhuis quemania —
Ca san ihquih Nictzoquihtia Nomemoria testamento yCa noCoCohCatlatol ymixpa noalBasea yhua notestigo ynit yenhuanti tlaneltilisque yxpatzico tt.^o^ D.s. ma y mochihua —
NoalBasea MaNuel silbestre Jues G.^or^ D Anto. de la Cruz Fiscal ^m.or^ de la santa ygelsia D Bernab. Anto testigo Anto. matias

female saints that fill heaven to pray for me to our lord God when I have died; may it be done. —
First of all, I order that my grave is to be opened outside the church, and my shroud will be the habit of holy San Francisco. And I make an offering of one real to Holy Jerusalem, and a mass with a responsory prayer is to be said for me; it will be the help of my soul. —
And I order that I leave this house including the lot to my wife Dominga María with a child of mine named Mariano Josef and, if God gives him health, he will be the householder. And I bought [*f. 46v*] half of this lot from don Marcos Juan; I gave him 5 pesos and 2 reales for [land] 12 varas wide, 40 long, and [the width of] 12 together with all my property makes 24;[1] no one is ever to say anything to them. —

And I order that I leave a lot at the Calvary in which 3 almudes of maize fit to my child Mariano Josef; no one is ever to say anything to him. —
And I order that I leave another piece of land at Hueiatlan [or at the large body of water] in which 3 almudes of maize fit to my wife Dominga María; no one is ever to say anything to her. And I order that there is a piece of land at Coyoacan in which half a fanega of maize fits; I leave to my wife [land] where three almudes of maize fit. I leave 3 almudes more to three nephews of mine, who are to take one almud each: Luis Antonio, Miguel Aparicio, and Máximo Antonio. No one is ever to say anything to them. —
And I order that I leave another piece of land where the stream bends, in which 4 almudes of maize fit, to my sister Felipa Antonia; no one is ever to take it from her. —
And I order that I leave another piece of land at Tlaxomolco in which a cuartillo and a half fits [*f. 47*] to my niece named Nicolasa Antonia; no one is ever to say anything to her. —
That is all. I conclude my memorandum of testament with my sick person's statement before my executor and my witness so that they will verify it before our lord God; may it be done. —
My executor is Manuel Silvestre. Judge-governor don Antonio de la Cruz. Fiscal mayor of the holy church don Bernabé Antonio. Witness Antonio Ma-

[1] I.e., Félix Juan had 12 too, and that plus the 12 he bought makes 24 wide, with the no doubt common length of 40.

tías.

Nehual oNitlaCuilo ytenCopa CoCohqui es.[no] Agustin diego

I wrote it by order of the sick person, notary Agustín Diego.

yhua Nitlanahuatia se binaCordia Nicahuilia noermana Felipa Antonia onehmocahuilitia notatzi moesticatca Axca yehual quimati tle quichihuilis noermana —

And I order that I leave a *binacordia* to my sister Felipa Antonia. My late father left it to me; now my sister will decide what to do with it. —

45. Lucas de la Cruz, San Pablo Tepemaxalco,[1] 1695

(AGN, Tierras 2303, exp. 1)[2]

HERE WE HAVE another testator with the second name de la Cruz, which we have seen to be very common in the altepetl of Tepemaxalco and shared by an entire dynasty of its governors. Lucas leaves his house to his wife María Angelina, saying that in it she is to raise their small children, and even contemplating the possibility that she will marry again, which is not found anywhere else in the corpus; if she does, both she and the children are to stay in the house, and it is to go to the latter once she dies. In addition, he leaves her two yokes of oxen, a horse with saddle, a chest, two axes, and all the saints, property very impressive in itself and a great deal to be left to a wife when children are around. Perhaps the intention is that María will pass it all on to the children, but that is not indicated anywhere; the only reference of that nature concerns a piece of land that she is to leave to a little daughter, but only when she dies, not when the daughter grows up, as is usually found. Thus the wife seems to have a prominent role here.

However, Lucas de la Cruz does provide for his children. To his son Diego he leaves a lot, two pieces of land, and 40 magueyes; to his little daughter Juana, another lot (bought for the tribute), two pieces of land, and a corncrib; and to another little daughter, Gertrudis, a corncrib and the piece of land that will come to her only when her mother should die. Thus it seems that Lucas treats Diego and Juana quite fairly, since they both get similar bequests, while Gertrudis is less fortunate, probably being the youngest one. It is unusual that all the children are listed with only a single name, maybe because they are very small, or maybe because a common second name, and in fact de la Cruz, is implicit. From an expression used after the mention of the corncribs, one wonders if perhaps the wife is to raise especially the two daughters, but in the first references all the children seem small and in need of raising.

There is also a note about Lucas not taking the inheritance of his brother Felipe de la Cruz from him (they share the same second name), a statement made to fend off claims from the brother and to justify Lucas's actions. Quarreling over inherited property was very common in eighteenth-century Nahua communities, and it was especially so when families were wealthy, as seems to be the case here. Though the estate of Lucas de la Cruz is not vast, it includes a variety of prestigious possessions, ranging from yokes of oxen to a riding horse to valuable tools and chests, as well as a stock of unnamed saints.

His funeral requests confirm Lucas's relatively high status, going beyond the usual to include burial inside the church and even a papal bull to help his soul, which is not commonly found. Note that the religious formulas here are quite long and complex (as well as conservative, corresponding to the date).

The witnesses are all public officers and bear the title don, something that could be expected given the relatively prominent position of the testator. What surprises here is that the executor is a woman, María de la Encarnación, a very rare phenomenon in the corpus, as we have already seen. The language leaves open the possibility, however, that some of the other witnesses are also executors although not specifically named as such. With so many implications of rank and status, Lucas de la Cruz may well be related to the gubernatorial family of the same

[1]Although the tlaxilacalli is not designated, it seems to be within the nucleated core of the double altepetl and could even have been Pasiontitlan like Jacinto de la Cruz (No. 40).

[2]The testament is accompanied by a contemporary Spanish translation. This translation and a transcription of the Nahuatl of the present testament are included in Rojas Rabiela et al. 1999–2002, 3: 398–403.

name in Nos. 39 and 40, but no concrete evidence appears.

It should not pass unnoticed that San Pablo Tepemaxalco, a proud and ancient altepetl, is here referred to as only a tlaxilacalli. We have already seen in the corpus, and will see again, hints of apparent confusion about the double-altepetl setup of Calimaya and Tepemaxalco. Whether or not the two altepetl are gradually merging in people's minds into one is not yet clear. One interpretation of the present instance could be that Calimaya and Tepemaxalco are each seen as subdivisions of a single larger entity, so that *tlaxilacalli* here would have the same meaning as Spanish *parcialidad*, a multiple-tlaxilacalli entity inside a complex altepetl. Or it may be that the portion of Tepemaxalco contained in the central settlement cluster (known today simply as Calimaya) was coming to be thought of as separate from the outlying tlaxilacalli such as San Lucas and Santa María de la Asunción, and thus was a large tlaxilacalli within Tepemaxalco, appropriating the name of the whole entity to itself.

There is some uncertainty about the notary, since it is not clearly stated who he is, but either the fiscal mayor, the past fiscal, or the temachti could have served in that capacity, as we have seen in other testaments. In any case, it can be said that the style is standard and many of the formulas older, in line with the early date of the testament.

[*f. 42*]
Jus ma^{a} y Joseph
Ma tlaçoyectenehualo yn itlaÇomahuiztoCatzin y dios tetatzin yn dios yntlaÇopiltzin yn dios espiritu Santo Ma y mochua Ame Jesus ma,^{a} y JosePh ett^{ra} —

Nicpehualtia Nodestamento Nehuatl NotoCa lucaz de la Cruz notlaxilaCalpan San pablo tepemaxalCo Axca mani metztli a 19 de otubre De 1695 años —
Ma quimatiCa yn ixquichtin quitasque ynin amatl Auh maçihui moCoCohua y Notlalo y noÇoquiyo Auh y noyolotzin y NoÇializ y notlalnamiquiliz y NotlaCaquia Amo quen Ca Ca pactiCa Auh Ca nicchixtiCa y miquiztli yn ayac huel ixpanpa yehuaz yn ayac huel quitlalCahuiz y notlalnaCayo[3] yuā yn iuh nictlalia y notestamento y Ça tlatzācca y Ca tlatzōnCo Notlanequilis ynic mopixtieyes mochipan yniC ayac quitlaCoz Ma y mochua Amen Jesus ma^{a} y Joseph ett^{ra} —

v Auh Ca yz Catqui yNic nicpehualtia huel achto nictlalia ymactzinCo Nictlalia yn tt^{o} dios noyoliatzin y nanimatzin Ca yehuatzin oquimochihuili oquimoyocolili yuā nicnotlatlauhtilia ynic nechmotlaoColiliz nechmotlapopolhuiliz yn ixquich notlatlacotl ynic nechmohuiquiliz yn itlatoCachantzinco yn ilhuiCatl itic yn iquac quitlalcahuiz y nonaCayo Ca ytech nicpohua yn tlali Ca ytech oquiz Ca tlali ca Çoquitl yuā notlanequiliztiCa Notlanequiliztica yez NoquimiliCa yez San Fra^{co} ytlaquetzin yuā ynic nic ninoCuitlalpiz San Fra^{co} yCordotzin Auh y noçepoltura onCa motlapos teopāCalitic oCa toctoz Notlalo noÇoquio yuā onCa mitoz centel missa yuā

[*f. 42*]
Jesus, Mary and Joseph.
May the precious revered name of God the father, God his precious son, and God the Holy Spirit be preciously praised; may it be done, amen. Jesus, Mary and Joseph, etc. —
I named Lucas de la Cruz begin my testament in my tlaxilacalli of San Pablo Tepemaxalco, today the 19th of the month of October of the year of 1695. —
May all who see this document know that, although my earthly body is ill, there is nothing wrong with my spirit, will, memory, and understanding; they are sound. I am awaiting death, from which no one can escape, which no one can leave behind. . . . my earthly body[3] . . . And I issue my testament, my last and final will, so that it will always be observed and no one will go against it; may it be done, amen. Jesus, Mary and Joseph, etc. —

v Here is how I start it: first of all, I place my spirit and soul in the hands of our lord God, for he made and created it, and I pray him that he grant me the favor of pardoning me all my sins, so that he will take me to his royal home in heaven when [my soul] abandons my body, which I assign to the earth, for it emerged from it, it is earth and clay. And by my will my shroud is to be the habit of San Francisco, and I will be girt with the rope of San Francisco. My grave is to be opened inside the church building; there my earthly body is to lie buried. And there a mass with a responsory prayer is

[3]The word "notlalnacayo," "my earthly body," is left without context in the original.

çe Responsos ypalehuiloCa yez y noyoliatzin y nanimatzin yuã Nichuenchihua çe tomintzin Jerusalen —

to be said; it will be the help of my spirit and soul. And I make an offering of one real to Jerusalem. —

v yNic çentlamantli nitlanahuatia yntla onechmocne[*f. 42v*]nelilitzino yn tt^{o} dios ynin nocha NicCahuilia noÇihuahuatzi yntoca ma^{a} Agelina niCa yez quihuapahuaz nopilhuantoto y[. . .]nel monamictiz niCa quihuapahuaz nopilhua Auh yn iquac quimolnamiquiliz dios quiCahuilitizaz nopilhua onca y[. . .]que Ayac quiquixtiliz —

v First, I order that when our lord God has befriended me [brought about my death], [*f. 42v*] I leave this home of mine to my wife named María Angelina; she is to be here and raise my small children. [Although?] she should get married, she is to raise my children here. When God remembers her [when she dies], she will leave it [the house] to my children; they are to be there. Nobody is to take it from her. —

v yNiC ontlamantli Nitlanahuatia y tlen inemac noerno pfelipe de la Cruz Ca amo nicquixtilia —

v Second, I order that I am not taking the inheritance of my brother Felipe de la Cruz from him. —

v ynic yetlamantli nitlanahuatia çe Çolar mani yCuitlapan teopa Ca yehuatl nicCahuilia nopiltzin ytoca diego yuã çe tlali onpa mani tepetonCo Ca Çano yehuatl nicCahuilia nopiltz[. . .] diego —

v Third, I order that I leave a lot behind the church to my son named Diego, and likewise I leave a piece of land at Tepetonco to my son Diego. —

v ynic nauhtlamantli nitlanahuatia oc no çe xolar onpan mani y[. . .]tlapan telpiloya Calimaya NicCahuilia nochpoxto ytoc[. . .] Juana yno xolar oticCoque itechCopa tlaCalaquili chicome p^{s} oticmaCaque Fra^{co} martinez ymixpan testigos tlatoq[. . .] yuã nicpie amatl amo aqui tle quitoz quemania yuã çe tlali onpan i Calimaya quactenCo yehuatl nicCahuilia noxp[. . .]chto Juana Amo aqui tle quitoz quemania yuã oc çe tlali mani cu[. . .]Cuextepec Çano yehual nicCahuilia noxpochto Juana amo aquiquixtiliz quemania —

v Fourth, I order that I leave another lot behind the jail of Calimaya to my little daughter named Juana; we bought that lot relating to the tribute [bought it for the tribute that was owed on it]; we gave Francisco Martínez 7 pesos before the rulers [the high officials of Tepemaxalco] as witnesses, and I have the document [showing the sale]; nobody is ever to say anything. And I leave a piece of land in Calimaya at the edge of the woods [or in Quauhtenco] to my little daughter Juana; nobody will ever say anything. And likewise I leave another piece of land at Cuecuextepec to my little daughter Juana; nobody is ever to take it from her. —

v yni maCuilamantli nitlanahuatia çe tlali onpan i puctla çaCamoli Ca yehual nicCahuilia nopiltzin diego yuã ome tecPantli metl Sano yehuatl nicCahuilia nopiltzin diego amo aquiquixtiliz quemania —

v Fifth, I order that I leave a piece of land at Poctla, with the ground recently broken, to my son Diego, and likewise I leave 40 magueyes to my son Diego; nobody is ever to take it from him. —

v ynic chiquaçentlamantli Nitlanahuatia ynon tlali onpan mantica Santiago ontenCo ca yehuatl nicCahuilia NoÇihuauhtzin ma^{a} angelina yn quemania quimolnamiqu[. . .]liz dios quiCahuilitiaz noxpochto Jetrudes ayac quiquixtiliz quemania —

v Sixth, I order that I leave that land at the side of the road to Santiago to my wife María Angelina; when God remembers her, she is to leave it to my little daughter Gertrudis; nobody is ever to take it from her. —

v yni choContlanmantli Nitlanahuatia ome yunta bueyes Ca yehuatl nicCahuilia noçiuh se Caballo ençillado yuã Caxa ome achas yuã mochi Santoz Santaz çe CuetzComatl nicCahuilia noxpochto Juana[4] yuãn oc çe cuetzcomatl nicCahuilia o çe noxpochto Jetrudes yc motlapielisque yntla quimonemictiliz dios amo aqui tle quimilhuiz quemania Ca

v Seventh, I order that I leave to my wife two yokes of oxen, a horse with saddle, a chest, two axes, and all the male and female saints; I leave a corncrib to my little daughter Juana,[4] and I leave another corncrib to another little daughter of mine, Gertrudis; they will store things in them if God gives them life. Nobody is ever to say anything to them. Their

[4]This passage can also be interpreted in the following way, though I think the rendering in the translation above is more likely: "Seventh, I order that I leave to my wife two yokes of oxen; to my little daughter Juana I leave a horse with saddle, a chest, two axes, all the male and female saints, and a corncrib."

yehual quihua[*f. 43*]huapahuaz ynātzin yuā Nitlanahuatia nechquixtilizque nobula chiCome xihuitl yc nechmopalehuilizque noanimantzin Ca san ixquich yc nictzonquixtia noCoCoxCatlatol yn imixpa nodestigohua yuā noabaseashua yn quineltilisque notenahuatil yxpantzinco yn tt^{o} dios, Nehuatl nitlaCuilohua yntenCopa CoCoxqui yuā nicneltilia yCa nofirma D^{n} Antonio de los S.tos fiscal ma^{or} de Sta ygleçia D^{n} Fra^{co} de la Cruz go^{or} pasado testigo D^{n} diego Gonsalez fiscal pasado Ma^{a} de la enCarnaÇion albasea D^{n} Andres de Stiago temachtin testigo

mother [*f. 43*] is to raise them. And I order that they are to get for me a papal bull good for seven years; with it they will help my soul. That is all with which I conclude my sick person's statement before my witnesses and my executors; they are to carry out [or verify] my commands before our Lord God. I write it by order of the sick person, and I authenticate it with my signature: Don Antonio de los Santos, fiscal mayor of the holy church. Don Francisco de la Cruz, past governor, witness. Don Diego González, past fiscal. María de la Encarnación, executor. Don Andrés de Santiago, temachti, witness.

46. Don Baltasar de los Reyes, San Lucas Evangelista, 1681

(AHAM, Box 65:39, Juzgado Eclesiástico de Toluca)[1]

BECAUSE OF ITS early date, twenty years before the main body of the corpus, the present document, like some others in the collection, gives us a notion of change and continuity across a longer time. In this case, the main lesson seems to be the extent to which trends of the time after 1700 were anticipated in the second half of the seventeenth century. The initial paragraph markers, the erratic periods or commas as punctuation, and an older formula or two are virtually all that point unambiguously to an earlier time. The language, the orthography, and most of the social practices illustrated here have ready parallels throughout the main corpus.

Don Baltasar de los Reyes, a wealthy man with a quite distinguished name,[2] is married to Francisca Leonor and has four children, two male and two female. The first to be mentioned, and in most ways the preferred heir, is Antonio de la Cruz, who gets the house and the saints, with an explicit, colorful note about the way he should worship them (similar instructions will be seen in some other wills from the tlaxilacalli of San Lucas); he also inherits a field, a corncrib, a yoke of oxen, and some money expected to come in from a lost axe. His brother Juan de la Cruz (note that he bears the same second name as his brother), though he must share with his mother, actually gets two pieces of land, one of which has been rented to don Baltasar's uncle, plus another yoke of oxen, but no corncrib or house. In all likelihood he is still very young and needs help in administering his property; however, the same can be said of Antonio de la Cruz, since at the beginning he is entrusted to the mother to raise; yet unlike Juan, he receives his possessions in his own name only. Most likely, despite being very young, the first-listed Antonio is the elder of the two and has a privileged position.

Although don Baltasar first says that Antonio gets the saints, he leaves an important altar to each son; Antonio is to take care of the altar of Santa María de la Asunción (patron of a tlaxilacalli of Tepemaxalco), and Juan of that of the Virgin of Guadalupe. To support their worship the sons are to cultivate jointly a field which is said to belong to the altars. The testator evidently has a special devotion to the Virgin Mary, displayed not only in the two altars but in the appeal to Santa María Nativitas in the preamble and even elsewhere, as will be seen below.

The two daughters, Melchora de los Reyes (the only one to preserve the testator's second name) and Angelina María, get only a cow each, though the latter also receives a bit of land close to the house where she can settle with her husband if they wish to. The daughters seem to be older than the sons, with at least one of them married; probably they have already left the household and received their share before, for which reason they get less property

[1]The testament is accompanied by a contemporary Spanish translation.

[2]Baltasar de los Reyes is one of the standard names based on the three Magi. The combination may have had special connotations in Tepemaxalco, where a don Baltasar de los Reyes had been governor in 1624 and 1647 (Lockhart 1992, p. 137).

here than they might have earlier.

Apart from renting out a field to an uncle, don Baltasar is also involved in renting and selling mules, even one to a past governor of Calimaya; in addition, he buys wine on credit, apparently from a Spaniard, and pays by lending some mules for transport or oxen for cultivation. These details allow a glimpse of the vitality of petty trade and the variety of activities that supported the daily economy of indigenous communities in the Toluca region.

This testament is quite odd when it comes to funeral arrangements in the sense that, very uncommonly for a relatively wealthy testator, only one detail is present, the burial in front of an image of Santa María de la Asunción, once again confirming the special devotion to the Virgin. Perhaps some earlier wills were less specific on such matters than those after 1700. Perhaps the testator was relying on his family or on his executor to arrange an appropriate ceremony. But we cannot be sure, since no executor is appointed, and witnesses and notary are not mentioned. It seems as if the last part of the will is missing, either because it was lost or the document was never completed.

As mentioned above, apart from the punctuation and a bit of formula, the testament is rich in traits normally found in eighteenth-century Toluca Valley language, in addition to illustrating some of the vocabulary used for Spanish animals.

Jesus ma^{a} y Joseph

v Ca nicnoneltoquitiya y dios tetatzin. y dios tepiltzin. yhua y dios espiritu santo ma y mochinhua ame Jesus maria, y Joseph. ma mochitin, quimactiyesque. yn aquique, quitasque ynin amal y nomemoria destamento, y nehual notoCa do baltasal, de lo reyes nica notlaxilaCalpa. Santo San luCas euāgelista, yntla onicnomasehui, yn itlasomiquilictzin y tt^{o} dios Yntla ycqui nopa mochihuas nicnotlaltactilia y notlasomahuisnatzin Sata maria, natibitas ma quimotlatlactilitzinnoc yn itlasomahuitzSenteConetzin, Jesu Christo ma quimohuiquilitzino y noyolian y naniman, yn itlatoCachantziCo yn ilhuiCactlitic, yn ōpan SemiCac, quimoyectenehuilis. yn igraciatzin. y tt^{o} dios ma y mochihuan —

v ynic sentlamantli. nitlanahuatitias. ỹtla oninomiquili Ca onpa toctiyec y notlalnaCayo yspantzinCo. notlaSomahuisnantzin Sata maria asuncion, Ca notlanequilis y nehual [. . .] niCoCoSqui —

v ynic, ontlamantli, nitlanahuatitias, notelpos, anton de la crus nicmaCatehua, Cali, yhuā Santonme, quinmotequipanilhuis, quintlacpanilis, quitlapopochhuitz, yhuan ynantzin quihuapahuas —

v ynic yectlamantli, nitlanahuatitias, nicCahuilitias notelpos, anto de la Crus, Se artar, Canpa mecticatqui Santa Ma^{a} aSunCion, quimotequipanilhuis —

v ynic nactlamantli, nitlanahuatitias, y notelpos ytoca Ju^{o} de la Crus, nicCahuilitias oc se artar quimotequipanilhuis Virgen de huadalope —

v ynic macuilamantli, nitlanahuatitias, mili, mani ystlahuaCan onicSaCamo, ynemac, ome artar, ConCahuisque, notelposhua ytoCa anton de la crus yuā se yto Ju^{o} de la crus, momesti, quiyelimiquisque yc

Jesus, Mary, and Joseph.

v I believe in God the father, God the son, and God the Holy Spirit. May it be done, amen. Jesus, Mary, and Joseph. May all who see this document, my memorandum of testament, know that my name is don Baltasar de los Reyes and my tlaxilacalli is here in holy San Lucas Evangelista. When I have attained the precious death of our lord God, if such a thing happens to me, I implore my precious revered mother Santa María Nativitas to pray to her precious revered only child Jesus Christ to take my spirit and soul to his royal home in heaven, where it will eternally praise the grace of our lord God. May it be done. —

v First I am ordering that when I have died my earthly body is to lie buried in front of my precious revered mother Santa María de la Asunción, for that is the will of me the sick person. —

v Second I am ordering that I leave to my son Antonio de la Cruz the house with saints; he is to serve them, to sweep for them, to provide them with incense, and his mother is to raise him. —

v Third I am ordering that I am leaving to my son Antonio de la Cruz an altar where Santa María de la Asunción is; he is to serve her. —

v Fourth I am ordering that I am leaving to my son named Juan de la Cruz another altar; he is to serve the Virgen de Guadalupe. —

v Fifth I am ordering that as to a cultivated field on the plain that I cleared, which is the inheritance of the two altars, my sons named Antonio de la Cruz and one named Juan de la Cruz are to share it; both

quitequipanosque — [*verso*]

v ynic maquilamantli sentel queccomal yc mopiyec tla[3]

v ynic chiquaSentlamantli nitlanahuatitias, notelpos ytoCa, anto de la Crus niCahuilitehua, Sentel mimili,[4] mani, Cuequestepec ytoCa lobotitla[5] —

v ynic chiContlamantli nitlanahuatitias. sano yehual, notelpos, anto de la Crus, Sentel, CuesComal ynemac yec, —

v ynic chiquentlamantli nitlanahuatitias. Ca Sāno yehual, notelpos, anto de la Crus. ynemac, Sē yonta, buyes —

v ynic chicnahuitlamantli, nitlanahuatitias. Sentel, achan. onecpolhuili, felipe de la Crus, quistlahuas, ynemac, yec, n notelpos anto de la Crus —

v ynic matlac, tlamantli, nitlanahuatitias, se nocpos ytoCa, merchora de lo reyes, nicmaCatehua Sentel, baca —

v ynic Sentlamantli, nitlanahuatitias, se nocpoc ytoCa angelina maria, ynemac, Sentel baca —

v ynic ontlamantli, nitlanahuatitias, sano yehual, nocpos angelina maria, nicmaCatehua yquintlapan Cali, yc temotica, yehual Conanas, yntla quinequi, ynamic mochantis onca no mochantis[6] —

v ynic yetlamantli, nitlanahuatitias, nosihuahuatzi, ytoCa fra.^{ca} leonor, yuā no telpos Ju^{o} de la Crus. ConCahuisque Sentel mili, mani tlapesCo —

v ynic nactlmantli nitlanahuatitia Sentel mili mani Canpa monepanohuā otli [*f.* 2] Ca San onictlanecti, notiyo, Calimāya, quitehuiquilia, quenta, ytla quitzaqua quenta quimaCas, nosihua yhua notelpos Ju^{o} de la Crus, ConCahuisque, yc quiChihuasque tequil —

v ynic maquitlamantli, nitlanahuatitias, se yunta buyes niquinmacatehua. sanno yehual, noCihua yhuā Ju^{o} de la Crus, ConCahuisque —

v ynic chiquaSentlam[. . .]li, nitlanahuatitias, Sentel machon, nechhuiquilia, don Ju^{o} de la crus G^{or} pasado, Calimāya, quixtlahuas, quinmacas nopilhua —

of them are to cultivate it and to serve [the altars] with [its proceeds]. — [*verso*]

v Fifth a corncrib that is to be kept . . .[3]

v Sixth I am ordering that I leave to my son named Antonio de la Cruz a cultivated field[4] at Cuecuextepec called Lobotitlan.[5] —

v Seventh I am ordering that a corncrib is likewise to be the inheritance of my son Antonio de la Cruz. —

v Eighth I am ordering that a yoke of oxen is likewise to be the inheritance of my son Antonio de la Cruz. —

v Ninth I am ordering that Felipe de la Cruz is to pay for an axe of mine that he lost; it is to be the inheritance of my son Antonio de la Cruz. —

v Tenth I am ordering that I leave a cow to my daughter named Melchora de los Reyes. —

v First I am ordering that a cow is the inheritance of my daughter named Angelina María. —

v Second I am ordering that I likewise give to my daughter named Angelina María [a bit of land on the lot] behind the house, as the land goes down; she is to take it; if her husband wants to make a home, he is to make a home there too.[6] —

v Third I am ordering that my wife named Francisca Leonor and my son Juan de la Cruz are to share a cultivated field at Tlapechco. —

v Fourth I am ordering that as to a cultivated field where the roads join, [*f.* 2] I rented [or lent] it to my uncle in Calimaya; he owes an accounting of it; when he closes the account he is to give it to my wife and my son Juan de la Cruz; they are to share it and with it do the duties. —

v Fifth I am ordering that I leave a yoke of oxen likewise to my wife and to Juan de la Cruz; they are to share it. —

v Sixth I am ordering that don Juan de la Cruz, past governor of Calimaya, owes me a male mule; he is to pay for it and give [the money] to my children.

[3]Erroneous partial entry.

[4]I interpret "mimili" as inadvertent repetition of the syllable *mi*, the intention being "mili" as in other cases in the document. However, since *i* occasionally appears in the corpus for standard *e*, an alternative interpretation could be *memilli*, a maguey field.

[5]Literally the word means "next to the wolf." It may be the name of an area and not just the field; however, the Spanish translator took it as the actual name of the field.

[6]The sentence could be interpreted differently, to mean that if she wants her husband to make a home there, he is to make a home there too; however, the Spanish translator says "si quisiere su marido que aga casa alli haga casa." The word *-namic* is translated as husband here because though only after about 1700 did it take on that meaning uniformly, the testator here already calls his wife exclusively *-cihuauh* or *-cihuahuatzin*, his woman.

v ynic chicontlamantli, nitlanahuatitias, S^r Ju^o de dios, onictlanecti, macho, oquihuicac, toloCaC, oquipoloc aparejo, yhuan Costalmen, Cargan, yhuan, arriatan yhuan llanso, yhuan silleyan omen yanquic, yuan aparejo, yanquic, gerga, mochin quixtlahuas amontle polictiyec Ju^o de d[. . .]

v yuan onectlaquiltin, vino, chiquaSentiCA, Ca oniquinmaCaC, omen yonta buyenyen, oyelimiquito, ymilpan, yuan yei mula oniquinmaCaC, oquinhuiCaC toloCaN, Ca yehuanti oquitzaquaque tomi amo tle nichuiquilia —

v niCa nictzonquistiyan. y noCoCoCCatlatol Y nehual, notoCan don baltasal de lo reyes, Ca chicactiyes y notlatol aya quixitinis. ayac quitlaCos, Axcan biernes [21?] dias del mes de abril[7]

—

v Seventh I am ordering that I rented a male mule to señor Juan de Dios; he took it to Toluca and lost the tackle, the sacks, the load, the lead rope [lariat], the tying rope [lasso], and two new saddles with new tackle of sackcloth. He is to pay for all of it; nothing is to be missing [. . .] Juan de [. . .]

v And he gave me on credit wine worth six reales. I gave him two yokes of oxen, and he went to plow his cultivated fields, and I gave him three female mules that he took to Toluca. They made up for the money; I owe him nothing. —

v Here I named don Baltasar de los Reyes conclude my sick person's statement. My statement is to be valid; no one is to undo it or go against it. Today Friday the 21st day of the month of April [of the year of 1681].[7]

[7]The paper is now torn at this point, but the Spanish translator gives the date as the 21st of the month of April, 1681.

47. Lucía María, San Lucas Evangelista, 1731

(AGN, Tierras 2541, exp. 9)[1]

LUCÍA MARÍA issues a short testament with relatively simple arrangements; the focal point is her daughter Feliciana de la Cruz, to whom she leaves her property, a small field and a corncrib. She makes no reference to her husband and relies on a brother to take care of her affairs, so she is probably a widow; in such a case she might usually possess the family house, but no mention of it appears in the will. In addition to the other bequests, she asks her brother don Francisco Martín to give 40 furrows of land to Feliciana, saying that it is her own inheritance; maybe it is part of a common property that the two siblings share, coming from their original family. Or maybe don Francisco acts here as an executor, even though Lucía does not formally appoint anyone as such.

The brother, it appears, will issue his testament a few years later (No. 48); here he is described at the end of the will as an alcalde, and he bears a don probably going with the office; in his own will he lacks both these attributes. The other witnesses also hold an office; in fact we find a fiscal, a mayordomo and a rector, the last two being uncommon in the present corpus, though they do appear in other documents from this tlaxilacalli. (The fiscal appears as alcalde in 1735 [No. 48].) From this, one would be inclined to rate Lucía María's connections as outstanding, but looking at the wills from San Lucas Evangelista as a whole, we will see that it was the custom there to have a combination of church and cabildo officers serve as witnesses, and no one else. Thus the witness lists tell us much about the tlaxilacalli and little about the testators. We do have two indications of somewhat high local status for Lucía María, the fact that an alcalde is her brother and that her daughter has the second name de la Cruz, which was much rarer in women than in men.

Apart from the rather elaborate formula at the beginning, with invocations of God, the Virgin, and the saints, the religious dispositions of the testament are very simple. For her funeral Lucía María only requests a mass with a responsory prayer that the priest is to administer. Once again, however, it seems that the tlaxilacalli custom overwhelms the individual case. All the wills from San Lucas Evangelista, after some impressive formulas, make only a similar request, often even without mentioning the responsory prayer.

The notary here has a very uncommon name, Anastasio de Benavides, his first name being somewhat rare and his second in the Spanish style. The implications for his standing are borne out when we

[1]The testament is accompanied by a contemporary Spanish translation.

see that in 1736 he was to be fiscal, with the don in front of his name (No. 49). His writing (though retaining some traditional punctuation) is very much in line with eighteenth-century Toluca Nahuatl, and in fact is an extreme example, having been used as the primary subject of an article on Toluca Valley orthography;[2] it is discussed in the introductory study (p. 42). Some of his spellings, such as *chu* for *hu*, are very unusual in notarial writings.

[*f.* 6]
Jesus Maria Johp.
Nica Ytl,^{a}So,MachuistoCatzin Y dios Tetatzin. Yn dios Ytl,^{a}Sonpiltzin. Yn dios Espiritu, S,^{n}to ma i mochichua Je^{S} maria Jos. ax^{C}a viernes a 15 de Junio de 1731 año Nica nichichua notestame^{to} nechual nicocoxiqui Notoca Lusia maria Ca ninotl,^{a}tl,^{a}tilia noteotzin, Notl,^{a}toCatzin, Y tt,^{o} dios nocYchua ninotl,^{a}tl,^{a}tilia notl,^{a}Somausnatzin Santa maria NocYchua ninotl,^{a}tl,^{a}tilia yn S,^{n}toti Ycha S,^{n}tati. Yn motemiltitiCate Ylchuicaqui Calitiqui nopa motl,^{a}toltisque Yn nechimotl,^{a}popolchuilisque Yn notl,^{a}tl,^{a}Col Ync onimoYoloytl,^{a}Calchuili Yn tt,^{o}cuio gesus Risto Ca ninoCemaquilitzin.nochua yn noyolia noanimatzin, y tl,^{a} ninomaCechuis yntl,^{a}Somiquilistzin, yn tutecuio dios ypallechuiloca noanimatzin Ce misa YnCa Resposos nopa mitos y ncehimopalechuilis noteopixicatzin padre ministro Ca Sann ixiquichi niSonquixitia nocococatl,atol Yxpa yaltepe,tzin, S,^{to} S,^{a} Lucas EnBangelista Ca yechuatzin,tzin, notestigos[3] —
Yni Centl,^{a}mali Nitl,^{a}nachuatitias Ce miltoli mani CuahutenCo nimacatias nu^{x}puchi YntuCa felisiana de la Ruz, ychua Ce CusComal ynema ies testigos —

yhua no niquituchua noermanotzin D,^{n} f,^{co} marti nechimaquilis nohipo, felisiana del + opuali Surco yxitl,^{a}huateco y[. . .]i nonemaqui nicocoxiqui

a~~ll~~de D,^{n} f,^{co} marti   Maiordomo Bernadino de S,^{n}tiago   fiscal del la S,^{a}ta yllesia D,^{n} leonisio Rafael Retor alxado Ju^{o} alexadro[4]
E,no anastasio de Benabides

[*f.* 6]
Jesus, Mary, and Joseph.
In the precious revered name of God the father, God his precious son, and God the Holy Spirit, may it be done. Jesus, Mary, Joseph. Today, Friday the 15th of June of the year of 1731, here I the sick person named Lucía María make my testament. I implore my deity and ruler our lord God; I also implore my precious revered mother Santa María; I also implore the male and female saints who fill heaven to speak for me and forgive me my sins through which I have offended our lord Jesus Christ, for I give him my spirit and soul entirely. If I attain the precious death of our lord God, the help of my soul will be that a mass with a responsory prayer will be said for me; my priest, the father minister, is to help me with it. That is all. I conclude my sick person's statement before the altepetl of holy San Lucas Evangelista. My witnesses are:[3] —

First I order that I am giving a small cultivated field at the edge of the woods [or in Quaxochtenco] to my daughter named Feliciana de la Cruz, and also a corncrib is to be her inheritance. Witnesses: —
And I also say that my brother don Francisco Martín is to give for me to my daughter Feliciana de la Cruz 40 furrows at the edge of the plain, the inheritance of me the sick person.
Alcalde don Francisco Martín. Mayordomo Bernardino de Santiago. Fiscal of the holy church don Dionisio Rafael. Rector Juan Alejandro.[4]
Notary Anastasio de Benavides.

[2]In Lockhart 1991, pp. 122–40, which contains a transcription of this very text and the two following ones. Some improvements on the earlier transcriptions and translations have been incorporated here, aside from the somewhat different conventions used.

[3]Here the testament has a strange format; it stops as if to introduce the witnesses, then fails to do so. After the first bequest it does the same thing. When the witnesses finally appear, nothing further is said about them.

[4]The form "alxado" may be a first attempt to write "alexandro."

48. Francisco Martín, San Lucas Evangelista, 1735

(AGN, Tierras 2541, exp. 9)[1]

AT THE TIME OF issuing his own will Francisco Martín does not use the title don with which he was introduced in the previous testament (No. 47), a few years before, probably because he is no longer alcalde. We can see in the corpus that most holders retained the title after leaving office, but it may be that some without the very best credentials did not do so. However that may be, the testator still remains a relatively prominent individual, at least in terms of possessions. He leaves the house with its lot, two fields, a mule and some tools to Agustín de los Angeles, doubtless his son, and also the testator of No. 49. He further gives him some saints, particularly the Señora de los Angeles to whom one of the fields is dedicated—a field that Francisco Martín inherited from his grandfather, who had the same name. A connection between the name of the son and that of the saint is most likely.

Agustín de los Angeles does not, however, receive everything. Bequests go to two males whose relation to the testator is not specified, but who in No. 49 turn out to be Agustín's sons, thus Francisco's grandsons. A few more saints and a corncrib are left to Juan Bautista, and an unclear, garbled passage seems to imply that the house is eventually to be his too. A saint and another corncrib go to Gerónimo Miguel, a younger son of Agustín's. Among the saints, note the predominance of various representations of the Virgin and of San Francisco, from whom the testator has taken his first name.

Finally, Francisco also leaves a field each to his wife, María Magdalena, and his nephew. No mention is made of the 40 furrows that his sister Lucía María (No. 47) had asked him to give to her daughter, so perhaps he had already dealt with the request. It is quite rare for a testator to give so much to grandchildren and others when there is a surviving male heir. Perhaps Agustín de los Angeles is already in bad health, and his death (which in fact is just a year in the future) is not unforeseen.

As we are learning is true for San Lucas in general, while the introductory formula is very rich, funeral arrangements are plain, and once again only a mass with a responsory prayer is asked for, to be celebrated by a Franciscan friar. The reference to San Pedro and San Pablo in the opening formula is typical of testaments from the Calimaya/Tepemaxalco area, for they were the patrons of the two paired altepetl.

As in testament No. 47, no executor is appointed, and almost all the witnesses bear the title don and hold a public office. We find again the mayordomo, an unusual witness in the corpus generally but common enough in San Lucas. Note also that don Dionisio Rafael, fiscal of the holy church in the previous testament, has now become alcalde.

The notary Leonardo de la Cruz shows many of the characteristics and difficulties of Toluca Valley Nahuatl in his writing, and he also commits numerous mistakes and syllable omissions. Peculiar to this testament is the use of an extra *a*, especially before *hu*, as in "nichiahua" for *nicchihua*, "I do it."[2] In this testament and some others, San Lucas is called both an altepetl and a tlaxilacalli, perhaps indicating a growing independence on the part of this entity, or perhaps an evolution in the meaning of the two words.

[*f. 33*]
Ju maria Jucph
Nn ica n itlasomaynstocatzin y dios tetatzin y dios ytlasop;itzin y dio epiritun santo ma y mochiahua ca neahual nichiahua notestamento noca fr^{co} martin ca ninoteltoquitia y noteotzi y notlatocatzi y dios no ihua notlasomaimaisnatzin Sata maria ma nopa motlatoltis quimotlatlalis yntlasomaisCenconetzin y ttyo Jesusto nehmopolpoluhuilis y notlacoli notla-

[*f. 33*]
Jesus, Mary, Joseph.
In the precious revered name of God the father, God his precious son, and God the Holy Spirit; may it be done. I named Francisco Martín make my testament; I believe in my deity and ruler God, and also may my precious revered mother Santa María speak for me and pray to her precious revered only child our lord Jesus Christ to pardon me my sins and evil

[1]The testament is accompanied by a contemporary Spanish translation.
[2]This document as well as No. 47 is included in Lockhart 1991, pp. 122–40, with some comment on its language and orthography.

pilchiahua niahua ninotlatlatilia Santomen y sa pedro y san pablo moxtitzitzi apostelo[mne] ma nopa motlatoltisq[. . .] y quinmoyquilis noyoliatzi noanimatzi quimoyetenechuilis yn ahuicatl itin ma y mochichia ame Jesus maria Jucph

Ca no yahua nopaleahuiloca noanimatzi centel misias yahua ce reposos nopa motlatoltzinno padre guardia nica ypan ialtepetzi Satun sa lucas Ebagelita notlaxilacalpa —

nin celtel ytlanahuatia ni Caltzintli nicati agustin de los ageles quimotelquipanilahuili santotin Cahueltzin Juan Bastista[3] Ca nema yes yhua solar quimochili mepapa tequtzit[li][4] —

cotlamatli nitlanahuatia ninomaquilia totlaxomaisnatzin de los ageles yahua santun sa fr^{co} ynemaquin agustin de los ageles —

yetlamatli nitlanahuatia totlasomaisnatzin de ahuadalope Ca ynemaqui Jua batista yahua o ce san fr^{co} yahua sann aniotonio =

y natlamatli nitanahuatia ninomaquiliatia totlasomaahuinatzi ecarnasio Ca ynemaqi geronimo miguel —

yn macuitlamatli nomaquilia Ce mili mani cuaxotenco calaqui xnaxtli yei almo ninomaquilia agustin de los agele quimochilis nepapa tequitzitli ca chicaties notlatol —

yn ChiquaCetlamatli nitlanatia Ce mili mani yxtlahuateco ynemaqui nosihua ytoca maria madalena — [*f. 33v*]

y chicotlamatli nitlanahuatia ce mili mani nixcahuila Cepoali surcu ynemaqui marcos nosobrino —

Chqueychicetlamatli nitlanahuatia Ce machio ninomaquilia Agustin de los ageles yehua ome acha yhua asasado —

Chinatlamatli nitlahuatia ce mili mani san anitzin Calbaroatit[. . .] tlapa onehmocalitia noCotzi catca ytoca D fr^{co} martin ninomaqulia agustin de los ageles quilemotequipanis yatzin S^{r}nora de s ageles opa quitias Cadela yhua xochil Ca chicaties notlatol —

yahua quecomal ynemaqui Juan bastia centel —

doing, and I implore the saints San Pedro and San Pablo and all the apostles to speak for me [so that he] will take my spirit and soul to praise him in heaven. May it be done, amen. Jesus, Mary, Joseph.

Also for the help of my soul, the father guardian is to say a mass with a responsory prayer for me here in the altepetl of holy San Lucas Evangelista, in my tlaxilacalli. —

First, I order that I am leaving Agustín de los Angeles [in] this house. He is to serve the saints, for Juan Bautista [cannot].[3] It is his inheritance. [And he is to have] the lot as well. He is to do the various duties.[4] —

Second, I order that I give our precious revered mother de los Angeles and holy San Francisco to Agustín de los Angeles as his inheritance. —

Third, I order that our precious revered mother de Guadalupe is the inheritance of Juan Bautista, along with another San Francisco and San Antonio. =

Fourth, I order that I am giving our precious revered mother Encarnación to Gerónimo Miguel as his inheritance. —

Fifth, I give a cultivated field at the edge of the woords [or in Quaxochtenco] where 3 almudes of seed fit to Agustín de los Angeles; he is to perform the various duties. My statement is to be valid. —

Sixth, I order that a cultivated field which is at the edge of the plain is the inheritance of my wife named María Magdalena. — [*f. 33v*]

Seventh, I order that a cultivated field at [Nixcahuillan?], of 20 furrows, is the inheritance of Marcos, my nephew. —

Eighth, I order that I give a male mule to Agustín de los Angeles, and two axes and a hoe. —

Ninth, I order that I give a cultivated field in San Antonio, next to the Calvary [or in Calvariotitlan], above, that my late grandfather whose name was don Francisco Martín left me, to Agustín de los Angeles. He is to serve the Señora de los Angeles; from there will come candles and flowers. My statement is to be valid. —

And a corncrib is the inheritance of Juan Bautista.

---

[3]Since we know from No. 49 that Juan Bautista, Agustín's son, is small, I have taken "Cahueltzin" as the equivalent of standard *ca ahuel*, "for he cannot." Another interpretation might be that "hueltzin" is lacking a possessive prefix as "nema" is and refers to permission. The Spanish translator rendered this passage as "para que sirua a los santos de consentimiento de Juan Bauptista que es su derecho."

[4]The Spanish translator gives this as "trauajos." See the remarks in the introductory study, pp. 26–27. The same ambiguity arises again below.

yahua geronimo miguel o ce quecomal ynemaquis —

Ca ytzoqutia nocococatlatol Ca yeahuatzi notestigo —

Dº llonisio Rafaell alld Dºn atonio de la Crzu fiscal de la ta lesia Dº Jua de los santos mayordo Dºn atonio de Sa Juan alld pasado nicolas de santia alsin

lleonardo de la crz esquiriban

A p 1 de Julio Axcan i xiahuil de 1735 años

—

And another corncrib is the inheritance of Gerónimo Miguel. —

I conclude my sick person's statement; these are my witnesses: —

Don Dionisio Rafael, alcalde. Don Antonio de la Cruz, fiscal of the holy church. Don Juan de los Santos, mayordomo. Don Antonio de San Juan, past alcalde. Nicolás de Santiago, alguacil.

Leonardo de la Cruz, notary.

Today, 1st of July, year of 1735.

49. Agustín de los Angeles, San Lucas Evangelista, 1736

(AGN, Tierras 2541, exp. 9)[1]

AGUSTÍN DE LOS ANGELES, the son of Francisco Martín (No. 48), dies only a year after his father, and he reports in his testament all the property that Francisco left him, dividing it up among his children and wife. Juan Bautista, no doubt the eldest, is to take the house with its lot, a field, a mule and an axe. The other son, Gerónimo (almost certainly the Gerónimo Miguel mentioned in Francisco Martín's will), gets a saint and an axe. Finally, his wife María de la Asunción takes a corncrib, as well as the Señora de los Angeles and, to provide for her worship, the same field that Agustín had inherited from his father and he from his grandfather before him. This shows a great continuity of the cult of the Virgin, with the image and its land in the family already for four generations and ready to go on for a fifth, for although Agustín gives his wife the responsibility rather than his son, it is probably only because the son is still too young.

Thus the testator assigns the core of his property to the eldest son, while some minor possessions go to the other son and to the wife. If we compare the assets listed here with what Agustín received from his father, only a hoe is left unmentioned; all the rest is recorded and bequeathed. The impression is that Agustín has even more saints than the two reported here and leaves them in the house, since in fact he asks Juan Bautista to perform there some activities that are related to worship, the classic sweeping and providing incense. Agustín apparently has a corncrib not mentioned in his father's testament, but otherwise, he seems to have virtually no assets other than those coming from the father; perhaps he lived in his father's house complex all his life.

Once again, the opening formula is quite elaborate, and this time it is accompanied by a few more details in terms of funeral arrangements. Agustín requests a burial inside the church, in a place that the Franciscan friar will designate for him, and a mass with responsory prayer.

Two executors, one of high standing, are appointed and entrusted with looking after the testator's children, which is quite unusual with the wife still alive. When it comes to the names of executors and witnesses, connections can be drawn with Nos. 47 and 48. One of the executors, Leonardo de la Cruz, was the notary of Francisco Martín's testament, while the fiscal don Anastasio Benavides was the notary of Lucía María's will. It seems that a limited set of individuals within the community is passing from one public office to the other, and that the officials as a group are staying in closer touch with the issuing of testaments than in most other tlaxilacalli represented in this book.

The notary Domingo Ramos also wrote another testament of the present corpus (No. 50) and is discussed in the introductory study (pp. 42–43).[2]

---

[1]The testament is accompanied by a contemporary Spanish translation.

[2]This document as well as Nos. 47 and 48 is included in Lockhart 1991, pp. 122–40, with some comment on its language and orthography.

[*f.* 35]

Jesu maria y Joseph

yn iCa yntoCatzin dios tetatzin yhua yn dios ytlasopiltzin yn dios espiritu Sato yhua notlaSomahuiznatzin Sata maria moChipa huel neli Yxpochtli ynic nopapan quimotlatlatiliatzinnos yn itlaSomahuizSeteConnetzin yn tt^{o} Jesu xto ynic nexmopopolhuilitzinnos y nanima noyolia yn ixquich i notlatlaCol y notlapilchihuaz yn itlatoCachatzinCon yn ilhuiCac yn opa CemiCac quimoyectenehuilistzinnos yeyCa axCan lunes a 23 de Julio de 1736 años y niCa nicchihua nomemoria testameto nehual notoCa agustin de losS ageles niCa notlaxilaCalpa yn iCuac dios quimonequiltitzinnos y nanima noyolia ytla ninomiquilis y notlalnaCayo onpa motoCa yn iteoynchatziCon dios yhuan ichatzinCon Sato Sa luCas euagelista no niquitohua yn itechConpan yn ipalehuiloCa y nanima noyolia Setel miSa yhua Se respossos y Capa nitoCos yc nexmopalehuilis notlaSoteopixCatzin padre guardia —

v ynic setlamatli nitlanahuatia notelpoch yntoCa Ju^{o} bactista nicnoCahuilia Cali quimoquitlahuiz tlacpanas tlapopoxhuiz yhua yni Solar ynemaqui ninomaquilia Ju^{o} bastista quimotequipanilhuiz Sata gelsia yhua yn mili mani yxtlahuateCon yc quacxuCu[3] nicnomaquili ju^{o} ba[. . .]tista yc quimochihuilis tequil yhua se macho ynemaqui yhua se acha

v yniC ontlamatli nitlanahuatia nosihua maria asosio nicnomaquilia se quesComal yhua totlaSonatzin de losS ageles quimotequipanilhuiz yhua se mili mani san atonio Carballotitla achi tlapaqui ayac aquixtili quemania onechmoCahuili notlaSotatzin OmestiCacCac

v ynic yetlamatli nitlanahuatia notelpoch ytoCa geronimo nicnomaquilia [. . .] frasiCon yhua Se acha ynem[. . .] geronimo yhua noalbasia leonardo de la Crus auh Ca quimoctilisque nopilhuatoto yhua no yehual noalbasia D^{n} diego de los Satos auh Ca ye nictzoquixtia noConCoxCatla[. . .] nehual niConCoxqui Ca yehuati ynique notestigohua ynique D^{n}n AstaSio benabides fisCal de Sata gelessia D^{n} sebastia niColas aƚƚde lifosi[4] de la Crus regidor mayor roque medosa mayordomo Ju^{o} pablo rafael retor nehual onitlaCuilo domigo ramos esnos[5]

[*f.* 35]

Jesus, Mary, and Joseph.

In the name of God the father, God his precious son, and God the Holy Spirit, and my precious revered mother Santa María, forever very true virgin, [I implore her] that on my behalf she pray to her precious revered only child, our lord Jesus Christ, to pardon my soul and spirit all my sins and evildoing so that it will praise him eternally in his royal home in heaven, wherefore today, Monday the 23rd of July of the year of 1736, here I named Agustín de los Angeles make my memorandum of testament here in my tlaxilacalli. When God wishes my soul and spirit, if I die, my earthly body is to be buried in the churchly home of God and the home of holy San Lucas Evangelista. I also say, concerning the help of my soul and spirit, that a mass with a responsory prayer [is to be said for me], and as to where I am to be buried, my precious priest the father guardian is to help me with it. —

v First, I order that I leave to my son named Juan Bautista the house; he is to take care of it, sweep up and provide incense, and I give him this lot as his inheritance. He is to serve the holy church, and I give Juan Bautista the cultivated field at the edge of the plain, at the border;[3] he is to perform the duties. And a male mule is his inheritance, and an axe.

v Second, I order that I give my wife María de la Asunción a corncrib and our precious mother de los Angeles—she is to serve her—and a cultivated field in San Antonio, next to the Calvary [or in Calvariotitlan], a bit above. No one is ever to take it from her; my late precious father left it to me.

v Third, I order that I give my son named Gerónimo [San] Francisco and an axe as his inheritance. And my executor is Leonardo de la Cruz; they are to see to my little children, and don Diego de los Santos is also my executor. I the sick person conclude my sick person's statement. These are my witnesses: don Anastasio Benavides, fiscal of the holy church; don Sebastián Nicolás, alcalde; Ildefonso[4] de la Cruz, regidor mayor; Roque de Mendoza, mayordomo; Juan Pablo Rafael, rector.

I did the writing, Domingo Ramos, notary.[5]

---

[3] *Ic quaxochco* is more definitely literal, "at the border," than the Quaxochtenco seen in many of these documents, which seems more a place name, but there may be some connection.

[4] The name was identified through the Spanish translation.

[5] At the back of the testament a note in Spanish, dated two days after the will, says that the mass was paid for.

50. Antonio de Santiago, San Lucas Evangelista, 1726

(AHAM, Box 65:39, Juzgado Eclesiástico de Toluca)[1]

IT IS PROBABLE that Antonio de Santiago is a widower, since there is no mention whatsoever of his wife, and he has four male children among whom he distributes all his property. Matías de Santiago seems to be the eldest, getting the house, two fields and some saints, particularly a San Antonio, following the name of his father (and possibly connected with the large Calimaya settlement of that name adjacent to San Lucas). Josef de Santiago and Bernardino inherit only some saints each, among which there is another San Antonio. Finally, Pedro Juan Pablo, the youngest according to the order in the testament, receives a field as well as some saints. Note that at least two children preserve the quite prestigious second name of their father; Bernardino likely uses Santiago as well, though it is omitted here. The three saint's names of the last son are unusual, but since they are repeated, they do not appear to be an error, and another such case or two occurs in the corpus. Antonio thus leaves the main property to his eldest son and gives some land to the youngest as well, while the others get only some saints.

When it comes to formulas and funeral arrangements, we find some traits that have already been seen in the previous testaments as typical of San Lucas Evangelista. The opening formula is complex and detailed (and quite archaic), with invocations of the Virgin and the Holy Trinity. Antonio requests burial in the parish church and a mass to be provided by the father guardian, so the role of the Franciscan friars is once again stressed.

Much as happens in other testaments from San Lucas, no executor is appointed, while all the witnesses are called don and occupy a church or civil office. Among them, note don Francisco Martín as a *maestro* (of the choir?), possibly the same who is to be found some years later in No. 47 as alcalde, and then issuing his own testament (No. 48).[2] As mentioned in the previous testament, it is apparent that the same set of individuals is circulating in the various offices within the community.

This testament and No. 49 were written by notary Domingo Ramos; an analysis of their characteristics appears in the introductory study, pp. 42–43. Here note the loan verb *cruzaroa*, "to cross."

Je[. . .] y Jose

v yn ica yntoCatzin dios tetatzin yn dios tepiltzin dios espiritu sato ma mochiti quimatiCa yn aquique quitasque ynin amal nehual notoCa anto de Satiago niCa noch[. . .] ynpan altepel Santo Sa lucas euagelista ytech nipo[. . .]tica y tlaxilaCalli Santo Sa luCas masihui y noCocotiCa nonaCa y noSoquio auh y notlamachilis y notlasicaCaquilis y notlalnam[. . .]lis auhque Ca Ca San huel pact[. . .]Ca chihuatiCa yCatzinCo dios yeyca ynn axCa niquitohua Ca huel nicnoseneltoquitia yn sa se huel neli dios y noteotzin y notlatoCatzin Catzin yn ixquich ihuelistzin dios y tetatzin dios tepil dios espiritu Sato yhua notlasomahuisnatzin yn sata marian mochipa hue[. . .]xpoc[. . .]tli ynic nopapan quimotlactilis yn itlasomahuizseteConetzin yn tt^{o} Jesus ~~xto~~ ynic nexmopopolhuilistzinnos yn ixquich i notlatlacol notlapilchihual auh quimohuiqui-[. . .]tzinnos y nanima y noyolia yn itlatochatzinCo yn ilhuiCa[. . .] yn opa SemiCac yn moyectene-

Jesus, [Mary], and Joseph.

v In the name of God the father, God the son, and God the Holy Spirit, may all who see this document know that I am named Antonio de Santiago, and my home is here in the altepetl of holy San Lucas Evangelista; I belong to the tlaxilacalli of the holy San Lucas. Although my earthly body is sick, there is nothing wrong with my cognition, full understanding, and memory, but they are very sound and strong through God, wherefore now I say that I very entirely believe in only one very true God my deity and ruler, omnipotent God, God the father, God the son, and God the Holy Spirit, and my precious revered mother Santa María, forever pure virgin, is to pray for me to her precious revered only child our lord Jesus Christ to pardon me all my sins and evildoing and to take my soul and spirit to his royal home in heaven where he will be eternally praised.

---

[1]The testament is accompanied by a contemporary Spanish translation.

[2]Also possibly his grandfather of the same name, mentioned in the body of No. 48.

huilitzinnos yeyCa yn axca[. . .] Sabado a 10 de agosto de 1726 años niCa nicchihua y nictecpana notestameto yn sa tlatzaccā notlanequilis nehual niCa notlaxilaCalpa Santo Sa luCa euagelista yni[. . .] Setlama[. . .] nitlanahuatia yn iCuac dios quimonequiltitzinnos yntla ninomiquilis notlanaCayo onpa mitos [?] yn itec[. . .]pa ychatzinCo dios yhua yChatzinCo Santo Sa luCas euagelista niCa tic altepel no niquitohua yntechCopa ypalehuiloCa y nanima noyolia nopa mitos Setel misa onCa teopa Capa nitoCos yc nexmopalehuilis noteopixCatzin padre guardia —

Therefore today, Saturday the 10th of August of the year of 1726, here I make and order my testament and last will, here in my tlaxilacalli of holy San Lucas Evangelista. First, I order that when God should wish that I die, my earthly body is to [be buried] at the home of God and the home of holy San Lucas Evangelista here inside the altepetl. I also say that concerning the help of my soul and spirit a mass is to be said for me at the church where I am to be buried; my priest the father guardian is to help me with it. —

v ynic Setlamatli nitlanahuatia nicmaCatia notelpoch yntoCa matiaS de Satiago nicmacatian Cali yhua yno mili yhua Satotin yey tlatoque yhua se san atonio quimotequipanilhuilis ayac aqui tle milhuis i quemania —

v First I order that I am giving to my son named Matías de Santiago the house and that cultivated field, and the saints, the Three Kings and a San Antonio; he is to serve them. No one is ever to say anything to him. —

v ynic otlamatli nitlanahuatia notelpoch yntoCa Joseph de Santiago nicmaCatia Se totemaxitisani[3] yhua se San atonio quimotequipanilhui ayac quixlis quemania

v Second I order that to my son named Josef de Santiago I am giving an [our Savior][3] and a San Antonio; he is to serve them. No one is ever to take them from him.

v ynic yetlamatli nitlanahuatia not[. . .]poch yntoCa bernardino niquinomaquilia omen satoti Sato temaxitia yhua Santissima Crus ayac aqui quemania quimilhuis —

v Third I order that I give to my son named Bernardino two saints, [our Savior] and the most holy Cross. No one is ever to say anything to him. —

v ynic natlamatli nitlanahuatia notelpoch yntoCa pedro Ju^{o} pablo y niquinomaquilia ometi Santoti se san isidro yhua se diotatzin ayac aqui tle quimilhui quemania —

v Fourth I order that I give to my son named Pedro Juan Pablo two saints, a San Isidro and a God the Father. No one is ever to say anything to him. —

v yni maquilatli y nitlanatia notelpoch pedro Ju^{o} pablo nicmaCatia Se mili mani Capa moCrusaro utli aya[. . .]qui quemania quixtoqui —

v Fifth I order that I am giving to my son Pedro Juan Pablo a cultivated field where the roads cross. No one is ever to claim it from him. —

v ynic chiquasetlamatli nitlanahuatia notelpoch yntoCa matias de satiago nicmaCa se mili tlapaqui utli calimaya yc chihuas mepapan tequil[4] ayac aquixtili quemani Ca ye nictzoquixtia notlatol niCoCoxqui Ca yehuati ynique notestigohua D^{n} Ju^{o} Corona allde D^{n} migel de satiago fisCal de s.^{ta} glesian D^{n} fra^{co} marti maestro D^{n} barta de lo reyes D^{n} Ju^{o} de la Crus regidor mayor

v Sixth I order that I am giving to my son named Matías de Santiago a cultivated field above the road to Calimaya, with which he is to perform the various duties.[4] No one is ever to take it from him. Now I the sick person conclude my statement. These are my witnesses: don Juan Corona, alcalde; don Miguel de Santiago, fiscal of the holy church; don Francisco Martín maestro [de doctrina? choirmaster?]; don Baltasar de los Reyes; don Juan de la Cruz, regidor mayor.

nehual onitlaCuilo domi[. . .]go ramos esnos

I did the writing, Domingo Ramos, notary.

---

[3]A very unusual form occurs here where one would expect *totemaquixticatzin*, "our savior or redeemer," and indeed the Spanish translation has "nuestro redemptor." "Totemaxitisani" would be impossible in normal Nahuatl grammar, because an agentive form in *-ni* cannot be possessed. In the bequest just below, "temaxitia" could be a normal finite verb, but an agentive is expected. Both forms appear to be based on a verb "maxitia," which with Tolucan substitutions could represent *machtia*, "to teach." Thus they might mean "our teacher" and "the teacher." Or *qui* could have been omitted both times, and "temaquixitia" would be a plausible form of "to save." My conclusion is that Domingo Ramos was simply very unfamiliar with how to write "our Savior" in Nahuatl.

[4]It is not certain whether work tasks or tribute duties are meant.

51. Ana Teresa, San Lucas Evangelista, 1759

(AGN, Civil 664, exp. 2)

THE TESTATOR IS apparently a widow, since no husband is mentioned at any time, and she has a grandchild and a daughter. A field and a small site to build a house go to a grandchild, Juan Aparicio. In addition, Ana Teresa gives a field to Teresa Rosa, her daughter (her first name being the second name of her mother). The status of another field is unclear; the Nahuatl seems merely to say that in case there is no heir, it is to go to a certain Lucas Vaina or his children, but no details are given about the relationship with him. Thus whether or not this property is somehow to go to the grandson, he as a male although another generation removed from the testator is being distinctly preferred over Ana Teresa's daughter, who is mentioned second and gets only one field. However, it is significant to note that it is a cultivated field, not a piece of land with no specified connection with agriculture, and this kind of land is not exclusively for male heirs. Ana Teresa owns three cultivated fields and some other land, which is quite impressive for an indigenous woman. No house is mentioned, though, probably because the house she lived in had been her husband's property and went to someone else.

The self-introduction is very detailed, giving not only the name of the tlaxilacalli but the parish and the jurisdiction, which is truly uncommon. The opening formula is quite complex and long, in line with other testaments from San Lucas, while funeral arrangements are once again very simple; only a mass is requested. And also as with other San Lucas wills, Ana Teresa appoints no executor but names three witnesses, all of them high officials, with impressive second names. Possibly the implication in these cases is that the officials take on some of the attributes of an executor.

The notary Pedro Martín shows the general characteristics of Tolucan Nahuatl, and his style and formulas are similar to those of another notary of San Lucas who wrote various testaments in the same period, Sebastián Fabián. We see a somewhat unusual Spanish loanword here in *heredero*, "heir," and the much rarer use of a whole Spanish phrase in a Nahuatl sentence in "en presente," "in the presence of," though it is not quite correct by Spanish standards (by which it would be *en presencia de*).

[*f. 38*]

Jeus maria y Jophe

Ahca martes : 24 de Julio xihhuil de 1759 a^{os} ma Yoqui quimatica yn aquique quitasque yni aMal nehual notoCa Ana teresa nica nocha notlaxilaCalpa Santo S, Lucaz EV,^{ta} nudotrina S,^{r} S. pedr^{o} y S, pablo Calimaya nuJuridicio metepec Ca mococohua notlalo nosoquio yhua noyolia aque ca Ca san huel pactica yCatzinco y tt,^{o} Dios yhua tla Yoqui nopa mochihuias nicnoMasehuis ytetlasotlalitzin y nuteotzin tt,^{o} X$^{\underline{to}}$ Ca senCa nicmotlatlanVctilia nuSenzixcanatzina Maria SS,^{a} ynic SemiCa yhpohtzintli yc quimotlatlantili ytlasomahuisSentecone-tzin yc nehmoselilis noYolia y nanimatzin yc nehmopopolhuilis yn ihquih notlapilchihual yc Nopan quimohuiquilis ytlatocachatzico y Gloria yc quimoYectenehuilis ytlasomahuistocatzin y Dios tetatzin y Dios ytlasopiltzin yhua Dios Espiritu Santo ma Ye mochihuan yCS,^{a} —

Ynic Sentlamantli nitlanahuatia Ca nopa mitos Sentel missa nopa mochihuas ypalehuiloca noYolia nanimantzin —

Ynic otlamantli nitlanahuatia Ca niccahuilia nuhhui

[*f. 38*]

Jesus, Mary and Joseph.

Today, Tuesday the 24th of July of the year of 1759, may those who see this document know that I am named Ana Teresa; my home is here in my tlaxilacalli of holy San Lucas Evangelista; my doctrina [parish] is lord San Pedro and San Pablo Calimaya, my jurisdiction Metepec. My earthly body is ill, and nothing is wrong with my spirit, but it is very sound through our lord God. And if it is to happen to me that I attain the love of my deity our lord Christ [that I die], I greatly implore my consummate mother María Santísima, eternally virgin, to pray to her precious revered only child to receive my spirit and soul and pardon me all my evildoing, so that he will take [my soul] to his royal home in glory, so that it will praise the precious revered name of God the father, God his precious son, and God the Holy Spirit. May it be done. Etc. —

First, I order that a mass is to be said for me; it is to be celebrated for me as a help to my spirit and soul. —

Second, I order that I leave to my grandchild named

ytoca Juan Apariio matlatlin Curco para ynahuac y-cha cimontzin yc motlalis amo aquixihtoquilis quemaria Ca chicahuaties notenahuatil —

Ynic lletlamantli nitlanahuatia Se nomil mantica barracatitla Yehual ynemac Juan Aparicio amo aquihtoquilis quemania Ca chicahuaties notenahuatil —

Ynic nactlamantli niquitua o se mili manti Sano opa mantica barraCatitla omonotihca[1] ytla Dios Cualquepas Se eredero ytehCaCopa yni tlalin San Cual-Yotica mocahuilis yni Lucas baina nusu aCa ypiltzin Cunanasque — [*f. 38v*]

Ynic maCuiltlamantli nitlanahuatia oc se mili ma-[. . .]tica tlapehco Calaqui xihnaxtlin tlaolin Se almo yn tlaco Ca Yehual ynemac noxpoh ytoca Teresa Ro[. . .] Amo aquihtoquilis quemania Ca chicahuaties n[. . .]tenahuatil —

Ca san ihquih nictzonquihtia nocochocatlatol Ca yMihpa notestigohua Ca nica mesticate en prensente Fiscal de Santa yGlecia D,^{n} Gergorio d[. . .] Cruz Gouernador bernardo de lo ReYes[2] Alde D,^{n} pedro de la Cruz

Es,^{no} de la Rep,^{ca} Onitlaquilo ytencopa cocohqui pedro martin

Juan Aparicio 10 furrows near the home of Simón, for him to settle on; no one is ever to claim it from him; my command is to be valid. —

Third, I order that a cultivated field of mine that is next to the ravine [or in Barrancatitlan] is the inheritance of Juan Aparicio; no one is ever to claim it from him; my command is to be valid. —

Fourth, I say that as to another cultivated field that is likewise next to the ravine [or in Barrancatitlan],[1] if God takes back an heir to this land [that is, if the heir to the land dies or there is no heir], it is properly to be left to Lucas Vaina, or some child of his; they are to take it. — [*f. 38v*]

Fifth, I order that another cultivated field that is at Tlapechco, in which an almud and a half of maize seed fits, is the inheritance of my daughter named Teresa Ro[sa?]; no one is ever to claim it from her; my command is to be valid. —

That is all. I conclude my sick person's statement before my witnesses, for they are present here: fiscal of the holy church don Gregorio de la Cruz; governor Bernardo de los Reyes;[2] alcalde don Pedro de la Cruz.

I, Pedro Martín, notary of the commonwealth, did the writing at the order of the sick person.

[1]Possibly the puzzling verb form "omonotihca" represents the same thing as standard *onmonotztica*, and the phrase would be interpreted as "at the place called Barrancatitlan." See the similar case in No. 53, where "quimonotilitzinnos" is quite clearly derived from *notza*.

[2]It would be extremely unusual for the governor of an altepetl not to bear the don during his period of office; here two lesser (though still high-ranking) officials properly bear it, and one would suspect a mistake in this case. The title is actually missing in the original, however, so the error would be of inadvertent omission on the part of the notary. It is also not clear what entity this person would have been governor of, though the altepetl of San Pablo Tepemaxalco would seem the most likely. Another problem is that if a governor had been present, surely he would have been listed first. Thus we seem to be dealing with a mistake in some dimension.

52. Marcela María, San Lucas Evangelista, 1759

(AGN, Civil 664, exp. 2)

AS WITH Ana Teresa in No. 51, here once again the testator seems to be a widow; unlike Ana Teresa, she follows the common practice of leaving all her property to her daughter, Micaela Gerónima, perhaps because no male heir is available or indeed any other heir at all. Micaela gets the house with its lot and the saints, accompanied by a note about their worship as often happens in this tlaxilacalli. In addition, Marcela María leaves her a field that she had inherited from her late father, and another piece left to her by her late mother, who bore the same (admittedly very common) second name. Thus the family of origin plays an important and acknowledged role here, providing all or virtually all of what the testator bequeaths, while no one on her husband's side appears in the will.

The testator requests burial in the church and a mass with responsory prayer, with the help of a señor Doctor who is to be found in other testaments from the same notary, and whose identity remains a mystery. The opening formula follows the style of San Lucas Evangelista, with a mention of the intercession of the Virgin.

While no executor is named, there is an impressive list of twelve witnesses, half of them with the title don and almost all with some sort of public office. Both the number and the quality of the witnesses may speak for the testator's connection with the tlaxilacalli elite, even if it was normal in San Lucas to use officials as witnesses. Although Ana Teresa (No. 51) issued her testament only a day after Marcela María, none of the officials are present in both documents. Between the two, we seem to have a good overview of the officialdom of San Lucas, higher and lower, in this year.

Finally, Sebastián Fabián was a very popular notary in San Lucas, at least judging from the number of testaments he wrote and that have reached us. His style is analyzed in the introductory study (p. 43). Here note especially that depending on the vowel in a stem, he is often inclined to write an extra *a* and sometimes an *e* rather than the more common *i* used to preserve syllable-final consonants.

[*f.* 32]
Ma mosequiyetenetzinno yn itlasomahuiztoCatzin yn Ds. tetatzin yhuan yntlasomahuizpilitzin yn Ds. espirito santon yhuan notlaSomahuiznatzin Santa marian mochipan hueli[e?] neli yn ichpochtli ynic nopapan quimotlatlauhtilitzinnos yn itlasomahuizseteConetzin yn tt^{o} Jesu x̃to ynic nechmopopolhuilitzinnos yn ixiquichi notlatlaCol y notlapilichihualan yhuan quimohuiquilitzinnos y nanima noyolian yn itlatoCachatzintzinCon ylhuiCac yn opa CemiCac quimoyetenehuilitzin niCachihua nomemoria testameto Ca notlanequilis nehuala notoCa marselan marian niCani notlaxilaCalpan pateron S^{r} S^{n} luCas luCas evagelistan [a?] yC aXCa domigo a 23 de Julio de 1759 a^{os} ynic Cetlamatlin nitlanahuatian ynqua dios quimonequilititzinos ytla nimomasehuiz yn itlaSomahuismiquilitzin y tt^{o} Ds. opa nimotoCas yn iteopachatzinCon y tt^{o} D^{s} opan mitos Cetele misan yhua setele resposos ye nmopalehuilis notlasotatzin Sr D.^{o}[1] Ca san iquixi nimotlatilian —

yniC otlamatli y nitlanhuatian Se nospos ytoCa migelan geronima ynema Cali yhua Colarar yhuan Santos quimotequipanihuiz tlapanas tlapohuiz quimotequipanihuiz ayaquitoquilis quemania Ca chiCaties notenhuatili [*f.* 32*v*]

yni yeytlamatli nitlanahuatian sano yeh[. . .]la nopos ytoCas miquelan geronima nimom[. . .]quilian Ce mili mantiCan ypan teopan ynemaCa mopos

[*f.* 32]
May the precious revered name of God the father, his precious revered son, and God the Holy Spirit be entirely praised; and my precious revered mother Santa María, forever very true virgin, will pray for me to her precious revered only child our lord Jesus Christ to pardon me all my sins and evildoing and take my soul and spirit to his royal home in heaven, where it will eternally praise him. I named Marcela María make my memorandum of testament, which is my will, here in my tlaxilacalli [of the] patron lord San Lucas Evangelista, today Sunday the 23rd of July of the year of 1759. First, I order that, when God desires it, if I attain the precious revered death of our lord God, I am to be buried in the churchly home of our lord God; there a mass with a responsory prayer is to be said, my precious father the señor doctor[1] is to help me. That is all that I request. —

Second, I order that a house and a lot are the inheritance of a daughter of mine named Micaela Gerónima, and she is to serve the saints; she is to sweep and dispense incense and serve them. No one is ever to claim it from her. My command is to be valid. [*f.* 32*v*]

Third, I order that I give likewise to my daughter named Micaela Gerónima a cultivated field that is facing the church; it is the inheritance of my daugh-

---

[1]The abbreviation "D.^{o}" here is puzzling, but some conclusions can be reached by taking all four of this notary's productions together. The form "D.^{o}" occurs virtually the same in No. 55, but in 53 it is "D.^{or}" and in 54 "D.^{r}." The intention must be "Doctor" in all four instances, considering that that title was normally preceded by *señor* and that Sebastián Fabián sometimes omits final *r*. A Franciscan friar would not bear the title of doctor, and we see in No. 42 that in 1736 a "father guardian," with a specifically Franciscan title, was in charge in San Lucas, but apparently between then and 1759 the local church had been secularized. In two of Sebastián Fabián's testaments, "señor" is followed by not one but two titles. The second one is given in No. 54 as "D.^{o}" and in 55 as "D.^{ro}." In the latter case, something has been marked out or smudged before the "ro," and the letter could have been *e*. The intention may be to specify an additional title of the priest. Often-seen possibilities such as *ministro* and *vicario* seem excluded. In the time just after the conquest the priest in charge of an indigenous parish had sometimes been called a *doctrinero*, which would fit the letters here well, but the term has not otherwise been seen in materials relating to eighteenth-century Toluca, and indeed by this time it had taken on a rather disrespectful tone and was used, if at all, for lay persons. Thus I am not attempting to interpret or translate this second abbreviation further.

miquelan geronima onemoCahuililiti notlasotatzin m[e]stiCatiCa aXCan nimomaquilia nopos ayaquiaXitocquil[. . .] quemania Ca chiCaties notenahuatili —

yni natlamatli nitlanahuatian ose mili mati[. . .] ytzitla loman san yeual nopos ytoCa miquelan gerniman notlasonatzin mestiCatatiCa onemoCahuilitia FransisCan marian tlaCon nemocah[. . .]ili tlaC[o][2] niCa nitzoquitian noCoCatlatol neu[. . .]la notoCan marsela maria niCoCosqui ymipa notestigohuan D^n Jergorio rapael alcad[. . .] D^n martin Carlos fisCala de la sata gelas D^n leo[. . .]rdo de la Cruz mayordomo leonardo Ju^o retor felipe de la Cruz regido mayor antonio basilio regido menor Salbador antonio merino mate[. . .] Ju^o alhuasili mayor marCos del Cruz topile D^n niColas aparisio alCde pasdo D^n Domigo migl [. . .] Dn Ju^o Cayetanos alCde pasdo testigos

nehuala onitlaquilon Sebastian Favan SS^n

ter Micaela Gerónima. My late precious father left it to me upon dying; now I give it to my daughter. Nobody is ever to claim it from her. My command is to be valid. —

Fourth, I order that another cultivated field that is below the slope I likewise [give] to my daughter named Micaela Gerónima. My late precious mother Francisca María left half to me upon dying.[2] Here I conclude my sick person's statement, I named Marcela María, the sick person, before my witnesses: don Gregorio Rafael alcalde; don Martín Carlos fiscal of the holy church; don Leonardo de la Cruz mayordomo; Leonardo Juan rector; Felipe de la Cruz regidor mayor; Antonio Basilio regidor menor; Salvador Antonio merino; Mateo Juan alguacil mayor; Marcos de la Cruz topile; don Nicolás Aparicio past alcalde; don Domingo Miguel [. . .]; don Juan Cayetano past alcalde, witnesses.

I did the writing, Sebastián Fabián notary.

[2]The original says *tlaco*, "half," two times, but still the meaning is not entirely clear. Is the field that the testator is leaving to her daughter half of a larger field, the other half having been left by her mother to someone else? Or is Marcela saying that she inherited from her mother only half of the field she is presently leaving to her daughter, having bought the other half later or inherited it from another relative? The second alternative seems somewhat more likely, especially if one assumes that the hanging second *tlaco* was meant to be followed by a statement saying how she acquired the other half, but the passage as it exists is inherently vague.

53. Felipe de Santiago, San Lucas Evangelista, 1759

(AGN, Civil 664, exp. 2)

THE TESTAMENT OF Felipe de Santiago is a model of one of the standard situations in terms of heirs and inheritance. He bequeaths all his property—consisting of a house, its lot, some saints, and a field—to his son, Benito Joaquín, while no other children are mentioned. Benito may be the only child, or the eldest, or maybe some other child has already left the household with his/her portion of the inheritance. Note that the field had been given to the testator by his late father don Lucas Damián. Felipe does not refer to his wife, so doubts remain about whether he is a widower.

The property just listed can be considered as average for an indigenous man in the eighteenth-century Toluca Valley, although later, almost as an afterthought, another holding, called a lot, enters into the picture. Felipe's late brother Domingo de Santiago left it to him, but it remains unclear what he intends to do with it. The most plausible conclusion would be that it too passes on to his son, but nothing is said to make that a certainty.

Notice the relatively high-status second name that the two brothers share, Santiago, although it is different from that of their father. Since the father was a don and doubtless held local office, it looks as if the expectation was the same for his sons, but whether because of a small property base or for some other reason, the expectation seems never to have been realized. The name of Felipe's son is also undistinguished and does not continue the Santiago.

In terms of funeral arrangements the testament is in line with the general practice of San Lucas, a burial in the church and a mass with responsory prayer, with the help of a señor Doctor who is present also in the other testaments by the same notary (Nos. 52, 54, and 55). In the same vein, the introductory formulas of the two testaments are basically identical.

Once again, there is no executor but a relatively long list of witnesses, all holding some public office, and three of them are dons. The names correspond almost exactly to those listed in the testament of Marcela María, No. 52, who died only a few days before Felipe; though some individuals who appear in No. 52 holding offices such as rector or merino are mentioned here without them, it can be assumed that they are still in office. The one remaining person, Simón de la Cruz, held an office too; in No. 54, also of the same year, he is called a topile. We learn here that the mayordomo who appears in some San Lucas wills is a cofradía official, so that at the indigenous level the civil corporation, the local church organization, and the cofradía are all in close cooperation.

This is another testament by notary Sebastián Fabián, who is discussed in the introductory study (p. 43). Notice the occurrence of the Spanish loan verb *cruzaroa*, "to cross," which seems to have been popular in San Lucas (see another instance, many years earlier and by a different notary, in No. 50).

[*f. 53*]
Jesus marian y Josph
Ma mosequisCayetenetzinno yn Ds. tetatzin yhua yn itlasomahuizpilitzin yn Ds. espiritu santo yhua notlasomahuiznatzin Sata marian mochipan huel neli yn ispotzintli yni nopapan quimotlatlatilitzinnos yn itlasomahuizCeteConetzin yn tt^{o} Jesû Xto yni nchmoponlhuilitzinnos yn ixiquich y notlatlaCol y notlapilichihuala yni quimohuiquilitzinnos yntlatoCachatzinCon y tt^{o} Ds. y nanima y noyolian —
AXCa Domigo a 29 de julio de 1759 a^{os} NiCa nichihuan nomemorian testameton nehual notoCan pelipe de S^{n}tiago niCa notlaxilaCapan Nuestro Pateron S.^{r} S^{n} LuCas evangelistan —
yni Cetlamatli nitlanhuatian yn iqua y tt^{o} Ds. quimonequilititzinnos yn itla nimomaCehuiz yn itlasomahuizniquilitzin yn tt^{o} Ds. y notlalanaCayon opan motoCas yn iteopanchantzinCon yn tt^{o} Ds. opan mitos Cetele misan yhuan Cetele respos yno y nimotlatlatilian yeuatzin Sr D.^{or}[1] y nemopalehuilistzinnos y quimotlatlatilitzinnos yn tt^{o} Ds. ypapan y noylia y noanimantzin yni quimonotilitzinnos y notlasomahuiztatzin yn Ds. —
yni Otlamatli nitlanhuatian Ce notepos ytoCan Benito guachi ynema nimomaquilian Colar yhua Santotin yhuan Santatin yhuan Calin tlapanasas tlaposhuizsis notepos Beniton guachi ayaquixtoquilis quemanian —
yni yeyetlamatli nitlanahuatian San yeuala notelpos Beniton guanquin nimomaquilian Ce mili matiCa Opan Capan moCruzara otli y ayaquiquitoquilis quemanian Ca chiCaties notenhuatitli onemomaquilitia notlasotatzin —
mestiCatiCa ytoCa Dn LuCas damian —
ini natlamatli nitlanhutia Ce noreman ytoCan Domigo de S^{an}tiago oquiCatia Ce solar mantiCan yztlahuateCon oneCahuilitia nehuala felipe de de Santiago niCosqui NiCa nitzoquitian noCostlatol neual niCoqui felipe de santiago — [*f. 53v*]

[1]See No. 52, n. 1.

[*f. 53*]
Jesus, Mary and Joseph.
May God the father, his precious revered son, and God the Holy Spirit be entirely praised; and my precious revered mother Santa María, eternally very true virgin, will pray for me to her precious revered only child our lord Jesus Christ to pardon me all my sins and evildoing, so that he will take my soul and spirit to the royal home of our lord God. —

Today, Sunday the 29th of July of the year of 1759, here I named Felipe de Santiago make my memorandum of testament, here in my tlaxilacalli of our patron lord San Lucas Evangelista. —
First, I order that, when our lord God desires it, if I attain the precious revered death of our lord God, my earthly body is to be buried at the churchly home of our lord God. There a mass with a responsory prayer is to be said. I implore the señor Doctor[1] to help me with that; he is to pray to our lord God for my spirit and soul, he is to call upon my precious revered father God. —

Second, I order that to a son of mine named Benito Joaquín I give as his inheritance a lot, the male and female saints, and a house; my son Benito Joaquín is to sweep and spread incense. No one is ever to claim it from him. —
Third, I order that likewise to my son Benito Joaquín I give a cultivated field that lies where the roads cross. No one is ever to claim it from him; my order is to be valid. My late precious father named don Lucas Damián gave it to me at death. —

Fourth, I order that a brother of mine named Domingo de Santiago left a lot at the edge of the plain; he left it to me, Felipe de Santiago the sick person, on dying. Here I the sick person Felipe de Santiago conclude my sick person's statement. — [*f. 53v*]

ymipan notestigohuan alld^{e} D^{n} Jregorio rpael fisCala de la santa gelesa D^{n} marti Carlos D^{n} leonardo del Cruz mayrdomo de la Cofradian [. . .][2] leonardo Ju^{o} felipe de la Cruz regido[. . .] mayor antonio basillo regidor menor Salvador antoni[. . .] mateo Ju^{o} alguasili mayor Simon de la Cruz marCos de la Cruz topilen —
Neuala onitlaquilon Sebastián Favan SS.^{n}

Before my witnesses, alcalde don Gregorio Rafael; fiscal of the holy church don Martín Carlos; don Leonardo de la Cruz, mayordomo of the cofradía; [. . .][2] Leonardo Juan; Felipe de la Cruz, regidor mayor; Antonio Basilio, regidor menor; Salvador Antonio; Mateo Juan, alguacil mayor; Simón de la Cruz; Marcos de la Cruz, topile. —
I did the writing, Sebastián Fabián, notary.

[2]Possibly the missing letters refer to the office of rector which is attributed to Leonardo Juan in No. 52.

54. Bernardino de Sena, San Lucas Evangelista, 1759

(AGN, Civil 664, exp. 2)

BERNARDINO DE SENA appears to be poor compared to many other testators in the corpus. In fact, as far as we can see he possesses only a small field that his late father left him; this he divides in two, leaving one half to his son Julián Dionisio and the other half to his little daughter María Felicia. No further possessions are listed, not even a house of residence, which may thus have been the property of his wife or of her family. He does not refer to his wife in the will, so we cannot be sure that she is alive. Quite unusually, Bernardino treats both his children in the same way even though one is an eldest son who could inherit the property, while the other one is female and still very young. Possibly the reason is the small worth of the total.

The testator's request for burial and mass is standard within the tlaxilacalli of San Lucas; somehow or other Bernardino can afford a mass, or someone else will pay for him. Once again we find the reference to a señor Doctor that is typical of the testaments written by Sebastián Fabián; this time it is accompanied by a traditional expression about kissing his hands and feet that was common in documents of the sixteenth and seventeenth centuries but rarer in the eighteenth. More generally, the opening formula follows Nos. 52 and 53 in practically every line.

By now we see that the fact of not appointing an executor but having numerous and important witnesses from the local official establishment is a well consolidated custom of San Lucas. As usual, those with the highest offices, bearing the don, come first, followed by other officeholders; the names here repeat those of testaments Nos. 52 and 53, issued in the previous month. The notary is again Sebastián Fabián, discussed in the introductory study (p. 43).

[*f. 43*]
Jesus Maria y Josph
Ma moCequisCayetenetzinno yn Ds. tetatzin yhuan yn itlaSomahuizpilitzin yni Ds. espiritu santo yhua notlasomahuiznatzin Sata marian mochipan huel neli yn tlatoCansipotzitli yni nopapan quimotlatlatilitzinnos yn itlasomahuizCeteConetzin yni tt^{o} Jes$\overline{ux}$to yni nchmoponpolhuilitzinnos yn ixiquich notlatlaCol y notlapilichihuala yni quimohuiquilitzinnos yn itlatoCachatzinCon y noteotzin y no y notemaquixtiCatzin yni tt^{o} Ds. y nanima y noliantzin —

[*f. 43*]
Jesus, Mary, and Joseph.
May God the father, his precious revered son, and God the Holy Spirit be entirely praised; and my precious revered mother Santa María, eternally very true royal virgin, will pray for me to her precious revered only child our lord Jesus Christ to pardon me all my sins and evildoing and take my soul and spirit to the royal home of my deity, my redeemer our lord God. —

aXCa Biernes a 17 de agosto de 1759 a^{o}s NiCan nichihuan nomemorian testameton nehual notoCan Bernadino de Sena niCa notlaxilaCalapa Nuestro Pateron S^{r} S^{n} LuCas evagelistan yni Cetlamatli nitlanahuatian ynqua Ds. quimonequilititzinnos yn

Today, Friday the 17th of August of the year of 1759, here I named Bernardino de Sena make my memorandum of testament, here in my tlaxilacalli of our patron lord San Lucas Evangelista. First, I order that when God desires it, if I attain the precious

itla nimomasehuis yn itlasomahuizmiquilitzin yn tt^{o} Ds yni notlanCayo y nosoquio opan motoCas yn iteopanchatzincon yni yn tt^{o} Ds. opan mitos Centel misan yhua setel resposos y nesemopalehuilistzinnos y notlasotatzin Sr Dr D.^{o}[1] nemotlalislis yn ipatzinCon y notlasomahuiztatzin yni Ds. Ca san iquixi nimotenamilia yn imatzin yhua yn ixitzin —
yniC ontlamatli nitlanhuatian Ce militotli onemomaquilitian notlasotatzin mestiCaCa aXCa niCahuilia se nopilitzin ytoCan gulian leonison tlaCo para y tlapa yhuan Se nopoton ytoCan marian felisan o tlaCo y tlatzintla tlaCon se alamo quitoCasque xinatli tlaoli —
niCa nitzoquitian noCoCatlatolo nehual niCoCosqui neual Bernadin de Sen ymizpan notestigohuan alCade D^{n} gergorion rapaele fisCal de la santa mader gelesian D^{n} martin Carlos D^{n} leonardo de la Cruz m[. . .]yordomo retor Leonardo Ju^{o} pelipe de la Cruz regidor mayor antonio basillo regidor menor mateon Ju^{o} alhuasile mayor simo de la Cruz Thopilen marCos de la Cruz
nehual onitlaquilon sebastian favan esSS.^{n}

[1]See No. 52, n. 1.

revered death of our lord God, my earthly body is to be buried in the churchly home of our lord God; there a mass with a responsory prayer is to be said; my precious father señor doctor [. . .][1] is to help me with it; he is to place me before my precious revered father God. That is all [with which] I kiss his hands and feet. —
Second, I order that as for a small cultivated field that my precious late father gave me, now I leave half of it, toward the upper part, to a son of mine named Julián Dionisio, and the other half below to a small daughter of mine named María Felicia; they are to sow 1 almud of maize seed. —
Here I the sick person, Bernardino de Sena, conclude my sick person's statement before my witnesses: alcalde don Gregorio Rafael; fiscal of the holy mother church don Martín Carlos; don Leonardo de la Cruz, mayordomo; rector Leonardo Juan; Felipe de la Cruz, regidor mayor; Antonio Basilio, regidor menor; Mateo Juan, alguacil mayor; Simón de la Cruz, topile; Marcos de la Cruz.
I did the writing, Sebastián Fabián notary.

55. Juan Clemente, San Lucas Evangelista, 1762
(AGN, Civil 664, exp. 2)

THE BEQUESTS OF Juan Clemente are very similar to those of the other male testators from San Lucas who a few years earlier used the same notary. He leaves to his son, Gerardo Josef, all his property, consisting of a house with the saints, a lot, a field, a corncrib, and a mare. Note that with notary Sebastián Fabián the mention of the saints is always accompanied by the same few words about their worship. However, contrary to what happens in the other wills, here we know for sure that Juan Clemente's wife is still alive, since he entrusts her with raising Gerardo, who is therefore still very small. The wife's name is not given, though, and she gets no bequest on her own, although she is probably to be in charge of Gerardo's inheritance until he grows up.

As can be expected by now with testaments from this tlaxilacalli, the introductory formula is quite complex and detailed, while the funeral rites mentioned afterwards are very simple, only a mass with responsory prayer and burial. A señor Doctor who is asked to help with it is still there, being a common feature of all the testaments by Sebastián Fabián. Moreover, here he is preceded by the term "precious father," so we can be sure that he is an ordained priest.

Lastly, and once again in line with the group of wills that I have been analyzing, there is no executor but a long list of witnesses who hold local public offices. A few years have passed since the previous testaments by this notary, and the names of the officials have changed; however, note that the mayordomo of the cofradía, don Leonardo de la Cruz, is still there holding the same post, and that Marcos de la Cruz has been promoted from topile (Nos. 52 and 53) to alguacil mayor.[1]

[1]The don Domingo Ramos listed as alcalde here could very well be the Domingo Ramos of San Lucas who appears twice as a notary (Nos. 49, 50), having acquired the don with the higher office. Advance from notary to the highest local offices is a normal phenomenon, though of course not all notaries advanced. The only problem is the interval of 26 years between the notary's last appearance and the first and only appearance of the alcalde. Domingo Ramos was a set combination of names based on Palm Sunday and therefore was rarely used for lineage *(cont'd)*

This is the last testament we have by Sebastián Fabián, bringing the total to four. Their analysis in the introductory study (p. 43) throws some light on the style of this interesting notary.

[*f.* 42]
Jesus maria y Josph
Ma moCequiCanyetenetzin yntlasomahuiztoCatzin yni D^{s}. tetatzin yhuan yn itlasomahuizpilitzin yni D^{s}. espirtu Santo yhuan notlaSomahuiznatzin Santa maria mochipan huel neli yn ispotzintli yni nopanpan quimotlatlatilitzinnos yn itlaSomahuizseteConetzin yni tt.^{o} D^{s}. Jesu x̂ton yni nchmopopolhuilitzinnos yn ixiquichi y notlatlaCol y notlapilichihualan yn quimohuiquilitzinnos ytlatoCanchantzinCon yni tt.^{o} Ds y naniman y noyolian yni quimohuiquilistzinnos yn itlatoCachantzinCon notlasomahuiztatzin yn D^{s}.[2] aXCa sabado a 23 denero de 1762 a^{os} niCan nichihuan notestameto neual notoCa Juan Celemeten y niCa notlaxilaCapan ypan yalatepetzin Nuestron Patron señor S^{n} luCas evagelistan —

yni setlamatli nitlanhuatian yn iqua D^{s}. quimonequilititzinos yn itlan ninomomaCehuiz yn itlasomahuizmiquilitzin y notlasomahuiztatzin y D^{s}. y notlalanaCayo nopan mitos setel misan yhua setel resposos Capan nitoties yno niquitohuan yn iteCaCopan yn ipalehuiloCa y n[. . .]yolia y noanimatzin yni nemopalehuilis y notlasotatzin Señor D^{o} D.^{ro}[3] —

yniC otlamatli nitlanhuatian se n[o]pilitzin ytoCan — Giraldo Josph nimomaquilitehuan yneman Cali yhua sato yhua satas tlaspanas tlapoposhuiz yhua solar ayaqui quixitoquilis quemarin Ca chiCaties notenhuatili —

yni yetlamatli nitlanhuatia sano yhual nopilitzin giraldo Josph ynemaC nimoCahuilitehua Ce mili matiCa Capan mestiCan satima Cruz y tlapa opa mani yno mili yhuan Ce quesComal yneman yhua Ce yehuana[4] san yehual ynema Jirado Josph ayaqui quixtoquilis quemania y quichihuas nepapa tequili[5] ytla D^{s}. chiCahuali yhuan quiuapahuas ynatzin yni

[*f.* 42]
Jesus, Mary, and Joseph.
May the precious revered name of God the father, his precious revered son, and God the Holy Spirit be entirely praised. And my precious revered mother Santa María, forever very true virgin, will pray for me to her precious revered only child our lord God Jesus Christ to pardon me all my sins and evildoing and take my soul and spirit to the royal home of our lord God [take it to the royal home of my precious revered father God].[2] Today, Saturday the 23rd of January of the year of 1762, here I named Juan Clemente make my testament, here in my tlaxilacalli in the altepetl of our patron lord San Lucas Evangelista. —

First, I order that when God desires it, if I attain the precious revered death of my precious revered father God, a mass with a responsory prayer is to be said for me where my earthly body is to lie buried ; that is what I say concerning the help of my spirit and soul. My precious father señor doctor [. . .][3] is to help me with it. —

Second, I order that to a child of mine named Gerardo Josef I give on dying as his inheritance a house and the male and female saints—he is to sweep and spread incense—and a lot; no one is ever to claim it from him; my command is to be valid.

Third, I order that I likewise leave on dying to my child Gerardo Josef as his inheritance a cultivated field where the most holy cross is, above—that cultivated field is there—and a corncrib as his inheritance, and likewise a [mare][4] is the inheritance of Gerardo Josef; no one is ever to claim it from him. With it he is to do the various duties[5] if God gives

---

continuity. The name was part of the standard repertoire but never extremely common in any one place.

The same considerations apply with the mayordomo don Leonardo de la Cruz, who might be the notary Leonardo de la Cruz of No. 48. In this case the interval would be 27 years. Since the name de la Cruz was often handed on across generations, the mayordomo might be a younger relative of the notary.

[2]At this point several words are inadvertently repeated in the original, so that the exact intention must be deduced.

[3]See No. 52, n. 1.

[4]The form "yehuana" is puzzling; "yehua" by itself could easily be interpreted as *yegua*, "mare," the problem being the additional *na*. Yet intrusive *n* is extremely common in the corpus, and Sebastián Fabián frequently adds a final *a*. Thus it seems likely, though not entirely certain, that his meaning here is "mare."

[5]It is not clear whether the reference is to work tasks or tribute duties.

giraldo Joph Ca sa niCa nitzoquitian noxcatlatol nehual notoCa gua Celemete niCoCosqui ayaquixitini notenhuati ymip notestigohuan alCade D^{n} Domigo ramos D^{n} leonardo del crus mayordomo D^{n} fran^{co} de satiago Bernabel de santiago regidor mayor marCos alegade regido menor leonardo martin merin marCos del Crus [der][6] aluasli mayo Luyz [Coasisa] topilen polito Casiano topilen [*f. 42v*]

nehuala onitlaquilo sebastian favan escrib^{ano} de la republiCan —

him health, and his mother is to raise Gerardo Josef. Here I the sick person named Juan Clemente conclude my sick person's statement; no one is to undo my commands. Before my witnesses: alcalde don Domingo Ramos; don Leonardo de la Cruz mayordomo; don Francisco de Santiago; Bernabé de Santiago regidor mayor; Marcos Alejandre regidor menor; Leonardo Martín merino; Marcos de la Cruz[6] alguacil mayor; Luis [. . . ?] topile; Hipólito Casiano topile. [*f. 42v*]

I did the writing, Sebastián Fabián, notary of the commonwealth. —

[6]The "der" is apparently what is left from another name that was marked out when it was corrected to "Crus."

56. Don Juan Alonso, Santa María de la Asunción, 1692

(AGN, Civil 664, exp. 2)[1]

DON JUAN ALONSO is another prominent testator of Tepemaxalco, with a title implying he has held high office, a great deal of land and livestock, and bequests to many children. He is reminiscent of don Baltasar de los Reyes (No. 46, 1681) or don Juan de la Cruz (No. 39, 1691), though not on so grand a scale. We do not know whether his wife is still alive or not, but all his children seem to be already grown up, which probably explains why the wife is not mentioned. The main heirs are two sons, Miguel and Nicolás, both of whom bear the same second name as the testator. They get a house, half the lot on which the home complex stands, a piece of land, and a yoke of oxen each. If we follow the general rule that children are mentioned in chronological order, Miguel should be the eldest son, and this is borne out. Though the two sons are treated quite equally, Miguel gets 9 almudes of land to his brother's 6, and he gets the primary residence of the father with all the saints.

Don Juan also has three daughters, who receive significant but lesser bequests. All three get one ox; Agustina and Martina Beatriz also receive a cow, while María de la Cruz gets a small piece of land instead. Martina seems to be the one preferred, since in addition to the stock she receives a somewhat larger piece of land and a sacred image, plus another piece of land to pass on to her son. The two properties together bring her portion within an almud of the land that Nicolás receives. The fact that the daughters only get a single ox, not a full yoke, is in line with the tendency to leave yokes to males to be used in agricultural tasks. Finally, a granddaughter receives 5 almudes of land, whereas a grandson, the son of Martina Beatriz, gets only an ox, although 3 almudes left to his mother are ultimately meant for him and seem to go to the mother because he is so little. Another grandchild, the testator of No. 57, goes unmentioned.

If we consider the totality of don Juan's property, his high-ranking position stands out quite clearly. Still further evidence is his possession of such an outstanding image of Nuestra Señora de la Asunción, the patron saint of the tlaxilacalli, that it is actually kept in the main church (apparently the large monastery church at the center of the altepetl) despite being his personal property, a point on which he insists strongly. Only very prominent individuals could afford the expense and be given such a privilege. He first charges his children in general with the worship, then specifies that Miguel Alonso, Nicolás Alonso, and another son, Felipe de la Cruz, are to take care of it. Felipe is not mentioned in the division of don Juan's property, per-

[1]AGN, Tierras 2533, exp. 3, contains at f. 9 a second copy of this Nahuatl will, a very unusual thing to find. The substance of the two agrees quite well; it would require a separate study to do justice to the implications of the existence of two copies and the nature of the differences between them. The copy in Tierras 2533 seems to be later, for example tending to adopt *s* for *ç* and final *z*. The preamble has some small omissions and additions. Most of the body of the will is identical in substance. The discussion of the image in the big church actually adds some phrases not in our version here, though they are in the same spirit.

haps because he has already left home and received his share. Thus only males are given this duty. When they die, they are to pass the worship on to their children in turn, perpetuating a tradition that seems to be very important within the family. A piece of land is left for candles and flowers, and don Juan once again strongly asserts that he was given the land by the municipal authorities and that it is not altepetl property. Clearly confusion between private and public property was a possibility where important sacred images were concerned, and don Juan wanted to be sure his rights were going to be acknowledged.

If the testament in general confirms that we are dealing with a prominent individual, the funeral arrangements are surprisingly sparse, consisting only of a mass with responsory prayer. Maybe don Juan is implicitly counting on his family to provide for a proper ceremony, shroud and burial. On the other hand, the religious formula at the beginning is quite elaborate, and includes a reference to the Virgin Mary that is typical of the tlaxilacalli, as we are going to see in the following testaments as well.

While no executor is mentioned, the three witnesses all hold some public office, and two of them are dons. The notary, don Bernardo de la Cruz, is also one of the few to bear the title don; his style is a mixture of standard, conservative traits and Toluca Valley elements. In the formulaic preamble he is quite prone to syllable omission. Note the curious variation of the plural in "santutzitzin" and "santasme," for male and female saints.

[*f.* 66]

Jesus maria Y Josep

Yca tlaçomahuistucatzin Y Dios tetatzin Yhua dios YtlaçuPiltzin Yhua Dios Espiritu san Ma Ye muchihua ame Jesus maria Y Jonsep Axca Martes a 14 de Nobienbre de 1692 años Nica nicpehualtia Notestametun Nehuatl nicucuxqui notuca D Juan aluço Nica nocha santa marian asupcion Ytla nopa muchihuas Yn içomaltzin Y tt^{o} Dios yhua Yehuatzin Y sihuapili sata maria Yhua mochititzitzin y santutzitzin Y santasMe Yn ilcac onuq̄ yhua Yehuatzin Noangeltzin Yhuan santu san Miguel arCajel Yhua santo San pedro San pablo Nopa mutlatultisq̄ ytla ninomiquilis ynic sentlamatli Nitlanahuatia nopa mitos Ce missa Yhua Ce respusos Y 2tli[2] Nitlanahuatia se nopiltzin Ytoca miguel aloço Nicahuilia Ce Cali Yca santotzitzin yhua tlaco solar yc tlacpac yhua se tlali mani yc calimaYan otli Calaqui tlaoli chicnahui almo yhua se Yota bueyes

Y 3tli Nitlanahuatia oc se Nopiltzin ytuCa Niculas aloço nicCahuilia oc tlaco sular Yhua se cali yhua se tlali mani yc quauhtla otli Calaqui tlaoli se media yhua se yota boeYes

Y 4tli Nitlanahuatia oc se nochpuch ytuca agostina Nicahuilia se bueye yhua ce baCa

Y 5tli Nitlanahuatia oc se nochpuch ytuCa Martina beatris Nicahuilia se tlali mani opa tepetuco sacamuli Calaqui tlaoli ome almo yhua se totlaçonatzin

[*f.* 66]

Jesus, Mary, and Joseph.

In the precious revered name of God the father, God his precious son, and God the Holy Spirit, may it be done, amen. Jesus, Mary, and Joseph. Today Tuesday the 14th of November of the year of 1692, here I the sick person named don Juan Alonso begin my testament; my home is here in Santa María de la Asunción. If the wrath of our lord God falls upon me, the lady Santa María and all the male and female saints who dwell in heaven, and my [guardian] angel, and holy San Miguel Arcángel and holy San Pedro and San Pablo are to speak for me if I die. First, I order that a mass with a responsory prayer is to be said for me. Second,[2] I order that I leave to a son of mine named Miguel Alonso a house with the saints and half a lot, the upper part, and a piece of land on the road to Calimaya where 9 almudes of maize fit, and a yoke of oxen.

Third, I order that I leave to another son of mine named Nicolás Alonso the other half of the lot and a house, and a piece of land on the road to Quauhtla where half a fanega of maize fits, and a yoke of oxen.

Fourth, I order that I leave to another daughter of mine, named Agustina, an ox and a cow.

Fifth, I order that I leave to another daughter of mine named Martina Beatriz a piece of land at Tepetonco, recently cleared, where 2 almudes of maize fit, and

---

[2] In numbering bequests this writer uses an Arabic number instead of writing out the number in Nahuatl as usual, and he elides most of the element *tlamantli*, "item." His "Y 2tli" corresponds to standard *ic ontlamantli*. This style was characteristic of Santa María de la Asunción; see No. 57 and others following.

huadalupe yhua se bueye yhua se baCa

Y 6tli oc se nochpuch Ytoca maria de la Crus NicCahuilia se bueYe yhua se tlali mani opa tepetoCo Y Caxtuli Cuemitl

7tli oc se noxhuiuh Ytuca Maria Nicolasan nicCahuilia se tlali mani yc quauhtla otli ynahuac tetl Calaqui tlaoli maCuili almon

Y 8tli oc se noxhuiuh ytuca niculas niCahuilia se vueye

Y 9tli oc se tlali mani sanopa tepetugo tituquaxochhuia D^{n} anttuño Juares yno tlali Calaqui tlaoli Yei almo nicCahuilia nochpuch Ytoca martina beatris ytla nemis yni ytelpuchto ytoCa niColas oc seppa yehuatl quiCahuilis

Yhua oc se tutlaçonatzin N.tra S^{ra} de la asupCion nicnotequipanilhuia opa metzticCa hueY teopan[3] axca Ca nitlanahuatia quenami nicnotequipanilhuia Yuh quimotequipanilhuisque nopilhua Xochitli Cadelan [*f. 66v*] AYc puhlihuis Ynahuactzico Yhua niquicahuilia se tlali Y caPa quistias Y tlen ic quiMotequipanilhuisque yno tlali MotuCa tlaoli se anega yno tlali onimaCoc amo q̄mania quitosq̄ altepehuaque aço yaxca altepetl yhua tutlaçonatzin amo yYaxCa Altepetl Nehuatl onicnoCohuili ypapan Niquimamaltia nopilhua p^{ra} quimotequipanilhuisq̄ miguel aloço Feliphe de la Cruz yhua niColas aloço Ytla mostla huiptla Momiquilisq̄ sano Yohqui quimamaltitiasq̄ ypilhua ynic quimotequipanilhuisque tlasucihuapili Yni tlali onechmomaquiliq̄ tlatuque Yehuatzin Gobernador D^{n} fran^{co} de la Crus D^{n} Ju^{o} fran^{co} alcalde D^{n} Ju^{o} rico alcalde avh Ca san ixquich onictzoquixti notestamento Ymixpan Notestigos D^{n} Mathias de la Crus fisCal de la santa Yglecia D^{n} fran^{co} diego alłde franc^{co} martin temachti

D^{n} bernal^{do} de la Crus ESCribano

an Our precious mother of Guadalupe, and an ox and a cow.

Sixth, I leave to another daughter of mine named María de la Cruz an ox and a piece of land at Tepetonco with 15 furrows.

Seventh, I leave to another grandchild of mine named María Nicolasa a piece of land on the Quauhtla road next to a rock, where 5 almudes of maize fit.

Eighth, I leave an ox to another grandchild of mine named Nicolás.

Ninth, I leave another piece of land likewise at Tepetonco, bordering [land of] don Antonio Juárez—3 almudes of maize fit in that land—to my daughter named Martina Beatriz. If her little son named Nicolás lives, she is to leave it in turn to him.

And I serve another Our precious mother Nuestra Señora de la Asunción which is at the great church.[3] Now I order that my children are to serve her as I have done; flowers and candles [*f. 66v*] are never to be lacking beside her. And I leave them a piece of land from which is to go along coming what they will serve her with; on that land a fanega of maize is sown. I was given that land; the [authorities? citizens?] of the altepetl are never to say that it is the property of the altepetl. And our precious mother is not the property of the altepetl; I bought her. Therefore I charge my children Miguel Alonso, Felipe de la Cruz, and Nicolás Alonso, to serve her. If they die in the future, they are likewise to charge their children with serving the precious lady. This land was given me by the rulers the governor don Francisco de la Cruz, the alcalde don Juan Francisco, and the alcalde don Juan Rico. That is all. I have concluded my testament before my witnesses: don Matías de la Cruz, fiscal of the holy church; don Francisco Diego, alcalde; Francisco Martín, temachti.

Don Bernardo de la Cruz, notary.

[3]The meaning is apparently the church of San Pedro and San Pablo, shared by the two altepetl of Calimaya and Tepemaxalco and located in the central settlement cluster of the paired altepetl.

57. Pascuala María, Santa María de la Asunción, 1762

(AGN, Civil 664, exp. 2)

THE TESTATOR HERE is the granddaughter of don Juan Alonso (No. 56), as will become clear later on, so she comes from a family prominent in Santa María de la Asunción. She says nothing about her marital status, but she has children and grandchildren, so she is presumably quite advanced in age and may be a widow. The preferred heir (though not overwhelmingly) is a grandchild, Pablo Antonio, who gets the house and half its lot, while the other half goes to a daughter of the testator, Martina Pascuala, who is no longer living in Santa María (note that her second name is her mother's first name); if she comes back the lot will be hers, but otherwise it is to be used by the children who are still present. In addition, Pascuala María has a large piece of land of 9 almudes, which is to be divided among Pablo Antonio, Martina Pascuala, and another daughter, Josefa María, at 3 almudes each. It is not entirely clear whether the testator had a son, since there is only a general reference to the children living locally, but it seems most likely that she has none surviving, since she seems to give preference to the first male heir available from the next generation.

At this point, Pascuala mentions two pieces of land that do not belong directly to her. The first parcel was the property of her sister, to whom it was left in her grandfather's will;[1] the sister had no children and seems to have died by now, so Pascuala gives it to her nieces and nephews. At the end of the testament, she remembers another piece of land, belonging first to her aunt Martina Beatriz and then to Pascuala's brother, who has died. She divides this parcel between a female and a male first cousin. It is the same piece of land that don Juan Alonso had left to Martina in his testament, asking that it go to his grandchild Nicolás at her death, if he lived. Apparently he did not, and the land went first to Martina's nephew, Pascuala's brother. Now Pascuala is giving it to two cousins, or if we read more closely, apparently gave it to them already when her brother died. Here Pascuala shows a great deal of initiative in administering property that does not belong to her; in addition, a female network seems to be in operation, involving Pascuala, a sister, and an aunt.

The full connection with don Juan Alonso is revealed by the impressive image of Nuestra Señora de la Asunción that Pascuala inherited from her father, don Miguel Alonso (note that he did not yet have the title in No. 56), and from her grandfather don Juan Alonso before him. Thus the request of don Juan has been carried out, and the image has been transmitted from one generation to the next, all the while remaining in the large church. Now Pascuala fears that the following generation is going to cause trouble for the arrangement, and she decides to leave the image to the altepetl authorities. In a sense, her request goes against what don Juan had been trying to assert, that the image was his property and not the authorities'. But she seems to fear not so much corporate appropriation as dissension among her relatives, probably over who is to be in charge of the cult and the land. Her deep devotion to the image can be perceived through her concern that its worship should be maintained.

As in No. 56, funeral arrangements are very basic despite the high rank of the testator, just a mass and an offering to the fund for Jerusalem. On the other hand, again as before, the religious formula at the beginning is long and complex, with invocations of various saints and of Nuestra Señora de la Asunción in particular. The formulaic elements seem to be specific to the tlaxilacalli Santa María de la Asunción, and if with her grandfather we could wonder whether the primary factor was the early time and its conservative usage, here we see much the same two generations later.

Our testator is a very good example of how status was shown in the name much more consistently with males, who received the don with high local office and more frequently bore prestigious second names, than with females. Pascuala María's name is different in nothing from that of the most humble indigenous woman in the area. One would have thought that at least she could have been called doña; but from indications in the corpus it may be that only wives of governors who belonged to dynasties, like the wife of don Juan de la Cruz, received the title. Yet it may be that there were subtle ways of emphasizing the female line through naming, as in the fact that Pascuala's daughter's second name is taken from her own first name and not from those of her husband or males in the direct line.

Pascuala follows the example of her grandfather also in the fact that she appoints no executor; this detail, together with very simple funeral rituals and the elaborate formulas of the preamble, reminds one of another set of testaments with similar characteristics, those of the tlaxilacalli of San Lucas Evangelista. In contrast, the witnesses are numerous and all prominent individuals bearing the title don. One is the present alcalde, don Pedro de la Cruz, possibly a descendant of the don Pedro de la Cruz who founded the gubernatorial dynasty, while all five of the others are past alcaldes. It appears that a concerted effort was made to assemble the entire corps of all

[1]In No. 56 the piece is 5 almudes, here 4. The identical descriptions in the two documents are so specific that we cannot doubt the same parcel is involved. It is possible either that 1 almud was given to someone else meanwhile, or that there has been a difference of opinion about the measurements.

those who had ever held the office in Santa María.

The numerous threads in the cluster of Nos. 56 and 57 allow us to reconstruct the situation over three generations of a prominent family and particularly to grasp the role of a woman, the testator here, in that context. In some fashion Pascuala María has for a time occupied the position of the head of an important lineage in the local society and economy; she has become, if she was not originally, the primary heir for her generation. Don Juan Alonso left 9 almudes of land to his son the future don Miguel Alonso; the primary 9 almudes that Pascuala María possesses must be the same land. The house she lives in is probably the same one that don Juan left to don Miguel.

The symbol of the line, the image of the patron saint in the great church, went not to a son of don Miguel but to her. One would think that it most likely would have been left first to her brother and later to her by default, but she says that her father gave it directly to her. However that may be, it appears that both her brother and her sister died before her and that she was left as the only adult member of her generation in the direct line, and no adult males survived in the next generation either. As the head of the family she not only administers the famous image of Santa María, but has been managing the inheritance of her deceased siblings, assigning properties to the collateral line as necessary. The solidarity of the larger group is seen not only in her allocations but in the fact that the name Nicolás/Nicolasa, prominent in the direct line, is found among the others as well. From the point of view of the disappearance of adult males in the direct line we can understand the female networking better, seeing that it is a very real phenomenon, but at the same time that it was brought about by necessity. Pascuala María herself has now moved to place a male, her grandson, in the central position again. Note however that though her husband must have been alive during a large part of her life, his role in inheritance allocation and family activities was negligible.

The present document in connection with No. 56 has suggestive if not definitive information on local jurisdictional matters and concepts. When don Juan Alonso spoke of the altepetl, since in the same breath he mentioned the governor, and in the whole of Tepemaxalco there was only one governor at a time, there can be no doubt that he was referring to the entire larger unit and its government. Pascuala María seems to be doing the same when she talks about giving the image to the altepetl authorities. But in other passages the word *altepetl* seems to be used differently. In the testaments from Santa María de la Asunción in general, Santa María is called neither a tlaxilacalli, as it traditionally had been and by rights still was, nor an altepetl (another ambitious tlaxilacalli, San Lucas, was occasionally referred to as an altepetl in its own documents). The issue is usually avoided, though in No. 60 Santa María is for once unambiguously called an altepetl. When Pascuala María speaks of relatives who live and work in the altepetl and can receive bequests, as opposed to others who do not and can receive bequests only if they return, we can hardly avoid the impression that Santa María specifically is meant, not the scattered Tepemaxalco overall. It is as though the word *altepetl* in addition to retaining its traditional meaning had also become a synonym for the Spanish *pueblo*, for no doubt the Spaniards would have called the settlement of Santa María a pueblo (for other similar instances see Nos. 58, 61, and 68). In any case, we see in these statements of the testator the ongoing conflict between people whose self-interest drove them far from their home entities, and those remaining, who tried to exert counterpressure to reverse the movement.

The situation with the notary is very unusual. Official notary don Antonio Silverio (see p. 44) entrusts a past notary, Luis Martín (see p. 43), with the writing; we will find quite a few testaments written by the latter in Santa María. The style is typical of the eighteenth-century Toluca Valley, and at times syllables are missing or repeated. Note the Spanish influence in the unusual expression "tlen oora," for "at whatever time." If we wonder why Luis Martín wrote for don Antonio, No. 67, done by plain Antonio Silverio in 1758 before he acquired the don, shows us that his writing skills were marginal, far below those of Luis Martín.

[*f. 61*]
Jesus Maria y Joephe
Ma muSenquisCayetenectzinno yn itlaSunMahuis-

[*f. 61*]
Jesus, Mary, and Joseph.
May the precious revered consummate name of God

SenquisCatocatzinCatzin yn dios tetantzin yhua dios ytlaSunpiltzin yhua dios espirito Santo yeititzintzin perSonas Ca San se huel neli teol dios yhua no yenhuatzin notlaSunmahuisNantzin Nra Senora de la Assump,^{on} quimotlactilis yn itlaSummahuisSenteConetzin yn tt,^{o} X̄p̄,^{o} ynic quimoSelilis noanimantzin noyoliantzin yntla yoqui nopa muChihuas ninomiquilis yhua San miguel arCanJel yhua S,^{n} p,^{o} yhua San pablo niquinotlatlactilia nicchihua notestamento nehual niCoCoxqui notuCa pasquala Maria niCa niChane Santa maria de la Assump,^{on} axCa Sabado a 24 de abril de 1762 años —

1 = huel achtopa nitlahuatia motemaCas se tomintzin JeruSalen yhuan se miSa nopa mintos Ca yehual ypalehuiloCa noanimantzin y noyoliantzin yes —

2 – tli nitlanahuatia Caltzintli yhua tlaCo Solar nicCahhuilia noxhui pablo antonio yhua oc tlanCo Solar niCahuilia noxpuh martina pasquala yntla dios quimoquenpilis tlen oora hualmuhuiCas nima nima Conas tlen iaxCa yhua tlaCamo yes quenami onCa yc tequipanosque ynique nopilhua yninque onCate yn altepetl neltis noCoCoxCatlantol yxpatzinCo dios ammaqui nechimaquilis netequipaCholi —

3 – tli nitlanahuatia Se tlali mani yc Calimaya ontli titoquasuchnamiqui D,^{n} antoni Salbador Calimaya[2] Calaqui tlaoli Chinahui almu nicCahuahuilia Canpa Calaqui yei almu tlaoli pablo antonnio yhua Oc yei almu nicCahuilia noxpoh Joepha maria yhua oc yei almu nicCahuilia oc se noxpoh yto martina pasquanla amo mostla huictla omotontopectinemisq̄[3] neltis noCoCoxCatlanto yxpatzinCo yn tt.^{o} D.^{s} —

4 – tli nitlanahuatia yehuatzin tutlasunmahuisnantzin Nra Señora de la Assump,^{on} nicnotequipanilhui onpa metztiCa huehui teopa oquimuCahuilintia noCultzin mestiCatCa D,^{n} Juan alonso oquimoCahuilili no[*f. 61v*]tantzin metztiCatCa D,^{n} miguel alonSo yeihuatzin onehmuCahuilili nicmotequipanilhui huā axCa para amu yes netequipaCholi yCa nopilhua yhua noSobrinoS yhua nosobrinas axCa yCa mochi nopaquilis niquinoCahuililia altepehuaq̄ yehuatzintzin quimotequipanilhuisq̄ anmo pulihuis xuchil Candela yhua Se miSa Cantada moChictiCa ypa Se xihuil ylhuitzin neltis noCoCoxCatlantol yxpatzinCo dios —

the father, God his precious son, and God the Holy Spirit, three persons but only one very true deity God, be entirely praised. And also my precious revered mother Nuestra Señora de la Asunción is to implore her precious revered only child, our lord Christ, to accept my soul and spirit if it should happen to me that I die, and I implore San Miguel Arcángel, San Pedro, and San Pablo. I the sick person named Pascuala María, citizen here in Santa María de la Asunción, make my testament today Saturday the 24th of April of the year of 1762. —

1. First of all I order that a real is to be given for Jerusalem, and a mass is to be said for me to be the help of my soul and spirit. —

2nd I order that I leave the house and half of the lot to my grandchild Pablo Antonio, and I leave the other half of the lot to my daughter Martina Pascuala. If God brings her back, at whatever time she comes back she is to take what belongs to her, and if not it will remain as it is; those of my children who are in the altepetl will use it. My sick person's statement is to be realized before God; no one is to give them grief for me. —

3rd I order that there is a piece of land on the Calimaya road bordering on [land of] don Antonio Salvador of Calimaya[2] into which fit 9 almudes of maize; I leave 3 almudes of maize to Pablo Antonio, 3 more I leave to my daughter Josefa María, and 3 more I leave to another daughter of mine named Martina Pascuala. They are not to go shoving one another around[3] in the future. My sick person's statement is to be realized before our lord God. —

4th I order that I have served our precious revered mother Nuestra Señora de la Asunción who is at the great church; my late grandfather don Juan Alonso left her; he left her to my [*f. 61v*] late father don Miguel Alonso, and he left her to me for me to serve her. Now so that there will not be trouble with my children, nephews, and nieces, now with great pleasure I leave her to the altepetl authorities. They are to serve her; flowers and candles are not to be lacking, and a high mass is to be performed every year on her feast day. My sick person's statement is to be realized before God. —

---

[2]This person would seem to be the wealthy don Antonio Salvador, citizen of Calimaya Teopantonco, who issued his will in this same year of 1762 (No. 82).

[3]In standard orthography this form would be *onmoto(h)topeuhtinemizque*.

5 – tli nitlanahuatia oc Se tlali mani ynahuac tel yc quactla ontli yaxCa noermana maria niColaSa Calaqui tlaoli nahui almu anmaqui quipien Se yCone axCa niquinCahuilia noSobrinos SenSe almū Juana niColasa se almu yhua petrona m,^{a} yhua tla hualas tequipanosq̄ ypilhua ypa altepetl Conanas yhua tlaCamo yes quenami oCatCa —

5th I order that there is another piece of land close to a rock on the Quauhtla road that is the property of my sister María Nicolasa, into which fit 4 almudes of maize; she had no children. Now I leave it to my nieces and nephews, 1 almud each: 1 almud to Juana Nicolasa and Petrona María, and if [their?] children come to work in the altepetl they are to take [their part], and if not it is to be as it was. —

6 – tli nitlanahuatia Ca san ixquih nictzoquixtia notestanmento yxpatzinCo yn tt,^{o} yhua notestigos fisCal de la Santa ygleSia D,^{n} miguel de Sa Ju^{o} motlaneltililisq̄ yehuātzintzin yxpatzinCo yn tt,^{o} D,^{s} alCalde auctual D,^{n} pe[. . .] de la Cruz D,^{n} antonio fransisCo alC^{e} pasado D,^{n} Jua aStasio AlC,^{e} pasado D,^{n} niCulas tolentino AlC,^{e} paSado Dn Jua Jocphe alC,^{e} pasado Dn Pedro antonio AlC,^{e} pasado

hua nehual onitlaCuylo ytenCopa esCribano hua CoCoxqui Luis Martin Ess,^{no} pasado

Ess,^{no} D.^{n} antonio Siberio

yhua oc Se onquilnamiqui oc Se tlali Calaqui tlaoli yei almu yaxCa notia martina beatriz yhua yhua yquac omuquili oquiCahuili noermano matias axCa y omumiquili noermano ypanpanno oniquixelhui noprimermana Gregoria m.^{a} [*f. 61 bis*] yhua noprimoermano niColas miguel[4]

6th I order that this is all; I conclude my testament before our lord and my witnesses, who will verify it before our lord God: fiscal of the holy church don Miguel de San Juan; present alcalde, don Pedro de la Cruz; don Antonio Francisco past alcalde; don Juan Anastasio past alcalde; don Nicolás de Tolentino past alcalde; don Juan Josef past alcalde; don Pedro Antonio past alcalde.

And I did the writing at the command of the notary and the sick person, Luis Martín past notary.

Notary don Antonio Silverio.

And I remembered another piece of land into which 3 almudes of maize fit, belonging to my aunt Martina Beatriz, and when she died she left it to my brother Matías. Now that my brother has died, because of that I divided it between my female first cousin Gregoria María [*f. 61 bis*] and my male first cousin Nicolás Miguel.[4]

[4]Don Juan Alonso of No. 56 originally instructed that on the death of Martina Beatriz the land go to her son Nicolás. That she gave it to a brother instead seems to tell us that her son Nicolás had meanwhile died and that the present recipient of half the land, Nicolás Miguel, though of the right generation, is not the same person as Martina Beatriz's son.

58. Alonso Cristóbal, Santa María de la Asunción, 1759

(AGN, Civil 664, exp. 2)

IN STRIKING CONTRAST with the cluster that we have just perused, the testator here appears to be a relatively poor man, at least from the property listed in his will. Only a single small piece of land (2 almudes or 20 quahuitl, the typical minimal or basic plot) is mentioned, going to his son Juan Martín, but no house or any other kind of possession. He states that he bought the land and can prove it through two notarial documents; he adds that whoever wants to attack his son's rights should verify them before God, the curate, and the alcalde mayor, thus invoking Spanish religious and civil authorities as well as the deity to protect his property. Such statements are not unheard of in Nahuatl documentation but are almost absent in the Calimaya/Tepemaxalco region as seen in the present corpus.

Alonso Cristóbal mentions no other children, so maybe Juan Martín is the eldest son, or the last one who is still waiting for his share of the father's estate, or again the only surviving one. The fact that the testator does not include any reference to his wife may not be meaningful, since, as we have already seen in many cases, it may just reflect the fact that there are no small children to take care of.

Juan Martín is called upon also for funeral arrangements and is to provide for shroud, burial and mass; this seems to confirm the impression that Alonso is poor and in need of his son's help. Following the style of the tlaxilacalli, the religious formula at the beginning is quite complex and includes an invocation of the Virgin.

No executor is appointed, while the witnesses all hold or have held a public office, and we find some names already familiar from the testament of Pascuala María (No. 57): don Pedro de la Cruz, who will be alcalde again a few years later (the date of No. 57 is 1762); don Miguel de San Juan, past alcalde (and frequent notary), who will become fiscal; and don Nicolás de Tolentino, in both testaments a past alcalde.

In most documents from Santa María de la Asunción the entity is neither put in any particular category nor described as within any larger jurisdiction. Here Santa María is seen as within the altepetl of "San Pedro and San Pablo Calimaya." Much evidence shows that Santa María was in fact a tlaxilacalli of San Pablo Tepemaxalco, not of San Pedro Calimaya. Here both parts of the overarching double altepetl are included in terms of patron saints, but in terms of Nahuatl names only Calimaya appears. This usage seems affected by the Spanish tendency to call the settlement Calimaya only. It is one of the many hints we see in the corpus of confusion about the original terminology and arrangements of the complex altepetl Calimaya/Tepemaxalco.

The notary Luis Martín's writing falls entirely within the eighteenth-century Toluca Valley style and is discussed in the introductory study (p. 43).

[*f. 69*]
Ma musenquisCayectenectzinno yn itlasummahuissenquisCatoCantzin yn dios tetantzin yhua dios ytlasunmahuizpiltzin yhua dios espirito Santo yn yeititzintzin teotlaCatzintzinti yn personas Ca Sa Çe huel neli teol y dios yhua no yenhuatzin notlansumahuisnantzin sihuapili Santa maria nicnotlatlactilia, ynic nopanpa quimutlatlactilis yn iSenteConetzin yn tt.^{o} x̄p̄o ynic quimoselilis noanimatzin y noyoliantzin yntla ycqui nopa moChihuas ninomiquilis nehual niCoCoxqui notuCa alonso Christobal maysihui huel muCoCotiCa notlallo nosoquio yhuā nanimantzin ca amu q̄ Ca Ca Sa pactiCa niChane Santa maria de la asump.^{on} nicchihua notestamento niCa yntic yni altepel Sr S.^{n} pedro y S.^{n} pablo Calimaya ypa yni tonali mierColes a 2 de mayo yhua xihuil de 1759 años — [*f. 69v*]
huel achtopa nitlanahuatia motemacas Se tomitzin JeruSalen yhua se misa nopa mintos yhua se responso Ca yehual ypalehuiloCa noanimantzin noyoliantzin yes —
2: tli: nitlanahuatia Ca yehual nopiltzin Jua[. . .] martin nechitas yhua nechquimilos yhu[. . .] nehtuCas yhua nehChihuilis nomiSa Ca n[. . .]ltis noCoCoxCatlantol yxpatzinCo y tt.^{o} d.^{s}
3: tli: nitlanahuatia sano yehual nopiltzin Juan martin nicCahuilia se tlaltotli mani ynahuac altepel[1] titoquanxunamiqui Dn Juan JoC̄p̄h Calaqui tlaoli om[. . .] almud notlaCual nicpie ome esCritura aqui mustla huictla tlen quintos yehual tlaneltilis yxpa

[*f. 69*]
May the precious revered consummate name of God the father, God his precious revered son, and God the Holy Spirit, three divine persons but one very true deity God, be entirely praised. I also implore my precious revered mother the lady Santa María to pray on my behalf to her only child our lord Christ to accept my soul and spirit if it should happen to me that I the sick person named Alonso Cristóbal should die. Although my earthly body is very ill, nothing is wrong with my soul, but it is sound. I, a citizen of Santa María de la Asunción, make my testament here in this altepetl [of the] lord San Pedro and San Pablo of Calimaya on this day of Wednesday, the 2nd of May in the year of 1759. — [*f. 69v*]

First of all I order that a real is to be given for Jerusalem, and a mass with a responsory prayer is to be said for me; that will be the help of my soul and spirit. —
Second I order that my child Juan Martín is to look after me, to shroud me, bury me, and have a mass said for me. My sick person's statement is to be realized before our lord God.
Third I order that I likewise leave to my child Juan Martín a little piece of land close to the altepetl,[1] bordering [land of] don Juan Josef, where 2 almudes of maize fit; I bought it, and I have two notarial documents. Whoever should say anything about it in

---

[1]Apparently the reference is to the settlement, the part with a concentration of houses, equivalent of Spanish *pueblo*, as in some other instances in the corpus. Since the document has just called the combined entities Calimaya and Tepemaxalco an altepetl, that settlement is most likely meant, but possibly the meaning is Santa María itself. See also the introduction to No. 57.

tzinCo dios yhua señor [. . .]ura noso señor alCalde mayor neltis noCoCoxCatlatol yxpatzinCo dios —

Ca san ixquih nictzoquihtia notestamento yxpatzinCo dios yhua notestigos fiscal de la Santa yglesia Dn Santiago martin D.^{n} pedro de la Cruz alCalde ordinario [*f. 70*] Rexidor mayor pasqual de la Cruz Dn Miguel de san Ju^{o} al^{e} pasado, D.^{n} niColas tolentino testigo alCalde pasado pablo albertu tepixqui

hua nehual nitlaCuyloa ytenCopa Cocoxqui luis martin es.^{no} de Rp.^{ca}

the future is to verify it before God and the lord curate or the lord alcalde mayor. My sick person's statement is to be realized before God. —

That is all. I conclude my testament before God and my witnesses, the fiscal of the holy church don Santiago Martín; don Pedro de la Cruz, alcalde ordinario; [*f. 70*] regidor mayor Pascual de la Cruz; don Miguel de San Juan, past alcalde; don Nicolás de Tolentino, witness, past alcalde; Pablo Alberto, tepisque.

And I am doing the writing at the order of the sick person, Luis Martín, notary of the commonwealth.

59. Marcelino de la Cruz, Santa María de la Asunción, 1759

(AGN, Civil 664, exp. 2)

HERE WE HAVE another case in which a testament is issued merely to set up the funeral; no property is listed at all. Marcelino de la Cruz has a son, Juan Santos, whom he asks to have a mass celebrated for his soul, and that is the only reference in the document to any family member. It would seem that the will was written in haste, when Marcelino was on the verge of death.

Funeral arrangements are relatively modest, a characteristic of all the testaments from Santa María, as we have already seen; they consist of the usual mass with responsory prayer and an offering to the fund for Jerusalem. On the other hand, the religious formula at the beginning is quite well developed and stands out compared to the simplicity of the rest of the will. It is basically the same preamble that is found in other testaments by this notary.

No executor is appointed, while there are three witnesses, all of them officials and two of them dons. The alcalde ordinario is once again don Pedro de la Cruz, as in No. 58. Note the continuing predominance of the famous de la Cruz family among the holders of public offices in Santa María; the alcalde and the regidor mayor share this same second name. Marcelino is possibly a poor relative of this group, but since the name was so common everywhere, no definite conclusions can be drawn.

The notary is once again Luis Martín, whose style is analyzed in the introductory study (p. 43).

[*f. 25*]

Jesus m.^{a} y Jo~~Cph~~

Ma moÇenquisCayectenectzinno yn itlasunmahuisSenquisCatoCantzin yn D.^{s} tetantzin yhua D.^{s} ytlasummahuispiltzin yhua dios espirito San yn lleititzintzin teotlaCatzintzinti San Se huel neli teol yn D.^{s} yhua nu yenhua notlanSummahuisnantzin Sihuapili Santa m.^{a} nicnutlatlactilia ynic nupapan quimutlatlactilis yn iSenteConetzin yn tt.^{o} JeSu christo ynic quimuSelilis noanimantzin nollolian-tzin nicChihua nomemoria testamento nehual niCoCoxqui niCa niChane Santa maria de la Assump.^{on} NotuCa marSelino de la Crus —

1: huel ahtopa nitlanahuatia motemacas Se tomintzin JeruSale yhua se misa yhua rrespos Ca huel ypalehuiloCa noannimantzin nolloliantzin yes —

2: tli nitlanahuatia hel ninotolia amu [*f. 25v*] tle ninopielia yhua nitlanahuatia nop[. . .]tzin Ju^{o}

[*f. 25*]

Jesus, Mary, and Joseph.

May the precious revered consummate name of God the father, God his precious revered son, and God the Holy Spirit, three divine persons but just one very true deity God, be entirely praised. And I also implore my precious revered mother lady Santa María to pray on my behalf to her only child our lord Jesus Christ to accept my soul and spirit. I named Marcelino de la Cruz, a sick person, citizen here in Santa María de la Asunción, make my memorandum of testament. —

First of all, I order that a real is to be given for Jerusalem, and a mass with a responsory prayer will be the great help of my soul and spirit. —

Second, I order that I am very poor, [*f. 25v*] I have nothing, and I order that my child Juan Santos is to

Santos yhua nechihuilis nom[. . .]Sa Ca san ixiquih nictzonquixtia notestamento AXCa biernes a 7 de disienbre yhua xihu[e]l de 1759 años yhua n[. . .]testigos AlCalde Ordinario D.^{n} pedro de la Crus Rexidor mayor D.^{n} pasqual de la Crus teopa topile paulin[o rio]
Ess.^{no} de la rrepublica luis martin

have a mass performed for me. That is all. I conclude my testament today, Friday the 7th of December of the year of 1759, and my witnesses are: alcalde ordinario don Pedro de la Cruz; regidor mayor don Pascual de la Cruz; church topile Paulin[o Río].

Notary of the commonwealth Luis Martín.

60. Juana María, Santa María de la Asunción, 1760

(AGN, Civil 664, exp. 2)

WITH THIS TESTAMENT the suspicion that at least some brief and simple wills were actually written after the death of the supposed testator is confirmed and becomes reality. The document contains a clear statement that Juana María is already dead and that some officials or notable persons of the tlaxilacalli are issuing the document for her. They speak in the first person and refer to her in the third. Her husband, Juan Gregorio, is still alive, but quite surprisingly he is not called upon to issue the testament as in other cases (see Nos. 20 and 34); he is referred to only where the mass is concerned.

Contrary to what happens in No. 59, here some property is mentioned. Juana María had a piece of land in San Antonio de Padua (a tlaxilacalli within Calimaya), which is to be shared by two children, Pedro Martín and Pascual Antonio. The land measures 2 almudes, so it is of the average size, but the one almud that each child receives is very little. The two children will most likely, however, get an additional inheritance from their father.

We know by now that a mass with responsory prayer and an offering to Jerusalem are standard features in Santa María, and so it is here as well; once again the opening religious formula is quite complex, very much in line with what we have already seen in the other testaments by this notary.

The testament ends with the names of the officials who are responsible for issuing it, the fiscal, the alcalde, and the regidor mayor, all of them with the title don. Note that the fiscal is the same as in No. 58, and the alcalde appears elsewhere more than once as past alcalde.

The notary is still Luis Martín (see p. 43), here with an addition to his name, de Francia, that does not appear in any other document. He seems to be beginning the process of signaling higher pretensions, thinking probably of something along the lines of the career of his local colleague the notary Miguel de San Juan (see pp. 43–44), who eventually became alcalde and fiscal and as such bore the don. "Don Luis Martín de Francia, fiscal of the holy church," may not be very many years in the future.

This is the one testament in the Santa María series that unambiguously calls the entity an altepetl, although it was traditionally a tlaxilacalli of Tepemaxalco and still functions within that framework at this time.

[*f. 26*]
Jesus m^{a} y JoCph
Ma moSenquisCayectenectzinno yn itlasummaahuisSenquisCayectenectzinno yn itlasummahuistoCantzin yn dios tetantzin yhua dios ytlasunmahuispiltzin yhua dios espirito Santo yeititzintzin teotlaCatzintzinti personas Ca Ca San Se huel neli ol dios[1] yhua no yehuatzin notlasummahuisnantzin Sihuapili Santa maria nicnutlatlactilia ynic nupanpa quimutlatlactilis yn isenteConetzin yn tt^{o} Xp̂^{o} ynic quimoselilis noanimantzin noyoliantzin yntla ycqui

[*f. 26*]
Jesus, Mary, and Joseph.
May the precious revered name of God the father, God his precious revered son, and God the Holy Spirit, three divine persons but just one very true deity God, be entirely praised.[1] And I also implore my precious revered mother lady Santa María to pray on my behalf to her only child our lord Christ to accept my soul and spirit; if it is done at his order he

---

[1]The writer started to put "his precious revered name" but became confused, and half way through the word began repeating the verbal phrase just preceding, then finally wrote "his precious revered name" after all.

ytenCopatzinCo moChihuas quimoselilis ma y mo-Chihua ame Jesus m$^{\underline{a}}$ y Jo~~Cph~~ —
1 = huel ahtopa moteCaS Se tomitzin JeruSalen yhua Se miSa nopa mintos yhua Se rrespoSo yehual ypalehuiloCa yanimantzin ylloliantzin yni mec-tzintli ytoCa Juana m$^{\underline{a}}$ ticchihuilia yn itestamento aXCa Sabado a 13 de Setienbre xihuil ypa 1760 años
2 = tlamantli ynamictzin Juan Gregorio quiChi-huislis misa yhua se tlali quipie onpa Santo S.^{n}n atoni de padua mani puetetitla Calaqui tlaoli ome almu quiCa[*f. 26v*]huilia omenti ypilhuatoto Se ytoca pedro martin yhua pasqual antonio quimone-patlaxelhuisq̄ sense almo [. . .]nasq̄ Ca San ixquih tictzonquixtia yn itestamento tehuati titlatequi-p[. . .]noCatzintzinhua yn tt$^{\underline{o}}$ D$^{\underline{s}}$ fiscal de [. . .] Santa yglesia D$^{\underline{n}}$ Santiago martín ALC$^{\underline{e}}$ autual D$^{\underline{n}}$ NiColas de tholentino Rexidor mayor D$^{\underline{n}}$ pablo masial

Ess=^{no} luis martín de fransia Ypa yni altepel Santa maria de la asunp$^{\underline{on}}$

will receive it. May it be done, amen. Jesus, Mary and Joseph. —
First of all a real is to be given for Jerusalem, and a mass with a responsory prayer is to be said for me; it is the help of the soul and spirit of this dead person named Juana María, whose testament we make for her today, Saturday the 13th of September of the year of 1760.
Second, her husband Juan Gregorio is to provide a mass for her. And she leaves a piece of land she has at [the settlement called] holy San Antonio de Padua, next to the bridge [or at Puentetitlan], in which 2 almudes of maize fit, [*f. 26v*] to her two little children, one named Pedro Martín and [the other] Pascual Antonio; they are to divide it equally; they are to get one almud each. That is all. we the servants of our lord God conclude her testament, fiscal of the holy church don Santiago Martín; present alcalde don Nicolás de Tolentino; regidor mayor don Pablo Marcial.
Notary Luis Martín de Francia in this altepetl of Santa María de la Asunción.

61. Francisco Javier, Santa María de la Asunción, 1762

(AGN, Civil 664, exp. 2)

FRANCISCO JAVIER follows the lines of the previous testaments by issuing a simple and relatively short will, but this time including the distribution of some property. He leaves the house with a saint and half the lot to his son Miguel Nicolás, while the other half is to be divided between two smaller children, Isidro Antonio and Julián Martín, for them to establish their homes there in the future. The two little sons also share a small piece of land and are entrusted to the care of Francisco's wife. Thus the testator distributes his property among his three male children, with the eldest being preferred; although the youngest two seem to get more land, the amount after division is so small as almost to be insignificant. It is interesting to note that Francisco wishes all his children to live on the same lot, building their houses there. The same tendency is seen elsewhere in the corpus. For people of modest means the policy seems almost inevitable; at the same time it tends to perpetuate the multi-family complex often seen among the Nahuas from the early sixteenth century forward. As often happens, the wife comes into the picture only to raise little children and does not get any property at all.

Francisco's funeral arrangements are the basic ones normal in this tlaxilacalli: a mass with responsory prayer and an offering to Jerusalem. Once again, the opening religious formula is quite long and contains an invocation of the Virgin Mary. While Francisco does not give the impression of being impoverished, he owns very little land outside the lot his house is on. No member of his family has a name of any distinction, nor do any of the names contain common elements. As usual in Santa María, no executor is appointed, but it seems meaningful that the only witness is the obligatory fiscal. We seem to see here a person with property below average and few or no ties with the higher-ranking portion of the community.

This is the last testament of the series by notary Luis Martín, who is commented on in the introductory study (p. 43).

[*f. 36*]
Jesus Maria y JoCphe
Ma muSenquisCayectenectzinno yn itlaSummahuisSenquiSCatoCatzin yn D.s tetatzin yhua D.s ytlasunmahuispiltzin yhua D.s espirito Santo yeititzintzin teotlaCatzintzinti personas Ca san Se huel neli teol dios yhua no yehuatzin nutlasumahuisnantzin Sihuapili Santa maria nicnutlatlactilia ynic nopanpa quimutlatlactilis yn iSenteConetzin yn tt,o Xp.o yntla ycqui nopa moChihuas yntla ninomiquilis nehual niCoCoxqui notuCa Frco xabiel nica niChane Santa maria de la Assump,on nicChihua notestamento nehual AxCa Juebes a 11 de febrero yhua xihuil de 1762 años —
1 = huel ahtopa nitlanahuatia motemaCas Se tomitzin Jerusalen yhua se miSa nopa mitos yhua Se rresponSo Ca yehual ypalehuiloCa noanimantzin noyoliantzin yes —
2 = tlamantli nitlanahuatia Caltzintli yhua Señor S antonio yhua tlaCo Solar para yc tlacpac nicCahuilia nopiltzin miguel niColas yhua oc tlaCo Solar para yc tlatzintla niquinCahuilia oc omenti nopilhuatoto ysidro antonio yhua Julia Martin para Canpa quiquetzasq̄ ynCha ytla dios quimochiCahuilis neltis noCoCoxCatlatol yxpatzinCo dios =
3 = nitlanahuatia oc Se tlaltotli mani ynahuac altepel[1] timocquaxuhnamiqui D.n blas difunto Calaqui tlaoli Se almo monepantlaxelhuis o yn omenti nopilhuatoto ysidro antonio yhua Julian martin yhua nitlahuatia noSihuatzin yehual nechimitilis nopilhuatoto nechihuapahuilis neltis noCoCoxCatlantol yxpatzinCo dios Ca san ixquih nictzoquixtia notestamento yxpatzinco dios yhua notestigos Fiscal de la Santa yglesia D.n Gaspar de los Reyes

Essno luis Martin

[*f. 36*]
Jesus, Mary, and Joseph.
May the precious revered consummate name of God the father, God his precious revered son, and God the Holy Spirit, three divine persons but one very true deity God, be entirely praised. And also I implore my precious revered mother, the lady Santa María, to pray on my behalf to her only child our lord Christ, if it happens to me that I die. I the sick person named Francisco Javier, citizen here in Santa María de la Asunción, make my testament today, Thursday the 11th of February of the year of 1762. —

First of all, I order that one real is to be given for Jerusalem, and a mass with a responsory prayer is to be said for me; it will be the help of my soul and spirit. —
Second, I order that I leave the house and señor San Antonio and half the lot, above, to my child Miguel Nicolás, and I leave the other half of the lot, below, to my two other little children Isidro Antonio and Julián Martín as a place to build their homes, if God gives them health; my sick person's statement is to be carried out before God. =
Third, I order that another small piece of land close to the altepetl[1] that borders on [land of] the deceased don Blas, in which 1 almud of maize fits, is to be divided in the middle for my two little children Isidro Antonio and Julián Martín, and I order that my wife is to look after my little children for me and raise them for me; my sick person's statement is to be carried out before God. That is all. I conclude my testament before God and my witnesses, fiscal of the holy church don Gaspar de los Reyes.
Notary Luis Martín.

[1]The way *altepetl* is used here does not correspond to the traditional sense of the whole area or jurisdiction of the sociopolitical unit, but seems to be the same as Spanish *pueblo*, meaning only the built-up settlement. The reference here is probably to Santa María specifically rather than to Tepemaxalco or Calimaya/Tepemaxalco. A similar instance occurs in No. 57; see the commentary there as well.

62. Guillermo Martín, Santa María de la Asunción, 1737
(AGN, Tierras 2301, exp. 9)[1]

WHAT DRAWS our attention about the present will is that the testator is not from Santa María de la Asunción but from Tenango del Valle further south in the valley. He married a local woman, however, and thus he is in Santa María when death comes upon him. His testament is not quite like those of citizens of the tlaxilacalli, for Santa María and the testator's affiliation are mentioned only at the end when the special circumstances are explained.

The unusual situation provides both insight and

[1]The testament is accompanied by a contemporary Spanish translation.

puzzles. One thing is certain, the people involved here have transcended the boundaries of tlaxilacalli and even of altepetl in their marital and also their economic life. What is not specified is whether the house and lands bequeathed are in Santa María or in Tenango del Valle. That Guillermo Martín's father is to take care of his children and that some of the land left to the children was lent to Guillermo's brother implies that everything is in Tenango, unless we are to imagine that the whole clan has migrated to Santa María, which seems highly unlikely. The piece of land left to Guillermo by his grandfather is surely in Tenango. Thus the general impression is that the assets are in Tenango and that the children are to continue to live there. The special charge to Guillermo's father may imply that the wife, Paula Inocencia, is expected to stay in Santa María or at least be there frequently. Whatever the reason, Guillermo is presently in Santa María, and Paula Inocencia and the children probably too.[2] From the Spanish dossier in which the will is contained, it emerges that in 1791 one of the people battling for the inheritance was a resident of San Lucas Evangelista, another Tepemaxalco tlaxilacalli and apparently located very close to Santa María, so that some parts of the family remained associated with the area after Guillermo Martín's death.

Except for giving his house and lot to his son, Guillermo treats the son and two small daughters equally as to both land and saints. Little can be deduced about the testator's status from the routine funeral arrangements and the request that the heirs be responsible for them. The only witnesses are two church officials whose presence is perhaps obligatory; that may be because Guillermo is from outside the tlaxilacalli and lacks connections in it. The testator's grandfather had earned the "don," but not his father; the father did, however, have a Spanish patronymic as a second name. Guillermo has neither, only the anonymous combination of two first or saints' names. From this, the family has been falling in rank. We know for sure only that Guillermo has somewhat more than the minimum in the way of property and that he has cross-altepetl interests in the Toluca Valley.

The style of the notary Miguel de San Juan (see pp. 43–44), though not without local traits, is unusually conservative for the time, with very few reuced and omitted syllable-final consonants. We also see the term *-teiccauh*, one's younger sibling or cousin of either gender, rather than the usual loanword *-hermano*. Yet the document contains an unusual and advanced loanword, "parejo" used almost as an adverb to mean "equally." Looking back to the testaments of Luis Martín, immediately preceding, we see that by their time Santa María de la Asunción had developed a strong common style or basic model for testaments, with the whole initial part so similar that one might imagine the same person had written them all, except that the orthography is different. Elements of the style go back as far as the will of don Juan Alonso (No. 56) in 1692, where we already see Arabic numbers at the beginning of bequests and a request for a mass and responsory prayer only, but the set formula for the preamble takes shape later.

Note that in "nechihuapahuilis," "he is to raise them for me," the first *i* is not inserted to preserve the consonant as so frequently in this corpus; here it is for *im/in*, representing the plural direct object when the indirect is also present—a subtle feature of Nahuatl grammar well preserved in Toluca Valley Nahuatl. The same construction occurs in "nechimictilis," standard *nechimittiliz*, "he is to look after them for me," where the *im* is more transparent.

[*f. 1*]
ma moçēquiscayectenectzinno yn itlaçomahuisyecthocatzin. yn dios tetatzin. yuā dios ytlaçomahuispiltzin, Yhua dios Espiritu santo yeitzitzin teotlacatzitzinti perçonas ca san se huel neli teotl dios yhua yehuatzin Sihuapili Santa maria nicnotlatlauhtilia ynic nopāpa quimotlatlauhtilistzinnos, yn itlaçomahuisçenteconetzin yn tt,[o] $\overline{xo}$, ynic quimoselilitzinos

[*f. 1*]
May the precious revered good name of God the father, God his precious revered son, and God the Holy Spirit, three divine persons but one very true deity God, be entirely praised. And I implore the lady Santa María to pray for me to her precious revered only child our lord Christ to accept my spirit

---

[2]Another theory would be that Paula Inocencia had died and Guillermo Martín had come to Santa María to settle her affairs. Here she is called Guillermo's wife as though she were still alive, but such statements are not quite as unambiguous as to time as similar ones in English or Spanish.

y noyoliatzin y nanimatzin, ȳtla yuhqui nopa mochihuas ytla ninomiquilis nehual nicocoxqui, gilermo marti, nicchihua nomemoria testamento axca ypa yni tonati miercules a 6 de febrerō de 1737 años —

huel achtopa nitlanahuatia se tomintzin mutemacas Jerusale yhua se missa nupa mitos yhua se rresponsos, ca yehual nutelpoch miguel marti nechchihuilis numissa —

2tli nitlanahuatia, nutatzin antonio ernādes, nechihuapahuilis nupilhua yhua satotzitzin quinxexelhuis parejo, amaqui muxicus

3tli nitlanahuatia nutelpoch miguel niccahuilia cali yhua çolar yhua se tlali onictlanecti [*f. 1v*] nutecca bartolo ypapa tlacalaquili[3] oniquitla quicahuilis nutelpoch miguel ca yehual nutatzin nechimictilis nupilhua quimamacas tle niquincahuilia, neltis y nococoxcatlatol yxpātzinco dios —

4tli nitlanahuatia oc se nuxpuchtu leonissa manuela niccahuilia se tlali ompa mani cuactenco tituquaxoxtia comunidad —

5tli nitlanahuatia oc se nuchpuchtu ytuca pasquala bisenta niccahuilia oc se tlaltutli onechcahuilitia nutlaçocultzin metzticatca D^{n} bartolo difun[. . .] ompa mani, cuactenco. yhua nitlanahuatia mucht[. . .] yeinti nupilhua miguel, yhua leonisa manuela yhua pasquala bisenta quiyecahuisque nechquimilusque yhua nechtucasque quixtlahu[. . .] yntierro, ca san ixquix nictzonquistia nomemoria testamento nehual nicocoxqui, gilermo martin chane tenanco del balle nica nitlacuilua santa maria assump,^{on} nica chane nusihua paula ynosensia neltis y nococoxcatlathol yxpantzinco y di[. . .] yhua no yehuatzintzin notestigos mutlaneltilisq[. . .] mustla huictla yxpatzin y tt,^{o} dios —

D^{n} Ju^{o} pedro fiscal de la santa yglesia temachti
D^{n} pasqual baylo
nehual nitlacuilua miguel de san Ju^{o} es,^{no}

and soul if it happens to me that I the sick person Gui-llermo Martín should die. I make my memorandum of testament today on this day of Wednesday, the 6th of February of the year of 1737. —

First of all I order that a real is to be given for Jerusalem, and a mass with a responsory prayer is to be said for me; my son Miguel Martín is to have a mass performed for me. —

Second I order that my father Antonio Hernández is to raise my children for me and to distribute the saints among them equally; no one is to show envy [the children are to be content with the saints that are given to them].

Third I order that I leave to my son Miguel the house and lot and a piece of land that I lent [*f. 1v*] to my younger sibling Bartolomé because of the tribute.[3] I have requested it [from him]; he is to relinquish it to my son Miguel. My father is to look after my children for me and distribute to them what I leave them. My sick person's statement is to be carried out before God. —

Fourth I order that I leave to another little daughter of mine, Dionisia Manuela, a piece of land at the edge of the woods [or in Quauhtenco] bordering on [land of] the community. —

Fifth I order that I leave to another little daughter of mine named Pascuala Vicenta another little piece of land that my late precious grandfather don Bartolomé, deceased, left me, that is at the edge of the woods [or in Quauhtenco]. And I order that all three of my children, Miguel, Dionisia Manuela, and Pascuala Vicenta, are to share shrouding and burying me and paying for the burial. That is all. I the sick person Guillermo Martín, citizen of Tenango del Valle, conclude my memorandum of testament. I write here in Santa María de la Asunción; my wife Paula Inocencia is a citizen here. My sick person's statement is to be carried out before God and also before my witnesses who will verify it in the future before our lord God. —

Don Juan Pedro, fiscal of the holy church. Don Pascual Bailón, temachti.
I am doing the writing, Miguel de San Juan, notary.

[3]The Spanish translator took it that, as is indeed probable, the intention was that the brother would use the produce of the land to pay his back tributes.

63. Josefa Trinidad, Santa María de la Asunción, 1752

(AGN, Civil 664, exp. 2)

ALTHOUGH THE preamble here is longer than in No. 62, in all else Josefa Trinidad's will is that of a poor and humble person and is issued almost purely to spell out funeral arrangements. The requests are standard but minimal and above all are left to the husband to carry out, with no mention of assets to support them. Rudimentary wills of this type may not always have been issued by indigent people, but in this case Josefa Trinidad specifically asserts that she has nothing and is very poor. It appears that she has no personal property of value. To what extent the poverty carries over to her husband Juan Jacinto is hard to say, but nothing indicates that the pair has any rank or connections. His name is of the most humble type, and the witnesses are the usual and obligatory ones. Her name is one slight step up from his, compressed from Josefa de la Trinidad; the names of such religious concepts had a somewhat higher profile than a second first or saint's name, but the difference is not great. It sounds here as if the couple had no children, but since Josefa had nothing to leave them, she might not have mentioned them even if she did have living children.

The notary Miguel de San Juan (see pp. 43–44) is the same as in No. 62; note that across fifteen years the first part of the preamble, up to the name of the testator, has stayed exactly the same except for the loss of one modifier, the addition of an "also," and a bit of orthographic evolution (the conservative *ç* has been abandoned in favor of the more up-to-date *s*). We see some other typical Toluca-style spellings, such as hypercorrect *-uh* for *-c* and "huictla" for *huiptla*, "the day after tomorrow," but the orthography remains mainly conservative.

[*f. 28*]
Jesus m,^{a} y JoCephe
ma mosenquiscayecteneuhtzinno yn itlasomahuistocatzin yn Dios te yuā Dios ytlasopiltzin yuā Dios espirito santo yeintzitzin teotlacatzitzinti personas ca san se huel neli teotl Dios, yuā no yehuatzin Çihuapili santa maria nicnotlatlauhtilia ynic nopanpa quimotlatlauhtilitzinnos yn itlasomahuissenteconetzin yn tt,^{o} $\overline{\text{xpo}}$ ynic quimoselilitzinnos y noyoliantzin y nanimantzin yntla yuhqui nopa mochihuas yntla ninomiquilis y nehual nicocoxqui Jocepha trinida masihui huel mococotica y notlalyo y nosoquiyo yuā noanimantzin camo quen ca ca san pactica nica nichane santa m^{a} assump,^{on} nicchihuan nomemoria testamento axca Juebes a primero de nobienbre yuā xihuitl de 1752 a^{os} huel achtopa motemacas se tomintzin Jerusale yuā se missa nopa mitos yuā se rresponsos ca yehual ypalehuiluca [*f. 28v*] nuanimantzin yes —
2tli nitlanahuatia ca yehuual nonamiuhtzin Ju^{o} xansinto nechtuCas yuā nechchihuilis nomissa neltis y notlatol yxpantzinco yn Dios, yuā ca niquitohua camo tle nicnopielia ca huel nimotolinia ca san ixquich nictzonquixtia y notlatol ymixpa notestigohua ca no yehuantzitzin motlaneltilisque mostla huictla yxpantzinco Dios —
Fiscal de la santa yglesia D,^{n} santiago martin tupile, anto^{nio} bitoriano
nehual nitlaCuiluhua Miguel de san Ju^{o} esn,^{o}

[*f. 28*]
Jesus, Mary, and Joseph.
May the precious revered name of God [the father], God his precious son, and God the Holy Spirit, three divine persons but one very true deity God, be entirely praised. And I also implore the lady Santa María to pray for me to her precious revered only child our lord Christ to accept my spirit and soul if it happens to me that I the sick person Josefa Trinidad should die. Although my earthly body is very sick, nothing is wrong with my soul, but it is sound. I am a citizen here in Santa María de la Asunción; I make my memorandum of testament today, Thursday the 1st of November of the year of 1752. First of all, a real is to be given for Jerusalem, and a mass with a responsory prayer is to be said for me; that will be the help of [*f. 28v*] my soul. —

Second, I order that my husband Juan Jacinto is to bury me and is to have a mass said for me. My statement is to be carried out before God. And I say that I have nothing; I am very poor. That is all. I conclude my statement before my witnesses; they are also to verify it before God in the future. —

Fiscal of the holy church don Santiago Martín. Topile Antonio Victoriano.
I am doing the writing, Miguel de San Juan, notary.

64. Ignacia Cristina, Santa María de la Asunción, 1759

(AGN, Civil 664, exp. 2)

AT FIRST GLANCE the present will gives the impression of being a direct copy of No. 63, issued seven years earlier by the same notary Miguel de San Juan, with only the names changed. In fact, there are a few minor differences, but the picture presented is again the same, that of a poor, humble woman without personal property making a will only to specify some modest funeral arrangements, for which the husband is made responsible. Children are again unmentioned, and again it is possible that one or more survived the testator anyway. The only thing at all different in the picture is that this time the testator's name shows not even a hint of distinction, while the husband is a de la Cruz, bearing a name of a higher category all over the valley and with very strong connotations of rank in Tepemaxalco and Santa María de la Asunción specifically. Yet the appearance of general poverty may be real. Another hint is that as of 1759 the mass had not been said. And only the fiscal serves as witness.

Nevertheless, one possible implication of the word-by-word similarity of Nos. 63 and 64 is that a set formula may be in operation and that one should not make too many deductions from the statement of poverty included. (We know that in some other cases it was pro forma and used at the end of wills of notably wealthy people.)

[*f. 31*]
Jesus m^{a} y JoCephe
ma mosenquisCayecteneuhtzinno yn itlasomahuistocatzin yn Dios tetatzin yuã Dios ytlasopiltzin yuã dios espirito santo, yeintzitzin teotlacatzitzintin personas ca san se huel neli teotl Dios, yhuan no yehuatzin Çihuapili santa m^{a} nicnotlatlauhtilia ynic nopanpa quimotlatlauhtilitzinnos yn itlasomahuissenteconetzin yn tt,^{o} x̄p̄o, ynic quimosclilis y noyoliantzin y nanimantzin yntla yuhqui nopa mochihuas yntla ninomiquilis y nehual niCoCoxqui notuCa ynasia christina masihui mocoCotiCa y notlalnacayo yhuan noanimantzin camo quen ca ca san pactica nicchihua nomemoria testamento, axca biernes a 5 de enero xihuitl de 1759 —
huel achtopa motemaCas sc tomintzin Jerusale yhuan se missa nopa mintos yhuan se rresponsos Ca yehual ypalehuiluCa nuanimantzin yes —
2 tli: nitlanahuatia Ca yehual nonamictzin antonio de la Crus ca yehual nechtuCas yhuan nechchihuiulis nomissa — neltis y nococoxcatlatol yxpantzinCo yn tt,^{o} Dios — [*f. 31v*]
3 tli: niquitohua camo tle nicnopielia yaxcatzin dios ca huel nimotolinia ca san ixquich nictzonquixtia y nococoxcatlatol yxpantzinco Dios, fiscal de la santa yglesia D,^{n} domingo esteba
miguel de san Ju^{o} es^{no}[1]

[*f. 31*]
Jesus, Mary, and Joseph.
May the precious revered name of God the father, God his precious son, and God the Holy Spirit, three divine persons but one very true deity God, be entirely praised. And also I implore the lady Santa María to pray on my behalf to her precious revered only child our lord Christ to accept my spirit and soul if it should happen to me that I the sick person named Ignacia Cristina should die. Although my earthly body is sick, nothing is wrong with my soul, for it is sound. I make my memorandum of testament today, Friday the 5th of January of the year of 1759. —

First of all, a real is to be given for Jerusalem, and a mass with a responsory prayer is to be said for me; it will be the help of my soul. —
Second, I order that my husband Antonio de la Cruz is to bury me and have a mass performed for me; my sick person's statement is to be carried out before our lord God. — [*f. 31v*]
Third, I say that I have none of the property of God, for I am very poor. That is all. I conclude my sick person's statement before God. Fiscal of the holy church, don Domingo Esteban.
Miguel de San Juan, notary.[1]

---

[1]In a note in Spanish dated 1759 it is reported that no mass was said; even more importantly, the note contains the name of the tlaxilacalli, Santa María de la Asunción, which is lacking in the testament.

65. Tomás de Aquino, Santa María de la Asunción, 1760

(AGN, Civil 664, exp. 2)

THE MOST REMARKABLE feature of the present will is that the only heir is a godchild. In this case the godchild did not grow up in the household of his biological mother and father, but was raised from infancy by his godfather the testator. Tomás de Aquino must have no other children at present, and possibly never did, so he leaves all he has to the godchild Isidro Serrano. It is not an impressive estate: a mere 3 almudes of land and a collection of saints. One wonders if a house containing the saints is implicitly included, but that is not established. The testator goes to some pains to warn others not to give trouble to the heir, as if fearing that he will be more vulnerable because he is not a blood relative. But the godchild is given the same duties with the testator's funeral as are often assigned to spouses and to heirs who are blood kin.

We have little with which to judge Tomás de Aquino's standing. He surely lacks wealth. There is no trace of any wife and children. His father's name is not distinguished and not the same as his. His own name is a bit ambiguous, more unusual than two first names, but of the type in which a saint's name is taken whole, in this case Thomas of Aquinas, and it is compatible with either high or low rank; lacking the don, he has apparently not played a leading role in the community. But there are some counterindications to this picture of relative humility. In other wills by this notary, the fiscal and a topile of the church are the only witnesses, but here a past and a present alcalde are added. The most impressive exhibit is the name of the godchild. Isidro is a quite rare name, while Serrano was perhaps the highest-ranking second name in the Tepemaxalco and Calimaya of this time. If he was godfather of a child so named and was able to adopt and raise him, Tomás must have had some good local connections.

We see by now that all of notary Miguel de San Juan's testaments (Nos. 62–66) are much alike, not only in wording and formulas but in the simple funeral requests and offerings. Advanced loans from Spanish continue to surface within the generally conservative framework; here "desde tepitzin" not only uses as a loan the preposition *desde*, but does so within an idiomatic loan phrase (calque). The phrase here is *desde pequeño*, "since (he was) little." The will also contains both of the main Nahuatl expressions for a godchild, a form of *teoyotica -coneuh*, "one's child through sacrament," and *-tlaquatequil*, "one's person who has been baptized."

[*f. 63*]
Jesus m,ª Y JoCephe
Ma mosenquizCayecteneuhtzinno yn itlaçomahuistocatzin yn dios tetatzin yhuā Dios ytlasopiltzin yhuan Dios espirito santo yeintzitzin teotlacatzitzintin personas Ca san se huel neli teotl dios yhuan no yehuatzin Çihuanpili Santa m,ª nicnotlatlauhtilia ynic nopanpa quimotlatlauhtilis yn itlasomahuissenteconetzin yn tt,º xp̄o ynic quimoselilis y noyoliantzin y nanimantzin yntla ninomiquilis y nehual nicocoxqui notuca tomas de aquino, maçihui huel mococotica y notlayo y nosoquiyo yhuan noanimantzin camo quen ca ca san pactica niCa nichane Santa m,ª Asumpon, nicchihuan notestamentento axca Domingo a 22 de Junio de 1760 años —
huel achtopa nitlanahuatia motemaCas se tomintzin Jerusalen yuā se missa nopa mitos yuā se rresponsos Ca yehual ypalehuiluca noanimantzin yes —
2 tli: nitlanahuantia ca yehual y noteoteticacune ysidro serrano, ca yehual nechitas nechquimilos yuā nechtuCas yhuan nechchihuilis y nomissa Ca yehual

[*f. 63*]
Jesus, Mary, and Joseph.
May the precious revered name of God the father, God his precious son, and God the Holy Spirit, three divine persons but one very true deity God, be entirely praised. And also I implore the lady Santa María to pray on my behalf to her precious revered only child our lord Christ to accept my spirit and soul if I the sick person named Tomás de Aquino should die. Although my earthly body is very sick, nothing is wrong with my soul, but it is sound. I am a citizen here in Santa María de la Asunción, and I make my testament today, Sunday the 22nd of June of the year of 1760. —

First of all I order that a real is to be given for Jerusalem, and a mass with a responsory prayer is to be said for me; that will be the help of my soul. —
Second I order that my godchild Isidro Serrano is to look after me, to shroud me, bury me, and have a mass performed for me. I have confidence in him

ytech nimotemachitia ypanpa ca oquimohuapahuilitzinno Dios yhuan quin oc tepa nehual Ca notlaquatequil desde tepitzin Onichuapahuan yhuã niquinnocahuililia nosantotzitzinhuan Ca yehual quinmotequipanilhuis yuã nicCahuilia se tlali Calaqui yei almo tlaoli ompa mani tlauhpac yuh Calimaya otli, yno tlali OnechmoCahuililitia notlasotatzin metzticatca asensio marti difunto, niquitua nehual nicocoxqui amaqui nechmaquilitinemis mostla huictla netequipacholi notlaquatequil neltis y notlatol yxpantzin[*f. 63v*]Con yn tt^{o} Dios, Ca sann ixquich nictzonquixtia y noCoCoxCatlatol yxpantzinco dios yuã ymixpantzitzin y notestigohua ca yehuantzintzin motlaneltilisque mostla huictla yxpantzinco yn tt,^{o} Dios, fiscal de la santa yglesia, D,^{n} Santiago martin Esteba de la Crus teopa tupile D,^{n} Ju^{o} martin al^{e} actual D,^{n} Ju^{o} astasion alcalde pasado
Miguel de san Ju^{o} es,^{no}[1]

because God and after that I myself raised him, for he is my godchild; I raised him since he was little. I leave him my saints, whom he is to serve, and I leave him a piece of land into which 3 almudes of maize fit; it is on the upper side, on the Calimaya road. My late precious father Asencio Martín, deceased, left that land to me. I the sick person say that in the future no one is to go about giving my godchild trouble for me. My statement is to be carried out before [*f. 63v*] our lord God. That is all. I conclude my sick person's statement before God and before my witnesses, who will verify it in the future before our lord God. Fiscal of the holy church don Santiago Martín. Esteban de la Cruz, church topile. Don Juan Martín, present alcalde. Don Juan Anastasio, past alcalde.

Miguel de San Juan, notary.[1]

[1]An annotation in Spanish says that a mass was performed in July 1760.

66. Pablo Marcial, Santa María de la Asunción, 1762

(AGN, Civil 664, exp. 2)

THE TESTATOR OWNS little and in addition directly tells us that he has nothing else, so his statement that he is very poor is credible. Since his two sons are small, he takes the common avenue of not explicitly bequeathing his house to anyone, instead "leaving his wife in it," that is, in charge of it, with the duty of raising the children. As in all such cases it is understood that the children will ultimately get the house. The land goes directly to the two boys, but it is a very small plot, a single almud to be divided equally between them. The plural verb used in describing the land's use to raise the children includes others in addition to the mother, but they are not named; as in this whole series of wills, no executor is appointed. The testator makes his sons responsible for his mass but seems to realize that it may be a long time before they can afford one.

Despite the poverty, some rather rare names are seen among the people here, including Marcial, Eugenia, and Luciano, while de los Reyes, second name of at least one of the children, has a certain cachet. It is possible, then, that our testator is the same person as the regidor mayor don Pablo Marcial seen in No. 60, issued in Santa María in 1760. The office of regidor mayor did not confer the don in the same automatic way as the higher offices of fiscal and alcalde, so it would not be unlikely that a person should abandon claim to the title after leaving office, particularly if having economic problems as the testator here seems to be.

No notary is named for this testament, but the extreme uniformity of the wills of Miguel de San Juan tells us that he is the writer. Our man is indeed present, but not as notary, and he is now titled, don Miguel de San Juan, having risen to the position of fiscal of the church like some other notaries in the corpus. He has also at some point been alcalde, as we see in No. 58. In other cases as well the fiscal functions as notary. The 1-almud plot here is called *tequitcatlalli*, an older term rare in the corpus meaning land that was subject to tribute, often in effect land which had not been in the hands of an owner or a family for long.

[*f. 67*]
Jesus M,^{a} y JoSephe
ma mosenquisCayectenectzinno yn itlasomahuisto-

[*f. 67*]
Jesus, Mary, and Joseph.
May the precious revered name of God the father,

catzin yn Dios tetatzin yuā Dios ytlasoPiltzin yhuan Dios Espirito santo yeintzitzin teotlacatzitzintin personas ca san se huel neli teotl Dios yhuan no yehuatzin Sihuanpili santa maria nicnotlatlauhtilia ynic nopanpa quimotlatlauhtilitzinnos yn itlasomahuissenteconetzin, yn tt,^{o} $\overline{xpo}$, inic quimoselilitzinnos y noioliantzin y nanimantzin yntla yuhqui nopa mochihuas yntla ninomiquilis y nehual nicocoxqui notoca pablo marseal masihui huel chicahuac moCoCotica y notlalyo y nosoquiyo yhuan nohanimantzin camo quen Ca Ca san pactiCa, niCa nichane Sa^{n}ta m,^{a} Assump,^{on} nicchihuan nomememoria testamento axca lunes a 27 de setiembre xihuitl de 1762 años —

God his precious son, and God the Holy Spirit, three divine persons but one very true deity God, be entirely praised. And I also implore the lady Santa María to pray on my behalf to her precious revered only child our lord Christ to accept my spirit and soul if it should happen to me that I the sick person named Pablo Marcial should die. Although my earthly body is very strongly ill, nothing is wrong with my soul, but it is sound. I am a citizen here in Santa María de la Asunción; I make my memorandum of testament today, Monday the 27th of September of the year of 1762. —

huel achtopa nitlanahuatia motemaCas se tomintzin Jerusalen yhuan se missa nopa mitos yuā se responsos ca yehual ypalehuiluca nohanimantzin yes —

First of all I order that a real is to be given for Jerusalem, and a mass with a responsory prayer is to be said for me; that will be the help of my soul. —

2 tli nitlanahuatia ca niccactia nosihua ogenia m,^{a} itic cali quinhuapahuas ypilhuantoto yhuan nitlanahuatia omenti notelpochhua bernaldo yuā lusiano de lo rreyes niquincahuilia se pedaso tlaltuntli Calaqui se almo tlaoli mani yxtlahuatenco tequitcatlali [*f.* 67*v*] quimonepantlaxelhuisque axCa ic quihuapahuasque ynantzin yhuan quenami Dios quinpalehuis nopilhuan nechchihuilisque nomissa camo tlen oc sequi nicmopielia Ca huel nimotolinia niquitua yxpantzinco Dios, yhuan imixpantzitzin y notestigohua ca yehuatzitzin motlaneltilisque mostla huictla yxpantzinco yn Dios, fisCal de la santa yglesia D,^{n} miguel de san Ju^{o} Ju^{o} astasio tupile

Second I order that I am leaving my wife Eugenia María inside the house; she is to raise her little children. And I order that I leave to two sons of mine, Bernardo and Luciano de los Reyes, a little piece of land where 1 almud of maize fits; it is at the edge of the plain and is tribute land. [*f.* 67*v*] They are to divide it in half. With it now their mother [and others] is to raise them, and accordingly as God should help them, my children are to have a mass performed for me, for I have nothing else and am very poor. I say it before God and before my witnesses, who will verify things in the future before God: fiscal of the holy church don Miguel de San Juan, and Juan Anastasio, [church] topile.

67. Gabriel de Santiago, Santa María de la Asunción, 1758

(AGN, Civil 664, exp. 2)

THE FIRST PROBLEM this testament presents is to determine where it was issued (on that point the notary says not a word), but within the context of the corpus the mystery is soon resolved. Don Juan Josef, present alcalde here, is past alcalde in No. 57, issued in Santa María de la Asunción in 1762. The notary here is Antonio Silverio; in No. 57 it is don Antonio Silverio, who must have acquired the title sometime during the intervening years. The connection is further strengthened by a combination of facts about this notary. In the present document, although he has a clear hand, Silverio shows himself far less skilled than his colleagues in Santa María and indeed one of the less skilled in the entire Toluca corpus; and then in No. 57, even though he was the official notary at the moment, Silverio had former notary Luis Martín write the document. Another factor in identification is that the preamble contains the same formulas as all the other testaments done in Santa María, merely a bit truncated and mutilated. The funeral dispositions are also those universal in the tlaxilacalli.

The human content of the will is slight. The testator, despite his quite impressive second name, appears to have no property and issues a will merely to specify the funeral arrangements and to request his son to take care of them. The son has a different and more humble second name than the father. The witnesses are very respectable. Perhaps we have here a person with good connections in the community who has fallen on bad times.

The phrases notary Antonio Silverio attempts are much like those seen in other wills of Santa María, but they are often mangled by missing words and syllables and disguised by his orthography. His writing not only is a rather strong example of characteristic eighteenth-century Toluca Valley traits but has some unique features, especially spelling the reverential syllable *-tzin* as "zn" and intruding *z* in unexpected places.

At the end of the document, the notary calls the local officials who serve as witnesses *notahuan*, "my fathers," a rare echo of the polite and elaborate speech more frequent in Nahuatl records of the sixteenth and early seventeenth centuries.

[*f.* 27]
Jus maria y Jopehe
ma moSequisCayeteneznno n itlaSumahustoCazn y Dios tetazn yhua Dios yntlasumahuspilzn ynhua Dios espirtu santo yezn teotlacaznti persunas Ca San Se hul neli teol Dios yhua no yhuazn sihuapil santa maria ninotlatilia yni nopapa quimotlatlatilis yn iseteconezn ytla yoqui nopa mochihuas nehual notoca garbiel de Santiago —
AxCa miercoles a quise de Fe de 1758 años nihihua nomeria testameto hul atopa nitlahuati motemacas se tomi geruSale yhua Se misa yhua Se respos nopa mitos nopilzn mateo atono nequimilos ne[h]toca ca sann ixiquichi oti nomomeria testameto ymipa notestigohuan — [*f.* 27*v*]

nehual nifiscal de la mader santi ygelsia D^{n} Juan na[. . .]rs ~~ald~~^{e} D^{n} matias ser[. . .]tes temati ~~ald~~^{e} D^{n} Juan Jocphe alcalde atual ~~ald~~^{e}[1]
ymixipazneo notahuan nehual onitlaquilo notoca atonio silberio

[*f.* 27]
Jesus, Mary, and Joseph.
May the precious revered name of God the father, God his precious revered son, and God the Holy Spirit, three divine persons but only one very true deity God, be entirely praised. And I also implore the lady Santa María to pray on my behalf to her only child if it happens to me that I named Gabriel de Santiago [should die].—
Today Wednesday the 15th of February of the year of 1758, I make my memorandum of testament. First of all, I order that a real is to be given for Jerusalem, and a mass with a responsory prayer is to be said for me; my child Mateo Antonio is to shroud me and bury me. That is all. [I have concluded] my memorandum of testament before my witnesses. — [*f.* 27*v*]

I am the fiscal of the holy mother church, don Juan Na[. . .]; don Matías [Cervantes?], temachti; don Juan Josef, present alcalde.[1]
I named Antonio Silverio did the writing before my fathers.

[1]Three times in this passage there occurs a stylized element ordinarily meaning *alcalde*, but I believe that as used by this notary it is simply a rubric accompanying the preceding name.

68. Don Felipe de Santiago, Santa María de la Asunción, 1783

(AGN, Tierras 2300, exp. 8)

THIS LAST TESTAMENT from the tlaxilacalli of Santa María de la Asunción closes the group the same way it opened, with a testator bearing the title don. Don Felipe de Santiago comes from a prominent family on his mother's side, for she is mentioned in the will with the title doña, and she bears the important second name de la Cruz. Everything that don Felipe has came from his mother, while his father goes unmentioned. The only name continuity we see is that one of don Felipe's sons has his grandmother's second name. Despite his title and his maternal heritage, don Felipe does not seem to have much property, not even a house and lot, which is unusual for a prominent individual; he mentions only two pieces of land, of which one at least is not of any notable size.

The eldest son, don Gregorio Martín, is already married and mature enough to have attained the don, so he has probably already held office, and his father, the testator don Felipe, must be quite advanced in age. Don Gregorio gets the first and doubtless larger piece of land; the other goes to the second son, Tomás de la Cruz, and to a daughter, Juana Paula. From the confusing wording it appears that if either of them should die without an heir, their land would go to don Gregorio.

The two sons are put in charge of funeral arrangements, which are not exceptional: a mass with responsory prayer, an unspecified shroud and burial, and an offering for Jerusalem. More precisely, don Gregorio Martín is to guide Tomás de la Cruz in this task, while the daughter is only implicitly included as well, almost as an afterthought. As usual in Santa María, no executor is appointed; the four witnesses are all officials and one of them, the fiscal, bears the title don and an important second name, Serrano, which is associated with the de la Cruz lineage of Tepemaxalco. This is a respectable showing, but not the collection of notable names sometimes seen with the wills of prominent testators.

The present testament was issued twenty years after any other document in this volume, at a time in fact when testaments in Nahuatl may have become rare in the Toluca region. Our first suspicion might be that the date is a mistake either of writing or of reading, but it is written out in letters, excluding any such error. One might even suspect a fake of some kind. But the document has nearly all the attributes of the other wills of the region and fits in well with them; also, little wealth is involved, so that there would be little incentive to deceive.

It is true that there are two almost suspiciously archaic traits in the writing. More than once the wives of men are called by the traditional term *-namic*, "spouse," instead of *–cihuahuatzin*, "woman, wife," which was normal in the Toluca Valley by the eighteenth century. The second instance has to do with a way of giving the date that is otherwise missing in the present corpus and in Nahuatl testaments in general. Unfortunately a crucial word is incomplete, but it is hard to devise another interpretation of "yei to[. . .]tli" than *yei tochtli*, "three rabbit," a year name in the preconquest 52-year cycle. This phrase appears here just before the normal Spanish designation of the year. Such calendrical indications are frequent in some genres of dubious factuality, the so-called primordial titles and the Techialoyan codices.

Nevertheless, nothing else here arouses suspicion, so we may begin to assess how the document compares with those of earlier in the century. The formula of the preamble is virtually the same as that of Miguel de San Juan and Luis Martín, Santa María's main notaries from the 1730s to the 1760s. Santa María's use of Arabic numbers to designate the items continues. The orthography of the notary Juan Bernardo is well within the limits of Toluca usage of the eighteenth century, with an unusual feature or two such as the use of *p* to represent the historical glottal stop, as in "itlasupmahuistucactzin", "his precious revered name." There are no signs of Spanish influence on the language beyond what we see twenty, thirty, or forty years earlier.

Note that not only, as shown above, is the testator a don himself, but he has a mother who was a doña, a rarity otherwise, and rarest of all, a son who is himself already don. And yet as we have also seen, our don Felipe de Santiago shows no sign of unusual wealth or influence. Possibly in the twenty years from 1763 to 1783 usage with the don and doña had loosened. On the other hand, the officials given as witnesses continue the style we already know: only the fiscal with don, the rest without.

[*f. 1*]

Jesus maria Y Josen

ma musenquiscaYecthenectzinno Yn itlasupmahuistucactzin y [. . .] thetactzin[1] Yhuan D.^{S} Espirito Santo Yeititzintzin theotla[. . .]tzintzin Personas san se huel neli theol D.^{S} ninunelt[. . .]tiatzinnuhua Yhuan nu Yechuatzin sihuapili Santa ma[. . .] nicmutlatlactilictzinnuhuan quimutlatlactilis Ysente[. . .]netzin tutheCuyo Jesu christo Yntla Ycqui

[*f. 1*]

Jesus, Mary, and Joseph.

May the precious revered name of [God] the father[1] and God the Holy Spirit, three divine persons but one very true deity God in whom I believe, be entirely praised. And I implore the lady Santa María to pray to her only child our lord Jesus Christ [on my behalf] if it happens to me that I should die. I the

[1]"God the son" or "God his son" is missing, no doubt through inadvertence.

nupa muchih[. . .] ninumiquilis nechual niCuCuxqui nutuca D^{n} felip[. . .] de santiago nica nichani Santa maria la Asump nunam[. . .] fransica maria Axca sabado mani metztli mayo Yei to[. . .]tli xihuil Ypan mil setesientos Y ochenta y tres años Nic[. . .]huan numemoria thestamento —

huel Axtupa nitlanahuantia muthemacas se thomi limosna de Jerusalen Yhuan se misa nupa mictos Yhuan se res[...]s nupa mictos ca yechual Ypalehuiluca nuanimantzin [. . .]huan noYoliantzin Yes —

2. tlamantli nitlanahuantia nupiltzin D^{n} Grigorio marti[. . .] quenamin Yacapantli Yechual quitas Yermano thomas [. . .] la Crus para quiYeccahuisque[2] tlen itheh puhui [. . .]quimilicca nuinthierro yhua numisan YhucQui muthemachictian YnahuactzinCo noD.^{s} Yhuan nupilhu[. . .] para Ypalehuiluca nuanimantzin noYoliantzin Yes —

3. tlamantli nitlanahuatia oc se[3] pedaso tlali nicpie hunehcmucahuililictia nutlasupnatzin metzticac[a] D.^{na} margarita de la Crus mecCatzintli Axca sanu Yhu[. . .]qui nitlanahuantia niccahuilia nupiltzin Dn Grigorio marti Yca inamictzin maria Antonia acmaqui mustla huictla quimixtoquitlis san Yhuiqui nelti — [*f. 1v*] nucucuxcatlactul Yxpantzinco D.^{s}

4. tlamantli nitlanahuantia oc se tlali mantiCa sanuc hunca Ynahuac altepel[4] Catlimaya octli calaqui tla oli tuctli hume almo Yhua Yei Cuartilio Yhuan tlacCu Cuartilio sanu humehmucahuililintia nutlasupnantzin metzticatica Axca niquincahuilia nupiltzin thomas de la Crus Yhuan nu[H?]uhpuh Juana Paula quimunepactlaxelhuis Yhuan tla mustla huictla in D^{s} quixtilis Ynemilis nupiltzin thomas de la Crus Yhuan acmo quipies se Ycone ca sanu Yhuiqui muCuepas Ca nupiltzin Yacapantli D^{n} Grigorio martin[5] Yhuiqui neltis nuCuCuxcatlactol YspantzinCo D.^{s} —

Ca san ixquix nictzonquixtia numemoria thestamento Ymixpan nutestigos Ca Yechuantzintzin mutlaneltililisque mustla huitlac Yxpantzinco tuthecuyo D^{s} —

fisCal de la Santa Yglesia D^{n} Basilo salbador se-

sick person named don Felipe de Santiago, citizen here in Santa María de la Asunción, my spouse being Francisca María, today the 3rd day of the month of May in the year three [rabbit], the year of 1783, make my memorandum of testament. —

First of all I order that a real is to be given in alms for Jerusalem, and a mass is to be said for me, and a responsory prayer is to be said for me, and that will be the help of my soul and spirit. —

Second, I order that my son don Gregorio Martín as the eldest should see to his brother Tomás de la Cruz so that the three of them can arrange[2] what pertains to my shroud, burial, and mass, as is confidently expected from my God and my children, to be the help of my soul and spirit. —

Third, I order that I have another[3] piece of land that my late precious mother, doña Margarita de la Cruz, deceased, left to me. Now likewise I order that I leave it to my son don Gregorio Martín along with his spouse María Antonia. No one is to claim it from him in the future; thus my sick person's statement is to be carried out [*f. 1v*] before God. —

Fourth, I order that there is another piece of land likewise close to the altepetl,[4] [on] the road to Calimaya, where 2 almudes and $3\frac{1}{2}$ cuartillos of maize seed fit, that likewise my late precious mother left me; now I leave it to my son Tomás de la Cruz and my daughter Juana Paula to divide equally. And if in the future God should take the life of my son Tomás de la Cruz and he should not have a child, [his part] will likewise be returned to the eldest child, my son don Gregorio Martín.[5] My sick person's statement is to be thus realized before God. —

That is all. I conclude my memorandum of testament before my witnesses, who will verify it in the future before our lord God. —

Fiscal of the holy church, don Basilio Salvador Se-

[2]Although the testator at this point has named only two children, he apparently includes here his daughter Juana Paula, mentioned below.

[3]At this point the text has "oc se," "another," even though no piece of land has been mentioned previously.

[4]Here we have another case in which the word *altepetl* is used in reference to a compact settlement rather than a whole unit with all its jurisdiction, as in Nos. 57 and 61. The meaning here seems to be Santa María, not the central settlement of Calimaya/Tepemaxalco.

[5]By the grammar alone, it could just as well be the whole piece that would be returned, but I am reluctant to think don Felipe would be so harsh with his daughter. Perhaps the intention, not fully put into words, was that if either Tomás or Juana died without an heir, that land would go to don Gregorio the eldest.

rrano Regidor maYor niculas tolentino Re^{dor} menor fran^{co} paulino theopan toPile Lasaro faustino
Es,^{no} de Rp,^{ca} Juan Bernardo

rrano. Regidor mayor, Nicolás de Tolentino. Regidor menor, Francisco Paulino. Church topile, Lázaro Faustino.
Notary of the commonwealth, Juan Bernardo.

69. Juan Andrés, San Pablo Tepemaxalco, San Juan Bautista Yancuictlalpan, 1737

(AGN, Civil 1120, exp. 7)[1]

THE WAY INHERITANCE is handled in the present will is unusual in several respects. First, despite having a child, Juan Andrés leaves his house and lot to his wife Petrona Felipa, with no mention of her handing it on to any children at a later date. Furthermore, a stepson, Juan Martín, his wife's child, and Juan Andrés's own daughter, María [Concepción], each receive the same bequest, one piece of land. We do not know the relative size and value of the two parcels, but it is already significant that a stepson and a daughter are treated so equally. The stepson may actually be preferred; he is named first, and experience shows that the preferred and elder heir is usually named first. Indeed, the stepson is probably older than the daughter.

Juan Andrés has a standard amount of property, a house with its lot plus two pieces of land. Otherwise he appears to rank as a humble person. Although the preamble of his testament is elaborate, not only is he to be buried outside of the church, he does not even request a mass, only a special shroud. His executor (not very clearly named as such) has a good second name but no don, and aside from the fiscal there are no other witnesses.

This is the only testament from the tlaxilacalli of San Juan Bautista Yancuictlalpan, which fails to appear among the eight districts of Tepemaxalco in the tribute lists for the 1650s and 60s.[2] Although strictly speaking the entire altepetl and all its territory belonged to San Pablo Tepemaxalco, it appears that outlying tlaxilacalli never used the altepetl name in primary unit identification in their documents, so that "San Pablo Tepemaxalco" was reserved for the tlaxilacalli within the core settlement of Calimaya/Tepemaxalco. If that is so, San Juan Bautista belongs to that core settlement.

No notary is given for the testament, so the writer is most likely the fiscal, don Diego Matías. Despite his high office he does not prove to be very skilled at writing. It is not so much that he is a rather extreme example of the peculiar orthographic tendencies of Toluca as that he omits a large number of syllables and does not always seem entirely familiar with the formulas of the genre. Thus whereas the norm is to leave one's soul in the hands of God, don Diego seems to have the testator leave it in the hands of the Virgin Mary and of his guardian angel.

Some of the rare features of the text are of considerable interest. The number "201" means not 200 plus 1 but 20 plus 1, 21, giving the traditional Nahua numerical structure with Arabic numbers; a few other examples are seen in the corpus. The most unusual aspect of the orthography is that the weakening of syllable-final [tl] to [l] has gone so far that by hypercorrection *tl* is freely used to represent [l] before a vowel, as in "de tla Cruz" for de la Cruz. Though the writer in general does not betray exceptional Spanish influence, he is unusual in using Spanish phrases to describe the Trinity rather than the normal Nahuatl terms.

In the corpus generally only the first of the pair of words *memoria testamento*, "memorandum of testament," is possessed, making them a unit, but here each one bears a possessive prefix.

[*f.* 7]
[. . .]Sus Maria Y Juseph
Ma moCequisCayectenehuatlo yn itlaÇomahuistoCatzin Santisima trinidad dios padre yhua dios hijo yhua dios espiritu Santo amen Jesus maria Y Juseph —

[*f.* 7]
Jesus, Mary, and Joseph.
May the precious revered name of the most holy Trinity, God the father, God the son, and God the Holy Spirit, be entirely praised, amen. Jesus, Mary, and Joseph. —

---

[1]The testament is accompanied by a Spanish translation from 1792.
[2]MNAH, Archivo Histórico, Col. Gómez Orozco 185.

niCa nicpehualtia nomemoria notestamento Ax Sanbado a 201 del mes de agosto de 1737 a^{os} nehual notoCa Juan adre niCa nocha San pablo tepemaxalco notlaxitlatlalpan San Ju^{o} ~~bhtt~~^{a} YaCuictlapan Ca San ixquih nicnotlatolchiyetlitlia yn itlaÇomiquitlitzi y notlaÇomahuistatzin dios Ca yCematzinCo nicnocahuitlia noyotliatzin yhua noanimatzin y notlaÇomahuisnatzin Santa maria yn ilhuiCa Cihuapitli y ynic nopapan motlatoltintzinosque yn opa yn ilhuicatl itic yn ixquihtic Santos yhua Santas Ynic nopapa motlatoltintzinosq̄ yhua notlaÇomahuisageltzin Ca yCematzico nicnoCahuitlia noyotliatzi yhua noanimatzin Y nopapa motlatoltitzinnos yn opa yn ilhuiCa ma y mochihua amen Jesus — Mari Y Juseph —

Yni Cetlamatli nitlanatia y noÇepoltura yes teopa quiahua YCa notlanequitlis —

yniC otlamatli nitlanahuatia noquimiliCa yes yn itlaquen notlasomahuistatzi Santo San F^{co} YCa notlanequilis —

Ynic yetlamali nitlanahuatia yni caltzitli nicCahuitlia noSihuahuatzi Ytuca petrona felipa para tlatequipanos Amo aqui tle quilhuis quemania YCa mohi Sotlar yCa notlanequilis —

Yni natlamatli nitlanahuatia Se tlatli mani Canpa moCutlohua al niCahuilia nochahuatelpox ytocan Juan martin Amo aquiquixtili Quemania yCa notlanequilis —

Yni macuiltlamali nitlanahuatia o Ce tlali mani CuateCon niCahui[. . .] nochpox ytoCa maria Cosisiana[?][4] YCa notlanequilis —

Can San ixquih nicSoquix noCoCoxCatlatol Ymixpa noalba[*f. 7v*]cea Yhua notestigos Salbador de tla Cruz fiscal mayor de Santa ygelsia D,^{n} Diego matias

Here I named Juan Andrés begin my memorandum and testament today Saturday the 21st of the month of August of the year of 1737; my home is here in San Pablo Tepemaxalco in my tlaxilacalli of San Juan Bautista Yancuictlalpan. I am just awaiting the precious death of my precious revered father God, and I leave my spirit and my soul entirely in the hands of my precious revered mother Santa María, the heavenly lady, so that all the male and female saints in heaven will speak for me; and I leave my spirit and my soul entirely in the hands of my precious revered [guardian] angel, who will speak for me in heaven. May it be done, amen; Jesus, Mary and Joseph. —

First, I order that my grave will be outside the church; it is according to my will. —

Second, I order that my shroud will be the habit of my precious revered father holy San Francisco; it is according to my will. —

Third, I order that I leave this house to my wife named Petrona Felipa, including the lot, in order to work [or serve] there. No one is ever to say anything to her; it is according to my will. —

Fourth, I order that I leave a piece of land where the stream bends to my stepson named Juan Martín. No one is ever to take it from him; it is according to my will. —

Fifth, I order that I leave another piece of land at the edge of the woods [or in Quauhtenco] to my daughter named María [Concepción?].[4] It is according to my will. —

That is all. I conclude my sick person's statement before my executor [*f. 7v*] and my witnesses. Salvador de la Cruz. Fiscal mayor of the holy church, don Diego Matías.

[4]The Spanish translator rendered the name thus.

70. Fabiana de la Cruz, San Pedro Calimaya, 1758

(AGN, Civil 664, exp. 2)[1]

THE PRESENT DOCUMENT is very simple in listing no property whatsoever or even hinting at any; the testator is issuing it principally to make dispositions about her funeral and burial. However, it is quite different from the general run of testaments, most often by women, that are confined to a brief display of funeral arrangements (see for instance the series from Santa María Nativitas, especially Nos. 90 and 92). In fact, Fabiana de la Cruz requests a full ritual: a mass with responsory prayer, an offering to Jerusalem, the habit of the Virgin of Carmen as a shroud, and burial (although outside the church). No specific relative is put in charge of it, so presumably either Fabiana has enough resources or she trusts

[1]The tlaxilacalli of the testator is not known, but by every indication it is in the central cluster.

that her family will take care of it.

The latter case is quite likely. Fabiana introduces herself as a widow, her late husband having been Juan de la Cruz. Note that they share the same second name, and one showing a relatively high status within Calimaya/Tepemaxalco. More men bore the name than women, so that it tends to mean even more in a woman. The executor (who would seem superfluous if there was no property, so maybe there was some not mentioned here) is a don with a highly prestigious second name who once was governor, and in fact acted three years earlier as the executor for the wealthy Agustín de la Cruz of No. 72. The witnesses also reveal the testator's good connections, being prominent individuals and officials, and some are also named de la Cruz.

The introductory formula is quite long and rich in invocations of saints, angels and the Virgin, in the typical style of notary de los Santos, this being the first in the volume (though not in time) of a series of documents by him. A full analysis of his writing can be found in the introductory study, p. 44. Here called don Hipólito de los Santos, he seems to have dominated the notarial profession in Calimaya for some years, eventually advancing to fiscal and acquiring the title don, which, however, he used only inconsistently for a time before adopting it definitively a little later. His preambles are of special interest for the saints they mention, an aspect which can best be discussed here, where we have a very full example. It is clear that some of the saints appear because they are patrons of entities in the Calimaya/Tepemaxalco complex. San Pedro, patron of Calimaya, and San Pablo, patron of Tepemaxalco, introduce the set. Next comes San Antonio de Padua, patron of San Antonio la Isla, a large outlying tlaxilacalli of Calimaya. It appears that there may have been a tlaxilacalli San Miguel in Calimaya, which would explain the presence a little further along of San Miguel Arcángel. However, I know of no tlaxilacalli corresponding to Concepción and San Rafael, who appear here as well, and reappear in other preambles of de los Santos. Indeed, rather similar collections of saints are also present in the preambles of other notaries of Calimaya.

Other preambles by de los Santos with the same array of saints in the same order are Nos. 72, 73, 74, and 82. His Nos. 71 and 76 are less elaborate. In the early example No. 81, dated 1738, his style seems to be still evolving.

[*f. 54*]
JeSus i Maria hi JoSphe
Ma moSenquisCayectenehualo in itlasomahuistocatzi Ds: tetatzi ihuan D:S in itlaSopiltzi ihua D.S. espiritu Santo
Axcan Juebes 21 de Setiembre de 1758 a^{os} ihuan Ca niCa nicpehualtia i nomemoria testamentt,^{o} nehual notoca Fabiana de la Crus ihuan notlasonamictzi catca in itoCa Juan de la Crus ihuan Ca nica nichane ipan iyaltepetzin Sor Sn P.^{o} Calimaya ihuan ca huel ahtopa niquitohua Ca intla yucqui nopan mochihuas in itlasomiquilistzi tt.^{o} D.S Ca iSenmactzinco nicnocahuilia i noyoliantzi noaniMantzi ihuan Ca hul nicnotlatlactilia notlaSotatzi Sor Sn P.^{o} ihuan yehuatzi Sor S.^{n} pablo ihuan yehuatzi notlaSotatzi Sor Sn Antt.^{o} de padua no ihuan nicnotlatlactilia yehuatzi notlaSoMahuisnantzi la linpia conSepSion ihuan yehuatzi notlaSotatzi Sor Sn Miguel arcanJel ihuan San Rafel no ihuan niquimotlatlactilia mohtintzitzi quexquih Santtos ihuan Santas in onpa motemiltitiCate in ilhuiCac inic nopan Motlatoltitzinosque in itlaSoixpantzinco tt.^{o} D.S Ma y mochihua —

[*f. 54*]
Jesus, Mary, and Joseph.
May the precious revered name of God the father, God his precious son, and God the Holy Spirit be entirely praised.
Today, Thursday the 21st of September of the year of 1758, here I named Fabiana de la Cruz begin my memorandum of testament; my late precious husband was named Juan de la Cruz, and I am a citizen here in the altepetl of lord San Pedro, Calimaya. And first of all, I say that if the precious death of our lord God happens to me, I leave my spirit and soul entirely in his hands; and I greatly implore my precious father lord San Pedro, and lord San Pablo, and my precious father lord San Antonio de Padua, and I also implore my precious revered mother la Limpia Concepción, and my precious father lord San Miguel Arcángel and San Rafael, and I also implore all the male and female saints that fill heaven to speak on my behalf in the precious presence of our lord God. May it be done. —

ihuan Ca inic SentlaMantli nitlanahuatia Ca intla oniMomiquili Ca Se Missa ihuan se Responsos nopan mictos in ipalehuiloCa yes noaniMantzi ca neltis notlanahuatil Mochihuas —

inic ontlamantli nitlanahuatia Ca noMortaJa yes in itlaquentzi notlaSomahuisnantzi la carme nicnohuiquilis Ca neltis notlactol mochihuas —

inic yectlamantli nitlanahuatia ca noSepultura Canpa motlap[o]s tiopan quiahua Yhua Ca nicteMaCatia se tomi huentzintli Santo Jerusalen Ca neltis notlanahuatil mochihuas —

ihuan Ca San ixquih niCa nictzonquixtia i noCoCoxCatlanahuatil imixpa noAlbasea ihua notestigos inic tlaneltilisque mostla huiptla —

NoAlbasea nicCahua D^{n} pablo de estrada testigo D^{n} Juan Antt.^{o} testigo Alcalde Dn Feliphe de S.^{n}tiago fiscal mayor de la Santa iglesia D.^{n} domingo de [S].tiago topile Antt.^{o} de la Crus topile Nicolas de la Crus [*f. 54v*]

Es.^{no} Actual de la republica D.^{n} hipollito de lo S.^{n}ttus

And first, I order that when I have died, a mass with a responsory prayer is to be said for me; it will be the help of my soul. My order is be carried out and done. —

Second, I order that my shroud will be the habit of my precious revered mother the [Virgen del] Carmen; I will wear it. My statement is to be carried out and done. —

Third, I order that where my grave is to be opened is outside the church, and I give an offering of one real for Holy Jerusalem. My order is to be carried out and done. —

And that is all. I conclude my sick person's order here before my executor and my witnesses so that they will verify it in the future. —

I leave as my executor don Pablo de Estrada. Witness don Juan Antonio. Witness alcalde don Felipe de Santiago. Fiscal mayor of the holy church don Domingo de Santiago. Topile Antonio de la Cruz. Topile Nicolás de la Cruz. [*f. 54v*]

Present notary of the commonwealth don Hipólito de los Santos.

71. Martina María, San Pedro Calimaya, Pasiontitlan, 1751

(Newberry Library, Ayer Collection 1477B [4])

THE TESTAMENT PORTRAYS an apparently common situation, one spouse leaving a house, lot, and saints to the other spouse and a child. But despite quite a few exceptions, most frequently a nuclear family's residence was owned by a man. Here we notice that Martina María, not her husband, is the owner of the house. She also owns a parcel of land well above the average size, half a fanega or 6 almudes. Another unusual element in the picture is that she does not give the name of the child, so that we do not even know its gender. The term *-coneuh* used here often refers to a very small child or infant. The lack of a name and the manner of the joint bequest leave us thinking that the child is indeed very small, with the husband to have control for now and at some point to pass everything on to the child.

A good part of the testament deals with funeral arrangements, which hint at a relatively high status for the testator. Although the preamble is quite abbreviated by this notary's standards, Martina requests a mass and the shroud of the Virgin of Carmen, makes an offering for Jerusalem, and is to be buried at San Josef, which may be a chapel at the main church or a shrine elsewhere. From a Spanish annotation we also learn that a high mass was performed for her. Martina apparently relied on her family to carry it all out.

The testator's name, as with so many women, tells us virtually nothing about her rank; the name of her husband stands out a bit more. Her executor has no particularly striking name; six witnesses, among whom there are two dons and some good second names (de la Cruz, Santiago, Pérez), are more than respectable, but they fall short of the sparkling collection we see in No. 72, for example. Her property is well above average for a woman. Overall, Martina and her husband seem to be people of high middling station.

The prominent notary Hipólito de los Santos is discussed in the introductory study, p. 44.

[*f. 5*]

Jesus i Maria i Josephe

Axcan lunes A 3 de Mayo de 1751 ihua niCa nic-

[*f. 5*]

Jesus, Mary, and Joseph.

Today Monday the 3rd of May of 1751, here I named

pehualtia i noMemoria testamento nehual notoCa Martina Maria nonaMic in itoCa Juan de D.^{s} ihua Ca niCa niChane in ipan ialtepetzi S,^{n} P,^{o} Calimaya ihua Ca nica nipuhui ipan tlaxilacali paxuctitla ihuan Ca huel axtopa niquitohua Ca intla yucqui nopa Mochihuas nicnoMasehuis in iMiquilistzi tt,^{o} D,^{s} Ca icenMactzinCo nicnoCahuilia i naniMantzi ihuan Ca huel niquinotlatlactilia Mohtintzi quexquih Santos ihuan Santas inic nopan Motlatoltitzinosque in itlaSoixpantzinco tt,^{o} D,^{s} Ma i mochihua —

inic SentlaMantli nitlanahuatia Ca intla oninoMiquili Ca Se missa nopan Mictos in ipalehuiloCa yes noaniMantzi Ca neltis notlatol —

inic ontlaMantli nitlanahuatia Ca nomortaJa in itlaquentzi notlaSonantzi del Carme Ca neltis notlanahuatil —

inic yectlaMantli nitlanahuatia Ca noSepultora onpa Motlapos San Josehe ihua nicteMaCatia Se tomi huentli Santo JeroSalen Ca neltis notlanahuatil mochihuas —

inic nactlamantli nitlanahuatia Ca ini nocha Caltzintli ihua ica mochi Solar ihua Santotzitzin ihua Ca yehual nicquinCahuilia nonaMic in itoCa Juan de D,^{s} imonehua noCone tlatequipanosque[1] Ca neltis notlanahuatil Mochihuas —

inic Maquiltlamantli nitlanahuatia Ca Se tlali onpa Mani Metepec otli timoquaxuhhuia Domingo de S,^{n}tiago ihua Calaqui Se Media tlauli yhua Ca Sano yechual nonaMic ihua nocone niquinCahuilia ca iCa notlanequilis Mochihuas —

ihua Ca San ixquih niCa nictzonquixtia NomeMoria testaMento ixpa noalbaSea ihua notestigos inic tlaneltilisque Mostla huiptla NoAlbaSea nicCahua Manuel Salbador testigo Josehe de la Crus oc Se notestigo D,^{n} matheo de S,^{n}tiago [*f. 5v*] fiscal Mayor de la Santa iglesia D,^{n} pasqual peres topile pedro de la Cruz Astasio de S,^{n}tiago[2]

Nehual onitlaquilo itenCopa CoCoxqui notoCa = ipolito de lo Santos, Es^{no} temahti[3] =

Martina María begin my memorandum of testament; my husband's name is Juan de Dios, and I am a citizen here in the altepetl of San Pedro, Calimaya; I belong to the tlaxilacalli of Pasiontitlan here. First of all I say that if it happens to me that I attain the death of our lord God, I leave my soul entirely in his hands, and I greatly implore all the male and female saints there are to speak for me in the precious presence of our lord God; may it be done. —

First I order that when I have died, a mass is to be said for me to be the help of my soul. My statement is to be carried out. —

Second I order that my shroud is to be the habit of my precious mother del Carmen. My order is to be carried out. —

Third I order that my grave is to be opened at San Josef, and I give a real as an offering for Holy Jerusalem. My order is to be carried out and done. —

Fourth I order that I leave this home of mine, the house along with the lot and the saints, to my husband named Juan de Dios, together with my child; they are to work with it.[1] My order is to be carried out and done. —

Fifth I order that I likewise leave a piece of land on the Metepec road, bordering [land of] Domingo de Santiago, where half a fanega of maize fits, to my husband and child. It is to be done by my will. —

And that is all. Here I conclude my memorandum of testament in the presence of my executor and my witnesses so that they will verify it in the future. As my executor I leave Manuel Salvador. Witness, Josef de la Cruz. Another witness of mine, don Mateo de Santiago. [*f. 5v*] Fiscal mayor of the holy church, don Pascual Pérez. Topile, Pedro de la Cruz; Anastasio de Santiago.[2]

I did the writing at the command of the sick person, I named Hipólito de los Santos, notary and temachti.[3]

---

[1]The meaning "to work with or use something," such as a tool, an animal, a field, usually requires *ic* or *ica* in addition to *tlatequipanoa*. The meaning may be "they are to serve" (especially the saints).

[2]Likely also a topile.

[3]Annotations in Spanish say that Martina María's husband Juan de Dios paid for a mass on May 24, 1751, and that the next day a mass was sung. Thus a high mass was performed although not specified in the testament. It is interesting that the husband paid for the mass even though there was an executor.

72. Agustín de la Cruz, San Pedro Calimaya, Pasiontitlan, 1755
(AGN, Tierras 2298, exp. 5)[1]

THE ESTATE OF Agustín de la Cruz is not overwhelming, but it is far above average: a house with several saint's images valuable enough to be listed separately, a lot and a half in town, and much other land. Though no one parcel is of outstanding size, his greatly scattered agricultural plots—9 holdings between 1 and 3 almudes in size—amount to $18^1/_2$ almudes. An implication is that Agustín is an active entrepreneur and has been accumulating land.

The testator's second name is so common that we cannot initially be sure it means he is connected with the famous family or lineage of wealthy officeholders of Calimaya/Tepemaxalco, but the overall combination of his property and his associations indicates that we do seem to have an authentic de la Cruz. Agustín's brother Pascual, with whom he shares a lot, also bears the same second name, so it is being used for the whole line, at least on the male side (his daughters are not de la Cruz).

His witnesses are maximum testimony to Agustín's standing, including the present governor of Calimaya (the most impressive possible witness) and the fiscal mayor, and in addition a person with the don and the prestigious second name Albarrán, which was the surname of a Spanish family prominent in the whole Toluca Valley across the centuries.[2] The executor (the same as for another de la Cruz in No. 70) also bears a name with implications of the highest standing and is a former governor. The funeral arrangements too point to relatively high status, going beyond the expected mass and offering for Jerusalem to being shrouded in the habit and rope of San Francisco and having a grave in the chapel of San Antonio.

Normally, in view of the fact that Agustín does not bear the don, we would think that he had not held high office, or perhaps only the ambivalent position of regidor mayor, which was sometimes associated with the don, sometimes not. A Calimaya land grant of 1750, however, includes a don Agustín de la Cruz, alcalde; the governor in the document was none other than the don Pablo de Estrada who is executor here.[3] In view of all the evidence of Agustín's position, one must conclude that he is most likely that same person, even though now he appears without title. In the corpus, alcaldes always bear the don while in office and almost always afterward as well. (Don) Francisco Martín of San Lucas in Tepemaxalco (Nos. 47, 48) was an exception, which could be explained, perhaps, by his not too impressive economic situation. Here that explanation would lack validity; nevertheless, the situation requires reporting.

Note that Agustín leaves his entire estate to his wife Vicenta Antonia together with two small daughters, María del Carmen and María Josefa, with the charge that the wife will later on divide everything between the daughters. No more remotely related male heirs are mentioned, as is sometimes seen in such cases; nothing is given to any male relative either as an inheritance or in a tutorial capacity. We will find Vicenta Antonia again in the corpus; in a 1712 will, No. 78, it is seen that she was the daughter of Francisco Juan, of Tlamimilolpan.[4] It is very interesting to see that she married a man belonging to Pasiontitlan, moving to live with him; this detail says much about the connections between tlaxilacalli in the central settlement of Calimaya/Tepemaxalco. The fact that Vicenta Antonia's father was wealthy and probably influential may help explain why her husband assigns her such a prominent role.

The notary is once again the prolific Hipólito de los Santos, described in the introductory study. The present text contains some special indications of the penetration of Spanish influence into his speech. "Nicchihuilia cargo," "I charge her with," is a calque or idiom translation originating in Spanish "le hago cargo"; the phrase is seen more than once in the texts of de los Santos. Note also the word *tlalme*, "lands." Nahuatl traditionally never puts a plural suffix on *tlalli*, "land," and that is generally true in the Toluca wills as well, but here we have an expression affected by Spanish *tierras*. (A few similar cases will be found here and there in the corpus.)

---

[1]The testament is accompanied by a contemporary Spanish translation.
[2]See Lockhart 1991, pp. 210–11.
[3]Lockhart 1991, p. 109.
[4]The present testament as well as Nos. 78 and 79 are all included in a file that was put together in 1794 for a suit to annul the 1779 testament of Vicenta Antonia (preserved only in Spanish).

[*f.* 22]

Jesus i Maria hi Josephe

Ma moSenquisCayectenehualo in itlaSomahuistoCatzi D.s. tetatzi ihua D.s in itlaSopiltzi ihuan D.s espiritu Santo Ma i mochihua =

Axcan Miercoles Mani Metztli A 22 de otubre de 1755 a^{os} ihuan Ca niCa nicpehualtia i noMemoria testaMento Nehual notoCa Agustin de la Crus ihuan nosihuahuatzi in itoca biSenta Antonia ihuan Ca niCa nichane ipan in ialtepetzi S,^{or} S,^{n} P,^{o} Calimaya ihuan Ca niCa nipuhui ipan tlaxilaCali[5] paxutitla ihuan Ca huel ahtopa niquitohua Ca intla yucqui nopa Mochihuas ihua nicnoMacSehuis in itlaSoMiquilistzi tt,^{o} D.^{s}. ihuan Ca iSenMactzinco nicnoCahuilia i noaniMantzi ihuan Ca huel nicnotlatlatlactilia notlasotatzitzihua[6] S,^{or} S,^{n} P,^{o} ihua yehuatzi S,^{r} S,^{n} Pablo no ihua nicnotlatlactilia yehuatzi notlaSotatzi S,^{or} S,^{n} Antonio [de] paduhua no ihua nicnotlatlactilia yehuatzi notlasoMahuisnantzi l[. . .]pia conSepSion ihuan yehuatzin S,^{or} S,^{n} Miguel ArCanjel ihuan San Rafel no ihua niquiMotlatlatlactilia Mohtintzitzi quexquih Santos ihuan Santas in onpa MotemiltitiCate in ilhuiCac inic nopa Motlatoltitzinosque in itlasoixpantzinco tt,^{o} D.s. Ma i mochihua —

inic SentlaMantli nitlanahuatia Ca intla onicnoMaSehui in itlasomiquilistzi tt,^{o} Je[?],^{tto} Ca Se misa nopan Mitos in ipalehuiloCa yes noaniMantzi Ca neltis notlanahuatil Mochihuas —

inic ontlaMantli nitlanahuatia Ca noMortaja yes in itlaquentzi notlasotatzi S,^{r} S,^{n} fr,^{co} ihuan iCordontzi nicnohuiquilis Ca neltis notlactol mochihuas =

inic yectlaMantli nitlanahuatia ca noSepultura Ca onpa Motlapos Capilla notlasotatzi S,^{or} S,^{n} Antonio ihuan Ca nicnoMaquilia Se mel no ihua Ca nicteMaca Se totomi huentzintli Santo Jerusalen Ca neltis notlactol mochihuas =

inic nactlamantli nitlanahuatia Ca ini nocha Caltzintli ihua ica Mochi solar ihuan ca yehual nicCahuilia noSihuahuatzi ihua ica omenti nopilhuantoto Se itoca Maria del CarMe ihuan oc Se itoca Maria JoSepha ihuan Ca nosihuahuatzi nicchihuilia Cargo quinhuapahuas ihuan intla D.s quiMonochilis Mostla huiptla quintlaxelhuilis oMenti nopilhuatoto Ca neltis notlactol Mochihuas = inic MaquiltlaMantli

[*f.* 22]

Jesus, Mary, and Joseph.

May the precious revered name of God the father, God his precious son, and God the Holy Spirit be entirely praised; may it be done. =

Today Wednesday the 22nd of the month of October of the year of 1755, here I named Agustín de la Cruz begin my memorandum of testament. My wife is named Vicenta Antonia, and I am a citizen here in the altepetl of lord San Pedro, Calimaya; I belong to the tlaxilacalli[5] of Pasiontitlan here. First of all I say that if it should happen to me that I attain the precious death of our lord God, I leave my soul entirely in his hands, and I greatly implore my precious fathers[6] lord San Pedro and lord San Pablo, and I also implore my precious father lord San Antonio de Padua, and I also implore my precious revered mother [la] Limpia Concepción and lord San Miguel Arcángel and San Rafael; I also implore all the male and female saints who fill heaven to speak for me in the precious presence of our lord God. May it be done. —

First I order that when I have attained the precious death of our lord Jesus Christ, a mass is to be said for me to be the help of my soul. My order is to be carried out and done. —

Second I order that my shroud is to be the habit of my precious father lord San Francisco, and I am to wear his rope. My statement is to be carried out and done. =

Third I order that my grave is to be opened in the chapel of my precious father lord San Antonio, and I give him a maguey. Also I give a real as an offering for Holy Jerusalem. My statement is to be carried out and done. =

Fourth I order that I leave this home of mine, the house including the lot, to my wife along with two small children of mine named María del Carmen and the other named María Josefa. I charge my wife to raise them, and if God summons her in the future, she is to divide things between my two small children. My statement is to be carried out and done. = Fifth I order that I likewise leave the saints who

[5]At this point the Spanish translation has "viuimos en la calle de Pashutitlan." It is unclear to me whether the translator merely rendered *tlaxilacalli* in an unusual and rather uninformed way, or whether what he says actually can help us understand the physical layout of the tlaxilacalli in this case.

[6]Only here and in No. 81 is this expression found in the plural, each time referring to these two saints.

nitlanahuatia Ca yehuantzitzi Santas [Santos?] ChaneCatzitzinti yehuatzi Señora de [Cuat?]alupe ihuan yehuatzi S,^{or} S,^{n} Juan yhuan yehuatzi Santo intiero ihuan yehuatzi Santa Maria Magdalena yhuan Ca Sano yehual niquiMoCahuililia noSihuahuatzi Ca iCa notlanequilis Ca neltis notlanahuatil Mochihua —

are resident [in the house], Nuestra Señora de Guadalupe, lord San Juan, the Santo Entierro, and Santa María Magdalena, to my wife, for it is by my will. My order is to be carried out and done. —

inic chiquaSentlaMantli nitlanahuatia[7] Ce tlali onpa Mani San Antt,^{o} octli ihua iteh Calaqui tlauli yei alMo ihua oc se tlali Mani San Miguel octli tiMoquaxuhhuia D,^{a} fr,^{ca} ihuan itech Calaqui yei almo tlauli ihua oc Se pedaSito Ca Sanonpa Mani para ic tlacpac Canpa Calaqui yei almo tlauli ihuan oc Se pedaSito tlali onpa mani ChiMalhuaca iteh Calaqui Se almo tlauli ihuan Ca sanonpa ChiMalhuacCa para ic tlacpac mani oc Se pedaso iteh Calaqui ome quartilios tlauli ihuan oc se tlali onpa Mani S,^{n} Lorenzo octli timoquaxuhhuia D,^{n} Antt^{o} de [. . .] reyes ihua iteh Calaqui oMe Almo tlauli ihuan oc Se tlali onpa Mantica quactenCo iteh Calaqui yei alMo tlauli = ihuan oc Se tlaltontli onpa Mantica ToloCa octli iteh Calaqui yei alMo tlauli ihuan oc Se Can onCa Mantica para ic tlacpac timoquaxuhhuia MarSel ihua iteh Calaqui Se almo tlauli = ihua nitlanahuatia Ca oc Se pedaSo Solar nican Mantica tlaMimilolpa ihuan ca tlacCo iyaxCa noerMano pasqual de la Crus ihuan oc tlacCo noaxca ihuan Ca quiCahuilis noSihuahuatzi Ca yehual nicCahuilia = no ihua nitlanahuatia Ca oc Se pedasito Solar niCan Mantica paxutitla Sentlapal octli ihuan Ca mochi tlalMe ihuan Solar ihuan Ca yehual nicCahuilia Nosihuahuatzi Ca yehual nicchihuilia Cargo para Mostla huiptla quintlaxelhuitias omenti nopil[*f. 22v*]huantoto Ca iCa notlanequilis Camo aqui tlen quitos queMania Ca neltis notlanahuatil mochihuas —

Sixth I order [that I leave to my wife][7] a piece of land on the road to San Antonio into which fit 3 almudes of maize; and another piece of land on the road to San Miguel bordering [land of] doña Francisca, into which fit 3 almudes of maize; and another little piece in the same place, above it, into which fit 3 almudes of maize; and another little piece of land at Chimalhuacan, into which fits 1 almud of maize; and likewise at Chimalhuacan, above it, another piece into which fit 2 cuartillos of maize; and another piece of land on the San Lorenzo road bordering [land of] don Antonio de los Reyes, into which fit 2 almudes of maize; and another piece of land at the edge of the woods [or in Quauhtenco], into which fit 3 almudes of maize; and another little piece of land on the Toluca road, into which fit 3 almudes of maize; and another in the same place, above it, bordering [land of] Marcel, into which fits 1 almud of maize; and I order that as to another piece of a lot here in Tlamimilolpan, of which half is the property of my brother Pascual de la Cruz and the other half is my property, he is to leave it [my half] to my wife, for I leave it to her. = I also order that I leave to my wife another little piece of a lot here in Pasiontitlan, with the road on one side. [I leave to her] all the lands and the lot, and I charge her in the future to divide everything gradually between my two small children, [*f. 22v*] for it is by my will. No one is ever to say anything. My order is to be carried out and done. —

Yhuan Ca San ixquih nica nictzonquixtia i noMemoria testamento imixpa noalbasea ihuan notestigos inic tlaneltilisque mostla huiptla in itlasoixpantzinco tt,^{o} D.^{s} Ma i mochihua —
NoAlbaSea nicCahua Dn Pablo de[s?] estrada
notestigo D,^{n} JoSephe[e?] de Albaran Jues i G,^{or} Actual D,^{n} Salbador Ramos fiscal mayor de la Santa iglesi D,^{n} Matheo de Santiago topile fr,^{co} de S,^{n}tiago topile DoMingo de la Cruz
ES,^{no} hipolitto de lo Santos temaxti

That is all; here I conclude my memorandum of testament before my executor and my witnesses, who will verify it in the future in the precious presence of our lord God. May it be done. —
I leave as my executor don Pablo de Estrada.
My witnesses are don Josef de Albarrán; present judge-governor don Salvador Ramos; fiscal mayor of the holy church don Mateo de Santiago; topile Francisco de Santiago; topile Domingo de la Cruz.
Notary Hipólito de los Santos, temachti.

[7]This passage is truncated and grammatically opaque, but in the end the intention becomes clear.

73. Lorenza de Subersa, San Pedro Calimaya, Pasiontitlan, 1759

(AGN, Civil 664, exp. 2)

FROM THE TESTAMENTS we have seen so far that were written by Hipólito de los Santos, we could form the impression that he caters to rather well-off clients. Here for the third time straight (Nos. 71 through 73) the testator is to be buried inside the church close to the image of a specifically named saint. In addition to the usual requests and offering, the rope of San Francisco is added to the frequent special shroud for women, a habit of Carmen. The witnesses include both the governor and the fiscal mayor. For the third time in these wills don Pablo de Estrada, the former governor, is named executor. Perhaps, however, that says less about Lorenza's status than one might think, for by this time it begins to look as if Estrada is almost a professional executor of wills, or that he and the notary have made some special arrangement. Lorenza's second name is rare (I have not yet identified its origin), and her husband had a Spanish second name. All of this seems to add up to relatively high status in the community.

The only property Lorenza lists is her house, which apparently contains a full complement of saints. It goes to a granddaughter. There is too little context to make any certain interpretation of the inheritance patterns in play here. The house could have been the main family residence left in the hands of Lorenza only because of the death of her husband and all her children. Or the rest of the family assets may have already gone to various heirs, and the granddaughter, María de la Encarnación, is the daughter of an heir who still had something coming. In any case, a substantial bequest here passes from female to female.

Notary de los Santos, so frequently seen in these pages, tends to follow a very uniform model. The saints mentioned here are exactly the same as in No. 70, and the whole preamble is nearly identical in both testaments; the first bequests are also very similar. Note the use of *barrio* for the same entity elsewhere called a tlaxilacalli (though in fact this equation is seen quite a few times in the central cluster of Calimaya/Tepemaxalco). By now we see that Hipólito de los Santos held the posts of notary and temachti simultaneously for several years.

[*f.* 52]

Jesus i Maria i JoSephe =

Ma moSenquisCayectenehualo in itlaSoMahuistoCatzi d.s. tetatzi ihuan dios in itlaSopiltzi ihua dios espiritu Santo = Axcan Juebes a 25 de otubre de 1759 a^{os} ihuan Ca niCa nicpehualtia i noMemoria testamento nehual notoCa LorenSa de SuberSa V,^{a} ihua notlasonaMictzi in itoca Mathias Sanches ihua ca nica tichaneque[1] ipan in ialtepetzi S,^{or} S,^{n} P,^{o} CaliMaya ihua Ca niCa nipohui ipan bario paxuctitla ihua ca intla yocqui nopan Mochihuas ihua nicnomaSehuis in itlaSoMiquilistzin tt,^{o} d.^{s}. Ca iSenMactzinco nicnoCahuilia i noyoliantzi noaniMantzi ihuan Ca huel nicnotlatlactilia yehuatzi notlaSotatzi S,^{or} S,^{n} P,^{o} ihua yehuatzi S,^{or} S,^{n} Pablo no ihua nicnotlatlactilia notlaSomahuistatzi S,^{or} S,^{n} Antt,^{o} de padua ihua yehuatzi notlaSoMahuisnantzi la linpia ConSepSion ihua yehuatzi notlaSotatzi S,^{n} Miguel arCanJel ihuan San Rafel no yhua

[*f.* 52]

Jesus, Mary, and Joseph. =

May the precious revered name of God the father, God his precious son, and God the Holy Spirit be entirely praised. = Today Thursday the 25th of October of the year of 1759, here I named Lorenza de Subersa, widow, begin my memorandum of testament. My precious husband was named Matías Sánchez, and we are[1] citizens here in the altepetl of lord San Pedro, Calimaya; I belong to the barrio of Pasiontitlan. If it should happen to me that I attain the precious death of our lord God, I leave my spirit and soul entirely in his hands, and I greatly implore my precious father lord San Pedro and lord San Pablo, and I also implore my precious revered father lord San Antonio de Padua and my precious revered mother la Limpia Concepción, and my precious father San Miguel Arcángel and San Rafael, and I also implore all the male and female saints that fill

[1]In Nahuatl equative statements are not verbal and have no time dimension, but are true in any time. In English we need to say that Matías Sánchez "was" Lorenza's husband, which is not part of the original, and there is no easy way to express the equation when one of the subjects is alive, the other dead, as with the deceased husband and the living widow being citizens of Calimaya.

niquiMotlatlactililia Mochi quexquch Santos ihuan Santas in onpan MotemiltitiCate in ilhuiCac inic nopan Motlatoltitzinosque in itlaSoixpantzinCo tt,^{o} Ds Ma y Mochihua —

heaven to speak for me in the precious presence of our lord God. May it be done. —

ihuan Ca inic SentlaMantli nitlanahuatia Ca intla oniMomiquili Ca Se missa ihuan Se ResponSoS nopan Mictos ni ipalehuiloCa yes noaniMantzi Ca neltis notlanahuatil Mochihuas —

And first I order that when I have died, a mass with a responsory prayer is to be said for me, to be the help of my soul. My order is to be carried out and done. —

inic ontlaMantli nitlanahuatia Ca noMortaJa yes in itlaquentzi notlaSomahuisnantzi del Carme nicnohuiquilis ihua in iCordontzi S,^{or} S,^{n} fr.^{co} ihuan Ca iCa notlanequilis Ca neltis notlanahuatil Mochihuas

Second I order that my shroud is to be the habit of my precious revered mother del Carmen that I will wear, and the rope of lord San Francisco. It is by my will; my order is to be carried out and done.

inic yectlaMantli nitlanahuatia Ca noSepultura Ca onpa Motlapos tiopanCalitic icpantzinCo notlaSoMahuistatzi S,^{or} S,^{n} diego No yhua Ca nicteMaCatia Se tomi huentzin Santo JeruSalen Ca neltis notlanahuatil Mochihuas —

Third I order that my grave is to be opened inside the church building in front of my precious revered father lord San Diego. I am also giving a real as an offering for Holy Jerusalem. My order is to be carried out and done. —

inic nactlamantli nitlanahuatia Ca ini nocha Caltzintli ihua iCa mohtintzitzi Santtos ihuan Santas ihuan Ca yehual nicCahuilia noxhui in itoca Maria de la EnCarnaSion Ca iCa notlanequilis Camo aqui tlen quitos queMania Ca neltis notlactol Mochihuas —

Fourth I order that I leave this home of mine, the house including all the male and female saints, to my grandchild named María de la Encarnación. It is by my will; no one is ever to say anything. My statement is to be carried out and done. —

ihua Ca San ixquih niCan nictzonquistia i noMemoria testamento iMixpa noalbaSea ihua notestigos inic tlaneltilisque in itlaSoixpantzinCo tt,^{o} D.^{s}. Ma y Mochihua —

That is all. Here I conclude my memorandum of testament in the presence of my executor and my witnesses who will verify it in the precious presence of our lord God. May it be done. —

NoalbaSea nicCahua D,^{n} pablo de Estrada testigo Manuel Antt,^{o} Jues i G,^{or} Actual D,^{n} Salbador Ramos fisCal mayor D,^{n} domingo de S^{n}tiago [*f. 52v*] Manuel Antt,^{o} topile = MarCos Antt,^{o} topile =
ES,^{no} hipolitto de lo Santos teMahtic =

I leave as my executor don Pablo de Estrada. Witness, Manuel Antonio. Present judge-governor don Salvador Ramos. Fiscal mayor don Domingo de Santiago. [*f. 52v*] Manuel Antonio, topile. Marcos Antonio, topile. =
Notary Hipólito de los Santos, temachti.

74. María Clara, San Pedro Calimaya, Pasiontitlan, 1763

(AGN, Civil 664, exp. 2)

THE EXACT SPECIFICATION of the size of María Clara's landholdings leaves us in no doubt that she owns well above the average: 12 almudes of scattered agricultural land, plus two pieces of lots in the central settlement and a house with many saints where she also may own the lot, though that is not stated. What María Clara possesses looks like an entire family estate; yet she names her husband, Francisco Javier. Does he have another entire similar set of lands and lots? Or is he deceased and María Clara became the heir of everything when the children were small? Francisco Javier is not mentioned again in any way.

María Clara divides her estate between a daughter, a son, and a grandchild. The daughter is preferred in being mentioned first and receiving the house, but otherwise the treatment is quite even-handed. The daughter gets 3 almudes of land, the son and grandson 4 each. The son also gets a piece of a lot and a substantial number of magueyes, what is left of them going to the grandson. (It is interesting that here as often a woman holds magueyes, but the number, though substantial, is not huge, and contrary to the pattern for maguey entrepreneurs she does own much land; also, the plants go to males, not to the female.) There are too many unknowns here to carry out further interpretation of the inheritance pattern. The daughter might be getting the house because she will help take care of the son and grandson, or the son could be grown up and already have a house. The grandson might be the child of either of the other two, or more likely stand in for a child of María Clara's who has died.

The situation with funeral arrangements is the same as with most of this notary's better-off and more influential clients, including burial in the church before a particular saint. The long preamble represents the notary's full treatment. This is a rare case in the corpus in which the testator orders that land, and indeed a specific piece, be sold for funeral expenses, though such instructions were common in other times and places. The fact that María Clara has in the past requested and received part of a lot in town from the altepetl authorities implies that she has considerable influence. The executor and witnesses are of the highest rank. Yet María Clara's estate does not represent a fortune; none of the names in her family have any hint of distinction, and there is no name continuity. Thus she and hers seem well off and well connected, but not at the top of local society.

María Clara has a large collection of saints, several mentioned by name, to be distributed among her heirs. The fact that the grandson gets the residue after those named are given out may imply that he is the child of María's daughter or at least will live in her house. The presence of so many saints calls for a bit of analysis. The saints mentioned in the preamble are not affected by any tendencies of the testator; they are the usual ones named by the notary de los Santos. Of María's six saints given with their names (counting each image, for the Señora de la Merced appears twice), five are female, only one male (although we are told that there are other saints both male and female). Four of those named are advocations of the Virgin Mary, perhaps indicating a special devotion corresponding to María's first name. She is to be buried before the image of another María, however: María Magdalena.

The frequently seen notary de los Santos has by 1763 definitively assumed the title don as don Hipólito. This particular text of his is notable for the unusual loan phrase *santo tribunal* at the end of the preamble; a frequent use of the loan particle *para*, including in hybrid idiom translations equivalent to Spanish *para abajo* and *para arriba*; and a rare loan verb, *constaroa*, from Spanish *constar*, to be evident, recorded, or confirmed.

[*f. 34*]

Jesus Maria hi JoSephe

Ma moSenquisCayectenehualo yn itlaSoMahuistoCatzi D.^{s} tetatzi yhua d^{s} ytlaSopiltzi yhua Ds. Espiritu Santto Ma y Mochihua =

AxCan doMingo A 2 de Julio de 1763 a^{os} yhua ca niCa nicpehualtia y noMemoria testamento nehual notoCa Maria Clara yhua notlaSonaMictzi ytoCa fr,^{co} Xabiel yhua Ca niCa niChane ypan yn ialtepetzi notlaSotatzi S,^{or} S,^{n} P.^{o} CaliMaya yhua Ca nica nipuhui ypan barrio paxuctitla yhua Ca yntla yucqui nopa Mochihuas yhua nicnoMacSehuis yn itlaSomiquilistzi tt.^{o} D.^{s} Ca ySenMactzinCo nicnoCahuilia noyoliantzi noaniMantzi yhua Ca huel nicnotlatlactilia yehuatzi notlaSotatzi S,^{or} S,^{n} P.^{o} yhua yehuatzi S.^{or} S,^{n} panblo yhua yehuatzi notlaSotatzi S.^{or} S,^{n} Antonio de paduhua yhua nicnotlatlactilia yehuatzi notlaSonantzi la linpia ConSepSion yhua yehuatzi Sn Miguel arCangel yhua S,^{n} Rafel no yhua niquinotlatlactilia Mochi quexquih Santos yhuan Santas yn onpa MotemiltitiCate yn ilhuicac ynic nopan motlactoltitzinosque ypan

[*f. 34*]

Jesus, Mary, and Joseph.

May the precious revered name of God the father, God his precious son, and God the Holy Spirit be entirely praised. May it be done. =

Today Sunday the 2nd of July of the year of 1763, here I named María Clara begin my memorandum of testament. My precious husband is named Francisco Javier, and I am a citizen here in the altepetl of my precious father lord San Pedro, Calimaya; I belong to the barrio of Pasiontitlan here. If it happens to me that I attain the precious death of our lord God, I leave my spirit and soul entirely in his hands, and I greatly implore my precious father lord San Pedro and lord San Pablo and my precious father lord San Antonio de Padua, and I implore my precious mother la Limpia Concepción, San Miguel Arcángel, and San Rafael, and I also implore all the male and female saints that fill heaven to speak for me at the holy Tribunal. May it be done. —

Santo tribunal Ma y mochihua —
ynic Sentlamantli nitlanahuatia Ca yntla onicnoMacSehui yn itlaSoMiquilistzi tt.^{o} Ds. Ca Se Missa yhua responsos nopan Mictos ypalehuiloCa yes noaniMantzi Ca neltis notlactol —
ynic ontlaMantli nitlanahuatia Ca noMortaga yes yn itlaquentzi yehuatzi notlaSonantzi del CarMe yhua in iCordontzi notlaSotatzi S,^{n} fr.^{co} nicNohuiquilis Ca neltis notlactol mochihuas =
ynic yectlaMantli nitlanahuatia Ca noSepultura Ca onpa Motlapos tiopanCalictic yxpantzinco notlaSonantzi Santa Maria Magdalena nicMotequipanilhuiya no yhua nitlanahuatia Ca Se toMi huentzintli Santo geruSalen Ca neltis notlanahuatil Mochihuas —
ynic nactlaMantli nitlanahuatia Ca yni noCha Caltzintli yhua Ca yehual nicCahuilia noxpoh MarSela fr.^{ca} Ca yCa notlanequilis nicCahuilia yhuan Santotzitzi nicCahuilia Señora de la Mersed yhua yehuatzi Santa getrudes yhua Santo EcSe omo yhua yehuatzi Señora de los dolores Ca neltis notlanahuatil MoChihuas —
no yhua nitlanahuatia Ca yehuatzi Señora de la MerSed yhua Ca yehual nicCahuilia nopiltzi JoSephe Antonio Ca yCa notlanequilis Ca neltis notlactol mochihuas —
No yhuan nitlanahuatia Ca noxhui ytoCa Josephe Mariano yhua Ca yehual nicquinMoCahuililia Mi Señora de huadaluphe yhua Mochi quexquih Santtos yhuan Santtas MoCactzinohua ypan caltzintli Ca yehual quiMotequipanilhuis ca neltis notlactol mochihuas — [*f. 34v*]
no yhua nitlanahuatia Ca Se tlali onpa Mani la ConSepsion octli yhua tiMoquaxuhhuia D,^{n} thoMas Alberto yhua yteh Calaqui MaCuili alMo tlauli yhua Ca tlacCo para yc tlatzintla Canpa Calaquis oMe alMo yhuan tlacCo nicCahuilia noxhui ytoCa JoSephe mariano = yhua para yc tlacpac Canpa Calaquis oc Ome alMo yhuan tlaco yhua Ca yehual nicCahuili nopiltzi ytoCa Josephe Antt.^{o} Ca yCa notlanequilis niquinCahuilia Ca neltis notlactol MoChihuas —
no yhua nitlanahuatia Ca Sanonpa la ConSepsion octli Ma oc Se tlali tiMoquaxuhhuiua D,^{n} fr.^{co} Antt.^{o} yhua yteh Calaqui yei alMo tlauli yhua Ca yehual nicCahuilia noxpoh MarSela fr,^{ca} Ca yCa notlanequilis nicCahuilia Ca neltis notlactol —

no yhua nitlanahuatia Ca oc Se tlaltontli mani Metepec octli tiMoquaXuhhuiya Dn Juan Aparisio yhua Calaqui Se alMo yhuan tlacCo yhua Ca yehual

First I order that when I have attained the precious death of our lord God, a mass with a responsory prayer is to be said for me to be the help of my soul. My statement is to be carried out. —
Second I order that my shroud is to be the habit of my precious mother del Carmen, and I will wear the rope of my precious father San Francisco. My statement is to be carried out and done. =
Third I order that my grave is to be opened inside the church building facing my precious mother Santa María Magdalena whom I serve; I order additionally one real as an offering for Holy Jerusalem. My order is to be carried out and done. —
Fourth I order that I leave this home of mine, the house, to my daughter Marcela Francisca; I leave it to her by my will, along with the saints. I leave her Señora de la Merced, Santa Gertrudis, holy Ecce Homo, and Señora de los Dolores. My order is to be carried out and done. —

In addition I order that I leave Señora de la Merced to my son Josef Antonio; it is by my will. My statement is to be carried out and done. —

In addition I order that I leave to my grandchild named Josef Mariano mi Señora de Guadalupe and all the [other] male and female saints that remain in the house; he is to serve them. My statement is to be carried out and done. — [*f. 34v*]

In addition I order that there is a piece of land on the la Concepción road bordering on [land of] don Tomás Alberto, into which fit 5 almudes of maize. I leave to my grandchild named Josef Mariano the lower half, into which $2^1/_2$ almudes fit, and I leave to my son named Josef Antonio the upper part, where another $2^1/_2$ almudes fit. By my will I leave it to them. My statement is to be carried out and done. —

In addition I order that likewise on the la Concepción road there is another piece of land bordering on [land of] don Francisco Antonio, into which fit 3 almudes of maize, which I leave to my daughter Marcela Francisca; I leave it to her by my will. My statement is to be carried out. —
In addition I order that there is another little piece of land on the Metepec road bordering on [land of] don Juan Aparicio, into which fits $1^1/_2$ almudes; I leave

nicCahuilia noxhui ytoCa Josephe Mariano Ca neltis notlactol mochihuas —

no yhua nitlanahuatia Ca oc Se tlaltontli Mani San Andres octli tiMoquaXuhhuiya D,^{n} pablo de Estrada yhua Calaqui Se alMo yhuan tlacCo yhua Ca yehual nicCahuilia Nopiltzi JoSephe Antt.^{o} Ca yCa notlanequilis nicCahuilia ca neltis notlactol Mochihuas —

No yhua nitlanahuatia Ca Se tlaltontli niCa mani ytenco baRanca timoquaXuhhuiya Matheo Astasio V.^{o} yhua yteh Calaqui Se almo tlauli yhua oc Se pedaso Solar niCan Mantica tiopantonCo yhua Ca yehual Nicchihuilia Cargo noAlbaSea para quinaMacas para noentiero ihua para noMissa Ca neltis notlanahuatil Mochihuas —

No yhua nitlanahuatia Ca oc Se pedaSo Solar niCan MantiCa tlaMimilolpa Santa Crustitla yhua Ca oniquitlanili AltepehuacCatzitzinti para nopiltzi JoSephe Antt^{o} quenaMe Costaros ypan Amal de poSeSion yhua Ca yCa notlanequilis nicCahuilia Camo aqui tlen quitos quemania ca neltis notlactol Mochihuas —

no yhua nitlanahuatia Ca Sempuali Mel yhuan chiCuaSen nicCahuilia nopiltzi Josephe Antt.^{o} Ca yCa notlanequilis nicCahuilia Ca neltis notlactol Mochihuas — [*f. 35*]

No yhua nitlanatia Ca quexquih Mel moCahuas Ca yehual nicCahuilia noxhui ytoCa JoSephe Mariano Ca yCa notlanequilis nicCahuilia Ca neltis notlanahuatil mochihuas —

yhua Ca San ixquih niCa nictzonquixtia y noCoCoxCatlactol noMemeMoria testaMento yMixpa notestigos ihua noAlbaSea ynic tlaneltilisque Mostla huiptla yn itlaSoyxpantzinCo D.^{s} Ma y Mochihua —

NoAlbaSea nicCahua Dn S.^{n}ttiago NiColas
testigo D,^{n} Manuel Antonio testigo D,^{n} Salbador NiColas D^{n} Julian de Santiago Jues y G.^{or} actual fisCal Mayor D,^{n} Esteban Ernandes
Es.^{no} D.^{n} hipolitto de lo Santtos

it to my grandchild named Josef Mariano. My statement is to be carried out and done. —

In addition I order that there is another little piece of land on the San Andrés road bordering on [land of] don Pablo de Estrada, into which fits $1^1/_2$ almudes; I leave it to my son Josef Antonio. I leave it to him by my will. My statement is to be carried out and done. —

In addition I order that there is a little piece of land at the edge of the ravine bordering on [land of] Mateo Anastasio, widower, into which fits 1 almud of maize, and another piece of a lot here at Teopantonco; I charge my executor to sell it for my burial and for my mass. My order is to be carried out and done. —

In addition I order that there is another piece of a lot here in Tlamimilolpan, at Santacruztitlan [or next to the holy cross], that I requested from the altepetl authorities for my son Josef Antonio, as will be confirmed in the document of possession; by my will I leave it to him. No one is ever to say anything. My statement is to be carried out and done. —

In addition I order that I leave 26 magueyes to my son Josef Antonio; I leave them to him by my will. My statement is to be carried out and done. — [*f. 35*]

In addition I order that I leave however many magueyes are left over to my grandchild named Josef Mariano; I leave them to him by my will. My order is to be carried out and done. —

That is all. Here I conclude my sick person's statement, my memorandum of testament, in the presence of my witnesses and my executor, so that they will verify it in the future in the precious presence of God. May it be done. —

As my executor I leave don Santiago Nicolás.
Witness don Manuel Antonio. Witness don Salvador Nicolás. Don Julián de Santiago, present judge and governor. Fiscal mayor don Esteban Hernández.
Notary don Hipólito de los Santos.

75. Dominga Melchora, Calimaya, Pasiontitlan, 1701

(AGN, Tierras 2541, exp. 11)[1]

THE PRESENT TESTAMENT is rather disjointed at some points, leaving out such crucial information as the relation of the testator to the recipients of the bequests, or whether a house on a lot with some ma-

[1]The testament is accompanied by a contemporary Spanish translation. The dossier also contains a Nahuatl land grant from later in the century definitely establishing that this is the Pasiontitlan in San Pedro Calimaya, not the one in San Pablo Tepemaxalco. That document has been published in Lockhart 1991, pp. 108–09.

gueyes on it belongs to the testator and is bequeathed. It seems to make sense, however, that the only heir mentioned, Josef de la Cruz, is the son of the testator, Dominga Melchora. Going just a bit beyond what is actually said in the will, one can deduce that Dominga leaves Josef not only a piece of agricultural land of unknown size but two lots in the central settlement, both with a few magueyes on them. A house on the second lot, apparently mentioned primarily to locate the magueyes, represents a true puzzle. The house that is the family home is usually the first bequest of substance in a testament. Not so here. Nor are any saints mentioned. Yet if a house is on the lot with the magueyes, it ought to belong to the testator and go to the heir along with the rest.

Nothing so far indicates any particular degree of wealth on the part of the testator, who is a widow; we can deduce that her husband made a testament and is thus deceased. The two jointly owned a horse, sometimes an indicator of participation in regional trade, but now the horse is to be sold for funeral expenses. Not a word is said about the funeral, however; even a request for a mass is absent. Perhaps it is the notary's fault again, or perhaps the testator relies entirely on the don Matías de San Francisco whom she appoints as executor. Dominga has high-ranking personal witnesses too, in addition to a complement of church officials. Not only does the son bear the good name of de la Cruz, but it emerges from the dossier containing the will that one of his grandchildren retained it. The overall interpretation seems to be of good connections within the community but not much wealth at present.

Issued in 1701, this document is over the dividing line of 1700, but still has characteristics of earlier decades. The formulas are not yet those of Hipólito de los Santos, who wrote so many wills in Calimaya from the late 1730s forward. Note *tlaçoichpochtli*, "precious maiden or virgin," in the preamble in reference to the Virgin Mary, which is an orthodox wording characteristic of Stage 2, whereas the later, more characteristically indigenous phrase seen generally in the corpus, *totlaçomahuiznantzin*, "our precious revered mother," is missing. Punctuation and indication of paragraphs are still in the older style, and generally speaking, final consonants are preserved better than in decades to come. I have already commented on the disjointedness or opaqueness of the notary, Tomás de Aquino.

Departing from the usual wording, Aquino places the soul of the testator entirely in the hands not of God but of intermediaries, here the Virgin Mary and the guardian angel, with doctrinal implications that are not clear. (For similar cases see Nos. 88 and 93.)

[*f.* 8]

Jesus m^{a} yn Juçeph

v Ma çequizcayectenehuallo yn itlamahuiztocatzin dioz tetatzin yoa. dioz tepiltzin. yoā. dios espiritu sancton ma i mochihuan ame jūs —

v Axucan. Domigo. mani. metztli 13 de febrero. 1701. anos nican nicpehualtia. nomemoria teztanmeton nehual notocan - domiga melchura. nican. notlaxicatlpa. Paxotitlan. tla ye nopa. mochihuas yn itlaçotlanequilitzin. tt^{o} Jesu x̄p̄ō. yoā. yehuatzin. tlaçoychpochtli S.^{t} m^{a} ma nopampa. motlatlauhtilitzino. yoā. mochtitzintzin. Sanctosme Sanctasme. yn ilhuicac - chanecatzintzintin. yoā. notlaçoageltzin ca ynçemactzin. nococahua noyolliatzin. nanimatzin. ma y mochihua —

v ynnic çetlamatli. nitlanahuatian. huei quauhtecon. tlallin. mani nicmacan. yn itocan. Juçeph de lla Crus. amo aqui. tlei quitos tla quemania. yoā [. . .][2]

[*f.* 8]

Jesus, Mary, and Joseph.

v May the precious revered name of God the father, God the son, and God the Holy Spirit be entirely praised. May it be done, amen. Jesus. —

v Today, Sunday the 13th of the month of February of the year of 1701, here I named Dominga Melchora begin my memorandum of testament, here in my tlaxilacalli of Pasiontitlan. If the precious will of our lord Jesus Christ is brought upon me [if I die], may the precious virgin Santa María pray for me, along with all the male and female saints who reside in heaven, and my precious [guardian] angel, for I leave my spirit and soul entirely in their hands; may it be done. —

v First I order that there is a piece of land at the edge of the big woods [or at Hueiquauhtenco] that I give to the one named Josef de la Cruz; no one is ever to say anything.[2]

---

[2]Almost two lines of the original are crossed out here.

v ynnic otlamatli. nitlanahuatia. mani çenxollal Paxiotitla oc oca chicome metl. cani. tlatica. amo a quiquixtiz tlei yc nitlanahuatia. yoā oc çe xollal. mani. teopantonco. sano chicometl. onca iquicāpa cali qui tlei quitos tla quemania yc quichihuaz tequitl. tlacalaquilli yntocan Juçeph de la Crus[3] yoā. nitlanahuatia. Sen. cabalon nonamic catca yc otlanahuatitia. ticocahuitiyesque. axcā niquitohua monamacas. calaquis teopan. ynotzin - tomi. ynpampan[4] yn imixpa. nodestigohua. Sen. yntocan. Do matheo ju^{o}res yoā. oc çe. ymn itoca. Do p^{o} de lla Crus Noallbasia yntocan Dō matias de Sa fr^{co}

v Second I order that there is a lot in Pasiontitlan with seven magueyes left where it ends; no one is to take away what I am ordering. And there is another lot at Teopantonco; there are likewise seven magueyes behind the house. No one is ever to say anything. The one named Josef de la Cruz is to do the tribute duties and pay the tribute with them.[3] And I order that as to a horse that my late husband ordered on dying that we two were to share, I now say that it is to be sold, and that that money be delivered to the church [for me].[4] Before my witnesses, one named don Mateo Juárez and another named don Pedro de la Cruz. My executor is named don Matías de San Francisco.

v fiscatl mayor do miguel de Sa Ju^{o} - de sancta yg^{a} v deputadon nicullas ernades v temachti Sebastia fabia v teopa topillen Abrosi Ju^{o}n

v Fiscal mayor of the holy church, don Miguel de San Juan. v Diputado, Nicolás Hernández. v Temachti, Sebastián Fabián. v Church topile, Ambrosio Juan.

v Es^{no} Domas de aquino

v Notary Tomás de Aquino.

[3]Despite the confused wording, if Josef de la Cruz is to do tribute duties on these properties, he must be receiving them as a bequest.

[4]The intention of "ynpampan" may have been "y nopampan," *in nopampa*, "for me, on my behalf," i.e., to pay for my funeral.

76. Juana de la Cruz, San Pedro Calimaya, Tlamimilolpan, 1758

(AGN, Civil 664, exp. 2)

JUANA DE LA CRUZ is a widow, to all appearances with no surviving children, since she leaves what she has in the hands of two grandchildren, Diego Paulino and Marcela Bernarda. Each of them gets a piece of land of 3 almudes, so that they are treated equally despite the gender difference. It is still possible that some of the testator's children actually survive and that she has already distributed most of her property among them, so that now at the time of her death she merely adds something for the grandchildren.

Although the two pieces of land are the only possessions Juana mentions, her second name, de la Cruz, and the fact that she shares it with her late husband Asencio hint that she may come from a relatively prominent set of people. Asencio could have been the major owner in the family, passing on to his children the house with saints, the lot, and other properties. In any case, the fact of a woman's owning two quite large pieces of land on her own is in itself a sign of some position.

The testator's funeral arrangements also speak of a comparatively high status. Juana requests not only the standard mass with responsory prayer and the offering for Jerusalem, but more importantly a shroud of the Virgin of Carmen and burial inside the church, before the Santo Entierro.

Finally, Juana appoints an executor, a don and former governor, and names six witnesses, who include the prestigious present governor, the fiscal mayor, and two lower officials, both named de la Cruz. This impressive display seems to show Juana's connections with some prominent individuals in the community and to be a further indication of her status.

The notary is once again Hipólito de los Santos, who is discussed in the introductory study (p. 44). He seems to have been so prominent in Calimaya that one must wonder if his influence was not more important than that of the testators in assembling some collections of high-ranking witnesses.

[*f.* 55]
Jesus i Maria hi JoSephe
Ma moSenquiscayectenehualo in itlaSomahuistocatzi D.s tetatzi ihua Ds in itlaSopiltzin ihua Ds espirito Santo
Axcan Martes a 7 de Nobiembre de 1758 a^{o} ihuan Ca nica nicpehualtia i nomemoria testamento nehual notoCa Juana de la Crus ihua nonamictzi catca in itoCa AsenSio de la Crus ihuan Ca niCa nichane ipan in ialtepetzi S,^{or} S,^{n} P.^{o} Calimaya ihuan Ca nica nipohui ipan tlaxilaCali tlamimilolpa ihuan Ca huel niquitohua Ca intla yucqui nopa mochihuas in itlaSomiquilistzi tt,^{o} D.s Ca iSenmactzinCo noniCahuilia i noaniMantzi ihuan ca huel nicnotlatlactilia yehuatzi notlaSomahuistatzi S,^{or} S,^{n} P,^{o} ihuan yehuatzi S,^{or} S,^{n} pablo no ihuan niquinMotlatlactilia mohtintzitzi quexquih Santtos ihuan Santas in onpa Motemiltiticate in ilhuiCac inic nopan motlactoltitzinosque in itlaSoixpantzinco tt,^{o} D.s Ma y mochihua —
ihuan Ca inic Sentlamantli nitlanahuatia Ca intla onimomiquili Ca Se misa ihuan se Responsos nopan mitos in ipalehuiloca yes noaniMantzi Ca neltis notlactol
inic ontlamantli nitlanahuatia ca noMortaja yes in itlaquentzi notlaSonantzi del Carme ninohuiquilis Ca neltis notlactol mochihuas —

inic yectlamantli nitlanahuatia Ca noSepultura Ca onpa MotlapoS tiopancalitic ixpantzinco Santo intiero no ihua Ca nictemaCatia Se tomi huentzintli Santo JeruSalen Ca neltis notlactol Mochihuas —

inic nactlamantli nitlanahuatia Ca Se tlali Mani Metepec octli iteh Calaqui yei almo tlauli ihua Ca yehual nicCahuilia noxhui in itoca Diego paulino ca neltis notlanahuatil mochihuas —
inic Maquiltlamantli nitlanahuatia Ca Sanonpa Metepec octli mani oc Se tlali ihua iteh Calaqui yei almo tlauli ihua Ca yehual nicCahuilia oc Se noxhui in itoCa Marsela Bernarda Ca neltis notlactol —
[*f.* 55*v*]
ihuan Ca San ixquih niCa nictzonquixtia i nomeria testamentto imixpa noAlbasea ihua notestigos para tlaneltilisque mostla huiptla —
NoAlbasea nicCahua D,^{n} Grabiel Juan G,^{or} pasado Miguel fr,^{co} testigo Julian fr,^{co} testigo

D,^{n} fr,^{co} Antt,^{o} G,^{or} Actual fisCal mayor D,^{n} domingo de S,^{n}tiago Antonio de la Crus topile

[*f.* 55]
Jesus, Mary, and Joseph.
May the precious revered name of God the father, God his precious son, and God the Holy Spirit be entirely praised.
Today, Tuesday the 7th of November of the year of 1758, here I named Juana de la Cruz begin my memorandum of testament. My late husband was named Asencio de la Cruz; I am a citizen here in the altepetl of lord San Pedro, Calimaya, and I belong to the tlaxilacalli of Tlamimilolpan here. And [first of all] I say that, if the precious death of our lord God should be brought upon me, I leave my soul entirely in his hands, and I greatly implore my precious revered father lord San Pedro and lord San Pablo, and I also implore all the male and female saints that fill heaven to speak on my behalf in the precious presence of our lord God. May it be done. —

And first, I order that when I have died, a mass with a responsory prayer is to be said for me, to be the help of my soul; my statement is to be carried out.

Second, I order that my shroud will be the habit of my precious mother [the Virgen] del Carmen that I will wear; my statement is to be carried out and realized. —
Third, I order that my grave is to be opened inside the church building, before the Santo Entierro, and I am also giving an offering of one real for Holy Jerusalem; my statement is to be carried out and realized. —
Fourth, I order that I leave a piece of land on the road to Metepec in which 3 almudes of maize fit to my grandchild named Diego Paulino; my order is to be carried out and realized. —
Fifth, I order that I leave another piece of land, likewise on the road to Metepec, in which 3 almudes of maize fit, to another grandchild of mine named Marcela Bernarda; my statement is to be carried out. —
[*f.* 55*v*]
And that is all; here I conclude my memorandum of testament before my executor and my witnesses so that they will verify it in the future. —
I leave as my executor don Gabriel Juan, former governor. Miguel Francisco, witness. Julián Francisco, witness.
Don Francisco Antonio, present governor. Fiscal mayor don Domingo de Santiago. Antonio de la

Nicolas de la Crus topile
ES,^{no} Actual de la Republica hipolito de lo San-
ttos

Cruz, topile. Nicolás de la Cruz, topile.
Present notary of the commonwealth, Hipólito de los Santos.

77. Josefa Encarnación, San Pedro Calimaya, Tlamimilolpan, 1759

(AGN, Civil 664, exp. 2)

AS IN THE PREVIOUS document, the testator here is a woman, in all probability a widow (though she does not specify her status), but in this case her will is more in line with expectations, since the bequest she makes is to two children of hers. As happened with Juana de la Cruz (No. 76), some land is all that Josefa seems to have; nothing else is mentioned. As in that case too, perhaps she has already distributed her property to her children at some time before, or her husband was the one to possess the house, lot and maybe more land, while she gives instructions only about what she owns personally.

The testator leaves a piece of land of 3 almudes to her sons Antonio Santos and Juan de la Cruz with the uncommon request (unique in the corpus) that they take turns sowing it for one year each as long as they should live. We are left uncertain whether this is an uncommon arrangement or was what was frequently meant by undefined instructions that land was to be shared.

Josefa has a less distinguished name than that of Juana de la Cruz of No. 76,[1] but her funeral arrangements are quite similar (possibly owing merely to common practice in the tlaxilacalli). She requests the same mass with responsory prayer and offering for Jerusalem, the same shroud of the Virgin of Carmen, and also a grave inside the church, although no specific place or image is given as in the other case. Note that one of her sons has the de la Cruz name. We see some elements of possible distinction, but nothing definitive.

The core of the witnesses is at first glance quite impressive, an array of officials. The fiscal mayor is the same as with Juana de la Cruz (No. 76), while the topiles have changed, and our famous Hipólito de los Santos the notary appears here as a temachti or teacher of doctrine and with the title don. They are all church officials, however, and could be here simply in the line of duty. Josefa's executor has a name with an unusual three elements, but otherwise not distinguished. The only other witness is someone quite unexpected, a woman, Juana Blasina. Women as witnesses had generally faded from view as early as 1700, if not before. Today we are delighted to see her, but for the time Juana Blasina would not have been a normal choice as one of the witnesses for a prominent person.

A notary is not named. One automatically suspects don Hipólito, who had often combined the posts of temachti and notary in his career. The handwriting superficially resembles his. But though we cannot be absolutely sure, there are strong reasons to think that someone else did the writing, perhaps the fiscal mayor, don Domingo de Santiago. In this document standard syllable-final *x* is mainly written as *h*, and some prevocalic *l* is written as *tl,* neither of which are common practices of de los Santos. Some strangely fragmented compound words are also not otherwise seen in the latter's work (see note 2 below). With the Virgin of Carmen we see the Spanish "mi señora" rather than the usual Nahuatl phrase of de los Santos.

What is really unusual in this document is the introductory formula, which is elaborate and full of complex invocations. The saints' names include several of the favorites of de los Santos, but they are not all the same nor in the same order. The Virgin Mary is called *huel motetlatlauhtiliani*, a "great implorer," a rare term. The role of the guardian angel is particularly strong here, and it is described with a terminology that is rarely seen in the corpus. Thus it seems that this preamble, which might be counted in favor of high status for the testator, may be instead the result of the style of a notary other than de los Santos. But without intense study it would be hard to be entirely sure.

---

[1]Names such as de la Encarnación, de la Concepción, etc., were intermediary between the higher-ranking indigenous second names and the low-ranking combinations of two Christian names. Omitting the "de la," as happens here, originally downgraded the name somewhat, but by this time that omission may have become so widespread that nothing can be deduced from it.

[*f. 45*]

Jesus Maria y Joseph = nican yaltepetzin Santo San Pedro y San pablo calimaya ====

AxCa Ma moSequisCayectenehualon yn itlasomahuistocatzi yn Dios tetatzin yhuan Dios ytlasopiltzin yhuan Dios espiritu Santo Ma i mochihua Amen Jesus = Axcan Juebes mani mestli 9 de agosto de 1759 aos = Nican nicpehualtia NomeMoria testamento Nehual notoca Josepha Encarnazion Nican NotlaXitlaCalpan tlaMimilolpan tla yocqui Nopa mochihuas yn itlasomahuisSenquisca yn itlanequilistzin[2] yn tt,o JeX,to Auc ca Sa niMosemaCasinohua yn itlaso ymihpantzinco yn tt,o Dios Yhua no yehuatzin Santa Maria Mochipa huel netli yhpohtzintli ca huel Motetlatlactiliani ynic noPanpa quiMotlatlactilis yn itlasoMahuisSenteconetzin yn tt,o JeX,to yc mochintintzitzin yn ilhuiCac chaneCatzitzinti Santosme yhuan Santasme yhuan NotlaSotatzi Santo San Migel arCangel yhua no Yehuatzi Santo San Rafael y Santo San Juan Bauctista yhuan Ca no huel nicnotlatlactilitzinohua NotlasoAngeltzin notePihcatzin Ca Amo nehmoCahuilis Ca sa nehmoteyhpantiliti[. . .?] Yn itlasoYhpantzinCo yn tt,o Dios nitlatlaCoani y noYoliatzi y noanimatzi ynic quiMomasehuis yn ilhuicac nequiltonolistli Papaquilistli yn Gloria Ma y mochihua = Yhuan ynic Sentlamatli nitlanahuatia Yntla Dios nehmocnelilis ypalehuiloCa yes noaniMatzin Sentel Misa Yhuan Sentetl Responso yhuan noSepoltura Yes teopanCalitic Motlapos Ca iCA notlanequilis yhua noquimilicCa yes nomortaJa ytlaquetzi Mi señora del Carme = yhuan Ca nicnoMaquilia Santo JeruSale Se tomitzin =====

[*f. 45*]

Jesus, Mary, and Joseph. = Here in the altepetl of holy San Pedro and San Pablo, Calimaya. ====

Today may the precious revered name of God the father, God his precious son, and God the Holy Spirit be entirely praised. May it be done, amen. Jesus. = Today, Thursday the 9th of the month of August of the year of 1759. = Here I named Josefa Encarnación begin my memorandum of testament here in my tlaxilacalli of Tlamimilolpan. If the precious revered perfect will of[2] our Lord Jesus Christ is to happen to me [if I die], I give myself entirely to the precious presence of our Lord God, and also Santa María, forever very true virgin, the great implorer, so that she will pray for me to her precious revered only child our lord Jesus Christ, and all the male and female saints that dwell in heaven, and my precious father holy San Miguel Arcángel, and also holy San Rafael and holy San Juan Bautista, and likewise I greatly implore my precious guardian angel that he not abandon me but present for me, a sinner, my spirit and soul in the precious presence of our lord God so that it will attain the celestial bliss and celebration called glory, amen. = And first I order that, if God befriends me [if I die], the help of my soul is to be a mass with a responsory prayer, and my grave will be opened inside the church building; it is by my will. And my shroud is to be the habit mi señora del Carmen. = And I give one real to Holy Jerusalem. =====

YniC ontlamantli nitlanahuatia Se tlatli Mani toluca otli Ca huel otenCo Para yc tlasintla calaqui Yey almo tlaotli yhuan Ca niQuinCahuilia omenti nopilhuan Se ytocan Antonio Santos yhuan oc Se ytoca Juan de la crus Ca niquinCahuilia ymonehuan quitocas Se xihuil tlamis oc sepa oc Se quitocas San yocqui QuimoMamacatiasque Mientras Dios quimochiCahuilis nopilhuan yhuan Ca yocqui nitlanahuatia [*f. 45v*] yca nocoCohcatlatol Ca ica notlanequilis Mochihuas = Ca san ihquih nica nicSonquihtia noMemoria testamento yMihpa noalBasea yhua notes-

Second, I order that I leave a piece of land on the road to Toluca, right at the edge of the road, on the lower side, in which 3 almudes of maize fit, to two children of mine, one named Antonio Santos, and the other named Juan de la Cruz. I leave it to them jointly; one is to sow it one year and stop, and the other is to sow it again; they are to go along giving it to each other that way while God gives my children health. Thus I order [*f. 45v*] through my sick person's statement; it is to be done by my will. = That is all. Here I conclude my memorandum of tes-

[2]Here we have a strange construction in which what should be one long possessed noun is divided into two parts and the possessive prefix is repeated in the middle, as though the writer had simply found it too long; "yn itlasomahuisSenquisca yn itlanequilistzin" should normally be "yn itlasomahuisSenquiscatlanequilistzin," "his precious revered perfect will." This construction is literally "his precious revered perfect his will." Just below something similar happens again: "yn itlaso ymihpantzinco," normally "yn intlasoihpantzinco," "in their precious presence."

tigo Para yc nopa Motlatoltitzinosque yc quimotlatlactilisque yn tt,o Dios yhuan tla yocqui = quimochihuilisque quiMotlahtlahuilmaquilitzinos yn tt,o Dios = noalBasea JuaN antonio Joseph testigo Juana Blasina

Fiscal manyor de la Santa yglesia D,n Domingo de santiago temahti D,n polito de los Santos topiles Marcos de la cruz Manuhel Joseph

tament before my executor and my witness so that they will speak for me and pray to our lord God, and if they do it our lord God will give them their reward. = My executor is Juan Antonio Josef. Witness Juana Blasina.

Fiscal mayor of the holy church don Domingo de Santiago. Temachti don Hipólito de los Santos. Topiles Marcos de la Cruz, Manuel Josef.

78. Francisco Juan, Calimaya, Tlamimilolpan, 1712

(AGN, Tierras 2298, exp. 5)[1]

THE TESTATOR HERE appears to be wealthy by indigenous standards, since he owns not only a house with its lot, but also six pieces of land, some of them very large, and a notable array of sacred images. Francisco Juan divides his property among his four children, leaving the house and lot to his son Juan Francisco, who by that token seems to be the favorite or the eldest, although he is not the first to be mentioned,[2] and the situation with land bequests remains unclear. Note that he bears the same names as his father, just reversed. He definitely receives 6 almudes of land. Another piece of 6 almudes, mentioned immediately thereafter, is left in limbo by a truncated sentence; if the intention was that it should also go to Juan Francisco, he would be dominant in all respects. The other son, Antonio de San Juan, gets two fields amounting to 7 almudes. Interestingly, his second name, de San Juan, is an expanded, more distinguished version of the father's second name, simple Juan.

Francisco also mentions two daughters, Benita Francisca and Vicenta Antonia (there is a recurrence of the names Francisco/a and Antonio/a in the family), to whom he leaves one piece of land each, of 3 and 5 almudes respectively. Vicenta Antonia later became the wife of Agustín de la Cruz (No. 72) in a marriage across tlaxilacalli of a woman from a wealthy family with a man who also acquired wealth.

All the children receive saints to worship. Two of these saints, the Señor de Chalma and San Antonio, have a specific piece of land of good size to be used to provide for incense and candles. The apparently most prestigious of them, the Señor de Chalma, with 6 almudes of land, goes to the preferred Juan Francisco, and San Antonio with 4 almudes is entrusted to his namesake Antonio. We can conclude overall that the two sons have a relatively privileged position compared to the daughters in terms of inheritance, although it is significant that Vicenta and Benita each get a piece of land of a good size.

The array of sacred images that Francisco Juan leaves behind is impressive. At least three saints—San Francisco, San Antonio, and San Juan—seem to correspond to a family devotion, since their names are found repeated in different ways in the names of the testator and the children. In addition, Francisco mentions a San Miguel, a San Nicolás, a San Diego, four crucifixes, the Virgin of Guadalupe, and above all, as we have seen, the Señor de Chalma. To the last the testator appears to have a special devotion, giving extra details about the worship and stressing the importance of the cult.

By now it is clear that Francisco Juan is a wealthy person; however, his requests in terms of funeral arrangements do not reflect it. There is the usual mass with responsory prayer and offering for Jerusalem, and while he requests a shroud and rope of San Francisco, no special burial is arranged for him; rather he actually says that the grave is to be outside the church, which was not common among wealthy individuals.[3] Despite the size of his estate, Francisco does not appoint any executor. His witnesses are

[1]The testament is accompanied by a contemporary Spanish translation.

[2]A possibility is that this notary, or the testator himself, has reversed the usual order of mention of the heirs, going from youngest to oldest rather than from oldest to youngest in the normal way. Note that in addition to the anomaly with Juan Francisco, the first of the two daughters to be mentioned gets less land than the second.

[3]The fact that the wealthy testator of this tlaxilacalli in No. 79 is also to be buried outside the church, and indeed has identical funeral arrangements despite the presence of a different notary, arouses the thought that such may have been the general practice in Tlamimilolpan. The other three wills from Tlamimilolpan are different, however.

very respectable; two are past high town officials, and the others are all representatives of the local church organization.

Notary Pedro de los Santos shows much Spanish influence in his language. A significant example is "tibesinos ticate" for "we are neighbors," in which he uses *vecino* in a meaning other than its usual one of "Spanish citizen" and employs the verb *ca* in an equative sense, something never done in normal Nahuatl. His "nicsonquixhtzia yca" "I conclude," seems based on *acabar con* in Spanish. Note also the plural of *milli*, "field" as "milme," another trace of Spanish usage, and the use of the rare Spanish loan *primeramente*. The initial formula contains some unusual expressions, but it is generally in the style of Calimaya/Tepemaxalco, with the mention of San Pedro and San Pablo and of the guardian angel. The orthography is quite extreme even by Toluca Valley standards, with much *tz* for normal *t* and much doubling of *o*.

It is tempting to imagine that Pedro de los Santos is the father or older relative of Hipólito de los Santos, the dominant notary of Calimaya later in the century, but any connection remains speculative.

[*f. 34*]
Ma moSenquisCayectenehualo yN itlasoMahuistocatzin i D,^{s} [. . .]tatzin in D.^{s} itlasoMahuispiltzin yhuan D^{s} espiritu Santo Ma y Mochihua Amen Jesus M^{a} y Josph —
Axca ypan yNi tonali Juebez A 2 de Junio de 1712 a^{os} Nica Nica Niccpechualtia Nomemoria testamento Nechual Notoca fran^{co} Juan NiCa NotlaxilaCalpan Barrio de tlamimilolopan ytla yoqui Nopan Mochihuas y NiynoMasehuis ini ytlasoMiqilistzin tt^{o} Jexp^{to} Ca SecMactzinCo NiConcahua Nocyoliantzin yhuan NuaniMantzin yhuan No yechuatzitzin NoAbogado niqimotlatlahutilia S^{r} S^{n} P,^{o} yhua Sr S^{n} Pablo yhua NotlasoAng^{l} de la Guarda Nopanpa qimotlatlahutzilisq̃ in tt^{o}yo Jexp^{to} para NechMotlapopolhuis in NotlatlaCol ihuan NechmoMaquilis Gloria yhuan ilhuiCac papaqilistli Amen —
YNicc Sentlamantli Nitlanahuatia intla yooqi Nopan mochihuas ninomiqilis ypalehuiloCa yecz NuanimantzinSentel Missa y Sentel ResponSos yhua Se tomin S.^{nto} Jerrosalen yoqi Mochihuas neltis No-[. . .]huatzil —
YNiC ontlaMantli No nitlaNahuatia y NoqimilicCa yecz ytlaquentzin Notlasotatzin Sr S.^{n} fran^{co} yhua yCordonsin Ninoquitlalpis yocqi Mochihuas Notlanahuatzil —
YNicc yecytlamantli No nitlanahuatzia Nosepoltura Motlapos teopa qiahuac yCa notlanequilis —
YNic Nauhtlamantli No nitlanahuatzia Ca niCahuilia Anton de Sa^{n} Juan Canpa Calaqui Se almo tlaolu Ca moCuasoctzia Maria Guilara yCa Notlanequilis Mochihuas notlaNahuatzil — [*f. 34v*]
YNich Maquiltlamantli No nitlanahuatzia Ca niCahuilia Noohpoh ytoca Venita fran^{ca} Sec Mili Calaqui yecy Almu tlaoli tooqili ompan matiCa SaCango otli AtlauteCo Ca yechual niiCa Niccahua

[*f. 34*]
May the precious revered name of God the father, God his precious revered son, and God the Holy Spirit be entirely praised. May it be done, amen. Jesus, Mary, and Joseph. —
Today on this day of Thursday, the 2nd of June of the year of 1712, here I named Francisco Juan begin my memorandum of testament in my tlaxilacalli, the barrio of Tlamimilolpan. If it happens to me that I attain the precious death of our lord Jesus Christ, I leave my spirit and soul entirely in his hands. And I also implore as my advocate lord San Pedro and the lord San Pablo and my precious guardian angel to pray on my behalf to our lord Jesus Christ to pardon me my sins and give me glory and heavenly rejoicing. Amen. —

First, I order that if it happens to me that I die, the help of my soul will be a mass with a responsory prayer, and one real [is to be given for] Holy Jerusalem. My order is to be thus carried out and realized. —
Second, I order that my shroud is to be the habit of my precious father lord San Francisco, and I will be girt with his rope. My order is to be thus realized. —
Third, I also order that my grave is to be opened outside the church; it is by my will. —
Fourth, I also order that I leave to Antonio de San Juan [land] into which fits 1 almud of maize; it borders on [land of] María Clara. It is by my will; my order is to be realized. — [*f. 34v*]
Fifth, I also order that I leave to my daughter named Benita Francisca a cultivated field in which fit 3 almudes of maize seed, on the road to Sacango, at the edge of the ravine. I leave it to her here by my

yCa Notlanequilis —
YNic chiCuasetlamantli No nitlanahuatzia Ca nichCahuilia NocOchpoh ytoca Visenta Antonia Calaqui Maquili Almu tlaoli Ompa mantiCa ypan loma chimalhuacCa yCa Notlanequiliz yooqui Mochihuas Notlanaguatzil —
Yc chiContlamantli No nitlanahuatzia Ca nic[h ?]-Cahuilia Sano yechual Notelpoh Anton de S,^{n} Juan Se mili Ma[ntica?] Mectecpech otli Calaqui Se media tlaoli Ca tinoCuasoshuia Mg.^{l} de S,^{ta} M,^{a} yhuan Mg.^{l} Antt^{o} tibesinos tiCate —
Yni chiCueytlamantli No nitlanahuatia Ca nichCahuilia Notelpoh ytoca Juan fran^{co} sec Mili Sano ompa Canpa Calaqui Se media tlaoli Mochihuas Notlanahuatzil —
YNi chiqueytlaMantli No nitlaNahuatzia Sec mili luis de Belasquez Calaqui Sano Se media tlaoli yCa notlanequilis yooqui Mochihuas Notlanahuatil[4] —

Ca san timoxtin tibesinos tiCate ytechCopan yni Milme Prim^{te} d,^{n} Esteban Ramos yhua Anton de la Cruz —
SaNo yooqui ytesCaCopan Caltzintli yhuan Santos[5] —

Prime^{te} yni Semtlamâtli No nitlanahuatia Caltzintli Ca sano yechual NichCahuilia Noteclpooch Juan fran^{co} yCa Mochi Solar yquiSayan tonali quipiec onpuali yhuan Chicome Baras de Suur y Norte quipie Onpuali yhuan Macuili Barras yCa notlanequiliz yooqui Neltzis Notlanahuatzil Mochihuas — [*f. 35*]
ynic ontlamantli No nitlanahuatia Ca no NicCahuilia Noochpooch ytoca Bisenta Antonia Sr San Mg.^{l} yhua Sr San Juan yca notlanequiliz Mochihuas Notlanahuatil —
yni yecxtlamantli No nitlanahuatia Ca no nicCahuilia Benita fran^{ca} Nahuintzitzin Crusificos yhuan Se Sr San fran^{co} para quiMotequipanilhuiis Ca popohtzli yhuan Candela tlatlaz yspantzinCo Ca yooqi neltzis Notlanahuatil —
yniyc Nauchtlamantli No nitlaNahuatia Ca niiCahuilia Notelpoxh Anton de Sa^{n} Juan Sec Sr S.^{n} NiColas yhuan Sr Sn Antt.^{o} yhuan Sr S^{n} Diego para quiMotequipanilhuis —
mochihuas Notlanahuatil —
Yni maquiltlamantli No nitlanahuatzia Ca nicahuilia

will. —
Sixth, I also order that I leave to my daughter named Vicenta Antonia [land] in which fit 5 almudes of maize, on the slope of Chimalhuacan. It is by my will; my order is to be thus carried out. —

Seventh, I also order that I likewise leave to my son Antonio de San Juan a cultivated field on the Metepec road where half a fanega of maize fits, bordering [land of] Miguel de Santa María and Miguel Antonio; we are neighbors. —
Eighth, I also order that I leave to my son named Juan Francisco a cultivated field at the same place, where half a fanega of maize fits. My order is to be carried out. —
Eighth, I also order that . . . a cultivated field . . . Luis Velásquez . . . where half a fanega of maize fits. It is by my will; my order is to be thus carried out.[4] —
For we are all neighbors concerning these cultivated fields, first don Esteban Ramos, and Antonio de la Cruz. —
The same concerning the house and the saints.[5] —

First, first I also order that I leave the house likewise to my son Juan Francisco, including the lot; it measures 47 varas to the east, and north to south it measures 45 varas. It is by my will; my order is to be thus realized and carried out. — [*f. 35*]

Second, I also order that to my daughter named Vicenta Antonia I also leave lord San Miguel and lord San Juan. It is by my will; my order is to be carried out. —
Third, I also order that I also leave to Benita Francisca four little crucifixes and a lord San Francisco, to serve them, for incense and candles are to burn before them. My order is to be thus realized. —

Fourth, I also order that I leave to my son Antonio de San Juan a lord San Nicolás, lord San Antonio, and lord San Diego, to serve them. —

My order is to be carried out. —
Fifth, I also order that I leave to my son named Juan

[4]The Nahuatl at this point lacks crucial grammatical elements and does not yield a sense without speculation; I have simply recorded the elements. The Spanish translation of the passage is also unclear. The reader will see that this item has the same number, eight, as the previous one.

[5]The full meaning of the last two sentences is obscure, and the Spanish translation does not help. Note that from here on the testament seems to start over, with entries numbered from one again.

notelpoxh ytoca Juan fran^{co} Mi Señora de Guadalupe yhua yechuatzin Sr de Chalma para quiMotequipanilhuis yca popooxtli yhua Candela para ySpantzinCo yooqui Mochihuas notlanahuatil —

Francisco mi señora de Guadalupe and the Señor de Chalma to serve them with incense and candles in front of them. My order is to be thus carried out. —

O Se tlali Mani Sn Mateotzili[6] yyaxCatzin yechuatzin Sr de Chalma Calaqui Se media tlaoli para ytectzinCo Monequi Ssese sihuil yahui quiMomaguisiotilia ytlatocachantzinco yhua quimochihuililia iMisa para Mientras yechuatzin tt.^{o} d^{s} quiMoChiCahuilis ypan yn itlaltzipach amo quiMolCahuilisq^{e} Siempre quichihuasq^{e} in iobligasion yhua o se tlali QuahutenCo Sano yechuatzin yyaxCatin Sr S^{n} Antt^{o} Calaqui Nahui Almu tlaoli —

There is another piece of land on the road to San Mateo[6] belonging to the Señor de Chalma, where half a fanega of maize fits, to be used for him; each year they go to honor him at his royal home and perform his mass for him as long as our lord God should give him [Juan Francisco] life on his earth. They are not to forget him; they are always to perform their obligation. And there is another piece of land at the edge of the woods [or at Quauhtenco] that belongs likewise to lord San Antonio, where 4 almudes of maize fit. —

Ca san ixquih Nica nicsonquixhtzia yCa nococox-Catlatol yhuan Nomemoria testam,^{to} Nechual notoCa fran^{co} Juan Ca yceixpan testigos Sec ytoCa D^{n} Nicolas felis pasado O se itoCA Sebastian fran^{co} Alcald^{e} pasado Ca yecantin tlaneltilisq^{e} Mostla huistla — q^{e}Name d^{s} Motlanahuatzilia [*f. 35v*]

That is all. Here I named Francisco Juan conclude my sick person's statement and my memorandum of testament in the presence all the witnesses: one named don Nicolás Félix, past [governor or alcalde?], another named Sebastián Francisco, past alcalde; they will verify it in the future as God orders. [*f. 35v*]

testigo fran^{co} pascual fiscal Mayor[7] testigo temaxti Sebastian fabian oc se teopan topile[8] fran^{co} de S.^{n}tiago oc se diego yNasio Moxtiti yNiique testigos =
ES^{no} Pedro de los Santtos =

Witness Francisco Pascual, fiscal mayor.[7] Witness temachti Sebastián Fabián. Another church topile,[8] Francisco de Santiago. Another, Diego Ignacio. All these are witnesses. =
Notary Pedro de los Santos.

[6]"Sn Mateotzili" is equivalent to standard *San Mateo otli.*

[7]Note that the names of a past alcalde and the fiscal mayor are given without don, showing that in this document of 1712 the notary adheres to an older, more conservative style of the use of that title than is seen in the majority of documents in the corpus.

[8]By saying "another" topile here, the notary implies that the temachti is also a topile.

79. Antonio de Santiago, Calimaya, Tlamimilolpan, 1734

(AGN, Tierras 2298, exp. 5)[1]

THIS TESTAMENT PRESENTS a very peculiar case in that the testator leaves all of his property to his brother-in-law, don Juan de la Cruz, mentioning nobody else in the will. It may be that Antonio de Santiago has no surviving children or wife or has never married at all; it is, however, uncommon for the entire inheritance to be entrusted to someone from outside the family of origin. Although the testator's sister or wife, source of the relationship, may have already died, it is also possible that she is alive but Antonio prefers to leave everything to his brother-in-law as the head of the family. In either case, conceivably some niece or nephew, living or not yet born, is intended as the ultimate recipient.

Note that the heir has an important second name combined with the title don, which together with Antonio's own second name, a bit above the average, implies a circle of people of some standing. Indeed, it will be seen in No. 80 that the governor of Calimaya in 1739 was a don Juan de la Cruz, and though the name is common, with the don it becomes rarer. If the don Juan here is a person of such outstanding influence and authority, it would become more understandable how Antonio would be willing simply to hand him everything and not mention his sister or any other relatives.

[1]The testament is accompanied by a contemporary Spanish translation.

Antonio leaves his brother-in-law a lot, a good number and variety of saints, and most importantly at least five pieces of land. (One piece is crossed out in the Nahuatl but present in the Spanish translation.) Apart from the lot, no measurements are given for the parcels, so it is difficult to place a value on Antonio's estate, but at least one can say that the number of holdings points to prominent status. At the end of the bequests to don Juan de la Cruz, Antonio is at pains to assert that no one is to say that he sold the land, that he rather left it to his brother-in-law. The document does not provide enough context to interpret this interesting statement with certainty. It actually seems to reverse a common trend. In Nahuatl testaments from various times and places it is seen that a testator leaves property to a relative and then says that in return the relative is to arrange the mass or funeral. It often then happened that the heir afterward claimed that the land was purchased, which gave the owner special rights to dispose of it. Here the testator seems concerned that no such claim should be made, for what reason is not at all clear.

The funeral arrangements indicate a person who is not impoverished but are otherwise a bit difficult to interpret. They go beyond the mass with responsory prayer and offering for Jerusalem to include the shroud and rope of San Francisco, but burial is to be outside the church. Though a grave in the churchyard tends to be less prestigious, by now we have seen various cases of relatively wealthy individuals in Calimaya/Tepemaxalco requesting it, and the arrangements of Francisco Juan of No. 78, who was even wealthier than Antonio de Santiago, were identical to those specified here in every respect. Thus under conditions we do not yet understand, an outside grave may have been a feature that did not really say anything about the status of the testator.

Antonio appoints an executor and two witnesses, all without title, two with plain names and the third a Santiago like himself. The others listed at the end of the testament are all church officials. As has been commented on before, listing church officials' names after finishing the will may have been a practice of the notary, or of some communities, and may not be related to the testator's standing.

The present testament belongs to a cluster including No. 78, Francisco Juan, of 1712, and No. 72, Agustín de la Cruz, of 1755, in that all three were inserted in the same dossier concerning Vicenta Antonia, the former's daughter and the latter's wife. Our Antonio de Santiago might be of an age to be a generation lower in the family of Francisco Juan, but no names seen in the other wills appear here, nor can any of the properties mentioned by Francisco Juan be identified in the will of Antonio. There are, however, properties in similarly named places in these two wills: on the Sacango road, on the Metepec road, in Chimalhuacan, almost too much for pure coincidence. Probably Antonio was indeed in some fashion a younger relative of Francisco Juan. If so, his first name could fit in with the Antonio/a repeated in Francisco Juan's family.

The notary here bears the don and is called "notary of the holy church," not of the municipality as often seen; he is also temachti, teacher of Christian doctrine. Thus he is quite reminiscent of (don) Hipólito de los Santos, the most prominent notary of Calimaya a little later. His name is the same as that of the fiscal mayor don Juan Francisco, but two individuals seem to be involved. His writing fully reflects the eighteenth-century Toluca Valley style. At times there are repetitions, omissions, or other mistakes. An unusual feature in the preamble is "motlasomahuistocatzin," "your precious revered name," instead of the standard *itlaçomahuiztocatzin*, "his precious revered name." This may be more than a simple mistake; it is repeated in No. 80, apparently by the same writer. The form may be a relic of another style, possibly with preconquest precedent, in which the speaker addressed the deity directly.

[*f. 19*]
Jesus Maria y Jesephe —
Ma mosenquisCayeteneNehual y MotlasoMahuistocatzin D.[s] Padro yhua D,[s] hijo y D,[s] Espiritu S.[n]to Ma y mochihua Amen Jesus Maria y Josephe —

Axcan Martes A 31 de Agosto de 1734 a[os] Nica Nicpehualtia y Nomemoria testaMento Nehual Ne-

[*f. 19*]
Jesus, Mary, and Joseph. —
May your precious revered name of God the father, God the son, and God the Holy Spirit be entirely praised. May it be done, amen. Jesus, Mary, and Joseph. —

Today, Tuesday the 31st of August of the year of 1734, here I named Antonio de Santiago begin my

hual Notoca Antt,^{o} de S,^{n}tiago Nicā NotlaXilacalpan tlaMimilopan yhua ytla yoqui y Nopan Mochihuas NimoMasenhuis NicMomaSehuis yn itlasoMiquilistzin y tt^{o} Xcp̄t̄o ca ycsema[. . .]con Nimocahuililia y noyoliatzin yhua NoaniMatzin y NotlasoMahuistatzin S^{n} Pedro yhua yehuatzin S^{n} Pablo yhua yechuatzin S,^{r} S,^{n} Antonio glorioso yhua yehuatzin S,^{n} miguel Arcangel yhua yehuatzin S,^{r} S,^{n} grabiele Arcangel yhua yehuatzin N,^{ra} S,^{ra} la lipia Consescion yhua yehuatzin y n[o?]tlasoAngeltzin yhua Mochitintzintzin y S,^{n}tosme yhua S,^{n}tasme yn ilhuicac ChanecCatzintzintin ynic Nocpan Motlatoltitzinnoq̄ ynic Momaquixtis y noyoliatzin yhua y noaniMatzin yn ixpantzincon y tt,^{o} D,^{s} Ma y moChihua aMen Jesus Maria y Josephe yhua No nictlanahuatia Nicmotemaquilia Se tomi S^{n}to gerusalem yhua No nitlanahuatia Sentel misa yhua Sentel Responsos Nopan Mitos yn iPalehuiloca yes y noyoliatzin [y?]hua Y noAnimatzin yhua No nitlaNahuatia Noquimilica yes yn itlaq̄tzin S,^{r} S,^{n} fran^{co} yhua yn iCordotzin yc nicMoquetlatictias yhua no Nitla[*f. 19v*]Nahuatia Nosepultura Motlapos teopan quiyahu[. . .] ca Notlanequilis yoqui Nitlanahuatia Ynic Sentlamatli NitlaNahuatia Sen Solar opan Mantican tlamiMiloPan quipie Senpohuali yhua Chiquasen Bara yc huiya yhua yc Patlahuac qui[. . .]ye Senpohuali Bara yhua maquili NicCahui[. . .] Nocuyado ytoca D,^{n} Juan de la Cruz yhuan NicCahuili Sen S,^{n}to xp̄t̄o yhua S,^{n}ta maria mada[. . .]Na yhua N,^{ra} S,^{ra} la cosecsion yhua Jesus Niño yhu[. . .] Mochin NiquiMocahuililia Para quiMotequ[. . .]Panilhuis Amo aquiquixtilis queMania yoqui n[. . .]tlanahuatia yca Notlatol Amo aqui quinmaca[. . .] NetequiPacholi y queMania —

memorandum of testament here in my tlaxilacalli of Tlamimilolpan. If it should happen to me that I attain the precious death of our lord Jesus Christ, I leave my spirit and soul entirely in his hands, [and I implore] my precious revered father San Pedro and San Pablo, and lord San Antonio glorioso, and San Miguel Arcángel, and lord San Gabriel Arcángel, and Nuestra Señora de la Limpia Concepción, and my precious [guardian] angel, and all the male and female saints who reside in heaven, so that they will speak for me so that my spirit and soul should be redeemed before our lord God. May it be done, amen. Jesus, Mary, and Joseph. And I also order that I give a real for Holy Jerusalem, and I also order that a mass with a responsory prayer is to be said for me to be the help of my spirit and soul. And I also order that my shroud is to be the habit of lord San Francisco, and as I go I will wear his rope. And I also order [*f. 19v*] that my grave be opened outside the church, for it is my will, and so I order. First I order that I leave a lot in Tlamimilolpan that measures 26 varas in length and 25 varas in width to my brother-in-law named don Juan de la Cruz, and I leave him a Santo Cristo, Santa María Magdalena, Nuestra Señora de la Concepción, and Jesús Niño. I leave them all to him to serve them. No one is ever to take it away from him; thus I order with my words. No one is ever to give him trouble. —

ynicC ontlaMatli No nitlaNahuatia Sen tla[. . .] Opan Mantica gui Atlateco metepec otli No nicCahuilia NoCuyado D,^{n} Juan de la Cruz yca Notlanequil[. . .] No nicahuilia Amo aquiquixtilis quemania —

Yhua No nitlaNahuatia o se mili NicCahuilia Opan MactiCan Sancan Otli Nocuyado D,^{n} Juan de la Cruz Amo aquiquixtilis quemaNia Yhua No nitlanahuatia O Sen tlali sannoPan Matica Sancan otli SanNo yehual Nocuyado D^{n} Juan de la Cruz No nicCahuilia Amo aq[. . .]quixtilis q̄maNia Yni yectlaMatli no nitlaNahuatia O Sen tlali OPan Mantican chiatla t[. . .]xocontitla SanNo yehual Nocuyado D^{n} Juan de la Cruz NicCahuilia yca notlanequilis Amo Aqui quiquixtilis q̄mania —

Second, I also order that I leave to my brother-in-law don Juan de la Cruz a piece of land at the edge of the large ravine [or at Hueiatlauhtenco] on the Metepec road. I leave it to him by my will; no one is ever to take it from him. —

And I also order that I leave another cultivated field on the Sacango road to my brother-in-law don Juan de la Cruz. No one is ever to take it away from him. And I also order that I am also leaving another piece of land likewise on the Sacango road to my brother-in-law don Juan de la Cruz. No one is ever to take it away from him. Third, I also order that I leave another piece of land in Chiauhtla, at Texocotitlan [or next to the tejocote], likewise to my brother-in-law don Juan de la Cruz. I leave it to him by my will. No one is ever to take it from him. —

Ynic Natlamatli No nitlaNahuatia O Sen tlali oPan Mantican chimalhuacā S^{n}N ō yehual Nocuy[. . .] D,^{n} Juan de la Cruz No nicCahuilia Amo aqui qui[*f. 20*]quixtilis q̄mania yoqui nitlaNahuatia ycan notlatol — [Yhua No nitlanahuatia O Sen tlali [ca] Opan Mantican Ahuehuetitla ymilteco Mateheo luys No nicCanhuilia Nocuyado D^{n} Juan de la Cruz Amo Aquin quiquiquixtilis y q̄mania —][2] Yoqui No nitlaNahuatia yca notlatol yhua No nitlaNatia yhua Niquitohua Amo Aquin tle quitos queMania Aso oNicNamaca yni solar yhua Milmen San oniNicahuili Nocuyado d^{n} Juan de la cruz Para y motequipan[. . .]huilis yhua yhua ye Nica Nictzonquixtiz [?] [. . .]tlatol yhua Notlahuali yxPan NoAlbasia ytoca lorenzo diego yhua omentin Notestigohua sen ytoca Antt^{o} lorenzo yhua o sen ytoca Juan de S,^{n}tiago yni oMotlaneltililiq̄ y mostla huictla yn ixPantzincon tt^{o} D,^{s} yhuan ixpātzinco y totatzin Cura Ministro —

Fourth, I also order that I leave another piece of land at Chimalhuacan likewise to my brother-in-law don Juan de la Cruz. No one is ever to take it from him; [*f. 20*] thus I order by my words. — [And I also order that I leave another piece of land at Ahuehuetitlan, at the edge of a cultivated field of Mateo Luis, likewise to my brother-in-law don Juan de la Cruz. No one is ever to take it from him. —][2] Thus I also order with my words. And I also order and say that no one is ever to say that I have sold this lot and cultivated fields; I have merely left it to my brother-in-law don Juan de la Cruz to work with, and here now I will conclude my statement and my commands before my executor named Lorenzo Diego and two witnesses of mine, one named Antonio Lorenzo and another named Juan de Santiago, so that they will verify it in the future before our lord God and before our father the curate and minister. —

yhua S,^{r} fiscal Mayor de la S,^{n}ta yglesia D,^{n} Juan fran^{co} Ħde teopan topille Juan Josephe Alhuasil Mayor Juan de la Cruz temaxtin y esCri,^{No} de la S,^{n}ta yglesia Dn Juan fran^{co}

The señor fiscal mayor of the holy church don Juan Francisco. [Alcalde?] Church topile Juan Josef. Alguacil mayor Juan de la Cruz. Temachti and notary of the holy church, don Juan Francisco.

[2]This bequest is crossed out in the Nahuatl but is included in the Spanish translation.

80. Pascuala de la Cruz, Calimaya, Tlamimilolpan, 1739

(Newberry Library, Ayer Ms 1477B[2])

MENTIONING A LITTLE daughter but no husband, the testator here is apparently a widow, for she relies on a nephew to take care of the daughter and the property the latter is going to inherit. The fact that the little girl is called only Petrona is a further hint of her tender age, since at times in the corpus very small children are referred to by only a single name. Pascuala de la Cruz is definitely a wealthy woman by indigenous standards, owning a town lot with two houses, a piece of another lot, an expensive saint, and five pieces of land (though two at least are considered small). She also has some magueyes; though the ones mentioned are not numerous, they may imply others.

In all, Pascuala leaves her daughter the home lot with two houses, the principal saint, two small fields, and another piece of land. Most of it goes directly to Petrona, but Pascuala's nephew Pascual Diego is made joint heir of the two little fields and receives specific instructions that doubtless apply also to everything else that Petrona gets. Pascual is to raise Petrona, with an eye to her eventual marriage, leaving the fields to her and her husband. Pascuala strongly urges Pascual Diego to do his duty by Petrona, as if she fears that the nephew is not going to fulfill her wishes, and she addresses him in the second person, a very unusual construction in a testament of this time, as if she is talking directly to him.

In addition, the testator leaves: a piece of a lot to two nieces, Bernarda de la Cruz and Margarita Pascuala; another piece of land to two nephews, one the already known Pascual Diego and the other a Juan de Santiago (who already has property next to the lot going to the nieces); and two magueyes to another niece, Lorenza Pascuala. She also leaves two more magueyes, but it is not entirely clear to whom. Although her daughter is the principal heir, Pascuala shows a great deal of attention to various nephews and nieces, a sign of her connections with an extended family.

It is of interest that Pascuala tells us that she bought Nuestra Señora de Guadalupe for 6 pesos, a significant if not overwhelming amount, probably putting the saint in an upper category for those kept in households. The testator seems afraid that someone will take something so valuable and prestigious from Petrona and tries to warn people off. Perhaps this saint was even of the type that might be appropriated for the altepetl and put in a church rather than a home.

The funeral arrangements are in line with high status, since over and above the usual mass with responsory prayer and the offering for Jerusalem, the testator requests the habit of the Virgin of Carmen and the rope of San Francisco as a shroud, and burial inside the church close to the image of Nuestra Señora de la Candelaria. An unusual feature is that Pascuala declares herself to be a member of a cofradía in Quauhtitlan (doubtless dedicated to the Sangre de Cristo as in No. 2) which is going to arrange and pay for everything for her funeral. Whether her confidence is justified we have no way of knowing. In some cases in the corpus appeal to a cofradía for burial expenses seems a measure of last resort, but Pascuala does not appear needy; perhaps she has already made significant investments in connection with the cofradía.

Note that the name Pascual/Pascuala seems to be very common in the family, and the locally prestigious second name de la Cruz is also present beyond Pascuala herself, appearing at the end of the testament as well. The executor is a de la Cruz and a don, holding the very important office of governor; this hints at very good connections between Pascuala and the local elite and probably with the well known powerful family de la Cruz in Calimaya/Tepemaxalco. The witness designated by Pascuala is also a de la Cruz. The three names added at the very end are of church officials who may be present just as a formality or as a common way of ending a testament in the tlaxilacalli, as seems to happen for instance in Nos. 78 and 79.

No notary is specifically indicated, but many points in common with testament No. 79 tell us that it is don Juan Francisco (see the introductory study, p. 45), who in this testament is called temachti only, but in 79 was notary as well as temachti. The fairly elaborate preambles of the two wills are nearly identical, saints and all, until the last few words. Note especially that God the father and the son are given in Spanish, that the same unusual form of the abbreviation for "Christ" occurs, and above all that there is the same rare use of the second person with the divinity, "your precious revered name" instead of "his precious revered name," as commented upon in No. 79. No other document in the corpus has all these features.

[*f.* 2]
Jesus mariã y Josephe
Ma mosenquiscayetenehualo y motlasomahuistocatzin y Dios Padre yhua Dios hijo yhua Dios espiritu S,^{n}to Ma y mochihua Amen Jesus Maria y Josephe —

Axca Domingo A 19 de mayo de 1739 a^{os} Nica nicpehualtia y nomemoria testamento Nehual notoca Pasquala de la cruz – Nica notlaxilacalpa tlamimilopan yhua ytla yoqui nopan moChihuas NimomaSehuis yn itlasomiquilistzin y tt,^{o} xc̄p̄to ca ye ysemactzinco Nimocahuililia y noyoliatzin yhua Noanimatzin y notlasomahuistatzin S,^{r} S,^{n} Pedro yhua yehuatzin S,^{r} S,^{n} Pablo yhua yehuatzin S,^{r} S,^{n} Antoni de Pauda yhua yehuatzin S,^{r} S,^{n} miguel arcangel yhua yehuatzin S^{r} S,^{n} grauiel Arcangel yhua yehuatzi N^{ra} S^{ra} la lipia ConSession yhua yehuatzin y notlasoAngeltzin yhua Mochitintzitzin y S,^{n}tosme yhua S,^{n}tasme yn ilhuicac Chanecatzintzintin yni nopã motlatoltitzinnosq̄ yn opãn yn itlatocayxpãtzinco y tt.^{o} xc̄p̄to Ma y mochihua

[*f.* 2]
Jesus, Mary, and Joseph.
May your precious revered name of God the father, God the son, and God the Holy Spirit be entirely praised. May it be done, amen. Jesus, Mary, and Joseph. —
Today Sunday the 19th of May of the year of 1739, here I named Pascuala de la Cruz begin my memorandum of testament; my tlaxilacalli is here in Tlamimilolpan. If it happens to me that I attain the precious death of our lord Christ, I leave my spirit and soul entirely in his hands. And my precious revered father lord San Pedro and lord San Pablo, and lord San Antonio de Padua, lord San Miguel Arcángel, lord San Gabriel Arcángel, Nuestra Señora de la Limpia Concepción, my precious [guardian] angel, and all the male and female saints who are residents of heaven are to speak for me in the royal presence of our lord Christ. May it be done, amen. Jesus, Mary, and Joseph. —

Amen Jesus Maria y Josephe —
ynic Sentlamatli nitlanahuatia Nimotemaquilia Se tomi S,^{n}to geruSallem = yhua no nitlanahuatia Setel misa yhua Setel Responsos Nopan mitos yn ipalehuiloca yes y noyoliatzin yhua noaniMatzin = yhua no nitlanahuatia noquimilica yes yN itlaquetzin N,^{ra} S,^{ra} del Carme yhua yn icordotzi S,^{r} S,^{n} fran^{co} ynic Moquitlapitiyas = yhua no nitlanahuatia Nosepultura motlapos teopācalitic yxpātzinco N,^{ra} S,^{ra} Candelaria yca notlanequilis mochihuas —

ynicC ontlamantli no nitlanahuatia yni Solar yca ome caltin y queNami oca NicCahuilia Noxpox ytoca Petrona Amo aqui quiquixtilis y quemania yoqui nitlanahuatia yca noccaracterístico

ynicC ontlamantli no nitlanahuatia yni Solar yca ome caltin y queNami oca NicCahuilia Noxpox ytoca Petrona Amo aqui quiquixtilis y quemania yoqui nitlanahuatia yca nococoxcatlatlatol yoqui mochihuas —
ynic yectlamatli No nitlanahuatia nicMocahuililia N,^{ra} S,^{ra} de guadalupe quimotequipanilhuis Noxpox Petrona amo aqui quimoquixtilis y quemania yoqui nitlanahuatia yhua can onicmoConhuili nuestra S,^{ra} de gudalupe yca chiquaSe peso amo aqui quimoyascatis y quemania yhua amo aquimacas netequipacholi [*f. 2v*] Noxpox y mostla huictla yCa yehuatzin nuestra S,^{ra} de guadalupe yoqui nitlanahuatia yca nococoxcatlatol yoqui mochihuas —
= Ynic natlamatli no nitlanahuatia Ca nihermano[1] opā quactitla ca opā hualas nomortaJa yhua tomi para noytierro yhua candela yhua Mochi tle notex monequis y para yc niMotocas yoqui nitlanahuatia Yca nococoxCatlatol yoqui mochihuas —

= Ynic maquiltlamatli no nitlanahatia o Se pedaSo Solar opan matica teopatoco y timoquaxotia nosobrino Juan de S.tiago ca niquiCahuilia noSobrinas ometi Se ytoca Brenalda de la cruz yhua o Se ytoca margarita pasquala moconcahuitiyes Amaqui quiquixtilis y q̄mania yoqui nitlanahuatia yca nococoxtlatol yoqui moChihuas —
= Ynic ChiquaSentlaMatli no nitlanahuatia o Se tlali opan matiCa s,^{n} miguel otli yhua o se tlali opan matiCa S,^{n} Andres otli ca Niccahuilia NoSobrino Pasqual Diego yhua nicahuilia noxpox Petrona yhua quihuapahuas yhua nexmoquitlahuilis yhua tla Dios quimolnamiquilis cana teCpaltzinco monamitis

First I order that I give a real for Holy Jerusalem. = And I also order that a mass with a responsory prayer is to be said for me to be the help of my spirit and soul. = And also I order that my shroud is to be the habit of Nuestra Señora del Carmen, and [my body] will go girt with the rope of lord San Francisco. = And also I order that my grave is to be opened inside the church building, facing Nuestra Señora de la Candelaria; it is to be done by my will. —

Second I also order that I leave this lot with two houses, just as they are, to my daughter named Petrona. No one is ever to take them from her. Thus I order by my sick person's statement; thus it is to be done. —
Third I also order that I leave Nuestra Señora de Guadalupe to my daughter Petrona; she is to serve her. No one is ever to take her from her; thus I order. And I bought Nuestra Señora de Guadalupe for 6 pesos; no one is ever to appropriate her, and no one is to cause trouble [*f. 2v*] for my daughter in the future about Nuestra Señora de Guadalupe. Thus I order by my sick person's statement; thus it is to be done. —
= Fourth I also order that I am a member[1] [of a cofradía] in Quauhtitlan; from there is to be brought my shroud, money for my burial, candles, and everything necessary with which I will be buried. Thus I order by my sick person's statement; thus it is to be done. —
= Fifth I also order that I leave another piece of a lot in Teopantonco, bordering on [land of] my nephew Juan de Santiago, to my two nieces, one named Bernarda de la Cruz and the other named Margarita Pascuala; they are to share it. No one is ever to take it from them. Thus I order by my sick person's statement; thus it is to be done. —
= Sixth I also order that I leave another piece of land on the San Miguel road and another piece of land on the San Andrés road to my nephew Pascual Diego, and I also leave it to my daughter Petrona. [Pascual Diego] is to raise her and take care of her for me, and if God remembers him [he dies], she is to get

[1]The original clearly says "nihermano," "I am a brother," not "nihermana," "I am a sister." The final line differentiating *a* from *o* in this writer's calligraphy is missing, and there is hardly even room for it. Usually when a Spanish word with gender differentiation was borrowed, it was taken in both the masculine and feminine genders as two separate words, and indeed that is what happened with this very word *hermano/hermana* when it refers to kinship. Here we are not dealing with a kinship term, as we can see in the fact that the word is not possessed. Either *hermano* in the sense of member of a sodality did not show gender, or the writer has simply made a mistake.

ca ticCahuilis[2] yno ome miltototi ca yc motequipanosque ynamic ytla Dios quimochicahuilis ypanpatzinco y tto Dios timochihuilis tinexictilis tinexmoquitlahuililis yhua timocmictis [?] yhua asta yqua tla omonamicti ticCahuilis ypanpatzincon y tt,o Dios timochihuilis yoqui nitlanahuatia yca nococoxCatlatol —

= Ynic chicontlamatli no nitlanahuatia oSe tlali opā matican quactecon quactla otli Nicahuilia Sanno yehual noxpox Petrona Amo aqui quiquixtilis y quemania yoqui nitlanahuatia yca noCocoxcatlatol —

= Yhua no nitlanahuatia o Sen pedaso Sacatitla Sannopa quactecon quactla otli niquicahuilia ome noSobrinos Se ytoca Pasqual Diego yhua o Se ytoca Juan de S,ntiago moconcahuitiyes Amo aqui quiquixtilis y quemania yoqui nitlanahuatia yca nococoxcatlatol — [*f. 3*]

= Yhua no nitlanahuatia ome mel nicahuilia NoSobrina lorenza Pasquala amo aqui quiquix y quemani yoqui nitlanahuatia yca y nococoxcatlatol —

Yhua no nitlanahuatia no nicahuilia ome mel no[bitori] amo aMo aqui quiquixtilis y quemani yoqui nitlanahuatia —

Yhua ye nica nitzonquixtia y nococoxCatlatol yxpa noalbasia S,r gouernadro D,n Juan de la Cruz yhuan testigo Bartolo de la cruz ynic nopan Motlatoltisque y mostla huictla ma y mochihua Amen Jesus Maria y Josephe —

Yhua ye nica titofirmatia y tinahuitic[3] ynic titlaneltilisque yn ixpātzincon y tt,o Dios S,r fiscal mayor de la S,nta yglesia D.n Josephe de S,ntiago teopan topicle MarSel Brenaldo temaxtin de la S,nta yglesia D,n Juan franco

married somewhere to someone. You[2] are to leave her those two little cultivated fields for her husband and her to work if God gives her health. For the sake of our lord God you are to do it, you are to look after and take care of her for me. [You will die ?,] and if by that time she has married, you are to leave them to her; you are to do it for the sake of our lord God. Thus I order by my sick person's statement. —

= Seventh I also order that I likewise leave another piece of land at the edge of the woods [or in Quauhtenco], on the Quauhtla road, to my daughter Petrona. No one is ever to take it from her. Thus I order by my sick person's statement. —

= And I also order that I leave another piece of [land] [among the grass], also at the edge of the woods [or in Quauhtenco], on the Quauhtla road, to two nephews of mine, one named Pascual Diego and the other one named Juan de Santiago; it is to be shared by the two. No one is ever to take it from them; thus I order by my sick person's statement. — [*f. 3*]

= And I also order that I leave two magueyes to my niece Lorenza Pascuala. No one is ever to take them from her; thus I order by my sick person's statement. —

And I also order that I leave two magueyes to my [Victorio? Victoria?]. No one is ever to take them away from [this person]; thus I order. —

And here I conclude my sick person's statement before my executor governor don Juan de la Cruz and the witness Bartolomé de la Cruz, so that they will speak for me in the future. May it be done, amen. Jesus, Mary and Joseph. —

And here we four sign,[3] so that we will verify it before our lord God. The señor fiscal mayor of the holy church, don Josef de Santiago. Church topile, Marcel Bernardo. Temachti of the holy church, don Juan Francisco.

[2]Here the testator begins to speak directly to Pascual Diego. Following older patterns, testators probably often made their oral statements in this form, and then they were put in third person in the written will.

[3]Although the text says that "we four" sign, only three "signatures" (all in the same hand as usual) are to be seen.

81. Félix de Santiago, Calimaya, Teopantonco, 1738

(Newberry Library, Ayer Ms 1477B [1])

THE WIDOWER Félix de Santiago leaves all his property to his only son (or the only one surviving), Martín León. The fact that Félix entrusts him to his godparents to be raised at their place tells us first of all that Martín is still very small, and second that Félix's wife is not available; in all probability she has already died. Godparents are not often found in the corpus, but when they are, they are a concrete sign of the extension of kin-style relationships beyond the family through the rite of baptism. Here the godmother seems to have prominence and bears an unusual second name, while the godfather probably gave Martín his first name.

The property that is left to Martín is considerable: a lot, five cultivated fields ranging from 1 to 4 almudes, 11 magueyes aside from some other little ones, a corncrib, and a notable array of saints. Clearly Félix was involved in agricultural activities and also in the production of beverages from the maguey plant. It is very unusual that despite being wealthy the testator mentions no house at all; actually his son is to be raised at his godparents' place.

As for the saints, Félix leaves a Virgin of Guadalupe, two Christs, a Santa Lucía, and a San Francisco; the latter may be the object of a special devotion, since we find him also in the funeral arrangements. In fact, the testator requests the shroud and rope of San Francisco, as well as the ordinary mass with responsory prayer and offering for Jerusalem, and burial outside the church. Thus the ritual suggests a somewhat middling status, but the saints rather more than that. In terms of religious formulas, this will follows the Calimaya/Tepemaxalco style in that there are invocations of the Limpia Concepción, San Miguel Arcángel, San Pedro and San Pablo.

Among the executor and the witnesses we find significant second names, such as Ramos, de Vega, and de la Cruz, although only the fiscal bears the title don. Once again, while Pedro de Vega and Gregorio Andrés are clearly indicated as witnesses, the fiscal and the topile may have been brought in more out of formality or notarial practice.

The notary is the famous Hipólito de los Santos, here introduced as notary of the church, not of the commonwealth, and without the title don. Full analysis of his style is included in the introductory study, p. 44. This is the earliest example of his work in the corpus, years before the rest. If the date were not written so clearly, one might suspect there had been some mistake. Looking closely, we see that his style was not yet fully mature; for example, later he would add a saint or two to the usual assembly and put them in a different order, and whereas later he usually said "I leave so-and-so as executor," here the phrase is simpler. Note the Spanish loan verb *mocruzaroa*, "to cross," and the compound relational word "juera de" (*fuera de*) for "aside from."

[*f. 1*]
Jesus Maria y Joseph
Ma moSenquisCayectenehualo yn itlaSoMahuisSenquisCatoCatzi d.s tetatzi d.s yn itlaSoMahuispiltzi yhua d.s Espiritu S^{n}tto ma y Mochihua —
AxCan Sabado Mani Metztli A 5 de Abril xihuil de 1738 a^{os} NiCan iPa yAltepetzi notlaSomahuistatzi S.^{n}tto Sn P.^{o} Calimaya niCa nichane yhua nipohui niCa ypan tlaxilaCali Bario tiopantongo, yhua niCa nicpehualtia y noMemoria testamento nehual notoCa felis de S.^{n}tiago v.^{o} yhua huel ahtopa niquitoa yntla yucqui nopa Mochihuas yn itlanahuatiltzi tt.^{o} d.s yntla oninoMiquili Ca ySemactzinco tt.^{o} Jexp.^{to} nicnoCahuilia y noyolia noaniMantzi yhua nicnotlatlactilia y notlaSoMahuisSenquis,Canantzi la linpia ConSecSion, no yhua nicnotlatlactilia y notlaSoMahuistatzi S,^{n} miguel ArCanJel yhua notlaSomahuistatzitzihua Patrones Sor Sn P.^{o} yhua yehuatzi S.^{n}tto Sn Pablo no yhua niquinnotlatlactilia quexquih S.^{n}ttos yhuan S.^{n}ttas MotemiltitiCate yn ilhuiCac yctic inic nopa Motlatoltictzinosque yn itlaSoyxpantzinCo tt.^{o} d.^{s} Ma y mochihua =
ynic ontlaMantli nitlanahuatia yntla oninoMiquili Se Misa yhuan Se responSos nopan Mitos ypalehuiloCa yes noaniMantzi neltis notlatol Mochihuas

[*f. 1*]
Jesus, Mary, and Joseph.
May the precious revered consummate name of God the father, God his precious revered son, and God the Holy Spirit be entirely praised. May it be done. —
Today Saturday the 5th of the month of April of the year of 1738, here in the altepetl of my precious revered father holy San Pedro, Calimaya, I named Félix de Santiago, widower, citizen here, begin here my memorandum of testament; I belong to the tlaxilacalli and barrio of Teopantonco here. First of all I say that if the order of our lord God should be so performed on me that I die, I leave my spirit and soul entirely in the hands of our lord Jesus Christ. And I implore my precious revered consummate mother la Limpia Concepción, and I also implore my precious revered father San Miguel Arcángel and my precious revered fathers the patrons lord San Pedro and holy San Pablo, and I also implore all the male and female saints who fill heaven to speak for me in the precious presence of our lord God. May it be done. =
Second I order that when I have died a mass with a responsory prayer is to be said for me to be the help of my soul. My statement is to be realized and car-

—

ynic yectlamantli nitlanahuatia noMortaJa yes ytlaquentzi notlaSoMahuistatzi S.^{n}tto S.^{n} fr.^{co} yhua ytlaSoCordontzi yc ninoquitlalpis neltis notlatol —

ynic nactlaMantli nitlanahuatia noSepultura onpa Motlapos tiopanquiahuac yhua nicteMaCa Se tomi - huentzintli JeruSalen neltis notlanahuatil MoChihuas =

ynic Maquiltlamantli nitlanahuatia onpa Mantica Se Solar yquitlapa telpiloya timoquaxohhuia d.^{n} bernardo Andres difunto ca yehual nicCahuilia notelpoh ytoCa Martin leon neltis notlatol mochihuas —

no yhua nitlanahuatia notelpoh Martin Leon Ca yehual nicCahuilia noCoMadre Maria de pelegrina yhua nocopadre Marselo Martin Ca yehuatzi ytlaSonantzi oquiMoquiMoquatequili onpa quiscaltisque yCa [*f. 1v*] tlen iyaxCa nicCahuilia neltis notlactol MoChihuas —

no yhua nitlanahuatia la VirJen de huadalupe yhua ome christotzitzi yhua S.^{n}tta lusia mohtintzitzi nicCahuilia notelpho ytoca Martin leon Neltis notlanahuatil Mochihuas —

yhua nitlanahuatia Se mili onpa Mani Sn Marcos quactenco Ca Sano yehual nicCahuilia notelpoh Martin leon neltis notlanahuatil moChihuas —

no yhua nitlanahuatia S.^{n}tto S.^{n} fr.^{co} Ca Sano yehual nicCahuilia notelpoh Martin leon neltis notlatol — no yhua nitlanahuatia Se miltontli onpa Mantica Metepec octli ynahuac tepetontli Calaqui Se almo tlauli Ca Sano yehual Martin leon nicCahuilia yhua Sano onpa Metepec octli Canpa MoCruSaroa octli para yc Sn Lorenzo onpa mantiCa oc Se Mili Calaqui nahui nahui almo tlauli Sano yehual nopiltzi martin leon nicCahuilia = yhua Sanonpa Metepec octli Mantica oc Se Mili Ca para yc [. . .]latzintla Calaqui yei almo tlauli Ca Sano yehual Martin [. . .]n nicCahuilia neltis notlatol —

No yhua nitlanahuatia oc Se mili onpa Mantica Sa mateo octli Calaqui nahui alMo tlauli Sano yehual nopiltzi nicCahuilia neltis notlanahuatil mochihuas — no yhua nitlanahuatia Se quesContontli quenami onCa Sano yehual notelpoh ytoCa Martin Leon nicCahuilia neltis notlatol mochihuas —

yhua Ca Nitlanahuatia Mactlactli yhua se Mel Juera de yno tepitzitzi Ca yehual nicCahuilia notelpoh

ried out. —

Third I order that my shroud is to be the habit of my precious revered father holy San Francisco, and I am to be girt with his precious rope. My statement is to be realized. —

Fourth I order that my grave is to be opened outside the church, and I give a real as an offering for Jerusalem. My order is to be realized and carried out. =

Fifth I order that I leave a lot behind the jail, bordering on [land of] don Bernardo Andrés, deceased, to my son named Martín León. My statement is to be realized and carried out. —

In addition I order that I leave my son Martín León to my comadre María de Peregrina and my compadre Marcelo Martín, for she is his precious mother who baptized him; they are to raise him there [at their place] with [*f. 1v*] the property of his that I am leaving him. My statement is to be realized and carried out. —

In addition I order that I leave la Virgen de Guadalupe, two little Christs, and Santa Lucía all to my son named Martín León. My order is to be realized and carried out. —

And I order that there is a cultivated field at San Marcos, at the edge of the woods [or in Quauhtenco], and I leave it likewise to my son Martín León. My order is to be realized and carried out. —

In addition I order that I likewise leave holy San Francisco to my son Martín León. My statement is to be realized. — In addition I order that I likewise leave a little cultivated field on the Metepec road, close to a little hill, where 1 almud of maize fits, to Martín León, and I leave another cultivated field likewise on the Metepec road, where the roads cross going to San Lorenzo, in which 4 almudes of maize fit, likewise to my child Martín León. = And likewise on the Metepec road there is another cultivated field, below, where 3 almudes of maize fit; I likewise leave it to Martín León. My statement is to be realized. —

In addition I order that I likewise leave another cultivated field on the San Mateo road, where 4 almudes of maize fit, to my child. My order is to be realized and carried out. — In addition I order that I likewise leave a small corncrib, as it is, to my son named Martín León. My statement is to be realized and carried out. —

And I order that I leave 11 magueyes, aside from the little ones, to my son Martín León, and if God

Martin leon yhuan tla d.s quiMohuapahuilis ynon tepitzitzi metotonti Sano yehua[ ] nicCahuilia Martin leon netis notlatol MoChihuas — yhua Ca san ixquih niCa nictzonquixtia y noMemoria testamento ymixpa noAlbaSea yhua notestigos ynic tlaneltilisque yn ixpantzinco tt.^{o} D.^{s} Ma y mochihua // AlbaSea Salbador Ramos testigo P,^{o} de Vega — oc Se testigo gregorio Andres
fisCal mayor de la S,^{n}ta yglesia Dn Antt^{o} de la Crus topile fr^{co} de la Crus
Nehual onitlaquilo ytenCopa CoCoxqui Es,^{no} de la S,^{n}ta yglesia hiPoLitto de lo S,^{n}ttos

should let those little magueyes mature, I leave them likewise to Martín León. My statement is to be realized and carried out. — And that is all. Here I conclude my memorandum of testament before my executor and my witnesses, who will verify it before our lord God. May it be done. // The executor is Salvador Ramos. Witness, Pedro de Vega; another witness Gregorio Andrés.
Fiscal mayor of the holy church, don Antonio de la Cruz; topile, Francisco de la Cruz.
I did the writing at the order of the sick person, notary of the holy church Hipólito de los Santos.

82. Don Antonio Salvador, Calimaya, Teopantonco, 1762

(AGN, Civil 1495, exp. 10)[1]

ONE MIGHT EXPECT the testament of a former governor of Calimaya, which don Antonio Salvador is, to be a long and complex document, but in fact the intricacy of the situation is beyond expectations. First let us consider the various major individual pieces of evidence. The will is in two separate parts; one section is dated 1762 and looks like a complete testament in every respect, while the other section, on a separate sheet, is simply appended to it with no explanation and no apparatus of date or witnesses, although it mentions a great deal of additional landed property and some additional heirs. The Spanish translation included in the file somewhat deceitfully integrates the two parts into a single consecutive testament, hiding the anomalous status of the second part. Crucial to an assessment of the testament is a memorandum issued in Spanish by the executor, don Antonio's brother don Julián de Santiago (on ff. 8–9). This statement shows us first that the method of adding up the two parts of the testament proper to understand the testator's intention is essentially correct, though it also points to some items of importance omitted from both sections of the will. Above all it gives us a different insight into who the heirs were.

Let us look at don Antonio's assets according to his compound testament. His holdings are not equal to those of some legendary governors, but far above average. In addition to a house with its saints on a lot he owns, he mentions four other pieces of lots in the "urban" area, two of them in tlaxilacalli other than his own (Pasiontitlan and Tlamimilolpan). His scattered nine parcels of agricultural land, some of it undeveloped, amount to 35 almudes, plus some pieces given without measurements. He specifically says that he bought two of the parcels, and we would suspect the same of some others as well. He also mentions four cows and some calves.

The executor's memorandum broadly agrees with this picture but defines it more sharply in some cases and also extends it a bit. The saints are seen to be very impressive. They are the only thing listed under household goods or furniture (*ajuar de casa*). Two are paintings two varas high, with another a vara and a half high; two are statues half a vara high, and there are also other "little pictures" (*cuadritos*). Some of the lots are contiguous to the house and to each other, and some of them have magueyes on them. The testator had also rented three other lots and planted on them a hundred magueyes or more each. Because of more precise measuring, the nine pieces of land amount to 39 almudes here, with a bit still unmeasured. There are six cows rather than four, plus two working donkeys with their equipment. In either version, the testator has been actively buying and developing land, and in the second version he is seen to be a substantial maguey entrepreneur.

In the two-section testament, don Antonio Salvador appears as a widower with at least four children, two male and two female, with other possible daughters as well. Antonia Guadalupe, who is called a grandchild in the first part, is called a child in the second part, and a Pascuala Dorotea del Espíritu Santo, with a name evoking religious pretensions, is included with Antonia among the children and

[1]The testament is accompanied by a contemporary Spanish translation.

later specifically called don Antonio's daughter ("noxpoh"). The heir to the house and lot, together with the saints, is the daughter Josefa de la Encarnación; she also gets a share of the other lands and a corncrib. A second daughter is of exceptional interest, called sor Felipa de la Purificación as if she were a nun. This is an extraordinary detail, placing the family at the highest level of indigenous society, and the only such case found in the corpus. Sor Felipa does not receive as much as Josefa, which might be because she is younger, but might also be because living in a convent she could not manage a house and lands. The apparent sons receive a good but not clearly predominant share of the lands, about equal amounts going to each. The grandchild or child receives a lot and shares a 6-almud plot with the mysterious Pascuala Dorotea, who gets another small plot on her own.

One is immediately inclined to speculate why the sons did not get more, and indeed there could have been very plausible reasons. The executor's statement, however, halts such speculation in its tracks, for the executor calls the first son mentioned, Josef Serrano, a nephew instead, while the second son, Asencio de Santiago, is called don Antonio's godchild. The rationale of don Antonio's allocations now becomes clear. He has no sons and is pressing a nephew and a godchild into that role, but not giving them the full predominance he would if they were his actual children. The executor also clears up the situation with Pascuala Dorotea del Espíritu Santo, saying that she receives what she does because she is the godchild of don Antonio's daughter sor Felipa de la Purificación. Probably Pascuala too is ambitious to become a nun. The status of sor Felipa herself becomes clearer, for the executor calls her "mother" and "nun."

After this we must examine exactly how don Antonio refers to the two male heirs. First he calls Josef Serrano "nopiltzi," literally "my child" and in actual meaning "my son" in contrast to Josefa, who is called "my daughter" ("noxpoh"). Asencio de Santiago appears first as one of "my children" or "my sons" ("nopilhua") along with Josef Serrano, and is later called "nopiltzi," "my child or son," as well. Did don Antonio actually intend to deceive anyone, or is he simply making a broader, affectionate use of kinship terminology, a manner of speaking that went far back in Nahuatl usage? At this distance in time it seems hard to say. Calling Antonia Guadalupe both child and grandchild may indicate that no deliberate deception was involved.

Don Antonio confirms his high status also in his funeral arrangements, though they are not on an unusual scale. Besides the expected mass with responsory prayer and offering for Jerusalem, he requests the shroud and rope of San Francisco, and burial in the chapel of San Antonio, showing a special devotion for the saint from whom he derives his name. One of the statuettes in his home was also a San Antonio.

The testator appoints as executor don Julián de Santiago, who, as emerges from the file in which the document was found, was don Antonio's brother. Apart from the two topiles, all the witnesses bear the title don, and one is the present governor, the person of maximum prestige in the community and another sign of don Antonio's important connections. Some of the names here are significant: Alcántara, Hernández, de la Cruz, and de Santiago, which was the second name of don Antonio's father and all his brothers (all of whom were don), as becomes clear in the executor's statement. We are moving within the highest stratum of indigenous society, and connections such as these are what we can expect from a past governor.

A word on land terminology in the will. It is worthy of note that all of don Antonio's parcels located either inside Teopantonco or in neighboring "urban" tlaxilacalli are called "pedaso solar," or "piece of lot." When he refers to a piece of land outside the core of tlaxilacalli, such as the one on the road to Metepec, for his daughter sor Felipa, don Antonio chooses the usual term *tlalli*, "land."

This is the last testament of the many in the present volume by the notary (don) Hipólito de los Santos. The orthography and language are in line with what is commented on in the other wills and in the introductory study (p. 44). Of special interest here is the notary's role in the preparation of this strange two-part testament. Seeing the two parts, it would be hard to know which was done first, but the form of the notary's name gives us a clue. In the will proper of 1762, he is styled don Hipólito de los Santos, in the fragment plain Hipólito. From other documents here we know that for most of his career he did not bear the don, that in 1758–59 he assumed it tentatively, and then by 1762 definitively. A plausible explanation of what happened in this case is that don Antonio Salvador had been very ill a couple of years earlier, and at that time de los Santos prepared a will for him, but don Antonio did not die. When a truly mortal illness came upon him, the notary made a new will but used the old sheet forming the second part as well, since most of what it said was still valid (one or two bequests were marked out). Such at least is a reasonable hypothesis.

Another question is whether the notary colluded in a false designation of the relationship of some of the heirs to the testator. With his position, de los Santos would have known don Antonio well and would have known that the male heirs were not literally his sons. Yet he wrote the words; perhaps he was merely repeating what the testator said and took no further responsibility.

[*f.* 2]

Jesus y Maria hi JoSephe

Ma moSenquisCayectenehualo yn itlaSoMahuistoCatzi D.S tetatzi yhua D.S in itlasopiltzi yhua D.S. Espiritu Santo Ma y mochihua =

AxCan Miercoles A 16 de diSiembre de 1762 a,^{os} yhua Ca niCa nicpehualtia y noMemoria testaMento nehual notoCa D,^{n} Antonio Salbador gobernador paSado yhua nosihuahuatzi CatCa NiColaSa pasquala yhua Ca niCa nichane ypan yAltepetzi notlasotatzi Sor Sn P.^{o} CaliMaya yhua Ca nica nipuhui ypan Barrio TiopantonCo yhua Ca huel ahtopa niquitohua Ca yntla yucqui nopa mochihuas ihua nicnoMacSehuis in itlaSoMiquilistzi tt.^{o} D.S. Ca iSenMactzinco nicnoCahuilia noaniMantzi yhua Ca huel nicnotlatlactilia notlasotatzi S,^{or} Sn P.^{o} yhua yehuatzi S,^{or} S,^{n} pablo yhua yehuatzi notlaSotatzi S,^{or} S,^{n} Antonio de paduhua yhua yehuatzi notlaSomahuisnantzi la linpia ConSepSion yhua yehuatzi S,^{n} Miguel arCangel yhuan S,^{n} Rafel no yhua niquiMotlatlactilia Mochi quexquih santtos yhua santtas i MotemiltitiCate yn ilhuiCac inic nopa Motlatoltitzinosque in itlaSoyxpantzinco tt,^{o} D.S. Ma y Mochihua Amen —

yhua Ca ynic Sentlamantli nitlanahuatia Ca yntla onicnoMacSehui yn itlaSoMiquilistzi tt.^{o} D.S. Ca Se Misa yhuan Responsos nopan mictos yn ipalehuiloca yes noaniMantzi Ca neltis notlactol =

ynic ontlaMantli nitlanahuatia Ca noMortaJa yes in itlaquentzi notlaSotatzi S,^{n} fr.^{co} yhua yn iCordontzi nicnohuiquilis Ca neltis notlanahuatil Mochihuas —

ynic yectlaMantli nitlanahuatia Ca noSepultura Ca onpa Motlapos Capilla notlasotatzi Sn Antonio no yhua Ca nicteMaCa Se tomi huentzintli Santo geruSalen Ca neltis notlactol mochihuas —

ynic NactlaMantli nitlanahuatia Ca ini noCha Caltzintli ihua yCa moChi Solar para yc tenanCopa yhua yehuatzitzi Santos quename MestiCate yhua Ca yehual nicCahuilia noxpoh in itoca JoSepha de

[*f.* 2]

Jesus, Mary, and Joseph.

May the precious revered name of God the father, God his precious son, and God the Holy Spirit be entirely praised. May it be done. =

Today, Wednesday the 16th of December of the year of 1762, here I named don Antonio Salvador, past governor, begin my memorandum of testament; my wife was Nicolasa Pascuala, and I am a citizen here in the altepetl of my precious father lord San Pedro, Calimaya, and I belong to the barrio of Teopantonco here. And first of all I say that if it happens to me that I attain the precious death of our lord God, I leave my soul entirely in his hands, and I greatly implore my precious father lord San Pedro, and lord San Pablo, and my precious father lord San Antonio de Padua, and my precious revered mother la Limpia Concepción, and San Miguel Arcángel, and San Rafael, and I also implore all the male and female saints who fill heaven to speak for me in the precious presence of our lord God. May it be done. Amen. —

And first I order that when I have attained the precious death of our lord God, a mass with a responsory prayer is to be said for me, to be the help of my soul; my statement is to be carried out. =

Second, I order that my shroud will be the habit of my precious father San Francisco, and I will wear his rope; my order is to be carried out and realized. —

Third, I order that my grave is to be opened at the chapel of my precious father San Antonio, and also I give an offering of one real for Holy Jerusalem; my statement is to be carried out and realized. —

Fourth, I order that I leave this home of mine, the house including the lot, in the direction of Tenango, and the saints as they are to my daughter named Josefa de la Encarnación, she is to work [or to serve]

la EncarnaSion Ca yehual tlatequipanos ypan Caltzintli Ca yCa notlanequilis nicCahuilia ca neltis notlactol mochihuas —

ynic Maquiltlamantli nitlanahuatia Ca oc Se pedaSo Solar niCa Mantica yquitlapa tiopaCaltzintli para yc tlacpac yhua Ca yehual nicCahuilia nopiltzi yn ito-Ca Josephe SeRano Ca yCa notlanequilis nicCahuilia Ca neltis notlactol Mochihuas =

yhua ca quin onimotlalnamicti ypa ini Solar quipie Senpuhuali yhua Mactlactli baras yc patlahuac ihua Ca omenti nopilhua Conanasque Ca huel quiMonepantlaxelhuisque Caxtoli bara Conanas Josephe Se-Rano yhua oc Caxtuli baras Conanas ASensio de Santiago ca iCa notlanequilis niquinCahuilia Ca neltis notlanahuatil Mochihuas — [*f.* 2*v*]

ynic ChiquaSentlamantli nitlanahuatia Ca oc Se pedaSo Solar nica Mantica ipa ini bario Tiopanton-Co timoquaxuhhuiya pablo de S.^{n}tiago yhua Ca sano yehuanti oMenti nopilhua niquinCahuilia Con-Cahuisque Josephe SeRano yhua ASenSio de S.^{n}tiago Ca yCa notlanequilis niquinCahuilia Ca neltis notlactol Mochihuas —

ynic chiContlaMantli nitlanahuatia Ca oc Se pedaSo Solar niCan Mantica bario paxiutitla Ca notlacohual yhua Ca yehual nicCahuilia noxhui Antonia huadaluphe ca yCa notlanequilis nicCahuilia Ca neltis notlactol mochihuas =

ynic ChiquetlaMantli nitlanahuatia ca oc Se pedaSo Solar niCan Mantica tlaMimilolpa ca tlaCohuali y-hua Ca yehual nicCahuilia noxpoh JoSepha de la EnCarnaSion Ca yCa notlanequilis Ca neltis notlactol Mochihuas —

ynic chicnactlaMantli nitlanahuatia Ca Se quesCo-Mal nicCahuilia noxpoh Josepha de la Encarnasion yhua oc Se quesComal nicCahuilia nopiltzin Josephe SeRano Ca yca notlanequilis niquinCahuilia Ca neltis notlactol Mochihuas

no yhua nitlanahuatia Ca Se tlali onpa Mani Metepec octli para yc tlacpac tiMoquaXuhhuiya D,^{n} Matheo yhua yteh calaqui Se media tlauli yhua Ca yehual nicCahuilia noxpoh Sor phelipha de la purifi-CaSion Ca neltis notlanahuatil Mochihuas —

yhua Ca San ixquih niCa nictzonquixtia noCoCox-Catlanahuatil nomeMoria testaMentto ymixpa noAl-baSea yhua Notestigo inic tlaneltilisque Mostla huiptla yn itlaSoyxpantzinco tt,^{o} D.S. Ma y mochihua —

NoAlbaSea nicCahua D,^{n} Julian de S,^{n}tiago

testigo D,^{n} pheliphe de S,^{n}tiago G,^{or} Actual Dn P.^{o} de Al.^{ra} fiscal Mayor Dn Esteban Ernandes

in the house; it is by my will that I leave it to her. My statement is to be carried out and realized. —

Fifth, I order that I leave another piece of a lot here at the back of the church building, above, to my son named Josef Serrano. It is by my will that I leave it to him; my statement is to be carried out and realized. =

And I just remembered about this lot that measures 30 varas in width; two of my children are to take it, they are to divide it right in half; Josef Serrano is to take 15 varas, and Asencio de Santiago is to take the other 15 varas. It is by my will that I leave it to them; my order is to be carried out and realized. — [*f.* 2*v*]

Sixth, I order that likewise I leave another piece of a lot here in this barrio of Teopantonco, bordering on [land of] Pablo de Santiago, to my two children, Josef Serrano and Asencio de Santiago; the two of them are to share it. It is by my will that I leave it to them; my statement is to be carried out and realized. —

Seventh, I order that I leave another piece of a lot here in the barrio of Pasiontitlan, that I bought, to my grandchild Antonia Guadalupe. It is by my will that I leave it to her; my statement is to be carried out and realized. =

Eighth, I order that I leave another piece of a lot here in Tlamimilolpan, that was bought, to my daughter Josefa de la Encarnación. It is by my will; my statement is to be carried out and realized. —

Ninth, I order that I leave a corncrib to my daughter Josefa de la Encarnación, and I leave another corncrib to my son Josef Serrano. It is by my will that I leave them to them; my statement is to be carried out and realized.

In addition I order that I leave a piece of land on the road to Metepec, above, that borders on [land of] don Mateo, and in which half a fanega of maize fits, to my daughter sor Felipa de la Purificación; my order is to be carried out and realized. —

And that is all. Here I conclude my sick person's commands, my memorandum of testament, before my executor and my witness so that they will verify it in the future in the precious presence of our lord God. May it be done. —

I leave don Julián de Santiago as my executor.

Witness don Felipe de Santiago. Present governor don Pedro de Alcántara. Fiscal mayor don Esteban

topile Josephe Antonio topile Juan de la Crus

Es,^{no} D^{n} hipolitto de lo Santtos [*f. 3*]

No yhua nitlanahuatia Ca Se pedaSo tlali Mani toloCa octli timoquaxuhhuiya tequimili del S.^{or} del perdon yhua yteh Calaqui Se media tlauli yhuan Ca niquinCahuilia oMenti nopilhua ConCahuisque Se ytoCa JoSephe SeRano yhuan oc Se ytoCa AsenSio de S.^{n}tiago Ca yCa notlanequilis niquinCahuilia Ca neltis notlanahuatil Mochihuas —

No yhua nitlanahuatia Ca oc Se pedaSo tlali Mani S,^{n} lorenSo otli timoquaxuhhuiya Martin Roque yhua yteh Calaqui Se media tlauli yhuan Ca niquinCahuilia omenti Nopilhua Concahuisque Se ytoCa Antonia huadaluphe yhua oc Se ytoCa paquala dorothea del Espiritu Santo Ca yCa notlanequilis niquinCahuilia Ca neltis notlanahuatil Mochihuas —

no yhua nitlanahuatia Ca oc Se pedaSo tlali Mani Sn Andres octli yhua yteh Calaqui Se Media tlauli yhua Ca yehual nicCahuilia noxpoh itoCa JoSepha de la EncarnaSion Ca yCa notlanequilis nicCahuilia Ca neltis notlanahuatil Mochihuas —

no yhua nitlanahuatia Ca oc tlaltontli niCa MantiCa toloCa octli Sentlapal baRanCa yhua yteh Calaqui Maquili quartillittos tlauli yhua Ca yehual nicCahuilia noxpoh pasquala dorothea Ca yCa notlanequilis Ca neltis notlactol mochihuas —

No yhua nitlanahuatia Ca oc Se pedaSo tlali onpa Mani pelaxtitla Ca notlaCohual yhua yteh Calaqui ome alMo tlauli yhua Ca yehual nicCahuilia nopiltzi AseSio de S,^{n}tiago Ca neltis notlactol —

No yhua nitlanahuatia Ca oc Se tlali Mani quactenCo otli S,^{n} Marcos yhua Ca yni tlali Ca ticnacCahuia entre tinahuinti tiErmanos yhua Ca yehual nicChihuilia Cargo NoAlbaSea para yehual quixelos Ca yucqui nitlanahuatia —

no yhua nitlanahuati Ca Sanonpa Mani quactenCo yhua Ca onicCohuili Martin de la Crus yhua yteh Calaqui Se media tlauli yhua Ca yehual nicCahuilia nopiltzin JoSephe SeRano para quiSaCaMos Ca yCa notlanequilis Ca neltis notlactol mochihuas =

no yhua nitlanahuatia Ca Sanonpa Mani oc se tlali yc tlatzintla ytenCo baRanCa yanquic SaCaMoli yhua Ca yehual nicCahuilia nopiltzi Asensio de Santiago Ca neltis notlactol — [*f. 3v*]

no yhua nitlanahuatia Ca ome baCas granisos yhua

Hernández. Topile Josef Antonio. Topile Juan de la Cruz.

Notary don Hipólito de los Santos. [*f. 3*]

In addition I order that I leave a piece of land on the road to Toluca that borders on the tribute field of the Señor del Perdón, and in which half a fanega of maize fits, to my two children, one named Josef Serrano and the other named Asencio de Santiago; the two of them are to share it. It is by my will that I leave it to them; my order is to be carried out and realized. —

In addition I order that I leave another piece of land on the road to San Lorenzo that borders on [land of] Martín Roque, and in which half a fanega of maize fits, to my two children, one named Antonia Guadalupe and the other named Pascuala Dorotea del Espíritu Santo; the two of them are to share it. It is by my will that I leave it to them; my order is to be carried out and realized. —

In addition I order that I leave another piece of land on the road to San Andrés, in which half a fanega of maize fits, to my daughter named Josefa de la Encarnación. It is by my will that I leave it to her; my order is to be carried out and realized. —

In addition I order that I leave another small piece of land here on the road to Toluca, on one side of the ravine, in which 5 little cuartillos of maize fit, to my daughter Pascuala Dorotea. It is by my will; my statement is to be carried out and realized. —

In addition I order that I leave another piece of land at Perastitlan, that I have bought, and in which 2 almudes of maize fit, to my son Asencio de Santiago; my statement is to be carried out. —

In addition I order that as to another piece of land at the edge of the woods [or in Quauhtenco] on the road to San Marcos, the four of us siblings share this land between us. I charge my executor with dividing it; thus I order. —

In addition I order that I leave [a piece of land] likewise at the edge of the woods [or in Quauhtenco] that I bought from Martín de la Cruz, and in which half a fanega of maize fits, to my son Josef Serrano for him to break the ground. It is by my will; my statement is to be carried out and realized. =

In addition I order that I leave another piece of land likewise at the edge of the ravine, below, with the ground newly broken, to my son Asencio de Santiago; my statement is to be carried out. — [*f. 3v*]

In addition I order that as to two dark-colored cows

Ca Se Conanas JoSephe SeRano yhua oc Se Conanas ASensio de S,^{n}tiago yhua in ipilhua MoCahuasque para Casimira yhua oc nome baCas Conanas Antonia huadaluphe yhua Se baCa huey yhua Se tepitzi Conanas noxpoh JoSepha de la EnCarnasion Ca neltis notlanahuatil mochihuas —[2]

Yhua Ca San ixquih niCa nictzonquixtia y noCoCoxCatlanahuatil noMemoria testamentto ymixpa noAlbaSea yhua notestigos inic tlaneltilisque Mostla huiptla Ma y mochihua —
ES.^{no} hipolitto de lo S.^{n}ttos

with white spots, Josef Serrano is to get one and Asencio de Santiago is to get the other, and its [their?] calves are to be left for Casimira; and as to two other cows, Antonia Guadalupe is to get the big one, and my daughter Josefa de la Encarnación is to get the little one; my order is to be carried out and realized. —[2]
And that is all. Here I conclude my sick person's commands, my memorandum of testament, before my executor and my witnesses, so that they will verify it in the future. May it be done. —
Notary Hipólito de los Santos.

[2]Five lines are marked out after this paragraph.

83. Antonia Espinosa, Calimaya, Teopanquiyahuac, 1759
(AGN, Civil 664, exp. 2)

THIS WILL WAS issued exclusively to give instructions about funeral arrangements, since there is no reference at all to any property or heirs. The only person mentioned other than the testator is Antonia's husband, but just as part of her self-introduction. Probably Antonia was a relatively poor, low-status woman, although her second name, Espinosa, strikes one in this context as rare and distinguished, a usual indication of some higher position within society. Another unexpected detail in this situation is related precisely to funeral arrangements. While they are generally standard or even less (for no responsory prayer is mentioned with the mass), the grave in front of an image of Nuestra Señora de la Candelaria stands out as something normally found in testaments of relatively wealthy individuals. Perhaps Antonia's family has some property after all, although she does not own anything personally and therefore nothing is included in her testament.

The low profile of the document continues also as far as the executor and the two personal witnesses are concerned: they all have common names and do not seem to hold any public office. The only one with a title is the fiscal, who represents the church.

Notary Pedro de la Cruz has a fairly standard style and orthography (especially retaining much final *n*), but still with some of the characteristic traits of the eighteenth-century Toluca Valley. In the preamble, note the presence of a bit of punctuation, a traditional feature not often seen this late. In terms of formulas, the will follows the standard of central Calimaya/Tepemaxalco, with mentions of all the relevant saints, much as in the work of Hipólito de los Santos.

[*f.* 68]
Ma senquiscayectenehuallo yn itlazomahuistocatzin yn dios tetatzin. yhuan yn dios ytlazopiltzin. yhuan y dios espirito Santo. Ma yuc mochia Amen. Jesus.
Axcan Martes a 6 de febrero Xihuil de 1759. nican nicpehualtia yn nomemoria testamento – nehual notoca Antonia espinoza. nonamictzin ytoca ynacio fran.^{co} yhuan ca nica nichane ypā yn ialtepetzin S,^{r} S,^{n} Pedro Calimaya. yhuan nica nipoi ypan tlaxilacali teopanquiahuac yhuā niquitoa tla onicnomasehui yn itlazomiquilitzin yn tt,^{o} dios Ca ysemactzinco nicnocahuilia y noyoliantzin y noanimantzin yhuan nicnotlatlactilia ȳ notlazomahuisnantzin la limpia consepsion yhuan S,^{r} Sn Pedro, y S.^{n}

[*f.* 68]
May the precious revered name of God the father, God his precious son, and God the Holy Spirit be entirely praised. May it be done, amen. Jesus.
Today Tuesday the 6th of February of the year of 1759, here I named Antonia Espinosa begin my memorandum of testament; my husband is named Ignacio Francisco, and I am a citizen here in the altepetl of lord San Pedro, Calimaya. I belong to the tlaxilacalli of Teopanquiyahuac here. And I say that when I have attained the precious death of our lord God, I leave my spirit and soul entirely in his hands, and I implore my precious revered mother la Limpia Concepción, lord San Pedro and San Pablo,

Pablo. yhuan yehuatzin S,^{r} S,^{n} Antonio de padua yhuan Sr Sn Miguel Arcangel yhuan y notlazoangeltzin yhuan quexquixtintzitzin Santos. yhuan Santas. yn ilhuicac motemiltiticate ynic nopāpa quimotlatlactilitzinosque yn tt.^{o} dios Ma y mochihua Amen Jesus Maria y Joseph. —
yhuan huel achto niquitoa Ca yntla oninomiquili Ca setel Missa nopan mitos yn ipalehuiloca yes yn noanimantzin neltis notlatol mochihuas —
ynic ontlamantli nitlanahuatia noSepultura motlapos yxpantzinco N,^{a} S,^{a} de la Candelaria, yhuan nictemaca Se tomintzin huentzintli Santo Jerusalen neltis notlatol. yhuan Ca san ixquix nican nictzonquixtia noMemoria testamento ymixpa noalbasea yhuan notestigos [*f. 68v*] ynic tlaneltilisque mostla y huictla noal[. . .] Juan chrisostomo testigo felix Juan oc se test[. . .] Pedro Martin
fiscal Mayor de la Santa yglesia D.^{n} domingo de [. . .] S^{n}tos topile Manuel Joseph
Pedro de la cruz escrivano

lord San Antonio de Padua, lord San Miguel Arcángel, my precious [guardian] angel, and all the male and female saints who fill heaven that they pray for me to our lord God. May it be done, amen. Jesus, Mary, and Joseph. —

First of all I say that when I have died, a mass is to be said for me to be the help of my soul. My statement is to be realized and carried out. —
Second I order that my grave is to be opened in front of Nuestra Señora de la Candelaria, and I give a real as an offering for Holy Jerusalem. My statement is to be realized. That is all. Here I conclude my memorandum of testament before my executor and my witnesses [*f. 68v*] so that they will verify it in the future. My executor is Juan Crisóstomo. Witness, Félix Juan. Another witness, Pedro Martín.
Fiscal mayor of the holy church, don Domingo de los Santos. Topile Manuel Josef.
Pedro de la Cruz, notary.

84. Rosa Francisca, San Pedro Calimaya, Teopanquiyahuac, 1760
(AGN, Civil 664, exp. 2)

IN THIS CASE the testator, a widow, mentions only one heir, her daughter Polonia Teresa, who is probably the only surviving child, or the only one left at home after others got married. Rosa Francisca says that she has nothing, and yet she leaves her daughter the house with the lot and a piece of land, the core of a family property. The answer to the puzzle is that Rosa's late husband only left her in charge of things, with the estate already destined to Polonia Teresa. We have seen many cases in which husbands left such directions, but few in which wives later openly acknowledge them in their own wills. The piece of land is of good size, 5 almudes, but it is said that a neighbor, Pedro Alcántara, has already appropriated an almud and a half; perhaps there had been a quarrel here, or part of the land was sold to him, or given to him to repay a debt. Note the distinguished second name of the neighbor.

As for funeral rituals, Rosa requests a mass, an offering for Jerusalem, burial in the church, and the shroud of the Virgin of Carmen. These arrangements already imply a certain status, but Rosa goes beyond the usual in that she is one of the very few in Calimaya/Tepemaxalco who specifically request a high mass, and she doubles the usual request for a responsory prayer. In view of the not very impressive property and Rosa's declaration of poverty, we must wonder how all this is to be paid for.

Rosa Francisca appoints her compadre, Hipólito Casiano, with a rare second name, as executor; of her two witnesses, one has an ordinary name, while the other from his title of don has probably held a high public office. The current officials of the church so often seen are missing here. The name of Rosa's late husband was undistinguished. The signs are thus somewhat ambiguous.

Pedro Hernández (see p. 42) is the same notary as in No. 43, issued two years later; he is the only known case of someone who officiated as notary in both Tepemaxalco and Calimaya. In No. 43 it is pointed out that his orthography and stock phrases make it certain that the same writer is involved in both cases. Here I can mention another common thread. In the present document he is one of the few to style himself "notary public"; in No. 43 he does the same and to raise his pretensions even higher adds "royal." His style and formulas have already been commented on in the previous testament; here notice the influence from Spanish in the expression "noconpadre motlalia por albasea," "my compadre is established as executor," making very idiomatic use of Spanish *por* in the sense of "as."

[*f. 37*]
Jesus M[. . .]
Axcan lunes ypan yn [. . .] tonati de [. . .][1] de 1760 años Ca nican nictlalia y nomemor[. . .] [. . .]toca Rosa fran^{ca} Viuda Ca nican nochan Santo San pedro calimaya yteh nipohui tlaxilacali yhuan Bario de tiopanquihuac huel ahtopa niconitohua yntla neh[. . .]lizinos yn tt.^{o} Dios y ninomiquilis ca san ymaczinco nicnocahuilia y noyolianzin noanimanzin yhuan senca nicmotlatlactilizinoa yn Sihuapili Santa Maria yhua Señor San pedro yhuan Sr San pablo Señor San Antonio glorioso yhuan San Miguel arcangel Yhuan mochintzinzizin Santos yhuan Santas yn ilhuiCal ytic motemiltizinotiCaten ynic nopan motlatoltizinosque yn ixpan.^{co} yn tt.^{o} Dios ynic momaquixtis noyolianzin noanimanzin = ett^{a}

yhuan yntla tt^{o} Dios nehmoyquilis nimomaSehuis yn itlazomiquiliszin noSepoltura motlapos tiopanCalitic onpa nimotocas yhuan nomortaxa ynic nimoquimilos yehual yn itlaquenzin nuestra S^{a} del Carme = yhuan nictemacatia Se tominzin Santo Jerozalen yhuan nomissa Cantada yCa ome noReponSos nopan mitos ypalehuililoca yes noyolianzin y nanimanzin = Ca neltis notlatol mochihua = Camo tlen nimopielia San niocnotlaCazintli = yxpanzinco noConpadre motlalia por albaSea = yhuan Ca niccahuilitia Se noxpox ytoca polonia teresa quenami tenectiCa ypan ytestamento nonamiczin moesticatca Pedro fran^{co} Conanas noxpox Cali yCa mochi Solar yhuan Se tlali Mantica metepec otli momilSalotica Pedro alcantara = yteh Calaqui MaCuili almo tlaoli xinaxtli Ca Se almo yhuan tlaco San oquimoyax[*f. 37v*]cati yhuan San oquimoquili Pedro alcantara = axca[. . .] Sano oc yey almo yhuan tlaco tlatoctli mili Ca yehua[. . .] Conanas noxpox polonia teresa = huan ca San yxqui[. . .] nican niczonquixtia y nomemoria yn iXpan^{co} noa[. . .]basea y notestigos Ca yehuanti tlaneltilisque yn ixpa[. . .] yn tt^{o} Dios yntla quimochihuilizinosque ca tt.^{o} D.^{s} qui[. . .]tlaxtlahuilizinos = ett^{a}
yPolito casiano albasea Dn Miguel fran^{co} testigo
Julian Antonio testigo
Nehual onitlaquili ytencopa CoCoxqui onextlatlac[. . .]que
Pedro hernandez Ess^{no} pu.^{co}

[*f. 37*]
Jesus, Mary, [and Joseph].
Today Monday on the [. . .] day of [. . .][1] of the year of 1760, here I named Rosa Francisca, widow, issue my memorandum [of testament]; my home is here in holy San Pedro of Calimaya, and I belong to the tlaxilacalli and barrio of Teopanquiyahuac. First of all I say that if our lord God [wishes] that I die, I leave my spirit and soul in his hands, and I greatly implore lady Santa María, lord San Pedro, lord San Pablo, lord San Antonio Glorioso, San Miguel Arcángel, and all the male and female saints who fill heaven to speak for me before our lord God so that my spirit and soul will be redeemed, etc.

And if our lord God should take me and I attain his precious death, my grave is to be opened inside the church building; there I am to be buried. And my shroud in which I am to be wrapped is the habit of Nuestra Señora del Carmen. = And I am giving 1 real for Holy Jerusalem. And a high mass is to be said for me with two responsory prayers, to be the help of my spirit and soul. = My statement is to be realized and carried out. = I have nothing; I am just a poor person before [God?]. = My compadre is established as executor. = And I am leaving to a daughter of mine named Polonia Teresa, as is mentioned in the testament of my late husband Pedro Francisco, and my daughter is to take, the house including the lot and a piece of land on the Metepec road bordering on a cultivated field of Pedro Alcántara, into which 5 almudes of maize seed fit. Pedro Alcántara already just made $1\frac{1}{2}$ almudes his property [*f. 37v*] and took it, and now my daughter Polonia Teresa is likewise to take the other $3\frac{1}{2}$ almudes of cultivated field planted in maize. = That is all. Here I conclude my memorandum in the presence of my executor and my witnesses. They will verify it before our lord God; if they do it our lord God will reward them, etc.
Hipólito Casiano, executor. Don Miguel Francisco, witness. Julián Antonio, witness.
I did the writing at the command of the sick person; they asked me.
Pedro Hernández, notary public.

---

[1] The day is illegible and the month nearly so in my copy; the month may be "Junio," but I cannot be certain.

85. Tomás de la Cruz, San Antonio de Padua, 1717

(AGN, Tierras 2539, exp. 4)[1]

THIS TESTAMENT IS issued by a married man who leaves all his property to his little son, while the wife comes in only to take care of the child and the property, a quite typical situation. Tomás leaves to Mateo Juárez (whose testament will follow as No. 86) the house with the saints and the lot, and also two rather small fields, of 3 and 2 almudes respectively. The testator seems to be truly worried that someone may take advantage of the situation, as is shown through various admonitions. He also appears to be less than confident in his wife Salvadora Juana, urging her not to do things wrong and not to get into disputes. Perhaps this anxiety is caused by the fact that Mateo is still very little.

As for funeral rites, Tomás is very unusual in not requesting a mass, alleging that he is very poor and only asking the father guardian (prior of the Franciscan establishment) to help with two responsory prayers. Nothing is said about burial, shroud or offerings. If we consider the property that he mentions in the will, Tomás does not seem unduly poverty stricken; perhaps, however, he and his family were stripped of cash. To begin to appreciate the situation we need to look ahead to the other two wills in this cluster, Nos. 86 and 87, also done in San Antonio, and observe that in both those cases as well a mass is missing and only a responsory prayer is requested. These do seem to be humble people, but for the same kind of request to occur three times, in the only three examples we have from San Antonio, may mean that we are dealing with some sort of special tlaxilacalli convention. We might think that the mass is implied even if not specifically mentioned, but a Spanish annotation to this testament speaks only of the performance of the responsory prayers, not mentioning a mass, and the same is true in No. 86.

There is no executor, and Tomás presents no special personal witnesses; instead, all four of the witnesses hold some kind of office linked to the church. It is true that three of them share the testator's second name, de la Cruz, but given the commonness of that prominent name, it could be a coincidence. Tomás shows no sign of belonging to the leading de la Cruz lineage, and he has not kept the name even for his son. The son's name Mateo Juárez has some aura of distinction, but less than one might imagine, for this was a set combination like Domingo Ramos; a majority of all men named Juárez had the first name Mateo, and it was not normally inherited. Overall, it seems that the testator is a humble person lacking any special connection with prominent individuals.

Note the rare mention of the Virgin of Rosario, who is not much seen in the corpus. She may have been especially prominent for this family and even in this tlaxilacalli as a whole, for in No. 87, issued by the testator's brother, we find a cofradía of the Virgin of Rosario mentioned.

Notary Diego Martín writes in a quite standard style, which is still relatively common in the early years of the eighteenth century, but he displays some signs of conservatism unusual even considering the date. Not only does he use the older fashion of indicating entries; several of the formulas of the preamble hark back to an earlier time. Most especially, Diego Martín does not join the by this time nearly universal trend to call a man's wife his *-cihuahuatzin*, his "woman or wife," but uses the older *-namictzin*, "spouse." But not everything is archaism. In *doctrina* for the larger parish this notary uses a quite rare loanword. He even gives us an example of the popular loan verb *cruzaroa*, "to cross."

[*f. 1*]
Jesus maria y Jocephe —
nicnoneltoquitia y dios tetatzi y dios tepiltzi yhua dios espiritu santo ma i mochihua ma iuhqui quimactieca yn aquique quitasque ynin amal nicchihua axca miercoles a 4 dias del mes de agosto de 1717 año niccentlalia y notestameto nehual notoca Tho-

[*f. 1*]
Jesus, Mary, and Joseph.
I believe in God the father, God the son, and God the Holy Spirit; may it be done. Let those who should see this document know that I am making it today, Wednesday, the 4th day of the month of August of the year of 1717. I named Tomás de la Cruz, married

[1]The testament is accompanied by a contemporary Spanish translation.

mas de la Crus ninamiqui ynahuac nonamictzi Salbadora Ju^{o}na nica notlaxilaCalpa San^{to} Sa^{n} Anio de padua yhua nodotrina Santo San pedro y San pablo Calimaya macihui Ca moCoCotiCa y notlalo nosoquio ahu i noyolia y nanimatzi Ca amo que Ca Ca san huel pactica auh ytla iuhqui nopa mochihuas ytla onicnomasehui yn itlaSomiquilitzi y noteotzi y notlathoCatzi y tt^{o} dios Ca huel senca nicnotlatlauhtilitzinohua y notlasomahuisnatzi y Santa maria del Rosario ynic nopapa quimotlatlauhtilitzinos yn itlasomahuisconetzi y tt^{o} Jesu Xpo ynic quimoselilis y noyolia y nanimatzi ynic quimohuiquilis yn itlathocachatzCo yn ilhuiCatl itic ynic onpa quimoyectenehuilis yn itlasomahuistocatzi ma y mochihua e^{ta} —

to my spouse Salvadora Juana, fully issue my testament here in my tlaxilacalli of holy San Antonio de Padua, and my parish is that of holy San Pedro and San Pablo of Calimaya. Although my earthly body is ill, nothing is wrong with my spirit and soul, but it is very sound. If it should happen to me that I have attained the precious death of my deity and ruler our lord God, I very greatly implore my precious revered mother Santa María del Rosario to pray on my behalf to her precious revered child our lord Jesus Christ to receive my spirit and soul and take it to his royal home in heaven to praise there his precious revered name. May it be done, etc. —

v ynic cetlamatli niquitohua nitlanahua yn ipalehuiloCa y noyolia y nanimatzi yc nechmopalehuilis y padre guardia ome Responsos Ca sa nimotolinia Ca amo tle nicnopielia —

v First I say that I order that as the help of my spirit and soul the father guardian is to help me with two responsory prayers, for I am poor and have nothing. —

v ynic otlamatli niquitohua nitlanahuatia y nocha nocalitic yhua santoti Ca yehual nicauhtias y notelpochto ytoca matheo Ju^{o}res quimoCuitlahuis yn cali yhua solar amo aqui quixtoquilis quemania yhua ynatzi quihuapahuas amo tlatlacos amo tle yes tlatoli yhua Ca nipie nomil matica huei otli quistica quaxoxtenco Calaqui tlaoli yei almo Ca niccahuilitia y notelpochto mateo Ju^{o}res yc tequipanos yhua se matica nomil Canpa moCrusadohua otli yc quaxoxtenco Calaqui tlaoli ome almo Ca sano yehual [*f. 1v*] ynemac mateo Ju^{o}res amo aqui quixtoquilis quemania ca chicahuaties y notenahuatil amo aqui qui[. . .]Cos Ca san ixqui y nocnotlatlaol Ca ye nictzonquixtia amo aqui quixitinis y notlanahuatil ca chicahuaties Ca yc ymixpa y notestigoshua Ca nican c[. . .]te y notestigos Don bernaldino de la Crus fiscal d[. . .] Santa yglesia Josep de la Crus teopa nemi marti gimenes teopa nemi antonio de la Crus themachti

v Second I say that I order that in my home, inside my house, with the saints, I am leaving my little son named Mateo Juárez. He is to take care of the house and the lot. No one is ever to claim it from him. And his mother is to raise him; she is not to do things wrong, there are to be no disputes [or suits]. And I have a cultivated field that comes out at the highway, along the border [or at Quaxochtenco], in which 3 almudes of maize fit; I am leaving it to my little son Mateo Juárez to work it. And there is a cultivated field of mine where the roads cross along the border [or at Quaxochtenco], in which 2 almudes of maize fit; that is likewise [*f. 1v*] the inheritance of Mateo Juárez. No one is ever to claim it from him, for my order is to be valid; no one is to act aggrieved over it. That is all of my humble statement, which I now conclude. No one is to undo my commands; they are to be valid. It [is done] before my witnesses; here are my witnesses: don Bernardino de la Cruz, fiscal of the holy church; Josef de la Cruz, who works at the church; Martín Jiménez, who works at the church; Antonio de la Cruz, temachti.

diego marti esno de rrepubliCa

Diego Martín, notary of the commonwealth.

86. Mateo Juárez, San Antonio de Padua, 1733

(AGN, Tierras 2539, exp. 4)[1]

FOLLOWING THE LINES of his father's testament (No. 85), Mateo Juárez leaves all his property to his little son, Hipólito Mateo, this time without mentioning any wife, so we do not know whether he is a

[1]The testament is accompanied by a contemporary Spanish translation.

widower or not. It is interesting to see that the testator passes on to his son the same house that he had inherited from his late father, and maybe also the same saints, although we cannot be sure, since the saints are not indicated by name in No 85. There is also a little field, no doubt one of the two that Tomás de la Cruz left to Mateo in 1717. It seems to be the smaller one of 2 almudes, since in both cases the field is said to be where roads cross; no clues are given about the other one in Tomás's will, of 3 almudes.

The similarity between the two wills is even more striking in terms of the funeral arrangements, since Mateo requests only a responsory prayer, nothing else, just like his father Tomás (although the latter asked for two of them). As was speculated there, perhaps it is a characteristic of the family or a common practice of the tlaxilacalli. Yet in this case even more than the other one, the testator seems genuinely poor.

Mateo also follows his father in not appointing any executor, and in having only witnesses who hold some church office (apparently including don Francisco de Santiago, though it is not explicit). Thus we are left not knowing whether they are connected with the testator or not. In any case, all the witnesses bear the title don and important second names such as de la Cruz and de Santiago. The second name Jiménez, present in the name of a church official in No. 85, is found here in the notary's name. As already pointed out in Tomás's will, the name of the testator here, though quite rare, was a set combination, so the Juárez is not passed on to his son, while the name Mateo is repeated, so that here the third generation has the least distinguished name.

Besides having an unusual and relatively high-status second name, the notary here also bears the title don. Don Bernardino Jiménez generally has a regular style, following traditional Nahuatl orthography, but there are also various misspellings and repetitions. At times he seems even more conservative than notary Diego Martín, of No. 85, for instance in avoiding the Spanish loan verb *cruzaroa*, "to cross," and using instead the pure Nahuatl *nepanoa*. He is also the only writer in the corpus to use the old term *teopantlacatl*, literally "church person," for a member of the indigenous church staff. Broadly speaking, the formulas in both testaments are very similar, probably reflecting local usage.

In both cases *doctrina* is used instead of *altepetl* to refer to the larger Calimaya/Tepemaxalco context. In a confusing formulation, here San Antonio seems to be called both an altepetl and a tlaxilacalli, the same ambivalence we saw with the outlying tlaxilacalli of Tepemaxalco, Santa María de la Asunción and San Lucas.

[*f. 5*]

Jesus maria Josepeh

yCa in itlasomahuistoCatzin y dios tetatzin y dios tepiltzin y dios espirito Santo ma y mochihua – ma mochitin – quimatinCa yn aquique quitasque ynin amal – nehuatl – notestameto – mateo Ju^{o}re[s] – niCa notlaxilaCalpa ypa yn ialtepetzin Sãto San atonio de padua yhua nodotrina Sato Sa pedro y Sa pablo Calimaya yhua [n]icnoSeneltoquitia y Sa huel neli teol dios y dios tetatzin y dios espirito Santo yhuan yn ixq̃[. . .] y quimoneltoquimoneltoquitia y tonatzin Santa ygleCia CantoliCa romana – yhua nicnotlaltactinli[. . .] y notlaSomahuiSnatzin y Santa maria mochipa huel neli ychpoctli – ynic quimotlatlactilitzinnoS yn itlaSomahuisSeteConetzin y t^{o} Jesus x^{o} ynic – nechmotlapopolhuililis – y notlatlaCol y notlapilchihual yhua noyoliatzin y nanimatzin Ca ySemactzinCo – noCotlalia – Ca noteotzin – Ca notlatoCantzin dios auh Ca opa quimo-

[*f. 5*]

Jesus, Mary, and Joseph.

In the precious revered name of God the father, God the son, and God the Holy Spirit, may it be done. – Let all who should see this document know that it is the testament of me, Mateo Juárez, that my tlaxilacalli is here in the altepetl of holy San Antonio de Padua, and my parish is that of holy San Pedro and San Pablo Calimaya. And I believe entirely in the very true deity God, God the father, God the Holy Spirit, and in all that our mother the holy Catholic Roman church believes. And I implore my precious revered mother Santa María, eternally very true virgin, to pray to her precious revered only child our lord Jesus Christ to forgive me my sins and evildoing. And I place my spirit and soul entirely in his hands, for he is my deity and ruler God, and he is to take it to his royal home in heaven, where it will eternally praise him along with all the male and

huiquilis yn itlatoCachatzinCo yn ilhuiCactl itic yn opa SemiCac quimoyêtenelis yhua ynn ixquichtin Santome y Santame – ma y mochihua –

— auh ynic Setlamatli y nitlanahuatia ytla nicnomaSehui yn itlaSomahuismiquilitzin y noteotzin – Can notlatoCatzin y dios yn ipalehuiloCa y noyolia y nanimatzin – Setel respoSoS – Ca huel Seca ninotolini[. . .]

YnicC otlamatli nitlanahua[. . .] dios quimochiCahuilia y notelpochto ytoC[. . .]to[2] mateo Ca yehuatl – nicnematia – nocha yno hu[. . .]Cali yn onech[no?]moCahuilitia y notlaSomahuis[. . .]in[3] – Ca yehua[. . .] quimotequipanilhuiS yehua y [. . .]tlaSomahuiSnatzin de guadalupe – yhua pad[. . .]an atonio de padua – amo aqui qixtoquililis quemania Ca no yhua Se miltotli – mani Capa monepanohua otli yc tiya[. . .] Calima – amo aquixtoquilis Ca huel chiCahuaties notenahua [*f. 5v*]

— auh Can San ixquich – niCa nictzoqūxtia y notzoquis[. . .]tenahuatil y nehuatl y niCoCos notoCa mateon ymixpatzin – notestingo — don atonio de la cruz fisCal S[. . .]leCia do fra^{co}sisco de Satiago do Berna[. . .]no ximenes esno do felipeh de S[. . .]tiago teopatlaCa

axCa lunes [9] dias del mes de marSo de 1733 años[4]

female saints. May it be done. —

— First I order that when I have attained the precious revered death of my deity and ruler God, the help of my spirit and soul is a responsory prayer, for I am very poor indeed.

Second I order that [if] God gives life to my little son named [Hipólito][2] Mateo, to him I bequeath my home, which is the [old, patrimonial] house that my precious revered [father][3] left me; he is to serve [my] precious revered mother de Guadalupe and [the patron?] San Antonio de Padua. No one is ever to claim it from him. And in addition [I give him] a little cultivated field where the roads join as we go to Calimaya. No one is to claim it from him; my command is to have full force. [*f. 5v*]

— That is all. Here I the sick person named Mateo conclude my final commands before my witnesses, don Antonio de la Cruz, fiscal of the holy church; don Francisco de Santiago; don Bernardino Jiménez, notary; don Felipe de Santiago, church attendant.

Today, Monday the 9th day of the month of March of the year of 1733.[4]

[2]The name Hipólito is not clear in the Nahuatl, but is readable in the Spanish translation.
[3]Again, the term "father" is readable only in the Spanish translation.
[4]An annotation in Spanish reports that a responsory prayer was in fact said.

87. Pablo Joaquín, San Antonio de Padua, 1737

(AGN, Tierras 2539, exp. 4)[1]

IN THE THIRD testament of this cluster (including No. 85 by the testator's brother Tomás de la Cruz and 86 by his nephew), Pablo Joaquín leaves all the property mentioned in the will to his two sons. Such is apparently his intention even though he calls only one son by name, Antonio de la Cruz, probably the elder, and leaves him a field of 4 almudes. (Here we see the name de la Cruz reappearing in the line even though it does not seem dominant.) Pablo also says that there is another field of his that he had given to his brother Tomás for a while to help feed him, and now that he is dead the field should be passed on to his children, seeming to mean the two sons, since no other children are mentioned. This would likely be the field of 3 almudes mentioned by Tomás in his 1717 will but not in the possession of his son Mateo (No. 86) in 1733. Yet we have nothing conclusive to indicate that the other field is the same one that Pablo is now claiming, nor what the status of the field of 3 almudes has been in the meantime. In any case, the field lent to Tomás has not returned firmly to the custody of Pablo, and one can sense controversy.

Thus once again we have a man who is not wealthy (no house or other kinds of property are mentioned, and the amount of land is small) and who leaves what land there is to a son. The pattern is similar in all the testaments of this cluster. And as in No. 86, the testator says nothing about his marital status. Pablo follows his relatives also as far as funeral arrangements are concerned; he too requests only a responsory prayer, with the help of the priest, while no indication is given of mass, burial and shroud.

[1]The testament is accompanied by a contemporary Spanish translation.

As in Nos. 85 and 86, no executor is appointed, but when it comes to the witnesses (all bearing the title don), the situation is different. While there is again someone linked to the church, the fiscal, Pablo includes also two men with high municipal offices, not only an alcalde but the governor, the latter occupying a very distinguished and influential position. The presence of the governor raises questions. Traditionally there was only one governor for all Calimaya, located in the central settlement and not likely to be in such a place as San Antonio. Could it be that San Antonio, a large settlement which in these years built a sumptuous church for itself, already had its own governor?

The notary Gregorio Juan has an unexpected and puzzling additional name, apparently Colidris, and is listed as affiliated not with the church or the municipality but with the cofradía of Nuestra Señora del Rosario (see comments in No. 85 on the Virgin of Rosario); this is the only case in the corpus of a notary stating that he works for a confraternity. The style is quite conservative, yet with some traits that recall eighteenth-century Toluca Nahuatl. Note again the presence of the loan verb *cruzaroa*, "to cross," as well as the particle *para*, "for, in order to." Formulas are very similar in this whole cluster; in particular, the opening formula of this testament closely recalls that of No. 85.

[*f. 14*]

Jesus ma,^{a}y Joseph

nicnoneltoquitia Y Dios tetatzin y Dios tepiltzin dios Espiritu santo ma y moChihua ma iuhqui quimatiCa yn aquique quictasque yni amal nicChihua nomemoria testamento axCa Juebes a 8 dias del mes de Junio de 1737 anõs notoCa pablo Juachin niCa nichane altepel notlaxilaCalpa santo san atonio de padua nudotrina S^{n} pedro S^{n} Pablo Calimaya Ca huel senCa moCoCotiCa y notlalo y nosoquio auh y noioliatzin aque Ca ca sa huel pactiCa yCatzinCo tt.^{o} dios yhua Ca nicnoneltoquitia y tonatzin S^{n}tta yglesia CatoliCa romana ypan tlaneltoquilistli ninomiquilis = auh ytla ycqui onicnomasehui yn itlasomiquilitzin y tt^{o}Jesus topo Ca huel senCa niquinotlactilia y santome yhua y santame yn opa yn ilhuiCa motemiltiCate ynic nopapa quimotlatlactilisque y tt^{o} Dios ynic quimohuiquilis yn ilhuiCa y noyoliatzin y nanimatzin ma y nochihua e^{ta} —

yNic sentlamatli niquitohua ytla onicnomasehui ytlasomiquilitzin tt.^{o} dios sentel Resposos yPalehuilo y noyolia y nanimatzin yc nehmopalehuilis y noteopixCatzin =

ynicC ontlamatli niquitohua yhua nitlanahuatia Ca nicpie se nomil mani Canpa moCrosaroa otli yc Calimaya yatiCa otli Calaqui xinahtli nahui almo Ca niquipie ometi notelpoxhua se ytoCa Antonio de la Crus Ca yehuatl nicCahuilia amo aquiquihtoquilis quemania Ca huel chicactiyes notenahuatil aya quitlaCos mostla huitla

ynic yetlamatli niquitohua yhua nitlanahuatia noermano tomas de la Crus Ca onicmaCa se pedaso tlali nomil para tlaquas quesqui tonali auh yn axCa Ca y omomiquili noermano tomas quiCahuasque mili pa-

[*f. 14*]

Jesus, Mary, and Joseph.

I believe in God the father, God the son, and God the Holy Spirit; may it be done. Let those who should see this document know that I named Pablo Joaquín make my memorandum of testament today, Thursday the 8th day of the month of June of the year of 1737. I am a citizen here in the altepetl and in my tlaxilacalli of holy San Antonio de Padua; my parish is San Pedro and San Pablo Calimaya. My earthly body is very ill indeed, but there is nothing wrong with my spirit, but it is very sound through our lord God. And I believe in our mother the holy Roman Catholic church; in [this] belief I will die. = And when I have attained the precious death of our lord Jesus Christ, I very greatly implore the male and female saints who fill heaven to pray on my behalf to our lord God to take my spirit and soul to heaven. May it be done, etc. —

First I say that when I have attained the precious death of our lord God, a responsory prayer is the help of my spirit and soul; my priest will help me with it. =

Second I say and order that I have a cultivated field where the roads cross on the road going to Calimaya, in which 4 almudes of seed fit, and I have two sons. One is named Antonio de la Cruz, and to him I leave it. No one is ever to claim it from him, for my command is to have full force and no one is to violate it in the future.

Third I say and order that I gave to my brother Tomás de la Cruz a piece of land, my cultivated field, for his sustenance for a while, and now, when my brother Tomás has died, they are to relinquish the

ra nopilhua ano aqui tle quitos quemania Ca huel chiCactiyes Y notenahuatl Ca ye ixquih Ca nictzoquihtia y noCoxCatlatol Ca chiCactiyes y notenahuitl Ca ye ymixpa testigos D^{n} andres miguel gouernador D^{n} ramos de la Cruz alCalde fisCal de la santa yglesia Dn Manuel ramos

nehuatl onitlaCuilo yteCopa Cocoxqui Gregorio [*f. 14v*] Juan [y colidris] Es.^{no} de la Cofradia de N.^{ra} S^{ra} del [. . .][2]

cultivated field for my children. No one is ever to say anything in this case either; my command is to be in full force. That is all. I conclude my sick person's statement; my command is to be valid. In the presence of the witnesses don Andrés Miguel, governor; don Ramos de la Cruz, alcalde; don Manuel Ramos, fiscal of the holy church.

I did the writing at the command of the sick person, Gregorio [*f. 14v*] Juan [y Colidris ?], notary of the cofradía of Nuestra Señora del Rosario.[2]

[2]The Spanish translation has "del Rosario" here, and something equivalent must once have been in the Nahuatl original, though now it is missing.

88. Antonio de la Cruz, Santa María Nativitas, 1678
(AGN, Civil 664, exp. 2)

BEING ONE OF THE EARLIER testaments in the corpus, the will of Antonio de la Cruz like the others of its time deserves especially close examination. As in other such cases, an older style of punctuation and indication of paragraphs is still prevalent here. Final consonants are better preserved than they would be later, but the *s* of Stage 3 has already taken over from the older final *z*. The old term *teiccauh*, the younger sibling of a male, of either gender, appears here rather than the *hermano/hermana* usually seen in later times. The formula of the preamble varies a bit from later; rarely in Toluca Valley texts of the eighteenth century would one see mention of "the children of God, the cantors."

Antonio de la Cruz does not seem to be a person of wealth. The assets he lists are: a lot, a saint's image, two fields he calls small, and another lot hocked to someone else and not yet redeemed. From a later passing reference it is clear that Antonio has a house on the first lot, making his estate quite respectable, and yet no house is mentioned in the bequest, apparently through the notable negligence of this particular notary, Francisco de la Cruz. There are two heirs and another person for whom the testator assumes responsibility, but the notary does not specify the relation between the testator and any one of the three. Nevertheless, it appears that Josef is the elder of two sons, Pascual the younger. The first bequest seems to go primarily to Josef, but Pascual is included too, and all other bequests go to the two of them. A girl named Antonia (possibly named after the testator) is likely their younger sister. Perhaps she is a mere infant, for she receives nothing, although she is to be raised in the house with the boys, who must be small themselves. The testator, using the verb *tlaelitta*, says that neither Pascual nor Antonia are to be abhorred—to be looked down upon, viewed with anger or disgust—apparently meaning here in effect that they are not to be neglected in favor of the first born.

The mother would be the natural person to raise the children, but Antonio does not mention her, and so it is likely that his wife has died, perhaps when Antonia was born. In the body of the will it is not specified who is to do the bringing up except that it is more than one person, likely the two executors who are mentioned in the witness list. As an addendum Antonio says that a Bartolomé de San Juan, perhaps a relative though again nothing is said, is to raise Pascual specifically.

It is hard to judge the funeral arrangements as a symptom of Antonio's status, for they may say more about the time than about the testator. An offering of 2 reales goes to the cantors and another of one real for the grave site—features of funerals that probably continued in the eighteenth century as a practice but are rarely mentioned in the testaments of that time. The statement about the shroud proclaims humility and poverty but may not be intended literally. A mass for the testator is not even mentioned, apparently being taken for granted as a benefit to be provided by Antonio's cofradía. For later years mentions of a cofradía providing such help are extremely rare and may be associated with testators in great need. In this earlier time the cofradías may have been more prominent in supplying death benefits to their members. The formulas of the preamble are rudimentary, but that may have been the normal style of this seventeenth-century notary. Thus we cannot with certainty deduce much about Antonio from the funeral arrangements.

Since he is a "de la Cruz" in Calimaya/Tepemaxalco, where so many prominent people had that name, Antonio may be well connected. No less than three witnesses are also de la Cruz, including the fiscal (titled don), the notary, and an executor; the fiscal has the same name as Antonio except for the don, which he would only have acquired recently. We are justified in assuming that our Antonio is somehow related to the others. Two people with the name de San Juan are also present, one with a lower office and one entrusted with raising one of Antonio's children; these too must be somehow connected with him. The person with whom he hocked the land, María Pérez, has a name tending to indicate that she either has high status within the indigenous community or is Spanish or of mixed descent. But despite his good connections, Antonio seems never to have held high office, owns quite little property, and is in economic straits, as shown by the unredeemed land, so his present status must be hardly above the average. His children, perhaps because small, are not called by a second name in the will, so we do not know whether or not they would later continue to proclaim the de la Cruz affiliation.

Francisco de la Cruz the notary is competent in his orthography, quite typical of his time, but he often leaves out words necessary to the sense and, more seriously, omits much crucial information virtually always included in a testament. An interesting passage toward the beginning of the will leaves us wondering if it is an example of his confusion about formulas or represents a special indigenous understanding of an aspect of Christianity. It is normal that he considers death to be bestowed by God (using the euphemism *icnelia*, "to befriend someone"), but he proceeds to include the Virgin Mary as also bestowing death. This passage could be taken to have the implication of a continuation of the indigenous tradition of equal and complementary male/female gods as opposed to the Christian concept of one all-powerful God, while the Virgin, for all her importance in the scheme, is merely a human saint and not part of the deity. We cannot forget, however, that these words are just as likely the product of a notary who is not in complete control of the formulas or who is distracted at the moment. (For similar cases see Nos. 88 and 93.)

For the evidence that Santa María Nativitas belongs to Calimaya/Tepemaxalco, see No. 89.

[*f. 56*]

Jesus Ma[a] y Juseph a 21 Julio de 1678 años

v Yn ica yn itocatzin, y dios tetantzin dios tepiltzin dios epu[to] ma y mochihua. niCan nicpehualtia y nomemoria testanmeto, nehuatl notoCan. atonio de la Cruz nica nichane. Sata ma.[a] natibitas. ytla onechmocnelilitzino. y notlaçotatzin. y dios. ytla onechmocnelilitzino y notlaçomahuiznatzin Can ytech. nipohui. y cofradia[1] ca nitlaoColilos – yhua niquitohua. noquimiliuhca notzotzoma.[2] nichuicas – neltis notlatol – y dios. yn ipilhuantzitzin. cantores. huetzintli. ome tomitzin. macosque. yhua nosepoltura. huetzitli. Se tomi. neltis notlatol, mochihuas. yhua niquitohua. niCahuilia. Setetl Solar ytoCan. Juseph.

[*f. 56*]

Jesus, Mary, and Joseph. On the 21st of July of the year of 1678.

v In the name of God the father, God the son, and God the Holy Spirit, may it be done. Here I named Antonio de la Cruz, citizen here in Santa María Nativitas, begin my memorandum of testament. When my precious father God has befriended me [brought about my death] and my precious revered mother has befriended me, I belong to the cofradía[1] and am to be favored [with the funeral benefits of the cofradía]. And I say that as my shroud I am to wear my rags.[2] My statement is to be realized. The children of God the cantors are to be given an offering of 2 reales, and the offering for my grave is 1 real. My statement is to be realized and carried out. And I say that

[1]The cofradía seems unnamed; perhaps there is only one in the tlaxilacalli, which might be dedicated to Santa María Nativitas. Perhaps "y cofradia," "the cofradía," should be "ycofradia," "her cofradía," that of Santa María.

[2]The normal name for worn-out clothing, rags, was *tzotzomatli*. When possessed, however, it could be a derogatory way of referring to one's everyday clothing. Thus the meaning here could be either that the testator will literally be buried in rags as a gesture of humility, or that he would wear ordinary clothing.

yhua pasqual. ca oca mohuapahuasque yn itecauh.[3] ca onechmacac Jues de la Cueta yhuan ocan onechitac. neltis notlatol. yhua yni quichinhuasque nepapa tequitl.[4] yhua Setetl miltontli tlapechco. calbariotitlan. yhua Se San FraSisco. Setetl miltotli ynic quichihuazque. tequitl. neltis notlatol. y mostla huiptla. yac quimixtoquilis. neltis notlatol mochihuas. yhua niquitohua. Setetl Solar. preda. onicauh San ixquich matlactomi. ycha maria peres neltis notlatol mochihuas yhua niquitohua ytoca atonian ocan mohuapasque. yn itic caltzintli. ayac quitlayelitas neltis notlatol. San ixquich nictzoquixtia y notestameto. nehuatl notoCa. atonio de la Cruz mochi tlacatl. ymixpa – don atonio de la Cruz. fiscal v nicolas de S Jua diputado – pe^{o} locas alBasea v fran^{co} de la Cruz es^{no} pablo de la Cruz alBasia [*f. 56v*]

I leave a lot to the one named Josef along with Pascual; he and his younger sibling are to be raised there.[3] The judge of accounts gave it to me and saw me there [inspected the place with me there?]. My statement is to be realized. And [it is] so that they will do the various duties.[4] And [I leave them] a little cultivated field at Tlapechco, at Calvariotitlan [or next to the Calvary]. And [I give them] a San Francisco. [I give them] the little cultivated field to do the duties. My statement is to be realized in the future. No one is to claim it from them; my statement is to be realized and carried out. And I say that I left a lot in hock for only 10 reales at the home of María Pérez [she gave me 10 reales and has the field in keeping]. My statement is to be carried out and realized. And I say that the one named Antonia is to be raised in the house with the others. No one is to abhor [neglect] her. My statement is to be realized. That is all. I named Antonio de la Cruz conclude my testament in the presence of everyone: don Antonio de la Cruz, fiscal; Nicolás de San Juan, diputado; Pedro Lucas, executor; Francisco de la Cruz, notary; Pablo de la Cruz, executor. [*f. 56v*]

v yhua niquitohua. ytocan pasqual quihuapahuas bartolome de S Jua, amo quitlayelitas y mostla huiptla. neltis mochihuas notlatol —

v And I say that Bartolomé de San Juan is to raise the one named Pascual; he is not to abhor him in the future. My statement is to be realized and carried out. —

[3]The translation here reflects the text as it is written. But if we consider how frequently *n* is omitted in the corpus, "yn itecauh" could be intended as having a plural possessive prefix. The meaning would then be: they and their younger sibling are to be raised there. The younger sibling might be the Antonia mentioned below.

[4]As in other documents in the corpus, doubt remains whether tribute duties are meant or just the tasks involved in cultivation. The same problem occurs again a few lines below. I take it that this is the same field just mentioned.

89. José de Alcántara, Santa María Nativitas, 1737

(AGN, Civil 664, exp. 2)

WE HAVE SEEN in the examples of San Lucas Evangelista and Santa María de la Asunción that in the Calimaya/Tepemaxalco complex, those tlaxilacalli which were outlying, distant from the core settlement cluster of the paired altepetl, tended in their documents not to mention the altepetl to which they belonged. Indeed, by the eighteenth century they often used the term *altepetl* for themselves, and that happens in this very document. It can thus be difficult to discover their affiliation. In five of the six testaments from Santa María Nativitas included in this volume, there is no clue that it belongs to Calimaya/Tepemaxalco, other than the fact that all six are found in AGN, Civil 664, exp. 2, which contains a major cache of testaments from Tepemaxalco and Calimaya. With the present document there are two different kinds of evidence. First is the fact that in the Spanish dossier in which this testament is included, Santa María Nativitas is stated to be in Calimaya parish (meaning the combined parish of both altepetl). Second is internal evidence. The testator here has a brother who is a resident or citizen of San Antonio de Padua (San Antonio la Isla), a major outlying Calimaya tlaxilacalli, and he leaves to him a piece of land located in a third such entity, San Miguel. All three tlaxilacalli must then be located in close proximity.

Since San Antonio belongs to Calimaya and a seventeenth-century tribute document gives a relatively complete understanding of the tlaxilacalli of

Tepemaxalco, at least as of that date, with no Santa María Nativitas included there, the likelihood is great that the latter belongs to Calimaya.[1] Yet since one Tepemaxalco tlaxilacalli has been identified that is not in the tribute book (San Juan Bautista Yancuictlalpan), the assignment to Calimaya cannot be considered definitive. For the time being I simply consider Santa María to belong to one of the two altepetl or the other.

The present testament is an unusual document. Although it begins with a quite well developed preamble full of traditional phrases, all the rest concerns a piece of land the testator has hocked and now leaves to his brother. No mass or offerings are mentioned, no other heirs or relatives, no executor, not even witnesses other than the notary. The testament seems to have been made either in haste or entirely for the special purpose of dealing with this single piece of land. The conclusions that one draws in somewhat similar cases—that the testator is poverty stricken, cannot afford a mass, has no other property or relatives—may not be justified here. The name Alcántara is quite rare and prestigious within the indigenous context; Luna, the second name of the brother, also has connotations of standing. Either could well be the surname of a Spaniard and even in that context would have a better tone than patronymics such as Hernández. The order or request to the brother to provide candles annually sounds as though the testator had been accustomed to use the land to support religious donations, something usually done by the relatively well off. Yet in a case where the only property mentioned has already been hocked, a traditional sign of economic trouble, one cannot draw any optimistic conclusions about the testator.

The notary Juan Antonio de Santiago, whose three-element name is quite pretentious, displays a mixture of standard and characteristic Toluca Valley traits (especially *c* for *uh*) in his writing, with an oddity or two such as writing "San" as "Can." It is worth noticing that although the beginning of this testament is not identical to that of No. 88, done in Santa María Nativitas in 1678, a general similarity can be observed after almost sixty years.

[*f. 65*]

gesus Maria y gosphe

ninononeltoquitia yn dios tetatzin yn dios tepiltzin yhuan dios espiritu santo yc yeyntzitzin personas can se uel neli teol dio ma y mochihua aCa martes a Catorse de mayo de mil seteCientos y treynta y ciete años niCan nicchihua notestamento nehual notoCa gose[2] de alcantara nichane ypa yn ialtepetzin notlasomahuisnantzi santa maria natibitas masihui mocohua yn notlalyo nosoquio ac yn noyolia yn nanimantzin aque Ca Ca san huel pacticCa yhuan tla yocqui quimonequiltitzinos yn noteotzin yn notlatoCatzin nicnomasehuis yn itlasomiquilictzin Ca huel cenca nicmotlatlactilia yn noteotzin y notlatocatzin yn dios ynic quimoselilis yn noyolia y nanimantzin ynic quimohuiquilis yn itlatocachantzinco ynic onpa quimoyectenehuilis en nonbre gesus maria y gose —

ynic centlamantli niquitohua yhuan nitlanahuatia noermo roque de luna chane ypa yn ialtepetzin S.^r

[*f. 65*]

Jesus, Mary, and Joseph.

I believe in God the father, God the son, and God the Holy Spirit, three persons but one very true deity God; may it be done. Today Tuesday the 14th of May of the year of 1737, here I named José[2] de Alcántara, citizen in the altepetl of my precious revered mother Santa María Nativitas, make my testament. Although my earthly body is sick, nothing is wrong with my spirit and soul, but it is very sound. If my deity and ruler should desire that I attain his precious death, I very greatly implore my deity and ruler God to accept my spirit and soul to take it to his royal home so that there it will praise him. In the name of Jesus, Mary, and Joseph. —

First I say and order that I leave to my brother Roque de Luna, citizen in the altepetl of lord San

[1]The fact that San Miguel is also not found in the Tepemaxalco tribute lists leads one, as with Santa María Nativitas, to speculate that it belongs to Calimaya. Note that Santa María, San Miguel, and San Antonio are all called altepetl in the text of the testament.

[2]In the corpus in general this name appears with final *phe, pe, p*, or *ph*. It is clear that the modern "José" was not yet common. In the present case, possibly there was an unwritten weak consonant at the end, but since the word appears twice as "gose," I use José in the translation. A few other examples of the name with no final consonant occur in the corpus.

Can antonio de padua nicCahuilia Ce tlali mani onpa ypa yn ialtepetzin Sr Can migel mani xolaltenco[3] quimopielia prenda don leonardo yntla oquitlami xihuil ma niman quicahuili no yhuan nitlanahuatia noermano roque de luna quitemaCatias censexihuil Se libra Cera ypan teocali[4] chicahuaties yn notenahuatil amo aquin quitlaCos mostla huictla ca san ixquix ye nictzonquixtia yn nocoxcatlatol yxpa testigo es̃no de republica Juan antonio de santiago

Antonio de Padua, a piece of land that is in the altepetl of lord San Miguel and that is at the edge of the lots.[3] Don Leonardo has it in hock; when he has completed a year let him relinquish it to [my brother]. I also order that my brother Roque de Luna is to go along providing a pound of wax candles every year for the temple.[4] My order is to be enforced; no one is to violate it in the future. That is all. I conclude my sick person's statement before the witness, the notary of the commonwealth Juan Antonio de Santiago.

---

[3]That is, apparently, at the edge of the nucleated settlement, a meaning that words with *xolal* can have today.

[4]The most frequent Nahuatl word for church came to be *teopan*, but *teocalli* always continued in use as well to some extent. It can mean a chapel as opposed to a full-scale church, and it can even refer to a devotional building in a private residence of the type earlier called *santocalli*, "saint-house." At other times, however, it is fully synonymous with *teopan* and is applied to any kind of church. The meaning here cannot be determined more precisely.

90. Antonia María, Santa María Nativitas, 1759

(AGN, Civil 664, exp. 2)

THE PRESENT DOCUMENT is the first of a series of four brief testaments from Santa María Nativitas, all issued by women and done primarily to specify arrangements for a mass. That so many come from the same place at close to the same time implies that at some level a local policy was formed at this time to put these matters in writing, which in turn implies that in other entities at other times many women who had little personal property at death may have had a mass said for them by relatives without making any formal testament.

In this case Antonia María explicitly proclaims her poverty and lack of property. The statement does not necessarily seem to apply to her husband, however, who is asked to arrange a mass and responsory prayer for her.

The orthography of the notary Agustín Matías falls well within the range of Tolucan documents of the time; he is one of those who often write *h* for standard *ch*. One unusual form does appear here, *imatitlantzinco* for the expected *imactzinco*, both meaning "in the hands of (God)." Even this abbreviated document begins in a way familiar from previous testaments issued in Santa María Nativitas.

[*f. 30*]

Jesus M,[a] hi Joseph yca ytocatzin y tentatzin y tepiltzin Dios espirito santo Ma y mochihuan Amen Jesus Maria y Joseph = Axca Domingo a 19 de Julio de 1759 a[o]s nictlalia nomemoria testamento nehual notoca Antt,[a] M,[a] nica nichane Santa Maria Nativitas ytla ninomiquilis ca san ymatitlatzinco nicnocahuilitia y noyoliatzin y noanimatzin y tt[o] Je X̄t̄o niquitoa ca amo tle nicnopielia ca huel nimotolinia ca nitlatlani ypampatzinco tt,[o] Dios nehtlaoculis nomissa yhua noresposo nonamictzin ytoca Juan de carme neltis notlatol mochihuas ca san ixquih onictzoquixtin y nomemoria testamento ymixpa oficiales de la santa Madre yglecia fiscal Don Josep Juan depotado felipe pascual teopan topile visente de Santiago

esCriuano Augustin Matias

[*f. 30*]

Jesus, Mary, and Joseph. In the name of the father, the son, and God the Holy Spirit, may it be done, amen. Jesus, Mary, and Joseph. = Today, Sunday the 19th of July of the year of 1759, I named Antonia María, citizen here in Santa María Nativitas, issue my memorandum of testament. If I die, I leave my spirit and soul in the hands of our lord Jesus Christ. I say that I have nothing; I am very poor. I request for the sake of our lord God that my husband named Juan del Carmen favor me with a mass and responsory prayer; my statement is to be carried out and realized. That is all. I have concluded my memorandum of testament before the officials of the holy mother church: fiscal don Josef Juan; diputado Felipe Pascual; church topile Vicente de Santiago.

Notary Agustín Matías.

91. Dominga María, Santa María Nativitas, 1759

(AGN, Civil 664, exp. 2)

THE TESTAMENT OF Dominga María belongs in the series of brief wills issued by women in Santa María Nativitas around this time, but here the testator is not entirely devoid of personal property as in some of the others. In addition to asking her husband to have a mass said for her, she makes some bequests, and the protestation of poverty is omitted. She also requests that an offering for Jerusalem be made. It appears that she or her family are on a somewhat different level than the women of Nos. 90 and 92.

Dominga María mentions no land, but she owns some small magueyes. This is not the only time that the phenomenon of landless or relatively landless women owning magueyes is seen in the corpus. The plants are scattered, at her home (which must belong to her husband) and elsewhere. She leaves them to four female persons and one male, who are identified only by their names, in some cases by one name only. We see here elements of a female network of some sort, and also the frequent (though not exclusive) association of women with magueyes. It is unlikely that the testator should have so many children and especially so many daughters; they could be a combination of daughters, perhaps a son or grandson, other relatives, and friends or business associates. The status of the testator is also shown as different from that of the women of Nos. 90 and 92 in that an executor is named.

The orthographic style of notary Felipe Juan (see the introductory study, p. 45) is very similar to that of Agustín Matías of No. 90, including the use of *h* for standard *ch*.

[*f. 39*]

Jesus Maria y Josephe —

Dios tetatzin yhuan Dios ypiltzin yhuan Dios espirito santo – Ma i mochihuan Amen Jesus Maria y ~~Jph~~^{e} — Axcan Sabado a 12 del Mes de mayo de 1759 a^{os} = Nica Nicpehualtia Notestamento Nehuatl Notoca Dominga Maria Nica nichane Santa Maria Nativitas Yhuan Niquitohuan yntla oninomiquili Ca ysemactzinco Nicnocahuilia Noyoliatzin yhuan Nohuannimantzin yhuan niquitoa Missan Nehchihualis Nonamictzin ytoca Lucas Josephe yhuan Niquitohuan se tomintzin Santo gerosale Nehmotlocolilisque Neltis Notlatol Mochihuas yhuan niquitohuan Metotoin Niccahuilia Visenta Maria Yhuan Juana yhuan Niquitohuan catltitla [t]eopa oncan mentototin Niccahuilia fransisca yhuan Maria yhuan Niquitoa Nica calitic metototin Niccahuilia Julia Joseph - Neltis notlatol mochihuas —

San ica Nictlamia notestamento Nehual Notoca Dominga Maria ymixpa oficiales de la santa madre yglecia — fiscal Don Joseph Juan tepotado felipe de la cruz topile manyor Vicente de santiago Eschribano Felipe Juan Albasia. Santiago Bentura

[*f. 39*]

Jesus, Mary, and Joseph.—

God the father, God his son, and God the Holy Spirit. – May it be done, amen. Jesus, Mary, and Joseph. — Today Saturday the 12th of the month of May of the year of 1759, here I named Dominga María, citizen here in Santa María Nativitas, begin here my testament. I say that when I have died I leave my spirit and soul entirely in the hands of [God], and I say that my husband named Lucas Josef is to have a mass performed for me. And I say that they are to favor me with a real for Holy Jerusalem. My statement is to be realized and carried out. And I say that I leave some small magueyes to Vicenta María and Juana. And I say that close to the church [I have] small magueyes that I leave to Francisca and María. And I say that here inside the house compound I leave small magueyes to Julián Josef. My statement is to be realized and carried out. —

With this I named Dominga María end my testament, in the presence of the officials of the holy mother church: fiscal don Josef Juan; diputado Felipe de la Cruz; topile mayor Vicente de Santiago; and notary Felipe Juan. The executor is Santiago Ventura.

92. Antonia Rufina, Santa María Nativitas, 1759

(AGN, Civil 664, exp. 2)

ANOTHER OF THE series of testaments done by women for funeral purposes, this will is quite close to being identical in content to No. 90 despite the fact that another notary is involved. The request for the husband to provide a mass is the same, the declaration of poverty is the same. Even the church officials who serve as witnesses are the same (and also in No. 91), showing that we can deduce nothing about the status of the testator from their presence. It seems that one of the two notaries virtually copied from the other (with a few idiosyncrasies), or they both used a common model.

The notary is Felipe Juan, as in Nos. 91 and 93, with the same orthographic and other characteristics.

[*f. 30*]
Jesus M,[a] hi Jo[?]ph Dios tetantzin Dios tepiltzin Dios espirito Santo Mari[. . .] hi Josep Amen —

AXca Martes a 3 del mes de Julio de 1759 a[os] nicpehualtia notestamento nehual notoca Antt,[a] Rufina nica nichane santa Maria Nativitas yhuan niquitoa tla ninomiquilis ca san ymactzinco nicnocahuililia noyuliatzin noanimatzin notlasotemaquixticatzin y tt,[o] Di[. . .] Je X[to] yhuan niquitoa nomisan nehtlaoColilis nonamic leonardo matias quichihuas neltis notlatol ca amo tle ninopielia ca hue[. . .] nimotolinia Ca san ixquih onitzoquiti nomemoria testamento ymixpa oficiales de santa Madre yglesia Don Joseph Juan fiscal depotado felipe de la cruz topile bisete de Santiago

esCriuano felipe Juan —

[*f. 30*]
Jesus, Mary, and Joseph. God the father, God the son, and God the Holy Spirit. Mary and Joseph. Amen. —

Today, Tuesday the 3rd of the month of July of the year of 1759, I named Antonia Rufina, citizen here in Santa María Nativitas, begin my testament, and I say that if I die, I leave my spirit and soul in the hands of my precious redeemer our lord God and Jesus Christ. And I say that my husband Leonardo Matías is to favor me with a mass for me; he is to do it. My statement is to be carried out. I have nothing, I am very poor. That is all. I have concluded my memorandum of testament before the officials of the holy mother church: don Josef Juan fiscal; diputado Felipe de la Cruz; topile Vicente de Santiago.

Notary Felipe Juan. —

93. Leonor María, Santa María Nativitas, 1760

(AGN, Civil 664, exp. 2)

IN THIS LAST of the series of four short women's wills, the testator once again lists no personal property, but she also does not declare poverty. She not only requests a mass but mentions being shrouded and buried, all of which is left in the hands of her three children, for she is a widow. The offering for Jerusalem also shows that resources are available. Despite the lack of property, an executor is appointed.

From the names of the children a good deal can be deduced. The eldest son is don Pablo Lorenzo, who from his title has already held local high office and must be economically comfortable, as such people almost invariably were. That don Pablo has already attained such a status means he must be mature himself, and thus Leonor María must be reasonably advanced in age. The second son also has the second name Lorenzo, a sign of a lineage with some pretensions. Leonor María's daughter shows the female version of name retention in the line, having her mother's name reversed, María Leonor. We can imagine that Leonor María's husband left the family house to don Pablo, but that Leonor has been living there ever since that time, perhaps in charge when the son was still small.

In previous testaments of this type for the year 1759, the fiscal had the second name Juan, the same as the notary of Nos. 91–93, Felipe Juan, but that could be coincidence. Now in 1760 a new set of church officials has come in, and we see that two of them also have the second name Juan, and so does the executor of the will. After this there can be no doubt that Felipe Juan belongs to a clan important in officeholding in Santa María Nativitas.

The style continues the same as in Felipe Juan's other testaments, but this time there is an interesting turn of phrase in the preamble. The testator is made to deliver her soul entirely into the hands, not of God as usual, but of Santa María Nativitas. As with an earlier document from this tlaxilacalli, No. 88 issued in 1678, the phrase could be construed as elevating the Virgin to the status of a parallel deity.

It could also merely hand the soul to Mary as an intercessor with God in a way compatible with orthodox belief. (For such a case see No. 75.) It may be that having a form of the Virgin as the patron saint of the tlaxilacalli invited special homage to her in the preambles of wills. It also may be that though, as we see throughout the corpus, the wording of preambles was primarily that of the officiating notary, Leonor María's special devotion had something to do with this passage.

Note the way of giving the day, "20 y 9," which, despite the Spanish conjunction between the numbers and the fact that the whole date phrase is in Spanish (as always with Felipe Juan), retains the traditional Nahuatl structure of 20, "one count," plus 9 in order to render 29. By now we have seen several such examples in the corpus. Other dates by this notary have the standard Spanish structure, however.

[*f. 44*]
Jesus Maria y Joseph Dios tetatzin yhuan Dios ytlasopiltzin yhã Dios espiritu santo Ma y Mochihuan Amen Jesus Maria y ~~Jph~~.^{e} — Axca Miercoles A 20 y 9 del Mes de octubre de 1760 años Nica Nicpehuatl Notestamento Nehuatl Notoca Leonor Maria V.^{a} Nica Nichane Sta Ma.^{a} Nativita yntla oninomiquili Ca ysemactzinco Nicnocahuilia Noyoliatzin yhuan Noanimantzin NotlasomaysNantzin Santa Maria Nativitas yhua Niquitoa Missa Nechihuilisq.^{e} NoPilhuan ytoca D.^{n} pablo lorenso yhuan tomas loreson yhuan Maria Leonor Nechquimilosq.^{e} Yhuan Nechtocasq.^{e} Neltis Notlatol Mochihuas yhuan Niquitohua se tomintzin santo gerosale — ca san ica Nictlamia Notetamento Nehuatl Notoca Leonor Maria Viuda —
Fiscal Don pedro Martin   tepotado Luis Juan
topile Miguel Juan   Albasia pedro Juan
Eschribano Felipe Juan

[*f. 44*]
Jesus, Mary, and Joseph. God the father, God his precious son, and God the Holy Spirit. May it be done, amen. Jesus, Mary and Joseph. — Today, Wednesday the 29th of the month of October of the year of 1760, here I named Leonor María, widow, citizen here in Santa María Nativitas, begin my testament. When I have died, I leave my spirit and soul entirely in the hands of my precious revered mother Santa María Nativitas. And I say that my children named don Pablo Lorenzo, Tomás Lorenzo, and María Leonor, are to arrange a mass for me; they are to shroud me and bury me. My statement is to be carried out and realized. And I say that a real is for Holy Jerusalem. — With this I named Leonor María, widow, end my testament. —
Fiscal don Pedro Martín. Diputado Luis Juan.
Topile Miguel Juan. Executor Pedro Juan.
Notary Felipe Juan.

94. Mateo Serrano, Santiago Apóstol Quaxochtenco, 1703

(AGN, Tierras 2523, exp. 5)[1]

ALTHOUGH THE TESTAMENT of Mateo Serrano does not tell us where it was issued, the dossier it is in allows identification of the place. The document is accompanied by an unusually rich documentation in Nahuatl, consisting of a bill of sale for a piece of land mentioned in the will and a memorandum on funeral expenditures by the testator's nephew, don Josef de la Cruz. The relationship between these two men indeed becomes the focus of our interest. Despite the fact that Mateo has direct heirs who receive bequests, the nephew don Josef seems to get the most, and is given the most responsibility. Yet don Josef does not simply inherit the two fields he receives. He has already "given" (in effect paid) money for one of the fields, and the bill of sale attached to the testament refers to its purchase several years earlier, in 1697. Thus Mateo's statement in his will about this parcel is not exactly a bequest, rather a sort of confirmation that the field is don Josef's property.

Another piece of land that goes to don Josef seems to be more like a simple bequest, yet when we look closely it too amounts to a trade. The arrangement is not made quite fully explicit, but it is clear that don Josef is to have a mass with responsory prayer said for Mateo *in return* for getting the land. Mateo goes on to say that he leaves the land to don Josef "so that he will remember me," which

[1]The testament and the bill of sale are accompanied by contemporary Spanish translations; the statement about funeral expenses is not. For a discussion of the status of Quaxochtenco, definitely in the Calimaya/Tepemaxalco district but with its more specific affiliation not yet determined, see the introductory study, p. 7.

seems a touching, sentimental phrase. But when we see in the later memorandum that don Josef continued to have rites performed for Mateo for a whole year and even as much as six years later, it seems that perhaps that was precisely the sort of remembering that Mateo hoped for in giving don Josef the land.

The situation with Mateo and don Josef is also our best clue about Mateo's general status and how he is presently doing. Other indications are present, of course. There seem to be quite a few cases of de la Cruz in the family, and Mateo passes his own second name, Serrano, on to one of the children. Serrano was a name with implications of high rank in Calimaya/Tepemaxalco, but did not necessarily assure that any given individual bearing it was at the top of local society. Mateo's property seems adequate but perhaps not too impressive; since the relative values of the furrow (surco) and the quahuitl have not yet been established, it is hard to assess his holdings. Though he has some saints, he does not mention a house. It is also hard to know just what to make of Mateo's six witnesses. Two are church officials, one is his son Pascual Serrano; surprisingly, three are women, which is very rare in the corpus and harks back to an earlier time. One of the women, indeed, may be Mateo's daughter Angelina María, but doubts remain, since only the first name is reported.

Despite the ambiguities, it surely puts Mateo close to the upper circles of the community to know that his nephew don Josef de la Cruz is presently alcalde and, as we see in the bill of sale, was fiscal of the church a few years earlier. The fact that he must rely so much on don Josef, however, who while not actually named executor acts like one, implies either that Mateo is in economic trouble or that none of his heirs can take over the funeral arrangements, whether because of poverty or because of their youth.

Bequests to the direct heirs look quite normal, although not all the relationships are specified. Mateo leaves three saints and a lot to Juana de la Cruz, without mentioning his relationship with her; in addition, he leaves 60 furrows of land to a Juan de la Cruz who could easily be the same Juana by a little mistake of the notary. What is sure is that Mateo has two children, Pascual Serrano and Angelina María, who get 60 and 37 furrows of land respectively, and who are mentioned right after Juana; this increases the suspicion that Juana is one of Mateo's children as well; the only other thing that seems at all likely is that she could have been his wife, with the children still very small.

The name of the first witness, the fiscal don Martín de la Cruz, is repeated at the very end of the testament, where the notary usually puts his name; since no notary is explicitly given, it may be that besides being a witness the fiscal also wrote the document. Whoever acts as notary, the style appears to be generally standard, with the peculiarity of *tz* used instead of standard *ç/z* on many occasions. One of the numbers given in the testament shows the traditional Nahuatl system still in use but affected by the Spanish decimal system; 37 is given as 20 + 10 + 7, whereas the traditional form would have been 20 + 15 + 2.

The bill of sale, dated 1697, in some ways resembles other documents of its kind, but the writer is reticent about using the actual term "to sell," using "give" instead, and does not mention a purchase or call the document a *carta de venta* as was usually done. It is remarkable but not untypical that despite this very clear legal document transferring the rights to the land to don Josef in perpetuity, it was felt necessary to repeat the gift or bequest in Mateo's will six years later. Here and in the other bequest of land to don Josef we see how in many cases, although indigenous people made free use of the mechanism of sale, it often still involved relatives and in such cases was not fully distinguished from a bequest. The text contains an unusual double loan, *ni . . . ni*, "neither . . . nor," which not only involves a Spanish particle but uses Spanish syntax in a Nahuatl phrase.

Don Josef's statement of expenditures for the funeral and for later rites in honor of Mateo is without parallel in the corpus and informs us of aspects probably common in death solemnities that are virtually never mentioned in testaments. We see not only the cost of the mass itself but what went for candles and above all for food: meat, salt, chile, pulque, chickens. Responsory prayers for Mateo were repeated later in the year, with another mass on the anniversary of his death. Still another mass was performed six years later. The prices of some of the masses show that they were done with some pomp. The expense of the primary funeral alone is listed as 10 pesos and 6 reales (2 reales more if we add it up), twice what one of the pieces of land cost. Yet none of this was actually specified in Mateo's will beyond the hint that he wanted don Josef to remember him. Much the same may apply to many other wills in the corpus.

The text of the memorandum has interesting features. We do not have other examples, so we do not know the conventions of the genre. At times don Josef is spoken of in the third person, at times he himself speaks, as in a will. The document is notarized, and part of it is authenticated by officials of the community. The writer, Francisco de la Cruz, apparently the same person who earlier did the bill of sale, has a few notable peculiarities, particularly his rows of three *l*'s in "polllo," "chicken," and "melllo," "medio, half a real." Apparently they are equivalent to [ly]. The form 206 is seen meaning 26, in a now familiar pattern. Mateo's name appears as "Mateotzin," with a reverential ending, something not uncommon in Nahuatl texts of earlier centuries but rare in the eighteenth century.

[*f.* 5]

y Jesus maria y Juseph — axcan mimierConles a 23 de mayo de 17003 yn iCa ytocatzin Y Dios tetatzi y Dios tepiltzi Dios espirito Santo y Ma semiCac quiyentenehualo yn itlatzomahuisyechipahualiutzi ytlatzomahuisnatzi y Santa maria la Compceio, y ma yec mochihua y Jesus maria y Juseph — y nehuatl Mateyo Serano, y nitlanahuatia, y mochian y memorial y destameto Y noteConpa y Santo San franCon niccanhuilia Juana de la crutz yhuan Santo San mateyo yhuan Santo christo ynic quimnotequipanilhuilitz yhuan ynicC omtlanmatli y nitlanahuatia, y nicCahuilia Sonlar yCuitlapa, teyopa Jua^{na} —

ynic entlamatli y nitlanahuatia, y Se nopiltzi, ytoca pascal senrano y niccahuilia yenpohualli Cuemill —

ynic natlamatli y nitlanahuatia y Se noxpochi ytocan angelina maria Sepohualli yhua matlatlin, yhua chiComen —

yhuan Juan de la crutz nicCahuilia yepohualli camo aqui, quiquixtilitz —

ynic Macuillamatlic Y nitlanahuatia yno milli, tequimilteCo,[2] y nicnomaquilia Y noSonbrino Do Juseph de la Crutz onexmomaquilli, maCuilli pe^{so} yhua nahui tomi, amo aqui, quemania y quiquixtilitinemitz —

ynic chiCuasetlamatli y nitlanahuaticyan y nosobrino Don Juseph de la Crutz nicCahuilia yno milli tenaCon[3] y noteConpa y nitlanahuatia, yhua setel missa quimochicuilitz yhua se respoçio, y note-Conpa Yn tlacuiloa Dō Juseph de la crutz alcalde San cepa NicCahuilia —

ynic nexmolnamiquilitz — Dō marti de la crutz fis-

[*f.* 5]

Jesus, Mary, and Joseph. — Today Wednesday the 23rd of May of 1703, in the name of God the father, God the son, and God the Holy Spirit, may the precious revered purity of his precious revered mother Santa María de la Concepción be eternally praised. May it be done. Jesus, Mary, and Joseph. — I Mateo Serrano order that this memorandum and testament are being made at my command. I leave holy San Francisco to Juana de la Cruz, along with holy San Mateo and Santo Cristo so that she will serve them. And second I order that I leave the lot behind the church to Juana. —

Third I order that I leave to a son of mine named Pascual Serrano 60 furrows [of land]. —

Fourth I order that [I leave] to a daughter of mine named Angelina María 37 [furrows]. —

And I leave to Juan de la Cruz 60; no one is to take it away from him. —

Fifth I order that I give that cultivated field at the edge of the tribute field[s][2] to my nephew don Josef de la Cruz; he gave me 5 pesos and 4 reales. No one is ever to go about taking it from him. —

Sixth I order that I leave to my nephew don Josef de la Cruz that cultivated field in Tenango;[3] I order it voluntarily. And he is to have a mass with responsory prayer performed [for me]. What is written is by my order. I leave it to don Josef de la Cruz, alcalde, [forever] so that he will remember me. —

Don Martín de la Cruz, fiscal of the holy church,

---

[2]*Tequimilli* traditionally meant a field or fields on which tribute was owed, often with the implication that the land had not been in the hands of the owner for long. The Spanish translator took the word in this sense, speaking of lands of the community. In the de la Cruz family papers, however, the word is employed meaning a special field used to produce revenue for something like the church choir or a cofradía (see Lockhart 1992, pp. 231, 233).

[3]Perhaps the reference is to Tenango del Valle in the south of the Toluca Valley, but Tenanco ("at the wall") was a very common Nahuatl place name.

Cal de la santa y yglenssia testigo ysabel maria — y PasCal de serano testigo Agustina maria — Agelina testigo — Matias miguel mātro

Don marti de la crutz fiscal santa yglesia testigon

[*f. 4*]

Axca martes a 17 de setiebre de 1697 años Nica momachiyotia mochihua ysgriptora ytehCaCopa se tlali nica tequimilteCo nehual notoCa mateo serano nicnomaquilian yc semi ayac aquiquixtilitinemis ni nopilhua ni aqui ayc tlamis semiCac yc semi nitemaCa notlatol yxpa testigos – Ju^{n} de la Crus – aloson de la Crus – notestigus – yca mahuili peso – 5 pesos – nictemaCa yno tlali yca notecocoya – nicnomaquilia d^{n} Juseph de la Crus fiscal sa yglesia ayc aqui moteCuepas Cuali quixtlahuas yxpa Justicia Ca san ixquih niCa titlacuilohua ypa mestli 17 de setibre teyxpa ymixpa notahua

dn marcos Ju^{n} aHdes Augusti de la Crus regidor mayor

nehual nica nitlaCuiloa fran^{co} de la Crus esCribano yteCopa notahua

nehual nican iba ninofirmatia mateon serano[4]

[*f. 10*]

Jesus maria y Josph

Axca sabado a 206 dias de Mayo de 1703 a^{os} Nica moMachiyotia Memoria ytexCopa MicCatzitli CacCa nitiotzin CacCa Mateotzin motlanahualitia onicchihuili miSan onictemaCa Nahui peso yō̄n nahui tomi onicnomaquili tlasoteopixCatzitli nica nesties —

v̲ Nima media libra Cadela yei tomi — 3 nes

oc se tomi ypatic Cadela onictemaca —

v̲ niMa Sachrista oniMaca se tomi —

v̲ Se tomi almorsar[5] —

v̲ Se Cuarto naCal ypatic yei peso yōnn ome tomi

niMa oc chiCuaSetica onechmaca yzteba sano opa omonec mochi omosetlali nahui pesos — 4 p —

witness. Isabel María. Pascual Serrano, witness. Agustina María. Angelina, witness. Matías Miguel, maestro [de doctrina].

Don Martín de la Cruz, fiscal of the holy church, witness.

[*f. 4*]

Today, Tuesday the 17th of September of the year of 1697, here is recorded and made a legal document concerning a piece of land here at the edge of the tribute field[s]. I named Mateo Serrano give it to [the buyer] forever. No one is to go about taking it from him, neither my children nor anyone else. [The agreement] will never end; it is eternal and forever. I give my word before the witnesses Juan de la Cruz and Alonso de la Cruz, my witnesses. For 5 pesos I give up that land [acquired by my effort]; I give it to don Josef de la Cruz, fiscal of the holy church. No one is ever to go back on his word. [If he does], he is to pay for it properly before an officer of the law. That is all. We are writing here on the 17th of the month of September in the presence of people, in the presence of my fathers [officials of the community].

Don Marcos Juan, alcalde. Agustín de la Cruz, regidor mayor.

I am doing the writing here, Francisco de la Cruz notary, by order of my fathers.

I sign here on [the paper], Mateo Serrano.[4]

[*f. 10*]

Jesus, Mary, and Joseph.

Today Saturday the 26th day of May of the year of 1703, here is recorded a memorandum concerning the late poor dead person who was my uncle, Mateo, who left orders for me to have a mass performed for him. I spent 4 pesos and 4 reales. I gave it to the precious priest, as will appear here. —

v̲ Then half a pound of candles, 3 reales. — 3 reales.

I spent another real, the price of candles. —

v̲ Then I gave the sacristan a real. —

v̲ A real for [breakfast?][5] —

v̲ A quarter of meat [of a steer?] at the price of 3 pesos and 2 reales.

Then Esteban gave me 6 reales more [of meat] that was likewise used there [at the funeral]; it all added up to 4 pesos. — 4 pesos.

---

[4]Despite this statement, the writing is the same as in the rest of the document.

[5]Spanish *almuerzo* and the corresponding verb *almorzar* originally referred to breakfast, a breakfast that grew later through time until it came to be lunch. Just where in that evolution the meaning of the present instance falls is a matter for speculation. The word "almorsar" is apparently the infinitive used as a noun, a type of loan seen often in the sixteenth century but less in later times.

v Chili setica yztal yetiCa niMa nectli Matlactomi —

v 1 real's worth of chiles, 3 reales' worth of salt, then 10 reales for pulque. —

ymixpa moxti huehueque y tle omotlanahuatilitia micCatzintli CacCa yehual onicchiuh mosetlalia matlactli peso yõn chiCuasSe tomi – 10 p – 6 nes nehual nitlaCuiloa fras^{co} de la Crus yca Jorameto

Before all the elders I did what the late poor dead person left ordered; it adds up to 10 pesos and 6 reales. — 10 pesos, 6 reales. I Francisco de la Cruz am doing the writing under oath.

v Don Joseph de la cruz quimochihuilian se resposos [. . .] Es^{no} ca nesties nahui tomi Ypa metztli de setienbre 21 de 17003 a^{os} ypa San atoyo Yilhuitzi – ypa todo santos onicchuhc resposio melllo – m^{o} –

v Don Josef de la Cruz has a responsory prayer performed [. . .] notary, as will appear, for 4 reales on the 21st of the month of September of the year of 1703, on the feast of San Antonio. On Todos Santos I had a responsory prayer performed: half a real. — 1/2 real.

v nima oc asi Cabo de añon onicchiuh misa resposio yõn sera se peso yõnn ChiuCuase tomi — 8 ps. 6 nes

v Then coming to the end of the year [after death] I had a mass with responsory prayer performed, [with] candles: 8 pesos and 6 reales. — 8 pesos, 6 reales.

v Axca Martes A diess i siete de setiebre de 1709 a^{os} nica nicchihuilia misa notiyotzin CacCa yntoca Mateo serano ymixpa moxti huehue[que] nica nesties fiscal Dn miguel de la Crus Dn thomas de la Crus aHte nica nesties quesqui motemaca ynpapa misa [*f. 10v*] yei peso — 3 ps — Nima resposio yei tomi – 3 nes – nima Cadela ypatic yei tomi — 3 nes — nima se polllo ynpatic se tomi — [orial][6] —

v Today Thursday the 17th of September of the year of 1709, here I have a mass performed for my late uncle named Mateo Serrano, as will appear here before all the elders, [including] fiscal don Miguel de la Cruz and alcalde don Tomás de la Cruz. Here will appear how much is spent on account of the mass: [*f. 10v*] 3 pesos. — Then for the responsory prayer, 3 reales. — Then the price of candles, 3 reales. — Then the price of a chicken, 1 real.[6] —

[6]The letters "orial" are quite clear, but their meaning is not. I have wondered if they could be in Spanish, equivalent to "o real," so that the meaning would be "1 tomín or real."

95. Baltasar de los Reyes, Santiago Apóstol Quaxochtenco, ca. 1730

(AGN, Tierras 2300, exp. 10)[1]

AS THE POSSESSOR of three pieces of land in addition to a house with saints and a lot, Baltasar de los Reyes is above average in wealth, assuming that the parcels are not unusually small. Everything goes to his son Juan Pedro, the only child mentioned and probably the only one surviving or still living at home. A wife is not mentioned either, and from the fact that Juan Pedro is charged with raising two orphans who are in the household, it would seem that she has already died. Orphans (here called by the Spanish loanword) were sometimes in fact the testator's children out of wedlock, but we have no way of knowing that in this case; they receive no bequest.

As a name, Baltasar de los Reyes, taken whole from one of the three Magi, stood out from the mass of double saints' names but did not necessarily in itself imply high status; it rarely became a lineage name. Baltasar has not achieved the don, and his son has a very unpretentious name, different from his father's; by 1762, however, the son was being called don, even in Spanish texts. Also, Baltasar has a nephew who is a don. His witnesses include a full complement of high-ranking local officials. His funeral requests do not go beyond the normal minimum and even seem to fall beneath it, for he makes no mention of an offering for Jerusalem. In other testaments issued in Santiago Apóstol, Jerusalem is missing as well, however, so apparently it is a matter of tlaxilacalli convention. Thus overall one may conclude that Baltasar was a person of considerable standing in the community.

We have seen that by the eighteenth century, terminology for the outlying entities in the Calimaya/Tepemaxalco region was wavering between *tlaxila-*

[1]The testament is accompanied by a contemporary Spanish translation. In the absence of a date in the testament itself, the approximate date is reckoned from a statement in the Spanish dossier containing the will that in 1762 the heir mentioned here had held one of the pieces of land he inherited for thirty years.

calli, the traditional word and the proper one given that they were constituent parts of the two true altepetl Calimaya and Tepemaxalco, and *altepetl*, implying greater independence. Here Santiago Apóstol is called both in almost the same breath.

The style of Juan Manuel de Constantino, who declares himself to be the municipal notary (rather than notary of the church as sometimes seen) contains typical Toluca Valley traits. He is quite prone to omitting and repeating parts of words. Although it seems in line with his awkwardness that he gives the Trinity in detail, with its attributes, two times in the same section, we find the same thing in the other wills from Santiago Apóstol (Nos. 96 and 97), even though written by different notaries, so it must be part of the tlaxilacalli style.

[*f. 1*]
J; y M. y J;
Yca ytocatzin Dios tetatzin Dios tepiltzin Dios espiritu S;^{to} yeintzitzin teotlacatzitzin Au san se huel neli teol D.^{s} ma mochintin quimatican yn aquiq̄; quitas ynin amatl; nomem[. . .] testamento nehual notoca blatezar de los Reyes nican nochan ypam yaltepetzin, Sr Santiago apostol ytec nipoctica yn, tlaxilacali au maccihuy moccomponica nonacayo Au notlanamiquilis Ca san huel pactica yCatzico yn to Dios Au nicnoneltoquitia yn Dios tetatzin Dios tepiltzin Dios espiritu S;^{to} yeintzitzin teotlacatzitzinn Au San se huel neli teol Dios Au ca ypam ynin tlaneltoquilistly ninomiquilia, ma y mochihua J; M; y Joseph —

yNic sentlamantly nitlanahuatia sentel Missa yhua sentel Responso nopampa motlatlatilis noteopiscatzin —

ynic ontlamatly nitlahuatia yehual Nopiltzin Ju;^{o} P;^{o} mocahua [ypa naci? ypan aci?][2] nehual para quimocuitlahuitzinos S;^{tos} Santas yhuan Caltzintly yCa solar yhuan quinhuapahuaspahuas ome huefanos yhuan quicalis nosobirno D;^{n} Sebastian ynahuac yChan nahuy Surco —

yNic yectlamantli nitlanahua oc se solar mani yna ychan bernardo no yehual nopiltzin nicahuilia —

ynic Nactlamantly nitlanahuatia [oc?] [*f. 1v*] se tlali mani yNahuac yChan Christoval no nicahuilia —

ynic macuiltlamantly o se tlali mani Cuaxosten[. . .][3] no nicahuilia —

Ca amo tel Nicnopielia Ca ycquimotlanelti[. . .] D;^{s} Notestigos —

fiscal D;^{n} Manuel de lo sã[. . .] Al;^{de} D^{n} Sebastian mate[. . .] M;^{ro} de Doctrin D;^{n} Est[. . .]van fran;^{co} D;^{n} Matias miguel Santiago ma[. . .]imiliano

[*f. 1*]
Jesus, Mary, and Joseph.
In the name of God the father, God the son, and God the Holy Spirit, three divine persons but one very true deity God, may all who see this document know [that it is] the memorandum of testament of me named Baltasar de los Reyes; my home is here in the altepetl of lord Santiago Apóstol, and I belong to the tlaxilacalli. Although my body is ill, my mind is very sound through our lord God. I believe in God the father, God the son, and God the Holy Spirit, three divine persons but one very true deity God, and in this belief I die. May it be done. Jesus, Mary, and Joseph. —

First I order that my priest is to be implored [to perform] a mass with a responsory prayer for me. —

Second I order that my child Juan Pedro is to be left [. . .][2] to take care of the male and female saints and the house with lot, and he is to raise two orphans, and he is to leave to my nephew don Sebastián four furrows close to his home. —

Third I order that I also leave to my child another lot close to the home of Bernardo. —

Fourth I order [*f. 1v*] that there is another piece of land next to the home of Cristóbal that I also leave to him. —

Fifth I also leave him another piece of land in Quaxochtenco.[3] —

I have nothing [else], as my witnesses will verify to God: —

Fiscal don Manuel de los Santos; alcalde don Sebastián Mat[eo]; maestro de doctrina don Esteban Francisco; don Matías Miguel; Santiago Maximi-

---

[2]Although the letters in the original are clear, I have not found a certain interpretation of them. The Spanish translation at this point has "como si llo fuera," "as if it were me."

[3]Although *quaxochtenco* literally means "at the edge of the boundary" and the Spanish translation is "en el lindero," since this very entity is named Quaxochtenco, I have taken it that the word is a proper name here.

ES;^{no} R;^{ca} Ju^{o} manuel de Constantino

liano.
Notary of the commonwealth Juan Manuel de Constantino.

96. Mateo Manuel, Santiago Apóstol Quaxochtenco, 1760

(AGN, Civil 664, exp. 2)

HERE IS ANOTHER example of a testator who mentions no property at all in his will, but issues it only to deal with funeral arrangements. As in other testaments from Santiago Apóstol, Mateo Manuel requests only a mass with responsory prayer; this time the person mentioned in this connection is not the priest but his father, Valeriano Antonio, who is to pay for it.

The introductory formula is striking in this context for being so long and complex compared to the simplicity of the testament. The reference to the Trinity is repeated twice, a peculiarity that we see in other testaments from this tlaxilacalli, and the generally conservative set of formulas is also common in Santiago.

Mateo names two witnesses at the end, the fiscal and an alcalde, both bearing the title don. We can infer no special connection between the testator and the witnesses, who are probably present in an official capacity only. Don Martín de la Cruz, the present alcalde, held some office in 1761 as well (No. 97). It is unlikely that he is the same person who was fiscal of the church in 1703 (No. 94); perhaps he is his descendant.

Notary Jacinto Pascual writes in a style typical of the eighteenth-century Toluca Valley, but distinguishes himself by the use of *h* to replace not only *ch* but also *tz* and *s*.

[*f. 62*]
Ycan ytocatzin yn Dios tetatzin yhuan Dios ytlazonpiltzin yhuan Dios Espiritu S^{to} Ma moChintin quiMatican yn aquique quictazque y NomeMorial testamento Yn nehual Nichihuan NotuCan Matheo Manuel Nica niChane Yn ipan yAltepetzin S,^{r} S,^{to} Santiago Apostol Maxihuin yn Mococohua yn Nonacayõ Yn Nosoquio Auh yn NotlamaChiliz yn notlacicacaquiliz Yn notlalnamiquiliz Aquen ca Ca san huel pactican Chicachtica Ycantzinco Yn Dios yehica Yn axca niquitoa Ca huel nicnocenNeltoquitia Yn San se huel neli Dios Yn noteotzin Notlatocatzin Yn ixquih yhuelitzin Dios tetatzin Dios ypiltzin Dios Espiritu S^{to} Auh yn Macihuin Yn yeintzitzin teotlacatzitzinti Ca san se huel neli Dios ypan Ynin tlaneltoquiliztli Ninomiquilia Yn axca huel ymactzinco NicnoCahuilia Yn Naniman Y notecuiyo Xpto ỹehica Ca huel ỹehuatzin OquimoChihuilitzino OquiMomaquixtilitzino Yca yn itlazollezotzin Miquilistica Ytech yn Sta Cruz No niquitoa Yn itehcacopa Yn ipalehuiloca Yn Naniman Nopan mitos Sentel Missa Ycan Sentel Responsos Yn Canpa nitocoz Auh yn huentzitli Ca quimotemaquiliz yn ỹehual Notatzin ytucan Baleriano Antonio Ca san ixquih Camo tle nicnopielia Can oca mehticate Notehtigos tlaneltilisque fisCal de la Sta [*f. 62v*] Dñ Simon Gregorio yhuan Alcalde Auh

[*f. 62*]
In the name of God the father, God his precious son, and God the Holy Spirit, let all who see my memorandum of testament know that I named Mateo Manuel, citizen here in the altepetl of lord saint Santiago Apóstol, make it. Although my earthly body is ill, nothing is wrong with my faculty of knowing, my complete understanding, and my memory, but they are very sound and strong through God, wherefore now I say that I believe entirely in only one very true God my deity and ruler, omnipotent God the father, God his son, and God the Holy Spirit, who although three divine persons are only one very true God. In this belief I die. Now I leave my soul very much in the hands of my lord Christ, because he himself made and redeemed it with his precious blood through death on the holy cross. I also say concerning the help of my soul that a mass with a responsory prayer is to be said for me where I am to be buried, and my father named Valeriano Antonio is to give the offering. That is all. I have nothing. There are my witnesses who will verify it, the fiscal of the holy [church] [*f. 62v*] don Simón Gregorio and the alcalde; our [alcalde] is don Martín

toa[. . .] Dn̄ Martin de la Cruz Axca Miercoles Mani m[. . .]tli Matlatli yhuan ỹey tonali Xictlapoa[. . .] de 1760 a^{os}
Nehual nitlaquiloa Es^{no} de la Rep^{ca} Jasinto Pasqual

de la Cruz. Today Wednesday the 13th day of the month of [. . .] of the year count of 1760.

I am doing the writing, the notary of the commonwealth, Jacinto Pascual.

97. Ventura Ramos, Santiago Apóstol Quaxochtenco, 1761

(AGN, Tierras 2538, exp. 4)

OWNER OF A house and lot with saints, a good-sized field of 4 almudes, and two other fields of average size, Ventura Ramos is not unusually wealthy, but also by no means poor by indigenous standards. We are not surprised to see that he leaves the house and lot jointly to his wife and son, who is doubtless small, and the large field directly to the son. It is more unusual that having a direct male heir and not possessing any superfluity of land, he leaves one of the other parcels to a nephew and a fourth of another to a niece, the son Luis Antonio getting only the remainder. Perhaps the son was also suffering from the epidemic disease of this year, from which, it is said in accompanying Spanish documents, the present testator died.

From those documents it also emerges that the testator's father was named Martín de la Cruz (probably connected to and perhaps even the same person as don Martín de la Cruz, fiscal in 1703 [No. 94]), and he had a brother named Juan Antonio Constantino (a Constantino was municipal notary in 1730 [No. 95]); the name Ramos itself is of middling connotations. From these facts we could say that Ventura belongs to a family with some pretensions; yet we also notice that the testator's name is less impressive than his father's, and his son's less impressive yet. Funeral requests seem minimal, though that may be the norm in this tlaxilacalli; possibly it means more for estimating his rank that the testator is to be buried in the church, and the preamble of the will is long and elaborate. The witnesses are very respectable. All in all, Ventura appears to be of upper middle rank in the community.

Comparing the preamble of this will with those in Nos. 95 and 96, we see a common model prevailing in the tlaxilacalli over some thirty years. The preamble of No. 94, however, done in 1703, is quite different. The notary Juan Pablo here displays many of the typical characteristics of eighteenth-century Tolucan Nahuatl writing; he is a little unusual in putting *c* for standard final *n* or simply intruding it, and the *ctz* he puts once for *ch* is unparalleled. In general there are no unusual loanwords, but the testament does contain a rare whole phrase in Spanish, *y demás oficiales de la república*, "and the other officers of the commonwealth (municipality)."

[*f.* 4]
J, M, Y, J, =
Ycan ytocatzin Dios tetatzin Dios ytlazopiltzin Dios espiritu S,^{to} Ma moChintin quimatica yn aquiq̃. quitasq̃ yni memoria tehtamento yn nehual niChihuan Bentura Ramos — nican nichane yn ipan yaltepetzin S.^{r} S,^{to} Santiago Apostol Masihuin yn Mocхарактер

[*f.* 4]
Jesus, Mary and Joseph. =
In the name of God the father, God his precious son, and God the Holy Spirit, may all who see this memorandum of testament know that I, Ventura Ramos, citizen here in the altepetl of lord saint Santiago Apóstol, make it. Although my earthly body is sick, there is nothing wrong with my cognition, my full understanding, and my memory, but they are very sound and strong through God, wherefore now I say that I very entirely believe in just one very true God, my deity and ruler, the omnipotent God the father, God his son, and God the Holy Spirit, who although three divine persons, are only one very true God; in this belief I die. Now I leave my soul in the hands of my lord Christ because it was truly

Xptho yehica Ca huel yehuatzin oquimoChihuilitzino oquimomaquixtilitzino yCa yn itlazoyezotzin Mi.quilistica yteh yn S,^{ta} Cruz, no niquitoa yn itehcopa yn ipalehuiloca yn nanima nopan mito[z?] Centel miza yCa Cen Responsos honca teopan Yn canpa nitocoz Auh yn huetzintli Ca quimotemaquiliz yê,hual Nusihua; maria, Antonia; yCan san nupilctzi; Luis Antonio = —

he who made it and redeemed it with his precious blood through death on the holy cross. I also say that concerning the help of my soul, a mass with a responsory prayer is to be said for me at the church where I will be buried. My wife María Antonia is to give the offering, with my child Luis Antonio. = —

yn Sentlamantli nitlanahuatia Nusihua yCan nupilctzic nicCahua; ypan cali yCan S,^{tos} yCan S,^{tas} yCa Sentel Solal nicCahuilia yn ontlamantli osen m[. . .]li mani ytenco Barãca nicCahuilia Nupilctzi Lu[. . .] Antonio Conanas Canpan Calaquic nahuic almo; tloli yn yêtlamantli nu nitlanauatia opuali surcos [*f. 4v*] NicCahuilia Manuel Martin nosobrino m[...]ni Calimaya otlin mumilsalua Marcelino de la Cruz:[1] —

First, I order that I leave my wife and my child in the house with the male and female saints, together with a lot that I leave to them. Second, I leave another cultivated field at the edge of the ravine to my child Luis Antonio, where 4 almudes of maize fit; he is to take it. Third, I also order that [*f. 4v*] to Manuel Martín, my nephew, I leave 40 furrows on the road to Calimaya, bordering on a cultivated field of Marcelino de la Cruz.[1] —

ync nactlamatlic nicCahuilia matlatli Surcos nicCahuia nuso;brino[2] Petrona Martina o Senpualic yhua matlatli conanas Luis antonioc —

Fourth, I leave 10 furrows to my niece[2] Petrona Martina; Luis Antonio is to take the other 30. —

Xan sann isquic nitlanahuatia Cantlen nicnopielia Conca Mesticate n[. . .]testigos tlaneltilique S,^{r} fiscal de la Santa iglesia D,^{n} Simon Gregorio S,^{r} Alcalde Autual D,^{n} fran,^{co} lionnardo hihua D,^{n} Martin de la Cru[. . .] y DeMas ofisiales de la R,^{ca} —

That is all that I order. I have nothing. My witnesses are there, they will provide verification: the señor fiscal of the holy church don Simón Gregorio; the señor present alcalde don Francisco Leonardo; don Martín de la Cruz; and other officials of the commonwealth. —

Es,^{no} Juan Pab[. . .]

Notary Juan Pablo.

Mani mestli Mayo ypan ctzihuase tonali Xitlapualic de 1761 a^{os}

The 6th of the month of May of the year count of 1761.

[1]This would appear not to be the Marcelino de la Cruz of No. 59, citizen of Santa María de la Asunción, who made his testament and presumably died in 1759, and at that time owned no land. However, in the corpus lands are sometimes associated with former owners now deceased.

[2]The original quite clearly has "sobrino," yet since a female is meant, perhaps a very faint line or flag near the end of the word should be interpreted as making it "sobrina." Gender differentiation in the Spanish style with these two words is otherwise entirely consistent in the corpus.

98. Tomás de la Cruz, Calimaya/Tepemaxalco, place unknown, 1760

(AGN, Civil 664, exp. 2)

ALTHOUGH THE tlaxilacalli where this testament was issued is not specified, it must have been somewhere in the area of the paired altepetl Calimaya and Tepemaxalco. The document is found among a large cache of wills from that jurisdiction, and the prominent mention of San Pedro and San Pablo, the patrons of the two altepetl, leaves no room for doubt. The mention of San Juan Bautista that follows could be a reference to the tlaxilacalli of San Juan Bautista Yancuictlalpan in Tepemaxalco, but there is no way of being sure. Some characteristics of the preamble hint strongly that the testament was issued in the central settlement of Calimaya/Tepemaxalco, whichever altepetl the testator was affiliated with.

The present testament is entirely devoted to funeral requirements. It is one of those in the corpus which are clearly issued after the death of the testator, apparently by a notary, perhaps in conjunction with the fiscal and some other officials. But in contrast to No. 60, where the named officials speak in the first person and refer to the "testator" in the third, here no notary, officials, or witnesses are named, and the dead testator is made to speak in the first person throughout. The only indication of the true situation—though a very definite one—is that he is suddenly described as deceased even though he is supposed to be talking at that very minute.

Since no property is bequeathed or mentioned, it would be natural to assume that Tomás de la Cruz dies in poverty. No relatives appear. Yet the arrangements for Tomás include not only being shrouded in style but being buried inside the church close to an important image, all of which will have to be paid for somehow even though the testator is made to say that he has nothing. Perhaps the official or officials who issued the will took it that they were responsible only for the church-related aspects, and matters of property and bequests were not their business. The will, then, does not give us a basis for assessing the status of Tomás de la Cruz. A dynasty of important people in Tepemaxalco and Calimaya had the same second name, but it was by no means exclusive to that lineage.

Whoever wrote the will, its style has a combination of standard and pronouncedly local Tolucan traits, and the writer was a trained notary.

[*f. 40*]

Jesus maria y Joh=

ma mosenquisCayectenehualo ytlaçomahuistoCatzin la santisma trenidad D.^{s} tetatzin D.^{s} tlaçopiltzin D.^{s} espirito sato = yeintzitzin teotlaCatzitzintin – Ca san se huel neli teol D.^{s} Ca se ymactzinCo – nictlalia nuanimantzin – yhua yehuatzin nosenquiscanantzin s.^{ta} maria mohipa huel neli xipottzintli – yhua yehuatzitzin apostoles s. pedro y s. pablo yehuatzin s.^{to} santo Juan bactista – yCa moxtintzitzin s.tos yhuan santas yn lihucac chaneCatzitzinti – Ca nihuan niquimotlatlactilia y nopa motlatoltisq̄. yxpantzinCo noteCoyo Jesu christo Ame Jesus

Ca nica nictemaCa se tomi. santo Jerusale – yhuan se misa nopa mitos – yhuan se Responsos nopa mitos ypalehuiloCa noanimactzin yes. yhuan. nosepoltura. motlapos teopaCalitic ynahuactzinco notlasonmahuistatzin s.to san Fran^{co} – yhuan ytlaquientzin notlaçomahuustatzin yehual ic ninoquimilos yn iCordontzin – ninolpis. Ca niCa nicçonquixtia. nomemoria ypa ynin tonatin lues 24 de nobievre. de 1760 a^{o}s – nehual notoCa thomas de la Cruz. defunto. yni memoria para ypalehuiloCa yes nanimantzin yes ipa[1] santa ygelsia Camo tle ninopielia Ca quimoctilis notiopixCatzin – ma ye i mochihuan —

[*f. 40*]

Jesus, Mary, and Joseph. =

May the precious revered name of the most holy Trinity, God the father, God [his] precious son, and God the Holy Spirit, three divine persons but just one very true deity God, be entirely praised. I place my soul entirely in his hands. And I also implore my consummate mother Santa María, forever very true virgin, and the apostles San Pedro and San Pablo, holy San Juan Bautista, with all the male and female saints who are resident in heaven, to speak for me before my lord Jesus Christ. Amen. Jesus.

Here I give a real for Holy Jerusalem, and a mass is to be said for me, and a responsory prayer is to be said for me, to be the help of my soul; and my grave is to be opened inside the church building close to my precious revered father holy San Francisco. - And I am to be wrapped in the habit of my precious revered father and to be girt with his rope. Here I named Tomás de la Cruz, deceased, conclude my memorandum on this day, Monday the 24th of November of the year of 1760; this memorandum will be for the help of my soul before[1] the holy church. I have nothing; my priest is to look after it. May it be done. —

---

[1]The intention of "ipan" seems to be standard *ixpan*.

Glossary

ALCALDE. A first-instance judge attached to a local municipal government. Sometimes *alcalde ordinario.*

ALGUACIL. Constable. The *alguacil mayor*, chief constable, is apparently always a municipal officer.

ALMUD. A Spanish dry measure, one-twelfth of a fanega, here used to indicate how much land can be sown by an almud of grain. Equivalent to 10 quahuitl.

ALTEPETL. Nahuatl word for any state, but here a local ethnic state. Traditionally refers to the sort of several-tlaxilacalli entity that in Spanish times would have a governor and a full municipal council, but here sometimes in addition denotes one of the tlaxilacalli, or affected by Spanish *pueblo*, any concentrated settlement.

CHIRIMÍA. A loud single-reed musical instrument.

COFRADÍA. Confraternity, lay sodality.

COMADRE. Female ritual coparent.

COMMONWEALTH. Translation here of *república*, the municipal government of an altepetl.

COMPADRE. Male ritual coparent.

CONSUEGRO. The father of one's child-in-law, one's fellow father-in-law.

CORNCRIB. Here, translation of *cuezcomatl*, the indigenous-style structure for storing maize and sometimes other foods.

CUARTILLO. One fourth of an almud. Here used to indicate the fine detail of land measurements.

DIPUTADO. Deputy. Here apparently an officer in a cofradía.

DOCTRINA. Spanish for Christian doctrine and indoctrination. Also used to denote an indigenous parish.

ESCARAMÁN. Today in parts of rural Mexico a heavy harrow pulled by oxen and used to prepare the soil for sowing (personal communication of Eliazar Hernández). Apparently the same in this corpus.

GOVERNOR. Here translates *gobernador*, the highest official of an altepetl.

JUDGE-GOVERNOR. Same as governor.

FANEGA. A Spanish dry measure often said to be equivalent to a bushel and a half. Used here mainly as a land measurement indicating how much land can be sown by a fanega of grain. Equivalent to 120 quahuitl.

FISCAL. Chief steward of a church, here always indigenous. Sometimes the distinction is made between *fiscal mayor*, chief fiscal, and *fiscal teniente*, deputy fiscal.

GUARDIAN. In the phrase father guardian, prior of a Franciscan establishment.

HUIPIL. Spanish form from Nahuatl *huipilli*, the sleeveless blouse-like upper garment worn by indigenous women.

MAESTRO. Master or teacher. Here apparently always refers to a teacher of the Christian doctrine, as when it is expanded to *maestro de doctrina*, much like or the same as the temachti. It is not excluded, however, that the word at times may mean choirmaster.

MAGUEY. The agave from which the juice for the alcoholic drinks pulque and tepache was extracted.

MAYORDOMO. Majordomo, steward. Here seems to refer to the chief officer of a cofradía.

MERINO. Holder of a lower office in municipal government.

METATE. Spanish from Nahuatl *metlatl*, grinding stone (principally for maize).

QUAHUITL. Literally "stick," one of the forms of the main traditional unit of measurement, often about seven feet or more, here used in Toluca area but not in Calimaya/Tepemaxalco.

REAL. Coin or value amounting to one-eighth of a peso.

REGIDOR. Councilman in municipal government. Here mainly *regidor mayor*, chief councilman, although *regidor menor*, lower councilman, occurs once.

REPÚBLICA. The formal governmental aspect of an indigenous altepetl, here translated as commonwealth.

TEJOCOTE. Spanish for Nahuatl *texocotl*, a kind of tree (Crataegus mexicana).

TEMACHTI. Literally teacher. Here an indigenous person assigned to teach the Christian doctrine locally.

TENIENTE. Deputy, as in fiscal teniente.

TEPISQUE. Spanish for Nahuatl *tepixqui*, "one who is in charge of people," a lower church official probably equivalent to the topile more frequently seen here.

TLAXILACALLI. One of the constituent parts or districts of an altepetl.

TOPILE. Used in Spanish from the same form in Nahuatl, meaning literally one with a staff; any official at an intermediary level. Here, always or almost always a low-level church official.

VARA. Spanish measurement, the Spanish yard, a little less than an English yard.

YOKE. A team of two oxen. Also, the amount of land that one yoke of oxen can plow.

Bibliography

Institutional abbreviations:

AGN. Archivo General de la Nación, Mexico City.

AHAM. Archivo Histórico del Arzobispado de México, Mexico City.

MNAH. Museo Nacional de Antropología e Historia, Mexico City.

Anderson, Arthur J. O., Frances Berdan, and James Lockhart, eds. 1976. *Beyond the Codices*. Berkeley: University of California Press.

Carochi, Horacio, S. J. 2001. *Grammar of the Mexican Language, with an Explanation of its Adverbs*. Bilingual edition by James Lockhart. UCLA Latin American Center Nahuatl Studies Series, 7. Stanford, Calif.: Stanford University Press and UCLA Latin American Center Publications.

Cline, S. L., and Miguel León-Portilla, eds. 1984. *The Testaments of Culhuacan*. UCLA Latin American Center Nahuatl Studies Series, 1. Los Angeles: UCLA Latin American Center Publications.

Cline, S. L. 1986. *Colonial Culhuacan, 1580–1600*. Albuquerque: University of New Mexico Press.

Florescano, Enrique, and Elsa Malvido, eds. 1992. *Ensayos sobre la historia de las epidemias en México*, 1: 171–76. México: Instituto Mexicano de Seguro Social.

Karttunen, Frances. 1983. *An Analytical Dictionary of Nahuatl*. Austin: University of Texas Press. (Reprinted in 1992 by University of Oklahoma Press, Norman.)

Karttunen, Frances, and James Lockhart. 1976. *Nahuatl in the Middle Years: Language Contact Phenomena in Texts of the Colonial Period*. University of California Publications in Linguistics, 85. Berkeley: University of California Press.

Karttunen, Frances, and James Lockhart, eds. and trans. 1987. *The Art of Nahuatl Speech: The Bancroft Dialogues*. UCLA Latin American Center Nahuatl Studies Series, 2. Los Angeles: UCLA Latin American Center Publications.

Kellogg, Susan, and Matthew Restall, eds. 1998. *Dead Giveaways: Indigenous Testaments of Colonial Mesoamerica and the Andes*. Salt Lake City: University of Utah Press.

Lockhart, James. 1991. *Nahuas and Spaniards: Postconquest Central Mexican History and Philology*. UCLA Latin American Center Nahuatl Studies Series, 3. Stanford, Calif.: Stanford University Press and UCLA Latin American Center Publications.

______. 1992. *The Nahuas After the Conquest*. Stanford, Calif.: Stanford University Press.

______. 1999. *Of Things of the Indies: Essays Old and New in Early Latin American History*. Stanford, Calif.: Stanford University Press.

______. 2001. *Nahuatl as Written: Lessons in Older Written Nahuatl, with Copious Examples and Texts*. UCLA Latin American Center Nahuatl Studies Series, 6. Stanford, Calif.: Stanford University Press and UCLA Latin American Center Publications.

Lockhart, James, ed. and trans. 1993. *We People Here: Nahuatl Accounts of the Conquest of Mexico*. UCLA Center for Medieval and Renaissance Studies. *Repertorium Columbianum*, 1 (gen. ed. Geoffrey Symcox). Berkeley: University of California Press.

Loera Chávez, Margarita. 1977. *Calimaya y Tepemaxalco. Tenencia y transmisión hereditaria de la tierra en dos comunidades indígenas. Epoca colonial*. México: Instituto Nacional de Antropología e Historia.

______. 1981. *Economía campesina indígena en la Colonia. Un caso en el Valle de Toluca*. México: Instituto Nacional Indigenista.

Márquez Morfín, Lourdes. 1993. "La evolución cuantitativa de la población novohispana: siglos XVI, XVII y XVIII." In *El poblamiento de Mexico. Una visión histórico-demográfica*, 2: 37–63. México: Ed. CONAPO.

Molina, fray Alonso de. 1970. *Vocabulario en lengua castellana y mexicana y mexicana y castellana*. México: Porrúa.

Pizzigoni, Caterina. 2002. "Between Resistance and Assimilation: Rural Nahua Women in the Valley of Toluca in the Early Eighteenth Century." Doctoral dissertation, University of London (King's College).

______. Forthcoming 2007. "Region and Subregion

in Central Mexican Ethnohistory: The Toluca Valley, 1650–1760." *Colonial Latin American Review.*

Restall, Matthew, trans. and ed. 1995. *Life and Death in a Maya Community: The Ixil Testaments of the 1760s.* Lancaster, Calif.: Labyrinthos.

Reyes García, Luis, Eustaquio Celestino Solís, Armando Valencia Ríos, Constantino Medina Lima, and Gregorio Guerrero Díaz, eds. and trans. 1996. *Documentos nauas de la ciudad de México del siglo XVI.* México, CIESAS/Archivo General de la Nación.

Rojas Rabiela, Teresa, et al., eds. 1999–2002. *Vidas y bienes olvidados: Testamentos indígenas novohispanos.* 4 vols. México: CIESAS/CONACYT.

Romero Quiroz, Javier. 1973. *La ciudad de Toluca. Su historia.* 2 vols. México: Gobierno del Estado de México.

Sousa, Lisa, Stafford Poole, C. M., and James Lockhart, eds. and trans. 1998. *The Story of Guadalupe: Luis Laso de la Vega's* Huei tlamahuiçoltica *of 1649.* UCLA Latin American Center Nahuatl Studies Series, 5. Stanford, Calif.: Stanford University Press and UCLA Latin American Center Publications.

Wood, Stephanie. 1991. "Adopted Saints: Christian Images in Nahua Testaments of Late Colonial Toluca," *The Americas,* 47: 259–93.

______. 1994. "Rural Nahua Women under Spanish Colonization: The Late-Colonial Toluca Valley. In *Mesoamerican and Chicano Art, Culture, and Identity / El arte, la cultura, y la identidad mesoamericana y chicana,* ed. by Robert Dash. *Williamette Journal of the Liberal Arts,* Supplemental Series, 6, pp. 78–103. Salem, Oregon: Willamette University.

______. 1997. "Matters of Life at Death: Nahuatl Testaments of Rural Women (Central Mexico), 1589–1801." In *Indian Women of Early Mexico,* ed. by Susan Schroeder, Stephanie Wood, and Robert Haskett, pp. 165–82. Norman: University of Oklahoma Press.

______. 2003. *Transcending Conquest: Nahua Views of Spanish Colonial Mexico.* Norman: University of Oklahoma Press.

Wood, Stephanie, and Robert Haskett. 1997. "Concluding Remarks." In *Indian Women of Early Mexico,* ed. by Susan Schroeder, Stephanie Wood, and Robert Haskett, pp. 313–30. Norman: University of Oklahoma Press.